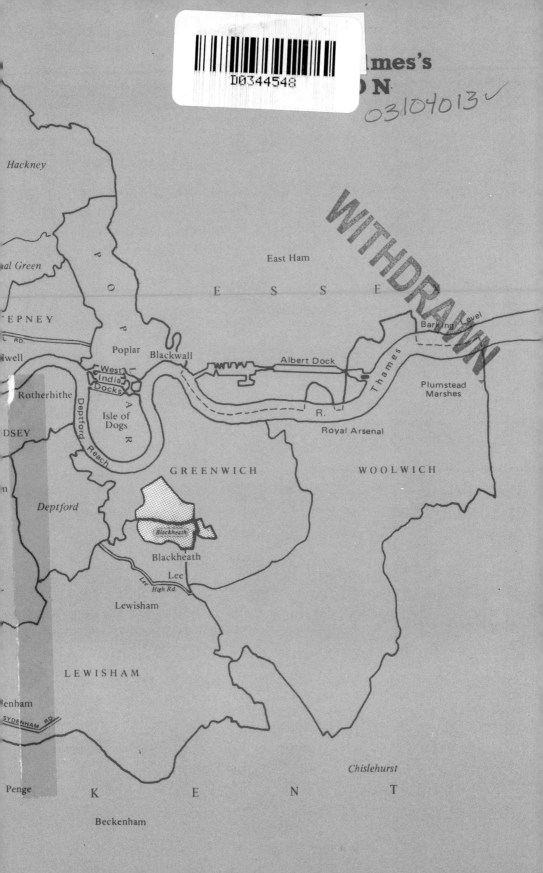

mes's
ON

Hackney

P
O
P
L
A
R

al Green

East Ham

E   S   S   E

EPNEY

Barking Level

L RD.

Poplar

Blackwall

Albert Dock

lwell

West
India
Docks

Plumstead
Marshes

Rotherhithe

A   R

Thames

Isle of
Dogs

R.

DSEY

Royal Arsenal

Deptford

Deptford Reach

R

GREENWICH

WOOLWICH

Blackheath

Blackheath

Lee

Lee High Rd.

Lewisham

LEWISHAM

enham

SYDENHAM RD.

Chislehurst

Penge

K   E   N   T

Beckenham

THE
Encyclopædia
Sherlockiana

THE
Encyclopædia
Sherlockiana

OR,

A Universal Dictionary
of the State of Knowledge

OF

SHERLOCK HOLMES

AND HIS BIOGRAPHER
JOHN H. WATSON, M.D.

Compiled and Edited by

JACK TRACY

Author of "Conan Doyle and the Latter-Day Saints,"
"The Second of August," "Old Woman Be Damned!," etc., etc.

PROFUSELY ILLUSTRATED

Doubleday & Company, Inc.
Garden City, New York
1977

Library of Congress Cataloging in Publication Data

Tracy, Jack W.
   The encyclopædia Sherlockiana.

   Bibliography: p. 405.
   1. Doyle, Arthur Conan, Sir, 1859–1930—Dictionaries,
indexes, etc.   I. Title.
PR4623.A3T7   823'.9'12
ISBN: 0-385-03061-4
Library of Congress Catalog Card Number 75–13394

For my Mother
and for Gomo

Introduction

Only twenty years ago a book like this would have been absurd. Anyone who grew up before World War II had any number of roots in the Victorian and Edwardian eras which serve as the settings for Sherlock Holmes; many of the people living in the 1930s and 1940s had been fully adult in Holmes's time, the physical and intellectual environments were not significantly different, and certainly attitudes and vocabularies had not changed much. It is those of us born and raised during and after the electronics revolution of the 1950s who need the thoroughly mechanistic, arrogantly optimistic nineteenth century explained to us.

It has been said that the Victorians were not so different from us after all, that today's institutions had most of their origins among the Victorians— but those who say so are the historians and sociologists who spent their own formative years before the computer and satellite communications changed the focus of everything. Perhaps thirty years ago we resembled the Victorians. We don't any more.

The truth is that the Victorians had almost nothing in common with us. They were the last of mankind—so far —to know real self-confidence, to thoroughly expect their world to endure. The brutal disillusionments of world war, depression, and nuclear uncertainty had not been divined. Their institutions, like their architecture and their artifacts, were designed to be perpetuated as the pinnacle of human accomplishment—a feat of ethnocentric hubris we'll not soon match. It is only now, after appalling delay, that the combined technology and social conscience of the twentieth century are finally dismantling the ponderous oppressions of the nineteenth.

The passing of Victorianism is not a thing to be mourned. Objectively viewed, our Victorian heritage is a remarkably negative one. The era's merits have been swept away in the stream of history, and we are left to cope with the remnants of an artificial age.

The Victorian has been called the era of compromise, and not without a great deal of justice. Nearly every significant concept identifiable as uniquely Victorian was the result of compromise —compromise between progress and tradition, science and religion, wealth and poverty, privilege and freedom, enlightenment and intolerance, conscience and hysteria. It was an operable solution a century ago, when resolution could be put off and forgotten. Our own generation, however, clearly can no longer afford to take refuge in compromise—particularly the kind of anachronistic, nonhumanist compromise we have inherited from the Victorians.

Such fundamental attitudes make us infinitely different from them, despite the superficial physical similarities of our worlds. If they enjoyed a strong sense of security and belonging, they did so at the cost of a rigid code of social behavior very much in conflict with our own concepts of personal liberty. If they had unparalleled cultural stability, it was at the expense of institutionalizing rather than solving the problems created by their own physical and economic expansion. If they lived at the center of a world-wide economic empire, it was through an exploitive system that forced them to rationalize the cruelest racial and cultural theories at the expense of both scientific and theological integrity.

It is a tribute of sorts to the Victorians' thoroughness and sense of commitment to their own shortsightedness that their institutions have stood so long, and that only in the face of the self-destruction they made inevitable have we begun to recognize how inapplicable they are to a society responsive to man and nature together.

The need to dissolve the Victorians' social models makes it all the more essential that we genuinely understand them if we are to do the job right. This is not always easy, for if we blind ourselves to their more unfortunate circumstances (an outrageously easy thing to do), the final twenty or thirty years of Victoria's reign are perhaps among the most genuinely romantic in history.

Any man with a little money and a lust for adventure had no trouble finding it. Every continent still teemed with whatever combination of danger and potential riches the mind could imagine. The maps of Africa and South America were still largely blank if you craved utterly primitive conditions and none of the distractions of civilized life, and Central Asia and the polar regions were perhaps less exotic but equally challenging. Australia, South Africa, and the American West offered adventure without the hardship of exploration. There were South Sea Islanders, East Indians, Red Indians, Africans, and Arabs ("niggers" all) to exploit the world over. Unless you were an officer the Army was for the lowest classes, but any battle-hungry Englishman could always find excitement fighting against (or with) filibusterers in Central America, slave-traders in the Sudan, or nationalists in the Balkans; or if you preferred, you could get a position as a war correspondent and join the jaunty campaigns against the crudely armed natives of Ashanti or the Indian frontier. It was the era of the "gentleman rankers"—the well-educated younger sons of the propertied classes who would never inherit at home and so went off abroad to fight, to settle, to plant, to administer, to explore, all for England and Empire.

It was the era too of the scientist and the civil engineer as hero. There was no popular anti-technology reaction in those days. There was disillusionment, to be sure; the promised utopia of the machine had not materialized, and the Victorians understood that gears and levers only served to make folly more efficient—but they did not fear their machines. The most limited mind could comprehend the workings of a steam engine, take apart grandfather's watch, smell the gas seeping from the jet, puzzle out lifts and derricks and pumping stations, and instantly recognize the sound of the toilet valve failing again. (Today we have no such advantage; we can't see an electron, and a circuit-card has no moving parts, and while intellectually we can grasp electronics theory, we just can't take the back off the pocket calculator and watch it for ourselves.) The Victorians believed creation to be orderly, uniform, and infinitely Newtonian. This concept of mechanistic simplicity they imposed upon everything, from cosmology to crime detection.

And for a brief flash of history, shorter than the span of a single human life, conditions were ideal for the emergence of a Sherlock Holmes.

Holmes's profession as a consulting detective depended on just the right combination of cultural elements—popular acceptance of scientific principles at a time when science was still in a stage which allowed a single individual a reasonable grasp of the whole; a stable society in which methods of observation, and deductive principles based on observation, could be formulated and applied faster than the data upon which they were founded changed; and the existence of a moneyed middle class from which clients could be drawn. But that is only half the story.

If the science of deduction and analysis, as Holmes claimed, existed only as a course of lectures, there would be no Sherlock Holmes saga. Fortunately Dr. Watson was a man of romantic and not of didactive bent.

For Holmes lived and worked at the very center of the largest colonial empire the world will ever know. In and out of that sitting-room in Baker Street came a succession of gold millionaires, African explorers, Government officials, and foreign dignitaries—all the trappings of Empire—colorfully blended

with representatives of the great British middle class, from tea-brokers to typewriter-girls to country doctors, for whom it was that the Empire existed (and here we must include the men of Scotland Yard, the existence of civil police being one sure sign of a dominant middle class); it was only toward the end of his career, having attained a reputation for discretion, that Holmes was consistently sought out by his own country's nobility. His necessarily pedantic attitude toward his profession may even have made him insensitive to its inherent romanticism—but happily for us all Watson was there, to put flesh and blood on the stark bones of detection and in so doing produce one of the most immortal series of tales in literature.

Today colonialism is a tired anachronism, cities as great centers of culture and finance are gone (though the illusion lives on), media diffuse culture as well as knowledge to all, and the victory of the middle class is long conceded—yet the fascination with Sherlock Holmes is as strong as ever. After the silly perversions of the Holmes image by such as William Gillette and Basil Rathbone (Holmes as tight-lipped derring-doer, Watson as comic sidekick, and performances all round by writers and actors who, if one didn't know better, you would swear never read a line of Holmes), there is a definite revival of interest in the great detective as a literary, and not a cinematic, figure.

The difficulty raised by this return to the original is the lack of familiarity with the Victorian milieu. Much of the vocabulary, institutions, and attitudes of the late nineteenth century have passed out of the modern American experience. For the reader who requires a fuller appreciation of Holmes through a reasonable understanding of the many allusions to Victorian lifestyle there is no longer easy access to definitions, explanations, and perspectives. So much has happened since Holmes's day that modern influences have crowded the nineteenth century right out of the dictionaries and encyclopædias. The information that Watson's readers took for granted is no longer available without a knack for the historical approach. Hence *The Encyclopædia Sherlockiana.*

Simply stated, then, this is a book about the historical background of the Holmes adventures. While it owes a great deal to the "Sherlockian" tradition, it is really not a part of it. It is based on the same prime assumption— that Sherlock Holmes and Dr. Watson were living historical personages, that the chronicles are based on actual incidents, and that Sir Arthur Conan Doyle acted as Watson's literary agent in placing them—and there the similarities end. The cult of "Sherlockiana" is a high-camp intellectual joke in which fact and fiction must be confused as thoroughly as possible. This work is established on precisely the opposite approach. It is not an "in" book, and it never speculates. In fact all references which are clearly imaginative are marked with an asterisk so that the reader immediately is made aware of the fact.

It is interesting (though not too surprising really) to observe that while Sherlock Holmes enjoys a world-wide popularity it is in the United States that his followers are most widespread, and that the bulk of Sherlockian scholarship has been done by Americans. Most of us are rather slavishly Anglophilic in the first place; we can idealize an England in which we don't live, yet when we choose to be we are far more objective observers of the British scene than the British themselves; and we don't have to read the stories in translation. So permit me to anticipate the criticism applied by so many English Sherlockians to American-written commentaries and point out that this is a book for Americans written by an American, and that it pretends to no other perspective.

Such an admission is perhaps more necessary than it would appear at first, for it has been my intention to produce a genuine companion-volume to the Holmes saga which a reader can consult comfortably as he reads. For this reason the language employed is a sort of Anglo-Victorian patois which to an Englishman may be stilted and even slightly comic, but to the American will blend with Watson's prose without distracting from the tone of the original. The style is carefully patterned on the reference works of the time, and the viewpoint assumed is a Victorian one.

Experimentation quickly shows that I cannot retain a period flavor to the language and at the same time provide a historical approach to the material. The solution is to present *The Encyclopædia Sherlockiana* as if it had been written during the first decade of the twentieth century by a denizen of that era, a device which both provides a unified point of view and achieves a roundabout historical perspective which in the aggregate is even more successful than I had envisioned.

As a result this book takes almost no notice of events which occurred after 1914 (the only exceptions are death dates and biographical details of persons mentioned in the saga). Naturally the viewpoint is not a consistent one, and the outcome is a synthesis of English society in the years 1880–1910, with accent on the 1890s, which represents the general state of knowledge prevailing in Holmes's time. Understand that no information is given herein which was not believed to be true by the Victorians themselves. (Where obligatory Sherlockian data occasionally is inserted, such as in the dating of the chronicles, it has been designated clearly as such.)

This technique has posed the danger of my inadvertently expressing nineteenth-century ideas in terms which did not exist then. To take the most apparent example, Watson alludes repeatedly to Holmes's "dual nature" as perhaps the outstanding facet of the detective's personality. Holmes clearly was a mild manic-depressive—yet the term is not found in general use in works of the period and will not be found in this one either.

Contrarily, I am well aware that a cheetah is not a leopard—but the state of zoological classification was not all that well refined in Holmes's day, and in the lay reference works of the time the cheetah was indeed defined as a variety of leopard, and so it is here. By a rigid adherence to such trivial standards can a reasonable atmosphere of authenticity be maintained.

While I have suppressed some Victorian attitudes, such as the blatantly racist allusions to non-Europeans, I have retained others, among them the practice of referring to wives and children under the names of their husbands and fathers, which not only saves space but also carries the right touch of nineteenth-century chauvinism. The use of population figures too is a simple and, in these overpopulated times, a rather profound indication of the gulf between ourselves and the Victorians; all figures for the United States are based on the 1900 census, and all other population statistics are as of 1901, unless otherwise specified.

Each entry herein ideally consists of three parts—the *definition,* the *exposition,* and the *reference.* The *definition* is a single sentence describing the subject. If further information is required for clarity or for Sherlockian interest, then the *exposition* is added; this can run from one sentence to several pages in length. Finally the *reference* provides a four-letter code to indicate in which story the item appears, often accompanied by a sentence putting it in context. Naturally this is not a universal practice; some subjects don't need definitions at all, and for others including an exposition or contextual sentence would be extraneous, clumsy, or distracting. In some articles, such as the one on Holmes himself, for example, or the one about SCOTLAND YARD, exposition and references are inextricably bound up with one another. A very few general terms too commonly used to specify contexts—POUND, for instance, or ENGLAND—carry no references at all; but these are kept to a minimum. Others consist of almost nothing but references, the entry entitled SERVANT being the most conspicuous example.

With some exceptions, items are entered just as they are worded in the stories to avoid confusion in looking them up, though in a few cases cross-references will direct the reader to a more serviceable heading. The work is liberally supplied with them whenever variant headings might suggest themselves, as well as among articles of related interest. This sort of thing reaches its logical extension in the article

LONDON, which in two thousand words of exposition contains not one story code and is effectively one long narrative cross-reference. To save space and to keep from interrupting the flow of information, cross-references are printed in SMALL CAPITALS without further designation.

Where Watson makes thinly disguised allusion to clearly identifiable places or things, either for literary purposes or through simple error, I have clarified the identification; but in adherence to the non-speculative nature of this book I have preferred to stay well on the conservative side and avoid making an identification if the evidence is not all but conclusive. Thus Watson's GREAT ORME STREET is declared to be the very real *Great Ormond Street* in Bloomsbury: but even though the overwhelming Sherlockian consensus is that STOKE MORAN is actually the Surrey hamlet of *Stoke D'Abernon,* I have declined to assert this identification in the absence of more direct evidence and have labeled Stoke Moran as fictitious. I will be criticized more for what I have left out than for what I have included, and the reader who feels his interest in the Sherlockian cult being kindled by this volume should keep that fact firmly in mind. Fictitious entries are preceded by an asterisk (*), important exceptions to this rule being the story characters, who are not so designated, along with other obviously imaginary items such as elements of Holmes's many cases, published and unpublished.

One important assumption which is strictly followed is that in all cases, in the absence of clear evidence to the contrary, it is assumed that Watson's observations and memory are accurate and that his recital of events is presented with complete honesty. Obvious contradictions of fact are pointed out and occasionally explained, always with the presupposition that inconsistencies are the result of error rather than dissimulation.

I have acted also on the presumption that no one is going to resort to a book such as this without having first read Sherlock Holmes purely for enjoyment. I have not scrupled to give away a story's secrets if it seems necessary. At the same time I have presumed that the reader knows nothing about Victorian England other than what common knowledge has taught him and what he has been able to deduce from reading the tales.

The more uninitiated reader may be dismayed to find that herein he will search in vain for any mention of a DEERSTALKER CAP, an INVERNESS CAPE, or a MEERSCHAUM PIPE, stereotypical symbols of Sherlock Holmes. All, alas, are apocryphal. They are a part of Sherlockian lore, but they are not part of Holmes as Watson depicted him. Sidney Paget, the famous illustrator of the stories for the *Strand* magazine, was fond of wearing the deerstalker (or "fore-and-aft"), and when he pictured Holmes in the provinces, he dressed him occasionally in one. But Holmes was always a man of propriety. The deerstalker is worn only in the country, and the Inverness is essentially a traveling-cloak to protect one from railway soot and road-mud. The image of Holmes prowling the gas-lit streets of London in this "traditional" garb is ludicrous. The tales themselves will tell you that when the detective went abroad in the metropolis, he donned tweeds or the oppressively respectable Victorian frock-coat.

The curved meerschaum can be at-

The deerstalker is worn only in the country, and the Inverness is essentially a traveling-cloak to protect one from railway soot and road-mud.

tributed to William Gillette, the American actor who originated Holmes on the stage in 1899. Gillette found that he could not keep his hands free for other business and keep the ever-present pipe, essential to any characterization of Holmes, clenched in his teeth at the same time. He solved the problem by making use of the more balanced meerschaum, which was far less of a strain on his jaw muscles. The American magazine illustrator Frederic Dorr Steele, who based his representations of Holmes on Gillette, perpetuated the image, and yet another cliché was born.

And you will never see the words, "Elementary, my dear Watson." Basil Rathbone may have been passionately fond of that expression, but Holmes never said it.

When we shed the mythology, however pleasant, and confine ourselves to the historical and cultural background of the Holmes saga, the first thing the researcher becomes aware of is the sheer mass of available material. The late Victorian and Edwardian eras may be the most minutely documented in history. Strikingly modern printing methods, cheap labor, a literate population, and a lack of competition from yet-to-be-invented media created a market for thousands of books on every conceivable subject. Economical photo-engraving processes developed around 1890 made the popular illustrated magazine such as the *Strand* possible. And today's "unabridged" dictionaries and "universal" encyclopædias are hardly worthy of the name compared to nineteenth-century standards. Reference works, of which there were many more then than there are today, could go into far greater detail for the simple reason that details did not change that radically from edition to edition—and when they did change they did so along what the lamenting scholars of the 1920s called "known lines of normalcy" and at generally predictable rates.

The material in this book is very largely derived then from what the Victorians had to say about themselves, and there is very little truly original research herein. Most of the information is there for the gathering—if, as I did, you care to spend six years seeking it out. I have done a lot of simplifying, reorganizing, and rewording, for most nineteenth-century reference works subordinated clarity to completeness and scrupulous accuracy, but for the most part I have chosen to intrude myself as little as possible on a particularly eloquent age. There are a few really original discoveries, especially those of a Sherlockian nature, among these pages, and they will be found in their proper places, but to call attention to them would be self-defeating. The ego trip involved here is not based on any one subject's prominence, but on the unity, accuracy, and unprecedented completeness of the work. Energy is nothing without method, and I have striven consciously for what Holmes himself called "that supreme gift of the artist—the knowledge of when to stop."

There is something undeniably appealing about an age—epitomized by the life and talents of Sherlock Holmes—whose inhabitants genuinely believed themselves in control of their environment, who were yet untouched by the long-term consequences of their technology, who were contentedly unaware of such twentieth-century preoccupations as nuclear proliferation, ecology, and shrinking energy reserves. Still, we're better off if we temper the nostalgia with a few coarse realities. Victorian England is a very real and very immediate place for me—one I can enjoy and sympathize with, but seldom one I can admire, and never one to which I would like to see us return.

It is true that there were in Holmes's day none of the likes of computers, frozen dinners, and other nemeses of the simple life. There were also no antibiotics, no food and drug laws, no sanitation to speak of, no civil rights, often no right to criminal appeal, no child labor laws, no trade unions, no social security, no minimum wage. It has been pointed out that during the sixty-three years of Victoria's reign Great Britain engaged in more than two hundred overseas wars, most of them against primitive tribesmen in Asia and Africa; but admittedly none of them were nuclear. Environmentally we merely have exchanged the pollution that causes emphysema for the pollution that causes typhoid. And when you find yourself yearning for that uncomplicated era before our homes were invaded by all those energy-consuming, indifferently constructed appliances, just remember that in Sherlock Holmes's day all routine labor was done by the hands of an underprivileged, underpaid servant class who knew nothing of comfort and little of self-respect; and if that doesn't move you, please consider that, given the relative size of the upper and mid-dle classes to the lower, you probably would have been one of them. The good old days have just begun.

Bloomington, Indiana
1 March 1977

Acknowledgements

This book owes a huge philosophical debt to the cult of Sherlockiana and particularly to the researches undertaken over the last forty years by the members of the Sherlock Holmes Society of London and of the Baker Street Irregulars and its dozens of scion societies all over the United States. The fact that I have made as little use as possible of Sherlockian publications (preferring, as described, to do my research among actual period sources) does not mean I haven't been guided and inspired every step of the way by the example of Sherlockian tradition. This "singular set of people" has been lovingly described by William S. Baring-Gould in his magnificent *The Annotated Sherlock Holmes,* a work which cannot be too heartily recommended.

Among Sherlockians to whom I owe special gratitude are H. B. ("Pete") Williams, my first and still favorite Irregular; Julian Wolff, M.D., editor of the *Baker Street Journal;* John Bennett Shaw and Ronald De Waal, who provided more encouragement than they knew; Andrew Page, Andrew Jay Peck, and Paul Cox, each of whom contributed in his own way.

For the many fine period illustrations I have to thank the largely anonymous staff people in the photograph library of the Greater London Council; R. A. Cecil of the Wallace Collection; the erudite K. C. Harrison, M.B.E., F.L.A., of the Westminster City Libraries; and David Tredinnick, head of the Department of Medical Illustration, St. Bartholomew's Hospital. Mike Daily, Edward Skager, and Sioux Hill are responsible for the excellent rephotography.

But more than anything I owe acknowledgement to the Indiana University library system and to its Victorian Studies collection in particular. It is no exaggeration to say that of the thousands of items included in these pages perhaps only twenty had to be sought elsewhere. Without that kind of comprehensive data pool at my disposal this book quite literally would not have been possible. All thanks to the main library reference staff and especially to Jim Greaves.

And finally my appreciation to all the people at Doubleday whose perception, understanding, and co-operation were truly remarkable.

KEY TO STORY TITLES

* Fictitious reference

Cross references in SMALL CAPITALS

U.S. population figures from 1900 census; all others 1901 except where noted.

A

A, the first letter in almost all alphabets. While copying out the *Encyclopædia Britannica,* Jabez Wilson spent eight weeks, he said, writing about Abbots, and Archery, and Armour, and Architecture, and Attica, until he hoped to get on to the B's before long (REDH).

Aback. The *Gloria Scott*'s fore-yard had been hauled aback during the mutiny (GLOR), that is, swung round so that the wind pressed its sail aft against the mast, in order to check the ship's progress.

*Abbas Parva, the Berkshire village where the Ronder circus was camped the night its owner was killed and Eugenia Ronder mutilated (VEIL). The name derives from the Latin *abbas,* meaning *abbot,* and *parvus,* meaning *small;* "parva" as an element in an English place-name denotes "little" or "lesser."

Abbey, The: see WESTMINSTER ABBEY.

*Abbey Grange, the house and estate of Sir Eustace Brackenstall, at Marsham in Kent (ABBE).

"Abbey Grange, The Adventure of the" (ABBE), a chronicle which appeared originally in the *Strand* magazine for September 1904 and *Collier's Weekly* of 31 December 1904 and was published in the collection entitled *The Return of Sherlock Holmes* the following year. It concerns Holmes's investigation of the murder of Sir Eustace Brackenstall. Watson dates the case as having taken place toward the end of the winter of 1897, and almost all authorities accept January 1897.

Watson writes that at one time he had intended "The Adventure of the Abbey Grange" to be the last of the exploits of Sherlock Holmes which he would ever communicate to the public (SECO).

*Abbey School: see PRIORY SCHOOL.

Abduction: see KIDNAPPING.

Abdullah Khan, one of the FOUR (SIGN).

Abel White (d. 1857), an Anglo-Indian indigo-planter who hired Jonathan Small as an overseer and was killed at the beginning of the Mutiny (SIGN). In some editions the name appears as *Abelwhite.*

Aberdeen, a city of eastern Scotland, pop. 153,503. Holmes knew of an instance here which had paralleled the St. Simon case (NOBL). Inspector MacDonald was from Aberdeen (VALL).

Aberdeen Shipping Company, properly **Aberdeen Steam Navigation Company,** a shipping company with offices in the City. Mrs. St. Clair went to the "Aberdeen Shipping Company" to pick up a parcel (TWIS).

Aberdonian, pertaining to ABERDEEN (VALL).

Abergavenny (*ab-er-gay'nee* or *ab-er-gah-ven'ee*), a town in the west of England, pop. 7,795. Holmes had been concerned with "the Abergavenny murder" (PRIO), which perhaps occurred here.

Abernetty, the name of a family involved in some "dreadful business" with which Holmes was involved. Holmes said that it was first brought to his notice by the depth which the parsley had sunk into the butter upon a hot day (SIXN).

Abet, in law, to encourage, counsel, incite, or assist in a criminal act. Sir Henry Baskerville decided, wrongly, that he and Watson were "aiding and abetting" a felony in not exposing Selden (HOUN); see COMPOUND.

Abrahams. Holmes insisted that he could not possibly leave London while old Abrahams was in mortal terror of his life (LADY).

Acetones, a class of carbon compounds used as solvents in manufacturing (COPP).

Achmet (d. 1857), the servant of a northern Indian rajah, murdered for the Agra treasure (SIGN).

Acid, the name popularly applied to a number of chemical compounds, many of which are organic, and a great many of which are known principally to chemists and prepared artificially.

Holmes's chemical table was acid-stained (EMPT, MAZA), and his hands were invariably discoloured with strong acids (STUD). John Clay had a white splash of acid upon his forehead (REDH). Bottles of acid stood in the corners of Bartholomew Sholto's laboratory (SIGN).

The smell of HYDROCHLORIC ACID told Watson that Holmes had been engaged in chemical work (IDEN). CARBOLIC ACID is much used in medicine (CARD, ENGR), and *sulphuric acid* is commonly called VITRIOL (BLUE, ILLU). Eugenia Ronder sent Holmes a bottle of PRUSSIC ACID (VEIL). See also NITRITE OF AMYL.

Acton, a wealthy businessman living near Reigate, whose house was burgled by the Cunninghams (REIG).

Acushla, an Irish term of endearment. John McMurdo so addressed Ettie Shafter (VALL).

Adair, Hilda: see MAYNOOTH, EARL OF.

Adair, Hon. Ronald (d. 1894), the second son of the Earl of MAYNOOTH, mysteriously murdered by Sebastian Moran (EMPT).

Adams, the culprit of the Manor House case (GREE).

Adder: see SWAMP ADDER; VIPER.

Addleton tragedy, a case Holmes investigated in 1894 (GOLD).

Adelaide, the capital of South Australia, pop. (1900) 162,200. Lady Brackenstall (ABBE) and Holy Peters (LADY) were from here.

*Adelaide-Southampton Company, the principal steamship company plying to Australia, with London offices "at the end of Pall Mall" (ABBE). The offices of the *Orient and Pacific Company* are "at the end of Pall Mall" in Cockspur Street, though Orient liners dock at Tilbury, in Essex, not at Southampton as the Adelaide-Southampton steamers were said to do.

Adler, Irene (1858–?1890), the well-known operatic contralto and adventuress, born in New Jersey. She sang at

La Scala and was prima donna of the Imperial Opera of Warsaw before retiring from the operatic stage. In Warsaw she became involved with the King of BOHEMIA, received several indiscreet letters, and was photographed with him. She threatened to use the photo to create a scandal which would end the King's wedding plans, and Sherlock Holmes then was engaged to procure it. She fled London with her newly-wed husband Godfrey NORTON, leaving a promise not to make use of the photograph (SCAN).

A precious snuff-box, given him by the King, served Holmes as a souvenir of the case, the only one in which Watson had known Holmes to fail (IDEN). Watson observed that the case had been free of legal crime (BLUE). Holmes identified himself to Von Bork as he who brought about the "separation" between Irene Adler and the King of Bohemia (LAST). He claimed to have been beaten four times by 1887—"three times by men and once by a woman" (FIVE).

To Sherlock Holmes, Irene Adler was always *the* woman (SCAN).

Admiralty, The, a department of the British Government, headed by a Cabinet minister, the *First Lord of the Ad-*

The original Admiralty building in Whitehall.

miralty. He and the other Lords Commissioners have the general management of maritime affairs, and of all matter relating to the Royal Navy. The Admiralty building in Whitehall, behind which new offices have recently been erected, was built 1722–26.

The Duke of Holdernesse had been a Lord of the Admiralty (PRIO). It was "buzzing like an overturned beehive" at the theft of the Bruce-Partington plans (BRUC), and it set down the *Gloria Scott* as having been lost at sea (GLOR). Von Bork declared that the Admiralty had unaccountably changed the naval codes upon the eve of the World War (LAST).

A.D.P. pipe, a smoking-pipe manufactured by the firm of Alfred Dunhill, the initials standing for *Alfred Dunhill Pipe.* An A.D.P. briar-root pipe was found in John Straker's pocket (SILV).

"Adventure of": for titles beginning thus, see the second element; e.g., for "The Adventure of the Speckled Band" see "SPECKLED BAND, THE ADVENTURE OF THE."

"Adventures of Sherlock Holmes, The," the first collection of Sherlock Holmes cases, published in 1892 and containing, in order of their first English magazine appearances, the following: "A Scandal in Bohemia" (SCAN), "The Red-Headed League" (REDH), "A Case of Identity" (IDEN), "The Boscombe Valley Mystery" (BOSC), "The Five Orange Pips" (FIVE), "The Man with the Twisted Lip" (TWIS), "The Adventure of the Blue Carbuncle" (BLUE), "The Adventure of the Speckled Band" (SPEC), "The Adventure of the Engineer's Thumb" (ENGR), "The Adventure of the Noble Bachelor"

(NOBL), "The Adventure of the Beryl Coronet" (BERY), and "The Adventure of the Copper Beeches" (COPP).

Adventuress, a woman engaged in or capable of enterprises of an equivocal moral character (SCAN). Isadora Klein had enjoyed "an interval of adventure." (3GAB).

Affaire de cœur, a love-affair (IDEN).

Afghan campaign: see AFGHANISTAN.

Afghanistan, a country in Asia, est. pop. 4,000,000. In part the boundaries are not well defined, and the country consists largely of bare, uninhabited table-lands, barren plains, ranges of snow-covered mountains, and deep valleys. The climate is intensely hot in the lower regions. The people are divided into a number of warlike tribes which are constantly engaged in dissensions among themselves. In religion they are Moslems of the Sunnite sect. See PATHAN.

The history of Afghanistan from the time of Alexander the Great to the first war against the British in 1839–42 consists of a series of conquests made by different nations. Shir Ali (1825–1879), who became emir in 1863, for a time maintained friendly relations with the British in India, but in 1878, in consequence of new Russian diplomatic overtures to Afghanistan, was invited to receive a British mission. His refusal precipitated the *Second Afghan War* of 1878–79, during the course of which Shir Ali died. His son Yakub Khan (1849–1923) shortly thereafter abdicated in favour of Shir Ali's nephew Abdurrahman (d. 1901).

In July 1880, Shir Ali's younger son Ayub Khan (1855–1914) led an uprising against his cousin's acceptance of British peace terms. He marched upon CANDAHAR and utterly defeated a British force, sent out from Candahar to meet him, at MAIWAND. He was finally defeated in September 1881 and Abdurrahman's rule confirmed.

On landing in India to join his regiment, Watson found that the Second Afghan War had broken out; he made his way to Candahar and was severely wounded at Maiwand (STUD). He did not get over the effects of the campaign for some time (NOBL, RESI,†️ SIGN), declaring that he had had enough noise and excitement in Afghanistan to last for the remainder of his natural existence (STUD).

Holmes's first words to Watson at their original meeting were: "You have been in Afghanistan, I perceive" (STUD).

Watson said that his experience of camp life had the effect of making him a prompt and ready traveller (BOSC) and rather more lax in his personal habits than befit a medical man (MUSG). He endeavoured to tell Mary Morstan some reminiscences of Afghanistan (SIGN) but failed to interest Percy Phelps (NAVA). Colonel Hayter had come under his professional care here (REIG).

Henry Wood wandered among the Afghans (CROO), and Colonel Sebastian Moran served in the Afghan campaign and fought at CHARASIAB, SHERPUR, and CABUL (EMPT).

See the map accompanying INDIA.

Africa. James Dodd and Godfrey Emsworth had served together in Africa (BLAN). Dr. Leon Sterndale was a famous African explorer (DEVI), and Ralph Smith went to

† This reference appeared in the original magazine and book publications of "The Resident Patient," but was omitted from the 1928 omnibus volume and all subsequent editions.

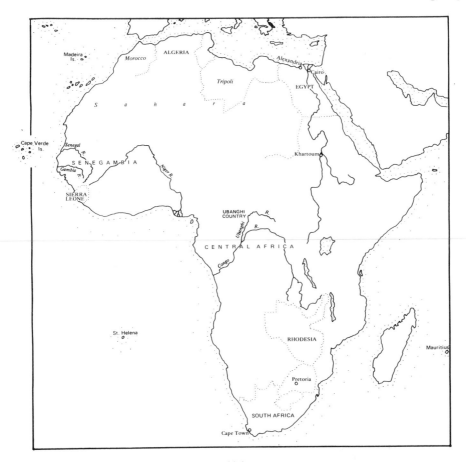

Africa.

Africa about 1870 (SOLI). The survivors of the *Gloria Scott* disaster believed themselves to be 700 miles west of the African coast (GLOR). The BUSHMEN are Africans (SIGN), and John Hebron was described as being of African descent (YELL).

See also CENTRAL AFRICA; NORTH AFRICA; SOUTH AFRICA; WEST AFRICA; also ALGERIA; CAPE DE VERDS; EGYPT; RHODESIA; SENEGAMBIA; SIERRA LEONE; UBANGHI COUNTRY. See also HOTTENTOT; NEGRO RACE; VOODOO.

After-hold, that part of a ship's hold aft of the mainmast and directly beneath the poop (GLOR).

Agar, Moore, the Harley Street physician who ordered Holmes's vacation of 1897. His original introduction to Holmes had been a dramatic one (DEVI). *Moore Agar* may be a compound surname.

Agate. There were sixty-one agates in the Agra treasure (SIGN).

Agatha, the housemaid of Charles Augustus Milverton, whom Holmes wooed to acquire information about her master (CHAS).

Agency, the term Holmes used (SUSS) in allusion to the "small, but very efficient organization" (LADY) which he assembled to assist him in his detective practice.

In the years before the Great Hiatus he seems to have worked alone, with occasional support from the BAKER STREET IRREGULARS (CROO, SIGN, STUD), and when help other than that for which he called upon Watson or his brother Mycroft was required, Holmes most often turned to children such as WIGGINS (SIGN, STUD), SIMPSON (CROO), and CARTWRIGHT (HOUN); exceptions being the hiring of the crowd of accomplices in the Irene Adler case (SCAN) and of several other "agencies" to help in the extensive search for the *Aurora* (SIGN).

A more formal organization grew up round the turn of the century, with such men as MERCER (CREE), Shinwell JOHNSON (ILLU), and Langdale PIKE (3GAB) rendering services on a somewhat regular basis. An unnamed agent of Holmes's wired to Josiah Amberley from Little Purlington (RETI), and Count Sylvius mistook Holmes himself in various disguises for agents of the detective (MAZA).

Agony column, in English slang, personal newspaper advertisements.

Holmes claimed to read nothing in the newspapers save the criminal news and the agony column, which he said was always instructive (NOBL), and he kept a great book in which he filed them day by day (REDC); see COMMONPLACE BOOK. He occupied much of his time in this way (COPP, ENGR) and amused himself by reading the cipher messages printed there (VALL). "Unmitigated bleat!" he said of them—"what a chorus of groans, cries, and bleatings! What a rag-bag of singular happenings! But surely the most valuable hunting-ground that ever was given to a student of the unusual" (REDC).

Holmes advertised for the *Aurora* in the agony column of the *Standard* (SIGN). He advertised in the evening papers for Henry Baker (BLUE) and for Joseph Harrison's cab-driver (NAVA), and the finding of Jefferson Hope's ring (STUD). Advertisements were tried and failed in the search for Lady Frances Carfax (LADY). Mycroft Holmes advertised for Paul and Sophy Kratides in all the London dailies (GREE).

The Countess of Morcar advertised in *The Times* her offer of a reward for the return of the blue carbuncle (BLUE), and the Sholtos sought Mary Morstan (SIGN) and Woodley and Carruthers advertised for Violet Smith (SOLI) here. Hugo Oberstein communicated with Colonel Walter through the agony column of the *Daily Telegraph* (BRUC), and Gennaro Lucca's messages to his wife appeared in the *Daily Gazette* (REDC). Mary Sutherland advertised for Hosmer Angel in the *Chronicle* (IDEN). Inspector Gregson advertised in all the papers for Joseph Stangerson (STUD), and the police sought Captain Morstan here on behalf of his daughter (SIGN). John Garrideb claimed to have advertised in the agony columns for more Garridebs (3GAR).

Agra, a city of north-central India, pop. 188,300. Located upon the Ganges, the city is one of the oldest in India and has several interesting structures, the best known being the celebrated Taj Mahal. During the Mutiny its sixteenth-century fort was a place of refuge for Europeans (SIGN). See also GREATHED, SIR EDWARD HARRIS; SHAHGUNGE.

Agra treasure, the object of the conspiracy of the FOUR, worth, it was said, some £500,000. Belonging originally to an Indian rajah, it was stolen suc-

The old fort at Agra, wherein its European defenders successfully resisted the three-month Sepoy siege until relieved by Col. Greathed upon 11 October 1857.

cessively by the Four, Major SHOLTO, and Jonathan SMALL. Small scattered the jewels into the Thames rather than have them fall into another's hands (SIGN).

Peter Jones observed that in the business of the Agra treasure, Holmes was more nearly correct than the official force (REDH).

Agriculture. Howard Garrideb was supposedly a constructor of agricultural machinery (3GAR).

Holmes mentioned the fall in agricultural prices between 1875, the year of Helen Stoner's mother's death, and 1883 (SPEC). This is a reference to the twenty-year period of agricultural decline 1873–94 which depressed prices to less than half their former amounts and ruined many English farmers. The immediate cause was the removal in 1873 of import duties on wheat, opening the British market to the cheap competition of American, Canadian, and Australian grain, compounded by long spells of bad weather, livestock epidemics, and rising labour costs owing to the enactment of compulsory education laws for children and the continuing population shift from the country to the town.

Holmes in retirement divided his time between philosophy and agriculture (PREF), particularly beekeeping (LAST, SECO).

Ague, or *malaria.* Jonathan Small suffered ague in the Andaman Islands (SIGN).

Ainstree, Dr., the greatest living authority upon tropical diseases, whom Watson wished to bring into Holmes's case (DYIN).

Airedale terrier, a variety of large, rough-coated terrier. Fitzroy McPherson's dog was an Airedale (LION).

Air-gun, a gun in which condensed air is used as the propelling agent. The bore of the barrel is connected with a reservoir, enclosed within or attached without the stock, into which air is forced by a piston or plunger fitted to the bore, or by an independent condenser. When the trigger is pulled, it operates a valve which permits the sudden escape of the whole or of a portion of the condensed air into the barrel at

Air-gun.

the rear of the ball or dart, thus projecting the latter. In some forms the propelling agent is a compressed spring freed by the trigger; the reactive force of the spring compresses the air between it and the projectile, and the air acts upon and projects the ball.

Holmes closed the shutters of Watson's consulting-room in fear of airguns (FINA), and Colonel Sebastian Moran murdered Ronald Adair and attempted to kill Holmes with Von Herder's invention, which fired a soft-nosed revolver bullet and which in the end embellished the Scotland Yard museum (EMPT). The air-gun made by

Straubenzee for Count Sylvius was never used for its intended purpose of murdering Holmes (MAZA).

Akbar, Dost, one of the FOUR (SIGN).

*Albemarle Mansion, the Kensington residence of Mr. Melville (WIST).

Albert chain, a heavy-linked watch chain. Hosmer Angel (IDEN), Jabez Wilson (REDH), and Enoch Drebber (STUD) wore Albert chains.

Albert Dock, part of the system of the *Royal Victoria and Albert Docks,* located in Essex and extending parallel to the Thames. The largest docking system of London's port, it accommodates all but the largest commercial steamers. James Browner was arrested at the Albert Dock (CARD), where the *Lone Star* was tied during her stay in London (FIVE). See the front endpaper map.

Albert Hall, properly **Royal Albert Hall of Arts and Sciences,** a vast assembly hall in south Kensington, constructed 1867–71 as a memorial to *Prince Albert* (1819–1861), royal consort of Queen Victoria. It is used for scientific and art assemblies, for political gatherings, and for musical fêtes and concerts on a large scale. Holmes attended a concert here (RETI). See the map of KENSINGTON.

Aldersgate Street Station, an Underground and suburban railway station in the northern part of the City. Holmes and Watson took the Underground to Aldersgate on their way to Saxe-Coburg Square ʼ(REDH). See Map I of LONDON

Aldershot, a city in north-eastern Hampshire, pop. 30,974. It was a mere village until 1855, when *Aldershot Camp* was established as the largest permanent military camp in Britain.

The great Albert Hall, one of the largest in the world, will comfortably seat more than eight thousand persons.

The camp is headquarters for a permanent defense force and has extensive facilities in its nine square miles for drilling, training, and maneuvering troops. As many as twenty thousand officers and men may be accommodated at one time.

Holmes and Watson crossed the border of Hampshire not far from Aldershot on their journey to Winchester (COPP). Holmes investigated the death of Colonel Barclay here (CROO). See the map of HAMPSHIRE.

Aldgate Station, an Underground and suburban railway station in the City, the eastern-most station of the Metropolitan line. Cadogan West's body was found near here (BRUC). See UNDERGROUND; see the map of the CITY.

Aldridge, a man who helped Holmes and Lestrade in the "bogus laundry affair" (CARD).

Alehouse, a beer-house; an establishment licensed for the sale of malt liquors only (SIGN). See also PUBLIC-HOUSE.

Alexandria, an ancient city and seaport in Egypt, at the north-west angle of the Nile delta, pop. (1902) 310,587. Founded by Alexander the Great in 332 B.C., it was long a great and splendid city, a centre of commerce and Greek learning and civilization, with a population at one time of perhaps 1,000,000. Nathan Garrideb preferred the coins of ancient Syracuse to those of Alexandria (3GAR). Ionides lived here (GOLD).

Alexis, a Russian Nihilist against whom Professor Coram testified and who was sentenced to a Siberian salt mine. It was in his interests that the woman Anna acted when she entered Yoxley Old Place (GOLD).

Algar, a member of the Liverpool police, to whom Holmes wired for information (CARD).

Algeria, a French colony in North Africa, pop. 4,774,042. Count Sylvius shot lions here (MAZA).

Alice, the maid and confidential servant of Hatty Doran (NOBL).

Alicia, the name of a cutter which sailed one spring morning into a small patch of mist from where she never again emerged, nor was anything further ever heard of herself and her crew (THOR).

Alienist, one engaged in the scientific study or treatment of mental diseases. Watson suggested that Professor Presbury's case was one for an alienist (CREE) and spoke of the modern French psychologists' conception of MONOMANIA (SIXN). See PSYCHOLOGY.

*Alison's, an establishment at which prizefights were presented, most likely a tavern or public house, at which Holmes fought McMurdo (SIGN).

Alkali, a term applied to the hydrates of the so-called alkaline earths of baryta, strontia, and lime; see the GREAT ALKALI PLAIN (STUD).

Alkaloid, a term applied to such compounds as morphine, quinine, and caffeine. **Vegetable alkaloids** are those which are obtained from plants, as distinguished from those that are extracted from viscera and stomach contents—the *animal alkaloids*. There is also a class of artificial alkaloids produced from COAL-TAR products. Among the alkaloids are the strongest poisons and the most powerful remedies known.

Young Stamford said he could imagine Holmes giving a friend a little pinch of the latest vegetable alkaloid— "not out of malevolence, you understand, but simply out of a spirit of inquiry" (STUD). Watson suggested that Bartholomew Sholto's death had been caused by some powerful vegetable alkaloid like STRYCHNINE (SIGN). Enoch Drebber died of an alkaloid extracted from a South American arrow poison (STUD), and a similar substance, perhaps CURARE, was used to poison the Ferguson infant (SUSS).

Allahabad (*ahl-lah-hah-bahd'*), an ancient city of India, capital of the North-west Provinces, pop. 172,032. Young Edwards was sent here (VEIL).

*****Allan Brothers',** the principal land agents at Esher (WIST).

Allan Water, the name of two rivers in Scotland, one in Perthshire, the other in Roxburghshire. John McMurdo sang "On the Banks of Allan Water" (VALL).

Allardyce, a London butcher at whose establishment Holmes experimented with a pig and a whaling harpoon (BLAC).

*****Allegro, The,** presumably a London theatre, at which Flora Millar was at one time a dancer (NOBL).

Allen, Mrs., the housekeeper at Birlstone Manor (VALL).

Almoner, a dispenser of alms or charity. Sir Charles Baskerville upon occasion made Stapleton his almoner (HOUN).

Alpenstock, a long, stout staff pointed with iron, originally used by Alpine mountaineers and now generally adopted by mountain-climbers (EMPT, FINA). In some editions this word appears as *Alpine-stock.*

*****Alpha Inn,** a small public-house near the British Museum. Henry Baker was a member of the goose-club organized here (BLUE).

Alps. Even in the homely Alpine villages, Watson writes, Holmes did not forget the shadow of Professor Moriarty (FINA).

Altamont, the alias used by Holmes in his guise as an Irish-American spy for the Germans (LAST).

Alton, a town in Hampshire, pop. 5,479. Mrs. Oldmore was from here (HOUN).

Aluminium or **aluminum crutch,** an article associated with a singular affair Holmes investigated before his meeting with Watson (MUSG).

Amalgam, any alloy or mixture of mercury and some other metal. Lysander Stark's gang were said to use a hydraulic press to form an amalgam which they supposedly used in their counterfeiting (ENGR).

*****Amateur Mendicant Society,** an organization who held a luxurious club in the vault of a furniture warehouse, and which Holmes investigated in 1887 (FIVE).

Amati (*ah-mah'tee*), a family of Cremona, Italy, who manufactured violins in the sixteenth and seventeenth centuries. STRADIVARIUS was their pupil. Holmes spoke of Cremona violins, and the difference between a Stradivarius and an Amati (STUD).

Amazon River. J. Neil Gibson met his wife upon the banks of the Amazon (THOR); see MANAOS.

Amberley, Josiah (b. 1835), the retired colourman who murdered his wife **Mrs. Amberley** (*c.*1855–98) and her lover Ray ERNEST, then engaged Holmes out of "pure swank" to investigate her disappearance. Holmes suggested that he should be sent to Broadmoor Asylum rather than the gallows (RETI).

America: see CENTRAL AMERICA; NORTH AMERICA; SOUTH AMERICA; SPANISH AMERICA. The term is also used frequently in reference to the UNITED STATES.

*****"American Encyclopædia,"** the reference work in which Holmes turned up the article on the KU KLUX KLAN (FIVE).

American Exchange, a money-changing firm which has its London office in the Strand. Two letters from the Guion Steamship Company, addressed to the American Exchange to be left until called for, were found upon the body of Enoch Drebber (STUD).

Ames, the butler of Birlstone (VALL).

Amethyst. The King of Bohemia presented Holmes with a gold snuff-box with a great amethyst in the centre of the lid (IDEN).

Ammunition boots, boots of military issue, so called from the former meaning of *ammunition* as any military store or provision. The old soldier Holmes and his brother observed in Pall Mall was wearing his ammunition boots (GREE).

*****Amoy River,** a river in southern China, in the banks of which the blue carbuncle was found (BLUE).

Amsterdam, the chief city of the Netherlands, pop. (1900) 510,850. Count Sylvius planned to have the Mazarin diamond cut up here (MAZA).

Amyl, in chemistry, a form of carbon and hydrogen believed to exist in many compounds, e.g., NITRITE OF AMYL (RESI).

Analysis, the separation of anything into its elements. In logic it is the mode of resolving a compound idea into its simple parts in order to consider them more distinctly and to arrive at a more precise knowledge of the whole. Holmes characterized analysis as "reasoning backwards" (CARD, STUD), an allusion to the ancient Latin logicians' distinction between *synthesis* as a progression from principles to conse-

quences and *analysis* as a "regression" from consequences to principles. Holmes maintained that there are fifty people who can reason synthetically for one who can reason analytically (STUD). See DEDUCTION AND ANALYSIS.

Anarchism, a revolutionary philosophy, distinct from NIHILISM and SOCIALISM, setting forth as the social ideal the extreme form of individual freedom. The anarchists hold that all government is injurious and immoral, that the destruction of every social form now existing must be the first step to the creation of a new and just society. Much of the political violence committed since the sect's emergence about 1872 has been attributed to them.

Morse Hudson declared that no one but an Anarchist would go about smashing statues (SIXN).

Anatomy. Watson rated Holmes's knowledge of anatomy as "accurate, but unsystematic" (STUD), and some years later humorously recalled his evaluation (FIVE). Holmes was struck by the anatomical similarities between the female ear in the cardboard box and that of Susan Cushing (CARD), and both he and Watson instantly recognized the human femur showed them by John Mason (SHOS). Nathan Garrideb's museum was crowded with geological and anatomical specimens (3GAR).

The field of **comparative anatomy** relates to the study of animals with a view to comparing their structure with that of the human body or of other animals. Professor Morphy occupied the chair of Comparative Anatomy at Camford University (CREE), and Dr. Mortimer and Sir Charles Baskerville spent "many a charming evening" discussing what Mortimer called "the comparative anatomy of the Bushman and the Hottentot" (HOUN).

For anatomical features see ANEU- RISM; AORTIC VALVE; CAROTID ARTERY; CONDYLE; FEMUR; HAM; MITRAL VALVE; PINNA; SUBCLAVIAN ARTERY; TENDO ACHILLIS.

See also CRANIOLOGY; also PATHOL- OGY. See also BERTILLON SYSTEM; FIN- GERPRINT.

*Ancient Order of Freemen: see SCOWRERS.

Andaman Islands, a chain of islands on the east side of the Bay of Bengal, 680 miles south of the mouth of the Ganges. The European population is about 15,000, some 14,250 of whom are convicts. The native inhabitants, who number no more than 2,000, are small, generally much less than five feet, well formed, and active. The islands have been used since 1858 as a penal settle- ment by the Indian Government, the settlement being at Port Blair.

Major Sholto and Captain Morstan became involved in the Agra mystery when Jonathan Small was sentenced to the colony; Tonga was an An- damanese, but the description of the islands' inhabitants found in Holmes's gazetteer (SIGN), which perpetuates centuries-old tales about these natives, is almost wholly erroneous. Watson ever associated the Thames with the pursuit of the Andaman Islander (GOLD).

Anderson (d. 1900), a companion of Godfrey Emsworth who was killed at Diamond Hill (BLAN).

Anderson, the Fulworth constable who investigated Fitzroy McPherson's death (LION).

Anderson murders, a case in North Carolina which Holmes said was analo- gous to the Baskerville affair (HOUN).

The Andaman Islands.

Andover, a town in Hampshire, pop. 6,509. There was a parallel case to that of Mary Sutherland here in 1877 (IDEN).

Andrews, a Scowrer (VALL).

*Anerley Arms, the Norwood hotel

where John Hector McFarlane spent the night (NORW).

Aneurism, in pathology, a localized enlargement of an artery due to the pressure of the blood acting upon a part weakened by accident or disease. Jefferson Hope suffered from an **aortic aneurism,** an aneurism of the main artery which issues from the left ventricle of the heart (STUD).

Angel, Hosmer: see WINDIBANK, JAMES.

***Anglo-Indian Club,** a club to which Colonel Sebastian Moran belonged (EMPT).

Anglo-Saxons, the name commonly given to the people formed by the amalgamation of the Angles, the SAXONS, the Jutes, and other German tribes who settled in Britain in the fifth and sixth centuries A.D. In the trek of the Mormons from the Mississippi to Utah, every impediment was overcome, it was said, with "Anglo-Saxon tenacity" (STUD).

Aniseed, the aromatic seed of the Mediterranean anise plant, or a derivative of this seed. Holmes sprayed aniseed upon the hind wheel of Leslie Armstrong's brougham, so that Pompey might follow it (MISS).

Anna: see CORAM.

Anne, Queen: see QUEEN ANNE.

Anstruther, a doctor who looked after Watson's practice when he was away (BOSC). Watson also refers to his "accommodating neighbour" (FINA, STOC) as *Jackson* (CROO).

Antecedents, the earlier events, circumstances, associations, conduct, or avowed principles of one's life. Wilson Kemp was said to be a man of the "foulest antecedents" (GREE), the keeper of the Bar of Gold of the "vilest" (TWIS). Madame Charpentier declared that her son Arthur's an-

tecedents forbade his being a murderer (STUD). Holmes said that the influence of one's trade upon the hand was of great practical interest to the scientific detective in cases of unclaimed bodies or in discovering the antecedents of criminals (SIGN).

Anthony, or **Antonio,** the man-servant to the Stapletons (HOUN).

Anthropoid, or *ape,* the family of tail-less, manlike monkeys. Professor Presbury took the mysterious "Serum of Anthropoid" supplied him by Lowenstein (CREE).

"Anthropological Journal," properly **"Journal of the Anthropological Institute of Great Britain and Ireland,"** the journal of a society formed in 1871, to which the prefix *Royal* was added in 1906. Holmes claimed to have published two short monographs on ears in the *Anthropological Journal* (CARD).

Antimacassar, an ornamental covering for the backs and arms of chairs and sofas (CARD).

Antiquities: see PREHISTORIC MAN.

Antonio: see ANTHONY.

Aortic aneurism: see ANEURISM.

Aortic valve, one of the three valves between the aorta and the left ventricle of the heart. Thaddeus Sholto expressed confidence in his (SIGN).

Apache (*ah-pah'chah*), a warlike tribe of American Indians inhabiting parts of the south-western United States and northern Mexico, about five thousand of whom remain. Francis Hay Moulton was captured by them while prospecting in New Mexico (NOBL).

Apaches (*ah-pash'*), the name applied to the street-ruffians of Paris. Le Brun was crippled by them (ILLU).

Apoplexy, or stroke, the sudden loss of consciousnes caused by rupture of blood vessels in the brain. Colonel

Barclay (CROO) and Trevor Senior (GLOR) died of apoplexy.

Appledore, Sir Charles, the father of the Duchess of HOLDERNESSE (PRIO).

*****Appledore Towers,** the Hampstead house of Charles Augustus Milverton (CHAS).

Aqua tofana (*ahk'wah tō-fah'nah*), the name given to a secret poison supposedly concocted about the end of the seventeenth century by a Sicilian woman named Tofana, who confessed that no fewer than six hundred persons had been killed with it. The *Daily Telegraph* alluded airily to *aqua tofana* in its editorial about the Drebber murder (STUD).

Arab, street: see STREET ARAB; BAKER STREET IRREGULARS.

"Arabian Nights, The," or *The Thousand and One Nights,* a celebrated collection of Eastern tales, supposedly derived from India by way of Persia. The men from the confectioner, having laid out the cold supper for Mr. and Mrs. Francis Hay Moulton, vanished away, Watson said, like the genii of the Arabian Nights (NOBL), and he remarked upon the "Arabian Nights drawing-room" belonging to Isadora Klein (3GAB).

*****Arcadia,** the name of Watson's favourite tobacco mixture (CROO).

Archie: see ROSS, DUNCAN.

Architecture, styles: see GEORGIAN; QUEEN ANNE; TUDOR; VICTORIAN. See also GOTHIC ARCH; GROIN; PALLADIO.

Arctic Ocean. Peter Carey had commanded in the Arctic seas, and Holmes as Captain Basil sought harpooners for an Arctic expedition (BLAC).

Argentine Republic, or *Argentina,* a country of South America, est. pop. 5,000,000. "Argentine" was a heading in the Neligan notebook (BLAC). See also TIERRA DEL FUEGO.

Arizona, a territory in the southwestern part of the United States, pop. 122,212. Francis Hay Moulton prospected here for a time (NOBL).

Arkansas (*ahr-kan'zus*) **River,** a river of the United States, rising in Colorado and flowing through Kansas, Oklahoma, and Arkansas into the Mississippi River. Alexander Hamilton Garrideb was said to have invested in land along the Arkansas in southwestern Kansas west of Fort Dodge (3GAR).

Armitage, a gentleman residing near Reading. His second son **Percy Armitage** probably married Helen Stoner following the death of Dr. Grimesby Roylott (SPEC).

Armitage, James: see TREVOR.

Arms: see HERALDRY.

Armstrong, Leslie, one of the heads of the Cambridge medical school. The friend and confidant of Godfrey Staunton, he did his best to frustrate Holmes's search for the missing man out of a mistaken belief that the detective was in the employ of Lord Mount-James (MISS).

Army: see BRITISH ARMY; INDIAN ARMY.

Army coach, a private tutor who prepares men for entrance examinations into the officer corps, and officers themselves for examinations for promotion. Moriarty set up in London as an Army coach (FINA).

Army Medical Department, the name given to the medical service corps of the British Army as established in 1873, consisting of the men of the Army Hospital Corps and the commissioned medical officers of the Army Medical Staff Corps who commanded them in the field and for administration and training at NETLEY. The name of the Army Hospital Corps was changed in 1884 to Army Medical Corps, and in 1898 the whole of the medical service was united under the name *Royal Army Medical Corps.*

Watson joined the Army Medical Department following his becoming an M.D. in 1878 (STUD) and afterward called himself a "retired Army surgeon" (RESI, SIGN). Colonel Hayter had come under his care in Afghanistan (REIG), and Watson himself recuperated from his wound at the base hospital at Peshawur (STUD). Holmes remarked in 1914 that Watson was rejoining his old service (LAST).

Arnsworth Castle business, a case with which Holmes was involved prior to 1888, in which he used a bogus alarm of fire to discover a hiding-place (SCAN).

Arson, in law, the malicious burning of a dwelling-house or outhouse of another. John Hector McFarlane was suspected of murder and arson (NORW). Moriarty's men set fire to the Baker Street rooms, doing no great damage (FINA).

Art. Holmes suggested spending some time in one of the Bond Street picture-galleries (HOUN). Baron Gruner was a collector (ILLU), and Thaddeus Sholto considered himself a knowledgeable one (SIGN). Holder & Stevenson loaned money to many noble families upon the security of their pictures (BERY), and the Duke of Balmoral was compelled to sell the family art collection (NOBL). Laura Lyons's husband had been an artist (HOUN). Morse Hudson was a picture-dealer (SIXN), and the St. Pancras case involved a picture-frame maker (SHOS).

Watson said that Holmes had only the "crudest ideas" of art, but the detective denied it (HOUN), and indeed

it was he who made use of "a little art jargon" to title *A Study in Scarlet* (STUD). Holmes himself was descended from the French artist Vernet, and remarked that "art in the blood is liable to take the strangest forms" (GREE).

For schools of art see BELGIAN PAINTING; FRENCH PAINTING. For individual artists see BOUGUEREAU; COROT; DEVONSHIRE, GEORGIANA CAVENDISH, DUCHESS OF (Gainsborough); GREUZE; KNELLER; RAPHAEL SANTI; REYNOLDS; ROSA, SALVATOR; VERNET; WAINWRIGHT (Wainewright).

See also LONDON, subheaded *Cultural Life;* also PORTALIS; also CHRISTIE AND MANSON'S; SOTHEBY'S. See also COLOURMAN. See also NARA.

See also ARCHITECTURE; CERAMICS.

Arthur, Lord Saltire: see HOLDERNESSE, DUKE OF.

Asia. Holmes said it was very surprising that Victor Savage should have contracted an obscure Asiatic disease in the heart of London (DYIN). The Vermissa *Daily Herald* referred to the "effete monarchies" of the East (VALL). Colonel Hayter maintained a little armoury of Eastern weapons (REIG), and Thaddeus Sholto possessed some Oriental vases and other suggestions of Eastern luxury (SIGN).

See AFGHANISTAN; ANDAMAN ISLANDS; CEYLON; CHINA; DUTCH EAST INDIES; INDIA; JAPAN; NEPAUL; PERSIA; SIAM; SINGAPORE; SYRIA; TIBET; TURKEY.

Assault and battery. In law, *assault* is an attempt to inflict bodily injury upon another; *battery* is the actual infliction of the injury, or the consummation of the assault. See also MURDER.

Holmes was assaulted by Joseph Harrison (NAVA), the Cunninghams (REIG), and Jack Woodley (SOLI), and was attacked in Regent Street by two men with sticks (ILLU). In resisting arrest, Jefferson Hope assaulted Holmes, Watson, Gregson, and Lestrade (STUD). Count Sylvius would not deny that he had intended to assault the detective (MAZA). James Windibank threatened Holmes with an action for assault and illegal constraint (IDEN).

Henry Baker was attacked by street roughs (BLUE), and Trevor Senior went about in fear of an attack (GLOR). Peter Carey had been summoned for assault (BLAC), and Ronder was often fined for it (VEIL), while Dr. Grimesby Roylott narrowly escaped the consequences of attacking the local blacksmith (SPEC). Jack Woodley and Williamson were convicted of abduction and assault upon Violet Smith (SOLI). Holmes said that wanton assaults and purposeless outrages reported in the newspapers could often be traced back to Professor Moriarty (NORW), and the Spencer John gang specialized in assaults and intimidation (3GAB). The Folkestone Court page was cold-bloodedly "pistolled" (HOUN). Bob Carruthers made a murderous assault upon Jack Woodley (SOLI), Lysander Stark upon Victor Hatherley (ENGR). Mrs. Ferguson twice struck her stepson Jack (SUSS).

Assizes, the periodical sessions held by superior court judges who are directed to take the *assizes,* or verdicts, of juries, in each of the counties of England and Wales, for the purpose of trying criminal cases. Such court sessions are popularly called **The Assizes,** and may be simply defined as judicial sessions during which criminal trials by jury are held.

The Gibson murder was referred to the Assizes (THOR). Inspector Baynes expected to bring Don Murillo before the Guildford Assizes (WIST). James McCarthy (BOSC) and John Douglas (VALL) were acquitted at the Assizes, and Abe Slaney was condemned at the winter Assizes at Norwich (DANC). The case against John Horner was said to be referred to the Assizes (BLUE).

See also POLICE COURT; QUARTER SESSIONS.

Asteroids, a numerous group of very small planetoids revolving round the sun between the orbits of Mars and Jupiter. Professor Moriarty was the author of a book entitled *The Dynamics of an Asteroid* (VALL).

Aston Manor, a north-eastern suburb of Birmingham, pop. 77,326. Howard Garrideb supposedly had offices in Aston (3GAR).

Astrakhan, a very fine wool originating in Persia and Syria, and deriving its name from a city in European Russia. Charles Augustus Milverton wore a shaggy astrakhan overcoat (CHAS). The King of Bohemia's coat was decorated with bands of it (SCAN), and Thaddeus Sholto's topcoat had an astrakhan collar and cuffs (SIGN).

Astronomy. Holmes at one time professed to know nothing of the theories of Copernicus or the composition of the Solar System, and Watson rated his knowledge of astronomy as "nil" (STUD), an evaluation he recalled with much humour some years later (FIVE, HOUN), for Holmes demonstrated a knowledge of astronomy upon several occasions, discussing the obliquity of the ECLIPTIC (GREE) and remarking upon the PERSONAL EQUATION (MUSG). He declared that a planet might as well leave its orbit as for Mycroft to come to Baker Street (BRUC).

Old Frankland was an amateur astronomer (HOUN), and Inspector MacDonald once had a conversation about eclipses with Professor Moriarty, who had written *The Dynamics of an Asteroid* (VALL).

Atavism, also called *reversion* and *intermittent heredity,* in biology, the exhibition of ancestral characteristics; in pathology, the recurrence of any peculiarity or disease of a remote ancestor.

Holmes and Watson discussed the question of atavism and hereditary aptitudes (GREE). It was Holmes's theory, which Watson considered rather fanciful, that the individual represents in his development the whole procession of his ancestors, and that a turn to good or evil stands for some strong influence in the line of his pedigree; the person becomes, as it were, the epitome of the history of his own family, or so Holmes said in an effort to explain Sebastian Moran's character (EMPT). He believed too that Moriarty had hereditary tendencies of the most diabolical kind, that a criminal strain ran in the Professor's blood which was increased and rendered infinitely more dangerous by his extraordinary mental powers (FINA). He characterized Stapleton as a THROW-BACK to Hugo Baskerville (HOUN), and apparently believed his theory to explain his own intellectual abilities and those of his brother (GREE).

Holmes said that there was "some strange, outlandish blood" in Ian Murdoch (LION). Violence of temper approaching to mania was said to be he-

reditary in the men of the Roylott family (SPEC). Dr. Mortimer was the author of "Some Freaks of Atavism" and "Is Disease a Reversion?" (HOUN). See also ANTECEDENTS.

Athene, or *Athena,* called *Minerva* by the Romans, in classical mythology, the goddess of the intellectual powers (CHAS).

Athens, the capital city of Greece, est. pop. 110,000. Paul and Sophy Kratides were from here (GREE).

Atkinson, brothers whose singular tragedy at Trincomalee was investigated by Holmes (SCAN).

Atlanta, the capital city of the state of Georgia, est. pop. (1904) 105,000. John and Effie Hebron had lived here (YELL).

Atlantic Ocean. The captain of the *Gloria Scott* was found dead with his head on a chart of the Atlantic (GLOR), and the barque *Lone Star* was lost in an Atlantic gale (FIVE). One of the London society papers protested humorously the marriage of girls from across the Atlantic into the noble houses of Great Britain (NOBL). John Ferrier was thought by many to have had an early affair with a girl who pined away on the shores of the Atlantic (STUD).

From a drop of water, Holmes maintained, a logician could infer the possibility of an Atlantic or a Niagara without having seen or heard of one or the other (STUD).

See also ARCTIC OCEAN.

At scratch: see SCRATCH.

Attaché, a member of the diplomatic service attached to an embassy or legation at a foreign court. Douglas Maberley was an attaché at Rome (3GAB).

Atwood, a Vermissa Valley ironworks-owner who was forced to sell out (VALL).

Auckland, a town of New Zealand, pop. 34,216. Mary Sutherland's uncle Ned apparently lived here until his death (IDEN).

*Audley Court, an unattractive quadrangle near KENNINGTON PARK GATE, where John Rance lived (STUD).

Aurora, the name of Mordecai Smith's steam launch (SIGN).

Australia, the smallest of the continents, pop. 3,600,000. Since 1901 it has

Australia and New Zealand.

been a federated commonwealth composed of its six former British colonies.

Lady Mary Brackenstall (ABBE) and Holy Peters (LADY) were Australians, and James Wilder promised to seek his fortune here (PRIO). The barque *Gloria Scott* was transporting

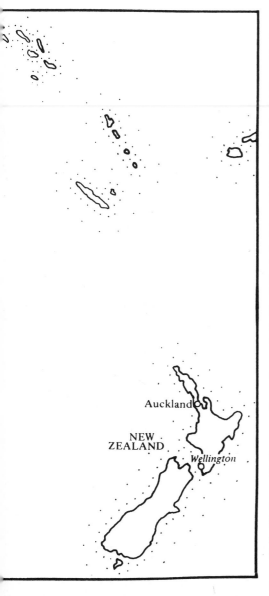

Auckland

NEW
ZEALAND

Wellington

convicts to Australia, where Trevor Senior and Beddoes prospered in the gold-fields (GLOR). Old Turner was once a prospector and then a bushranger here, where he first met Charles McCarthy (BOSC). The Earl of Maynooth was governor of one of the Australian colonies in 1894 (EMPT).

See also SOUTH AUSTRALIA; VICTORIA; also ADELAIDE; BALLARAT; MELBOURNE; SYDNEY.

Austria-Hungary, a dual kingdom situated in the south-eastern part of Europe, pop. (1900) 45,359,204. The Austro-Hungarian monarchy consists of two separate governments, whose only bond of union, practically speaking, is the ruler, FRANZ JOSEPH, who is at once Emperor of Austria and King of Hungary. See the map of EUROPE.

The letter from Lowenstein to Professory Presbury bore an Austrian stamp (CREE), and Baron Gruner was himself an Austrian (ILLU). BUDA-PESTH is in Hungary (GREE). "Vampirism in Hungary" was an entry in Holmes's index (SUSS). See also PRAGUE; also BOHEMIA; TRANSYLVANIA.

Automobile: see BENZ; FORD; see also CHAUFFEUR.

Aveling, the mathematical master at the Priory School (PRIO).

Avenging Angels: see DANITES.

Ayrshires, a Stock Exchange term referring to the stock of the *Glasgow and South-Western Railway* (STOC).

Azof (*ah-zof'*), or **Azov, Sea of,** an arm of the Black Sea lying east of the Crimea. Admiral Green had commanded the Sea of Azof fleet in the Crimean War (LADY).

Azure, in heraldry, the colour blue (NOBL); see HERALDRY.

B

B, in Baker Street address: see BAKER STREET.

B Division, one of the twenty-two administrative divisions of the Metropolitan Police. Its 5.17 square miles include parts of south Kensington and the south-western section of Westminster; see the map accompanying SCOTLAND YARD. Inspector Bradstreet was assigned here (BLUE).

B Squadron, the squadron of Middlesex Corps, Imperial Yeomanry, in which James Dodd and Godfrey Emsworth served (BLAN).

Baboon, a common name applied to a division of Old World monkeys and apes, almost all of which are confined to Africa. Dr. Grimesby Roylott had a passion for "Indian" animals, and kept a baboon which wandered freely over the grounds at Stoke Moran (SPEC). Watson writes that Beppo's face resembled that of a baboon (SIXN) and that Enoch Drebber had a "baboon-like" countenance (STUD).

Back, in Rugby, a position behind the line of forwards, or a player in this position, called a *half-back, three-quarter-back,* or *full-back,* according to the distance from the forwards. "The back," however, is the *full-back,* a single individual who maintains the last line of defense, either to tackle an opponent who has managed to get through the other players, or, more usually, to catch and return long kicks. Robert Ferguson had had a "fine turn of speed which had carried him round many an opposing back" (SUSS). See HALF-BACK; THREE-QUARTER.

Back, injury: see HACK.

Backgammon, a common board game (FIVE).

Backwater, Lord, a guest at the wedding of Lord Robert St. Simon, to whom he recommended Holmes (NOBL). He was the owner of the Capleton stables, and his horse Desborough was beaten in the Wessex Plate by Silver Blaze (SILV).

Baden, a celebrated health-spa in the grand duchy of Baden, near the Rhine, pop. (1900) 15,700. Lady Frances Carfax made the acquaintance of the Shlessingers here (LADY).

Badger. There was a badger at old Sherman's (SIGN).

*Bagatelle Card Club, the London club, of which they were members, where Ronald Adair and Colonel Sebastian Moran played whist upon the evening of Adair's murder (EMPT).

Bain, Sandy, a jockey at the Shoscombe stables (SHOS).

Baize, a very light, coarse woollen material with a nap on one side, dyed in plain colours and used for table-covers, curtains, and draperies. The inner doors of St. Luke's College were decorated with green baize (3STU), the practice of covering door-panels with the material formerly having been greatly in fashion. A "green baize," possibly a PORTIÈRE, possibly a baized door, marked Don Murillo's bedroom (WIST).

Baker, Henry, a member of the Alpha Inn's goose-club, whose Christmas goose, unknown to him, had the blue carbuncle in its crop. His wife **Mrs. Henry Baker,** according to Holmes, had ceased to love him (BLUE).

Baker Street, the most famous of all London streets, the residence of Sherlock Holmes from the beginning of the 1880s to 1903, during the greater part of his professional life as a consulting detective.

Baker Street is situated in the heart of the West End, in the metropolitan borough of St. Marylebone, and extends approximately north and south for just over a quarter of a mile. Its southern continuation *Orchard Street* extends to Oxford Street. To the north it bears the names *York Place* and then *Upper Baker Street* before reaching Regent's Park. It consists of large, closely built, flat-fronted, four-storey Georgian houses which are now divided between residences and business establishments. The street is known commercially for the large numbers of photographers who have their studios here.

Baker Street was laid out late in the eighteenth century by a Dorsetshire businessman and speculator, *Edward Berkeley Portman* (1771–1823), whose son *Edward Berkeley, 1st Viscount Portman* (1799–1888) and grandson *William Henry Berkeley, 2nd Viscount Portman* (1829–1919) continue to own the land upon which much of this

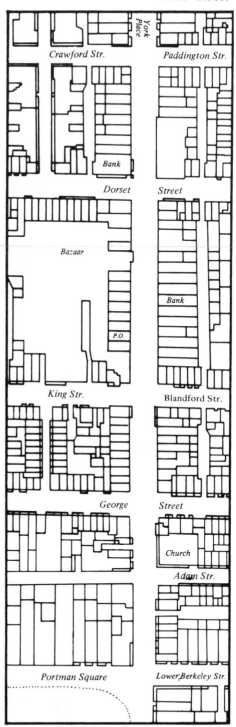

Baker Street.

The view northward along Baker Street from the corner at Dorset Street.

quarter of London is built. The thoroughfare is named for a Dorsetshire baronet and friend of the Portman family, *Sir Edward Baker* (*c.* 1763–1825).

The houses here are numbered consecutively, south to north, from No. 1 to No. 42 upon the east side and southward from No. 44 to No. 85 upon the west. There is no No. 43, nor is there a No. 221. Sherlock Holmes's legendary address, **221b Baker Street,** is clearly a disguise for the actual number. The B represents the French designation *bis,* meaning that the address is a subsidiary one, in this case on an upper floor, Holmes's landlady Mrs. HUDSON being in residence upon the ground floor.

Holmes and Watson first met to go partners in the Baker Street rooms (STUD), for which the detective's payments, it was said in later years, were "princely" (DYIN). The quarters were set fire to by Moriarty's men, doing no great damage (FINA), and Mycroft Holmes kept them up during his brother's absence from England (EMPT). The details given in the telling of the Mazarin diamond case (MAZA) would seem very untrustworthy.

See also BOW-WINDOW; FANLIGHT; LUMBER-ROOM; also ELECTRICITY; GAS; TELEPHONE.

For household furnishings see BASKET CHAIR; COAL-SCUTTLE; GASOGENE; PERSIAN SLIPPER; SIDEBOARD; SPIRIT-LAMP; STUDENT LAMP; see also BEAR (bearskin hearthrug); CHEMISTRY; DEAL (chemical corner); COCAINE; TOBACCO (Holmes's bedroom); JACK-KNIFE; PIPE (mantelpiece); V.R. See also BEECHER, HENRY WARD; GORDON, GEN. CHARLES GEORGE. See also CAMDEN HOUSE; PLANE TREE.

See also HUDSON, MRS.; TURNER, MRS.; also BILLY; PAGE.

See also Maps I and III of LONDON.

Baker Street Irregulars, a group of street Arabs recruited by Holmes for searching London. They found Jefferson Hope's cab (STUD) and the steam launch *Aurora* (SIGN), and watched over Henry Wood at Aldershot (CROO). He paid them a shilling a day with a guinea bonus to the one who found the object of their search, plus expenses (SIGN), and said there was more work to be got out of them and their leader Wiggins than out of a dozen of the official force (STUD). "The mere sight of an official-looking person seals men's lips," he said (STUD). These youngsters, however, "go everywhere, see everything, overhear everyone" (SIGN). All they wanted, said Holmes, was organization (STUD), and this he provided them to his own advantage. See AGENCY.

Baker Street Station, a London railway station, located at the northern end of Baker Street. Operated by the METROPOLITAN RAILWAY line, the station nonetheless practically ranks among the larger termini, since one may travel some distance into the Midlands from here. Watson observed Alexander Holder coming down Baker Street from the direction of the Metropolitan station, where Holder had arrived after taking the UNDERGROUND from Scotland Yard (BERY).

Baldwin, Ted, a Scowrer. Imprisoned through the efforts of Birdy Edwards, he sought later to murder Edwards in England but was himself killed (VALL).

Baldwin Club, a club in Pall Mall. Ronald Adair was a member (EMPT).

Ballarat, a city and gold-field in Victoria colony, Australia, the centre of one of the richest gold-yielding regions in the world, pop. of the district 44,766. Watson had been here (SIGN), and John Turner had been

known as "Black Jack of Ballarat" (BOSC).

Ballarat Gang, the gang of bushrangers to which John Turner belonged (BOSC).

Balmoral, Duke of, an English peer, of the *St. Simon* family, at one time Secretary for Foreign Affairs. The family were somewhat impoverished, and Balmoral in later life was compelled to sell the family art collection (NOBL). His horse Iris ran in the Wessex Cup but finished a bad third (SILV). He apparently did not attend the wedding of his second son Lord Robert ST. SIMON, though his wife the **Duchess of Balmoral,** his third son **Lord Eustace St. Simon,** and his daughter **Lady Clara St. Simon** were present (NOBL). Ronald Adair won a large sum at cards from *Lord Balmoral* (EMPT), which is improper terminology when referring to a duke.

Balmoral Castle is a favourite residence of Queen Victoria, built 1854 in Scotland, some forty-five miles west of Aberdeen.

Balzac, Honoré de (1799–1850), the greatest of French novelists, author of the series of novels called *The Human Comedy.* Hosmer Angel quoted him in one of his letters to Mary Sutherland (IDEN).

Bang, drug: see BHANG.

*Bangalore Pioneers: see FIRST BENGALORE PIONEERS.

Bangor, a seaport in the north of Wales, pop. 11,269. There are extensive slate-quarries nearby. Carston Castle was here (PRIO).

Bank. Trevor Senior entered a London banking-house as a young man (GLOR). Elias Openshaw left some £14,000 to his credit at the bank (FIVE), and Watson referred Baron Gruner to his bankers (ILLU). Blessington did not believe in bankers and said he would never trust one, possibly because he was a former bank robber (RESI). Lord Mount-James put his plate in the bank (MISS).

A once-depleted bank-account (CARD)† perhaps explains Watson's cheque-book being locked in Holmes's desk (DANC). Holmes examined Jonas Oldacre's bank-book (NORW). A random sample of Moriarty's cheques showed them to be drawn upon six different banks, and Holmes suspected he had twenty accounts (VALL).

The firm of *Holder & Stevenson* was the second largest private banking concern in the City (BERY), and *Dawson & Neligan* was a Cornish banking-house (BLAC). Lady Frances Carfax banked at *Silvester's* (LADY). Holmes thwarted the robbery of London's *City and Suburban Bank* (REDH). CROSBY was a banker (GOLD).

See also BANK OF ENGLAND; BANK OF FRANCE; CAPITAL AND COUNTIES BANK; COX & CO.; CRÉDIT LYONNAIS; DEUTSCHE BANK; POST OFFICE SAVINGS BANK.

See also LOMBARD STREET; also AMERICAN EXCHANGE; COOK'S TOURIST OFFICES.

Bank of England, the most important banking institution of England, incorporated in 1694 as a joint-stock association. It is the only bank in London which has the power to issue paper money, and it acts as the principal business agent for the Government. The Bank building in the City, fronting upon Threadneedle Street, was opened in 1834. See the map of the CITY.

There was £1,000 in Bank of Eng-

† This allusion is inserted in "The Resident Patient" in some editions.

land notes in Elsie Cubitt's hand-bag (DANC). Killer Evans said that no one could tell a Prescott counterfeit note from a Bank of England (3GAR). See the bottom photograph on p. 75.

Bank of France, the national bank of France, established in 1800 upon a basis similar to that of the Bank of England. The City and Suburban Bank stengthened its resources by borrowing £30,000 from the Bank of France (REDH).

Bannister, the servant to Hilton Soames. He had once been Sir Jabez Gilchrist's butler and so attempted to shield his former employer's son from a charge of cheating (3STU).

Bar, to object to a person or action. James Dodd said that he "barred" Colonel Emsworth (BLAN).

Barberton, a town of the South African Republic, or the Transvaal, pop. (1904) 2,433. The chief town of a district of the same name, it was founded in 1886 and owes its existence to the discovery of gold in the region. Philip Green made his money here (LADY).

Barcarolle, the name given in English to a song sung by Venetian *barcaruoli,* or boatmen, as they pole their gondalas; or a song or piece of music composed in imitation of such songs; e.g., the HOFFMANN BARCAROLLE (MAZA).

Barcelona, a port and one of the chief cities of Spain, pop. (1900) 533,000. Don Murillo had stayed here (WIST).

Barclay, Colonel James, a British soldier who rose from sergeant to command of his regiment. During the Indian Mutiny he betrayed to the Sepoys a rival in love, Henry WOOD, and was struck dead with apoplexy at Wood's reappearance thirty years later. His wife **Nancy Barclay,** the former *Nancy*

Devoy, was the daughter of a regimental colour-sergeant, and it was for her that Barclay betrayed Wood (CROO).

Barclay Square: see BERKELEY SQUARE.

Bardle, an inspector in the Sussex constabulary, assigned to investigate the death of Fitzroy McPherson (LION).

Barelli, Augusto, a well-known Italian lawyer and deputy. His daughter Emilia married Gennaro LUCCA (REDC).

Bari, a seaport of southern Italy, pop. 77,478. The Luccas were married here (REDC).

Baritsu, properly **Bartitsu,** the system of self-defense introduced from Japan into England by *E. W. Barton-Wright,* after whom the method is called, in 1899. Holmes defeated Moriarty at Reichenbach through his knowledge of "baritsu, or the Japanese system of wrestling" (EMPT). While Moriarty's death predated the Barton-Wright system by eight years, Japanese techniques were known at the time, and publication of "The Adventure of the Empty House" in 1903 followed shortly after the first notice of "Bartitsu" in *Pearson's* magazine for March and April 1899, resulting in Watson's commission of an anachronism in authoring the tale. The name "Bartitsu" is a clever variation of *bujitsu,* the Japanese word for martial arts.

Bark, ship: see BARQUE.

E. W. Barton-Wright, shown at left, demonstrates the way to overthrow an assailant through a sound knowledge of balance and leverage as applied to human anatomy. The defensive art of "Bartitsu" is an elaboration of Japanese methods, and these photographs, first published in Pearson's magazine for April 1899, were taken in Japan.

Barker, a London private detective, Holmes's friend and "hated rival upon the Surrey shore." He was engaged by Ray Ernest's family to investigate Ernest's disappearance (RETI).

Barker, Cecil James, a long-time friend and former partner of John Douglas, and a conspirator in the Birlstone affair (VALL).

Barking Level, the largely uninhabited Essex bank of the Thames immediately below the Albert Dock. The police launch caught the *Aurora* between Barking Level and the Plumstead Marshes (SIGN). See the front endpaper map.

Barnes, Josiah, the keeper of the Green Dragon Inn (SHOS).

Barney, in English slang, a prizefight in which there is some element of chicanery or unfairness; hence, any conflict in which one of the participants is at a disadvantage. James Dodd said that he and Colonel Emsworth had "a bit of a barney" (BLAN) in the colonel's study.

Barnicot, Dr., a London practitioner, both of whose Napoleonic busts were smashed by Beppo (SIXN).

*Bar of Gold, The, the riverside opium den in the City from which Neville St. Clair vanished (TWIS).

Barometer. Holmes consulted the barometer at the Hereford Arms, remarking that the glass kept high (BOSC). An oak barometer was stolen from the house of old Acton (REIG), and Watson was impressed by the tranquillity suggested by the barometer at Mrs. Cecil Forrester's (SIGN).

Baron, in Great Britain, the title of a nobleman holding the lowest rank in the PEERAGE (MAZA, PRIO). On the Continent, too, especially in France, Germany, and Austria, a baron is a member of the lowest order of hereditary nobility (ILLU, LAST, REIG).

Baronet, a British title of hereditary rank next below that of a baron, and thus not conferring a peerage. A baronet is addressed in the same manner as a knight. The order was founded by James I in 1611. Sir Eustace Brackenstall (ABBE) and Sir Robert Norberton (SHOS) were baronets, as were the Baskervilles (HOUN) and possibly the Falders (SHOS).

Barouche (*bah-roosh'*), a four-wheeled carriage having a low body, two inside seats facing one another front-to-back, and an outer seat for the

Barouche.

driver. It has a folding top for the passengers which may be lowered in fine weather. Lady Beatrice Falder kept a barouche (SHOS).

Barque (*bark*), a type of three-masted sailing-ship. The *Gloria Scott* was such a vessel (GLOR), as were the *Lone Star* and *Sophy Anderson* (FIVE). In some editions the word is Americanized *bark*.

Barraud & Lunds, a London watchmaking firm. A Barraud watch was found upon the body of Enoch Drebber (STUD).

Barrel, rifle: see STOCK.

Barrett, the London police-constable who discovered the body of Eduardo Lucas (SECO).

Barrister, in England, the term applied to a member of the highest class of lawyers who have the exclusive right to plead in the superior courts and at the Assizes. The particular business of the barrister is the advocacy of causes in open court, and, except in criminal cases, he may not undertake a case without the intervention of a SOLICI-TOR, who acts as the medium between the barrister and the general public and who actually prepares the cause for trial. Every barrister must belong to one of the four ancient societies known as the *Inns of Court*—Gray's Inn, Lincoln's Inn, the Middle Temple, or the Inner Temple; see TEMPLE, THE.

Joyce Cummings was a rising barrister (THOR). Since Godfrey Norton was a lawyer whose chambers were in the Inner Temple it is certain that he too was one (SCAN). Both Holmes (HOUN) and Watson (ILLU) remarked upon the barrister's power of intense mental concentration.

Barrow, a mound of earth or stones raised over a grave, among the most important monuments of primitive antiquity. Dr. Mortimer excavated a Dartmoor barrow (HOUN). The singular contents of an ancient British barrow seem associated with the Addle-

Long barrow.

ton tragedy (GOLD). There were a number of "irregular mounds" upon the moors of Cornwall (DEVI).

Barrymore, John, the butler of Baskerville Hall, son of the old caretaker, whose family had looked after the Hall for four generations. His wife **Eliza**

Barrymore was the sister of the convict SELDEN (HOUN).

Barton, the Scotland Yard inspector who took charge of the St. Clair case (TWIS).

Barton, Dr. Hill, Watson's alias in his interview with Baron Gruner (ILLU).

*****Barton's Crossing,** one of the towns of Vermissa Valley (VALL).

Barts, or **Bart's:** see ST. BARTHOLO-MEW'S HOSPITAL.

Baryta, in chemistry, an oxide of barium. **Bisulphate of baryta,** a sample of which Holmes claimed to analyse (IDEN), cannot exist.

Basalt, a variety of rock the tendency of which to crystallize in columns gives a peculiar character to the scenery in which it is found. John and Lucy Ferrier, led by Jefferson Hope, passed long basaltic columns during their escape from Utah (STUD).

Basil, Captain, the alias used by Holmes in his investigation of the Peter Carey murder (BLAC).

Baskerville, a Devonshire family residing at BASKERVILLE HALL on Dartmoor. A family legend held that **Hugo Baskerville** (d. *c.*1647) was killed by an agent of the devil in the form of a gigantic hound, and the tale was perpetuated by a descendent **Hugo Baskerville** (*fl.* 1742), who wrote out the legend as a moral lesson for his sons **Rodger Baskerville** and **John Baskerville,** with a caution to say nothing to their sister **Elizabeth Baskerville.** Later **Rear-Admiral Baskerville** (*fl.* 1782) served in the West Indies, and **Sir William Baskerville** (*fl.* 1800) sat in the House of Commons. Sir William may have been the first baronet.

Sir Charles Baskerville (d. 1889) restored the lost fortune of the Baskervilles and lived at Baskerville Hall for only a short time before his death. His two younger brothers were both dead; one had lived on the south coast of England, and the youngest, **Rodger Baskerville** (d. 1876), had gone to Central or South America. Sir Charles was succeeded by a Canadian nephew, **Sir Henry Baskerville,** son of Sir Charles's younger brother, in whose interests Holmes acted as he pursued STAPLETON, who was himself the son of Rodger Baskerville (HOUN).

*Baskerville Hall, the ancestral home of the Baskervilles, located on Dartmoor, not far from the hamlet of Grimpen. The prosperity of the countryside depended upon a tenant of the Hall, which Sir Charles Baskerville had been rebuilding (HOUN).

Baskervilles, Hound of the, the devilish hound said to have killed Hugo Baskerville and thereafter to be responsible for the sudden, bloody, and mysterious deaths which supposedly plagued the Baskervilles. STAPLETON used the legend to murder Sir Charles Baskerville and attempt murder upon Sir Henry Baskerville. The hound he purchased for this purpose, said to be a cross between a mastiff and a bloodhound, was shot by Holmes (HOUN).

Basket chair, a chair made of wickerwork. There was a basket chair at Baker Street (BLUE, NOBL), at Mrs. Cecil Forrester's (SIGN), and at The Cedars (TWIS). See the illustration on p. 248.

Basle, properly **Basel,** a city in the north of Switzerland, located on the Rhine, pop. (1900) 109,169. Holmes and Watson made their way into Switzerland by way of Basle (FINA).

*Bass Rock, the steamer commanded by Captain Jack Croker (ABBE).

Bates, Marlow, the manager of J. Neil Gibson's estate, who warned Holmes against his employer (THOR).

Bath-chair, an invalid's chair on wheels, intended to be pushed by an attendant (GOLD).

The three-wheeled Bath-chair, so named from the resort town where it originated, may be pushed by an attendant or with minor modifications may be drawn by a pony.

Bathing-cot, a small boat used by ocean-bathers (LION).

Bathsheba, in the Bible (*II Sam.* 11), the wife of URIAH, taken into the harem of King David after her husband's death, and later mother of Solomon. Holmes referred to the story of David and Bathsheba (CROO).

Battery, the smallest division of artillery for tactical purposes, consisting generally of four to eight guns, and commanded by a captain. There was a battery of artillery at Agra (SIGN), and half a battery at Bhurtee (CROO).

Baxter, Edith, the maid of John Straker (SILV).

Baxter, Richard (1615–1691), an

eminent Nonconformist divine. Holmes claimed to be thinking of Baxter's words when he said: "There, but for the grace of God, goes Sherlock Holmes" (BOSC). Holmes's words, however, were actually a paraphrase of the remark traditionally ascribed to *John Bradford* (1510–1555), Protestant preacher and martyr.

Bay, a reddish or brownish-red horse (SILV).

Bay, The, the **Bay of Biscay,** that part of the Atlantic Ocean which lies between France and Spain. Before the *Gloria Scott* had crossed "the Bay" almost all the convicts on board were aware of the mutinous conspiracy (GLOR).

Bayard, a horse belonging to Colonel Ross, scratched from the Wessex Cup (SILV). The name derives from *bayard,* a bay horse.

Baynes, Inspector, an official of the Surrey constabulary. His investigation of the Wisteria Lodge case was at least as successful as Holmes's (WIST).

Bayswater bus, the name applied to any of the London omnibuses plying a number of routes between the East End and Hammersmith. The name derives from the fashionable quarter of *Bayswater,* once the western-most end of the line. Lord Mount-James took a Bayswater bus to Bentley's private hotel (MISS).

Bay window, a window forming a bay or recess in a room, projecting outward and rising from the ground or basement on a straight-sided plan. There was a bay window in the study of Appledore Towers (CHAS). See also BOW-WINDOW.

Beagle. Pompey appeared to be something between a beagle and a foxhound (MISS).

Bear. Jefferson Hope found signs of bear in the Utah wilderness (STUD). There was a bearskin hearthrug at Baker Street (PRIO). The *grizzly bear,* one of the largest and most savage of the family, was one of the few inhabitants of the Great Alkali Plain (STUD).

Beat, in sailing, to make progress against the wind by a series of alternate tacks in a zigzag line; see TACK. Jonathan Small said he and Tonga were "beating about" the Bay of Bengal for ten days before they were picked up (SIGN).

*Beauchamp (*beech'm*) **Arriance,** a lonely wood near Poldhu Bay in Cornwall, where Leon Sterndale spent his days between his African expeditions (DEVI).

Beaune (*bōn*), a red Burgundy wine. Watson drank it at lunch (SIGN).

Becher, Dr., the accomplice of Colonel Lysander Stark, and owner of the house at Eyford. He was introduced to Victor Hatherley as *Ferguson* (ENGR).

Beckenham (*beck'en-um*), a suburb of London, pop. 26,331. Located in Kent, it retains some of its rural character. Harold Latimer lived here (GREE). See the back endpaper map.

Beddington, the name of two brothers who attempted a daring stock robbery. While one kept Hall PYCROFT in Birmingham under the aliases of *Arthur Pinner* and *Harry Pinner,* the other Beddington impersonated Pycroft in London and attempted to rob Mawson & Williams' of £100,000 in bonds, murdering the watchman in the attempt. The robber was captured, and his brother then attempted suicide (STOC).

Beddoes, a country squire residing in

Hampshire. His real name was *Evans*. He survived the destruction of the *Gloria Scott* and prospered with TREVOR SENIOR in the Australian goldfields before returning to England. Blackmailed by the sailor HUDSON, he disappeared when he believed himself betrayed. His open-code note to Trevor caused the latter's death by apoplexy (GLOR).

Bedford, the county-town of Bedfordshire, pop. 35,144. The south midland county of **Bedfordshire,** pop. 171,-240, is mostly agricultural. Tuxbury Old Park was in Bedfordshire near the city (BLAN).

Bee, specifically the *honey-bee*. Holmes retired to study and bee-farming upon the South Downs (SECO) and penned the *Practical Handbook of Bee Culture* (LAST). Crusts of beeswax round his lips helped him appear to be dying (DYIN).

The bee is often held to be the very type of the busy worker or of industrious endeavour; e.g., COMPOUND OF THE BUSY BEE AND EXCELSIOR (CREE). The Mormons chose the bee, to them too a symbol of industry, for their emblem (STUD).

Beech. The largest tree in the neighbourhood of Boscombe Pool was a great beech (BOSC). A young beech stood in the grounds of Pondicherry Lodge (SIGN). There were many upon the estate at Hurlstone (MUSG), and the Birlstone Manor park was famous for its beeches (VALL). Jephro Rucastle's home took its name from the COPPER BEECH (COPP). There were HAZEL trees near Wisteria Lodge (WIST).

Beecher, Henry Ward (1813–1887), a noted American preacher. He is best remembered in England for his moderating influence upon the British atti-

Henry Ward Beecher.

tude toward the North during the American Civil War. Watson possessed an unframed portrait of him (CARD).†

Beer, in England, any malt liquor; on the Continent and in America, lager beer only. Holmes and Watson drank beer at the Alpha Inn (BLUE), and Holmes declared his wish for beer after a day on the Irene Adler case (SCAN). Mrs. St. Clair was a brewer's daughter (TWIS). Grant Munro was a hop merchant (YELL). See also ALEHOUSE; HALF-AND-HALF.

Beeswax: see BEE.

Beeswing (*beez'wing*), a shining, filmy crust formed in port and some other wines, indicative of age, so called from its gauzy resemblance to bees' wings (ABBE).

Befrogged: see FROGGED.

Beige (*baij*), a variety of thin wool. Violet Hunter was asked to wear a blue beige dress (COPP), and Mary Morstan wore a dress of sombre greyish

† This allusion is inserted in "The Resident Patient" in some editions.

beige when she first called upon Holmes (SIGN).

Belfast, a seaport of northern Ireland, pop. 348,965. The cardboard box was mailed from here (CARD).

Belgian painting, modern, the works of the modern Belgian school, exhibiting a strong sense of contrast or harmony of colouring, and characterized by a free, bold style of brushwork in a revival of the traditions of the old Flemish school. Holmes was entirely absorbed in the pictures of the modern Belgian masters (HOUN).

Belgium, a lowland kingdom of Europe, pop. (1900) 6,815,054. Baron Von Herling considered the possibility that England might leave Belgium to her fate when the Germans invaded upon 4 August 1914, this despite the treaty which since 1839 had guaranteed Belgian neutrality (LAST). See the map of EUROPE.

Belgrade, the capital city of the Balkan kingdom of Serbia, pop. (1900) 69,097. A memorandum from Belgrade was in Trelawney Hope's dispatch-box (SECO). See the map of EUROPE.

Belladonna, a poisonous plant native to Great Britain. Watson rated Holmes's knowledge of botany "variable" but said he was "well up in belladonna, opium, and poisons generally" (STUD). Holmes put belladonna in his eyes to enhance the appearance of illness by dilating the pupils and producing a glistening appearance which gives the illusion of deep fever (DYIN).

Bellamy, Tom, a Fulworth businessman in partnership with his son **William Bellamy.** His daughter **Maud Bellamy** was secretly engaged to Fitzroy McPherson (LION).

Belle dame sans merci, an expression meaning, literally, *fair lady without*

mercy. It is the title of a long poem by the French writer Alain Chartier (*c*.1385–*c*.1433), the English translation of which, appearing in 1532, was long attributed to Chaucer. A dialogue between a tormented lover and the cruel lady whom he adores, "La Belle Dame sans Merci" set a literary fashion and inspired a work of the same title by the English poet John Keats (1795–1821) which was first published in 1888. Holmes characterized Isadora Klein as "the *'belle dame sans merci'* of fiction" (3GAB).

Bellinger, Lord, the second-term Premier who called upon Holmes to recover the stolen Trelawney Hope document (SECO).

Belliver Tor, properly **Bellever Tor,** a Dartmoor tor (HOUN).

Belminster, Duke of, the father of Lady Hilda Trelawney Hope (SECO).

Belmont Place, a group of houses at the corner of the Wandsworth Road and Nine Elms Lane. Holmes and Watson passed here in pursuit of Jonathan Small (SIGN). See Map IV of LONDON.

Benares (*beh-nahr'ez*), a city in India, located on the left bank of the Ganges, pop. 209,331. It is the headquarters and most holy city of the Hindu religion, and is famous for the textiles and jewellery produced here. The Agra treasure was in a chest of Benares metal-work (SIGN).

Bench of bishops, a collective designation of the bishops who represent the Church of England in the House of Lords. Watson writes that Baron Gruner's butler "would have adorned a bench of bishops" (ILLU), an allusion either to his costume or to his solemnity.

Bender (d. 1847), a member of the Ferrier wagon party, the first to die when the party became lost on the Great Alkali Plain (STUD).

Benefit club, an association for the purpose of forming a fund for the assistance of members in sickness, or of their families in case of death. The Ancient Order of Freemen was in part a benefit club (VALL).

Bengal, Bay of, that portion of the Indian Ocean which lies between the Indian and the Indo-Chinese peninsulas. The Andaman Islands are situated here (SIGN).

Bengal Artillery, a regiment of the Bengal Army prior to the Indian Mutiny. It ceased to exist in the military reorganization which followed the Mutiny, artillery duties in India being transferred directly to the British Army. Major-General Stoner served with the Bengal Artillery (SPEC). There was a BATTERY of artillery at Agra (SIGN), half a battery at Bhurtee (CROO). See also INDIAN ARMY.

Bengal Fusiliers: see THIRD BENGAL FUSILIERS.

*Bengalore Pioneers: see FIRST BENGALORE PIONEERS.

*Benito Canyon, a canyon in California, where Cecil Barker and John Douglas were partners in a mining claim (VALL).

Bennett, Trevor ("Jack") (b. 1873), the assistant and secretary to Professor Presbury, and fiancé of Edith Presbury, who consulted Holmes over his employer's singular behaviour (CREE).

Bentinck Street, a short street in the West End, running between Marylebone Lane and Welbeck Street. Holmes was nearly run down by a van at the corner of Bentinck and Welbeck streets (FINA). See Map III of LONDON.

*Bentley's, a private hotel in London, located near the Strand, where the Cambridge Rugby team stayed (MISS).

Benz, a German make of automobile manufactured 1885–1926 by *Karl Benz* (1844–1929), who designed and built the first practical internal-combustion engine automobile in 1885 (LAST).

Beppo, the former sculptor and known ne'er-do-well who hid the black pearl of the Borgias in the plaster bust of Napoleon, and who killed Pietro Venucci during his efforts to recover it (SIXN).

Berkeley (*bark'lee*) **Square,** a square in Westminster, noted for its plane trees and fine houses, nearly every one of which has some historical association. General de Merville lived here (ILLU), and Admiral Sinclair lived at "Barclay Square" (BRUC). See Map III of LONDON.

Berkshire (*bark'shur*), a southern county of England, pop. 256,509. It is almost entirely under cultivation, the only manufacturing centre of any great importance being READING. The estates of Shoscombe Old Place (SHOS) and Crane Water (SPEC) were in Berkshire, as were EYFORD (ENGR) and ABBAS PARVA (VEIL). The Roylott estate at one time extended over the borders of Surrey into Berkshire and Hampshire (SPEC). See also WINDSOR.

Berkshires, The, properly **Princess Charlotte of Wales's Royal Berkshire Regiment,** an infantry regiment of the British Army, composed of the former 49th and 66th Foot, which were united to form the Berkshires in 1881. Six companies of the 66th fought at MAIWAND and were overrun by the Afghans while acting as a rear-guard for the retreat. Of 488 members engaged, only 216 survived the battle, 33 of whom were wounded. Watson served with them at Maiwand (STUD).

Berkeley Square.

Berlin, the largest city in Germany, capital of Prussia and of the German Empire, pop. (1900) 1,884,150. The personnel of the Embassy in London were bound here (LAST).

Bermondsey (*ber′mun-zee*), a southeastern metropolitan borough of London, pop. 130,760. It is a poor district embracing the ROTHERHITHE docks and inhabited by factory-labourers and dockworkers. Hall Pycroft introduced Holmes to Harry Pinner as being from here (STOC).

Bermuda Dockyard. James McCarthy's barmaid-wife revealed a previous husband working in the Bermuda Dockyard (BOSC). This allusion may be to the fictionalized name of a dockyard round Bristol and the mouth of the Severn, for many English docks are named for the areas of the world to which their ships originally plied; or it may refer to the actual dockyard located upon Bermuda Island, in the West Indies, directly across the harbour from the city of Hamilton.

Bernstone, Mrs., the housekeeper to Bartholomew Sholto (SIGN).

Bertillon (*bahr-tee-yoN′*), **Alphonse** (1853–1914), a French criminal expert. At first a mere police clerk, in 1879 he developed the **Bertillon system** for the identification of criminals, known generally as *bertillonnage*. The system consists of a series of anthropometrical measurements of the body, especially of the bones, as well as descriptive data, which are classified and filed. Since about 1900 *bertillonnage* has been superseded by fingerprint identification. While Holmes was very jealous of Bertillon's reputation (HOUN), he was an admirer of the man and his system (NAVA).

Beryl. The King of Bohemia's cloak was secured by a brooch which consisted of a single, blazing beryl (SCAN). There was a great variety of beryls in the Agra treasure (SIGN), and the BERYL CORONET was encrusted with them (BERY). See also EMERALD.

Beryl Coronet, one of the most precious possessions of the Empire, fashioned of gold and encrusted with thirty-nine enormous beryls. Given to Alexander Holder as security for a £50,000 loan, it was nearly stolen in an attempt which resulted in its mutilation and the disappearance of three of the gems, which Holmes was able to recover (BERY).

"Beryl Coronet, The Adventure of the" (BERY), a chronicle which appeared originally in the *Strand* magazine for May 1892 and was published in the collection entitled *The Adventures of Sherlock Holmes* the same year. It concerns Holmes's investigation of the attempted theft of the Beryl Coronet, and the case is variously dated as having occurred between 1881 and 1890.

Beverley, Baron, an inferior title of the Duke of Holdernesse (PRIO). *Beverley* is a town in the east of Yorkshire.

*Bevington's, a pawnshop in the Westminster Road, where Holy Peters pawned one of Lady Frances Carfax's jewels (LADY). In some editions the name is spelled *Bovington's*.

Bhang, dried hemp leaves smoked as a drug in India (SIGN). It is spelled *bang* in many editions.

*Bhurtee, a town in India, where Henry Wood's regiment was besieged by the Sepoys (CROO).

Bible. Holmes confessed his Biblical knowledge to be a trifle rusty (CROO), and claimed he could not name any book less likely to lie at the elbow of one of Moriarty's associates

(VALL). The author of the Baskerville manuscript appealed to Holy Writ (HOUN). Jack Prendergast swore by the Book (GLOR), as did Jonathan Small (SIGN) and James Ryder (BLUE). Hosmer Angel made Mary Sutherland swear eternal faithfulness to him with her hands on the Testament (IDEN).

See also BATHSHEBA; DAVID; GABRIEL; SAMUEL; SOLOMON; URIAH; also BROKEN REED; COALS OF FIRE; DANITES; MIDIANITES; MORMONS. See also HOLY LAND.

Bicycle: see RUDGE-WHITWORTH; see also DUNLOP; PALMER.

Biddle, one of the WORTHINGDON BANK GANG (RESI).

Big Ben, the name given to the great bell which hangs in the Clock Tower of the Houses of Parliament. It is one of the largest known, weighing no less than thirteen tons. Watson writes that it was twenty-five to eight as he and Holmes passed the Clock Tower, which stands upon the north side of Parliament next to Westminster Bridge, and that the bell struck eight as they rushed down the Brixton Road on their way to save Lady Frances Carfax (LADY).

Bighorn sheep, or *Rocky Mountain goat,* the wild sheep of the Rocky Mountains. Jefferson Hope shot a bighorn for food (STUD).

Bijou, any object of beauty or charm of small size. Holmes described Briony Lodge as a "bijou villa" (SCAN).

Bile-shot, ill-tempered. Watson described Dr. Grimesby Roylott's eyes as such (SPEC).

Bill, the small boy who assisted Mr. Breckinridge, possibly his son (BLUE).

Billet, a stick of wood cut for firewood (MUSG).

Billet, in English slang, a situation or

position of employment (REDH, STOC, STUD).

Billiards. Watson was fond of the game, which he played with his friend THURSTON (DANC). There was a billiard-room at the house of Trevor Senior (GLOR), at the Abbey Grange (ABBE), Baskerville Hall (HOUN), Hurlstone (MUSG), and possibly at Appledore Towers (CHAS). It was said that Lord Mount-James "could chalk his billiard-cue with his knuckles" (MISS), an allusion to his GOUT. A **billiard-marker** is a servant at a commercial billiard-room who attends upon players and records the progress of the game (GREE).

Billy, the page at Baker Street at the end of the 1880s (VALL).

Billy, the "young but very wise and tactful" (MAZA) page at Baker Street round the turn of the century. He announced Marlow Bates (THOR) and assisted Holmes in the case of the Mazarin diamond (MAZA).

Billycock, a BOWLER hat (BLUE).

Bi-metallism, the system of money in which coins of both silver and gold are legal tender to any amount; that is, the concurrent use of coins of two metals as a circulating medium, the ratio of the two being arbitrarily fixed by law. It is contended by advocates of the system that by fixing a legal ratio between the value of gold and silver, and using both as legal tender, fluctuations in the value of the metals are in part avoided, and the prices of commodities are therefore rendered more stable. Mono-metallists reply that the cheaper metal will always drive the dearer from use, whatever the legal ratio. The *bi-metallic question* was one of Mycroft Holmes's specialisms (BRUC).

Binomial Theorem, in mathematics,

the theorem devised by Sir Isaac Newton for raising a binomial, that is, two terms connected by the sign $+$ or $-$, to any power, or for extracting any root of it by an approximating infinite series. Thus:

$$(x+y)^2 = x^2 + 2xy + y^2$$
$$(x+y)^3 = x^3 + 3x^2y + 3xy^2 + y^3$$
$$(x+y)^4 = x^4 + 4x^3y + 6x^2y^2 + 4xy^3 + y^4$$

or, in general:

$$(x+y)^n = x^n + nx^{n-1}y + \frac{n(n-1)}{2}x^{n-2}y^2$$
$$+ \frac{n(n-1)(n-2)}{2.3}x^{n-3}y^3 +, \text{ etc.}$$

Professor Moriarty wrote a treatise upon the Binomial Theorem, which had a European vogue (FINA).

Biology: see ANATOMY; BOTANY; PATHOLOGY; ZOOLOGY.

*Birchmoor, a small estate belonging to Lord Robert St. Simon (NOBL).

Bird. Holmes and Watson were "rejoicing in the music of the birds" as they walked through Surrey (SOLI), and the detective suggested giving a few hours "to the birds and the flowers" during the Peter Carey case (BLAC). Young Master Rucastle showed remarkable talent, it was said, in the capture of birds (COPP), and a shocking story of how Jonas Oldacre turned a cat loose in an aviary demonstrated his "brutal cruelty" (NORW). Old Sherman was a bird-stuffer (SIGN). In his disguise as an old bibliophile Holmes carried a volume entitled *British Birds* (EMPT). Folk who were in grief came to Mrs. Watson, her husband said, "like birds to a lighthouse" (TWIS). A small bird-bow hung in the South American weapons collection at Cheeseman's (SUSS).

See also BITTERN; BUZZARD; CA-

NARY; CORMORANT; CURLEW; DUCK; GROUSE; GULL; OWL; PARTRIDGE; PHEASANT; PLOVER; RAVEN; STORMY PETREL; VULTURE; WHIP-POOR-WILL; WOODCOCK. See also COVERT; GRASS; PHEASANT MONTHS; PRESERVE; PUT UP; SHOOTING.

Bird, Simon, a victim of the Scowrers (VALL).

Bird's-eye, an English style of cut tobacco. Holmes compared the "white fluff" of the bird's-eye ash to that of the Trichinopoly (SIGN).

*Birlstone, a small village on the northern border of Sussex, a short distance from the rise known as **Birlstone Ridge,** which Holmes said offered a remarkable view over the Weald. Half a mile from the village is the ancient **Birlstone Manor House,** where Holmes

investigated the supposed murder of John Douglas (VALL).

Birmingham, a large manufacturing city in the North Midlands, pop. 522,204. Trevor Senior's daughter died of diphtheria while on a visit to Birmingham (GLOR), and Steve Dixie protested that he was training here when young Perkins was killed (3GAB). Holmes and Watson journeyed here to investigate the Hall Pycroft mystery (STOC), and Howard Garrideb supposedly had offices in the suburb of Aston (3GAR).

Bishopgate, more commonly *Bishopsgate,* a London thoroughfare running north from the City. Holmes and Athelney Jones were associated with the Bishopgate jewel case (SIGN). See the map of the CITY.

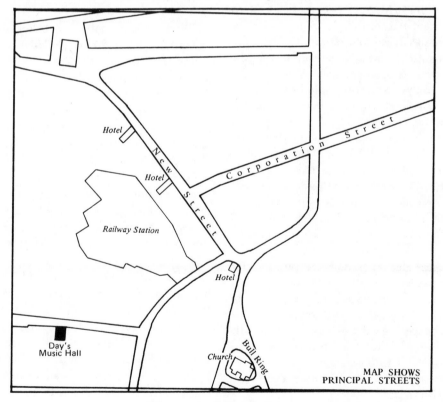

The centre of Birmingham.

Bishops, bench of: see BENCH OF BISHOPS.

Bison, or *buffalo,* the North American wild ox. The dust cloud raised by the trekking Mormons upon the Great Alkali Plain might have led an observer to the conclusion that a great herd of bison was approaching (STUD). Holmes made use of the expression "a herd of buffaloes" (BOSC, STUD). See BUFFALO.

Bisulphate, in chemistry, a salt of sulphuric acid, in which one-half of the hydrogen of the acid is replaced by a metal. Holmes spent the second day of the Sutherland case analyzing a sample of bisulphate of BARYTA (IDEN).

Bit, a morsel of food. Jefferson Hope said he had had no time for "bit or sup" (STUD), a common expression meaning *food or drink.* In some editions this phrase appears as *bite or sup.*

Bittern, a wading bird of the heron family, remarkable for its curious booming cry. Stapleton said the strange noise Watson heard in Grimpen Mire may have been a bittern booming (HOUN).

Bittern.

Blackfoot, a tribe of American Indians once living in the United States and Canada north of the Yellowstone River (STUD).

*Black Formosa corruption, a disease Watson confessed he had never heard of (DYIN).

Black Gorgiano: see GORGIANO, GIUSEPPE.

Blackheath, a pleasant residential district of Lewisham, lying to the north of Lee and south of the famous common from which it takes its name. John Hector McFarlane lived at Blackheath with his parents (NORW). Both Watson (SUSS) and Godfrey Staunton (MISS) at one time had played for the *Blackheath Football Club,* the premier Rugby club of England. Watson took a train from Lewisham at **Blackheath Station** for London Bridge (RETI). See the front endpaper map.

Black Jack of Ballarat: see TURNER, JOHN.

Black-letter edition, a book printed in *black-letter,* a name now given to the Gothic or Old English style of lettering, which was introduced into England about the middle of the fourteenth century and was the character

𝔚illiam 𝔆axton brought printing to 𝔈ngland

Black-letter.

generally used in the first printed books (REDH, SIGN). See also GERMAN CHARACTERS.

Blackmail, money extorted from persons under threat of exposure for an alleged offense.

Holmes seems to have considered blackmail a particularly despicable crime (CHAS). He said that Moriarty stood at the head of the criminal chain which ended with the minor criminal such as the blackmailer (VALL), and he called Charles Augustus Milverton the "king of the blackmailers" (CHAS).

John Turner was blackmailed by Charles McCarthy (BOSC), and Eduardo Lucas blackmailed Lady Hilda Trelawney Hope into stealing a document from among her husband's papers (SECO). At the time of the Baskerville case, one of the most revered names in England was being besmirched by a blackmailer (HOUN). Patrick Cairns attempted blackmail upon Peter Carey (BLAC), the sailor Hudson upon Beddoes and Trevor Senior (GLOR), and William Kirwin upon his employers the Cunninghams (REIG). Irene Adler attempted to blackmail the King of Bohemia, but relented (SCAN).

Holmes was of the opinion that Effie Munro was being blackmailed (YELL), and Watson thought that perhaps Lady Frances Carfax was being blackmailed (LADY). Isadora Klein did not fear blackmail from Barney Stockdale (3GAB). The decent citizens of Vermissa Valley were terrorized by the Scowrers into paying blackmail through corrupt government (VALL). The funds of the Red Circle were raised through blackmail and EXTORTION (REDC).

Black pearl of the Borgias: see BORGIA.

Black Peter: see CAREY, PETER.

"Black Peter, The Adventure of" (BLAC), a chronicle which appeared originally in the *Strand* magazine for March 1904 and *Collier's Weekly* of 27 February 1904 and was published in the collection entitled *The Return of Sherlock Holmes* the following year. It concerns Holmes's investigation of the murder of Peter Carey in July 1895.

Black Sea. The barque *Gloria Scott*

was pressed into service for transporting convicts to Australia owing to the use of the regular convict ships as troop transports in the Black Sea during the Crimean War (GLOR). See the map of EUROPE.

Blacksmith, a smith who works in iron. Dr. Grimesby Roylott threw the blacksmith of Stoke Moran over a parapet into a stream (SPEC). A lad worked the smithy at the Fighting Cock Inn (PRIO). A FARRIER saw the Hound of the Baskervilles upon the moor (HOUN).

Black Steve: see DIXIE, STEVE.

Black Swan Hotel, an inn of repute in Winchester. Holmes met with Violet Hunter here (COPP).

Blackthorn, a European thicket-shrub, the hard wood of which is much favoured for walking-sticks and tool-handles (ABBE).

Black Tor, a Dartmoor tor (HOUN).

Blackwall, a district of Poplar, lying on the Thames immediately below the West India Docks. Once famous as the point from which Continental steamers departed, it is today the site of a considerable dry dock. The *Aurora* was pursued past here (SIGN). See the front endpaper map.

Blackwater, Earl of, the father of one of the Priory School boys (PRIO). *Blackwater* is the common name given to several rivers and towns in Ireland, Scotland, and England.

Blair Island, properly **South Andaman Island,** the southern-most of the three principal ANDAMAN ISLANDS. Jonathan Small was imprisoned here (SIGN).

Blaker, a mine or colliery foreman against whom the Scowrers planned revenge (VALL).

"Blanched Soldier, The Adventure

of the" (BLAN), a chronicle which appeared originally in the *Strand* magazine for November 1926 and *Liberty* magazine of 16 October 1926 and was published in the collection entitled *The Case Book of Sherlock Holmes* the following year. It concerns Holmes's interest in the mysterious seclusion imposed upon Godfrey Emsworth. The story has the distinction of having been written by Holmes himself, who dates the case as having occurred in January 1903.

Blandford Street, a short West End street connecting Manchester Street with Baker Street. Holmes led Watson down Blandford Street on their way to Camden House (EMPT). See Map III of LONDON.

Blasé, in French and English, jaded or calloused (STUD).

Blazoning, in heraldry, the art of describing armorial bearings; the description itself in the technical language of arms; and, in general, the coat-of-arms itself. Reginald Musgrave compared the Musgrave Ritual to his family's "blazonings and charges," as something of little importance to him (MUSG). See also CHARGE; HERALDRY.

Blessington, the worst, according to Holmes, of the WORTHINGDON BANK GANG, who was hanged by his former accomplices in a way calculated to appear as suicide. His real name was *Sutton* (RESI).

Blondin (*blōN-daN'*), **Charles** (1824–1897), the assumed name of *Jean François Gravelet,* a noted French gymnast, renowned for having crossed Niagara Falls on a tight rope several times. Holmes jokingly compared himself to Blondin (SIGN).

Bloodhound. Chester Wilcox kept bloodhounds as watch-dogs (VALL). Stapleton's giant hound seemed to be a combination of the bloodhound and

the mastiff (HOUN). Watson mentioned bloodhounds as an example of dogs used in detective work (CREE). See also SLEUTH-HOUND.

Blood stains. The identification of blood stains is an important medicolegal question, Holmes maintained, and one which he believed himself to have solved by discovering a reagent which was precipitated by hæmoglobin and by nothing else, a method he considered superior to the old GUAIACUM TEST (STUD).

Bloody footprints were found in the empty Howe Street tenement (REDC) and at Birlstone Manor (VALL). Beppo's knife bore traces of recent blood (SIXN). Some slight blood stains were found at Deep Dene House, upon John Hector McFarlane's stick and upon one wall in the form of a bloody thumb-print (NORW). Holmes found a slight smudge of blood upon the wall round Pondicherry Lodge (SIGN). There were numerous splashes of blood in the room where Enoch Drebber's body was found, and in Joseph Stangerson's hotel room, as well as the word *"Rache"* written in letters of blood upon a wall at both places (STUD). There was a large blood stain upon the carpet where Eduardo Lucas lay murdered, but it did not correspond with the stain upon the floor beneath (SECO). Drops of blood were found in the room where Neville St. Clair was last seen (TWIS), upon the seat of the chair in which Lady Brackenstall had been bound (ABBE), and upon Lower Gill Moor (PRIO). There were blood marks at Hugo Oberstein's house, but no indication of bleeding upon the railway line where Cadogan West's body was found (BRUC).

Bloomsbury, a region of central London centred about the British Museum. Within easy reach of the City, the West End, and the great railway termini, it is more favoured by visitors than any other part of London, and there are many hotels and boarding-houses. The Alpha Inn was in Bloomsbury (BLUE), as was the Warrens' boarding-house (REDC). See Map I of LONDON.

Blount, a student at Stackhurst's coaching establishment (LION).

Blue, one who has been chosen to represent Oxford or Cambridge in athletic contests. The term derives from the distinctive colours adopted by the students of these institutions, *dark blue* for Oxford and *light blue* for Cambridge.

The defeat of the Light Blues in the Rugby match with Oxford was attributed to the absence of Godfrey Staunton (MISS). Gilchrist had received his Blue for the hurdles and long jump (3STU), and Harold Stackhurst had been a well-known rowing Blue in his day (LION).

*Blue Anchor, the name of a hypothetical inn or public-house, from whose female employees Holmes said Watson might have got valuable information about the Amberley case (RETI).

Bluebottle, in zoology, a variety of common fly having a blue abdomen (BLAC).

Blue carbuncle, the priceless gem belonging to the Countess of Morcar, stolen by James Ryder and ultimately recovered by Holmes. The reward offered for its return was £1,000, which Holmes said was not a twentieth part of its market value (BLUE). See also CARBUNCLE.

"Blue Carbuncle, The Adventure of the" (BLUE), a chronicle which appeared originally in the *Strand* magazine for January 1892 and was published in the collection entitled *The Adventures of Sherlock Holmes* later that year. It concerns the theft of the Countess of Morcar's blue carbuncle by James Ryder and the gem's strange passage from Ryder to Henry Baker to the commissionaire Peterson and finally to Holmes in the crop of a Christmas goose. The case is variously dated as having taken place in 1887, 1889, and 1890.

Watson recalled the case as having begun with a mere whim (COPP).

Blue ribbon, the badge, consisting of a bit of blue ribbon worn in a buttonhole, of the *Blue Ribbon Army,* a society pledged to total abstinence from the use of intoxicating drinks; hence, the state or condition of abstinence. James Browner said he was "blue ribbon" at the beginning of his marriage (CARD).

Blymer estate, the estate left to Count Sylvius by old Mrs. Harold, which he rapidly gambled away (MAZA).

Boar. Boars' heads were on the arms of the Baskervilles (HOUN).

Board school, formerly a public elementary school under the management of a locally elected school board. Board schools were so called 1870–1902, during the term of the Elementary Education Act. Holmes spoke enthusiastically of their rôle in framing England's future (NAVA).

Boat: see BATHING-COT; LIGHTER; PUNT; SKIFF; WHERRY; YAWL; see also AURORA; RIVER POLICE; WATERMAN; WHARFINGER. For nautical terms see SHIP.

Bob (d. 1847), the natural brother of Lucy Ferrier, who died when the

Ferrier wagon party became lost upon the Great Alkali Plain (STUD).

Bob, in English slang, a SHILLING (SIGN).

Boccaccio (*boh-kah′cho*), **Giovanni** (1313–1375), an Italian novelist and poet. A pocket edition of Boccaccio's *Decameron,* a collection of one hundred ribald tales written 1348–53, was found upon the body of Enoch Drebber (STUD).

Boers, the name given to the South African colonists of Dutch descent (BLAN).

Boer War: see SOUTH AFRICAN WAR.

Bogus laundry affair: see ALDRIDGE.

Bohemia, a principality of northwestern Austria, pop. (1900) 6,318,280. The inhabitants are principally Czechs and Germans, who control the social and political life of the country, and both languages are maintained. The capital is PRAGUE. Dorak was a Bohemian (CREE), and Holmes was able to be of service to the "King" of Bohemia (SCAN). See the map of EUROPE.

Bohemia, King of, properly **Wilhelm Gottsreich Sigismond von Ormstein** (b. 1858), the Grand Duke of CASSEL-FELSTEIN and hereditary King of Bohemia. It was he who engaged Holmes to recover certain compromising letters and a photograph from the adventuress Irene ADLER (SCAN). The King gave Holmes a valuable snuff-box as a token of gratitude, though the case was the only one in which Watson had known the detective to fail (IDEN). Many years later Holmes identified himself to Von Bork as he who brought about the "separation" between Irene Adler and the King (LAST).

Bohemian, a person who leads a free and unconventional life, is irregular in his habits, or has little regard for ordinary society.

Watson claimed to possess a natural Bohemianism of disposition (MUSG), but Holmes was the true Bohemian (ENGR) who "loathed every form of society with his whole Bohemian soul" (SCAN) and characterized social invitations as "those unwelcome social summonses which call upon a man either to be bored or to lie" (NOBL). Watson called the house in which Nathan Garrideb lived "the abode of Bohemian bachelors" (3GAR) and skipped over the pages of Henri Murger's *Vie de Bohème* (STUD).

Bombay, the chief seaport of the west coast of India, pop. 776,006. Watson landed at Bombay when he first arrived in India to join his regiment (STUD).

*Bombay Infantry: see THIRTY-FOURTH BOMBAY INFANTRY.

Bond Street, more correctly *New Bond Street* and *Old Bond Street,* a thoroughfare in Westminster, extending from Oxford Street to Piccadilly. It is a street of fashionable shops and several picture-galleries. Holmes suggested spending some time in one of the Bond Street galleries (HOUN), and Madame Lesurier's milliner shop was here (SILV). See Map III of LONDON.

Bond Street, a short street in Lambeth, running between Upper Kennington Lane and Miles Street. Holmes and Watson passed down Bond Street in pursuit of Jonathan Small (SIGN). See Map IV of LONDON.

Bon vivant, a jovial companion (SIGN).

Boodle, in American slang, money or property. Holmes as Altamont demanded his "boodle" from Von Bork (LAST).

"Book of Life, The," the "somewhat ambitious" title of an article Holmes wrote for an English magazine, attempting to show how much an observant man might learn by an accurate and systematic examination of all that came in his way (STUD).

Boom, in America, to promote vigorously, as a commercial product or a political candidate (THOR).

Boone, Hugh: see ST. CLAIR, NEVILLE.

Boots, the servant in a hotel who blacks the boots of guests and runs errands for them. See HOTEL SERVANTS.

There was a boots at Halliday's Private Hotel (STUD). Sir Henry Baskerville could not "get sense" out of the boots at the Northumberland Hotel, who may have been bribed to steal Sir Henry's footwear, and who is probably identifiable as the "German waiter" with whom Sir Henry spoke (HOUN).

Bordeaux (*bor-dō'*), a major city and port of south-western France, pop. (1906) 237,707. James Windibank was said to be in Bordeaux, where his company had its French offices, at the time of Mary Sutherland's wedding (IDEN).

Borgia, the name of a family prominent in Italian politics during the fifteenth and sixteenth centuries. The name has been attached to the so-called "black pearl of the Borgias" which was stolen from the Prince of Colonna and finally recovered by Holmes (SIXN).

Borough, The, properly **Southwark,** a central metropolitan borough of London, pop. 206,180. It is located directly across the Thames opposite the City, with which its history is intimately connected, and it has kept its familiar title *The Borough* for more than five hundred years. It is today a poor and crowded district, its population employed mostly in the riverside wharves and in manufactories. John Clayton lived in the Borough (HOUN). See the front endpaper map and the map of the CITY.

*Boscombe Valley,** a country district in Herefordshire, where the Boscombe Valley tragedy occurred. A small lake called the **Boscombe Pool** is formed by the spreading-out of the stream which runs down the valley. John Turner owned the **Boscombe Valley Estate** and apparently lived in *Boscombe Hall* (BOSC).

"Boscombe Valley Mystery, The" (BOSC), a chronicle which appeared originally in the *Strand* magazine for October 1891 and was published in the collection entitled *The Adventures of Sherlock Holmes* the following year. It concerns Holmes's investigation of the murder of Charles McCarthy. The case is commonly dated as having taken place in 1889.

Boss, the stud or knob at the centre of an ancient shield. Watson describes the town of Tavistock as lying in the centre of Dartmoor "like the boss of a shield" (SILV), an utterly erroneous statement in that Tavistock lies upon the western edge of the moor.

Boswell, James (1740–1795), the friend and biographer of the eminent author and conversationalist Dr. Samuel Johnson (1709–1784), and whose *Life of Samuel Johnson* (1791) is universally admitted to be the best piece of biography in the English language. Holmes jocularly remarked of Watson: "I am lost without my Boswell" (SCAN).

Botany. Watson rated Holmes's knowledge of botany as "variable" (STUD), an evaluation he recalled some years later with much humour (FIVE). Holmes carried about an elementary book on the subject as he investigated Aloysius Garcia's neighbours (WIST), and the Stapletons professed strong tastes for botany and zoology (HOUN).

Bouguereau (*boo-gro'*), **Adolphe William** (1825–1905), a French painter of religious and mythological scenes. Thaddeus Sholto possessed a Bouguereau (SIGN).

Boulevards, The, a series of broad and magnificent thoroughfares of Paris, constructed in the reign of Louis XIV (1643–1715) on the site of the ancient *boulevards,* or fortifications, which formerly surrounded the city. They are divided by the Seine into a northern and a southern half. The streets of the northern semicircle, commonly known as "The Boulevards," are nowhere surpassed for their imposing handsomeness. HURET was known as "the Boulevard assassin" (GOLD), which may well refer to this series of streets.

Bourgeois (*ber-jois'*), a size of printing-type.

> This line is set in bourgeois.

Holmes remarked that *The Times* made use of *leaded bourgeois* (HOUN), that is, bourgeois type separated or spaced by the insertion of thin strips of type-metal between the lines.

*Bovington's: see BEVINGTON'S.

Bowery, The, a street in New York City, and the name given to that part of Manhattan through which it passes. Genarro Lucca saved Tito Castalotte from some ruffians here (REDC).

Bowler, a stiff, round, low-crowned felt hat. Dr. Kent wore a bowler (BLAN), and Henry Baker's hat was a battered BILLYCOCK (BLUE).

Bow Street, a street in Westminster, in which is located London's principal police-court. Holmes and Watson hurried here to examine Hugh Boone (TWIS). See Map II of LONDON.

Bow-window, a window built so as

Bow-window.

to project from a wall; specifically, one that is in plan a segment of a circle. A bow-window is distinct from a BAY WINDOW in that it is neither straight-sided nor need it extend to the building's foundation, though in the popular mind the terms are generally interchangeable.

There was a bow-window at Baker Street (BERY, MAZA); Holmes spied Dr. Mortimer from "the recess of the window" (HOUN), from which Watson and Percy Phelps watched Holmes arrive (NAVA), Watson "sat in the window" reflecting upon his first meeting with Mary Morstan (SIGN), and Helen Stoner was found "sitting in the window" (SPEC). There was a bow-window at the Diogenes Club (GREE) and in Nathan Garrideb's flat (3GAR), and Langdale Pike spent his waking hours in the bow-window of a St. James's Street club (3GAB).

Box, the driver's seat on a carriage (SIGN, STUD).

Boxer cartridge, any kind of centre-fire cartridge, so called from *Col. Edward Mourrier Boxer* (1822–1898), the British Army ordnance designer who perfected this kind of ammunition. Holmes reportedly used Boxer cartridges in his HAIR-TRIGGER (MUSG).

Boxing, a combative art which has fallen into disrepute in more recent years. Prizefighting is now illegal in England.

Sam Merton (MAZA) and Steve Dixie (3GAB) were prizefighters, as McMurdo and Williams had been (SIGN). Watson described Cecil Barker as possessing a "prizefighter" face (VALL). Trevor Senior had boxed in his youth (GLOR), and Von Bork (LAST) and Sir Robert Norberton (SHOS) participated in the sport.

Holmes himself had boxed at college (GLOR) and was said to be a fine boxer for his weight (YELL). Watson described him as an "expert" (FIVE, STUD) whose skill was of service in his encounters with a street rough (FINA), Joseph Harrison (NAVA), and Jack Woodley (SOLI). He attended professional contests and at least once engaged in a benefit match (SIGN). See also ALISON'S; BARNEY; BRUISER; DO DOWN; FANCY, THE; TRIM.

Box-room, a room for storing boxes, trunks, and the like; a LUMBER-ROOM (BERY, HOUN, REDC). Holmes compared his own mind to a "crowded box-room" of randomly acquired knowledge kept without any scientific system (LION).

Box the compass, to name the points of the compass in their order; hence, figuratively, to make a complete turn or round. Inspector Bradstreet laughed that he, Watson, Victor Hatherley, and the Berkshire plain-clothes man had boxed the compass among them in

their opinions of the direction of Dr. Becher's house from Eyford (ENGR).

Bracken, a FERN (HOUN).

Brackenstall, Sir Eustace (1856?–97), an English baronet, murdered for his brutality by his wife's lover, Captain CROKER. The wife, **Lady Mary Brackenstall,** the former *Mary Fraser,* had been cruelly used and was not exposed by Holmes when he deduced the solution to the case (ABBE).

Brackwell, Lady Eva, Holmes's client in the Milverton case (CHAS).

Bradford, a city in Yorkshire, pop. 279,767. Mason committed his crimes here (STUD).

Bradley, the name of Watson's tobacconist (HOUN).

"Bradshaw's Railway Guide," the most complete of the numerous British railway guides, published monthly. Holmes did not believe that the coded message from Porlock could be keyed to Bradshaw (VALL). Watson looked up the trains to Winchester here (COPP).

Bradstreet, Inspector, a Scotland Yard official who joined the force in 1862. When Holmes and Watson arrived at the Bow Street police-court, they found Bradstreet on duty here (TWIS), which is in the E Division of Scotland Yard. Shortly thereafter, apparently, in June 1889, he was assigned to the case of the blue carbuncle while serving in B Division, according to the newspapers (BLUE), and in that same summer of 1889 he accompanied Holmes to Eyford in the Hatherley case (ENGR), revealing himself to be assigned most likely to the central headquarters staff. See SCOTLAND YARD.

Brain fever, in medicine, an inflammation of the brain attended with acute fever and delirium; thus, in popular usage, any delirium or frenzy. Brain fever was suffered by Sarah Cushing (CARD), Alice Rucastle (COPP), Mrs. Barclay (CROO), Rachel Howells (MUSG), and Percy Phelps (NAVA).

Bramble, any rough, prickly shrub (DEVI, FINA, SPEC).

***Brambletye Hotel,** the hotel where Holmes and Watson stayed during the Peter Carey case (BLAC). *Brambletye* is a rural district of Sussex lying to the north-west of Forest Row.

Brandy, the liquor obtained by the distillation of wine, or the refuse of the wine-press. Brandy is nearly one-half alcohol and is often used in medicine as a stimulant.

Dr. Grimesby Roylott attempted to stimulate Julia Stoner with brandy (SPEC). Constable MacPherson hurried to get brandy for the woman who fainted at the sight of Eduardo Lucas's blood (SECO), Lestrade gave brandy to Sir Henry Baskerville and to Mrs. Stapleton (HOUN), and Hilton Soames gave brandy to his servant Bannister (3STU). Ian Murdoch shouted for brandy to ease his pain, and a bottleful seems to have saved the life of J. G. Wood (LION).

Holmes and Watson gave brandy to James Ryder (BLUE), Victor Hatherley (ENGR), Percy Phelps (NAVA), Thorneycroft Huxtable (PRIO), and John Scott Eccles (WIST). An empty brandy bottle was found at The Myrtles, but Watson found some with which to revive Mr. Melas (GREE). Holmes helped himself to some of Colonel Hayter's brandy after being attacked by the Cunninghams (REIG) and gave Watson brandy when the doctor fainted (EMPT).

There was a tantalus containing brandy and whisky in Peter Carey's cabin (BLAC). Elias Openshaw drank a great deal of it (FIVE), and Trevor Senior fortified himself with brandy at his reunion with the sailor Hudson, who himself reeked strongly of it (GLOR).

Brazil, a republic of South America, est. pop. 15,000,000. Maria Gibson was a Brazilian (THOR), and Jonathan Small planned to escape to "the Brazils" (SIGN), once a common form of the name.

Breckinridge, a dealer in geese at Covent Garden Market. BILL may have been his son (BLUE).

Brewer, Sam, a London money-lender whom Sir Robert Norberton once horsewhipped upon Newmarket Heath. It was the belief that Brewer would not extend his credit that prompted Sir Robert to conceal his sister's death (SHOS).

***Briarbrae,** the Phelps home at Woking (NAVA).

***Brickfall & Amberley,** a manufacturer of artistic materials, of which Josiah Amberley was junior partner (RETI).

Bridge, The: see LONDON BRIDGE.

Brig, a type of two-masted sailing vessel (GLOR).

Brilliant, the form in which the diamond and other precious stones are cut when intended to be used as ornaments. There are many possible modifications, but the general shape of all brilliants is that of two pyramids united at their bases, the upper one being so truncated as to give a large

Brilliant.

plane surface, the lower one terminating almost in a point. The cut considered most perfect displays fifty-eight facets. A remarkable brilliant decorated a ring given Holmes by the reigning family of Holland (IDEN). A silver-and-brilliant pendant belonging to Lady Frances Carfax was pawned in the Westminster Road (LADY).

Brinvilliers (*braN-vil-yay'*), **Marquise de** (*c.*1630–1676), an infamous French murderess, born *Marie d'Aubray,* said to have poisoned several members of her own family with AQUA TOFANA before she was found out and hanged. The *Daily Telegraph* alluded airily to the "Marchioness de Brinvilliers" in its editorial about the Drebber murder (STUD).

*Briony Lodge, the home of Irene Adler in St. John's Wood (SCAN). The *bryony* is a common European plant known for its medicinal properties.

Bristol, a port city in Gloucestershire, in the south-west of England, pop. 328,945. James McCarthy had been away here for three days before his father's death (BOSC).

British Army. Watson joined the Army in 1878, trained as an Army surgeon at Netley, and served with the Fifth Northumberland Fusiliers and with the Berkshires; severely wounded at the battle of Maiwand, he was granted a wound pension (STUD). He later called himself a retired Army surgeon (RESI, SIGN) and remarked that his summer quarters were once near Shoscombe (SHOS). He said that his experience of camp life in Afghanistan had the effect of making him a prompt and ready traveller, and Holmes remarked upon his "military neatness" (BOSC). Holmes declared that he would never pass as a pure-

bred civilian as long as he kept the habit of carrying his handkerchief in his sleeve (CROO), an Army practice which results from the fact that uniform tunics do not have pockets. He remarked that Watson was rejoining his old service in the German war (LAST).

James Dodd carried his handkerchief in the military manner, but his beard showed that he had not served in the regular Army (BLAN). The gardener Mortimer was an Army pensioner (GOLD), and Jonathan Small joined the Army as a young man (SIGN). Holmes and his brother observed an old soldier in Pall Mall (GREE). Colonel Emsworth had been the greatest martinet in the Army in his day (BLAN).

See also ARMY MEDICAL DEPARTMENT; BERKSHIRES; COLDSTREAM GUARDS; FIFTH NORTHUMBERLAND FUSILIERS; FUSILIERS; GUARDS; IMPERIAL YEOMANRY; MARINES; ROYAL ARTILLERY; ROYAL MALLOWS; ROYAL MUNSTERS; THIRD BUFFS; VOLUNTEERS.

See also ALDERSHOT; NETLEY; WOOLWICH. See also INDIAN ARMY.

See also AMMUNITION BOOTS; CANTEEN; COMMISSIONAIRE; GOOSE-STEP; HALF-PAY; MARTINI-HENRY RIFLE; ORDERLY; SAPPER; SHILLING; V.C.; also ROBERTS, FREDERICK SLEIGH, EARL ROBERTS.

"British Birds," the title of a book carried by Holmes in his disguise as an old bibliophile (EMPT).

British Broken Hills, an Australian mining company listed on the London Stock Exchange (STOC).

British Empire. Watson called London "that great cesspool into which all the loungers and idlers of the Empire are irresistibly drained" (STUD). The Beryl Coronet was one of the most precious public possessions of the Empire (BERY). Certain colonial developments angered a foreign sovereign, resulting in the explosive document stolen from Trelawney Hope's residence (SECO).

For British colonies and other possessions see AUSTRALIA; CANADA; CEYLON; EGYPT; MAURITIUS; NEW ZEALAND; RHODESIA; ST. HELENA; SIERRA LEONE; SINGAPORE; SOUTH AFRICA; SOUTH AUSTRALIA; VICTORIA. See also COLONIAL OFFICE.

The Indian Empire is politically and administratively distinct from the rest of the British Empire; see INDIA.

British India: see INDIA.

British law. Holmes had a strong, practical knowledge of British law (FIVE, STUD), which was the peculiar passion of old Frankland (HOUN).

Watson observed that the Mary Sutherland, Neville St. Clair, and Irene Adler cases had been free of legal crime (BLUE, COPP), and that the St.

Simon affair as well had been outside the pale of the law (COPP).

For legal terms see ABET; ASSAULT AND BATTERY; BLACKMAIL; BURGLARY; COMMUTE; COMPOUND; CONSPIRACY; COUNTERFEITING; EMBEZZLEMENT; ENTAIL; EXTORTION; FORGERY; FRAUD; INTIMIDATION; KIDNAPPING; LARCENY; LIBEL; LIFE INTEREST; MURDER; MUTINY; REMAND; REVERSION; ROBBERY; SUICIDE; see also LOCUS STANDI; SOLATIUM; also PEINE FORTE ET DURE; TRANSPORTATION.

See also ASSIZES; COMMUNAL RIGHTS; COURT OF QUEEN'S BENCH; DOCK; DOCTORS' COMMONS; JUSTICE OF THE PEACE; MANORIAL LAW; POLICE-COURT; QUARTER SESSIONS; TEMPLE, THE.

"British Medical Journal," the journal of the British Medical Association. Watson read it (STOC), and Holmes wished to determine if Godfrey Emsworth's "keeper" was reading it (BLAN).

British Museum, the great national

The British Museum.

The Reading Room of the British Museum, ingeniously constructed 1855–57 out of the Museum's inner quadrangle.

museum and library in London, founded by Sir Hans SLOANE in 1753.

Holmes had rooms in Montague Street, "just round the corner from the British Museum," when he first began his practice in London (MUSG). The Alpha Inn was near the Museum, where Henry Baker and his friends were to be found during the day (BLUE), and Great Orme Street too was nearby (REDC). Holmes investigated Stapleton's reputation (HOUN) and read up on voodooism (WIST) at the British Museum.

See also BLOOMSBURY; see Maps I and II of LONDON.

Brixton, a middle-class district of central Lambeth. Holmes and Watson traversed the area in pursuit of Jonathan Small (SIGN), and the newspapers termed the Drebber murder the "Brixton Mystery" (STUD). Stanley Hopkins (BLAC) and the Tangeys (NAVA) apparently lived here, where Poultney Square was situated (LADY), and Nathan Garrideb was last heard of in a nursing-home here (3GAR). The name **Lower Brixton** or *North Brixton* is given to the region just north of Brixton proper, where J. Davenport lived (GREE) and Dr. Barnicot's branch surgery was to be found (SIXN). Mrs. Merrilow's boarding-house was in **South Brixton** (VEIL), the elevated district better known as *Brixton Hill.*

Brixton bus, the name given to any of the London omnibuses plying a particular route between Regent Street and the Brixton Road. The agony column of the *Daily Gazette* carried an advertisement for "the lady who fainted in the Brixton bus" (REDC).

Brixton Road, a thoroughfare in Lambeth, mostly residential in character. The body of Enoch Drebber was found at Lauriston Gardens, off the Brixton Road (STUD). Maggie Oakshott lived here (BLUE), and Holmes and Watson tore down the Brixton Road in a hansom on their way to save Lady Frances Carfax (LADY).

When Inspector Lestrade said that Dr. Barnicot had a branch surgery in the *Lower Brixton Road* (SIXN), he presumably meant the lower or northern-most extremity of the Brixton Road, for there is no Lower Brixton Road. See Map IV of LONDON and the front endpaper map.

*Brixton Workhouse Infirmary, the institution where Holy Peters found Rose Spender (LADY). See WORK-HOUSE.

Broadcloth, a finely finished woollen cloth, commonly black, used in making men's garments (STUD).

Broadmoor Asylum, a prison for criminal lunatics in the south-east of Berkshire. Holmes suspected that Josiah Amberley's destination was more likely to be Broadmoor than the scaffold (RETI).

Broads, The, a district of low, level land in the east of Norfolk, bordering the sea, so called from the shallow lagoons formed here by the broadening out of the lower courses of the rivers.

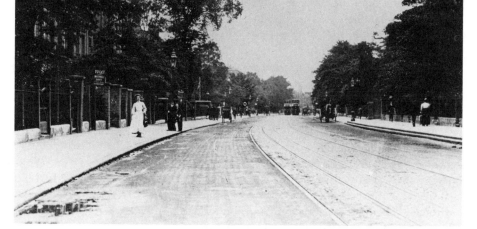

The Brixton Road, one of the principal thoroughfares upon the Surrey side.

A Norfolk broad.

Holmes found good duck shooting and fishing in the country of the Broads (GLOR).

Broad Street, a short street in Lambeth, the western extremity of Princes Road, opening onto the Thames. Mordecai Smith's landing-stage was at the foot of Broad Street (SIGN). See Map IV of LONDON.

*Broderick and Nelson's, a timber yard in Nine Elms Lane, into which Toby led Holmes and Watson (SIGN).

Broken reed, a weak or ineffectual person, so called from *Isa.* 36:6: "Thou trustest in the staff of this broken reed." Holmes so characterized the lawyer Sutro (3GAB).

Broker, a bill-collector (NAVA).

Bromley Brown, Lieutenant, an officer of the Andaman Islands garrison (SIGN).

Bronze, an alloy of copper and tin. As a stage of culture, the use of bronze by a people comes between the use of stone and the use of iron. Stapleton said that neolithic man mined tin with which to make bronze (HOUN).

Brooklyn, a borough of New York City, situated upon the western extremity of Long Island, pop. 1,166,582. Nearly three-fourths of the inhabitants are foreign-born or the children of immigrants. The Luccas were among these (REDC).

Brooks, one of fifty men who had reason for taking Holmes's life (BRUC).

Brook Street, a street in Westminster. Dr. Percy Trevelyan had his practice here (RESI). See also CLARIDGE'S HOTEL. See Map III of LONDON.

*Brotherhood, The, or **The Order,** names used by Professor Coram's wife

Anna in speaking of the Nihilist organization to which they had belonged (GOLD).

Brougham (*brōm*), a four-wheeled, closed carriage, with a single seat inside for two persons, and with a raised driver's seat, named after the British statesman *Henry, Lord Brougham* (1778–1868), who popularized this sort of conveyance.

Brougham.

By examining the wheel marks in the mud, Holmes satisfied himself that Enoch Drebber had arrived at Lauriston Gardens in a four-wheeled cab, which, he said, is considerably less wide than a gentleman's brougham (STUD). Watson was driven to Victoria Station in one (FINA), they were kept by Sir Leslie Oakshott (ILLU), Leslie Armstrong (MISS), Dr. Percy Trevelyan (RESI) and the King of Bohemia (SCAN), and Sir James Damery rode in his client's brougham, the arms of which Watson recognized (ILLU).

Brown, Bromley: see BROMLEY BROWN.

Brown, Josiah, a purchaser of one of the Napoleonic busts (SIXN).

Brown, Sam, a Scotland Yard inspector. He and his partner were aboard the police launch in its pursuit of the *Aurora,* and his partner accompanied Watson to Mrs. Cecil Forrester's (SIGN).

Brown, Silas, the manager of Capleton, who found and hid Silver Blaze (SILV).

Browner, James, a steam-packet steward who murdered his unfaithful wife **Mary Browner,** the former *Mary Cushing,* and her lover Alec Fairbairn. He then mailed a severed ear from each of his victims to Mary's sister Sarah CUSHING, but the package reached her elder sister Susan instead, and brought the police and Holmes upon the scene. Browner was arrested aboard his ship and freely confessed his crimes (CARD).

"Bruce-Partington Plans, The Adventure of the" (BRUC), a chronicle which was published originally in the *Strand* magazine for December 1908 and *Collier's Weekly* of 18 December 1908 and appeared in the 1917 collection entitled *His Last Bow.* It concerns the theft of the plans for the Bruce-Partington submarine and the accompanying murder of Arthur Cadogan West. Watson dates the case as having occurred in November 1895.

Bruce-Partington submarine, one of the most jealously guarded of all Government secrets. It was said that naval warfare became impossible within the radius of its operation, and when some of the plans for the submarine were stolen from Woolwich Arsenal, Holmes was called upon to recover them (BRUC).

Bruce Pinkerton prize, the distinguished medical prize won by Dr. Percy Trevelyan for a monograph upon obscure nervous lesions (RESI).

Bruise. Holmes raised comment by beating the corpses in the dissecting-rooms at St. Bartholomew's Hospital with a stick, to verify how far bruises may be produced after death (STUD).

Bruiser, a boxer (3GAB).

Brunton, Richard, the butler of Hurlstone, whose death at the hands of Rachel Howells came about as a result of his solving the riddle of the Mus-grave Ritual (MUSG).

Brussels, the capital of Belgium, pop. (1900) 183,686. Holmes and Watson made their way into Switzerland by way of Brussels (FINA), and the Franco-Midland Hardware Company supposedly had a branch here (STOC).

Buck, a fashionable man or dandy. A Baskerville ancestor was a Regency buck (HOUN), and Watson said that Sir Robert Norberton should have been a buck in the days of the Regency (SHOS).

Buckboard, in the United States, a four-wheeled carriage in which a long, somewhat flexible board or frame is used in place of body, springs, and other gear (3GAR).

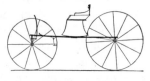

Buckboard.

Buda-Pesth, or *Budapest,* the capital of the kingdom of Hungary, pop. (1900) 716,476. It is made up of two cities on either side of the Danube, *Buda* upon the right bank and *Pesth* upon the left bank, which were united in 1873. Sophy Kratides apparently killed Harold Latimer and Wilson Kemp here (GREE). The only other specimen of the devil's-foot poison in Europe was in a laboratory at Buda (DEVI).

Buddha. The hasp of the Agra treasure chest was wrought in the image of a sitting Buddha (SIGN). Holmes sat upon the floor like some strange Buddha as he consulted his pile of commonplace books (VEIL).

Buddhism of Ceylon, or *Hinayana,*
the simpler, more ancient form of Buddhism as practised in Burma and Ceylon; as opposed to *Mahayana,* the Buddhism of China and Nepaul, of which LAMAISM is an influential sect. Holmes spoke as if he had made a special study of the Buddhism of Ceylon (SIGN).

Buffalo. Holmes's use of the expression "a herd of buffaloes" upon two occasions (BOSC, STUD) has led to speculation that he had some association with the United States before his meeting with Watson. See also BISON.

Buffalo, a city of the United States, located in New York, pop. (1905) 376,587. John McMurdo had lived in Buffalo (VALL), and Holmes as Altamont joined an Irish secret society here (LAST).

*****Buffelsspruit,** a dry creek-bed near Pretoria, where Godfrey Emsworth was wounded during the South African War (BLAN).

Buffs: see THIRD BUFFS.

Bughouse, in American slang, a lunatic asylum. When Holmes as Altamont said that spying was "enough to make a man bughouse" (LAST), he meant enough to make a man mad.

*****Bull, The,** the hotel at Esher where Holmes and Watson stayed (WIST).

Bull, John: see JOHN BULL.

Bulldog. A gold pin, designed as a bulldog's head with rubies as eyes, was found upon the body of Enoch Drebber (STUD). Watson claimed to keep a BULL PUP (STUD).

Bull pup, a young bulldog. At his first meeting with Holmes, Watson said that he kept a bull pup (STUD), but the animal is never mentioned again. *To keep a bull pup,* in Anglo-Indian slang, means to have fits of quick temper.

Bull Ring, The, a large open area near the centre of Birmingham, lying north and east of the ancient Church of St. Martin's. Steve Dixie protested that he was training here when young Perkins was killed (3GAB). See the map of BIRMINGHAM.

Bull's-eye, a lantern possessing a focusing lens (SIGN). See DARK LANTERN and the illustration on p. 83.

Bull-terrier, a common variety of dog, originally a cross between the bulldog and the terrier. Holmes made Victor Trevor's acquaintance when Trevor's bull-terrier bit him severely upon the ankle (GLOR).

Bully, good or fine. John Ferrier said that little Lucy would feel "bullier" if she would rest against him (STUD).

Bumper, a cup or glass filled to the brim, especially when drunk as a toast (SIGN).

Bunsen burner, or **Bunsen lamp,** a form of gas burner especially adapted for heating, used in chemical laboratories (NAVA, SIGN, STUD).

Burberry, a well-made and expensive type of waterproof coat (LION).

Burglary, the breaking and entering by night into the dwelling-house of another with the intent to commit a felony. Burglary is distinguished from LARCENY and ROBBERY in the common law. The carrying of burglary-tools upon the person at night is in itself a crime.

The Randalls (ABBE) and Beddington (STOC) were well-known burglars, and Mr. Blessington became agitated when, he said, he read of a West End break-in (RESI). Peter Jones said that John Clay would crack a CRIB in Scotland one week and be raising money to build an orphanage in Cornwall the next (REDH). Holmes suspected Stapleton of four major West-country burglaries (HOUN), and burglars in the pay of the King of Bohemia

twice ransacked the house of Irene Adler in search of the compromising photograph (SCAN). Inspector MacDonald asked if Professor Moriarty got his money from burglary (VALL).

The Mazarin diamond was stolen in a burglary committed by Count Sylvius and Sam Merton (MAZA). There was an attempted break-in at Briarbrae (NAVA). Beppo committed burglary in his search for the black pearl of the Borgias (SIXN), Pondicherry Lodge was burgled for the Agra treasure (SIGN), and the Three Gables for Douglas Maberley's novel (3GAB). Holmes remarked that John Hopley Neligan was a very poor burglar (BLAC). The house of old Acton was burgled by the Cunninghams, who later disguised the murder of their coachman as the result of an attempted break-in (REIG). The murder of Sir Eustace Brackenstall was made to appear incidental to a burglary (ABBE), and Don Murillo thought to kill Garcia as a burglar (WIST). It was at first believed that the murderer of John Douglas had intended to burgle the manor house (VALL).

Reginald Musgrave thought first of burglars when he saw a light in the Hurlstone library (MUSG). The sight of the mastiff Carlo was more chilling to Violet Hunter than any burglar (COPP). Arthur Holder expressed the fear that his father's house might be broken into (BERY), but Baron Gruner (ILLU) and Nathan Garrideb (3GAR) had no such fears for their own non-saleable possessions. The confidential office where the Bruce-Partington plans were kept was said to be burglar-proof (BRUC), a claim Josiah Amberley made for his strong-room (RETI).

Colonel Emsworth was prepared to

treat with Holmes and James Dodd as if they were burglars (BLAN), and Holy Peters called Holmes a common burglar (LADY). Indeed, Holmes remarked that burglary was an alternative profession at which he surely would have excelled (RETI), a statement borne out by his successfully burgling the homes of Hugo Oberstein (BRUC), Charles Augustus Milverton (CHAS), Baron Gruner (ILLU), and Josiah Amberley (RETI). He cautioned Watson not to drop the tools they carried for the Oberstein episode (BRUC) and was threatened with a charge of burglary, which however did not come about, in the matter of Baron Gruner (ILLU). See also CANARY; CRACKSMAN.

Burnet, Miss: see DURANDO.

Burnwell, Sir George, a gambling acquaintance of Arthur Holder's. He induced Arthur's cousin Mary to steal for him the Beryl Coronet and, when the attempt failed, fled with the girl after his confrontation with Holmes (BERY).

Bus, properly **omnibus,** a four-wheeled, enclosed carriage with a long body and seats along the sides and on top for passengers, drawn by a team of two horses and plying regular routes within a city. Mrs. Tangey (NAVA) and Mr. Warren (REDC) each took a bus home. See also BAYSWATER BUS; BRIXTON BUS. See the photograph on p. 225.

Bushmen, a race of nomadic people who dwell in the western part of South Africa. They are exceedingly small in stature, as Holmes's gazetteer pointed out (SIGN). Dr. Mortimer and Sir Charles Baskerville spent "many a charming evening," Mortimer said, discussing "the comparative anatomy of the Bushman and the Hottentot" (HOUN).

Bushranger, in Australia, a criminal, generally an escaped convict, who takes to the bush or woods and leads a predatory life. John Turner had been a bushranger in his youth (BOSC).

Busy Bee: see COMPOUND OF THE BUSY BEE AND EXCELSIOR.

Butler, the head man-servant of a household, whose principal duty is to take charge of the liquors and the plate, and generally to have supervision of the other household servants. See SERVANT.

Holmes said that Mr. Henderson's house was full of butlers and other servants (WIST). The sailor Hudson was promoted to butler when the post of gardener did not suit him (GLOR). BANNISTER had once been butler to Sir Jabez Gilchrist (3STU). Thaddeus and Bartholomew Sholto each kept a KHITMUTGAR (SIGN), and Dr. Grimesby Roylott had beaten his native butler to death in India (SPEC).

Old Ralph was the butler of Tuxbury Old Hall (BLAN), BARRYMORE of Baskerville Hall (HOUN), Richard BRUNTON of Hurlstone (MUSG), Stephens of Shoscombe Old Place (SHOS), and Ames of Birlstone (VALL). Culverton Smith's butler was named Staples (DYIN), Dr. Leslie Armstrong's was John (MISS), and the butler of the Trelawney Hopes was Jacobs (SECO). Anthony was man-servant to the Stapletons (HOUN), José to Don Murillo (WIST). Butlers were employed by Sir James Walter (BRUC), Baron Gruner (ILLU), Aloysius Doran (NOBL), Thorneycroft Huxtable (PRIO), and Colonel Hayter (REIG).

Butter, parsley sunk into: see ABERNETTY.

Butterfly: see LEPIDOPTERA.

Buzzard, specifically the *turkey buzzard,* the commonest of American vultures. The buzzard was one of the few inhabitants of the Great Alkali Plain, and the three who waited for the deaths of John and Lucy Ferrier were frightened away by the Mormons (STUD).

C

Cab: see FOUR-WHEELER; HANSOM; see also CAB-YARD; JARVEY; OFFICIAL REGISTRY; also BUS.

Cabaret, a French word meaning *tavern* (LADY).

Cabinet, the select council of a sovereign, or of an executive government; the collective body of ministers who direct the government of a country. In Great Britain, though the executive government is vested nominally in the Crown, it is practically in a committee of ministers called **The Cabinet,** the members of which are the chief Secretaries of State who direct the Government departments and initiate most legislation in Parliament. It is headed by the majority party leader as PRIME MINISTER.

See also ADMIRALTY; COLONIAL OFFICE; FOREIGN OFFICE; HOME OFFICE; INDIA; TREASURY.

The Government Office Building, housing the Colonial Office, the Home Office, the Foreign Office, and the India Office, viewed from Whitehall. At right may be seen the entrance to Downing Street, to the left Charles Street.

At the time of the Drebber case a Liberal administration was in power, and the *Daily Telegraph* admonished the Government to keep a closer watch over foreigners in England (STUD). The papers reported an impending change of Government in 1895 (BRUC). Each member of the Cabinet was aware of the contents of the Trelawney Hope document, and during the crisis Holmes received almost hourly reports from the Government (SECO). The approach of the German war of 1914 caused Holmes to put his skills at the disposal of the Government in the area of counter-espionage (LAST, PREF).

Officially, Mycroft Holmes audited the books in some of the Government departments (BRUC, GREE), but in reality his ability to order and systemize data meant that upon occasion he *was* the British Government (BRUC).

Many a Cabinet had cowered before the fierce gleam of Lord Bellinger's eyes (SECO). The Duke of Balmoral (NOBL), the Duke of Holdernesse (PRIO), Lord Holdhurst (NAVA), and Trelawney Hope (SECO) were members of the Cabinet, and Baron Von Herling recalled a week-end spent at the country house of an indiscreet minister (LAST). Charles Augustus Milverton's assassin had been the wife of a great nobleman and statesman (CHAS).

See also CONSERVATIVE PARTY; ESTI-MATES, THE; LIBERAL PARTY; P.C.; RT. HON.; WHITEHALL.

Cabinet, the name for a photograph of a size 3⅞″×5½″. The compromising photo of Irene Adler and the King of Bohemia was a cabinet (SCAN).

Cabul (*kah-bool'*), or *Kabul,* the capital of Afghanistan, est. pop. 60,000. It was captured by the British in 1879

during the Second Afghan War, following the siege of SHERPUR. Colonel Sebastian Moran was present at the taking of the city (EMPT).

Cab-yard, a yard where cabs are kept when off duty, usually maintained by a *cab-owner* who leases his cabs to licensed drivers who work for a percentage of the fares collected (HOUN, STUD).

Cadet, the younger branch of a family. Reginald Musgrave belonged to a cadet branch of the Musgraves (MUSG).

Cadogan West, Arthur (1868–95), a clerk at Woolwich Arsenal who observed the theft of the Bruce-Partington plans and was murdered by Hugo Oberstein. His mother **Mrs. Cadogan West** was of no help in the investigation (BRUC).

Café noir, a French phrase meaning *black coffee,* that is, coffee drunk without milk or cream (MUSG).

Café Royal, properly **Grand Café Royal,** a celebrated French restaurant in Regent Street. Holmes was attacked outside the Café Royal by roughs who escaped through the restaurant and out into the street behind it (ILLU).

Cairn, a man-made heap of stones, erected in prehistoric times as a BAR-ROW or to commemorate an event or serve as a landmark. There were cairns upon Dartmoor (HOUN).

Cairns, Patrick, the harpooner who saw Peter Carey murder the elder Neligan. When Carey refused to be blackmailed, Cairns killed him (BLAC).

Cairo, the capital of Egypt, situated upon the right bank of the Nile, est. pop. 570,000. Holmes asked Mary Maberley if she would like to visit here (3GAB).

Calcutta, the capital of British India and of Bengal, situated upon a branch

A Calcutta street-scene.

of the Ganges, pop. 949,144. Dr. Grimesby Roylott established a large practice at Calcutta (SPEC), and Jonathan Small suggested that a boat could be found here with which to escape from the Andamans (SIGN).

Calhoun, Captain James (d. 1887), an American sea-captain and member of the Ku Klux Klan, who engineered the murder of three members of the Openshaw family and apparently was lost at sea when his ship the *Lone Star* broke up in an Atlantic gale (FIVE).

California, one of the far-western states of the United States, pop. 1,485,-053. Salt Lake City prospered on the trail the gold prospectors took to California (STUD). Birdy Edwards made his fortune and changed his name here (VALL), where Jefferson Hope had been a pioneer (STUD). Aloysius Doran retired to San Francisco (NOBL).

Caltrop, formerly a military instrument with four iron points disposed in such a manner that, three of them being on the ground, the fourth

pointed upward. They were scattered upon the ground to impede the progress of cavalry. Caltrops were repre-

Caltrop.

sented upon Lord Robert St. Simon's arms (NOBL) ; see HERALDRY.

Cam, the river upon which Cambridge is built (MISS).

Camberwell, a southern metropolitan borough of London, pop. 259,339. It is mainly residential, and there are many parks.

The Charpentier boarding establishment was in Camberwell (STUD), as were the homes of Mary Sutherland (IDEN) and Miss Dobney (LADY). Holmes sent Porlock money addressed to the Camberwell post-office, and the letter from him was posted here (VALL). Holmes and Watson traversed the borough in pursuit of Jonathan Small (SIGN). PECKHAM is in Camberwell (STUD). Mrs. Cecil Forrester lived in **Lower Camberwell** (SIGN), an allusion to the older, more northerly part, the region to the south having been built upon a number of hills. See the front endpaper map.

Holmes investigated the **Camberwell poisoning case** in 1887, in which he was able, by winding up the dead man's watch, to prove that it had been wound up two hours before, and that therefore the deceased had gone to bed by that time—a deduction which was of the greatest importance in clearing up the case (FIVE).

Camberwell Road, a thoroughfare in

south London, in which the establishment of John Underwood was located (STUD). See Map IV of LONDON.

Cambridge, the seat of Cambridge University, pop. 38,379. It is the county-town of **Cambridgeshire,** pop. 190,682, one of the chief agricultural counties of the kingdom, nearly nine-tenths of its area being under cultivation. Holmes called Cambridge a "venerable" but "inhospitable" town and remarked that the Cambridgeshire scenery did not lend itself to concealment (MISS).

Cambridge University, one of the two ancient English universities, dating at least from the thirteenth century. The university comprises twenty col-

Cambridge and vicinity.

leges serving about three thousand undergraduate students.

Willoughby Smith attended Cam-

The view up Trumpington Street, Cambridge's busiest thoroughfare. The Græcian-style building at left is an art museum, and beyond it, on both sides as the street curves away to the right, stand the many handsome collegiate buildings. Though considered less picturesque in appearance than Oxford, Cambridge does possess charms peculiar to itself, notably the "Backs," a system of tree-fringed lawns and walkways lying behind the colleges.

bridge (GOLD), where Percy Phelps had had a "triumphant" career (NAVA), and nearly all the principals of the Godfrey Staunton case were Cantabrigians (MISS). The university which Holmes attended (GLOR, MUSG), the one at which he pursued his researches into Early English charters (3STU), and the one thinly disguised by Watson as "Camford" (CREE) might be either Oxford or Cambridge. See also BLUE; TRINITY COLLEGE.

*Camden House, the house opposite Holmes's rooms in Baker Street, from which Sebastian Moran attempted to shoot him (EMPT).

Cameo, an engraving in relief upon a gem, hard stone, or shell. Holmes was involved with the case of the Vatican cameos (HOUN).

*Camford, the university at which Professor Presbury resided, the city of which Holmes called "this charming town" (CREE).

Camp bed, a folding bed (SPEC).

Campbell, Sir Colin, Lord Clyde (1792–1863), a famous British soldier. During the Indian Mutiny he relieved Lucknow, and is credited with crushing the rebellion, for which he was made a peer (SIGN).

Campden House Road, a street in Kensington, into which Pitt Street opens. Horace Harker's bust of Napoleon was found here (SIXN). See the map of KENSINGTON.

*Campden Mansions, the Notting Hill address of Louis La Rothière (BRUC).

Canada, the largest and most important British colony, pop. 5,371,315. Sir Henry Baskerville had farmed in Canada (HOUN), upon which Mycroft Holmes was an expert (BRUC). See also NOVA SCOTIA; TORONTO.

Canadian Pacific Railway, the great transcontinental railway of Canada, begun in 1871 and completed in 1886, the construction of which was a matter of international financial concern and which is credited with being the most prominent feature of the westward development of the country. "C.P.R." was a heading in the Neligan notebook, and Holmes suggested that the letters stood for "Canadian Pacific Railway" (BLAC).

Canary. Henry Wood's mongoose Teddy tried to get at the Barclays' canary (CROO).

The arrest of Wilson, "the notorious canary-trainer," removed a "plague-spot" from the East End of London (BLAC). While a thriving trade in singing-birds is indeed carried on in the East End, the word canary, in criminal slang, also refers to a female sentry posted in the street during a burglary to "sing out" if danger approaches.

Candahar (kahn-dah-hahr'), or Kandahar, a town of considerable commercial and strategical importance in the south of Afghanistan, est. pop. 25,000 to 50,000. It was occupied by the British during the Second Afghan War, and here Watson succeeded in joining his regiment (STUD).

Cane. Holmes took a thin cane with him to the vigil at Stoke Moran (SPEC). He carried one to Thor Bridge (THOR), as did Watson to Shoscombe Old Place (SHOS). Sir Henry Baskerville (HOUN) and the retired sergeant of Marines (STUD) carried a cane. See WALKING-STICK.

Cannon Street Station, a London railway station, located in the City. It is the terminus, with Charing Cross Station, of the South Eastern Railway. Neville St. Clair commuted to the City from Lee each day via Cannon Street (TWIS). See the map of the CITY and the top photograph on p. 226.

Cannula, a small tube used by surgeons to drain fluids from a body cavity or tumor (CREE).

Canteen, a place in a military reservation where alcoholic drinks are sold to enlisted men by permission of the military authorities (CROO).

Canterbury, a city in Kent, pop. 24,889. It is especially famous for its cathedral, built between the eleventh and fifteenth centuries, and is the seat of the Archbishop of Canterbury. Holmes and Watson changed their route to the Continent here (FINA).

Cantlemere, Lord, the government official, representing "the very highest interests," who opposed employing Holmes in the case of the Mazarin diamond (MAZA).

Cantonment, in India, a permanent military station forming the nucleus of the European quarter of a city. Henry Wood's regiment was in cantonments when the Mutiny broke out (CROO).

Cap, a percussion cap. Watson's smoke-rocket was fitted with a cap at either end to make it self-lighting (SCAN), that is, upon impact when thrown.

Cape de Verds, properly **Cape Verde Islands,** an island group some 150 miles west of Africa's western-most point. The survivors of the *Gloria Scott* disaster believed themselves 500 miles south of "the Cape de Verds" (GLOR). See the map of AFRICA.

Cape Town, a seaport and capital city of the Cape of Good Hope colony, and the chief city of the British possessions in South Africa, est. pop. 167,000. The Douglases sailed for Cape Town in the *Palmyra* (VALL), and Godfrey Emsworth was hospitalized here during

the Boer War (BLAN). See the map of SOUTH AFRICA.

Capital and Counties Bank, an English banking firm with its home offices in London and branches in many of the more important provincial cities of England. Holmes banked at the Capital and Counties (PRIO), as did Neville St. Clair (TWIS) and Arthur Cadogan West (BRUC).

*Capleton, the racing establishment belonging to Lord Backwater, on Dartmoor, where Silver Blaze was hidden by Silas Brown (SILV). In some editions this name appears as *Mapleton.*

Carbine, a kind of fire-arm, shorter than a musket or rifle, used in place of a side-arm by cavalry, artillery, and other non-infantry troops (SIGN). The prison guards who sought Seldon upon Dartmoor carried "short rifles" (HOUN).

Carbolic acid, an acid obtained from coal-tar. It is an ill-smelling, colourless liquid used in medicine as a disinfectant and preservative. Holmes said that carbolic or rectified spirits would be the preservatives which would suggest themselves to the medical mind (CARD). Watson dressed Victor Hatherley's wound with carbolized bandages (ENGR).

Carbonari (*kahr-bō-nah′ree*), a secret political society which flourished in Italy and France in the early years of the nineteenth century. Anti-monarchical, anti-clerical, and pro-democratic in philosophy, they were suppressed in the 1830s. The Red Circle was said to be allied to the old Carbonari (REDC), and the *Daily Telegraph* alluded airily to them in its editorial about the Drebber murder (STUD).

Carboy, a glass bottle protected by

an outside covering of basket-work. Carboys of acid stood in the corners of Bartholomew Sholto's laboratory (SIGN).

Carbuncle, a gem of a deep red colour with a mixture of scarlet, found in the East Indies. Blue carbuncles are unknown, but the Countess of Morcar possessed a BLUE CARBUNCLE (BLUE). There were forty carbuncles in the Agra treasure (SIGN).

"Cardboard Box, The" (CARD), a chronicle which appeared originally in the *Strand* magazine for January 1893 and in *Harper's Weekly* of 14 January 1893. It was published variously in the 1894 collection entitled *The Memoirs of Sherlock Holmes* and the 1917 collection *His Last Bow,* having been omitted or removed from editions of the *Memoirs* because of its discussion of adultery. For this reason the famous "mind-reading" incident with which "The Cardboard Box" begins has been transferred in many editions of the *Memoirs* to "The Resident Patient" and actually opens both tales in the American omnibus edition. The case concerns Holmes's investigation of the murder by James Browner of his wife and her lover, and is dated as having occurred between 1885 and 1891.

Cardsharper. Holmes said that Moriarty stood at the head of the criminal chain which ended with the minor criminal such as the cardsharper (VALL).

Carère, Mademoiselle, the French woman believed murdered by her stepmother, but discovered later alive and married in New York (HOUN).

Carey, Peter (1845–95), known as *Black Peter,* a seal and whaling captain who retired in 1884 and was murdered by Patrick Cairns when he re-fused to be blackmailed. His wife and his daughter (b. 1875) did not mourn him (BLAC).

Carfax, Lady Frances, the sole survivor of the direct family of the Earl of Rufton. Abducted by Holy Peters for her jewellery, she was the object of an extensive search by Holmes and her own lover Philip Green (LADY).

Carina, a singer whom Holmes interrupted his investigation of the Amberley case to hear perform at Albert Hall (RETI).

Carlo, the mastiff belonging to Jephro Rucastle, killed by Watson (COPP).

Carlo, the spaniel belonging to the Fergusons (SUSS).

Carlsbad (*kahrls'baht*), or *Karlsbad,* a town and famous health-spa in Bohemia, pop. (1900) 14,640. Egria was not far from here (SCAN).

Carlton Club, the premier Conservative political club of England, located in Pall Mall. The Diogenes Club was a few doors away from the Carlton (GREE), to which Sir James Damery belonged (ILLU).

Carlton House Terrace, an exclusive street in Westminster, just south of Pall Mall. The German Embassy is here (LAST), as was the London residence of the Duke of Holdernesse (PRIO). See Map III of LONDON.

Carlton Terrace: see CARLTON HOUSE TERRACE.

Carlyle, Thomas (1795–1881), an eminent British man of letters, born in Scotland. Upon Watson's quoting Thomas Carlyle, he said, Holmes inquired in the naïvest way who he might have been and what he had done—and shortly thereafter paraphrased Carlyle's most famous aphorism: "They say that genius is an infinite capacity for taking pains" (STUD). Watson said he had worked back to RICHTER through him (SIGN).

Carnaway, Jim (d. 1875), a Scowrer killed in carrying out the work of the lodge. A pension was paid to his widow (VALL).

Carolinas: see NORTH CAROLINA; SOUTH CAROLINA.

Carotid artery, one of the two great arteries which convey blood from the aorta to the head and brain. Willoughby Smith died of a divided carotid artery (GOLD), and Professor Presbury's had been narrowly missed by his wolf-hound's teeth (CREE).

Carpetbaggers, in American history, the name given to northern politicians who took up residence in the southern states in order to become representatives of those states in Congress following the Civil War. The name is now especially applied to those northern adventurers who settled in the South and who 1865–76 attempted to control the southern states by becoming leaders of the Negro voters. Elias Openshaw took a strong part in opposing the "carpet-bag politicians" (FIVE).

Carriage: see BAROUCHE; BROUGHAM; BUCKBOARD; BUS; DOG-CART; DRAG; FOUR-WHEELER; GIG; HANSOM; LANDAU; TRAP; WAGONETTE; see also BOX; FOUR-IN-HAND; JARVEY; OFFICIAL REGISTRY.

McFarlane's carriage-building depot backed on to Jabez Wilson's pawnshop (REDH).

***Carriton's,** a house in Sussex (SUSS).

Carruthers, Bob, the employer of Violet SMITH and partner of Jack WOODLEY. He participated in the plan to acquire the girl's fortune, but fell in love with her and finally acted in her own interests. His daughter (b. 1885) was Miss Smith's charge (SOLI).

Carruthers, Colonel. Holmes and Watson locked up Colonel Carruthers shortly before the Wisteria Lodge case (WIST).

Carson City, a city of the United States, now capital of the state of Nevada, pop. 2,100. John and Lucy Ferrier, led by Jefferson Hope, fled Salt Lake City toward Carson City (STUD) at a time when the town was the western-most settlement of the Territory of UTAH.

Carstairs, a town in the south of Scotland, pop. (1891) 477. Edith Woodley was from here (EMPT).

Carston, Earl of, an inferior title of the Duke of Holdernesse (PRIO).

***Carston Castle,** the hereditary seat of the earls of Carston, at Bangor in Wales (PRIO).

Carter, the treasurer of the Scowrers (VALL).

Cartwright (b. 1875), a district messenger-boy. Holmes dispatched him in search of the cut *Times,* and he brought Holmes's supplies to the moor (HOUN).

Cartwright, one of the WORTHINGDON BANK GANG (RESI).

Case-book, a small book in which Holmes recorded the details of his cases. He consulted it upon the mention of Mrs. Farintosh by Helen Stoner (SPEC). He referred to the notes upon the Baskerville case under the heading *B* in his "indexed list of cases" (HOUN) and looked fondly through the letter *V* in the index volume which recorded his old cases (SUSS); see also COMMONPLACE BOOK; DIARY; NOTEBOOK.

"Case Book of Sherlock Holmes,

The," the fifth and final collection of Sherlock Holmes cases, published in 1927 and containing, in order of their first English magazine appearances, the following: "The Adventure of the Mazarin Stone" (MAZA), "The Problem of Thor Bridge" (THOR), "The Adventure of the Creeping Man" (CREE), "The Adventure of the Sussex Vampire" (SUSS), "The Adventure of the Three Garridebs" (3GAR), "The Adventure of the Illustrious Client" (ILLU), "The Adventure of the Three Gables (3GAB), "The Adventure of the Blanched Soldier" (BLAN), "The Adventure of the Lion's Mane" (LION), "The Adventure of the Retired Colourman" (RETI), "The Adventure of the Veiled Lodger" (VEIL), and "The Adventure of Shoscombe Old Place" (SHOS).

"Case of Identity, A" (IDEN), a chronicle which appeared originally in the *Strand* magazine for September 1891 and was published in the collection entitled *The Adventures of Sherlock Holmes* the following year. It concerns the vanishing of Mr. Hosmer Angel from the cab conveying him to his wedding with Mary Sutherland, and of her plea to Holmes to locate her affianced. It is variously dated as having taken place in 1887, 1888, 1889, or 1890.

Watson himself dates it by implication in 1890 (REDH) and observed that the case had been free of legal crime (BLUE, COPP).

*Cassel-Felstein, the grand duchy ruled by the King of Bohemia (SCAN). In some editions it appears as *Cassel-Falstein.*

Castalotte, Tito, a New York fruit importer, senior partner of the firm of **Castalotte & Zamba,** who befriended Gennaro Lucca and defied the Red Circle (REDC).

Castor-oil, a mild purgative (SIGN).

Cat. Large black cats were kept by Von Bork's housekeeper Martha (LAST) and at the cottage where little Lucy Hebron stayed (YELL), and there was a cat at Appledore Towers (CHAS). A shocking story of how Jonas Oldacre turned a cat loose in an aviary demonstrated his "brutal cruelty" (NORW).

Catalepsy, a condition in which a person suddenly becomes unconscious and remains rigidly fixed in the attitude which he had assumed when the attack seized him. Dr. Percy Trevelyan had excited considerable interest by his research into the pathology of catalepsy, yet was unable to discern the fraud when a member of the Worthingdon Bank Gang imitated a cataleptic attack; but Holmes said that it was an easy complaint to imitate, and that he had done it himself (RESI).

Cataract, a disease of the eye, in which the lens becomes opaque and causes partial or total blindness. It is treated by different surgical operations, all of them consisting of removing the diseased lens from its position opposite the transparent cornea. Lady Maynooth returned to England for a cataract operation (EMPT).

Cataract knife, a small, delicate knife used in the removal of the lens of the eye in cataract surgery. A cataract knife was found in John Straker's hand (SILV).

Cathedral, The, Winchester: see WINCHESTER.

Catholic: see ROMAN CATHOLIC CHURCH.

Catkin, in botany, the scaly spike of a unisexual flower. Holmes said that it was pleasant to see the catkins on the hazels once again (WIST).

Catkin.

Cat's-eye, a variety of quartz from which a gem of considerable value is cut. There was a great variety of cats'-eyes in the Agra treasure (SIGN).

Catullus (*kuh-tuhl'luhs*), **Gaius Valerius** (*c.*87–54 B.C.), a famous Roman lyric poet. In his disguise as an old bibliophile, Holmes carried a volume entitled *Catullus* (EMPT).

*Caulfield Gardens, the Kensington address of Hugo Oberstein, which backed onto a Metropolitan railway cutting (BRUC).

Caunter, a classmate of Lord Saltire (PRIO).

Cause célèbre, a French phrase meaning *famous case,* that is, a well-publicized occurrence (COPP).

Caution, in slang, something extraordinary. Jefferson Hope remarked that the way Holmes kept on his trail was "a caution" (STUD).

Cavalier, the name applied to a partisan of CHARLES I in his conflict with Parliament, as opposed to the *Roundheads,* the name given to the adherents of the Parliamentary cause. Sir Ralph Musgrave was a prominent Cavalier (MUSG), as was Hugo Baskerville (HOUN).

Cavendish, tobacco which has been pressed into cakes and sweetened with syrup or molasses, for chewing or smoking (SILV).

Cavendish Club, a London club located in Regent Street. Ronald Adair was a member (EMPT).

Cavendish Square, a square in the West End, at the heart of the doctors' quarter of London. Dr. Percy Trevelyan complained that a medical specialist who aims high is compelled to start in one of a dozen streets in the Cavendish Square quarter, all of which entail enormous rents and furnishing expenses (RESI). The circuitous route taken on foot to Camden House by Holmes and Watson began at Cavendish Square (EMPT), and the two of them passed through the doctors' quarter on their way to the Alpha Inn (BLUE). See also HARLEY STREET; QUEEN ANNE STREET. See Map III of LONDON.

Cawnpore, a city in India, situated on the Ganges, pop. 197,000. The European inhabitants of the city, after a heroic attempt to defend themselves against the besieging Sepoys during the MUTINY, capitulated on the sworn promise of NANA SAHIB that he would

The river steps at Cawnpore, where the European garrison was treacherously massacred in June 1857 by the Indian mutineers under Nana Sahib.

allow them to retire unmolested; but as they were embarking, they were set upon and indiscriminately slaughtered. The women and children were carried back to Cawnpore and kept until the approach of the relieving British force, when they were all put to death (SIGN).

C.B., the abbreviation for *Companion of the Bath,* the lowest class of the order of knighthood known as the *Knights of the Bath.* The order was supposedly instituted by Henry IV in 1399 and takes its name from the ritual purification bath taken the evening before dubbing. The present order was begun by George I in 1725. Sir Augustus Moran was a C.B. (EMPT).

Cecil Forrester, Mrs., a lady whom Holmes once helped. She was Mary Morstan's employer (SIGN).

*****Cedars, The,** the villa belonging to Neville St. Clair, located near Lee (TWIS).

Celts (*kelts*), the earliest Aryan settlers in Europe, according to the common theory. Holmes spoke of Celtic intuition (SIGN) and claimed that Rachel Howells, being of Welsh blood, possessed a passionate Celtic soul (MUSG). Dr. Mortimer said Sir Henry Baskerville possessed the rounded head of the Celt, and with it the Celtic enthusiasm and power of attachment (HOUN). See also GAEL; IVERNIAN.

The **Celtic language** is divided into two great dialects, widely differing from each other but belonging to the same stock. One is the *Gaelic,* represented by the Highlanders of Scotland and by the Irish; the other is the *Cymric,* represented by the Welsh and the inhabitants of Brittany and CORNWALL. Holmes believed that CHALDEAN roots were to be traced in

the Cornish branch of the Celtic speech (DEVI).

Celts (*selts*), prehistoric weapons or other implements of stone or bronze. Holmes discoursed upon them to Watson (DEVI).

Central Africa, or the *Congo,* that part of Africa which is drained by the Congo River and its tributaries, generally congruent to the central portion of the continent. Leon Sterndale intended to bury himself here (DEVI). See also UBANGHI COUNTRY.

Central America. Rodger Baskerville had gone to Central America as a young man (HOUN), and Don Murillo's name was a terror throughout the region (WIST). See also COSTA RICA; SAN PEDRO; also SPANISH AMERICA.

Central Press Syndicate, properly **Central News Agency,** an English association for the collection and distribution of news to newspapers subscribing to its services. Horace Harker worked for the "Central Press Syndicate" (SIXN).

Ceramics: see CROWN DERBY; EGG-SHELL PORCELAIN; MIDDLE AGES (mediæval pottery); MONOGRAPH (Baron Gruner). For Chinese porcelain see HUNG-WU; MING; SUNG; TANG; TANG-YING; WEI; YUAN; YUNG-LO.

Ceylon, an island and British crown colony of the Indian Ocean, located just off the southern point of India, pop. 3,576,990. Holmes had made a special study of the BUDDHISM of Ceylon (SIGN). See also TRINCOMALEE; see the map of INDIA.

Chaffer, to bargain or haggle (BERY).

Chair, the position or office of a professor at a university, so called because in the mediæval universities the lecturer alone sat in a chair, his listeners upon benches or the floor. Moriarty's treatise upon the Binomial Theorem won him the mathematical chair at a small English university (FINA). Professor Morphy occupied the chair of Comparative Anatomy at Camford University (CREE).

Chairman of Committees, in either House of Parliament, the member appointed to preside over it whenever it resolves itself into a committee of the whole. Sir William Baskerville had been Chairman of Committees of the House of Commons under Pitt (HOUN).

Chaldea, a district south-east of Babylonia, on the Persian Gulf. The Chaldean dynasty of Babylonian rulers occupied the throne from the end of the seventh century B.C. to 556 B.C. and included the famous Nebuchadnezzar. The **Chaldean language,** also known as *Aramaic,* was one of the principal varieties of the ancient Semitic, closely allied to the Hebrew and Phoenician, and was spoken in Syria and Palestine following its importation to the west by Jews returning from the Babylonian captivity. In Palestine it supplanted Hebrew after the sixth century B.C., and it was the tongue of the Jews in the time of Christ. Holmes had conceived the idea that the ancient Cornish language was akin to the Chaldean and had largely derived from the Phoenician traders in tin (DEVI).

Chalk, a soft white rock, comprising very conspicuous formations in the south of England and northern France. The NORTH DOWNS are chalk (VALL), and Holmes writes that in the vicinity of his retirement home the Sussex coast-line is composed entirely of chalk cliffs (LION). Von Bork's house stood upon a chalk cliff overlooking Harwich (LAST). Joseph Openshaw

died from a fall into a chalk-pit (FIVE), and there was one near Abbas Parva (VEIL).

Champagne. John McGinty served champagne to McMurdo and Baldwin (VALL).

Chancellery, the office or court of a *chancellor,* who is, broadly speaking, the chief officer of a monarchy, charged with the direction of state affairs and responsible to the King (SECO).

Chancellor, the chief executive of the German Empire, appointed and removed at will by the KAISER. His duties very approximately correspond with those of Britain's Prime Minister. Baron Von Herling spoke of the heavy-handedness of the Chancellor (LAST), who 1909–17 was *Theobald von Bethmann-Hollweg* (1856–1921), known for his honesty and good intentions but also for his lack of diplomacy.

Chandler: see CORN-CHANDLER.

Chandos, Sir Charles. Ames had been with Sir Charles for ten years before becoming the butler of Birlstone (VALL).

Channel, The: see ENGLISH CHANNEL.

Chaparral bush, any low scrub growing in arid parts of the western United States. *Chaparral* refers to the clump or grove of bushes rather than to the type of the plant itself. Dwarfish chaparral bushes dotted the Great Alkali Plain (STUD).

Chapel. Holmes was bitten by Victor Trevor's dog on his way to attend chapel at his college (GLOR). Lady Beatrice Falder was entombed in the crypt beneath the ancient chapel of Shoscombe Old Place (SHOS).

Chaplet: see CORONET.

Charasiab (*kah-rah-see-ahb'*), or *Charasia,* a town of Afghanistan, twelve miles south-west of Cabul. A battle fought here on 6 October 1879 during the Second Afghan War was a British victory which opened the way to the capture of the Afghan capital. Colonel Sebastian Moran fought in the battle of Charasiab, and his bravery was cited in the official dispatches (EMPT).

Charge, in heraldry, any device borne upon a coat-of-arms. Reginald Musgrave compared the Musgrave Ritual to his family's "blazonings and charges," as something of no practical use (MUSG). See also BLAZONING; HERALDRY.

Charing Cross, the official centre of metropolitan London, an open area on the south side of Trafalgar Square, between Whitehall and the Strand. Harold Latimer took Mr. Melas through Charing Cross (GREE), where Cox & Co. was located (THOR) and in the neighbourhood of which young Cartwright searched for the mutilated copy of *The Times*

The view down the Strand from Charing Cross. Trafalgar Square is to the extreme left. At centre is the building in which the Charing Cross Post Office is located, and across the Strand rises the curved façade of the Grand Hotel, with Northumberland Avenue entering in the fore-ground upon the far right.

(HOUN). Holmes declared that he deserved to be "kicked from here to Charing Cross" for his slowness in solving the St. Clair case (TWIS). See Map II of LONDON and the map of WHITEHALL.

Charing Cross Hospital, a hospital in the Strand near Charing Cross, which serves as a medical school for London University. Dr. Mortimer had been house-surgeon here (HOUN), and Holmes was carried here after he was attacked in Regent Street (ILLU). See Map II of LONDON.

Charing Cross Hotel, the hotel adjacent to Charing Cross Station, fronting upon the Strand. The trap for Hugo Oberstein was set in the smoking-room here (BRUC). See the photograph of the STRAND and Map II of LONDON.

Charing Cross Post Office, a post-office at the intersection of Charing Cross and the Strand. Both Holmes (ABBE) and John Scott Eccles (WIST) sent wires here, and the mysterious letter to Sir Henry Baskerville bore the Charing Cross postmark (HOUN). See the photograph of the STRAND and Map II of LONDON.

Charing Cross Station, the London terminus, with Cannon Street Station, of the *South Eastern Railway,* constructed in 1864 between the Strand and the Embankment. Holmes and Watson departed for Marsham (ABBE) and for Chatham (GOLD) from Charing Cross, and Irene Adler and her husband left London from here (SCAN). Madame Fournaye attracted much attention here by her appearance and gestures (SECO). Holmes said that a man named Matthews had knocked out his left canine tooth in the Charing Cross waiting-room (EMPT). Watson writes that it was between here and the Grand

Hotel that he saw the news of the attack upon Holmes (ILLU). See the photograph of the STRAND and Map II of LONDON.

Charles, Kings of Great Britain and Ireland, of the Stuart house.

Charles I (1600–1649) succeeded to the throne in 1625. After nearly twenty years of conflict with Parliament over funds, and in the midst of Scottish insurrection, open warfare between Charles and Parliament erupted, resulting finally in the King's capture and execution. Coins of Charles I were found hidden at Hurlstone along with the ancient Stuart crown, and the "he who is gone" in the Musgrave Ritual refers to him (MUSG). It was said that he had been concealed at Birlstone Manor for several days during the Civil War (VALL), and Holmes remarked that Charles's head was still firm on his shoulders when the volume *De Jure inter Gentes* was struck off in 1642 (STUD). See also CAVALIER.

His son, **Charles II** (1630–1685), spent his young manhood in exile and finally was restored to the throne in 1660. Sir Ralph Musgrave was an intimate companion of the King in his wanderings, and the "he who will come" in the Ritual refers to Charles II (MUSG).

"Charles Augustus Milverton, The Adventure of" (CHAS), a chronicle which appeared originally in the *Strand* magazine for April 1904 and *Collier's Weekly* of 26 March 1904 and was published in the collection entitled *The Return of Sherlock Holmes* the following year. It concerns Holmes's efforts to recover the letters used by Charles Augustus Milverton to blackmail Holmes's client Lady Eva Brackwell, and the tragic events which followed his and Watson's attempt to bur-

gle Milverton's house. Watson states his intention to conceal the date and other facts by which one might trace the actual events, and opinions as to the case's date range from 1882 to 1899.

Charles Street, a short street in Westminster, running along the south side of the government office building which houses the Foreign Office. Percy Phelps rushed into Charles Street after the stolen naval treaty (NAVA). See the map of WHITEHALL and the photograph on p. 56.

*Charlington, a region of western Surrey, near Farnham. Chiltern Grange was located here, and between Chiltern Grange and the high road to Farnham lie **Charlington Heath** and the nearby **Charlington Hall,** where Jack Woodley lived, which is surrounded by the magnificent **Charlington Wood** (SOLI).

Charpentier, a family residing in Camberwell. **Madame Charpentier** was the proprietress of **Charpentier's Boarding Establishment,** where Drebber and Stangerson stayed, and Drebber's brutish conduct toward her daughter **Alice Charpentier** caused Alice's brother **Arthur Charpentier,** a British naval officer, to pursue Drebber and attempt to thrash him (STUD).

Chart: see MAP.

Charter: see EARLY ENGLISH CHARTERS.

Charwoman (*chair'woman*), a woman hired by the day to do odd jobs of household work (NAVA). The Amberleys employed a woman who came in by the day (RETI).

Charybdis: see SCYLLA AND CHARYBDIS.

Chasing, a design engraved upon a metallic surface. The price of the gold chasing on the Beryl Coronet was said to be incalculable (**BERY**).

Chatham (*chat'm*), a city of Kent, pop. 37,057. Yoxley Old Place was not far from here (GOLD). See the map accompanying SUSSEX.

Chauffeur. Baron Von Herling's car was chauffeured (LAST).

*****Cheeseman's,** the name of Robert Ferguson's home in Sussex (SUSS).

Cheetah, or *hunting leopard,* a variety of leopard found in northern India. Dr. Grimesby Roylott had a passion for Indian animals and kept a cheetah which wandered freely over the grounds at Stoke Moran (SPEC).

Chemist, a registered seller of drugs, poisons, and pharmaceuticals (ILLU, SILV).

Chemistry. Watson called Holmes's knowledge of chemistry "profound" (STUD) yet "eccentric" (FIVE) and complained that the Baker Street chambers were always full of chemicals (MUSG). Holmes often performed experiments and analyses (COPP, DANC, IDEN, NAVA, RESI,† SIGN, STUD) in his own chemical corner (EMPT, MAZA) and at St. Bartholomew's Hospital (STUD), and Watson writes that without his chemicals Holmes was an uncomfortable man (3STU). Holmes and Watson first met in the chemical laboratory of St. Bartholomew's (STUD), and Holmes maintained that he would devote himself to chemical researches when he retired (FINA).

When Holmes heard of the murder of John Douglas, his face showed "the quiet and interested composure of the chemist" who watches the results of an experiment (VALL). Bartholomew

† This reference appeared in the original magazine and book publications of "The Resident Patient" but was omitted from the 1928 omnibus volume and all subsequent editions.

Sholto's chamber had been fitted up as a chemical laboratory (SIGN). Jefferson Hope had been janitor at the laboratory of York College (STUD).

For chemical apparatus see BUNSEN BURNER; CARBOY; LITMUS-PAPER; PIPETTE; RETORT; see also MICROSCOPE.

That division of chemistry which treats of the carbon compounds is called **organic chemistry.** Holmes worked on some experiments in organic chemistry after his first visit to Donnithorpe (GLOR) and believed he had discovered a test for blood stains superior to the old GUAIACUM TEST (STUD). He called a demonstration of the DEVIL'S-FOOT ROOT a "chemical experiment" (DEVI) and conducted some researches into COAL-TAR derivatives during the Great Hiatus (EMPT).

See also ACETONES; ACID ALKALI; ALKALOID; AMALGAM; AMYL; BARTYA; BISULPHATE; CARBOLIC ACID; HYDRO-CARBONS; HYDROCHLORIC ACID; IODO-FORM; NITRATE; NITRITE OF AMYL; PHOSPHORUS; PRUSSIC ACID; REAGENT; RECTIFIED SPIRITS; SPIRITS OF WINE; VITRIOL. See also NARCOTIC; POISON.

*****Chequers,** the inn at Camford where Holmes and Watson stayed (CREE).

*****Chequers,** the inn or hotel at Lamberley where Holmes and Watson stayed (SUSS).

Chesterfield, a town in Derbyshire, pop. 27,185. The father of Neville St. Clair was a schoolmaster here (TWIS), where Reuben Hays was arrested (PRIO).

Chesterton, an urban district to the north of Cambridge, pop. 9,591. Holmes sought Godfrey Staunton here (MISS). See the map of CAMBRIDGE.

Chestnut. There were chestnut trees at Wisteria Lodge (WIST) and in the Park (YELL).

Chevy, in English slang, to chase

about or vex. Watson and his play-mates used to chevy Percy Phelps with a wicket (NAVA).

Chianti (*kyahn'tee*), a red wine made in Tuscany. Thaddeus Sholto offered Mary Morstan a glass (SIGN).

Chicago, the second largest city in the United States, situated at the head of Lake Michigan in the state of Illinois, pop. 1,698,575.

Old Patrick and Abe Slaney were members of a Chicago gang, and Slaney was described to Holmes as "the most dangerous crook in Chicago" (DANC). Killer Evans was a native of this city, where Alexander Hamilton Garrideb was said to have made part of his fortune (3GAR). Birdy Edwards came to Vermissa Valley from Chicago and returned here after the suppression of the Scowrers, was married here, and was driven from the city by his enemies (VALL). Holmes began his own penetration of Von Bork's organization here (LAST).

Chicago Central, the Central Division of the Chicago Police Department, with headquarters in City Hall. Captain Marvin was spoken of as "Marvin of the Chicago Central" (VALL).

Chicken, in English slang, a child. Lestrade said he was no chicken (STUD).

Chief, in heraldry, the upper third of a shield. The caltrops upon Lord Robert St. Simon's arms were **in chief** (NOBL), that is, borne upon the upper third of the shield; see HERALDRY.

Chief. Inspector Gregson referred the Lucca affair to his Chief (REDC), that is, to one of the several Chief Inspectors at SCOTLAND YARD to whom the other detectives are responsible.

Chief constable, in England, the head of a county police force. The chief constable of Kent sent for Scotland Yard in the Willoughby Smith murder case (GOLD).

Chief Constructor, in the Admiralty, the officer charged with the general supervision of construction for the Navy (BRUC).

Chief Secretary of State: see CABINET.

Chilian Wallah, or *Chillianwallah*, a village in the Punjaub. In a battle fought here 13 January 1849 during a war with the Sikhs, the British forces won a tactical victory which led to the conquest of the Punjaub. Mahomet Singh and Abdullah Khan had fought against the British here (SIGN).

*Chiltern Grange, the house occupied by Bob Carruthers (SOLI).

China, or *The Chinese Empire,* the largest empire of Asia and third largest in the world, est. pop. 350,000,000. PEKING is the capital.

The blue carbuncle was found in the banks of a river in southern China (BLUE), and the *Gloria Scott* had been built for the coastal tea trade (GLOR). Holmes deduced that Jabez Wilson had been in China from the tattoo above his wrist and the Chinese coin upon his watch-chain (REDH). Before falling ill Holmes had been working among some Chinese sailors in the London dock region (DYIN). Baron Gruner was an authority upon Chinese pottery (ILLU). The code Birdy Edwards was said to use might as well have been written in Chinese (VALL).

For Chinese dynasties see MING; SUNG; TANG; WEI; YUAN; for emperors see HUNG-WU; YUNG-LO. See also IMPERIAL PALACE OF PEKING; TANG-YING; TIBET; also COOLIE; CYCLICAL DATES. See also GORDON, GEN. CHARLES GEORGE.

Chinchilla beard, a long beard which is gathered into little tufts resembling chinchilla fur. Dr. Becher had such a beard (ENGR).

Chin China coaster, the term used by Jack Prendergast in speaking of the *Gloria Scott* (GLOR). *Chin China* is a diffusive term probably derived from the former use by Europeans of *Chin* as a name for China. This expression is omitted from some editions.

Chip-box, a small box made of thin wood (STUD).

Chislehurst Station, the railway station adjacent to the London suburb of *Chislehurst,* located in Kent but within the Metropolitan Police District. It is centred in a beautiful, well-wooded district occupied by a number of exclusive estates. Holmes and Watson detrained at Chislehurst Station for Marsham and the Abbey Grange (ABBE). See the back endpaper map.

Chiswick (*chiz'ick*), an urban district of Middlesex, suburban to London, pop. 29,809. It is largely residential. Josiah Brown lived here (SIXN). See the back endpaper map.

Chloroform. Lady Frances Carfax was drugged with chloroform (LADY), Mary Maberley was chloroformed during the burgling of her house (3GAB), and Holmes chloroformed Von Bork (LAST).

Chokey, or *choky,* an Anglo-Indian word for a guard-house, police station, or lock-up; thus, in English slang, a prison (SIGN).

Chopin (*shō-paN′*), **Frédéric François** (1809–1849), a celebrated pianist and musical composer. Holmes mused upon one of the Chopin pieces played by Norman-Néruda (STUD).

Chowdar, Lal, a servant of Major Sholto (SIGN).

Christie and Manson's Auction Rooms, the well-known rooms off St. James's Square, celebrated for sales of valuable art objects. The chief sales take place on Saturdays in the London season. Nathan Garrideb occasionally drove to Sotheby's or Christie's (3GAR). Holmes said that no finer piece than the Ming saucer he borrowed had ever passed through Christie's, where Watson was to suggest it be appraised (ILLU).

Christmas. The case of the blue carbuncle occurred upon the second day after Christmas (BLUE). Julia Stoner met a half-pay major of Marines at her aunt's during Christmas 1880 (SPEC).

Chronicle, London newspaper: see DAILY CHRONICLE.

Chubb lock, a lock of a special type devised by the English inventor *Charles Chubb* (d. 1845). There was a Chubb lock on the door of Briony Lodge (SCAN) and on Professor Coram's bureau (GOLD).

Church of England. Watson described Scott Eccles as a Churchman (WIST). Dr. Grimesby Roylott's death-cry was heard at the Stoke Moran parsonage (SPEC). J. C. Elman (RETI), Parker (DANC), Roundhay (DEVI), and the vicar assaulted by Peter Carey (BLAC) were Church of England clergy, as presumably were James Desmond (HOUN), Joshua Stone (WIST), Elias Whitney (TWIS), the minister who performed the wedding between Irene Adler and Godfrey Norton (SCAN), and the defrocked Williamson (SOLI). Holmes turned up Elman in his CROCKFORD (RETI).

See also ST. GEORGE'S; ST. PAUL'S; ST. SAVIOUR'S; WESTMINSTER ABBEY; also CANTERBURY; KENSINGTON; WINCHESTER; also BENCH OF BISHOPS;

CHAPEL; LIVING; PARISH; PARSONAGE; VICAR. See also MORMONS; NONCONFORMIST; ROMAN CATHOLIC CHURCH.

Church Row, a residential street in Hampstead. Holmes and Watson took a hansom as far as Church Row on their way to burgle Appledore Towers (CHAS).

Church Row, Hampstead.

Church Street, a street in Kensington, lying to the west of Hyde Park. Holmes in his disguise as an old bibliophile claimed to have a bookshop here (EMPT). See the map of KENSINGTON.

Church Street. The Napoleonic busts were made in a sculptor-works in "Church Street, Stepney" (SIXN). There is a Church Street in Stepney, in the Thames-side region known as *Wapping,* but it is short and mean, not "a broad thoroughfare, once the abode of wealthy City merchants."

C.I.D.: see SCOTLAND YARD.

Cigar. Holmes kept his cigars in the coal-scuttle (MUSG). He made a special study of cigar ashes and believed he could distinguish at a glance the ash of any known brand of either cigar or tobacco (STUD); he was the author of a monograph upon the subject (BOSC, STUD) entitled "Upon the Distinction Between the Ashes of the Various Tobaccos" (SIGN). He deduced that the killer of Charles McCarthy smoked Indian cigars which he cut with a blunt penknife and smoked with a cigar-holder (BOSC), and said that the cigar-ends found in Blessington's fireplace were of the sort imported by the Dutch from their East Indian colonies, while Blessington's own were Havanas (RESI). Dr. Grimesby Roylott also smoked strong Indian cigars (SPEC). Dr. Mortimer deduced how long Sir Charles Baskerville had stood at the Yew Alley gate by the ash which had dropped from his cigar (HOUN).

See also HAVANA; LUNKAH; TRICHINOPOLY; also CIGARETTE; PIPE; TOBACCO.

Cigarette. Cigarette tobaccos were included in Holmes's monograph upon tobacco ashes (BOSC, SIGN). Dr. Mortimer made his own (HOUN). Professor Coram smoked an enormous number, which were made for him by Ionides of Alexandria (GOLD), and Watson's cigarettes bore the name of his tobacconist Bradley (HOUN).

Cipher: see CRYPTOGRAPHY.

Circus, the space formed at the intersection of two streets by making the buildings at the angles concave so as to give the form of a circle; e.g., REGENT CIRCUS (CHAS, GREE).

City, The, properly the **City of London,** the commercial centre of the me-

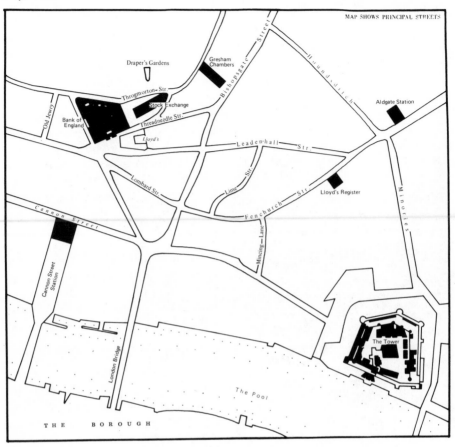

The City.

tropolis, forming the nucleus of the EAST END. The resident population is 26,923. It is the most ancient part of London, standing upon the site of the original Roman town, and embraces the many offices of merchants, money-changers, brokers, bankers, and underwriters, as well as the BANK OF ENGLAND, the STOCK EXCHANGE, the Central Post Office, the legal corporations of the Inns of Court (see TEMPLE), and ST. PAUL's cathedral. Legally the City is a separate municipality, distinct even from the administrative county of London, having an ancient civic corporation of its own, at the head of which is the Lord Mayor.

John Hector McFarlane's office was in the City (NORW), as were the firms of Holder & Stevenson (BERY), Westhouse & Marbank (IDEN), Jabez Wilson's pawnshop (REDH), and the infamous opium-den called the Bar of Gold (TWIS). Hall Pycroft was a City man (STOC), and Hugh Boone was a familiar figure in the busy streets (TWIS). Grant Munro's business often took him here (YELL). Church Street, Stepney, had once been the abode of wealthy City merchants (SIXN).

Holmes commenced his investigation

The view westward over the City, dominated by the dome of St. Paul's.

The traditional centre of the City, from which radiate its most important streets.
The building shown is the Bank of England. At right lies Threadneedle Street.

of the Openshaw case in the City (FIVE), which the police launch passed on its way to the Tower (SIGN).

See also BOROUGH, THE; CITY POLICE; COCKNEY.

*City and Suburban Bank, the London banking firm whose Coburg branch office was the target of a burglary foiled by Holmes (REDH).

City Police, the police organization of the City of London, distinct from Scotland Yard. The force's strength in 1893 was 893. Members of the City Police captured Beddington (STOC).

Civil War, American, the great struggle of 1861–65 between the Northern and the Southern states of the Union. Elias Openshaw fought for the South under JACKSON and HOOD, and the Ku Klux Klan was formed in reaction to Northern reconstruction policies following the war (FIVE). Chester Wilcox had served in the war (VALL), and his portrait of Henry Ward Beecher turned Watson's mind to it (CARD).†

Civil War, English, also called The Great Rebellion, the conflict between the supporters of Parliament and of CHARLES I in 1641–49. Charles was concealed at Birlstone for several days during the war, and a Parliamentary colonel took the manor in 1644 (VALL). Hugo Baskerville's death occurred during the Great Rebellion (HOUN).

Clapham (clap'm) Junction, the most important railway station in South London, and a major junction through which twelve hundred trains pass daily, notably those serving Victoria and Waterloo stations. Mr. Melas

† This allusion is inserted in "The Resident Patient" in some editions.

took a train for Victoria at Clapham Junction (GREE), and the trains from Woking (NAVA) and Winchester (SILV) passed through here. See the front endpaper map.

Clarendon, Edward Hyde, Earl of (1608–1674), a chancellor of England, in 1668 forced to take refuge in France owing to the disfavour of Charles II. His *History of the Great Rebellion* (1702) was recommended by the author of the Baskerville manuscript (HOUN).

Claret, the name given in English to the red wines of France, excluding Burgundy wines. Holmes and Watson talked together over a bottle of claret (CARD), Holmes refreshed himself with a glass after the taking of Culverton Smith (DYIN), and James Windibank travelled for a claret importing firm (IDEN).

Claridge's Hotel, one of the more famous London hotels, located in Brook Street in Westminster. J. Neil Gibson stayed here while in London (THOR), and Holmes told his agent Martha to report to him here (LAST). See Map III of LONDON.

Clay, John (b. c.1860), the fourth smartest man in London, according to Holmes, and the third most daring, whose scheme to rob the City and Suburban Bank was frustrated by the detective (REDH).

Clayton, John, the cab-driver who drove the disguised Stapleton about London (HOUN).

Clear, in sailing, to leave port having satisfied the customs authorities and procured the necessary permissions to depart (FIVE).

*Cleft Tor, a Dartmoor tor (HOUN).

Clerk (clark). Percy Phelps and Charles Gorot were clerks at the Foreign Office (NAVA), and Cadogan

West and Sidney Johnson at Woolwich Arsenal (BRUC). Hall Pycroft was a stockbroker's clerk (STOC). Hosmer Angel was supposedly a cashier in a Leadenhall Street office and spoke of the firm's "other clerks" (IDEN). Victor Hatherley employed a clerk (ENGR), and John Hector McFarlane's witnessed Jonas Oldacre's will (NORW). Clerks were employed at Holder & Stevenson (BERY), and the clerk or secretary of the firm of Morrison, Morrison, and Dodd had the initials E.J.C. (SUSS). A volunteer force of clerks and merchants had been formed to help defend Agra during the Mutiny (SIGN). See also HOTEL SERVANTS; SERVANT, subheaded *Professional and Commercial Servants.*

Cleveland, a city of Ohio, pop. 381,768. Enoch Drebber and Joseph Stangerson resided in Cleveland until the arrival of Jefferson Hope, and Holmes solved Drebber's murder largely by wiring here for information about the victim (STUD).

Clipper, the swiftest of all sailing-ships, of a type developed by American builders after 1832. They declined after 1860 in the face of improved steamships, but by 1855 the *Gloria Scott* had lost much of her trade to them (GLOR).

Clog, a kind of shoe with a very thick sole and high heels, in common use until about 1840. Holmes said that "the clogs of curious peasants" would have obliterated the clues in the Yew Alley (HOUN).

Clubfoot, a congenital deformity of the foot, set awry from the ankle, imperfect in shape, and often undersized. Ricoletti had a club foot (MUSG).

Clubs, London: see ANGLO-INDIAN; BAGATELLE; BALDWIN; CARLTON; TANKERVILLE; see also PALL MALL; ST.

JAMES'S STREET. Watson spent a day at his club (HOUN).

For sporting clubs see HURLINGHAM; PRINCE'S; see also RUGBY; also LONDON, subheaded *Streets and Parks.*

Coach, a private tutor, especially one employed in preparing for a particular examination. Harold Stackhurst's coaching establishment was not far from Holmes's retirement villa (LION). Professor Moriarty was an ARMY COACH (FINA).

Coachman: see SERVANT.

Coal and Iron Police: see POLICE.

Coal-scuttle, a metal or more commonly wooden box or container for the carrying and keeping of coal for the fireplace. Holmes kept his cigars (MUSG), as well as his pipes and tobacco (MAZA), in his coal-scuttle.

Coals of fire. Culverton Smith made reference to the expression *to heap coals of fire upon one's head* (DYIN), that is, to render good in return for the evil done one by another, in obedience to the Biblical injunction: "If thine enemy hunger, feed him; if he thirst, give him drink; for in so doing thou shalt heap coals of fire on his head" (*Rom.* 12:20).

Coal-tar, a dark, viscid, ill-smelling, organic compound obtained during the distillation of coal for the manufacture of illuminating gas. In recent years a great number of valuable products have been derived by distillation from coal-tar, such as ammonia, naphtha, CREOSOTE, CARBOLIC ACID, benzine, and a series of dyes and ALKALOID products. Holmes spent some months in a research into the coal-tar derivatives during the Great Hiatus (EMPT). He detected the "tarry odour" of disinfectant upon the butler's gloves at Tuxbury Old Hall (BLAN), and Watson remarked upon the "tarlike odour" of creosote in Bartholomew Sholto's laboratory and the garret above it (SIGN).

Coat-of-arms: see HERALDRY.

Cob, a strong, thick-set horse. The Baskervilles' wagonette was pulled by a pair of cobs (HOUN).

Cobb, John, the groom employed by Charles McCarthy (BOSC).

Cobbler's wax, a resinous substance which is rubbed on shoemakers' thread to facilitate the stitching of leather (REDH).

Cobra. Henry Wood had a fangless cobra which his mongoose Teddy caught to please the audiences at the canteens (CROO). Holmes said that *Cyanea capillata* could be as dangerous to life as the bite of a cobra (LION).

*Coburg Square: see SAXE-COBURG SQUARE.

Cocaine, a white, crystalline drug prepared from the leaves of the South American coca plant. It has a stimulating and exhilarating effect upon the user which is followed later by depression, and its use tends to breed a dangerous habit.

During their early association, Watson dismissed the suspicion that Holmes was addicted to the use of some narcotic (STUD), but for many years Holmes was a *habitué* of cocaine (FIVE, SCAN, SIGN, TWIS, YELL), alternating between the "drowsiness" of the drug and "the fierce energy of his own keen nature" (SCAN). Watson often favoured him with his medical views of the taking of cocaine (TWIS), calling him a "self-poisoner" (FIVE), and Holmes admitted that the influence of the drug was physically a bad one (SIGN). A litter of syringes was scattered over the mantelpiece in his bedroom (DYIN), for he took it subcutaneously (SIGN). For years Watson weaned him from the drug

mania, but he was well aware that the fiend was not dead but sleeping; and that the sleep was a light one, and the waking near, during periods of idleness (MISS).

Watson writes that in 1897 Holmes's constitution showed signs of giving way in the face of constant hard work and "occasional indiscretions of his own" (DEVI), and that he was himself an institution in Holmes's life like the violin, the shag tobacco, the index books, "and others perhaps less excusable" (CREE). See also MORPHINE; also HOLMES, SHERLOCK, subheaded *Character*.

Cock. A white cock was sacrificed in the mulatto's voodoo ritual (WIST). The sign of a game-cock hung above the door of the Fighting Cock Inn (PRIO).

Cockney, a native or permanent resident of the City of London. Hall Pycroft was a Cockney (STOC).

Coconut, or **cocoanut.** There were coconuts growing in the Andaman Islands (SIGN). The floor-matting at Yoxley Old Place was of coconut fibre (GOLD), as was that which served as a stair-carpet at Pondicherry Lodge (SIGN).

Code: see CRYPTOGRAPHY.

Coffin notice, a death-threat. Coffin notices were hung outside William Hales's door by the Scowrers (VALL).

Coin: see DOLLAR (crown); FARTHING; FLORIN; GUINEA; HALF-CROWN; HALFPENNY; HALF-SOVEREIGN; PENNY; SHILLING; SIXPENCE; SOVEREIGN; THREEPENCE; TWOPENCE; see also BIMETALLISM; COUNTERFEITING; also FRANC; MOIDORE; NAPOLEON; RUPEE; also ALEXANDRIA; SYRACUSE.

Coiner, in English slang, a counterfeiter of silver money (ENGR, SHOS).

Coldharbour Lane, a street in south

London, forming part of the boundary between Lambeth and Camberwell. Holmes's party passed along Coldharbour Lane on their way to meet Thaddeus Sholto (SIGN). See Map IV of LONDON.

Coldstream Guards, the oldest regiment of the British Army, dating from 1650. Tangey had served with the Coldstream (NAVA).

Colin: see CAMPBELL, SIR COLIN.

College of Surgeons, properly **Royal College of Surgeons of England,** an association of surgeons, created in 1800 but tracing its ancestry to 1540, incorporated by royal charter for the purpose of examining and licensing practitioners in surgery. While government supervision of medical qualifications began in 1858, and though the great universities now dominate the realm of medical education in Great Britain, the College still retains its privileges. Its buildings near the western border of the City include the admirable **Museum of the Royal College of Surgeons,** dating from 1793 and devoted to natural history. Dr. Mortimer visited the Museum and was an **M.R.C.S.,** that is, a *Member of the Royal College of Surgeons,* revealing him to be a qualified surgeon but not having pursued his education to the extent of acquiring the degree of Doctor of Medicine, and so deserving to be addressed as "Doc-

The Royal College of Surgeons.

tor" by courtesy only (HOUN); see also JACKSON PRIZE. See Map II of LONDON.

Colliery, a coal-mine (VALL).

Colonial Office, a department of the British Government headed by a Cabinet minister, the *Secretary of State for Colonial Affairs.* Lord Robert St. Simon was Under-Secretary for the Colonies (NOBL). Certain colonial developments had angered a foreign sovereign, resulting in the explosive document stolen from Trelawney Hope's residence (SECO). See also BRITISH EMPIRE.

The Indian Empire is administered through the *India Office,* not the Colonial Office; see INDIA.

Colonna, Prince of, the owner of the black pearl of the Borgias. The pearl was stolen by the maid of the **Princess of Colonna,** Lucretia Venucci (SIXN). *Colonna* is a promontory of eastern Greece.

Colorado River, a river of the United States, which forms the Grand Canyon in the state of Arizona (STUD).

Colourman, one who prepares and sells *colours,* or paints, and other artists' materials. Josiah Amberley was a retired colourman (RETI).

Colour-sergeant, a sergeant who has charge of battalion or regimental colours. Nancy Barclay was the daughter of a colour-sergeant (CROO), and Chester Wilcox had been a colour-sergeant in the American Civil War (VALL).

"Columbine's New-fangled Banner," the subject, according to Constable Rance, of Jefferson Hope's song as Hope feigned drunkenness to escape arrest (STUD).

Comet wine, wine made in any of the years in which notable comets have been seen, and which are superstitiously believed to have a superior flavour in consequence. Having heard Hall Pycroft's story, Holmes behaved like a connoisseur who had just taken his first sip of a comet vintage (STOC).

Commercial hotel, a hotel managed particularly for the accommodation of commercial travellers; e.g., the EAGLE COMMERCIAL (VALL).

Commercial Road, an important East End thoroughfare extending from the City through Stepney to the West India Docks. Dorak kept a general store here (CREE). See the front endpaper map.

Commissionaire, a member of the uniformed establishment of retired soldiers of good character, called the *Corps of Commissionaires,* organized in 1859. They are convenient and trustworthy messengers for the conveyance of letters and parcels, act as guides and escorts, and perform a variety of other tasks by the hour or the day.

A commissionaire delivered the message to Holmes from Inspector Gregson (STUD), and a commissionaire was one of Holmes's witnesses in the Mazarin diamond case (MAZA). PETERSON was a commissionaire (BLUE), as was TANGEY (NAVA).

Common, a tract of ground belonging to the public; e.g., OXSHOTT COMMON (WIST); WANDSWORTH COMMON (GREE).

Commonplace book, a book in which things especially to be remembered or referred to are methodically recorded. Holmes maintained an extensive series of commonplace books, consisting of all manner of knowledge which came to his attention. They apparently became so large and comprehensive that he was obliged to keep a separate index for them, though when speaking of his "index" Holmes often seems to be referring to the commonplace books themselves.

Watson mentions the formidable "scrap-books" at Baker Street (EMPT, REDC, 3STU), which would seem to be identifiable with Holmes's commonplace books. Conceivably a separate "index of biographies" was maintained containing biographies only (EMPT, SCAN), and in yet another set of volumes he appears to have filed, day by day, the AGONY COLUMN of the various London papers (REDC).

Holmes spent hours compiling and cross-indexing his books (BRUC, FIVE, MUSG, REDC). He consulted his commonplace book for the notice of Jeremiah Hayling's disappearance (ENGR) and for the Abbas Parva tragedy (VEIL), and said there were in his index parallel cases to that of Mary Sutherland (IDEN). He sought Irene Adler here, finding her biography sandwiched between that of a Hebrew Rabbi and that of a staff-commander who had written a monograph upon deep sea fishes (SCAN). He turned up the Duke of Holdernesse in volume *H* of "his encyclopædia of reference" (PRIO), but since the passage quoted does not conform to the accepted form of such works, this volume too is possibly of Holmes's own composition. He browsed through the collection of *M*'s in his book of biographies as he turned up the entry for Sebastian Moran (EMPT) and consulted the *S* volume in vain for the name of Godfrey Staunton (MISS).

He spoke of the notes upon the Baskerville case under the heading *B* in his "indexed list of cases" (HOUN), looked fondly through the letter *V* in the index volume which recorded his old cases (SUSS), and consulted his CASE-BOOK for the details of his service to Mrs. Farintosh (SPEC). See also DIARY; NOTEBOOK.

Watson writes that he too became an institution in Holmes's life like the index books and others (CREE).

Commons, House of: see PARLIAMENT.

Communal rights, those rights, conferred through custom as well as law, held in common by the members of a community. Old Frankland was learned in old MANORIAL and communal rights (HOUN).

Commute, in law, to exchange one penalty or punishment for another of less severity. Selden's death sentence was commuted to a term of imprisonment (HOUN), as were those of Abe Slaney (DANC) and Jonathan Small (SIGN).

Holmes said that in the case of James Ryder he would have to commute a felony and let Ryder go free in exchange for the return of the blue carbuncle (BLUE); see COMPOUND.

Company, The, the **East India Company,** the great English company, chartered in 1600 and dissolved in 1874, which conquered and ruled India until the powers of government were withdrawn in 1858 (SIGN).

Comparative anatomy: see ANATOMY.

Comparative pathology: see PATHOLOGY.

Compass. The survivors of the *Gloria Scott* disaster had a compass (GLOR). Holmes took the cardinal points with his pocket compass before stepping off the distances indicated by the Musgrave Ritual (MUSG). The Ferrier wagon party became lost upon the Great Alkali Plain due to errors in compasses or maps (STUD). Inspector Bradstreet laughed that his party had

managed to BOX THE COMPASS among them (ENGR).

Competence, property, means of substance, or income sufficient to furnish the necessaries and conveniences of life without superfluity. Joseph Openshaw was able to retire upon a handsome competence (FIVE). Holmes said that Josiah Amberley had a competence (RETI), and Jefferson Hope possessed a small one (STUD).

Compositor, a type-setter. One of Holmes's monographs dealt with the hands of compositors (COPP, SIGN). The compositors of the Vermissa *Daily Herald* were unable to identify editor Stanger's assailants (VALL).

Compound, in law, to agree, for a consideration, not to prosecute or punish a wrong-doer. Holmes said that in the cases of the Mazarin diamond (MAZA) and of Isadora Klein (3GAB) he would have to "compound a felony," an erroneous use of the word, as was his use of COMMUTE (BLUE) and CONDONE (PRIO) and Sir Henry Baskerville's use of ABET (HOUN) in the same context. The crime committed in each of these cases was *misprision of felony,* that is, criminal neglect in response to the crime of another, especially a passive complicity, as by concealment, which however falls short of the guilt of a principal or accessory.

Compound of the Busy Bee and Excelsior. Holmes characterized the sentiment expressed by Watson's remark "We can but try," as a "compound of the Busy Bee and Excelsior" (CREE), that is, typifying the aspirations suggested by the image of the "busy bee" and the motto EXCELSIOR.

Conceit, a fanciful, strained, or farfetched turn of thought; an affectation of thought or style. Holmes remarked that conceits such as Jonathan Small's leaving the sign of the four upon the bodies of Batholomew Sholto and his father were common enough in the annals of crime (SIGN).

Condone. Holmes accused the Duke of Holdernesse of having "condoned a felony" (PRIO). In this sense the word is not a legal term; see COMPOUND.

Conduit Street, a street in Westminster, extending between Bond Street and Regent Street. Colonel Sebastian Moran lived here (EMPT). See Map III of LONDON.

Condyle, in anatomy, a protuberance on the end of a bone serving to form an articulation with another bone. John Mason showed Holmes and Watson what Watson called "the upper condyle of a human femur" (SHOS), there being no such part, the condyle of the femur, or thigh-bone, being at the lower extremity, at the knee. Watson seems to have been simply applying the word loosely to the proximal, or upper, extremity of the bone.

Confederate States of America, the confederation formed 1861–65 by the eleven states which seceded from the United States. According to the *American Encyclopædia* the Ku Klux Klan was created by ex-Confederate soldiers (FIVE).

Conk-Singleton forgery case, a case Holmes took up immediately following the recovery of the black pearl of the Borgias (SIXN).

Conqueror, a steam packet of the Liverpool, Dublin, and London Steam Packet Company (CARD).

Conquistadors, the Spanish conquerors of America. Isadora Klein was descended from them (3GAB).

Conservative Party, the party in British politics opposed to the LIBERAL PARTY. The name came into use about

1832 as the reactionary Tory party, which had disapproved of change in the ancient constitution and supported the claims of the King, Church, and aristocracy, began to moderate its policies and declare its willingness to support "judicious reforms." Lord Holdhurst was a Conservative (NAVA), and Watson so described John Scott Eccles (WIST).

For Conservative newspapers see EVENING NEWS; EVENING STANDARD; GLOBE; MORNING POST; PALL MALL GAZETTE; STANDARD; see also TIMES, THE. See also CARLTON CLUB.

Conspiracy, in law, a combination of two or more persons, by some concerted action, to accomplish some criminal or unlawful purpose, or to accomplish some purpose not in itself criminal or unlawful by criminal or unlawful means. The term was formerly used in English law more specifically to designate an agreement between two or more persons falsely or maliciously to indict, or procure to be indicted, an innocent person of felony. Jonas Oldacre and his housekeeper were charged with conspiracy (NORW).

Constable, a uniformed policeman; in London, a member of the uniformed branch of SCOTLAND YARD. Specifically a *constable* is a member of the lowest rank in the Metropolitan Police, under the supervision of a *sergeant*.

Every man James Ryder met, he said, seemed to be a policeman or detective (BLUE). Mrs. St. Clair happened to meet a number of constables in Fresno Street (TWIS). The police were in possession of the Three Gables (3GAB), and Watson writes that the silence of south London at night was broken only by the footfall of the policeman (TWIS).

A constable, one of three within call,

A London police-constable walks his beat. Observe the bull's-eye lantern worn at the belt. The pouch from which the night-stick hangs also contains the rattle used to summon assistance before the introduction of the police-whistle.

showed Holmes about Deep Dene House, and the night-constable there was shown the thumb-mark upon the wall (NORW). Three constables searched The Haven for the bodies of Mrs. Amberley and her lover (RETI). An inspector and two officers guarded the door to Jabez Wilson's pawnshop, where they presumably intercepted Duncan Ross (REDH). Two constables saluted Holmes at the door of the Bow Street police-court (TWIS), and two uniformed policemen accompanied Lestrade to Baker Street (EMPT, NORW).

A constable accompanied the inspector assigned to the case of the Beryl Coronet (BERY). A sergeant and a constable escorted Holmes and Watson from Holy Peters's house, and the ser-

geant called at Baker Street later to report on what he had observed (LADY). A police-constable was left at Pondicherry Lodge (SIGN). A stalwart constable leaned against the wall at Lauriston Gardens (STUD). The smashing of the Napoleonic bust at Morse Hudson's shop was reported to the constable on the beat (SIXN). Watson kept watch for a policeman while Holmes broke into Hugo Oberstein's house (BRUC). A policeman was at the Whitehall end of Charles Street (NAVA) and came to assist Horace Harker (SIXN). A policeman was killed in the St. Pancras case (SHOS).

Watson writes that Constable Rance's police-whistle brought Murcher and two other constables to Lauriston Gardens (STUD) ; but while the Drebber case is dated early in the 1880s, whistles were not used by policemen on London night duty until 1887, constables up until that time making use of a special rattle to summon help.

See also constables BARRETT; COOK; MACPHERSON; MURCHER; RANCE.

Sergeant Tuson and Constable Pollock were members of the CITY POLICE (STOC).

Colonel Emsworth threatened to send for the county constables (BLAN), and the Barclays' coachman sought a policeman (CROO). A constable was on duty at Ridling Thorpe Manor, and two more arrived to take Abe Slaney to Norwich (DANC). A county constable had been on duty upon the road east of the Priory School (PRIO). A Surrey constable guarded the kitchen door of the Cunningham house, and at least one more was on the premises (REIG) ; and three Surrey constables arrived at Charlington Hall (SOLI). A burly Sussex policeman assisted Holmes at Hurlstone (MUSG), a policeman was assigned to remain in John Openshaw's house (FIVE), and it was said that every constable in Sussex was looking for a stranger with wet trousers (VALL). See also ANDERSON; COVENTRY; DOWNING; EVANS; WALTERS; WILSON.

See also CHIEF CONSTABLE; POLICE.

Constabulary: see POLICE.

Constructor: see CHIEF CONSTRUCTOR.

Consulting detective, the profession of Sherlock Holmes. He supposed he was the only one in the world (SIGN, STUD). When government or private detectives found themselves baffled, Holmes said, they consulted him, and he generally managed to put them on the proper scent: "They lay the evidence before me, and I am generally able, by the help of my knowledge of the history of crime, to set them straight" (STUD). He often served private clients, and so performed as a private detective, but he for ever thought of himself primarily as a consulting detective; he remarked upon his extensive consulting practice (HOUN), and the newspapers referred to him as "the well-known consulting expert" (SIXN).

He served GREGSON and LESTRADE in the Drebber case (STUD) and was retained by Lestrade in the Boscombe Valley mystery (BOSC), the cardboard box murder (CARD), the recovery of the black pearl of the Borgias (SIXN), an early forgery case (STUD), and possibly the "bogus laundry affair" (CARD). He refused to consult with Lestrade in the murder of Charles Augustus Milverton (CHAS). In return for the criminal news that Lestrade would bring on his visits to Baker Street, Holmes was always ready to listen to the details of any case upon which the Scotland Yarder was engaged, and was able occasionally to give some hint or suggestion drawn from his own vast knowledge and experience (SIXN).

Stanley HOPKINS consulted him in the deaths of Sir Eustace Brackenstall (ABBE), Peter Carey (BLAC), and Willoughby Smith (GOLD). He looked into the St. Pancras case at the request of Merivale of the Yard (SHOS), and Inspector MacDonald introduced him to the murder of John Douglas (VALL). He was consulted by Inspector Forrester of the Surrey constabulary (REIG) and by François le Villard (SIGN), and in the case of the Mazarin diamond he was consulted by the Home Secretary himself

(MAZA), presumably on behalf of Scotland Yard. Holmes remarked that in the case of the blue carbuncle he was not retained by the police "to supply their deficiencies" (BLUE).

Inspector Gregory asked Holmes to enter the Silver Blaze case, but so too did Colonel Ross, and Holmes seems to have been acting for the latter and not in his consulting capacity (SILV)'. His private clients, in the early days at least, were mostly referred by private inquiry agents (STUD), but the police inspector who was assigned to the case of the Beryl Coronet suggested him to Alexander Holder (BERY), Stanley Hopkins referred Cyril Overton (MISS), and Josiah Amberley was sent on by the Yard (RETI).

See also HOLMES, SHERLOCK, subheaded *Methods*.

Consumption, or *tuberculosis,* a widespread, highly infectious disease caused by a bacillus. Watson was summoned back to Meiringen to comfort a consumptive Englishwoman (FINA). The tutor Fraser was a consumptive (HOUN), and Godfrey Staunton's wife died of consumption of the most virulent kind (MISS).

Continent, The: see EUROPE.

"Continental Gazetteer," the reference work in which Holmes turned up the entry for Egria (SCAN).

"Cooee," the call or cry (*"kooooo-ee!"*) used as a signal by the Australian aborigines and adopted by the colonists in the bush (BOSC).

Cook, the London police-constable who found the body of John Openshaw (FIVE).

Cook: see SERVANT.

Cook's Tourist Offices, a firm of travel-agents and money-changers, with branches throughout Europe. Watson was able to trace Lady Frances Carfax through the Cook's office in Lausanne (LADY).

Coolie, an East Indian or Chinese labourer employed under contract for menial work. Holmes claimed to suffer from a coolie disease from Sumatra (DYIN). Abel White hired Jonathan Small to oversee his coolies (SIGN).

Cooling medicine, any preparation believed to be capable of lowering the temperature of the blood (SIGN).

*Coombe Tracey, a town on Dartmoor (HOUN). A *coombe* is a narrow valley or ravine.

Cop, in criminal slang, to ensnare or to take unfair advantage. Sam Merton called Holmes's ruse of the bust and violin recording "a fair cop" (MAZA). See also FAIR.

Copenhagen, the capital and largest city of Denmark, pop. 400,757. Enoch Drebber and Joseph Stangerson fled to London from here (STUD).

Copernican Theory, the hypothesis, since proven, that the sun is the centre round which the earth and the other planets revolve, first proposed by the Polish monk and astronomer *Nicholas Copernicus* (1473–1543). Holmes professed to know nothing of the Copernican theory (STUD), but nonetheless demonstrated a knowledge of ASTRONOMY on a number of occasions.

Copper. Holmes was able to trace a counterfeiter by the zinc and copper filings in the seam of his cuff (SHOS).

Copper, in English slang, a PENNY (DANC, SCAN, TWIS).

Copper beech, a variety of common beech tree possessing a red sap in its leaves which gives them a metallic copper colour. Jephro Rucastle's home took its name from the copper beeches before the door (COPP).

*Copper Beeches, The, the country home of Jephro Rucastle (COPP).

"Copper Beeches, The Adventure of the" (COPP), a chronicle which appeared originally in the *Strand* magazine for June 1892 and was published in the collection entitled *The Adventures of Sherlock Holmes* that same year. It concerns Holmes's involvement with the strange experiences of Violet Hunter and her employer Jephro Rucastle. The case is variously dated as having taken place in 1885, 1889, 1890, or 1891.

Many years after the event, Holmes referred back to this case (CREE).

Copts, a class of people, resident in Egypt, who observe a rude form of the Christian religion and who are supposed to be a relic of the old Egyptian race. Professor Coram said that his analysis of the documents found in the Coptic monasteries of Syria and Egypt would cut deep at the very foundations of revealed religion (GOLD). Holmes was preoccupied with the case of the two Coptic patriarchs, which came to a head the same day he was consulted by Josiah Amberley (RETI).

Coram, Professor, the name used by a former Russian Nihilist while living in England. His real name was *Sergius.* He betrayed his revolutionist companions and his own wife **Anna** (d. 1894) to the Russian government. Later, in attempting to retrieve important documents from his home, Anna accidentally killed her husband's secretary Willoughby Smith, then committed suicide when exposed (GOLD).

Cords, breeches or trousers (SOLI).

Cork-cutter, one whose trade is the cutting and fashioning of cork for commercial purposes. One of Holmes's monographs dealt with the hands of cork-cutters (SIGN).

The clips of the golden pince-nez were lined with cork (GOLD), and the point of John Straker's cataract knife was guarded by a cork disc (SILV).

Cormac, Tiger, a Scowrer (VALL).

Cormorant, a large diving bird found throughout the world. The Chinese and Japanese have for many centuries trained the cormorant to fish for them by tying a cord about the bird's neck which prevents it from swallowing, it obediently bringing the unmutilated fish back to its masters. Watson's notes of Holmes's cases included that of "the politician, the lighthouse and the trained cormorant" (VEIL).

Cormorant.

Corn-chandler, a grain-merchant. The Duke of Holdernesse had sacked Reuben Hays, so Hays said, "on the word of a lying corn-chandler" (PRIO).

Cornelius, an alias of Jonas Oldacre, used by him to transfer moneys (NORW).

Cornwall, the south-western-most county of England, pop. 322,334. Its main sources of wealth are fishing and mining. The failure of the Dawson & Neligan bank ruined half the families of Cornwall (BLAC). Holmes and Watson vacationed here in 1897

(DEVI). Peter Jones said that John Clay would crack a crib in Scotland one week and be raising money to build an orphanage in Cornwall the next (REDH). See also FALMOUTH; HELSTON; REDRUTH; ST. IVES; TREDANNICK WOLLAS; also POLDHU BAY. See the map accompanying DEVONSHIRE.

The ancient **Cornish language** survives in a few words still in use in the fishing and mining communities, as well as in the names of persons and places, but the last persons who spoke it died toward the end of the eighteenth century. It belonged to the Cymric division of CELTIC, in which Welsh is also included. Holmes had conceived the idea that it was akin to the CHALDEAN, and had been largely derived from the Phoenician traders in tin (DEVI).

Coronet, a crown representing a dignity inferior to that of the sovereign. In the Middle Ages, small coronets called *chaplets* were popular with both men and women.

Coronet.

The BERYL CORONET was one of the most precious public possessions of the Empire (BERY). A gold chaplet was in the Agra treasure, and the Sholtos sent Mary Morstan six of the pearls which decorated it (SIGN). The arms of the Falders carried a griffin and coronet (SHOS).

Corot (*koh-rō'*), **Jean Baptiste Camille** (1796–1875), a French artist known chiefly for his subtle woodland scenes. Thaddeus Sholto possessed a Corot (SIGN).

Corporation Street, one of the main thoroughfares of Birmingham, full of handsome, modern buildings. The Franco-Midland Hardware Company's offices were here (STOC). See the map of BIRMINGHAM.

Correspondence. Dr. Mortimer was a corresponding member of the Swedish Pathological Society (HOUN).

Holmes remarked that his correspondence had the charm of variety, and that the humbler were usually the more interesting (NOBL), though he was somewhat upon his guard against any packages which reached him (DYIN). It was his habit to keep his unanswered correspondence transfixed by a jack-knife into the very centre of his wooden mantelpiece (MUSG).

Cosmopolitan, hotel: see HOTEL COSMOPOLITAN.

Costa Rica, a republic of Central America, est. pop. (1903) 322,600. Beryl Stapleton was a Costa Rican (HOUN), and "Costa Rica" was a heading in the Neligan notebook (BLAC).

Coster, or *costermonger,* a hawker of fruits and vegetables (REDH). See the photograph on p. 225.

Cot, boat: see BATHING-COT.

Cotton grass, a rush-like plant common in swampy places, possessing spikes which resemble tufts of cotton. White cotton grass grew upon Dartmoor (HOUN).

Cottonwood, the name given to several species of poplar tree native to the United States. Holmes's gazetteer apparently stated that cottonwoods grew in the Andaman Islands (SIGN).

*Council of Four: see SACRED COUNCIL OF FOUR.

Count, a title of nobility in some European countries (LAST, MAZA, RESI, SCAN), corresponding to earl in Great Britain. The wife or daughter of a count is styled a **countess,** as is, in the British peerage, the wife or widow of an earl. The Countess of MORCAR (BLUE) and the Countess d'Albert (CHAS) may have been either British or Continental.

Counterfeiting. It was for the Prescott counterfeiting outfit, particularly the bank-note plates, that Killer Evans lured Nathan Garrideb away from his rooms (3GAR). Holmes was able to trace a COINER by the zinc and copper filings in the seam of his cuff (SHOS), and Lysander Stark and his gang were coiners on a large scale (ENGR). John Clay was said to be a SMASHER (REDH), and John McMurdo claimed to SHOVE THE QUEER in Chicago (VALL). Henry Wood's landlady took an Indian rupee for a "bad florin" (CROO).

Counterpane, a quilt or bed-cover; specifically, a coverlet woven of cotton with raised figures (SPEC).

Countess: see COUNT.

"Country of the Saints, The": see "STUDY IN SCARLET, A."

Coup-de-maître, a French phrase meaning *master-stroke* (FINA, SIGN).

Coursing, the sport of pursuing game with greyhounds; hence, hunting by pursuit. Watson said he had coursed "many creatures in many countries" (SIGN). See FOX-HUNTING.

See also DRAGHOUND; DRAW A COVER; SWING TO THE LINE; VIEW-HOLLOA.

Court of Queen's Bench, a subdivision of the British supreme court. It was formerly the supreme court of common law, called *Queen's* or *King's*

Bench because the sovereign once presided in person. *Frankland* v. *Morland* was tried here (HOUN).

Cove, in English slang, a man; a fellow (MAZA, STUD).

Covent Garden Market, the chief wholesale vegetable, fruit, and flower market of London, situated in the extreme eastern part of Westminster, north of the Strand. Mr. Breckinridge dealt in geese at Covent Garden (BLUE), though poultry is seldom if ever sold here. See Map II of LONDON.

The Covent Garden market-days are Tuesdays, Thursdays, and Saturdays, during which an enormous business is transacted here.

Covent Garden Theatre, or *Royal Italian Opera House,* a celebrated theatre in Westminster, located in Bow Street near Covent Garden Market. Dating from 1858, the house was originally devoted exclusively to Italian opera, but it is now used for concerts and dress balls as well as opera of all sorts. Holmes and Watson attended a Wagner performance here (REDC). See Map II of LONDON.

Coventry, a midland city of England, located in Warwickshire, pop. 69,978. Joseph Openshaw had a small factory here (FIVE), and Cyril Morton was employed here by the Midland Electric Company (SOLI).

Coventry, Sergeant, an official of the Hampshire constabulary, who was assigned to investigate the apparent murder of Maria Gibson (THOR).

Cover, in hunting: see DRAW.

Covert, a thicket or other cover for game. Holmes said that the agony column was his "favourite covert for putting up a bird" (3GAR); see also PUT UP.

Cowper, a Mormon residing at Salt Lake City, to whom Jefferson Hope had rendered services (STUD).

Cox & Co., a London banking firm, located in Charing Cross. Watson's tin dispatch-box (CREE, THOR, VEIL) was kept in the vaults of Cox & Co. (THOR).

Coxon, senior partner of **Coxon & Woodhouse,** stockbrokers for whom Hall Pycroft worked (STOC).

Coyote, one of the few inhabitants of the Great Alkali Plain (STUD).

C.P.R.: see CANADIAN PACIFIC RAILWAY.

Crabbe, a victim of the Scowrers (VALL).

Crack a crib, in underworld cant, to commit a burglary (REDH, REIG).

Cracksman, in underworld cant, a burglar (STOC).

*Crane Water, apparently the house or country estate, near Reading, of Mr. Armitage (SPEC).

Craniology, that branch of anatomy

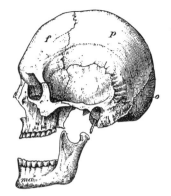

The human skull, viewed from the side: f, frontal bone; ma, maxillary or jawbone; o, occipital bone; p, parietal bone.

which deals with the study of human skulls. Craniology was Dr. Mortimer's special hobby (HOUN), and Professor Moriarty remarked upon Holmes's skull (FINA). See also MAXILLARY CURVE; OCCIPITAL BONE; PARIETAL BONE; SUPRA-ORBITAL; also DOLICHOCEPHALIC; PROGNATHOUS; also CROMAGNON; HEIDELBERG MAN; NEANDERTHAL.

Craven Street, a short street in Westminster, extending from the Strand to the Embankment, where it meets Northumberland Avenue. The Stapletons stayed in a hotel here (HOUN). See Map II of LONDON.

Cream-laid paper, a heavy, cream-coloured writing-paper characterized by a ribbed texture. The note to Aloysius Garcia was written upon such paper (WIST). J. Davenport wrote to Mycroft Holmes on **royal cream paper** (GREE), meaning that the sheet measured 19″×24″.

Crédit Lyonnais (*creh'dit lee-on-naiz'*), one of the great joint-stock banks of France. Holmes suspected that Moriarty kept the bulk of his fortune here (VALL), and Count Sylvius denied forging a cheque on the Crédit Lyonnais (MAZA). Marie Devine cashed the cheque from Lady Frances Carfax at the Montpellier branch (LADY).

"Creeping Man, The Adventure of the" (CREE), a chronicle which appeared originally in the *Strand* magazine and *Hearst's International* for March 1923 and was published in the collection entitled *The Case Book of Sherlock Holmes* in 1927. It concerns Holmes's investigation of the remarkable behaviour of Professor Presbury of Camford University. Watson dates the case as having occurred in September 1903 and states that it was one of the very last cases handled by Holmes before his retirement from practice.

Cremona, a city of northern Italy, especially famous as the residence of the AMATI family and of STRADIVARIUS, est. pop. 40,000. Holmes "prattled" of Cremona violins (STUD).

*Crendall, a town in Berkshire, near which the Green Dragon Inn was located (SHOS).

Crenellated, broken in square projections and depressions. The twin towers of Baskerville Hall were crenellated (HOUN).

Creole (*kree'ohl*), the name originally given to all descendants of Spaniards or Frenchmen born in the southern United States or the West Indies. Madame Fournaye was of creole origin (SECO).

Creosote, an oily, ill-smelling substance made from wood products. It is used to treat wood against rotting and has medical and other chemical applications. Holmes and Watson tracked the murderers of Bartholomew Sholto across London by following the scent of creosote in which one had stepped (SIGN).

Crest, in heraldry, a figure borne above the shield in a coat-of-arms and used separately upon articles of personal property such as plate and notepaper. Lord Robert St. Simon's crest appeared upon his stationery (NOBL). See HERALDRY.

Crewe, a city and important railway junction of north-western England, in Cheshire, founded in 1841, pop. 42,074. Helen Stoner's mother was killed in a railway accident near here in 1875 (SPEC).

Crib, in English slang, a situation or position of employment (REDH, STOC).

Crib, in underworld cant, any house, shop, warehouse, or public-house. To **crack a crib** means to commit burglary (REDH, REIG).

Cricket. Gilchrist was a cricket player (3STU). See also INNINGS; WICKET.

Crimea, a peninsula of southern Russia, between the Sea of Azof and the Black Sea. It was the principal scene of the **Crimean War,** the struggle fought 1853–56 between England, France, and Turkey upon the one hand, and Russia upon the other. Colonel Emsworth had earned the V.C. in the Crimea (BLAN), where Colonel Barclay's regiment (CROO) and the gardener Mortimer (GOLD) had served. The *Gloria Scott* was pressed into service for transporting convicts to Australia owing to the use of the regular convict ships as troop transports during the war (GLOR), in which the Hon. Philip Green's father commanded the Sea of Azof fleet (LADY).

Criterion, a sumptuous restaurant, bar, and variety theatre, located in Regent Circus, Piccadilly. The bar is on the American pattern and is referred to as the *Long Bar* or the *American Bar*. It was here that Watson met young Stamford (STUD). See Map III of LONDON.

Croaker, one who complains unreasonably or takes a desponding view of things; an alarmist. Jack McGinty said old Morris had always been a croaker (VALL).

Crocker, Jack: see CROKER.

"Crockford's Clerical Directory," an annual directory published since 1858. Holmes turned up J. C. Elman in his Crockford (RETI).

Crocodile. Jonathan Small lost his leg to a crocodile while swimming in the Ganges (SIGN). Elsie Cubitt possessed a crocodile-skin hand-bag (DANC).

Crocus. A bed of crocuses lay beneath Ronald Adair's window (EMPT), and Holmes commented to Grimesby Roylott that the crocuses promised well (SPEC).

Croker, Jack, the first officer of the liner *Rock of Gibraltar,* aboard which he met Mary Fraser; later captain of the *Bass Rock.* After Mary's marriage to the brutal Sir Eustace Brackenstall, Croker killed Brackenstall to free her from him. Holmes refused to expose him (ABBE). In many editions the name appears as *Crocker.*

Cromagnon, properly **Cro-Magnon** (*krō-mah-nyōn'*), a prehistoric race of Europe, characteristic remains of which were found in the cave of Cro-Magnon in south-western France. The type is distinguished by a very long head, low forehead, and tall stature. Nathan Garrideb possessed a Cromagnon skull (3GAR).

"Crooked Man, The" (CROO), a chronicle which appeared originally in the *Strand* magazine for July 1893 and *Harper's Weekly* of 8 July 1893 and

was published in the collection entitled *The Memoirs of Sherlock Holmes* the following year. It concerns Holmes's investigation of the death of Colonel James Barclay, and the case is commonly dated as having occurred in 1888 or 1889.

Crooksbury Hill, a wooded eminence in the west of Surrey, just east of Farnham. The Farnham high-road passes nearby (SOLI).

Crop: see HUNTING-CROP.

Cropper, in English slang, a fall, as from a horse; hence a failure in an undertaking (STOC).

Croquet lawn, a well-tended, close-cropped lawn upon which the game of croquet is played; any lawn resembling one tended for this purpose; a TENNIS LAWN. There was a croquet lawn round the Tredannick Wollas vicarage (DEVI).

Crosby (d. 1894), a banker whose terrible death was associated in Watson's mind with a red leech (GOLD).

Cross, in English and American underworld slang, a thief; anything false, dishonest, or illegal. Thus to be or live **on the cross** is to live by illegal means (DANC).

Cross, to write the name of a banking company across the face of a cheque between two parallel lines provided for that purpose. A crossed cheque can be used only by depositing it into the bank mentioned. Holmes requested the Duke of Holdernesse to cross his cheque with the name of the Oxford Street branch of the Capital and Counties Bank (PRIO).

Cross Street, properly **Cross Road,** a short street in Croydon. Susan Cushing lived here (CARD), though it is by no means a "very long street" as described.

Crowder, William, a gamekeeper in the employ of John Turner (BOSC).

*Crow Hill Mine, a large Vermissa mine whose management opposed the Scowrers, and whose manager and engineer were murdered by them (VALL).

Crown, coin: see DOLLAR; HALF-CROWN.

Crown Derby, the name given to the fine porcelain manufactured at Derby in the late eighteenth and early nineteenth centuries, so called from the inclusion of a crown in the potters' marks. Mary Maberley remarked that she owned nothing more valuable than a Crown Derby tea set (3GAB).

Crown diamond: see MAZARIN STONE.

*Crown Inn, an inn at the village of Stoke Moran, where Holmes and Watson stayed (SPEC).

Crown Prince, the eldest son or other heir-apparent of a monarch (SCAN).

Croydon, a great residential city of Surrey, suburban to London, pop. 133,895. Susan Cushing lived here (CARD).

Crusade, first, the first of the wars between the Christians and Moslems for possession of the Holy Land, fought 1095–99. The original Birlstone Manor dated from the first crusade (VALL).

Crutch: see ALUMINIUM CRUTCH.

Cryptography, the art of secret writing. A cryptograph is anything written in a secret manner as well as the system used. Forms include codes, ciphers, invisible writing, and other devices which make the true meaning incomprehensible except to those who possess the proper key. A *cipher* consists of letter groups made up by transposition of letters within the message or substitution of one letter for another or of a number or symbol for a letter. A *code* properly is a form of secret writing in which one word, number, or symbol is made to stand for a whole word or phrase.

Aside from a word-puzzle which was not properly a cryptograph (MUSG), Holmes was called upon to solve four secret messages—three codes and a cipher.

He solved an *open-text code* sent by Beddoes to Trevor Senior (GLOR), the codetext of which read: "The supply of game for London is going steadily up. Head-keeper Hudson, we believe, has been now told to receive all orders for fly-paper and for preservation of your hen pheasant's life." He quickly deduced that the plaintext message could be revealed by reading every third word, beginning with the first: "The game is up. Hudson has told all. Fly for your life."

He read the light-flash message sent by Gennaro Lucca to his wife by counting the number of flashes—one for A, two for B, and so on—to observe the warning: "ATTENTA! PERICOLO!" —"Beware! Danger!" (REDC).

He deduced the key of a *book code* sent him by his informant Porlock in which a series of numbers represented the order of words in a book both Holmes and Porlock would possess—an almanack. The message warned of the planned murder of John Douglas, but Holmes received it too late to prevent the crime (VALL).

He solved a *simple substitution cipher* in which a series of stick figures, made to look like a child's innocent scrawl, represented the letters of the alphabet:

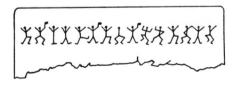

The plaintext reads: "AM HERE. ABE SLANEY." The flags held by the figures represent the last letters of words. With this message and others like it Holmes deciphered the cryptograph by means of *frequency analysis,* but his solution came too late to save the life of Hilton Cubitt (DANC).

Holmes professed himself "fairly familiar" with all forms of secret writings (DANC) and would beg for the opportunity to examine "the most obstruce cryptogram" to put him in his own proper intellectual atmosphere (SIGN). He amused himself reading the ciphers in the agony column (VALL) and was the author of a "trifling" monograph in which he analyzed 160 separate ciphers (DANC). As Altamont he claimed to have acquired the new naval codes for Von Bork (LAST).

A cipher telegram was dispatched to the impetuous sovereign who wrote the Trelawney Hope document (SECO).

Birdy Edwards was said to send daily messages out of Vermissa Valley in code (VALL).

Crystal Palace, a large building, constructed chiefly of glass and iron, erected in Hyde Park for the universal exhibition of 1851. It was subsequently re-erected at Sydenham, near London, as a permanent institution for public instruction and entertainment. Grant Munro went for a walk in the Crystal Palace grounds (YELL). Watson believed he heard the "Palace" clock strike three (SIGN), but there is no chiming clock here.

Cubitt, Hilton, a Norfolk squire, murdered in defense of his wife **Elsie Cubitt,** the former *Elsie Patrick,* who had fled America to escape the criminal gang led by her father. She was followed to England by her suitor **Abe** SLANEY, who killed her husband and caused her to attempt suicide (DANC).

Culverton Smith, the murderer of

In summer the Crystal Palace is the scene of many great festivals and gatherings.

his nephew Victor Savage, who attempted to murder Holmes as well (DYIN).

Cummerbund, a large, loose sash worn as a belt, common in the East (SIGN).

Cummings, Joyce, the barrister for Grace Dunbar (THOR).

Cunard (*kyoo-nard′*) **Line,** the most prestigious of the transatlantic steamship lines, founded in 1838 by *Samuel Cunard* (1787–1865). Baron Gruner was to leave Liverpool in the *Ruritania* upon a Friday (ILLU), despite the fact that Cunard liners sail for New York only upon Tuesdays, Thursdays, and Saturdays.

Cunningham, a Surrey country squire. He and his son **Alec Cunningham** murdered their coachman William Kirwin and atttempted to kill Holmes when he discovered evidence against them (REIG).

Cup, a cup-shaped or other vessel of precious metal, or by extension any elaborately wrought piece of plate, offered as a prize to be contended for in horse-racing and other sports. Silver Blaze won the Wessex Cup (SILV).

Curaçao (*koo-rah-sō′*), a liquor prepared from a peculiar kind of bitter oranges growing on the Dutch West Indian island of *Curaçao.* Holmes and Watson drank curaçao at Goldini's restaurant (BRUC).

Curare (*koo-rah′ree*), the well-known arrow poison of the Indians of southern Brazil. It is the juice of a tree, and its properties are such that if the poison is introduced into a scratch or puncture of the skin, it causes death by paralysis of the nerves of the respiratory organs. It may, however, be swallowed in relatively small amounts without injury. Holmes suggested that the Fer-

guson baby had been poisoned with curare or a similar drug (SUSS).

Curb, a chain or strap attached to the bit of a bridle, used in controlling an unruly or high-spirited horse. Jefferson Hope caught Lucy Ferrier's frightened horse by the curb (STUD).

Curlew, a bird related to the woodcock. Watson observed a gull or curlew above Dartmoor (HOUN), and Holmes said that the plover and the curlew were the only inhabitants of Lower Gill Moor (PRIO).

*Curzon Square, presumably a square in London, from which Don Murillo vanished (WIST).

Curzon (*kur′zohn*) **Street,** a street in Westminster, extending eastward from Park Lane to Half Moon Street. Sam Brewer lived here (SHOS). See Map III of LONDON.

Cusack, Catherine, the maid to the Countess of Morcar, who with James Ryder stole the blue carbuncle (BLUE).

Cushing, Susan, a maiden lady living at Croydon, the eldest of three sisters. She received in the mail a carboard box containing two human ears, intended for her sister **Sarah Cushing,** whom James BROWNER blamed for the failure of his marriage with their youngest sister Mary (CARD).

Cutter, a type of small, single-masted sailing-ship. The ALICIA was a cutter (THOR).

Cuvier, Georges Léopold Chrétien Frédéric Dagobert, Baron (1769–1832), a distinguished French naturalist. Holmes opined that as Cuvier could correctly describe a whole animal by the contemplation of a single bone, so the observer who has thoroughly understood one link in a series of incidents should be able accurately to state all other ones, both before and after (FIVE).

Cyanea capillata, also called *lion's*

Cyanea.

mane, the name given to a variety of common jellyfish, possessing a severe sting, which inhabits the waters of the Atlantic. Fitzroy McPherson was killed and Ian Murdoch attacked by *Cyanea capillata* (LION).

Cyclical dates, properly the **sexagenary cycle,** also called the *Chinese cycle,* a method of computing time based entirely upon multiples of the number 60, in use throughout the Chinese Empire and the countries receiving their cultures from China. A vestige of this system, transmitted to Europe through the ancient middle-eastern civilizations, survives in the division of the hour into sixty minutes. Watson read up on "cyclical dates" as he prepared for his interview with Baron Gruner (ILLU).

Cyclopides, the name formerly given to a genus of butterfly now called *Hesperia,* consisting of a number of small black-and-white species known popularly as *skippers.* Stapleton pursued what he called a Cyclopides upon Dartmoor (HOUN).

D

D, the symbol for PENNY.

Dace, a small fresh-water game-fish (SHOS).

*Dacre Hotel, the London hotel at which the Prince of Colonna was staying when the black pearl of the Borgias was stolen (SIXN).

Daily Chronicle, a London morning newspaper, independently Liberal in tone, established 1877, which has swiftly taken rank among the leading London dailies. Watson read accounts of the cardboard box (CARD) and the Silver Blaze (SILV) affairs in the *Daily Chronicle,* and Mary Sutherland advertised for Hosmer Angel here (IDEN).

*Daily Gazette, the newspaper asked for by Emilia Lucca, in the agony column of which her husband's messages appeared (REDC).

*Daily Herald, the Vermissa newspaper, edited by James STANGER, which opposed the Scowrers (VALL).

Daily News, a London morning newspaper, the champion of Liberal ideas and principals, founded in 1846. An editorial in the *Daily News* observed that there was no doubt as to the murder of Enoch Drebber being a political crime (STUD). Mycroft Holmes advertised for Paul and Sophy Kratides here (GREE).

Daily Telegraph, a London newspaper, begun in 1855, published in the mornings. In politics it was consistently Liberal up to 1878; since 1886 it has represented Unionist opinions. It led the way in capturing a large and important reading public from the monopoly of *The Times* and became the great organ of the middle classes, distinguished for its enterprise in many fields.

Holmes read the *Telegraph* (COPP), which carried accounts of Jonas Oldacre's apparent murder (NORW) and the Silver Blaze affair (SILV). A story here, filed from Paris, raised the veil which hung round the murder of Eduardo Lucas (SECO). An editorial remarked that in the history of crime there had seldom been a tragedy which presented stranger features than the Drebber murder, and that all evidence pointed to its perpetration by political refugees and revolutionists (STUD). Hugo Oberstein communicated with Colonel Walter through the agony column of the *Daily Telegraph* (BRUC).

D'Albert, Countess. Charles Augustus Milverton's assassin posed as a servant of the Countess d'Albert (CHAS).

Damery, Sir James, the intermediary between Holmes and the ILLUSTRIOUS

CLIENT who took an anonymous interest in Violet de Merville's welfare (ILLU).

"Dancing Men, The Adventure of the" (DANC), a chronicle which appeared originally in the *Strand* magazine for December 1903 and *Collier's Weekly* of 5 December 1903 and was published in the 1905 collection entitled *The Return of Sherlock Holmes.* It concerns Holmes's decipherment of the "dancing men" cipher and his use of it to trap the murderer of Hilton Cubitt. The case occurred the year following the JUBILEE, dating it in 1888 or 1898, though all authorities prefer 1898.

Dancing men cipher: see CRYPTOGRAPHY.

Danites, properly **The Sons of Dan,** a secret society of Mormons, organized in Missouri in 1838 by Dr. Samson Avard, a recent convert to the Church. Its members vowed vengeance upon those who actively opposed Mormonism, upon apostates, and upon whoever might reveal the group's secrets. The name derives from *Dan,* one of the twelve tribes of Israel, described oracularly in the Testament of Jacob: "Dan shall be a serpent by the way, an adder in the path, that biteth the horse heels, so that his rider shall fall backward" (*Gen.* 49:17). In addition Dan was the tribe of the Biblical hero Samson (*Jud.* 13:25), whose namesake Dr. Avard was.

The society never engaged in any of its avowed activities, for its existence was quickly discovered by Joseph Smith, who dissolved the organization and excommunicated Avard. Nonetheless the depredations of "the Danite Band, or the Avenging Angels" (STUD) were featured in anti-Mormon literature for another fifty years

following its abolition. There is no evidence that the society ever existed in Utah.

Danseuse (*daN-sez′*), a woman dancer or ballerina. Flora Millar was a *danseuse* at the Allegro (NOBL).

Danton (*dahN-tahN′*), **Georges Jacques** (1759–1794), a leader in the French Revolution. His moderate policies were opposed by ROBESPIERRE, and he was executed. John McGinty was compared with him (VALL).

Dantzig, or *Danzig,* a seaport in western Germany, pop. 140,000. Fritz von Waldbaum was a criminal specialist here (NAVA).

Darbies, or **derbies,** in English slang, handcuffs (CARD, REDH).

Darbyshire, William: see STRAKER, JOHN.

Darjeeling, a military station of British India, in the hill region of northern Bengal, pop. 16,924. Henry Wood escaped his Sepoy captors near here (CROO).

Dark horse, in racing, a horse whose capabilities are not generally known, and concerning whose chances of success in a pending race little or no information is to be had. Shoscombe Prince was a dark horse (SHOS).

Dark lantern, a lantern so constructed as to permit the light to be shut off without extinguishing the flame, and possessing a lens which allows the focusing of the beam. A single moveable shutter acts as the reflector when moved behind the flame, and as a shade which shuts off the light when moved between the lens and the flame. A POCKET LANTERN is of similar design.

Dr. Grimesby Roylott lit a dark lantern to remove the swamp adder from his safe (SPEC). A dark lantern was used in the vigil in the City and Suburban Bank vault (REDH), and Holmes borrowed a police sergeant's BULL's-EYE lantern (SIGN). He asked Watson to bring a dark lantern with the other burglars' tools to Kensington (BRUC) and carried one in breaking into Appledore Towers (CHAS), as did Beppo in burgling Laburnum Villa (SIXN).

See the illustration on p. 83.

Darlington, a town in the north of England, in the county of Durham, pop. 44,511. Holmes investigated a case he called the *Darlington Substitution Scandal* (SCAN), which may refer to this town.

Dartmoor, an open, bleak plateau of south-west Devonshire, about two hundred square miles in extent. The wild expanse of moor, crested with broken tors, contrasts strongly with the more gentle scenery of the well-wooded lowlands surrounding it. There is little or no cultivation, and the more elevated regions are traversed only in part by a few rough tracks. The events of the Baskerville (HOUN) and Silver Blaze (SILV) cases took place on Dartmoor.

See also BOSS; TAVISTOCK; also MOOR; NORTH DEVON LINE; PRINCETOWN PRISON; TIN; TOR; also BELLIVER TOR; BLACK TOR; CLEFT TOR; VIXEN TOR. See the map of DEVONSHIRE.

Dartmoor, prison: see PRINCETOWN PRISON.

Darwin, Charles Robert (1809–1882), a noted English naturalist, the first to propose the theory of evolution and natural selection. Holmes referred

On Dartmoor.

to Darwin's comments in *The Descent of Man* concerning music; the *Daily Telegraph* alluded airily to the Darwinian theory in its editorial about the Drebber murder (STUD).

Daubensee, a small lake of southwestern Switzerland, located near the summit of the Gemmi Pass. An attempt was apparently made upon Holmes's and Watson's lives as they walked along the shore (FINA). See the map of SWITZERLAND.

Daulat Ras: see RAS.

Davenport, J., an acquaintance of Sophy Kratides (GREE).

David, a king of Israel, who died *c.*1000 B.C. Mrs. Barclay reproached her husband by comparing him to David, in reference to the story of David and BATHSHEBA (CROO).

Davos Platz, a hamlet of eastern Switzerland, the chief community of the Davos Valley, pop. of the valley (1900) 8,089. Its excellent climate makes it much frequented by consumptives. The consumptive Englishwoman was said to have come from here (FINA). See the map of SWITZERLAND.

Dawson, the senior partner of the banking firm of **Dawson & Neligan.** He was retired when the firm failed and Neligan fled from England (BLAC).

Dawson (d. 1857), the manager of the Abel White plantation. He and his wife **Mrs. Dawson** (d. 1857) were killed at the outset of the Indian Mutiny (SIGN).

Dawson, a groom at the Capleton stables (SILV).

Day's Music Hall, a music hall in Birmingham which Harry Pinner recommended (STOC). See the map of BIRMINGHAM.

D.D., the abbreviation for *Doctor of*

Divinity, the degree of one who is empowered to teach theology (TWIS).

Deal, a board or plank. The name is applied chiefly to planks of pine or fir above seven inches in width and of various lengths exceeding six feet. Holmes's chemical table was deal-topped (EMPT). A small deal box containing children's bricks was found in the room where Neville St. Clair was last seen (TWIS). Duncan Ross sat behind a deal table in the Pope's Court office (REDH), the furniture was of deal at the offices of the Franco-Midland Hardware Company (STOC), and the floor of the Howe Street tenement was of deal boards (REDC).

"Decameron": see BOCCACCIO, GIOVANNI.

De Capus, Hugo (*fl. c.*1095), presumably a Norman nobleman, to whom Birlstone was granted by William Rufus, and who built the original manor house (VALL).

De Croy, Philippe (*fl. c.*1642), the publisher of the volume *De Jure inter Gentes* (STUD).

Deduction, the method of thought which begins with general truths or *a priori* principles such as definitions and rules, and proceeds to apply them to particular facts. It creates individual ideas under general laws, and is the reverse of *induction*. Deduction is known as SYNTHESIS when it progresses directly from principles to consequences, as ANALYSIS when the logical syllogism is "regressive" from consequences to principles. See DEDUCTION AND ANALYSIS.

Deduction and Analysis, the science professed by Sherlock Homes. The most complete portrayal of the Science of Deduction and Analysis is set forth in his "Book of Life" (STUD) and is extensively amplified in his projected volume upon the "whole art of detection" (ABBE). See ANALYSIS; DEDUCTION; SYNTHESIS; also HOLMES, SHERLOCK, subheaded *Methods*.

Holmes was pleased that Watson chose to chronicle those incidents which gave room for deduction and logical synthesis, though he maintained that the inobservant public did not care about the finer shades of analysis and deduction (COPP).

The same powers which Holmes turned to the detection of crime, his brother Mycroft used for his own particular services to the British Government (BRUC), and he maintained that Mycroft possessed these faculties in a larger degree than he himself did (GREE).

*Deep Dene House,** the Norwood residence of Jonas Oldacre. The *Daily Telegraph* reported it located "at the Sydenham end of the road of that name" (NORW), which seemingly could refer either to the SYDENHAM ROAD or to *Deepdene Road,* which is, however, in Brixton and not in Lower Norwood.

Deer. There were deer's heads upon the walls of the Abbey Grange's dining-room (ABBE).

"De Jure inter Gentes" (*On the Law of Nations*), the title of a "queer old book" Holmes picked up at a London bookstall (STUD).

Delhi (*del'ee*), a city of northern India, pop. 208,385. The scene of a bloody massacre during the MUTINY, the city was relieved by WILSON (SIGN).

De Merville, General, a famous British soldier "of Khyber fame" who became a broken man when his daughter **Violet de Merville** came under the

power of Baron GRUNER. At the urging of Sir James DAMERY, Holmes acted to prevent the impending marriage (ILLU).

Dene, a vale or narrow, wooded valley between two hills; see DEEP DENE HOUSE (NORW).

Denmark, a kingdom of northern Europe, pop. 2,464,770. Enoch Drebber and Joseph Stangerson learned in Copenhagen that Jefferson Hope was in Europe (STUD). A Dane acted as an assistant at the Bar of Gold (TWIS). See the map of EUROPE.

Dennis, the non-existent couple fabricated by the man who impersonated Mrs. SAWYER. She claimed the ring held by Holmes to belong to her daughter **Sally Dennis,** whose husband **Tom Dennis** was a steward aboard a Union boat (STUD).

De novo, a Latin phrase meaning *anew;* afresh or unbiased (ABBE).

Deptford (*det'ford*) **Reach,** that part of the Thames lying on the southwest of the Isle of Dogs (SIGN). See the front endpaper map.

Deputy, in Italy and some other European countries, a member of the Chamber of Deputies, the lower house of the national legislature. Augusto Barelli had been a deputy for Posilippo (REDC).

De Quincey, Thomas (1785–1859), a well-known English author. He was addicted to opium for many years and published *Confessions of an English Opium Eater,* his chief contribution to literature, in 1821. Isa Whitney acquired the opium habit after reading some of De Quincey's works (TWIS).

Derbies: see DARBIES.

Derby (*dahr'bee*), the county-town of Derbyshire, a northern midland county of England, pop. 114,848. The Birlstone murderer was reported from

Derby and nineteen other places (VALL).

Derby, The, the most important annual horse-race of England, founded in 1780 by the 12th Earl of Derby, and run at Epsom, in Surrey, each year toward the end of May. Sir Robert Norberton's horse Shoscombe Prince won the Derby (SHOS).

Derbyshire, William: see STRAKER, JOHN.

De Reszke (*deh-resh'kee*), **Jean** (1850–1925), a celebrated Polish operatic tenor. His brother **Édouard De Reszke** (1855–1917) became even more famous as a bass with New York's Metropolitan Opera Company. Holmes asked Watson if he had heard the De Reszkes (HOUN).

Desborough, a racing-horse belonging to Lord Backwater, which finished second in the Wessex Cup (SILV).

Desmond, James, an elderly clergyman, a distant cousin to the Baskervilles. He stood to inherit the Baskerville fortune in the event of Sir Henry's death (HOUN).

Detective: see CONSTABLE; CONSULTING DETECTIVE; POLICE; PRIVATE DETECTIVE; SCOTLAND YARD.

Detroit, a city in Michigan, pop. (1904) 317,591. John McMurdo had lived in Detroit (VALL).

Deutsche Bank, properly the **Reichsbank,** also known as the *Imperial Bank of Germany,* the German national bank. Holmes suspected that Moriarty kept the bulk of his fortune here (VALL).

De Vere. Lord Robert St. Simon's full name was Robert Walsingham de Vere St. Simon (NOBL), suggesting kinship with the ancient family of *Vere,* Earls of Oxford 1142–1703, often considered the most illustrious line in all of English history.

"Devil's Foot, The Adventure of the" (DEVI), a chronicle which appeared originally in the *Strand* magazine for December 1910 and the U.S. edition of the *Strand* for January and February 1911 and was published in the collection entitled *His Last Bow* in 1917. It concerns Holmes's investigation of the macabre deaths of members of the Tregennis family while vacationing in Cornwall in March 1897.

Devil's-foot root, in Latin *radix pedis diaboli,* the name given to an obscure ORDEAL poison of West Africa, the term deriving from the shape of the root from which the reddish-brown powder is extracted. The poison, when burned, produces fumes which bring on insanity and then death. Mortimer TREGENNIS used it to murder his relatives and then was killed with it by Leon STERNDALE, who had brought a sample with him to England (DEVI).

Devine, the French sculptor who created the bust of Napoleon reproduced in the Stepney factory (SIXN).

Devine, Marie, the maid of Lady Frances Carfax (LADY).

***Devon County Chronicle,** a West-country newspaper, in which an account of Sir Charles Baskerville's death appeared (HOUN).

Devonshire, or **Devon,** a south-western county of England, pop. 661,314. It is valuable pasture and cattle country, and the fisheries are important. The events of the Baskerville (HOUN) and Silver Blaze (SILV) cases took place here, on DARTMOOR. See also COOMBE TRACEY; EXETER; FERNWORTHY; GRIMPEN; PLYMOUTH; TAVISTOCK. See the map on the following page.

Devonshire, Georgiana Cavendish, Duchess of (1757–1806), the first wife of the 5th Duke of Devonshire (1748–1811), famous for her beauty,

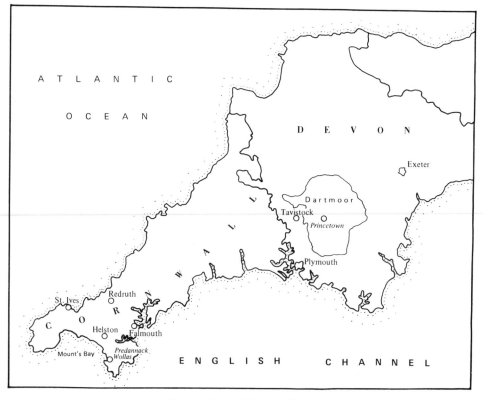

Cornwall and Devonshire.

wit, and social influence. Watson described Mary Sutherland's broad-brimmed hat as being "tilted in a coquettish Duchess-of-Devonshire fashion over her ear" (IDEN), an allusion to the celebrated portrait of the Duchess by Thomas Gainsborough.

Devoy, Sergeant, the colour-sergeant of Henry Wood's regiment during the Indian Mutiny. His daughter Nancy married James BARCLAY (CROO).

Diabetes. John Turner had suffered from diabetes for years, and presumably died of it (BOSC).

Diadem, a crown (BERY, MUSG).

Diamond. Charles Augustus Milverton commiserated that a woman's marriage would be ruined because she would not turn her diamonds into paste; and the photograph of Milverton's assassin showed her wearing a diamond tiara (CHAS). Lady Frances Carfax inherited some remarkable diamonds, for which she was abducted by Holy Peters (LADY), and Jack Woodley offered Violet Smith diamonds if she would marry him (SOLI). Peterson believed at first that the BLUE CARBUNCLE was a diamond (BLUE). The MAZARIN STONE was a diamond (MAZA), and there were 143 diamonds of the first WATER in the Agra treasure, among them the GREAT MOGUL (SIGN).

Holmes's monograph on hands included lithographs of the hands of diamond-polishers (SIGN).

See also BRILLIANT; KIMBERLEY.

Diamond Hill, one of a series of mountainous plateaus in the Transvaal some twenty miles east of Pretoria, astride the Pretoria-Delagoa Bay railway line. It was the principal scene of action in the *Battle of Diamond Hill,* a scattered and largely indecisive engagement of the South African War, fought 11–12 June 1900, when the British, advancing from recently captured Pretoria, attacked the strong Boer entrenchments atop the ridges and forced them to withdraw. The withdrawal was effected in complete order and with virtually no loss of life, and both sides claimed the victory. Godfrey Emsworth

Gainsborough's portrait of the Duchess of Devonshire. Nicknamed "The Stolen Duchess," it was famous during the last quarter of the nineteenth century, having been daringly stolen from a Bond Street picture-gallery in 1876. It was recovered by Pinkerton detectives in Chicago in 1901 and shortly thereafter was sold to the American millionaire J. Pierpont Morgan.

was wounded in the battle (BLAN). See the map of SOUTH AFRICA.

Diary. Elias Openshaw kept a register and diary of his days with the Ku Klux Klan which the society was anxious to recover (FIVE), and Professor Coram had stolen his wife's diary (GOLD).

Holmes refers to his own diary (BLAN), which may be identical with his case-book. Watson recorded the details of the Baskerville case in his diary (HOUN); see also JOURNAL; NOTEBOOK; PORTFOLIO; SCRAPBOOK; YEARBOOK.

Dibbs, in English slang, money (GLOR).

Dieppe, a seaport town of France, located on the English Channel, pop. 22,503. Holmes and Watson landed at Dieppe (FINA).

Digger Indians, the name given to several tribes in California and Nevada who live almost solely upon roots which they dig from the ground. Holmes's gazetteer stated that the Digger Indians were exceedingly small in stature (SIGN).

Diggings, in English slang, one's residence (STOC, STUD).

Dime novel, in America, the common name for a type of cheap, sensational literature, cheaply printed and sold for a dime or less (HOUN, VALL).

***Dingle, The,** the house belonging to Lord Harringby (WIST). A *dingle* is a closely wooded hollow or DENE.

***Diogenes Club,** a London club begun for the convenience of what Holmes called the most unsociable and unclubbable men in town. Mycroft Holmes was one of the founders (BRUC, GREE).

Diphtheria, an infectious and exceedingly dangerous disease. Trevor

Senior's daughter died of it on a visit to Birmingham (GLOR).

Directory, probably either *Kelly's Post Office Directory,* a thick annual volume of some three thousand pages listing the residences and commercial establishments of London, or the similar but less extensive *Morris's Directory.* Holmes doubted that Mr. Haines-Johnson would be found in the Directory (3GAB). Holmes selected for young Cartwright the names of twenty-three hotels near Charing Cross from what he called the "Hotel Directory" (HOUN), also probably identifiable with one of the two established directories.

"Disappearance of Lady Frances Carfax, The" (LADY), a chronicle which appeared originally in the *Strand* and *American* magazines for December 1911 and was published in the collection entitled *His Last Bow* in 1917. It concerns Holmes's search for the missing Lady Frances Carfax, and the case is dated as having occurred in any of several years between 1894 and 1903.

Diseases and disorders: see PATHOLOGY.

Disjecta membra, a Latin phrase meaning *scattered parts* (BLUE).

District, of Western Sussex: see PARLIAMENT.

District Messenger Service Co., a service operating throughout London and its suburbs at rates which are twice those charged by the Post Office for similar express deliveries by special messenger.

Mr. Wilson managed the district messenger office at which young Cartwright worked (HOUN), and the letter to Baron Gruner was dispatched with a district messenger (ILLU). Holmes sent a letter to Josiah Barnes by "express messenger" (SIXN), his use of the term echoing a previous allusion to a District Messenger Service branch as an "express office" (HOUN). His note to Watson was delivered by messenger (BRUC), and he declared that nothing less than attempted murder would hold the London message-boy from keeping on his way (SIXN).

Dixie, Steve, whom Holmes called *Black Steve,* a prizefighter hired by Isadora Klein to intimidate Holmes (3GAB).

Dixon, Jeremy, owner of the draghound Pompey (MISS).

Dixon, Mrs., the housekeeper to Bob Carruthers (SOLI).

Dobney, Susan, the old governess of Lady Frances Carfax, who first consulted Holmes in the case (LADY).

Dock, the place in a courtroom where the accused stands during his trial (COPP, CROO, DYIN, EMPT, ILLU).

Doctor, in common use, a word synonymous with *physician* or *surgeon.*

Watson took his degree of Doctor of Medicine at the University of London in 1878 (STUD) and served as an Army surgeon (RESI, SIGN, STUD) before returning to civil practice; see WATSON, JOHN H.

Holmes was not following any systematic medical studies at St. Bartholomew's Hospital (STUD), though he occasionally made use of medical expressions (SIGN). Dr. Leslie ARMSTRONG was one of the heads of the Cambridge medical school (MISS). Holmes remarked that when a doctor goes wrong he is the "first of criminals," having both nerve and knowledge, and he cited PALMER and PRITCHARD as he spoke of Dr. Grimesby ROYLOTT (SPEC). Trevor BENNETT had a medical degree (CREE), and Dr. BECHER (ENGR) and Dr. Leon STERNDALE (DEVI) were perhaps medical men. Dr. James MORTIMER repudiated the title, stating that he was only an M.R.C.S. (HOUN).

There was a doctor aboard the *Gloria Scott* (GLOR). A doctor had treated Lady Beatrice Falder for dropsy (SHOS), and Nathan Garrideb's physician lectured him about never going out (3GAR). Godfrey Emsworth was treated by the doctor in charge of a South African leper hospital (BLAN). Jefferson Hope went to a doctor about his aneurism while in London (STUD). The local surgeon treated Elsie Cubitt (DANC), and Baron Gruner's family surgeon and a specialist arrived to treat the baron (ILLU). A doctor saw Rachel Howells (MUSG) and was summoned to the Red Bull Inn (PRIO), and the North Walsham station-master (DANC) and Godfrey Staunton (MISS) both mistook Holmes and Watson for doctors. Watson suggested that a first-class surgeon see Professor Presbury (CREE). The bogus letter to Watson said that the consumptive Englishwoman refused to see a Swiss physician (FINA), and Holmes would not permit Mrs. Hudson to get a doctor for him when he fell ill (DYIN).

The Barclays' coachman obtained the help of a medical man; and the medical evidence at the inquest showed conclusively that Colonel Barclay died of apoplexy (CROO). A surgeon's deposition was read at the inquest into Charles McCarthy's death (BOSC). A doctor was sent for who examined Fitzroy McPherson's body (LION), Maria Gibson's body was examined before it was moved (THOR), and a

doctor examined the bones found at Wisteria Lodge (WIST).

While a specialist assured Holmes that Sir Henry Baskerville's nervous collapse would be a temporary one (HOUN), the doctors held out no hope that Madame Fournaye would reestablish her reason (SECO); see ALIENIST; BROADMOOR ASYLUM.

Other medical men associated with Holmes and Watson were Moore AGAR (DEVI), Ainstree (DYIN), ANSTRUTHER (BOSC), Barnicot (SIXN), Ray ERNEST (RETI), Farquhar (STOC), Ferrier (NAVA), Penrose Fisher (DYIN), Fordham (GLOR), Horsom (LADY), Jackson (CROO), Kent (BLAN), Sir Jasper Meek (DYIN), Sir Leslie Oakshott (ILLU), Richards (DEVI), Sir James Saunders (BLAN), Somerton (SIGN), Percy TREVELYAN (RESI), VERNER (NORW), Willows (BOSC), and Wood (VALL).

See also "BRITISH MEDICAL JOURNAL"; BRIXTON WORKHOUSE INFIRMARY; CANNULA; CAVENDISH SQUARE; COLLEGE OF SURGEONS; DRESSER; HARLEY STREET; JACKSON PRIZE; "LANCET"; MEDICAL DIRECTORY; MEDICAL OFFICER OF HEALTH; M.R.C.S.; QUEEN ANNE STREET; RED LAMP; also CHARING CROSS HOSPITAL; KING'S CROSS HOSPITAL; ST. BARTHOLOMEW'S HOSPITAL. See also ARMY MEDICAL DEPARTMENT; NETLEY; PESHAWUR. See also ANATOMY; PATHOLOGY.

Doctors' Commons, the name formerly applied to a society of ecclesiastical lawyers in London, dissolved in 1857, and to the building near St. Paul's occupied by this corporation. Here records of marriage licenses, divorces, and wills were kept until the building was demolished in 1867. In 1874 these archives were transferred to *Somerset House,* a great palace on the Strand begun in 1547 and not completed until 1856, which now contains many government offices as well as King's College. Holmes examined the will of the late Mrs. Stoner at "Doctors' Commons" (SPEC). See Map II of LONDON and the photograph on p. 116.

Doctors' quarter, of London: see CAVENDISH SQUARE.

Dodd: see MORRISON, MORRISON, AND DODD.

Dodd, James M., a London stockbroker whose efforts to locate his wartime friend Godfrey Emsworth brought him to Holmes (BLAN).

Do down, in English prizefighters' slang, to "punish" badly; to severely beat an opponent. Sam Merton said of Holmes that he would "do him down a thick 'un" (MAZA); see THICK 'UN.

Dog. Holmes gave serious thought to the writing of a monograph upon the use of dogs in the work of the detective (CREE).

See also BEAGLE; BLOODHOUND; BULLDOG; DRAGHOUND; FOXHOUND; LURCHER; MASTIFF; NEWFOUNDLAND; SLEUTH-HOUND; SPANIEL; STAGHOUND; TERRIER; WOLF-HOUND. See also COURSING; FOX HUNTING.

Dog, more commonly *cat,* a double tripod with six legs, formed by three bars joined in the middle and so arranged that it always rests on three of its legs, set before an open fireplace and used as a toasting-stand. High iron dogs stood before the fire at Baskerville Hall (HOUN).

Dog, to follow pertinaciously (DANC, FINA, HOUN, MAZA, MISS, STUD).

Dog-cart, a light pleasure-cart with two seats placed back to back. The cart derives its name from the box under the rear seat which originally was used for carrying dogs.

Helen Stoner took a dog-cart from Stoke Moran to Leatherhead (SPEC). Inspector Martin arrived at Ridling Thorpe Manor (DANC) and White Mason at Birlstone (VALL) in dogcarts. They were kept by Jephro Rucastle (COPP), vicar Roundhay (DEVI), the Trevors (GLOR), and Reginald Musgrave (MUSG). Reuben Hays (PRIO), Bob Carruthers (SOLI), and Neville St. Clair (TWIS) each owned a dog-cart which was referred to as a TRAP, and Dr. Mortimer's was also spoken of as a GIG (HOUN).

Dog-grate, a fire-grate of the general shape of a basket, supported on andirons known as *fire-dogs,* hence the name. There was a dog-grate at Wisteria Lodge (WIST).

Dog-lash, or dog-whip, a whip used for training or controlling dogs (SPEC, WIST).

Dogs, Isle of: see ISLE OF DOGS.

Dog-whip: see DOG-LASH.

Dolichocephalic, pertaining to a long head. Dr. Mortimer said he had not expected Holmes's skull to be so dolichocephalic (HOUN).

Dollar, the unit of the monetary system of the United States. It is equivalent to .205 English pound sterling; 5.18 French francs, Italian lire, or Spanish pesetas; 4.2 German marks; 3.73 Danish, Swedish, and Norwegian crowns; 1.94 Russian rubles.

Dollar, in British slang, a five-shilling piece, or *crown.* At first James Browner's marriage was, he said, "bright as a new dollar" (CARD). Sir Henry Baskerville believed that "house, land, and dollars" must go together in the Baskerville estate (HOUN). Neville St. Clair wavered before devoting himself to begging, but "the dollars won at last" (TWIS).

Dolores, the maid and companion of Mrs. Ferguson (SUSS).

Dolsky, a man who was murdered at Odessa by the forcible administration of poison (STUD).

Don, a Spanish title, formerly confined to men of high rank, but now applied in courtesy to all of the better classes. It is prefixed to a man's Christian name; thus Watson's allusion to Don Juan MURILLO as "Don Murillo" (WIST) is improper.

Doncaster, a town in Yorkshire, pop. 28,932. Horace Harker recalled that he had been unable to write the story of the stand which fell here (SIXN).

Don Juan, the hero of a Spanish legend, recklessly immoral in character (MUSG).

Don Murillo: see MURILLO.

*Donnithorpe, a hamlet in Norfolk, at which Trevor Senior had his estate (GLOR).

Dorak, A., the London agent for Lowenstein (CREE).

Doran, Aloysius, the American millionaire and former gold prospector whose daughter **Hatty Doran** vanished after her wedding to Lord Robert St. Simon (NOBL).

Dorking, Colonel, a victim of Charles Augustus Milverton (CHAS).

Doss-house, a cheap lodging-house (ILLU).

Dost Akbar, one of the FOUR (SIGN).

Double league, in European diplomacy: see TRIPLE ALLIANCE.

Douglas, Ivy: see EDWARDS, BIRDY.

Douglas, John: see EDWARDS, BIRDY.

Dove-colour, a warm gray with a tone of pink or purple (SILV).

Dovercourt, Earl of, the intended husband of Lady Eva Brackwell (CHAS). *Dovercourt* is a seacoast town of Essex immediately south of Harwich.

"Do We Progress?" the title of an article Dr. Mortimer wrote for the *Journal of Psychology* (HOUN).

Down, a hilly region not covered by forests; e.g., NORTH DOWNS; SOUTH DOWNS. Watson referred to the "undulating downs" of Dartmoor (HOUN) and to the "rolling moors" of Cornwall (DEVI); see MOOR.

Down: see HELM.

Downing, the Surrey constable who was injured in the capture of the mulatto (WIST).

Downing Street, a short street in Westminster, opening into Whitehall, between the Treasury and the Government Office Building. No. 10 is the residence of the Prime Minister. Holmes spoke with Lord Holdhurst in the Foreign Office chambers in Downing Street (NAVA). See the map of WHITEHALL and the photograph on p. 56.

Downs, The, uplands: see NORTH DOWNS; SOUTH DOWNS.

Downs, The, a sheltered anchorage for shipping, between the coast of Kent and the GOODWINS. Holmes suspected a ship might be waiting in the Downs for Jonathan Small (SIGN). See the map of ENGLAND.

Dowson, Baron, he who said upon the night before he was hanged that in Holmes's case the law had gained what the stage had lost (MAZA).

Doyle, Sir Arthur Conan (1859–1930), the famous English physician, novelist, patriot, and literary agent, born in Edinburgh and educated at the University of Edinburgh. From 1882 to 1890 he practised medicine at Southsea, but the success of some early attempts at fiction led him to give up his profession for a literary career. He

Dr. A. Conan Doyle in 1886.

is known to have acted as literary agent for Dr. John H. WATSON in the placing for publication of Watson's adventures with Sherlock Holmes. It is generally agreed that he also wrote the American retrospectives in *A Study in Scarlet* and *The Valley of Fear,* and possibly the third-person narratives "His Last Bow" and "The Adventure of the Mazarin Stone."

Among Conan Doyle's own works are the historical novels *Micah Clarke, The White Company,* and *Sir Nigel,* and the volumes of short stories *Round the Red Lamp* and *The Stark Munro Letters.* He served in the South African War as a physician, and upon his return to England he wrote *The Great Boer War.* He was knighted in 1902 as a reward for his services during the war and for his defense of British policy in *The War in South Africa: Its Causes and Conduct.* His last years were devoted to the cause of spiritualism.

Drag, a carriage resembling a stage-coach, with seats inside and on top, and drawn by four horses. Colonel Ross's party drove to the Wessex Cup in a drag (SILV).

Draghound, a hound trained to follow an artificial scent, usually that of a bag of aniseed dragged along the ground, which is substituted for a fox in riding to hounds. Holmes called Pompey "the pride of the local drag-hounds" (MISS) and remarked that if a pack could "track a trailed herring across a shire" then Toby could follow the creosote scent through London (SIGN).

Drapers' Gardens, a small court in the City just north of Throgmorton Street and the Stock Exchange. The firm of Coxon & Woodhouse was located here (STOC). See the map of the CITY.

Draughts (*drafts*), a common board game, also called *checkers* (FIVE).

Draw, in hunting, to force game from cover; thus, to **draw a cover** is to hunt through it. In seeking Captain Croker, Holmes said, he would first "draw the larger cover" of the Adelaide-Southampton line (ABBE), and he looked to Watson like a foxhound drawing a cover as he dashed about the Tredannick Wollas vicarage (DEVI).

Drebber, one of the four principal elders of the Mormons. His son **Enoch J. Drebber** was instrumental in the persecution and murder of John FERRIER,

A drag drawn by a four-in-hand.

whose daughter Lucy became his eighth wife. In company with his secretary Joseph STANGERSON he fled the vengeance of Jefferson HOPE but eventually was murdered by Hope in London (STUD).

Dresser, a surgeon's assistant. Young Stamford had been Watson's dresser at St. Bartholomew's Hospital (STUD).

Dressing-gown, a long lounging-robe. Holmes had at least three dressing-gowns, one blue (TWIS), one purple (BLUE), and one mouse-coloured (BRUC, EMPT). He wore them often (BERY, CARD, ENGR, FINA, HOUN, LADY, MAZA, RESI, VALL) and draped them about the wax busts of himself (EMPT, MAZA).

Dressing-gowns were worn by Lady Brackenstall (ABBE), Professor Presbury (CREE), Paul Kratides (GREE), Reginald Musgrave (MUSG), Horace Harker (SIXN), and Mrs. Douglas (VALL). Holmes found the evidence to implicate the Cunninghams in the pocket of young

Holmes in dressing-gown.

Alec's dressing-gown (REIG). Hilton Cubitt's body was dressed in a dressing-gown (DANC), as were those of Dr. Grimesby Roylott (SPEC) and John Douglas (VALL).

Dribble, in Rugby, to move the ball by repeated short kicks in such a way as to progress quickly downfield (MISS).

Drop, in Rugby, to score a goal with a drop-kick or punt, for four points, without first scorning a try (MISS).

Dropsy, in medicine, the morbid accumulation of watery fluid in any cavity of the body or in the tissues. Lady Beatrice Falder died of dropsy, with which she had suffered for many months (SHOS).

Drug: see BHANG; COCAINE; MORPHINE; OPIUM; see also CHEMIST.

Drugget, a coarse woollen material, either of one colour or printed upon one side, and used either as a protection for a carpet or as a rug covering the middle portion of a floor (SECO).

Drying-room: see TURKISH BATH.

Dublin, the capital and chief city of Ireland, pop. 290,638. James Browner's ship touched here (CARD).

Dubuque, a member of the Paris police, to whom Holmes demonstrated the true facts of the case of the second stain (NAVA). In some editions the name appears as *Dubugue*.

Duchess, in Great Britain, the wife or widow of a duke (NOBL, PRIO). See PEERAGE.

Duck. Holmes enjoyed wild-duck shooting in the fens round Donnithorpe (GLOR).

Duke, in Great Britain, the highest rank of hereditary nobility (NOBL, PRIO, SECO, SILV, 3GAB); see PEERAGE. For names beginning thus, see the second element; e.g., for the *Duke of Balmoral* see BALMORAL, DUKE OF.

A **Royal Duke** is a duke who is a member of the royal family. John Clay was said to be the grandson of a Royal Duke (REDH).

See also GRAND DUKE.

Duke of York's steps, properly **Waterloo Steps,** a broad flight of steps in Westminster, descending from Carlton House Terrace into St. James's Park. The German Embassy adjoins these stairs, which Baron Von Herling called "the Duke of York's steps" (LAST) because at their top stands the *York Column,* a granite column and statue erected in 1833 in memory of George III's second son *Frederick Augustus, Duke of York* (1763–1827). See the map of WHITEHALL.

The view from St. James's Park toward the York Column and the "Duke of York's steps." The building at left is the German Embassy, and behind it lies Carlton House Terrace.

*Dulong, hotel: see HOTEL DULONG.

Du Louvre, Hôtel: see HÔTEL DU LOUVRE.

Dunbar, Grace, the governess of J. Neil Gibson, whom he came to love. She was implicated in the apparent murder of Gibson's wife and cleared of suspicion by Holmes (THOR).

Duncan Street, a short street in the City, near the border of Stepney. "Mrs. Sawyer" claimed to live here (STUD).

Dundas separation case, a case in which Holmes was engaged in clearing up some small points; the wife complained of her husband's conduct in winding up every meal by taking out his false teeth and hurling them at her (IDEN).

Dundee, a city and seaport of southeastern Scotland, pop. 161,173. The whaler *Sea Unicorn* sailed from here (BLAC), and Joseph Openshaw's death notice bore a Dundee postmark (FIVE).

Dunlop Pneumatic Tyre Co., an English manufacturer of bicycle tyres. James Wilder's bicycle was fitted with them (PRIO).

Dunn, Josiah H. (d. 1875), the manager of the Crow Hill Mine, murdered by the Scowrers (VALL).

Dupin, C. Auguste, the detective created by Edgar Allen POE for his stories "The Murders in the Rue Morgue" (1841), "The Mystery of Marie Rogêt" (1842), and "The Purloined Letter" (1845). Holmes considered him a "very inferior fellow" (STUD), though later he called the character a "close reasoner" (CARD).†

Durando, Victor, minister of San Pedro in London before being recalled and shot by order of Don Murillo. His wife, **Signora Victor Durando,** an Englishwoman, later became governess to Don Murillo's children under the name *Burnet* and conspired against the ex-dictator's life (WIST).

† This allusion is inserted in "The Resident Patient" in many editions.

Dutch, people: see NETHERLANDS; see also BOERS.

Dutch East Indies, a name given to the possessions of the Netherlands in the Malay archipelago.

Two of the Worthingdon Bank Gang smoked cigars which Holmes said were imported by the Dutch from their East Indian colonies (RESI). Holmes declared too that John Turner's murderer had smoked "an Indian cigar, of the variety which are rolled in Rotterdam" (BOSC), suggesting another allusion to *Netherlands India,* as the Dutch East Indies are officially named.

See also COOLIE; LASCAR; MALAY; SUMATRA.

"Dying Detective, The Adventure of the" (DYIN), a chronicle which appeared originally in the *Strand* magazine for December 1913 and *Collier's Weekly* of 22 November 1913 and was published in the 1917 collection entitled *His Last Bow.* It concerns Holmes's entrapment of Culverton Smith by pretending to fall victim to Smith's death-trap. It is variously dated as having taken place between 1887 and 1890.

Dynamics, that branch of physics which deals with the laws of force. Professor Moriarty was the author of *The Dynamics of an Asteroid* (VALL).

"Dynamics of an Asteroid, The," a book written by Professor Moriarty, which ascended to such rarefied heights of pure mathematics, Holmes remarked, that it was said there was no man in the scientific press capable of criticizing it (VALL).

Dyspnœa, in pathology, difficulty in breathing. Sir Charles Baskerville suffered from it (HOUN).

E

E, Greek: see GREEK E.

*Eagle Cañon, or Eagle Ravine, a ravine not far from Salt Lake City (STUD).

*Eagle Commercial, a hotel at Tunbridge Wells, where Ted Baldwin took a room (VALL).

Earl, a British title of nobility (CHAS, EMPT, LADY, PRIO); see PEERAGE. For names beginning thus, see the second element; e.g., for the *Earl of Maynooth* see MAYNOOTH, EARL OF. The wife or widow of an earl is called a *countess*.

Early English charters, instruments granting rights and privileges under seal, written generally in Latin and dating from the Early English period, *c.*1066–1500. Holmes spent some weeks in one of the great University towns pursuing some laborious researches in Early English charters which, it was said, led to some striking results (3STU).

Earth. Holmes maintained that if the earth travelled round the sun or round the moon it would not make a pennyworth of difference to him or his work (STUD), and years later Watson recalled this indifference (HOUN).

East Anglia, an ancient English kingdom, corresponding to the modern counties of Norfolk and Suffolk, which flourished between the sixth and ninth centuries (DANC).

Eastbourne, a seacoast city of Sussex, pop. 43,344. Holmes's retirement villa was some five miles from here (PREF).

East End, The, that part of London which lies to the east of the Temple, embracing the CITY and the dock regions; see LONDON. The arrest of Wilson, the notorious canary-trainer, removed a plague-spot from the East End (BLAC), and Holmes said he believed that he had contracted an Asiatic disease while working among the Chinese sailors here (DYIN). Holmes spent some days in the East End pursuing the Peter Carey case (BLAC). See the front endpaper map.

Eastern Empire, The: see INDIA.

Eastern railway line, in the Transvaal, the line of the *Delagoa Bay and East Africa Railway,* opened in 1895 and running from Pretoria eastward to Delagoa Bay in Portuguese East Africa. Godfrey Emsworth was wounded near the line in the battle of Diamond Hill (BLAN). See the map of SOUTH AFRICA.

East Ham, a city in Essex, pop. 96,018. Geographically it is part of the eastward extension of London, and the city is in the main an industrial one.

The streets of London's East End present an aggregation of meanness and monotony unparallelled anywhere in the world.

The Birlstone murderer was reported from East Ham and nineteen other places (VALL). See the back endpaper map.

East Indies: see DUTCH EAST INDIES.

East London, the designation given to the postal district which embraces London east of the City and north of the Thames, including much of the dock region (FIVE). See the postal map of LONDON.

East Ruston, a parish of Norfolk, located some six miles south-east of North Walsham. Elrige's farm was in East Ruston (DANC).

E.C. (*East Central*), the designation given to the London postal district which embraces the City (CREE, NORW, STOC). See the postal map of LONDON.

Écarté, a game of cards played by two persons. Sir Henry Baskerville and Dr. Mortimer played écarté (HOUN).

Eccles, John Scott: see SCOTT ECCLES.

Echo, a London evening newspaper, Liberal in politics. It was never in sound financial condition and changed its ownership twice before coming to an end in 1905. Holmes and Watson read of Jefferson Hope's death in the *Echo* (STUD), and Holmes advertised for Henry Baker here (BLUE).

Eckermann, the author of *Voodooism and the Negroid Religions,* which Holmes consulted in connection with the Wisteria Lodge case (WIST).

Ecliptic, the great circle in which the sun appears to describe its annual course across the sky. Holmes discussed the changes in the *obliquity* of the ecliptic (GREE), that is, the angle at which the ecliptic stands to the earth's equator, which has been diminishing for about four thousand years at the rate of some fifty seconds of arc in a century.

Edgware Road, a thoroughfare in the West End, running north-westerly from Oxford Street. The church of St. Monica was here (SCAN), and the firm of Holloway and Steele was located in the Edgware Road, from which Little Ryder Street was one of the major offshoots (3GAR). In some editions the name is misspelled *Edgeware*. See the front endpaper map and Map I of LONDON.

Edinburgh, the capital of Scotland, pop. (1904) 331,977. Mary Morstan was raised here (SIGN).

Edison: see SWAN AND EDISON.

*Edmonton Street, presumably a street in London, from which Don Murillo vanished (WIST).

Edmunds, a member of the Berkshire constabulary, who investigated the Abbas Parva tragedy (VEIL).

Edwards, Birdy, a detective with the Pinkerton agency, originally from Ireland. Under the name *John ("Jack")* *McMurdo* he infiltrated the SCOWRERS and brought about their suppression, following which he settled in Chicago. After two attempts upon his life there he fled to California, where he made his fortune in the gold-fields under the name *John ("Jack") Douglas,* then fled again, this time to England, where another murder attempt failed. He was lost overboard during an ocean voyage two months later, probably a victim of the Moriarty organization.

He was twice married. **Ettie Edwards,** the former *Ettie Shafter,* whom he wed in Chicago in 1875, died of typhoid in California. His second wife, known as **Ivy Douglas,** he married in England, and she survived him (VALL).

Eel. Holmes and Watson spoke with Josiah Barnes upon eels and dace (SHOS).

Egan, a Scowrer (VALL).

Egg-shell porcelain, a porcelain of extreme thinness and translucency, originally made in China. Watson took to his appointment with Baron Gruner an egg-shell saucer of the Ming dynasty (ILLU).

*Eglonitz, an entry in Holmes's *Continental Gazetteer* (SCAN).

*Eglow, an entry in the *Continental Gazetteer* (SCAN).

Egria, properly **Eger,** a town of Bohemia, pop. (1900) 23,665. It lies in the centre of a German district distinguished from the surrounding Czech population by language, manners, and customs. WALLENSTEIN was assassinated in what is now the town house. The King of Bohemia's note-paper was made in "Egria," which Holmes found described in his *Continental Gazetteer* (SCAN).

Egypt, a country in the north-eastern part of Africa, pop. (1897) 9,734,405. Nominally a Turkish dependency, it has been practically under British control since 1882. There was a pigeon-hole in Von Bork's safe marked "Egypt" (LAST).

Professor Coram said that his analysis of documents found in the Coptic monasteries of Syria and Egypt would cut deep at the very foundations of revealed religion (GOLD).

The golden plates delivered to Joseph Smith by the angel Moroni, containing the *Book of Mormon,* were said to be written in "Egyptian letters" (STUD) ; see MORMONS.

See also ALEXANDRIA; CAIRO; SUEZ CANAL.

E.J.C., the clerk or secretary of the firm of Morrison, Morrison, and Dodd (SUSS).

Elder, a subordinate officer of the Mormon church (STUD).

Electricity. Cyril Morton was an electrician, that is, an electrical engineer, employed by the Midland Electric Company and later senior partner of Morton and Kennedy (SOLI). Holmes, in his feigned delirium, wondered how a battery feels when it pours electricity into a non-conductor (DYIN), and Watson writes that the blue carbuncle twinkled like an electric point (BLUE). There were electric call-bell systems at Holdernesse Hall (PRIO) and at Baker Street (MAZA), and electric light at St. Luke's College (3STU) and in the homes of Charles Augustus Milverton (CHAS), Culverton Smith (DYIN), Von Bork (LAST), and Isadora Klein (3GAB). Sir Henry Baskerville proposed to install a SWAN AND EDISON electrical system at Baskerville Hall (HOUN).

Eley Bros., a manufacturer of fire-arms ammunition. Holmes's reference to Watson's "Eley's No. 2" (SPEC) is most probably an allusion to the *Webley No. 2* revolver, for which Eley cartridges are made.

Elise, the woman who helped Victor Hatherley escape from Lysander Stark (ENGR).

Elizabethan, pertaining to *Elizabeth* (1533–1603), Queen of England 1558–1603, or her reign. A Baskerville ancestor was an Elizabethan knight (HOUN). The name **Elizabethan architecture** is given to the style of the late TUDOR period (BLAN, PRIO).

Elm. An elm figured prominently in the Musgrave Ritual (MUSG). Birlstone's village street was lined with pollarded elms (VALL), and there were elms round the Abbey Grange (ABBE) and in the Park (YELL).

Elman, J. C., the vicar of Little Purlington (RETI).

Elrige, a Norfolk farmer, owner of **Elrige's Farm,** where Abe Slaney stayed (DANC).

Embankment, The, properly **Victoria Embankment,** a magnificent London thoroughfare extending from the Houses of Parliament along the northern bank of the Thames into the City. The river is held in check by a solid granite embankment through which, at intervals, steps give access to steamers. John Openshaw apparently was decoyed onto the Embankment and thrown into the river (FIVE). See the photograph on the following page.

Embezzlement, the fraudulent appropriation of the personal property of another, held in the capacity of agent, servant, or trustee. Trevor Senior was sentenced to transportation for embezzlement (GLOR).

Emerald, a precious stone of pure green colour, a variety of BERYL. Holmes was presented with an emerald tie-pin by Queen Victoria (BRUC), and the King of Bohemia offered him an emerald snake ring as a reward for his services (SCAN). There were ninety-seven emeralds in the Agra treasure (SIGN).

***Eminent Order of Freemen:** see SCOWRERS.

Empire, The: see BRITISH EMPIRE; INDIA.

"Empty House, The Adventure of the" (EMPT), a chronicle which appeared originally in the *Strand* magazine for October 1903 and *Collier's Weekly* of 26 September 1903 and was published in the 1905 collection entitled *The Return of Sherlock Holmes.* It

The Victoria Embankment, constructed 1864–70 upon the left bank of the Thames. The obelisk, brought from Egypt and erected here in 1878, is called "Cleopatra's Needle." The bridge is Waterloo Bridge, and the long, low building immediately beyond it is Somerset House ("Doctors' Commons").

concerns Holmes's trapping of Colonel Sebastian Moran and his return to his detective practice in April 1894.

Emsworth, Colonel, a retired Army officer, living with his wife at Tuxbury Old Park in Bedfordshire. Their son **Godfrey Emsworth** was believed to have contracted leprosy in South Africa and was kept secluded until, through the efforts of his friend James Dodd and of Holmes, it was discovered that he was a victim of ICHTHYOSIS (BLAN).

"Encyclopædia Britannica," the best-known and most comprehensive of English-language encyclopædias, established in 1768. The monumental ninth edition, in twenty-four volumes, appeared 1875–89. Jabez Wilson's duties with the Red-Headed League was to copy out the *Encyclopædia Britannica* (REDH).

Endell Street, a short street of central London, reaching northward from near Covent Garden. Holmes and Watson passed down here on their way to the market (BLUE). See Map II of LONDON.

Endowment (*on-dew′ment*) **House,** formerly a small two-storey building in Salt Lake City, originally built as a temporary place of worship, where Mormons received the gift of ordination, or *éndowment,* into certain priestly orders. The sealing of husbands and wives in eternal marriage was a part of the ceremony, and all polygamous marriages were required to be performed here (STUD).

"Engineer's Thumb, The Adventure

of the" (ENGR), a chronicle which appeared originally in the *Strand* magazine for March 1892 and was published in the collection entitled *The Adventures of Sherlock Holmes* that same year. It concerns Holmes's interest in the strange experience of and the murderous assault upon Victor Hatherley, and Watson dates the case as having occurred in the summer of 1889.

England, the chief political division of Great Britain and of the United Kingdom, pop. 30,807,232. The name is often commonly used in speaking of GREAT BRITAIN itself.

See also BEDFORDSHIRE; BERKSHIRE; CAMBRIDGESHIRE; CORNWALL; DEVONSHIRE; ESSEX; HALLAMSHIRE; HAMPSHIRE; HEREFORDSHIRE; KENT; LANCASHIRE; LONDON; MIDDLESEX; NOR-FOLK; NORTHUMBERLAND; SURREY; SUSSEX; WESTMORLAND; WORCESTERSHIRE; YORKSHIRE.

See the map on the following page.

*Englischer Hof, the hotel in Meiringen where Holmes and Watson stayed (FINA).

Englischer Hof, a well-recommended hotel at Baden. Lady Frances Carfax made the acquaintance of the Shlessingers here (LADY).

English Channel. Holmes's Sussex villa commanded a view of the Channel (LION). There was a pigeon-hole in Von Bork's safe marked "The Channel" (LAST).

English Charters: see EARLY ENGLISH CHARTERS.

Entail, in law, the limitation of land to a particular family or line of de-

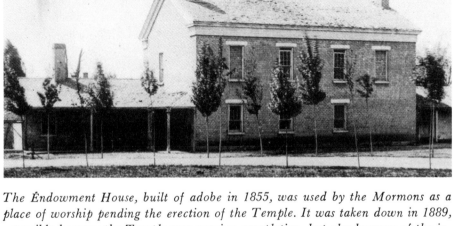

The Endowment House, built of adobe in 1855, was used by the Mormons as a place of worship pending the erection of the Temple. It was taken down in 1889, ostensibly because the Temple was nearing completion, but also because of the infamous reputation it had acquired.

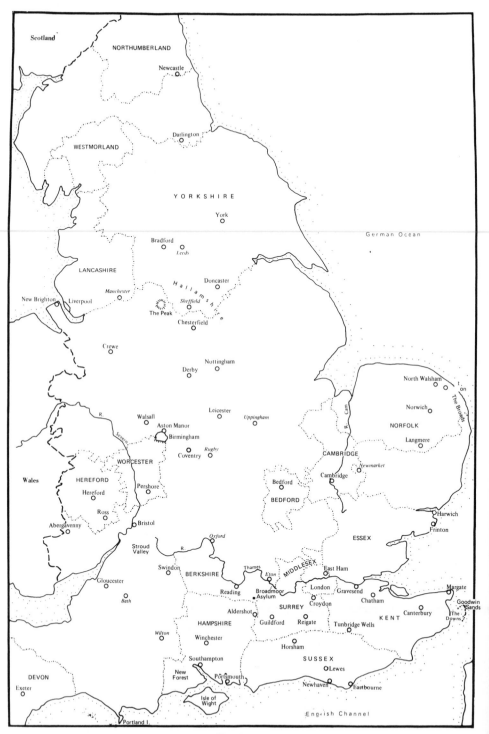

England.

scent, prohibiting the division or sale of the property. The Baskerville estate was entailed (HOUN), and James Wilder attempted to force his father, the Duke of Holdernesse, to break the entail upon his estates and leave them to Wilder by will (PRIO).

Enteric fever: see TYPHOID FEVER.

Entomology, the branch of zoology which treats of insects. Stapleton was devoted to the discipline, and his alias *Vandeleur* was given to a variety of moth which he was the first to describe (HOUN). Young Master Rucastle showed remarkable talent in the capture of insects (COPP). See also BEE; BLUEBOTTLE; CYCLOPIDES; LEPIDOPTERA.

Epilepsy, or *falling sickness,* a disease of the nervous system, causing unconsciousness, either with or without convulsions. Jefferson Hope, in resisting arrest, appeared to have the convulsive strength of a man in an epileptic fit (STUD).

Epithelial scales, dandruff flakes. Such scales were visible in the microscopic field Holmes showed Watson (SHOS).

Equinoctial gales, storms which are observed generally to take place about the time of the sun's crossing the equator, that is, at the vernal and autumnal equinoxes in March and September. The equinoctial gales were long and severe in 1887, and the barque *Lone Star* apparently was lost with all hands in an Atlantic gale in September of that year (FIVE).

Ernest, Ray (d. 1898), a London physician, the lover of Mrs. Amberley, who was murdered with her by her husband. His family hired Holmes's rival Barker to investigate his disappearance (RETI).

Erysipelas, in medicine, an infectious disease characterized by inflammation of the skin accompanied by fever and other general discomfort. There was a report of erysipelas in the newspaper accounts of Holmes's condition (ILLU).

Escott, the alias used by Holmes in his wooing of Charles Augustus Milverton's housemaid Agatha (CHAS).

Escurial: see HOTEL ESCURIAL.

Esher, a residential district of northwestern Surrey, pop. 9,489. Wisteria Lodge was near here (WIST). See the back endpaper map.

*Esmeralda, a ship in which Jonathan Small planned to escape to Brazil (SIGN).

Esquimaux, or *Eskimo.* Dr. Mortimer claimed that he could tell the skull of a Negro from that of an Esquimaux (HOUN). In some editions the word appears in the more grammatically correct singular form *Esquimau.*

Essex, an eastern county of England, pop. 1,085,771. While the county is highly agricultural, it nonetheless possesses extensive industries in the south-west and south, in the vicinities of London and the lower Thames. Holmes sent Watson and Josiah Amberley on a wild goose chase into Essex so that he might burgle Amberley's house (RETI). See also EAST HAM; FRINTON-ON-SEA; HARWICH. See the endpaper maps and the map of ENGLAND.

Estimates, The, the accounts presented annually to Parliament, showing the probable amount of expenditure on the several administrative departments for the current year. The appropriation for the Bruce-Partington submarine was smuggled through the Estimates (BRUC).

Ether. Injected ether was used to revive Lady Frances Carfax (LADY), a common treatment for overdoses of anæsthesia, since ether, subcutaneously injected, constitutes perhaps the most rapid and powerful cardiac stimulant known.

Etherege, a man whom Holmes easily found when the police had given him up for dead. His wife **Mrs. Etherege** recommended Holmes to Mary Sutherland (IDEN).

Eton College, one of the famous schools of England, at *Eton* in Buckinghamshire. Established in 1440, the school originally was intended for the sons of poor but worthy Englishmen, but it has now become the school of the gentry and nobility. The enrollment is about one thousand. Colonel Sebastian Moran (EMPT) and John Clay (REDH) were educated here.

Eton jacket, a short coat of distinctive cut worn by schoolboys. The Priory School suit consisted of a black Eton jacket and dark gray trousers (PRIO).

Euclid (*fl. c.*300 B.C.), a distinguished Greek mathematician. Holmes claimed that the conclusions of one trained to observation and analysis would be as infallible as so many propositions of Euclid (STUD), and he complained that for Watson to tinge his cases with romanticism produced much the same effect as if he had worked a love-story or an elopement into the fifth proposition of Euclid (SIGN).

Europe, also called **The Continent** by the English. Holmes and Watson fled to the Continent to escape Professor Moriarty (FINA). Holmes said that Moriarty's treatise upon the Binomial Theorem—or perhaps the theorem itself—had a European vogue, that is, was popular or fashionable among the Continental scholars (FINA). An editorial in the *Daily*

Eton College, as seen from its famous playing-fields.

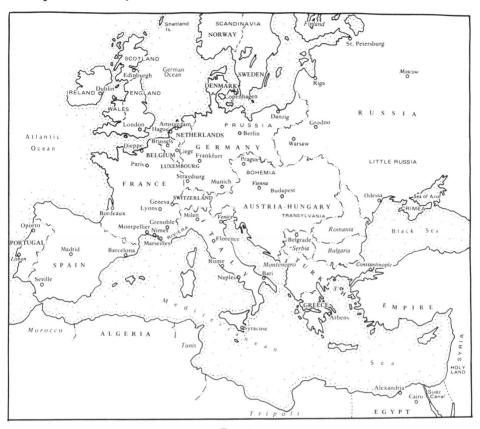

Europe.

News observed that the Continental governments were animated by despotism and hatred of Liberalism (STUD), and the *Vermissa Herald* made reference to the despotisms of Europe (VALL).

The whole of Europe was an armed camp, said Lord Bellinger, Great Britain holding the scales of power between the two European alliances; if Britain were driven into war with one camp, it would assure the supremacy of the other, and thus the publication of the letter written by the indiscreet foreign sovereign assumed a potential for European complications of the utmost moment (SECO) ; see TRIPLE ALLIANCE.

To Watson's knowledge Holmes at the time of the naval treaty theft had acted on behalf of three of the reigning Houses of Europe in very vital matters (NAVA), these being the royal families of BOHEMIA, SCANDINAVIA, and the NETHERLANDS. Later Holmes was of service to the POPE, the Sultan of TURKEY, and the republic of FRANCE.

See also AUSTRIA-HUNGARY; BELGIUM; DENMARK; GERMANY; GREECE; ITALY; LUXEMBOURG; NORWAY; PORTUGAL; PRUSSIA; RUSSIA; SPAIN; SWEDEN; SWITZERLAND.

*European Secretary: see FOREIGN OFFICE.

Eustace, Lord: see BALMORAL, DUKE OF.

Euston Station, a railway station in

Euston Station, constructed in 1837, is the oldest of the major London termini. The great hall pictured here was added in 1849.

St. Pancras, London terminus of the *London and North Western Railway.* Holmes's party entrained for Tuxbury Old Park at Euston (BLAN), and Enoch Drebber and Joseph Stangerson proposed to depart here for Liverpool (STUD). Thorneycroft Huxtable was of the belief that trains for the Peak country departed from Euston (PRIO), but the nearby *St. Pancras* would be the correct station. See Map I of LONDON.

Evans: see BEDDOES.

Evans (d. 1875), a Vermissa policeman who was murdered when he ventured to arrest a Scowrer (VALL).

Evans, Carrie: see NORLETT.

Evans, "Killer" (b. 1868), a notorious American criminal whose real name apparently was *James Winter;* another alias was *Morecroft.* He came to London in 1893 and was imprisoned for shooting the counterfeiter Rodger Prescott. Under the name *John Garrideb* he lured Nathan GARRIDEB from the rooms where Prescott's printing outfit was hidden, but he was taken by

Holmes and Watson in a struggle in which Watson was superficially wounded (3GAR).

Even date, a legal expression meaning *the same date;* today's date (SUSS).

Evening News, a London newspaper, politically Conservative, founded in 1881. Holmes advertised for Henry Baker here (BLUE).

Evening Standard, a London newspaper, the evening edition of the STANDARD. Watson read the account of the London stock robbery and murder here (STOC), and Holmes advertised for Henry Baker in the evening edition of the *Standard* (BLUE).

Excelsior, a Latin motto meaning *higher,* that is, as an expression of incessant aspiration after higher attainment (CREE).

Exeter, the county town of Devonshire, pop. 47,185. Holmes and Watson took a train for Exeter from Paddington (SILV). See the map of DEVONSHIRE.

Express messenger: see DISTRICT MESSENGER SERVICE CO.

Extortion, the act or practice of wresting anything from another by force, duress, menace, or any undue exercise of power. The funds of the Red Circle were raised through blackmail and extortion (REDC), and the Scowrers extorted money from the large firms of Vermissa Valley (VALL). See also BLACKMAIL; ROBBERY.

*****Eyford,** a village in Berkshire, where Dr. Becher lived. Railway service to nearby Reading was provided at **Eyford Station** (ENGR).

F

Faber, Johann (1817–1896), a Nuremberg lead-pencil manufacturer. The pencil used to copy out the passage of Thucydides was made by his firm (3STU).

Facer, in English slang, a sudden blow upon the face; hence any sudden, staggering check. Captain Morstan had had a "nasty facer" at cards (SIGN).

Fair, free from obscurity or doubt; clear, distinct, and direct. Sam Merton called Holmes's ruse of the bust and violin recording "a fair cop" (MAZA), and Holmes as Altamont said that John Bull would be "fair ramping" within a week (LAST). See COP; RAMP.

Fairbairn, Alec, the lover of Mary Browner, killed by her husband (CARD).

*Fairbank, the house of Alexander Holder (BERY).

Fait accompli, that which has already been done (NOBL).

Falder, an ancient English family, dating apparently from Saxon times, who maintained their seat at Shoscombe Old Place. Several members appear to have borne the names **Hugo Falder** and **Odo Falder** under the Normans. **Sir William Falder** and **Sir Denis Falder** flourished in the eighteenth century, and **Sir James Falder** died toward the end of the nineteenth

century. His widow **Lady Beatrice Falder,** the sister of Sir Robert NORBERTON, held a life interest in Shoscombe Old Place, which reverted to her late husband's brother upon her own death. Because of the existence of the reversion, Sir Robert attempted to conceal her death until after the running of the Derby (SHOS).

Falmouth (*fal'muth*), a port in Cornwall, pop. 11,789. The *Gloria Scott* sailed from here (GLOR). See the map accompanying DEVONSHIRE.

"Family Herald," a family-interest magazine established in 1842. Holmes called it an "excellent periodical" and said that the condition of his breakfast might not be unconcerned with the arrival of the *Family Herald* the day before (THOR).

Fancy, The, in English sporting slang, the fraternity of prizefighters, or the art of boxing in general (SIGN).

Fanlight, a window in the form of an open fan situated over a door in a semicircular-shaped opening; any window over a door. The house at 221B Baker Street possessed a semicircular fanlight (BLUE, DYIN, ILLU), and there were fanlights over the doors at Camden House (EMPT) and Laburnum Villa (SIXN).

Fareham (*fair'um*), a town in Hampshire, pop. 8,246. Joseph Openshaw was murdered on his way from here to Portsdown Hill (FIVE).

Farintosh, Mrs., a client of Holmes before Watson's time, who mentioned him to Helen Stoner (SPEC).

Farnham (*farn'um*), a town in Surrey, pop. 6,124. Chiltern Grange was near here (SOLI).

Farquhar, the practitioner from whom Watson purchased his Paddington practice (STOC).

Farrier, a BLACKSMITH (HOUN).

Farringdon Street, a street in the City. Holmes's party passed down the street on its way to the City and Suburban Bank branch (REDH). See the map of the CITY.

Farthing, a common English bronze coin, equal to a fourth part of a penny (BERY).

Fates, in Greek and Roman mythology, the three sisters who spun the thread of human life (REIG).

Femur, in anatomy, the thigh-bone (SHOS).

Fen, a marsh or tract of wet, boggy land, often containing extensive pools. Holmes enjoyed duck shooting in the fens round Donnithorpe (GLOR).

Fenchurch Street, a street in the eastern part of the City, one of the busiest commercial thoroughfares in London. The firm of Westhouse & Marbank was here (IDEN). See also LLOYD'S. See the map of the CITY.

Fencing, the art of attack and defense with sword or rapier, no shield being used. Holmes participated in the sport at college (GLOR), and Watson described him as an "excellent" swordsman (FIVE, STUD). See also SINGLESTICK.

Fender, a metal guard placed before an open fire to keep live coals from falling on the floor (CROO).

Ferguson: see BECHER.

Ferguson, the secretary of J. Neil Gibson (THOR).

Ferguson, the retired sea-captain who owned the Three Gables before Mary Maberley purchased it (3GAB).

Ferguson, Robert, a London teabroker, senior partner of **Ferguson & Muirhead.** A former Rugby player, he was a widower with a fifteen-year-old son, **Jack Ferguson,** who had become deformed in a childhood fall. When Ferguson married a Peruvian lady and they had a baby boy, Jack's hatred of the infant compelled him to poison it. Mrs. Ferguson's sucking the poison from the wound led her husband to suspect her of vampirism, and Holmes was called upon to investigate (SUSS).

Feringhee (*feh-ring'gee*), a word used by the inhabitants of India and some other Asian countries to refer to a European (SIGN).

Fern. The Dartmoor countryside was heavy with BRACKEN (HOUN) and ferns (SILV). HART'S-TONGUE ferns also grew upon Dartmoor (HOUN), and there were ferns in Hampshire (THOR). The brambles and ferns which fringed the Reichenbach chasm were torn and bedraggled from the Holmes-Moriarty death-struggle (FINA).

*Fernworthy, a village on Dartmoor (HOUN).

Ferrers Documents, a case upon which Holmes was engaged when asked to investigate Lord Saltire's disappearance (PRIO).

Ferrier, Dr., the physician who attended Percy Phelps (NAVA).

Ferrier, John (d. 1860), an American frontiersman and farmer, who embraced the Mormon faith but was persecuted and finally killed by the DANITES for his refusal to adhere to strict doctrine. His adopted daughter **Lucy Ferrier** (1842–60) was forcibly married to Enoch Drebber as his eighth wife and died within a month. Their deaths caused Lucy's betrothed Jefferson HOPE to devote his life to vengeance (STUD).

Fess, in heraldry, a band covering the middle third of a shield (NOBL); see HERALDRY.

Fetish, in primitive cultures, any material object regarded as having mysterious powers residing in it, and from which supernatural aid may be expected (WIST).

Ffolliot, Sir George: see FOLLIOT.

Fifth Northumberland Fusiliers, an infantry regiment of the British Army, originally designated the *5th Regiment of Foot.* It was raised in 1674 and officially named the *Northumberland Fusiliers* in the Army reorganization of 1881. Watson joined the Fifth Northumberland Fusiliers in Afghanistan, but was removed from that regiment and attached to the Berkshires (STUD).

*Fighting Cock Inn, the country inn kept by Reuben Hays, where Lord Saltire was held after his abduction (PRIO).

"Final Problem, The" (FINA), a chronicle which appeared originally in the *Strand* and *McClure's* magazine for December 1893 and was published in the collection entitled *The Memoirs of Sherlock Holmes* the following year. It concerns Holmes's campaign against the criminal organization headed by Professor MORIARTY, his flight from England to avoid a determined effort to assassinate him, and his apparent death at Moriarty's hands on 4 May 1891.

Fingerprint, the impression of the finger-tip. Such markings are individual in character and permanent throughout life. They are used for purposes of identification according to a system devised by Francis Galton (1822–1911), and its gradual substitution for the previously used BERTILLON system of criminal identification has since been carried out. Scotland Yard adopted fingerprint identification measures in 1901.

James Oldacre attempted to implicate John Hector McFarlane as a murderer by duplicating his thumb-mark in blood upon a wall at Deep Dene House (NORW). Holmes opined that a corner had been torn from the instructions to Mrs. Warren to eliminate a thumb-print or other mark which might identify her mysterious lodger (REDC). The inspector assigned to the Three Gables burglary kept the sheet from Douglas Maberley's novel because there was "always the chance of finger-marks or something" (3GAB). There were no finger impressions upon Hilton Soames's galley slips (3STU). Two thumb-marks were found upon the cardboard box sent to Susan Cushing (CARD). The letter from Neville St. Clair to his wife was posted by a man with a dirty thumb (TWIS), and Holmes remarked that the thumb-print on the envelope of the letter to Mary Morstan was probably the postman's (SIGN).

Finn, a native of the Russian duchy of *Finland.* With the exception of Captain Calhoun and his two mates, the crew of the *Lone Star* were Finns and Germans (FIVE).

Fir. The Dartmoor countryside was dense with fir (HOUN), and there were fir-woods round Woking (NAVA). There was a grove of SCOTCH FIR near Grant Munro's home (YELL).

*Firbank Villas, the address, presumably in south London, of Dr. Horsom (LADY).

Firelock, a flintlock rifle (SIGN).

*First Bengalore Pioneers, the Indian Army regiment from which Colonel Sebastian Moran was forced to resign (EMPT). In some editions this appears as *1st Bangalore Pioneers,* and *Bangalore* is one of the principal cities of southern India.

First Folio, the first published collection of the plays of William Shakespeare, printed in London in 1623. Holmes humorously asked Mary Maberley if she perhaps possessed a First Folio Shakespeare (3GAB).

First reserve, in Rugby: see RESERVE.

First water, of diamonds: see WATER.

Fish. Holmes's index contained the biography of a staff-commander who had written a monograph upon deep sea fishes (SCAN). Holmes enjoyed fishing in the Broads near Donnithorpe (GLOR) and visited Shoscombe in the guise of a fisherman (SHOS). See also DACE; EEL; HERRING; JACK; PIKE; SHARK; TROUT.

Fisher, Penrose, one of the best medical men in London, whom Watson wished to bring to Holmes (DYIN). *Penrose Fisher* may be a compound surname.

Fishing: see FISH.

Fishmonger, a seller or dealer in fish (NOBL).

"Five Orange Pips, The" (FIVE), a chronicle which appeared originally in the *Strand* magazine for November 1891 and was published in the collection entitled *The Adventures of Sherlock Holmes* the following year. It concerns the mysterious persecution and systematic murder of members of the Openshaw family, and Holmes's failure to prevent the last of the tragedies. Watson dates the case as having taken place in September 1887, though some authorities prefer 1888 or 1889.

Holmes referred several years later to the case (WIST).

Flap-window, a kind of window with the hinges on the bottom and the latch at the top, opening outward (SIGN).

Flaubert (*flō-bair'*), **Gustave** (1821–1880), a French writer and novelist, regarded as the master of naturalism. Holmes quoted Flaubert's letter to George Sand: *"L'homme n'est rien, l'œuvre—tout"*—"The man is nothing, the work everything" (REDH) —which he mistakenly rendered as: *"L'homme c'est rien—l'œuvre c'es tout."*

Fleet Street, a busy commercial street in the City, the eastern continuation of the Strand, celebrated for its newspaper, printing, and publishing offices. Holmes and Watson took a stroll through London the night the Blessington case opened, watching the kaleidoscope of life as it ebbed and flowed through Fleet Street and the Strand (RESI). The offices of the Red-Headed League were off Fleet Street, which was choked with red-headed folk following the appearance of the League's advertisement (REDH). See Map I of LONDON.

Flier, that which is capable of great speed (MISS, SIGN).

Florence, a celebrated city of Italy, pop. 204,950. Holmes fled to Florence from Reichenbach (EMPT).

Florida, one of the southern states of the United States, pop. 528,542. Elias Openshaw became a successful planter here, where Holmes's *American Encyclopædia* stated the Ku Klux Klan had been particularly active (FIVE).

Florin, an English silver coin equal to two shillings, or one tenth of a

Looking down Fleet Street, home of newspaper offices, book publishers, and printers of every description, toward St. Paul's. Immediately at left may be seen the offices of the Daily Telegraph, *to the right the headquarters of the* Daily Chronicle.

pound, introduced in 1849 in a short-lived effort at the decimalization of British currency. Henry Wood's landlady mistook an Indian rupee for a "bad florin" (CROO).

Flowers, Lord. A note from Lord Flowers was in Trelawney Hope's dispatch-box (SECO).

Flushing, properly **Vlissingen,** an important seaport of the Netherlands, pop. (1900) 18,893. Von Bork's wife and household crossed from England to Flushing the day before he himself was arrested (LAST).

Flutter, in English slang, a wager (STOC).

Folding-door, a double door. A massive folding-door formed the entrance to Culverton Smith's house (DYIN).

*Folkestone Court, the West-country site of a considerable burglary in May 1889, one of a series in which Holmes suspected Stapleton to be the culprit (HOUN).

Folliot, Sir George, a neighbour of Aloysius Garcia (WIST). In some editions the name curiously appears as *Ffolliot.*

Foment, to bathe with warm water or medications. Theresa Wright fomented the bruise upon her mistress's brow (ABBE).

Foolscap, a writing-paper, measuring about 12″×15″ in size, so called from its former watermark, the outline of a fool's head and cap, for which other devices are now substituted (CARD, HOUN, REDC, REDH, SIXN, 3GAB, 3GAR). Holmes referred to Watson's chronicling his cases as "laying out his foolscap" (BRUC, NORW).

Football: see RUGBY.

Footman, a man-servant in livery employed chiefly to attend the carriage and wait at table. Holmes said that Charles Augustus Milverton had once paid £700 to a footman for a note two lines in length (CHAS). Milverton (CHAS), General de Merville (ILLU), the Duke of Holdernesse (PRIO), and Isadora Klein (3GAB) each employed a footman. There were two at Hurlstone (MUSG), and Baron Gruner had several (ILLU), as did Don Murillo (WIST). Two plain-clothes policemen posed as Aloysius Doran's footmen (NOBL). See SERVANT.

Footstep, or *footprint,* the mark or impression of a foot. Holmes maintained that there was no branch of detective science which was so important and so much neglected as the art of tracing footsteps (STUD), and he penned a monograph upon the subject (SIGN). He forcefully argued that so long as a criminal remains on two legs he must leave behind some indentation, some abrasion, some "trifling displacement" which can be detected by the scientific researcher (BLAC) or the expert observer (PRIO), though he confessed that he could not undertake to recognize Watson's footprint amid all the footprints of the world (HOUN).

Bloody footmarks were found in the empty Howe Street tenement (REDC) and upon a window-sill at Birlstone Manor (VALL). The intruders into Blessington's room left footprints upon the carpet (RESI), and Holmes examined the strange footsteps left in Bartholomew Sholto's chamber (SIGN). He could find no signs in the lawn round Deep Dene House, though he observed footmarks in the carpet inside (NORW), and he examined the prints within and without Lauriston Gardens (STUD).

Barrymore and Dr. Mortimer examined the footmarks in the Yew Alley, and Mortimer noticed the print of Stapleton's giant hound (HOUN). The police had the footmarks Holmes and Watson left outside Appledore Towers (CHAS) and examined Mary Maberley's geranium beds (3GAB). There were footmarks outside Ridling Thorpe Manor (DANC), and those round Dr. Becher's house told how Victor Hatherley had been saved (ENGR). The Sholtos found a single footmark outside Pondicherry Lodge the night of their father's death (SIGN).

Both Stanley Hopkins and Holmes searched for footmarks round Yoxley Old Place (GOLD). Holmes sought footprints round Tredannick Wartha and the vicarage, and followed the tracks made by Leon Sterndale (DEVI). He examined the marks where John Straker's body was found, and trailed Silver Blaze across the moor to Capleton despite Inspector Gregory's inability to find any tracks (SILV). He found some remarkable footmarks in the lawn at Lachine (CROO), and he and Watson found and followed a remarkable collection of tracks between the Priory School and the Fighting Cock Inn, particularly those left by a set of horse-shoes which made impressions like those of a cow (PRIO). He examined the tracks all round Boscombe Pool (BOSC), in the snow outside Fairbanks (BERY), and outside Wisteria Lodge (WIST). He observed the footprints upon the path Fitzroy McPherson had taken, and McPherson's dog's spoor upon the beach (LION), and examined those left by the Briarbrae burglar (NAVA).

No footmarks were found at Woodman's Lee (BLAC), near Joseph Openshaw's body (FIVE), in the ditch near the Cunningham house (REIG), upon the linoleum at the Foreign Office (NAVA), or in Hilton Soames's study (3STU). James Browner declared that he thought more of his wife's footmark in the mud than of Sarah Cushing's "whole body and soul" (CARD).

Forbes, the Scotland Yard detective assigned to the case of the naval treaty (NAVA).

Ford, a make of automobile manufactured by the American company founded in 1903 by *Henry Ford* (1863–1947). The British models manufactured in Manchester since 1911 are right-hand-drive versions of the American Models A and T. Watson chauffeured Holmes to Von Bork's in a Ford (LAST).

Fordham, the lawyer who drew up Elias Openshaw's will (FIVE).

Fordham, Dr., the physician who attended Trevor Senior and was with him at his death (GLOR).

Fordingbridge, a town in Hampshire, where Beddoes had his estate (GLOR).

Forecastle (*fōk's'l*), that section of a merchant ship where the seamen have their quarters, generally situated toward the bow. The Bar of Gold looked to Watson like the forecastle of an emigrant ship (TWIS). James Browner said that Alec Fairbairn once must have known more of the POOP than the forecastle (CARD).

Foreign Office, a department of the British Government headed by a Cabinet minister, the *Secretary of State for Foreign Affairs.*

The Duke of Balmoral was at one time Secretary for Foreign Affairs (NOBL), and the Rt. Hon. Trelawney Hope was "Secretary for European Affairs" (SECO). Percy Phelps had received a good position at the Foreign Office and served under his uncle Lord Holdhurst, who was Foreign Minister (NAVA). Holmes communicated the results of his visit to Khartoum to the Foreign Office (EMPT), and said that he was asked to take on his counter-espionage assignment by the Foreign Minister (LAST), who 1905–16 was *Sir Edward Grey* (1862–1933), a Liberal.

Sir Augustus Moran had once been the British minister to Persia (EMPT), and Douglas Maberley had been an attaché at Rome (3GAB).

Forest Row, a village of Sussex, near which Woodman's Lee was located (BLAC).

Fore-yard, the lower spar on the foremast of a square-rigged sailing vessel (GLOR).

Forgery, at common law, the fraudulent making or alteration of a writing or instrument, to the prejudice of another man's rights. Lestrade consulted Holmes in a forgery case (STUD), Holmes investigated the Conk-Singleton forgery case (SIXN), and he said he felt Moriarty's presence in a number of such cases (FINA, VALL). Count Sylvius denied forging a cheque on the Crédit Lyonnais (MAZA). Evans's crime had been forgery (GLOR), and John Clay was said to be a forger (REDH), as were Beddington (STOC), Archie Stamford (SOLI), Victor Lynch (SUSS), and Arthur H. Staunton (MISS).

*Formosa corruption: see BLACK FORMOSA CORRUPTION.

Forrester, Cecil: see CECIL FORRESTER.

Forrester, Inspector, an officer of the

Surrey police, who engaged Holmes to join in the search for William Kirwin's murderers (REIG).

Fortalice, a small fort. The original Birlstone Manor was built as a fortalice (VALL).

Fort Dodge, a town of south-western Kansas, located upon the north bank of the Arkansas River about four miles below Dodge City, pop. (1870) 427. Alexander Hamilton Garrideb was said to have invested in land west of Fort Dodge (3GAR).

*Fortescue Scholarship, the scholarship for which Gilchrist, McLaren, and Daulat Ras vied (3STU).

*Forton Old Hall, the house belonging to James Baker Williams (WIST).

*Foulmire, a Dartmoor farm-house (HOUN).

Four, The, the name applied to themselves by Jonathan SMALL, Mahomet Singh, Abdullah Khan, and Dost Akbar. Together they murdered the rajah's servant Achmet and stole the AGRA TREASURE, but were exposed and imprisoned. Small escaped and sought the treasure in the name of the Four. The words "the sign of the four" accompanied the map of Agra's fort and were found upon the bodies of Major Sholto and his son Bartholomew (SIGN).

While Mahomet Singh, Abdullah Khan, and Dost Akbar are represented as being SIKHS, the names *Mahomet, Abdullah Khan,* and *Dost Akbar* are all Moslem, only *Singh* being genuinely Sikh.

*Four, Council of: see SACRED COUNCIL OF FOUR.

Four-in-hand, a team of four horses matched for the purpose of drawing a single vehicle driven by one person (LAST). See the illustration accompanying DRAG.

Fournaye: see LUCAS, EDUARDO.

Four of gin hot, in English slang, a cold- or wet-weather drink of gin mixed in hot water and served with a lemon, sold for fourpence the quart. (STUD).

Four-wheeler, officially known as a *clarence cab,* the enclosed, four-wheeled cab, drawn by a single horse, commonly in use in English cities (BLAC, BLUE, GREE, IDEN, NAVA, NORW, PRIO, SIGN, SIXN, STOC, STUD). In slang it is called a *growler* (STUD).

A London four-wheeler.

One blast upon a London cab-whistle summons a four-wheeler, two a hansom. Watson whistled for a cab (DYIN).

Fowler, the suitor and future husband of Alice Rucastle (COPP).

Fox. Holmes said that Selden's body could not be left upon the moor for the foxes and the ravens (HOUN).

Foxhound. Pompey appeared to be something between a beagle and a foxhound (MISS). See also STAGHOUND.

Fox hunting, or *riding to hounds.* Birlstone Manor had seen three centuries of the meetings of fox hunters, and John Douglas always turned out for the local meets, though his friend Cecil James Barker did not ride (VALL). Hugo Baskerville's hounds were set loose after the yeoman's daughter (HOUN). Watson declared he had coursed "many creatures in many countries" (SIGN) and mistakenly believed that Dr. Mortimer belonged to a HUNT (HOUN). See also DRAGHOUND; DRAW A COVER; MEET; SWING TO THE LINE; VIEW-HOLLOA.

Franc, a silver coin and money of account of France, Belgium, and Switzerland. Its value is about 9½d. in English money and a little more than 19¢ in American money. Holmes said that a Greuze had sold in 1865 for 1,200,000 francs (VALL). This reference is missing from some editions. See also NAPOLEON.

France, a republic in the southwestern part of Europe, pop. 38,961,-945.

Holmes was engaged by the French government in the spring of 1891 upon a matter of supreme importance (FINA). The tracking and arrest of Huret, the Boulevard assassin, in 1894, won for him an autograph letter of thanks from the French president (GOLD), who in 1894 was *Marie François Sadi Carnot* (1837–1894) until his assassination upon 24 June of that year by an Italian anarchist; he was succeeded by *Jean Paul Pierre Casimir-Périer* (1847–1907), who resigned seven months later. NAPOLEON was Emperor of the French 1804–15 (SIXN). Baron Von Herling considered the possibility that England might leave France to her fate in the German invasion of 1914 (LAST).

Holmes spent the latter part of the GREAT HIATUS in the South of France (EMPT), where the Duchess of Holdernesse lived (PRIO), and through which Watson trailed Lady Frances Carfax (LADY). James Windibank's business often took him to France (IDEN), where the Franco-Midland

Hardware Company supposedly had 134 branches (STOC).

The French police made the important discoveries in the Lucas murder case (SECO). Watson spoke of the modern French psychologists (SIXN). Mlle. Carère and, presumably, her stepmother were French (HOUN), as were Le Brun (ILLU), Tavernier (MAZA), BERTILLON (NAVA), Madame Fournaye (SECO), François le Villard (SIGN), the sculptor Devine (SIXN), and the artist VERNET (GREE).

See also BORDEAUX; DIEPPE; GRENOBLE; LYONS; MARSEILLES; MONTPELLIER; NARBONNE; NÎMES; PARIS; RIVIERA.

The **French Embassy** in London is situated upon the southern border of Hyde Park; see the map of KENSINGTON. It was said that the embassy would pay an immense sum for the stolen naval treaty (NAVA).

See the map of EUROPE. See also FRENCH LANGUAGE; FRENCH MUSIC; FRENCH PAINTING.

France, Bank of: see BANK OF FRANCE.

*Franco-Midland Hardware Company, Limited, the bogus company created by the Beddingtons to deceive Hall Pycroft (STOC).

Franco-Prussian War, the conflict between France and Germany 1870–71. Holmes knew of an instance paralleling the St. Simon case which occurred in Munich the "year after" the war (NOBL).

Frankfort, properly **Frankfurt-am-Main,** a city of western Prussia, pop. (1900) 289,000. The Von Bischoff case occurred in "Frankfort" (STUD). There is also a *Frankfurt-am-Oder,* in eastern Prussia, pop. 62,000.

Frankland, an eccentric neighbour of

the Baskervilles. Laura LYONS was his daughter (HOUN).

Franz Joseph (1830–1916), the Emperor of Austria 1848–1916. Von Bork's Tokay was said to be from Franz Joseph's special cellar at the Schoenbrunn Palace (LAST).

Fraser, the maiden name of Lady Mary Brackenstall, and presumably the name of her brother, with whom Theresa Wright threatened Sir Eustace (ABBE).

Fraser, the tutor who helped Stapleton establish St. Oliver's school (HOUN).

Fraser, Annie, the accomplice of Holy PETERS, who played the rôle of his wife *Mrs. Shlessinger* (LADY).

Fratton, a suburban district of Portsmouth. Holmes as Altamont said he lived "down Fratton way" (LAST).

Fraud, an act or course of deception, deliberately practised with the view of gaining an unlawful or unfair advantage and resulting in legal injury to another. Jack Prendergast obtained huge sums of money from the leading London merchants by an ingenious system of fraud (GLOR).

Fred, a son of old MORRIS (VALL).

Freebody, Major, the commander of a fort in Hampshire, whom Joseph Openshaw visited upon the day of his death (FIVE).

Freemasonry, the name commonly given to a secret fraternal organization of ancient origin, calling themselves *Free and Accepted Masons.* Jabez Wilson was a Freemason (REDH), as were John Hector McFarlane (NORW), the detective Barker (RETI), and Enoch Drebber (STUD).

*Freemen, Ancient Order of: see SCOWRERS.

Free Trade, the term applied to na-

tional commerce when relieved from restriction by laws or tariffs. Free trade has not been adopted by any nation except Great Britain, where it dates from 1846. The mysterious letter to Sir Henry Baskerville was constructed from a *Times* leader in favour of Free Trade (HOUN). One of the London society papers protested humorously the principle of free trade in the marriage market (NOBL).

French Embassy, in London: see FRANCE.

French language. The stolen naval treaty was written in French (NAVA), the international language of diplomacy. Thaddeus Sholto remarked that the French had a "very neat way" of putting things (SIGN). François le Villard was translating some of Holmes's monographs into French (SIGN), though from his remark that a Frenchman could not have written the note from the King of Bohemia (SCAN), his French ancestry (GREE), and his frequent use of French words and phrases, it may be presumed that Holmes himself spoke the language well. Violet Hunter spoke a little French (COPP), in which Madame Fournaye screamed her jealous accusations (SECO). The clerk Gorot was suspected of stealing the naval treaty because of his French name (NAVA).

French music. Holmes said that German music was more to his taste than Italian or French (REDH).

French painting, modern school of, a philosphy of art exhibiting in active operation the various styles that have at different periods prevailed in that country, sometimes modified or adapted to the taste and feeling of the times. It is often called the *eclectic* school, characterized as it is by the selection, combination, and tolerance of all schools, even foreign ones. Thaddeus Sholto said he was partial to the modern French school (SIGN).

French window, a glass-paned window having two halves at the sides, and opening in the middle. There were French windows at the Abbey Grange (ABBE), Lachine (CROO), and Deep Dene House (NORW).

*Fresno Street, a street in the City, branching out of Upper Swandam Lane, where the offices of the Aberdeen Shipping Company were located (TWIS).

*Friesland. Watson writes that the shocking affair of the Dutch steamship *Friesland* nearly cost him and Holmes their lives (NORW).

Frinton-on-Sea, a town in Essex, pop. 644. Holmes said that Little Purlington was not far from Frinton (RETI).

'Frisco, a familiar name for the city of SAN FRANCISCO (NOBL).

Fritz: see STARK, COLONEL LYSANDER.

Frock-coat, a body-coat, usually double-breasted and with a full skirt, worn by men. Holmes wore a frock-coat (EMPT, HOUN, NORW), as did Hosmer Angel (IDEN), Henry Baker (BLUE), Sir James Damery (ILLU), Enoch Drebber (STUD), Alexander Holder (BERY), old Lawler (VALL), Mr. Merryweather (REDH), Dr. Mortimer (HOUN), Professor Presbury (CREE), Colonel Ross (SILV), Dr. Grimesby Roylott (SPEC), Lord Robert St. Simon (NOBL), Dr. Percy Trevelyan (RESI), and Jabez Wilson (REDH).

Frogged, ornamented or fastened with *frogs,* which are fastenings for the front of a garment, often made ornamental by the use of embroidery or braiding, and consisting generally of

Frock-coat

spindle-shaped buttons attached by a cord and corresponding with loops on the opposite side of the garment. Inspector Bradstreet wore a frogged jacket (TWIS), and Thaddeus Sholto a befrogged top-coat (SIGN).

Frontal, in craniology: see SUPRAORBITAL.

Fulham (*ful'm*) **Road,** a West End thoroughfare extending from just south of Hyde Park almost to the Thames in the borough of Fulham. It serves as the southern boundary of the borough of Kensington. The firm of Ross and Mangles was here (HOUN). See the map of KENSINGTON and the front endpaper map.

Fuller's earth, a variety of clay

which is useful in the cleansing of cloth, as it absorbs the grease and oil used in preparing wool. Lysander Stark claimed to be processing fuller's earth in his hydraulic press (ENGR).

*Fulworth, a seaside town of Sussex, situated upon **Fulworth Cove,** some miles from Holmes's retirement cottage (LION).

Furies, in Greek mythology, certain deities who pursued all criminals who had escaped from the law and drove them mad with remorse. Baron Von Herling claimed for the Germans credit for England's "window-breaking Fu-

ries" (LAST), an apparent allusion to the labour unrest which immediately preceded the German war.

Furlong, a measure of length equal to one-eighth of a mile (SILV).

Furze, a GORSE bush (GREE, SILV).

Fusiliers, infantry soldiers who originally carried a *fusil,* an improved type of flintlock rifle. The name is still borne by some of the British Army infantry regiments; e.g., the FIFTH NORTHUMBERLAND FUSILIERS (STUD). See also ROYAL MUNSTERS; THIRD BENGAL FUSILIERS.

G

*Gables, The, the name of Harold Stackhurst's coaching establishment (LION).

Gaboriau (*gah-bō-ryō'*), **Émile** (1832–1873), a French novelist, creator of the fictional detective LECOQ. Holmes had no respect at all for his work (STUD).

Gabriel, in the Bible, the archangel whose duty it was to announce to man the will and purpose of God. He appeared to Daniel as the interpreter of a vision (*Dan.* 8:7) and heralded the births of John the Baptist (*Luke* 1:19) and Jesus Christ (*Luke* 1:26). Compared to her husband, the strong-man Leonardo seemed to Eugenia Ronder "like the Angel Gabriel" (VEIL).

Gael (*gail*), a branch of the CELTS. Dr. Mortimer said that Sir Charles Baskerville's head was half Gaelic, half Ivernian in its characteristics (HOUN).

Game-cock, a cock bred and trained for cock-fighting (PRIO).

Gamekeeper, one who is employed upon an estate to look after game and to protect it from poachers. John Turner had a gamekeeper (BOSC), and there was a staff of them at Hurlstone (MUSG). Maria Gibson's body was found by one (THOR). White Mason looked more like a retired gamekeeper than a policeman (VALL).

Ganges (*gan'jeez*), the most important river of India, both in size and in religious significance to the Hindus. Jonathan Small lost his leg to a crocodile while swimming here (SIGN).

Garcia, a high dignitary of San Pedro, apparently wronged by Don Murillo. His son **Aloysius Garcia** sought to murder Murillo in England but was himself killed (WIST).

Garçia, Beryl: see STAPLETON.

Gardener: see SERVANT.

Garrideb, Alexander Hamilton, the fictitious benefactor of Garridebs, created, along with the equally non-existent **Howard Garrideb** of Aston, by Killer Evans in his guise as **John Garrideb,** as a part of his scheme to lure Nathan Garrideb from his rooms (3GAR).

Garrideb, Nathan (b. *c.*1840), the antiquarian who occupied rooms in which the counterfeiting outfit of Rodger PRESCOTT was hidden. He was lured away by the remarkable ruse perpetrated by Killer EVANS, but only after he had engaged Holmes. The shock of not realizing the fortune promised him cost him his reason (3GAR).

Garrotter, or **garroter,** one who commits street robbery by first rendering his victim insensible by strangling (EMPT).

Gas, illuminating, a gas made from bituminous coal or oil and used for illuminating purposes.

Gas was laid on at Baker Street (COPP), and when Culverton Smith turned up the gas in Holmes's bedroom he unwittingly signalled the police (DYIN). The streets of London are extensively gaslit (BLUE, REDC, REDH, RESI, SCAN, SIGN), as is Cambridge (MISS). Vermissa was gaslit (VALL). Gas was laid on at the homes of Alexander Holder (BERY), Harold Latimer (GREE), Holy Peters (LADY), and Dr. Percy Trevelyan (RESI), and Holmes deduced that it was not laid on in Henry Baker's house (BLUE). Grant Munro was in the habit of lighting his pipe at gas-jets (YELL). There was a gas flare on one of the Covent Garden Market stalls (BLUE), and Jacobson's Yard was gaslit (SIGN). Josiah Amberley murdered his wife and her lover by suffocating them with gas (RETI). Some work had been done on the gas in Watson's house (CROO), and Joseph Harrison hid the naval treaty in a floor-recess at Briarbrae made for plumbers to get at the gas-pipes (NAVA). See also COAL-TAR; GASFITTER; PLUMBER.

Gasfitter, one whose business is the fitting up of buildings with all the apparatus for the use of illuminating gas (IDEN); see also PLUMBER.

Gasogene, an apparatus for manufacturing aërated water on a small scale for domestic use, by the action of an acid upon an alkali carbonate, generally used to make "soda" for alcoholic drinks (MAZA, SCAN).

Gatekeeper: see LODGEKEEPER.

Gazetteer, a geographical dictionary. Holmes used his *Continental Gazetteer* to turn up the entry for Egria

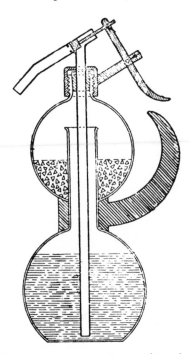

The gasogene generally consists of two glass globes, one above the other, the lower containing water and the upper the chemicals for producing the aërated liquid, the two globes being connected by a glass tube. When water is gently introduced into the upper chamber from the lower by inclining the vessel, chemical action takes place, and carbonic acid is produced. This descends and gradually saturates the water in the lower globe. When aëration has occurred, the liquid can be drawn off by opening a valve or stopcock at the top, which is connected with the lower chamber by a second tube. The water, now under pressure, forces its way through a nozzle into the receptacle provided.

(SCAN), and he looked up the ANDA-MAN ISLANDS in his new gazetteer (SIGN).

*Gelder & Co., a sculptor-works in Stepney, where the Napoleonic busts had been manufactured (SIXN).

Gemmi (*gehm'mee*) Pass, a much-frequented mountain pass in south-western Switzerland, elevation 7,641 feet. Holmes and Watson made their way over the pass, where an attempt seems to have been made upon their lives (FINA). See the map of SWIT-ZERLAND.

Gems: see JEWELS.

*General Iron: see WEST WILMER-TON GENERAL MINING COMPANY.

Geneva, a town in the extreme west of Switzerland, pop. (1900) 105,710. Holmes and Watson passed through Geneva on their journey to Reichen-bach (FINA). See the map of SWITZERLAND.

Genii, or *jinn,* in Islamic mythology, a class of spirits exercising supernatural influence over mankind for both good and evil. The men from the confec-tioner, Watson observed, having laid out the luxuries for Holmes's supper for Mr. and Mrs. Francis Hay Moulton, vanished away "like the genii of the Arabian Nights" (NOBL).

Genius loci, the presiding divinity of a place; hence, the pervading spirit of a place. Holmes said humorously that he was a believer in the *genius loci* (VALL). John Ferrier might have been "the very genius or demon" of the Great Alkali Plain (STUD), and Wat-son wrote that the tall, thin man he ob-served on Dartmoor might have been "the very spirit" of the moor (HOUN).

Gentile, among MORMONS, one who is not of the Mormon faith (STUD).

Gentry, in England, the class of peo-ple of means or leisure below the rank of the nobility, sometimes called the "upper middle class." The term is also applied in ironical civility to persons of an inferior sort (SIXN).

Geology. Watson rated Holmes's knowledge of geology as "practical, but limited" (STUD), an evaluation he later recalled with much humour (FIVE). Holmes was able to tell at a glance different soils from one another (FIVE, SIGN, STUD). Nathan Gar-rideb's museum was crowded with geo-logical and anatomical specimens (3GAR).

George II (1683–1760), King of Great Britain and Ireland 1727–60. He visited Birlstone Manor during his reign (VALL).

George III (1738–1820), King of Great Britain and Ireland 1760–1820. The American Revolution occurred during his reign, and increasing fits of insanity after 1810 brought about the REGENCY. Holmes declared himself to be one of those who believed that the folly of a monarch and the blundering of a minister (see PRIME MINISTER) in far-gone years would not prevent suc-ceeding generations from being some day citizens of the same world-wide country under a flag which would be a quartering of the Union Jack with the Stars and Stripes (NOBL).

Georgia, one of the south-eastern states of the United States, pop. 2,216,329. The Ku Klux Klan had branches here, and the *Lone Star* was registered out of SAVANNAH (FIVE). See also ATLANTA.

Georgian architecture, the style pre-vailing in England during the reigns of the four Georges 1714–1830, called in the United States the *Colonial* style. It was an adaptation to English requirements and tastes of the Italian neo-classical fashion of PALLADIO. The house at Thor Place was half Tudor and half Georgian (THOR), and Nathan Garrideb lived in an Early Georgian building (3GAR).

Geranium. There were geranium beds round the Three Gables (3GAB).

German characters, a form of BLACK-LETTER printing characteristic of the Germans. Holmes said part of the word *"Rache"* had been printed after the German fashion (STUD).

𝕾𝖕𝖊𝖈𝖎𝖒𝖊𝖓 𝖔𝖋 𝕲𝖊𝖗𝖒𝖆𝖓 𝕿𝖊𝖝𝖙.

German Embassy, in London: see GERMANY.

German language. Holmes remarked that though unmusical, German was the most expressive of all languages (LAST), and he quoted GOETHE in the original (SIGN). He declared that the Germans are "most uncourteous" to verbs when writing in English; and the King of Bohemia spoke with a thick German accent (SCAN). The word *"Rache,"* the German for *revenge,* was found scrawled in blood near the bodies of Enoch Drebber and Joseph Stangerson (STUD). Violet Hunter spoke a little German (COPP), there were German books at Dr. Becher's (ENGR), and Heidegger was the German master at the Priory School (PRIO).

German music. Holmes remarked that German music was more to his taste than Italian or French (REDH); see MENDELSSOHN; WAGNER.

German Ocean, The, the North Sea (DANC).

Germany, or *The German Empire,* a country of central Europe, pop. (1900) 56,367,178.

A note on the Russo-German grain taxes was in Trelawney Hope's dispatch-box (SECO). The *Daily Telegraph,* in its article about the Drebber murder, was of the opinion that the German name of the victim and the sinister inscription upon the wall pointed to its perpetration by political refugees and revolutionists (STUD). Von Bork master-minded a German spy organization in England during the years 1910–14 (LAST), and the approach of the German war caused Holmes to put his skills at the disposal of the British Government in the area of counter-espionage (LAST, PREF). Not even the German VEHMGERICHT was able to put a more formidable machinery in motion than the DANITES of Utah (STUD).

Holmes described BOHEMIA as a German-speaking country (SCAN), and Professor Presbury brought back from Prague a carved wooden box which his assistant associated with Germany (CREE).

With the exception of Captain Calhoun and his two mates, the crew of the *Lone Star* were Finns and Germans (FIVE). The blind Von Herder was a German (EMPT), as were Lysander Stark (ENGR), the attendant at the Northumberland Hotel (HOUN), Von Bork (LAST), Heidegger (PRIO), the manager of Gelder & Co. (SIXN), and old Klein the sugar king (3GAB). In some editions Jacob Shafter and his daughter Ettie are said to be German (VALL).

The **German Embassy** in London is in CARLTON HOUSE TERRACE, and Von Bork's name had been filed as one of the personal suite of the Ambassador (LAST), who 1912–14 was *Prince Karl Max Lichnowsky* (1860–1928), a very able and understanding diplomat

whose anti-war opinions finally resulted
in his exile to Switzerland in the after-
math of the World War.

See also PRUSSIA; SAXE-MENINGEN;
also   BADEN;   BERLIN;   DANTZIG;
FRANKFORT; MUNICH; STRASBURG. See
also CHANCELLOR; KAISER. See also GER-
MAN LANGUAGE; GERMAN MUSIC.

See the map of EUROPE.

Ghazi (*gah'zee*), a veteran soldier of
Islam, the title given to a warrior
champion or hero renowned for war-
ring against infidel forces. Watson
would have fallen into their hands at
the battle of Maiwand had he not been
saved by his orderly Murray (STUD).

Giant rat of Sumatra: see SUMATRA.

Gibson, J. Neil, called the *Gold
King,* an American Senator and gold
millionaire. His wife **Maria Gibson,** the
former *Maria Pinto,* by whom there
were two small children, committed suicide in such a way as to implicate their
governess Grace DUNBAR as a murderess
(THOR).

Gig, a light, one-horse carriage with
a single pair of wheels. Dr. Mortimer
drove a gig which Watson also refers to
as a DOG-CART (HOUN).

Gila (*hee'luh*) **monster,** the name
commonly given to a lizard found in
the southwestern part of the United
States. It is the only venomous lizard
known, and its bite is rapidly fatal to
small mammals and birds and is very
injurious, though seldom fatal, to man.
The remarkable case of a "venomous
lizard, or gila" was entered in Holmes's
index (SUSS).

Gilchrist, Sir Jabez, a gambler who
ruined himself on the turf. His son
Gilchrist, whose Christian name Watson neglects to mention, was the guilty
party in the Fortescue Scholarship
cheating case (3 STU).

Gill, a narrow valley or ravine, espe-

cially one with a rapid stream running
through it; e.g., LOWER GILL MOOR
(PRIO).

*Gilmerton, the coal and iron region
of the United States, located round the
Gilmerton Mountains, where the
Scowrers waged their war against big
business (VALL).

Gin. Enoch Drebber stopped at a
"gin palace" the night of his death
(STUD), and the Bar of Gold was located next a gin shop (TWIS). John
Rance longed for a FOUR OF GIN HOT as
he walked his beat in the rain
(STUD).

Gipsies, a wandering nation. Dr.
Grimesby Roylott had no friends save
bands of gipsies whom he would give
leave to encamp upon the Stoke Moran
estate and accept in turn the hospitality
of their tents, wandering away with
them sometimes for weeks on end; and
who were at first suspected of being
implicated in Julia Stoner's death because of her dying allusion to a "speckled band" (SPEC). MURPHY was a
gipsy (HOUN), and others lived upon
Dartmoor (HOUN, SILV). Lord Saltire's cricket-cap was found by them
(PRIO). John Clay said a gipsy had
pierced his ears for ear-rings when he
was a lad (REDH). In many editions
the word is Americanized *gypsy.*

Glad hand, in American slang, the
hand extended in greeting. Holmes as
Altamont declared that Von Bork
could give him "the glad hand" for acquiring the wanted naval codes
(LAST).

Gladstone bag, a large leather trav-
elling-bag or portmanteau (TWIS).

Glass, a BAROMETER (BOSC).

Glass, magnifying: see LENS.

Glasshouse Street, a street in Westminster, extending from Regent Street
to Piccadilly Circus. Holmes's attackers

escaped into Glasshouse Street (ILLU). See Map III of LONDON.

Glen, a narrow valley (STUD).

Globe, the oldest of existing London evening newspapers, founded in 1803. At one time the principal Whig organ, it was converted by purchase in 1866 into a Conservative paper. A rumour of Lord Saltire's abduction had reached the *Globe* (PRIO), and Holmes advertised for Henry Baker here (BLUE).

*Gloria Scott, the barque in which Trevor Senior was transported to Australia, destroyed in an explosion following a mutiny of the convicts on board (GLOR).

"Gloria Scott, The" (GLOR), a chronicle which appeared originally in the *Strand* magazine for April 1893 and *Harper's Weekly* of 15 April 1893 and was published in the collection entitled *The Memoirs of Sherlock Holmes* the following year. It is the story of the first case in which Sherlock Holmes was ever engaged, that of Trevor Senior and the voyage of the *Gloria Scott,* and it is told in the form of a monologue in which Holmes relates the details to Watson many years after the event. It is variously dated as having occurred in the summer of any of the years between 1872 and 1876.

Watson writes that the share Holmes himself took in determining the causes of this case was less pronounced than he as a biographer could wish (RESI). Holmes recalled the affair (MUSG) and said that he was unable to congratulate Watson upon his telling of it (SUSS).

Gloucester (*glos'ter*), a port and commercial city of western England, the county-town of Gloucestershire, pop. 47,955. Mr. Oldmore had once been mayor here (HOUN).

Gloucester Road, a West End street which extends south from Hyde Park into Kensington. Goldini's Restaurant was here (BRUC). See the map of KENSINGTON.

Gloucester Road Station, a station of the Underground, situated in the Gloucester Road. A number of suburban lines branch off nearby. Holmes walked along the line from here (BRUC). See the map of KENSINGTON and the map accompanying UNDERGROUND RAILWAY.

Goal, in Rugby, a kick over the goalposts for two additional points following the scoring of a TRY (MISS).

Godno: see GRODNO.

*Godolphin Street, a street in Westminster, south of the Abbey, where Eduardo Lucas resided (SECO).

Goethe (*gehR'teh*), **Johann Wolfgang von** (1749–1832), a German man of letters, perhaps the greatest figure in German literature. Holmes quoted from the first part of his *Faust* (1790): *"Wir sind gewohnt, dass die Menschen verhöhnen/Was sie nicht verstehen"*—"We are accustomed to seeing man despise what he does not understand"—with the remark that Goethe "is always pithy" (SIGN). Later he quoted the *Xenian* (1796): *"Schade dass die Natur nur einen Mensch aus dir schuf,/Denn zum würdigen Mann war und zum Schelmen der Stoff"*—"It's a pity that Nature made only *one* person out of you, for there was material for a good man and a rogue" (SIGN).

Gold. Aloysius Doran made his millions through a gold strike near the Rocky Mountains (NOBL), and John Douglas had made his fortune in the California gold-fields with Cecil Barker (VALL). J. Neil Gibson, the "Gold King," was the "greatest gold-mining magnate in the world" (THOR). Salt Lake City prospered from its position upon the overland route to California after the discovery of gold there (STUD).

Trevor Senior and Beddoes prospered in the gold-fields of Australia (GLOR), and old Turner also made his money in Australia, but not in the gold-fields as he claimed (BOSC). Ralph Smith made a fortune in South African gold (SOLI), but Watson did not propose to invest his money there (DANC). Baron Gruner's house had been built by a South African gold king (ILLU).

"Golden Pince-Nez, The Adventure of the" (GOLD), a chronicle which appeared originally in the *Strand* magazine for July 1904 and *Collier's Weekly* of 29 October 1904 and was published in the collection entitled *The Return of Sherlock Holmes* the following year. It concerns Holmes's investigation of the murder of Willoughby Smith, the secretary of Professor Coram, and Watson dates the case as having occurred in November 1894.

*Goldini's Restaurant, an establishment in the Gloucester Road where Holmes and Watson dined (BRUC).

Golf. Holmes had a knowledge of golf clubs (GREE), and John Hopley Neligan came to the Brambletye Hotel on the pretext of playing golf (BLAC).

Goodge Street, a shabby street in the south of St. Pancras. The incident between Henry Baker and the street roughs happened at the corner of Goodge Street and the Tottenham Court Road (BLUE). See Map III of LONDON.

Goodwins, The, properly **Goodwin Sands,** a dangerous line of shoals at the entrance to the Strait of Dover from the North Sea, about six miles

from the coast of Kent. By the time Holmes was certain that the barque *Lone Star* was the ship he was seeking in the Openshaw case, she had already left London and was past the Goodwins (FIVE). See also DOWNS, THE.

Goose. The Countess of Morcar's blue carbuncle was found in the crop of a Christmas goose (BLUE). When Peter Jones compared himself to an old dog upon the chase, Mr. Merryweather gloomily hoped that a wild goose might not be the end of it (REDH). See also PÂTÉ-DE-FOIE-GRAS PIE.

Goose, in English slang, a foolish person or simpleton (BLUE).

Goose-step, in the British Army, the marking of time by raising the feet alternately without making progress; "marching in place" (SIGN).

Gordon, Gen. Charles George (1833–1885), a British soldier, known as *Chinese Gordon,* who made his fame in the Chinese War of 1860 and was killed at KHARTOUM by the forces of the insurgent known as the Mahdi.

Gen. Charles George Gordon.

Watson possessed a picture of him (CARD).†

Gordon Square, a square in central London, not far from the British Museum. Mr. and Mrs. Francis Hay Moulton took refuge in lodgings here (NOBL). See Map I of LONDON.

Gorgiano, Giuseppe, called *Black Gorgiano,* a leader of the Red Circle, killed by Gennaro Lucca (REDC).

Gorot, Charles, one of Percy Phelps's fellow clerks in the Foreign Office (NAVA).

Gorse, a low shrub growing in barren, heathy districts. There was gorse upon Lower Gill Moor (PRIO), Charlington Heath (SOLI), and Oxshott Common (WIST). There was FURZE upon Wandsworth Common (GREE), and John Straker's overcoat was found upon a furze bush on Dartmoor (SILV).

Gothic arch, an arch which is pointed rather than rounded at its apex. The door to Hilton Soames's rooms was Gothic arched (3STU), and a Gothic archway opened into the Shoscombe crypt (SHOS). See also VICTORIAN ARCHITECTURE.

Gout, the name rather vaguely given to a constitutional disorder which manifests itself by inflammation of the joints. Lord Mount-James suffered from gout, and it was said that he "could chalk his billiard-cue with his knuckles" (MISS), an allusion to the so-called *chalk-stones* which in chronic cases frequently form round the affected joints and are upon occasion exposed by the splitting of the skin.

Governess. Mary Morstan was a governess (SIGN), as were Violet Hunter (COPP), Violet Smith (SOLI), Grace

† This reference is inserted in "The Resident Patient" in some editions.

Dunbar (THOR), and Miss Burnet (WIST). Miss Dobney was Lady Frances Carfax's old governess (LADY). Westaway's agency for governesses was in the West End (COPP).

Government, The: see CABINET.

Governor, in English slang, one's father (GLOR).

Governor-General, formerly the title given to the head of the government of INDIA, appointed by the Crown for a tenure of five years. Since 1858 he has been called the *Viceroy.* Jonathan Small suggested that he tell his story to the Governor-General, meaning the Indian authorities (SIGN).

Gower, a Scowrer (VALL).

Goyal, in west-country dialect, a deep gully. Hugo Baskerville died in a Dartmoor goyal (HOUN).

Grafenstein, Count Von und Zu, the elder brother of Von Bork's mother, whom Holmes saved from the Nihilist Klopman (LAST).

***Graham & McFarlane,** the law firm of which John Hector MCFARLANE was junior partner (NORW).

Gramophone, an instrument for the reproduction of sound, differing from the *graphophone* and the *phonograph* in that it makes use of a disc record instead of a cylinder. Holmes made use of a gramophone to recover the Mazarin diamond (MAZA).

Grand Duke, the ruler of a *grand duchy,* a sovereign territory holding precedence next below that of a kingdom. The King of Bohemia was Grand Duke of Cassel-Felstein (SCAN).

Grand Hotel, one of London's newer hotels, located in Charing Cross. Watson writes that it was between here and Charing Cross Station that he saw the news of the attack upon Holmes (ILLU). See the photograph of

CHARING CROSS and Map II of LONDON.

Grand National, an annual steeplechase run at Aintree, a suburb of Liverpool. Despite his "huge" stature, Sir Robert Norberton seems to have ridden in the Grand National and finished second (SHOS).

Grange, a house situated at a distance from other houses or villages; e.g., the ABBEY GRANGE (ABBE); CHILTERN GRANGE (SOLI). Holmes called High Gable a Jacobean grange (WIST).

Grass, to throw upon or bring down to the ground, as a bird shot on the wing or a fish caught from the water. Holmes said he twice had to "grass" Joseph Harrison (NAVA), that is, knock him down. In some editions this word is misspelled *grasp.*

Gravesend, a city in Kent, pop. 27,196. Situated upon the south bank of the Thames some twenty-five miles below London Bridge, it is a popular resort in addition to having some shipping. Mrs. Smith said that her husband often took his barge as far as Gravesend (SIGN), and the letter from Neville St. Clair to his wife was posted from here (TWIS).

Holmes wired here for news of the *Lone Star* (FIVE), for Gravesend is the recognized limit of the port of London, and the place at which most of the Thames river-pilots are taken on and put off sea-going ships, and it was therefore the point farthest down river at which information might be obtained from the customs authorities. The *Esmeralda,* as Holmes suspected, was waiting for Jonathan Small at Gravesend (SIGN), thereby avoiding scrutiny by the customs. See the back endpaper map.

Gray's Inn Road, a dingy and unattractive London thoroughfare extending northward from Holborn to King's Cross. Holmes and Watson took a cab up Gray's Inn Road to King's Cross Station (MISS). See Map I of LONDON.

*Great Alkali Plain, the arid and repulsive desert occupying the central portion of the North American continent (STUD).

Great Britain, geographically, the largest island of Europe; politically, the *United Kingdom of Great Britain and Ireland,* pop. 41,458,721.

See ENGLAND; IRELAND; SCOTLAND; WALES; see also BRITISH EMPIRE. See also CABINET; PARLIAMENT; PRIME MINISTER; VICTORIA.

Great George Street, a short commercial street in Westminster, lying between the government offices and West-

Gravesend.

minster Abbey. Adolph Meyer lived here (BRUC). See the map of WHITEHALL.

Greathed, Sir Edward Harris (1812–1881), a lieutenant-colonel in the British Army during the Indian Mutiny, who commanded the column which relieved Agra (SIGN).

Great Hiatus, the name applied by scholars to that portion of Holmes's life between his apparent death at Reichenbach in May 1891 and his return to active practice in April 1894. By his own word he travelled for two years in Tibet under the name Sigerson, crossed Persia to Mecca and thence to Khartoum, and spent the remainder of the time in the South of France (EMPT). In the absence of supporting evidence, an enormous number of alternate theories have been formed to account for Holmes's activities during this period, each more outrageous than the others.

*Great Mire: see GRIMPEN.

Great Mogul, an Indian diamond, said to have been seen at the imperial Indian court in 1665, and to have weighed 280 carats. Jonathan Small claimed that one of the diamonds in the Agra treasure was the Great Mogul (SIGN).

Great Mutiny: see MUTINY, THE.

Great Orme Street, properly **Great Ormond Street,** a street in central London, lying just to the north-east of the British Museum. The Warrens' house was here (REDC). See Map I of LONDON.

Great Peter Street, a street in the south of Westminster. Holmes sent a wire at the Great Peter Street post-office (SIGN). See Map IV of LONDON and the map of WHITEHALL.

Great Rebellion: see CIVIL WAR, ENGLISH.

Great Salt Lake, the great inland sea of Utah (STUD).

Greece, a kingdom of south-eastern Europe, pop. (1896) 2,433,806. Mr. Melas was of Greek extraction; and although Paul and Sophy Kratides were Greek, the **Greek legation** in the southwest of Westminster was unable to assist Mycroft Holmes in locating them (GREE).

The **Greek language** has undergone many changes in the 3,500 years of its existence, but while classical and modern Greek differ considerably as spoken tongues, the integrity of the written language has been preserved to a remarkable degree. Mr. Melas was an interpreter of Greek (GREE). Hilton Soames's subject was Greek, and the first of the Fortescue Scholarship examinations was a translation of Thucydides (3STU).

Greek e, the letter *e* written in the shape of the Greek letter epsilon (ϵ). Holmes's interest in HANDWRITING included the observation of Greek *e*'s (REIG, SIGN, VALL).

"Greek Interpreter, The" (GREE), a chronicle which appeared originally in the *Strand* magazine for September 1893 and *Harper's Weekly* of 16 September 1893 and was published in the collection entitled *The Memoirs of Sherlock Holmes* the following year. It concerns the strange experience of Mr. Melas and Holmes's subsequent investigation. The case has been dated variously between 1882 and 1890.

Watson recalled Holmes's explanation of Mycroft's profession at the time of this case (BRUC).

Greek language: see GREECE.

Greek legation: see GREECE.

Green, Admiral, the commander of the Sea of Azof fleet during the Crimean War, who apparently later was ennobled. His son the **Hon. Philip Green,** the beloved of the Lady Frances Carfax, made his money in South Africa and returned to England in time to assist Holmes in his search for the missing Lady Frances (LADY).

*Green Dragon, the inn near Shoscombe Old Place, where Holmes and Watson stayed (SHOS).

Green room, a room near the stage in a theatre, to which actors retire during the intervals of their parts in the play, so called from the traditional colour of the walls (TWIS).

Greenwich (*grin'ij*), a south-eastern metropolitan borough of London, pop. 95,770. It is most notable for the Royal Observatory, built in 1675, through which the prime meridian passes by international agreement. Victor Hatherley had been apprenticed to a Greenwich firm of hydraulic engineers (ENGR). Holmes said that the *Aurora* could be anywhere on the Thames between Millbank and Greenwich, and she was pursued past here by the police launch in the wild chase down the river which climaxed the Sholto case (SIGN). See the front endpaper map.

Gregory, Inspector, a police detective, presumably of Scotland Yard, who asked Holmes's co-operation in the Silver Blaze case (SILV).

Gregson, Tobias, an inspector at Soctland Yard. While Holmes said that he was normally out of his depth (SIGN), he nonetheless called Gregson "the smartest of the Scotland Yarders" (STUD), and Watson praised his courage (REDC). He was assigned to the Melas case (GREE) and, in partnership with his rival Lestrade, to the Drebber murder, in which he consulted Holmes (STUD). He assisted Leverton in his pursuit of Giuseppe Gorgiano (REDC) and helped Inspector Baynes

in the London search for John Scott Eccles (WIST).

Grenoble, a town in the South of France, pop. (1906) 58,641. Oscar Meunier lived here (EMPT).

Gresham Buildings, also called *Gresham House* or *Gresham Chambers,* a large office block in the City. The firm of Graham & McFarlane was here (NORW). See the map of the CITY.

Greuze (*grooz*), **Jean Baptiste** (1725–1805), a French artist, known for his painting of everyday life and morality scenes, and for the delicacy of his portraiture. Professor Moriarty owned a Greuze, and Holmes remarked that in 1865 a Greuze entitled "La Jeune Fille à l'Agneau" ("Young Girl with a Lamb") fetched £40,000 at the PORTALIS sale (VALL). This figure is revised to £4,000 in some editions.

A painting depicting a young girl holding a lamb, entitled "Innocence" and believed to be by Greuze, was purchased at the sale for 100,200 francs

"Innocence" by Jean Baptiste Greuze, a copy of which was sold at the Pourtalès sale for £4,000.

—or £4,000—by an anonymous buyer. When it came on to the open market again in 1918, the picture was shown to be a copy, by a hand other than his, of the Greuze "Innocence" now in the possession of the Wallace Collection in London.

Greyminster: see HOLDERNESSE, DUKE OF.

Grice Paterson, apparently the name of a family, expedition, or organization which experienced some singular adventures in the island of UFFA, an affair Holmes looked into in 1887 (FIVE).

Griffin, a fabled monster, common in heraldry, usually represented with the body, feet, and claws of a lion and the head and wings of an eagle. Heraldic griffins topped the Shoscombe Park gates, and many of the coffin-plates in the Shoscombe crypt were adorned with the griffin and coronet of the Falders (SHOS).

Griggs, Jimmy, a clown travelling with the Ronder circus (VEIL).

Grimm, the name of two German philologists, brothers, who were associated in the joint authorship of several works, the best known in English being a collection of fairy tales published 1812–15. Their full names were *Jakob Grimm* (1785–1863) and *Wilhelm Grimm* (1786–1859), of whom the latter was the chief collaborator in the children's stories. Holmes said that he and Watson seemed to have been switched on to a Grimm's fairy tale (SUSS).

*Grimpen, a hamlet on Dartmoor, the nearest settlement to Baskerville Hall. It was located in **Grimpen parish,** of which Dr. Mortimer was medical officer, as were the **Grimpen Mire,** where Stapleton hid his hound and apparently met his end, and the **Grimpen**

Road, which lay between Merripit House and Baskerville Hall (HOUN).

Grizzly bear: see BEAR.

Grodno, a city of eastern Russia, capital of an administrative region of the same name, pop. 41,736. Holmes said that an incident in Grodno, Little Russia, in 1866 was analogous to the Baskerville case (HOUN). Grodno is not, however, in LITTLE RUSSIA, and in some editions the name appears as *Godno*.

Groin, in architecture, the curve or edge formed by the intersection of two arched ceilings crossing one another at right angles. The Shoscombe crypt possessed an "arched and groined roof" (SHOS). See also VICTORIAN ARCHITECTURE.

Groining.

Groom: see SERVANT.

*Gross and Hankey's, presumably a jewellers' establishment in Regent Street, to which Godfrey Norton hurried, no doubt to buy a ring for his wedding with Irene Adler (SCAN).

*Grosvenor Buildings, presumably an office block at Aston, where Howard Garrideb was said to have offices (3GAR).

Grosvenor (*gro'veh-nor*) **Hotel,** a London hotel, located at Victoria Station and owned by the London, Chatham, and Dover Railway. Peter Steiler the elder had been a waiter here (FINA). See Map IV of LONDON and the photograph of VICTORIA STATION.

Grosvenor Mansions, a block of flats in Victoria Street, Westminster. Lord Robert St. Simon dated his letter to Holmes from here (NOBL). See Map IV of LONDON.

*Grosvenor mixture, the tobacco smoked by Grant Munro (YELL).

Grosvenor Square, a square in Westminster. Isadora Klein lived here (3GAB). Holmes remarked that the case of "the Grosvenor Square furniture van" was obvious from the first (NOBL). See Map III of LONDON.

Grouse. Holmes served a brace of grouse to Watson and Athelney Jones (SIGN).

Growler, in English slang, a FOUR-WHEELER (STUD).

Gruner, Baron Adelbert (d. 1860), an Austrian murderer, speculator, philanderer, and art collector. It was to prevent his marriage to Violet de Merville that Holmes acted in behalf of Sir James Damery's illustrious client, believing as he did that the Baron had murdered his first wife. He was mutilated by vitriol thrown by Kitty Winter (ILLU).

Guaiacum (*gwī'uh-kuhm*) **test,** the test universally used for the presence of blood in certain liquids, utilizing the resin of the South American *guaiacum* tree. A single drop of tincture of guaiacum is added in a test-tube to an inch or so of the liquid under examination. A solution of ether, dissolved in hydrogen peroxide, is then poured gently into the test-tube, and a deep blue coloration is produced along the line of contact if hæmoglobin is present. Holmes

considered the guaiacum test clumsy and uncertain, and believed he had discovered a superior test (STUD).

Guards, the household troops of the British Army, specially employed to guard the person of the sovereign. Two of Holmes's hired accomplices before Briony Lodge were dressed as guardsmen (SCAN). Mr. Tangey had served with the COLDSTREAM GUARDS (NAVA).

Guides, in the Bengal Army, a native regiment, known as the *Corps of Guides,* organized in 1846 for purposes of scouting and reconnoitring (SIGN).

Guildford, the county-town of Surrey, pop. 15,938. Inspector Baynes expected to bring Don Murillo before the Guildford Assizes (WIST). See the back enpaper map.

*Guild of St. George, a Roman Catholic charity, formed at Aldershot for the purpose of supplying the poor with cast-off clothing, with which Mrs. Barclay had interested herself (CROO).

Guinea, a former English gold coin, worth twenty-one shillings. It was last coined in 1813 and withdrawn from circulation in 1817, being superseded by the SOVEREIGN, but it is still customary to estimate professional fees in guineas (ENGR, HOUN, MISS, RESI, SCAN, SIGN, SILV).

Guion Steamship Company, a British transatlantic steamship line, founded in 1866 by *Stephen Barker Guion* (1820–1885), an Anglo-American businessman. Two letters from the Guion Line, referring to the sailing of their boats from Liverpool to New York, were found upon the body of Enoch Drebber (STUD).

Gull. A gull or curlew flew above the moor (HOUN).

Guttered, channeled by the flow of melted tallow or wax, as a candle (BLUE, DEVIL, HOUN). The fact that the candle had not guttered showed that the window through which Hilton Cubitt was shot had been open for only a short time (DANC); otherwise a gutter would have been created atop the candle to correspond with the slanting of the flame by the draught; in some editions this reference is misspelled *gutted*.

Guy, to jeer at or make fun of. Old Sherman complained that he was "guyed at" by the children (SIGN).

Gypsies: see GIPSIES.

H

H Division, one of the twenty-two administrative divisions of the Metropolitan Police, very generally analogous to the metropolitan borough of Stepney. Police-Constable Cook was assigned to H Division (FIVE), yet was on duty nearby when John Openshaw was killed near Waterloo Bridge and the Embankment, which are in *E Division*. See the map accompanying SCOTLAND YARD.

Hack, in Rugby, the bruise produced by a kick on the shin. Godfrey Staunton was once laid up with a hack (MISS). This appears misprinted in some editions as *back*.

Hæmoglobin, a substance found in the red corpuscles of the blood. Holmes believed himself to have discovered a reagent which was precipitated by hæmoglobin and by nothing else (STUD).

Hafiz (d. *c.*1389), a celebrated Persian writer, one of the most famous lyric poets of all time. Holmes quoted a Persian saying, which he attributed to Hafiz: "There is danger for him who taketh the tiger cub, and danger also for whoso snatches a delusion from a woman" (IDEN).

Hague, The, the capital of the Netherlands, pop. (1902) 218,029. There was a parallel case to that of Mary Sutherland here the preceding year (IDEN).

Haines-Johnson, the name used by the sham house-agent hired by Isadora Klein to purchase the Three Gables (3GAB).

Hair-trigger, an old-fashioned kind of fire-arm possessing a secondary trigger which is very delicately adjusted. Very slight pressure upon the hair-trigger releases the main trigger and fires the weapon. This sort of gun is practical only for target- and trick-shooting. Holmes used his hair-trigger to adorn the wall of the Baker Street sitting-room with a patriotic *V.R.* done in bullet-pocks (MUSG).

Hales, William, a Gilmerton mine-owner who was killed by the Scowrers (VALL).

*Hales Lodge, the Hampstead residence of Cecil James Barker (VALL).

Half, in Rugby, a HALF-BACK (MISS).

Half-and-half, a mixture of malt liquors, especially a mixture of porter and ale. Holmes received a glass of half-and-half for helping the Serpentine Mews ostlers in their work (SCAN).

Half-back, in Rugby, one of two players positioned between the forwards and the three-quarters (MISS); see BACK.

Half-crown, an English silver coin of half the value of the crown (see DOLLAR), that is, 2*s*.6*d*. Lysander Stark and his gang were counterfeiting half-crowns (ENGR).

Half Moon Street, a short street in Westminster, lying between Curzon Street and Piccadilly. Watson pretended to live here in his alias as Dr. Hill Barton (ILLU). See Map III of LONDON.

Half-pay, the reduced pay of an Army or Navy officer who is not on active service. Watson was said to be on half-pay (SIGN). Julia Stoner became engaged to a half-pay major of Marines (SPEC).

Halfpenny (*hay′p′nee*), an English bronze coin of the value of half a penny (TWIS).

Half-sovereign, an English gold coin, equivalent to 10 shillings, one half of a pound sterling, or about $2.433 in United States money (BLAC, HOUN, SCAN, SIGN, STUD). See SOVEREIGN.

Halifax, the capital of Nova Scotia, pop. 40,832. Colonel Spence Munro received an appointment here (COPP).

*Hallamshire, the English county of which the Duke of Holdernesse was Lord-Lieutenant, and where the Priory School was located (PRIO). The ancient district of Hallamshire encompassed the PEAK COUNTRY; see the map of ENGLAND.

Hallé, Sir Charles (1819–1895), a British pianist and concert director, born *Karl Hallé* in Westphalia, Germany. In 1861 he began Hallé's Popular Concerts at St. James's Hall in London. In 1888 he was knighted in recognition of his many contributions to the popularizing of fine music in the British Isles, and in the same year he married his star performer, Wilhelmine NOR-MAN-NÉRUDA. Holmes took time out from the Drebber investigation to attend a Hallé concert (STUD).

*Halliday's Private Hotel, the hotel in Little George Street where Joseph Stangerson was murdered (STUD).

Halter, a hangman's noose. Holmes said Jonathan Small did not wish "to put his head in a halter" (SIGN).

Ham, in anatomy, the area behind the knee. The body of Richard Brunton was squatted upon his hams when found (MUSG). John Straker intended to lame Silver Blaze by nicking the horse's ham with a knife (SILV).

Hammerford Will case, an affair handled by Sir James Damery (ILLU).

Hammersmith, a western metropolitan borough of London, pop. 112,239. It is mainly residential, but there are many manufactures as well. John Mitton was visiting a friend here the night his employer was murdered (SECO). Holmes's commonplace book held some reference to "Vigor, the Hammersmith wonder" (SUSS). See the front endpaper map.

Hammersmith Bridge, a bridge spanning the Thames between the London borough of Hammersmith and the county of Surrey. It is the western-most of the bridges giving egress from London, and so when Watson remarks that CHISWICK is "at the other side of Hammersmith Bridge" (SIXN) he means beyond the bridge to the west, and outside the county of London, for Chiswick is upon the Middlesex side of the river, as is the West End, and crossing the bridge was unnecessary. See front endpaper map.

Hampshire, properly **Southampton** after 1888, a southern county of England, principally agricultural in character, pop. 797,634. Jephro Rucastle

Hampshire and the Isle of Wight.

(COPP), Beddoes (GLOR), and J. Neil Gibson (THOR) lived here. The Roylott estate at one time extended over the borders of Surrey into Berkshire and Hampshire (SPEC).

See also ALDERSHOT; FAREHAM; FORDINGBRIDGE; NETLEY; PORTS-MOUTH; SOUTHAMPTON; SOUTHSEA; WINCHESTER.

Hampstead, a north-western metropolitan borough of London, pop. 81,942. It is mainly residential. Charles Augustus Milverton lived here (CHAS), as did Hall Pycroft (STOC) and Cecil James Barker (VALL).

Included within the boundaries of the borough is **Hampstead Heath,** an open space of diverse topography which, with its several adjacent commons, to a great extent preserves its natural characteristics unaltered. Holmes and Watson fled across the Heath after the murder of Milverton (CHAS), and Mr. Warren's captors released him here (REDC). See the front endpaper map.

Handwriting. Holmes seems to have been a keen student of handwriting regarded as an expression of the writer's character, and he claimed that the deduction of a man's age and health from his writing was a science which had been brought to consid-

Hampstead Heath, with its broken heights and wild, furze-covered expanses, is the most popular of London's public areas among the lower classes.

erable accuracy by experts (REIG). He studied Annie Harrison's handwriting (NAVA) and easily recognized Porlock's hand (VALL). He analyzed the writing in Jonas Oldacre's will (NORW) and studied that upon the letter to Mary Morstan in comparison with the pearl-box's address (SIGN). His examination of a fragment of the note sent by the Cunninghams to William Kirwin was important in solving Kirwin's murder (REIG).

James Windibank feared that Mary Sutherland would recognize even the smallest sample of his handwriting (IDEN). The Beddingtons were anxious to get a sample of Hall Pycroft's writing (STOC). The style of writing enabled Holmes to fix the date of the Baskerville manuscript (HOUN). Holmes declared that a TYPEWRITER has quite as much individuality as a man's handwriting (IDEN).

Hanover Square, a square in Westminster. The church of St. George's is here (NOBL). See Map III of LONDON.

Hansom, a two-wheeled covered carriage drawn by a single horse, so called from *J. A. Hansom* (1803–1882), its patentee (CHAS, CREE,

The hansom holds two persons besides the driver, who is mounted upon an elevated seat behind the body of the carriage, and has a high dashboard and folding half-doors, pictured open.

CROO, DANC, EMPT, ENGR, FINA, GREE, HOUN, IDEN, ILLU, LADY, NAVA, REDH, SCAN, STUD, TWIS, VEIL).

Many Londoners carry a distinctive-sounding cab-whistle, one blast of which summons a four-wheeler, two a hansom. Watson whistled for a cab (DYIN) and heard Holmes whistling for a hansom (FINA).

Hard down: see HELM.

Harden, John Vincent, the well-known tobacco millionaire whose peculiar persecution Holmes investigated in 1895 (SOLI).

Harding, a proprietor of **Harding Brothers,** the shop at which Horace Harker purchased his bust of Napoleon (SIXN).

Hardy, the foreman of the Sutherland plumbing firm (IDEN).

Hardy, Sir Charles. A report from Sir Charles was in Trelawney Hope's dispatch-box (SECO).

Hardy, Sir John, a member of the Bagatelle Card Club, with whom Ronald Adair played upon the night of his death (EMPT).

Hare, John (1844–1921), a well-known English actor, knighted in 1907, who specialized in character rôles. Holmes's appearance as an amiable and simple-minded Nonconformist clergyman, said Watson, was such as only John Hare could have equalled (SCAN).

Hargreave, Wilson, an official of the New York police, with whom Holmes often exchanged information (DANC).

Hargrove, the alias of Ted Baldwin while in England (VALL).

Harker, Horace, apparently a reporter for the Central Press Syndicate, whose house was burgled for a Napoleonic bust. Pietro Venucci was murdered upon his doorstep in Kensington, and at Holmes's word he inserted an unwittingly false statement in his published account of the incident which was intended to ease the murderer's mind (SIXN).

Harley Street, a street in the West End, inhabited largely by consulting physicians and specialists. Holmes and Watson walked through Harley Street on their way to the Alpha Inn (BLUE) and on their way home from Brook Street (RESI). Dr. Moore Agar lived here (DEVI). When John Mason said he believed that his employer had gone mad, Holmes reminded him that he was in Baker Street, not Harley Street (SHOS). Watson writes that White Mason regarded Holmes as a village practitioner regards a Harley Street specialist (VALL). See also CAVENDISH SQUARE. See Map III of LONDON.

Harmonium, a kind of small musical organ (BLAC, ENGR).

Harness cask, a cask or tub fastened to the deck of a ship in which is kept the salt-meat for the day's consumption (GLOR).

Harold, Mrs., a woman whose death seems to have been due to Count Sylvius (MAZA).

Harraway, the Scowrers' secretary (VALL).

Harringby, Lord, a neighbour of Aloysius Garcia (WIST).

Harris, the alias Holmes used in his interview with Harry Pinner (STOC).

Harrison, a Northumberland ironmaster. His daughter **Annie Harrison** was engaged to Percy Phelps, and his son **Joseph Harrison** stole the naval treaty (NAVA).

Harris tweed, a hand-made cloth manufactured upon the Hebrides island of Lewis-with-Harris, and enjoying a considerable reputation for excellence (IDEN).

Harrow-on-the-Hill, a city in Middlesex, celebrated for its famous public school, pop. 10,220. A considerable extension has taken place to the north of the city as an outer residential suburb of London and embraces such semi-rural districts as HARROW WEALD. Steve Dixie warned Holmes that it was not safe "out Harrow way" (3GAB), and Honoria Westphail lived here (SPEC). See the back endpaper map.

Harrow Weald, an urban district of Middlesex, lying to the north of Harrow. Mary Maberley lived here (3GAB). See the back endpaper map.

Hart's-tongue, a variety of fern possessing long, fleshy fronds (HOUN).

Harvey, a Shoscombe stable-boy (SHOS).

*Harvey's, a house in Sussex (SUSS).

Harwich (*har′ij*), a seaport town in Essex, pop. 10,070. The harbour is one of the best in England, and Harwich is one of the principal ports for passenger traffic to Holland and Germany, as well as the base for the British destroyer and submarine fleets on the eve of the German war. Von Bork's house overlooked Harwich and its harbour (LAST).

Hatherley, Victor (b. 1864), the hyraulic engineer called upon by the mysterious Colonel Lysander Stark to examine a hydraulic "stamping" machine which was, in reality, apparently a press used in a process of counterfeiting. Here two murderous assaults were made upon him, one of which caused his thumb to be severed from his hand. Escaping his assailants, he found his way to Watson's consulting-room and thence to Holmes. His father died in 1887 (ENGR).

*Hatherley Farm, the farm at which the McCarthys lived (BOSC).

Havana, a cigar made from genuine Cuban tobacco (RESI).

*Haven, The, the Bellamys' home at Fulworth (LION).

*Haven, The, the Lewisham house belonging to Josiah Amberley (RETI).

Hayling, Jeremiah (1862–?1888), a hydraulic engineer, presumably murdered by Lysander Stark (ENGR).

Haymarket Theatre, a theatre in Westminster, where drama and English comedy are regularly presented. Josiah Amberley claimed to have attended a performance here the evening of his wife's disappearance (RETI). See Map III of LONDON.

The Haymarket Theatre.

Hays, Reuben, the landlord of the Fighting Cock Inn. He assisted in the abduction of Lord Saltire and was the murderer of Heidegger, the German master. His wife **Mrs. Hays** was a kindly woman, it was said, but entirely under the control of her brutal husband (PRIO).

Hayter, Colonel, a British military officer who had come under Watson's professional care in Afghanistan and some years later invited Holmes and the doctor for a rest at his house near Reigate (REIG).

Hayward, one of the WORTHINGDON BANK GANG (RESI).

Hazel, a small tree belonging to the beech family (WIST).

Head: see MAKE HEAD.

Head Llama: see LAMA.

Heart: see ANEURISM; AORTIC VALVE; CAROTID ARTERY; MITRAL VALVE; see also ETHER; NITRITE OF AMYL; RHEUMATIC FEVER.

Heath, The: see HAMPSTEAD HEATH.

Heather tweed, a fabric woven of *heather-wool,* which is mottled in various shades and produces a tweed of mixed or speckled colour (ENGR).

Heath Newton, owner of The Negro (SILV).

*"Heavy Game of the Western Himalayas," a book written by Colonel Sebastian Moran, published in 1881 (EMPT).

Hebrew Rabbi: see Rabbi

Hebron, John, a Negro lawyer of Atlanta, who died of yellow fever. His widow later became Mrs. Grant MUNRO (YELL).

Hectic, in medicine, referring to heightened colour associated with fever and emaciation. Watson observed a hectic flush upon either cheek when he arrived at Holmes's sickbed (DYIN).

Heeled, in American slang, armed with a pistol (DANC, VALL).

Heidegger, the German master at the Priory School, murdered when he attempted to follow Lord Saltire's abductors (PRIO).

Heidelberg man, a species of prehistoric man represented by a single jawbone found near Heidelberg in southern Germany, characterized by a thoroughly ape-like mandible in which are set altogether human teeth. Watson writes that Nathan Garrideb possessed a skull labelled "Heidelberg" (3GAR), an impossibility in that the Heidelberg specimen was not discovered until 1907, while Watson clearly dates the Garrideb case as having occurred in 1902.

Heinrich, the cousin of Von Bork who was Imperial Envoy in 1889 (LAST).

Helm, the wheel or tiller of a ship or boat. Watson writes that it was only by putting the police launch's helm "hard down" that they were able to avoid a collision (SIGN), meaning that the helm was turned fully to one side so as to turn the launch's bow away from the direction from which the wind was blowing.

*Helmdale, one of the towns of Vermissa Valley (VALL).

Helston, a town in Cornwall, pop. 3,088. The Tregennis brothers were conveyed here in their madness (DEVI). See the map accompanying DEVONSHIRE.

Henderson: see MURILLO.

*Henrietta Street, a street in south London (STUD).

*Herald: see DAILY HERALD.

Heraldry, the science of the forms, terms, and laws which pertain to the use of armorial bearings, or coats-of-arms. A *coat-of-arms* consists of the figure of a shield, marked and coloured in a variety of ways with figures known as *charges,* so as to be distinctive of an individual, a family, or a community. The shield represents the original used in war, upon which arms were anciently borne.

The art of *blazoning,* or describing, arms makes use of an extensive technical vocabulary. Thus the arms of Lord Robert St. Simon were blazoned: *Azure, three caltrops in chief over a fess sable* (NOBL). This means, with

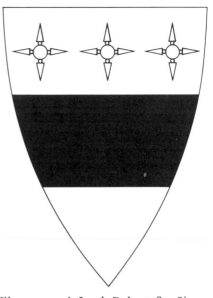

The arms of Lord Robert St. Simon: Azure, three caltrops in chief over a fess sable.

reference to the rendering above, that the shield itself is blue (*azure*), and that three caltrops are represented in the upper third (*three caltrops in chief*) over a black band drawn across the middle third (*a fess sable*).

Reginald Musgrave compared the Musgrave Ritual to his family's "blazonings and charges," as something of no practical use (MUSG). Boars' heads were upon the arms of the Baskervilles, and there were coats-of-arms upon the inside and outside walls of Baskerville Hall (HOUN). Heraldic griffins topped the Shoscombe Park gates, and many of the coffin-plates in the Shoscombe crypt were adorned with the griffin and coronet of the Falders (SHOS). Heraldic emblems surmounted the stone side-pillars of the main gateway to Charlington Hall (SOLI), and the pillars before Birlstone Manor House bore "a shapeless something which had once been the rampant lion of Capus of Birlstone" (VALL).

Sir Eustace Brackenstall's stationery bore his coat-of-arms (ABBE), as did that of the Duke of Holdernesse (PRIO), and Lord Robert St. Simon's crest appeared upon his (NOBL). There was a coat-of-arms upon the envelope showed Holmes by Charles Augustus Milverton (CHAS). Baron Gruner's arms were stamped in gold upon the cover of the book which Holmes called Gruner's "lust diary" (ILLU), and Watson recognized the arms of Holmes's illustrious client (ILLU).

For heraldic terms see AZURE; BLAZONING; CALTROP; CHARGE; CHIEF; CORONET; CREST; FESS; GRIFFIN; RAMPANT; SABLE.

Hercules, the most celebrated among the Greek heroes or semi-divine persons, whose strength and prowess have become legendary. Dr. Percy Trevelyan described one of the Worthingdon Bank Gang as possessing the limbs and chest of a Hercules (RESI), and Watson described the King of Bohemia in those same words (SCAN).

Hereford (*her'eh-furd*), the county-town of Herefordshire, pop. 21,382. James McCarthy was imprisoned here (BOSC).

*Hereford Arms, the hotel at Ross where Holmes and Watson stayed (BOSC).

Herefordshire, a western inland county of England, pop. 114,380. Cattle-raising is the primary industry. Boscombe Valley was here, not far from ROSS (BOSC). See the map of ENGLAND.

Herring, the name given to a number of economically important salt-water fishes (SIGN); see DRAGHOUND.

Higgins, the treasurer of the Scowrers' Merton County Lodge (VALL).

*High Barrow, the Devonshire parish for which Dr. Mortimer was medical officer (HOUN).

*High Gable, the house belonging to Don Murillo in his alias as Mr. Henderson (WIST).

High Holborn, the name given to the western extremity of HOLBORN. The firm of Marx & Co. was located here (WIST). See Maps I and II of LONDON.

*High Lodge, the Alton home of Mrs. Oldmore (HOUN).

High Street, a street in Kensington. The shop of Harding Brothers was here (SIXN). See the map of KENSINGTON.

High Street, Kensington.

High Street, one of the principal streets of Winchester. The Black Swan Inn is located here (COPP).

High Street Station, an Underground railway station located in the Kensington High Street (SIXN). See the map of KENSINGTON.

High tea: see TEA.

*High Tor, a Dartmoor farm-house (HOUN).

Hill, Inspector, a Scotland Yard inspector who made a specialty of Saffron Hill and the Italian quarter (SIXN).

Himalaya Mountains, the great mountain chain which separates Tibet from India. Colonel Sebastian Moran was the author of *Heavy Game of the Western Himalayas* (EMPT). Trevor Bennett's manual of zoology stated that the langur was to be found upon the Himalayan slopes (CREE).

Hindu, a word used in various senses: (1) one of the people speaking the Hindi dialect of the North-west Provinces; (2) one of the Aryan inhabitants of northern India; (3) one who professes the Hindu religion.

Hinduism as a religious and social system is the most prevalent among the Indians, and is also called *Brahmanism* because it was developed and expounded by the priestly class known as the Brahmans. Its chief characteristic is the notorious caste system which originally represented distinctions of race, but intermarriages, giving rise to a mixed people, and the variety of employments in modern times, have greatly modified caste so that there are now thousands of castes built upon innumerable minor distinctions.

With the exception of Jonathan Small, Holmes believed that the FOUR were Hindus or Mohammedans, though in reality they were Sikhs; Abdullah Khan did not believe that a Hindu would keep an oath; and Thaddeus Sholto's servant was a Hindu (SIGN). The spelling *Hindoo* appears in many editions.

Hippocratic smile: see RISUS SARDONICUS.

"His Last Bow" (LAST), subtitled *"The War Service of Sherlock Holmes"* and *"An Epilogue of Sherlock Holmes,"* a chronicle which appeared originally in the *Strand* magazine for September 1917 and *Collier's Weekly* of 22 September 1917 and was published in the collection entitled *His Last Bow* later that year. The story is written in the third person and concerns the taking of the German spymaster Von Bork upon the evening of 2 August 1914 after two years on Holmes's part of counter-espionage work in America, Ireland, and England.

"His Last Bow," the fourth collection of Sherlock Holmes cases, published in 1917 and containing, in order of their first English magazine appearances, the following: "The Adventure of Wisteria Lodge" (WIST), "The Adventure of the Bruce-Partington Plans" (BRUC), "The Adventure of the Devil's Foot" (DEVI), "The Adventure of the Red Circle" (REDC), "The Disappearance of Lady Frances Carfax" (LADY), "The Adventure of the Dying Detective" (DYIN), and "His Last Bow" (LAST). It contains too a short preface (PREF) written by Dr. Watson and concerning Holmes's life in retirement. Most editions include "The Cardboard Box" (CARD).

Histon, a village to the north of Cambridge, where Holmes sought Godfrey Staunton (MISS). See the map of CAMBRIDGE.

Hobbs, Fairdale, a lodger of the Warrens, whom Holmes once helped (REDC). *Fairdale Hobbs* may be a compound surname.

*Hobson's Patch, one of the towns of Vermissa Valley (VALL).

Hoby, Sir Edward, a Norfolk squire and neighbour of the Trevors, who was attacked by a gang of poachers he had helped bring to justice (GLOR). In some editions the name appears as *Sir Edward Holly.*

Hoffmann Barcarolle, the barcarolle from the opera *Les Contes d'Hoffmann* (*Tales of Hoffmann*) by the French composer of light opera Jacques Offenbach (1819–1880), which was first performed in 1881. The song, an empassioned duet to love and the night, opens the second act. Holmes played a recording of a solo violin performance of "the Hoffmann Barcarolle" to dupe Count Sylvius and Sam Merton (MAZA). In some editions the name is misspelled *Hoffman.*

Hogshead, a large cask. The *May Day* turned back to Liverpool because a loose hogshead dislocated a hull plate (CARD).

Holborn, an eastern continuation of Oxford Street, extending from the West End into the City. It contains many office buildings as well as some of the oldest houses in London, and there are many historical and literary associations. The Alpha Inn was located at the corner of one of the streets running from near the British Museum down into Holborn, which Holmes and Watson crossed on their way to Covent Garden Market (BLUE), and the firm of Marx & Co. was in HIGH HOLBORN (WIST). See Map I of LONDON.

Holborn, The, an extensive and elaborate restaurant in High Holborn. Watson and Stamford lunched here following their meeting at the Criterion Bar (STUD). Young Perkins was killed outside the "Holborn Bar" (3GAB), which is conceivably an allusion to this establishment. See Map II of LONDON.

Holder, Alexander, the senior partner of **Holder & Stevenson,** the second largest private banking concern in the City. He accepted the Beryl Coronet as security for a loan and blamed his wastrel son **Arthur Holder** for its attempted theft. Arthur's silence was intended to protect his cousin **Mary Holder,** who fled with Sir George BURNWELL when Holmes recovered the missing gems (BERY).

Holder, John, an Army sergeant who saved Jonathan Small from drowning (SIGN).

Holdernesse, Duke of, a famous English peer, the sixth of his line, one of the richest and most influential subjects of the Crown. His wife the **Duchess of Holdernesse,** the former *Edith Appledore,* was estranged and living in France. Their heir and only child *Arthur,* called **Lord Saltire,** was abducted from the Priory School by the Duke's secretary and illegitimate son James WILDER in an effort to acquire the ducal property (PRIO). Many years later Holmes wrote of "the case which my friend Watson has described as that of the Abbey School, in which the Duke of Greyminster was so deeply involved" (BLAN), most certainly an allusion to Holdernesse. Save in this case, Watson said, Holmes seldom claimed a large reward for his services (BLAC).

The *Holderness* is a peninsula in the east of Yorkshire.

***Holdernesse Hall,** the seat of the Duke of Holdernesse, near Mackleton in Hallamshire (PRIO).

Holdhurst, Lord, the Foreign Minister of Britain at the time the naval treaty was stolen (NAVA).

Holland: see NETHERLANDS, THE.

Holland Grove, a short residential street just east of the Brixton Road in south London. Constable Murcher had the Holland Grove beat (STUD). See Map IV of LONDON.

Hollis, a member of Von Bork's spy ring, who was arrested, probably upon Holmes's information (LAST).

*Holloway and Steele, the firm of house-agents in the Edgware Road through which Nathan Garrideb leased his rooms (3GAR).

Holly. Holmes concealed himself behind a holly-bush by the Shoscombe Park gates (SHOS).

Holly, Sir Edward: see HOBY.

Holmes, Mycroft, the brother of Sherlock Holmes. Seven years Sherlock's senior, he ostensibly audited the books in some of the Government departments (GREE), but in actuality, in Sherlock's words, Mycroft occasionally *was* the British Government: "The same great powers which I have turned to the detection of crime he has used for this particular business. The conclusions of every department are passed to him, and he is the central exchange, the clearing-house, which makes out the balance. All other men are specialists, but his specialism is omniscience. We will suppose that a Minister needs information as to a point which involves the Navy, India, Canada and the bi-metallic question; he could get his separate advices from various departments upon each, but only Mycroft can focus them all, and say off-hand how each factor would affect the other. They began by using him as a short-cut, a convenience; now he has made himself an essential. In that great brain of his everything is pigeon-holed, and can be handed out in an instant. Again and again his word has decided the national policy. He lives in it. He thinks of nothing else save when, as an intellectual exercise, he unbends if I call upon him and ask him to advise me on one of my little problems" (BRUC).

Holmes insisted that his brother had even better powers of observation and deduction than he had himself, but that Mycroft had no ambition and no

Mycroft Holmes.

energy and would rather be considered wrong than take the trouble to prove himself right (GREE). "Mycroft has his rails and he runs on them," Sherlock remarked. "His Pall Mall lodgings, the Diogenes Club, Whitehall— that is his cycle" (BRUC). He visited Baker Street only twice (BRUC, GREE), though he drove the brougham in which Watson rode to Victoria Station (FINA), and he was Holmes's one confidant during the Great Hiatus, providing his brother with money and maintaining the Baker Street rooms (EMPT).

Watson was struck particularly by Mycroft's "sharpness of expression" and "far-away, introspective look," which he had in common with Sherlock (GREE). "Heavily built and massive, there was a suggestion of uncouth physical inertia in the figure, but above this unwieldy frame there was perched a head so masterful in its brow, so alert in its steel-gray, deep-set eyes, so firm in its lips, and so subtle in its play of expression, that after the first glance one forgot the gross body and remembered only the dominant mind" (BRUC).

Holmes, Sherlock, the world's first and only CONSULTING DETECTIVE.

The descendant of country squires and the grandson of a sister of the French artist VERNET (GREE), Holmes called himself "middle-aged" about 1889 (BOSC) and was described as being sixty years of age in 1914 (LAST), thus suggesting a birth-date *c.*1854. It was during the two years he spent at college, he said, that upon the advice of a classmate's father he realized that "a profession might be made out of what had up to that time been the merest hobby" (GLOR), and so "during my last years at the university there was a good deal of talk there about myself and my methods" (MUSG).

Since he retired late in 1903 or in early 1904 (CREE), and it is known that he was in active practice for twenty-three years (VEIL), it can be

The "official" portrait of Sherlock Holmes by Sidney Paget.

determined, having subtracted the three years of the GREAT HIATUS, that he began his professional career as a detective in or about the year 1878. His partnership with Dr. Watson began no later than 1882 (FIVE); see WATSON, JOHN H.

While his practice began slowly (MUSG, STUD), by 1889 he could claim to have investigated some five hundred cases "of capital importance" (HOUN) and a thousand in all by 1891 (FINA). From late in the 1880s (VALL) to April 1891 (FINA) he devoted himself to exposing and breaking up the criminal organization of Professor MORIARTY, though this does not precisely correspond with Holmes's remark that the investigation took three months, or Moriarty's statement that their paths first crossed upon 4 January, presumably of 1891 (FINA).

He returned to active practice in 1894 (EMPT) and during 1894–1901 handled hundreds of cases (SOLI). It was apparently during this period that Watson at last weaned him from the "drug mania which had threatened once to check his remarkable career" (MISS); see COCAINE. His services to England earned him a private audience with Queen Victoria in 1895 (BRUC), and he refused the offer of a knighthood in June 1902 (3GAR).

He retired in 1903 or 1904 (CREE) to the solitude of the Sussex coast (LAST, LION, PREF, SECO), where apparently he turned his energies to a review of the records of his cases and the destruction of those which might compromise his more exalted clients (THOR). "The approach of the German war caused him, however, to lay his remarkable combination of intellectual and practical ability at the disposal of the government" (PREF)

with the result of communicating much false intelligence to the Germans and the arrest of the Prussian spymaster Von Bork (LAST).

APPEARANCE AND CONDITION

The most immediately striking feature of Holmes's appearance seems to have been his tallness (BOSC, HOUN, LAST, MAZA, STUD, TWIS, VALL) and his thinness (BERY, BOSC, DANC, DYIN, EMPT, HOUN, ILLU, LAST, MAZA, REDC, REDH, SCAN, SIGN, 3GAR, TWIS, VALL, YELL). "I am six feet high," he said (3STU), but Watson put him "rather over six feet, and so excessively lean that he seemed to be considerably taller" (STUD). His face was a narrow one (BERY, GOLD), his forehead large (HOUN), his hair black (DANC), his brows dark and heavy (BRUC, LADY, VALL), his nose thin and hawk-like (REDH, STUD), his lips thin (EMPT) and firm (3GAR). His eyes were gray (HOUN, MAZA, RETI, THOR, 3GAR) and particularly sharp and piercing (BOSC, GREE, RETI, STUD, TWIS), taking on a "far-away introspective look" when he exerted his whole powers (GREE—THOR). He possessed a quick (CARD), high (CARD, STOC), "somewhat strident" (STOC) voice.

Seldom a man who took exercise for its own sake (YELL), still he was "always in training" (SOLI), a good runner (HOUN), and possessed of a strength with which, Watson said, one would hardly credit him (STUD). "I am exceptionally strong in the fingers," he declared (BERY), and had a "grasp of iron" (LAST) which he put to use in straightening the poker bent by Dr. Grimesby Roylott (SPEC). Watson asserted that few men were capable of

"Few men were capable of greater muscular effort, and he was undoubtedly one of the finest boxers of his weight that I have ever seen; but he looked upon aimless bodily exertion as a waste of energy, and he seldom bestirred himself save where there was some professional object to be served."

greater muscular effort (YELL). He had too "an abnormally acute set of senses" (BLAN) and an "extraordinary delicacy of touch" (STUD).

A man whose "frugal" (PRIO) habits were "simple to the verge of austerity" (YELL), he took little interest in his own comfort (HOUN). He complained that "idleness exhausts me completely" (SIGN) and from time to time would spend whole days in bed (3GAR). He was a late riser as a rule (SPEC), "save upon those not infrequent occasions when he was up all night" (HOUN—COPP), but he was up early on a case (BLAC, HOUN, PRIO, RETI, 3STU), during which he

was vigorous and untiring (PRIO, YELL), going for days, or even a week, without rest (MISS, REIG, TWIS). His diet, spare at the best of times (YELL), was abandoned altogether when he was working (FIVE, MAZA, MISS, VALL), for he had conceived that starving himself increased the supply of blood to his mind: "I am a brain, Watson. The rest of me is a mere appendix" (MAZA). Watson lamented that the state of his health "was not a matter in which he took the faintest interest" (DEVI). His wiry, iron constitution (DEVI, ILLU) suffered a breakdown from nervous prostration in the spring of 1887 (REIG), and he was ordered to take a complete rest in March 1897 if he wished to avert another in the face of "constant hard work of a most exacting kind, aggravated, perhaps, by occasional indiscretions of his own" (DEVI). In retirement he was somewhat crippled by occasional attacks of rheumatism (PREF) but took up swimming nonetheless (LION).

He seemed to know little or nothing of amateur sport (MISS) or of the Turf (SHOS), and claimed to have few athletic tastes himself (GLOR); see BARITSU; BOXING; FENCING; FISH; GOLF; SINGLESTICK.

Dress. It was said that he had a "catlike love of personal cleanliness" (HOUN) and affected a certain quiet primness of dress (MUSG). While he normally dressed in conventional tweeds or FROCK-COAT, and occasionally donned an ULSTER, in the privacy of his rooms he preferred a DRESSING-GOWN. In the country he assumed a "long gray travelling-cloak" (BOSC) and the familiar close-fitting, ear-flapped, cloth "travelling cap"

(BOSC, HOUN, SILV); see the illustration on page xiii. See also *Methods: Disguises*, below.

See also BAKER STREET; MONTAGUE STREET; also CORRESPONDENCE; FRENCH LANGUAGE; HONOURS LIST; HUNTING-CROP; LEGION OF HONOUR; PERSIAN SLIPPER; PIPE; TELEGRAPH; TELEPHONE; TOBACCO; TURKISH BATH; WALKING-STICK.

CHARACTER

The most pronounced of Sherlock Holmes's traits was the "dual nature" of his personality (BOSC, BRUC, DEVI, MUSG, PRIO, REDH, REIG, RETI). "Nothing could exceed his energy when the working fit was upon him; but now and again a reaction would seize him, and for days on end he would lie upon the sofa in the sitting-room, hardly uttering a word or moving a muscle from morning to night" (STUD). "I never remember feeling tired by work," he confessed, "though idleness exhausts me completely" (SIGN). "Just let me alone, and I'll soon be right" (STUD). During these moods he turned to drugs for stimulation, alternating "between cocaine and ambition, the drowsiness of the drug and the fierce energy of his own keen nature" (SCAN). Then an even blacker depression took him in reaction to the narcotic (SIGN), from which he could be rescued only by a case.

His own powers became irksome to him when they were not in use (VALL). "My mind rebels at stagnation," he insisted (SIGN), and he chafed and brooded over "the insufferable fatigues of idleness" (WIST—BRUC, MISS). "My mind is like a racing engine, tearing itself to pieces because it is not connected up with the work for which it was built" (WIST—DEVI). "Was there ever such a dreary, dismal, unprofitable world?" he demanded (SIGN). "My life is spent in one long effort to escape from the commonplaces of existence" (REDH) which he said surrounded him (SIGN). The days of the great cases were past, he lamented (COPP, SIGN, STUD), and he upbraided the London criminal as "certainly a very dull fellow" (BRUC). "Life is commonplace; the papers are sterile; audacity and romance seem to have passed forever from the criminal world" (WIST).

When presented with an intellectual problem, however, his mood and behaviour changed, and he was seized with an "animal lust for the chase" (BOSC). "The man is nothing, the work everything," he insisted (REDH). "Work is the best antidote to sorrow" (EMPT); "a change of work is the best rest" (SIGN). Working and living as he did solely for the love of his art (BLAC, BRUC, COPP, NAVA, NORW, PRIO, REDC, RETI, SIGN, SPEC, THOR, VALL), it was during his cases that he demonstrated his masterful manner (BRUC, DANC, DYIN, HOUN, SIGN, TWIS) and his love of all that was complex and out of the common (PRIO, SIXN).

Like all human beings, Holmes was complex and often contradictory in both character and attitudes. While he frequently impressed those about him as unemotional (GREE, ILLU, SCAN, SIGN, SOLI, VALL) and introspective (BLUE), as scientific approaching to cold-bloodedness (STUD) or as an inhuman automation (SIGN) possessed of a "red-Indian composure" (CROO,

NAVA) who "loved above all things precision and concentration of thought" (SOLI), Watson made constant reference to his restlessness (REDH, SIGN, THOR) and impatience (BRUC, EMPT, STUD, 3STU, VALL, YELL), his nervousness (ILLU, LADY, SIGN) and excitability (DANC, NORW, REIG, STOC, THOR), his eager nature (BERY, ENGR, HOUN, PRIO, SCAN), his habit of biting his nails when restless or preoccupied (BRUC, STOC), his concern with his own pride (FIVE) and self-respect (CHAS, HOUN), and a certain petty selfishness (NAVA).

"I cannot agree with those who rank modesty among the virtues," he said. "To the logician all things should be seen exactly as they are, and to underestimate one's self is as much a departure from truth as to exaggerate one's own powers" (GREE). Yet he could claim bitterly that "what you do in this world is a matter of no consequence. The question is, what can you make people believe that you have done?" (STUD). He was egotistical (BOSC, COPP, ILLU, LAST, NOBL, RETI, SIGN, STUD) and didactic (SIGN) and was said to be "as sensitive to flattery on the score of his art as any girl could be of her beauty" (STUD—REDC). One of his "most obvious weaknesses" was his impatience with "less alert intelligences than his own" (BLUE), and he could be openly contemptuous of his mental inferiors (BOSC, CARD, SIGN, STUD) and those of whom he disapproved (MAZA, THOR). His behaviour was most often particularly annoying to Watson (COPP, HOUN, MUSG, SIGN, VALL).

Though he left the credit in his cases to the police (CARD, EMPT, NAVA, NORW, RETI, SIGN, THOR,

VALL), he chafed at lack of recognition (STUD) and always retained the option of acting independently (BOSC, DANC, SILV, SIXN, VALL, WIST). "Local aid is always either worthless or else biased," he said (BOSC). "I go into a case to help the ends of justice and the work of the police. If I have ever separated myself from the official force, it is because they have first separated themselves from me. I have no wish ever to score at their expense" (VALL). He was fond of twitting the official detectives by deliberately pointing out clues but neglecting to explain their significance (BOSC, CARD, SIGN, SILV), though he would not tamper with evidence (DEVI), and his eyes were "sparkling with mischief" as he dangled the evidence in the Birlstone tragedy before a thoroughly puzzled Watson (VALL). He could upbraid himself, too, however, for his own slowness in solving his problems (ABBE, CREE, LION, THOR, TWIS).

He could go to extremes in his love of attention (STUD) and of admiration and applause (SIXN). "The same singularly proud and reserved nature which turned away with distain from popular notoriety was capable of being moved to its depths by spontaneous wonder and praise from a friend" (SIXN). Just as, he said, he had found it wise to impress clients with a sense of power (BLAN), he confessed to a love of surprising those around him (HOUN). "Some touch of the artist wells up within me, and calls insistently for a well staged performance," he admitted. "The blunt accusation, the brutal tap upon the shoulder—what can one make of such a *denouement*? But the quick inference, the subtle trap, the clever forecast of coming events, the triumphant vindication of bold theories —are these not the pride and the justification of our life's work?" (VALL). "I never can resist a touch of the dramatic" (NAVA—MAZA, NORW, SILV, SIXN).

His conceited, dramatic nature, combined with his unofficial status, created in him a tendency to private judgement (ABBE, BLUE, BOSC, DEVI, 3GAB) as well as to private vengeance (FIVE, 3GAR). "Once or twice in my career I feel I have done more real harm by my discovery of the criminal than ever he had done by his crime" (ABBE). He condoned private revenge in others (CHAS) and confessed that his being indirectly responsible for Dr. Grimesby Roylott's death was not likely to weigh heavily upon his own conscience (SPEC). He did not hesitate to use illegal methods in a "morally justifiable" cause (CHAS) and often expressed the idea that he would have made a highly efficient criminal had he turned his energies against the law (BRUC, CHAS, RETI, SIGN), a proposition with which even Scotland Yard heartily agreed (GREE); see BURGLARY; COMPOUND; see also BLACKMAIL. "It's a wicked world," he shrugged (SPEC).

"Like all great artists," Watson said of him, "he was easily impressed by his surroundings" (THOR), and he humorously professed a belief in the GENIUS LOCI (VALL), though apparently only between problems, for during a case he "could rise superior to petty influences" (SIGN) and had, "in a very remarkable degree, the power of detaching his mind at will" (HOUN—DEVI, REDH). He took little care for his own safety once his mind was absorbed in an investigation (THOR)—though he did assert that "it is stupidity rather than courage to refuse to recog-

nize danger when it is close upon you" (FINA)—and he greatly resented anything which distracted his attention (SOLI, STUD, 3STU, VALL). "Intense mental concentration has a curious way of blotting out what has passed," he said of another of his mental peculiarities, and as a consequence he would never permit cases to overlap (HOUN).

Professionally Holmes "stood alone in Europe, both in his gifts and in his experience" (VALL). For this reason he refused the commonplace (SPEC). "I am the last court of appeal," he boasted (FIVE, MUSG). Described as unworldly and capricious in his choice of cases (BLAC), he declared that "the status of my client is a matter of less moment to me than the interest of his case" (NOBL). "To the man who loves art for its own sake, it is frequently in its least important and lowliest manifestations that the keenest pleasure is to be derived" (COPP). "Education never ends, Watson. It is a series of lessons with the greatest for the last" (REDC). He refused to act if not in his client's complete confidence (ILLU, SECO, THOR), and accordingly the records of many cases, Watson wrote years after his retirement, "involve the secrets of private families to an extent which would mean consternation in many exalted quarters if it were thought possible that they might find their way into print" (THOR). "The discretion and high sense of professional honour which have always distinguished my friend are still at work in the choice of these memoirs, and no confidence will be abused" (VEIL).

"Without having a tinge of cruelty in his singular composition, he was undoubtedly callous from long overstimulation," Watson wrote (VALL).

Holmes described himself as "never a very sociable fellow" (GLOR). Except for Watson, he said, he had no friends and did not encourage visitors (FIVE), he exhibited a disinclination to form new friendships (GREE), seldom went anywhere save upon professional business (STOC), and lived in an air of loneliness and isolation (MAZA); see BOHEMIAN.

He affected a "carelessness of manner" (DYIN) and a "half-humorous, half-cynical vein which was his habitual attitude to those about him" (DEVI), but harshness was foreign to his nature, said Watson (SOLI), who made mention of Holmes's kindness (REDC) and the "somewhat sinister cheerfulness" that characterized his lighter and more imp-like moments (THOR). He was remarkable for his "easy courtesy" (IDEN), "a past-master" in the art of putting the humble at ease (MISS), and possessed of "an almost hypnotic power of soothing when he wished" (REDC). "I suppose every one has some little immortal spark concealed about him," he remarked (SIGN). See also *Character: Emotional Qualities,* below.

He demonstrated himself to be a keen judge of human character (BERY, BOSC, CARD,† COPP, ILLU, THOR). He displayed a propensity to categorize persons (BLUE, CHAS, EMPT, IDEN, REDH), but not to underestimate his foes (EMPT, FINA, HOUN, ILLU, REDH), and showed a tendency in fact to inflate their abilities (MISS), claiming to appreciate the challenge of a good foeman (PRIO). While it was said that

† The "mind-reading" incident in "The Cardboard Box" is inserted in "The Resident Patient" in many editions.

he was more prone to understatement than exaggeration (MAZA), he nonetheless tended to over-rate the importance of some of his cases (BRUC, SECO). He was angry when crossed or thwarted, but his innate good humour usually reasserted itself quickly (CHAS, STUD, VALL) in "that half comic and wholly philosophical view which was natural to him when his affairs were going awry" (MISS). "There is nothing more stimulating than a case were everything goes against you," he rationalized (HOUN).

"There was a curious secretive streak in the man which led to many dramatic effects, but left even his closest friend guessing as to what his exact plans might be. He pushed to an extreme the axiom that the only safe plotter was he who plotted alone"

"The gap of loneliness and isolation which surrounded the saturnine figure of the great detective."

(ILLU). "Partly it came no doubt from his own masterful nature, which loved to dominate and surprise those who were around him. Partly also from his professional caution, which urged him never to take any chances" (HOUN). Even to Watson he would not talk about his relations, save his brother Mycroft, and hardly ever about his own early life (GREE). He was notoriously reticent, though he could be "communicative enough" (STUD). "I am not often eloquent," he admitted (ILLU), but his biographer declared that he "could talk exceedingly well when he chose" (SIGN), and his conversation, Watson said, was characterized by a "keen observance of detail and subtle power of inference" (RESI).

"Life is full of whimsical happenings, Watson," he said (MAZA), and despite the assertion that he rarely laughed (HOUN, MAZA, SUSS), he laughed, smiled, and joked incessantly, though his ideas of humour were called "strange and occasionally offensive" (LADY) and even "perverted" (MAZA) and were often manifested in wry irony or outright sarcasm (CREE, HOUN, LADY, MISS, RETI, SOLI, SUSS, THOR, VALL).

"He was a man of habits," Watson wrote of him, "narrow and concentrated habits" (CREE). During their early association he considered those habits regular and not difficult to live with (STUD), but he quickly reassessed them as eccentric and irregular (DYIN, MAZA), characterizing Holmes as "one of the most untidy men that ever drove a fellow-lodger to distraction" (MUSG—EMPT, MAZA), an almost studied Bohemian who engaged in indoor pistol practice, who

had "a horror of destroying documents," and who kept "his cigars in the coal-scuttle, his tobacco in the toe end of a Persian slipper, and his unanswered correspondence transfixed by a jack-knife into the very centre of his wooden mantelpiece" (MUSG). "His incredible untidiness, his addiction to music at strange hours, his occasional revolver practice within doors, his weird and malodorous scientific experiments, and the atmosphere of violence and danger which hung around him made him the very worst tenant in London" (DYIN). He craved seclusion and solitude (HOUN), and "without his scrapbooks, his chemicals, and his homely untidiness, he was an uncomfortable man" (3STU).

"Appreciation of nature found no place among his many gifts, and his only change was when he turned his mind from the evil-doer of the town to track down his brother of the country" (CARD).† He took no interest in natural objects (NAVA), and "neither the country nor the sea presented the slightest attraction to him" (CARD),† yet he claimed in retirement to give himself up entirely "to that soothing life of Nature for which I had so often yearned during the long years spent amid the gloom of London" (LION).

Emotional Qualities. "All emotions," Watson wrote of Holmes, "were abhorrent to his cold, precise but admirably balanced mind" (SCAN). He remained unsentimental (SOLI), saturnine (MAZA), and uneffusive (SCAN), his emotions dulled by exposure to the world's woes (VALL). "The emotional qualities are antagonistic to clear reasoning," he insisted

† These passages are inserted in "The Resident Patient" in many editions.

(SIGN). "I use my head, not my heart" (ILLU). Grit in a sensitive instrument, or a crack in one of his high-powered lenses, Watson asserted, "would not be more disturbing than a strong emotion in a nature such as his" (SCAN). Often he impressed Watson as "a brain without a heart, as deficient in human sympathy as he was preëminent in intelligence" (GREE).

It was, however, in his attitudes toward women and love that he was particularly remarkable, for it was claimed that he never felt any emotion that was "akin to love" (SCAN). Love, he said, "is an emotional thing, and whatever is emotional is opposed to that true cold reason which I place above all things. I should never marry myself, lest I bias my judgment" (SIGN).

But his feelings ran deeper, as he admitted: "I am not a whole-souled admirer of womankind," he confessed (VALL—CHAS, IDEN). He had in fact a positive aversion to them, said Watson (GREE), "never spoke of the softer passions, save with a gibe and a sneer" (SCAN), and refused to abide in any but a bachelor establishment (REIG). "Women are never to be entirely trusted—not the best of them" (SIGN).

Nonetheless he had, when he liked, a "peculiarly ingratiating" way (GOLD) and "a remarkable gentleness and courtesy in his dealings with women. He disliked and distrusted the sex, but he was always a chivalrous opponent" (DYIN). "Woman's heart and mind are insoluble puzzles to the male," he complained (ILLU). "Their most trivial action may mean volumes, or their most extraordinary conduct may depend upon a hair-pin or a curling-tongs" (SECO).

"I have seen too much not to know

that the impression of a woman may be more valuable than the conclusion of an analytical reasoner," he said in 1889 (TWIS). "I value a woman's instinct," he commented in 1907 (LION). In both cases, however, he was addressing bereaved and distrait women to whom he had reason to be kind.

"He used to make merry over the cleverness of women," Watson remarked, but he seemingly stopped such cavalier thinking after his defeat at the hands of Irene Adler (SCAN). He remained insensitive to Mary Morstan's charms (SIGN), and despite his attentiveness to Violet Hunter, "rather to my disappointment," Watson wrote, he manifested no further interest in her "when once she had ceased to be the centre of one of his problems" (COPP). Yet his landlady Mrs. Hudson was genuinely fond of him (DYIN, SIGN), and he successfully wooed Charles Augustus Milverton's housemaid in the guise of Escott the plumber (CHAS).

The only intimacy he permitted himself was that which he shared with Watson (EMPT, FINA, ILLU, YELL), yet even here he seldom permitted his feelings to show (BRUC, DEVI, EMPT, 3GAR). "I was nearer him than anyone else, and yet I was always conscious of the gap between," the doctor wrote (ILLU). Only once did Holmes's mask fall away completely, and "for the one and only time I caught a glimpse of a great heart as well as of a great brain" (3GAR). See WATSON, JOHN H.; also *Attitude to Watson's Writings,* below.

In all, however, is no evidence for doubting Holmes's own words: "I have never loved" (DEVI).

Friends and Acquaintances. See ALGAR; BARKER; HARGREAVE, WILSON;

HUDSON, MRS.; MARTHA; SHERMAN; STACKHURST; STAMFORD; VERNER; VILLARD, FRANÇOIS LE; also AGENCY; BAKER STREET IRREGULARS; CONSULTING DETECTIVE; SCOTLAND YARD; also HOLMES, MYCROFT; WATSON, JOHN H.

Hobbies. See ART; BEE; BLACK-LETTER EDITION; BUDDHISM OF CEYLON; CORNISH LANGUAGE; EARLY ENGLISH CHARTERS; LASSUS; MIDDLE AGES; MIRACLES PLAYS; see also *Methods: Knowledge,* below.

Publications. See MONOGRAPH.

Sports and Athletics. See *Appearance and Condition,* above.

Drug Addiction. See COCAINE; MORPHINE; see also NARCOTIC; OPIUM.

Music. Watson wrote that Holmes was "an enthusiastic musician, being himself not only a very capable performer but a composer of no ordinary merit" (REDH) who was fond of extemporaneous playing upon his violin (STUD). He was both a concert lover (REDH, RETI, STUD) and a patron of the opera (HOUN, REDC). German music, he said, was more to his taste than Italian or French (REDH). See also VIOLIN.

Philosophy and Religion. While he possessed a certain native optimism (LAST, NAVA), Holmes's philosophical beliefs seem to have been pessimistic and uncertain: "Why does fate play such tricks with poor, helpless worms?" he asked (BOSC). "The ways of fate are indeed hard to understand. If there is not some compensation hereafter, then the world is a cruel jest" (VEIL). "But is not all life pathetic and futile? . . . We reach. We grasp. And what is left in our hands at the end? A shadow. Or worse than a shadow—misery" (RETI).

He seemed impressed with the anti-Christian ideas of Winwood READE

(SIGN), agreed with RICHTER that "the chief proof of man's real greatness lies in his perception of his own smallness" (SIGN), firmly refused to believe in the supernatural (DEVI, HOUN, SUSS), and quoted DARWIN (STUD). "When one tries to rise above Nature one is liable to fall below it," he remarked (CREE). "The example of patient suffering is in itself the most precious of all lessons to an impatient world" (VEIL). See also BIBLE.

"There is nothing in which deduction is so necessary as in religion. It can be built up as an exact science by the reasoner," he maintained (NAVA). But he seems never to have found solace: "What is the meaning of it, Watson? What object is served by this circle of misery and violence and fear? It must tend to some end, or else our universe is ruled by chance, which is unthinkable. But what end? There is the great standing perennial problem to which human reason is as far from an answer as ever" (CARD).

When he retired at last to the solitude of the south coast of England, it was, after all, for the study of philosophy (PREF).

ATTITUDE TO WATSON'S WRITINGS

"I suppose, Watson, we must look upon you as a man of letters," Holmes joked (WIST). "I am lost without my Boswell," he said (SCAN), and his view of Watson as his biographer (BLAN, BRUC, MUSG, TWIS) and his frequent uncritical allusions to the stories (CARD, FINA, HOUN, IDEN, LION, NORW, SIXN, THOR, WIST) indicate that they were an accepted part of his life.

Though Watson claimed that Holmes was "indifferent" to the publication of his cases (HOUN, STUD),

"I am lost without my Boswell."

in truth the detective was much concerned over them, labelling the accounts "superficial" (BLAN) and accusing Watson of seeking to embellish his experiences (COPP, REDH) and to tinge them with romanticism (SIGN). He told the doctor that he was "unable to congratulate you" upon these sketches (SIGN, SUSS), declaring their effect to be "entirely meretricious, depending as it does upon your retaining in your own hands some factors in the problem which are never imparted to the reader" (CROO).

"Detection is, or ought to be, an exact science and should be treated in the same cold and unemotional manner," he declared (SIGN), taxing Watson with "pandering to popular taste instead of confining himself rigidly to facts and figures" (BLAN). "You have erred perhaps in attempting to put colour and life into each of your statements instead of confining yourself to the task of placing upon record that severe reasoning from cause to effect which is really the only notable feature about the thing" (COPP). He accused his biographer of "telling a story backward" (THOR). "Your fatal habit of looking at everything from the point of view of a story instead of as a scientific exercise has ruined what might have been an instructive and even classical series of demonstrations. You slur over work of the utmost finesse and delicacy, in order to dwell upon sensational details which may excite, but cannot possibly instruct, the reader" (ABBE). "You have degraded what should have been a course of lectures into a series of tales" (COPP).

Blundering, too, he added, was "a more common occurrence than anyone would think who only knew me through your memoirs" (SILV), and he complained that the accounts gave "an exaggerated view of my scientific methods" (SUSS); see *Methods: Failures and Errors*, below. Watson in some asperity challenged Holmes in the face of his criticism to write his own narratives (ABBE), which many years later he in fact did (BLAN, LION).

"In choosing a few typical cases which illustrate the remarkable mental qualities of my friend, Sherlock Holmes," Watson wrote, "I have endeavoured, as far as possible, to select those which presented the minimum of sensationalism, while offering a fair field for his talents" (CARD). Even Holmes concurred that "you have some power of selection, which atones for much which I deplore in your narratives" (ABBE), and he approved of the prominence given "not so much to the many *causes célèbres* and sensational trials in which I have figured but rather to those incidents which may have been trivial in themselves, but which have given room for those faculties of deduction and of logical synthesis which I have made my special province" (COPP).

"To his sombre and cynical spirit all popular applause was always abhorrent, and nothing amused him more at the end of a successful case than to hand over the actual exposure to some orthodox official, and to listen with a mocking smile to the general chorus of misplaced congratulation" (DEVI). Despite his affectation of disdain for notoriety (SIXN), he gained considerable fame through Watson's writings (GREE, HOUN, NAVA, RETI, 3GAR, VALL, VEIL), as, incidentally, did Watson himself (ILLU, VALL). A chronicler, he admitted, "is always of use" (TWIS), and he not only told Watson of some of his early experiences (GLOR, MUSG), he invited him to join in his investigations in the particular expectation of finding material for his annals (CARD, STOC). No memoir seemingly was released without his specific prior approval (VEIL), and he actually suggested some of the cases he wished to see written up (CREE, DEVI).

Holmes prohibited the publication of

any of his cases, with the single exception of *The Hound of the Baskervilles*, from the time of his return in 1894 until 1903, just before his planned retirement (EMPT, NORW, SIXN). Even then he was reluctant to see them continued (DEVI, SECO). "So long as he was in active professional practice the records of his successes were of some practical value to him," Watson remarked in 1904, "but since he has definitely retired from London and betaken himself to study and bee-farming on the Sussex Downs, notoriety has become hateful to him" (SECO). During 1887–1904 no fewer than forty of his cases were first published over a period of seventeen years; in the twenty years 1908–1927 just twenty cases appeared, only sixteen of which came from Watson's pen.

FINANCES

It was the oft-repeated principle of Holmes's that he worked rather for the love of his art than for the acquirement of wealth (SPEC). "My professional charges are upon a fixed scale. I do not vary them, save when I remit them altogether" (THOR). He told one client that she was "at liberty to defray whatever expenses I may be put to, at the time which suits you best" (SPEC).

A few cases, though, yielded high fees. Rewards of £1,000 were offered for the return of the missing piece of the Beryl Coronet (BERY) and for the Countess of Morcar's blue carbuncle (BLUE), and he received the same amount in expense-money from the King of Bohemia (SCAN). He collected £12,000 from the Duke of Holdernesse in what can be described only as a bribe (PRIO), and Watson said he never knew Holmes to "claim any large reward" save in the Holder-

nesse case (BLAC). His services to the royal house of Scandinavia and to the French republic, he said, had by 1891 left him with enough money to retire (FINA). No sum was to be spared by Lady Frances Carfax's family in locating her (LADY), and Holmes apparently kept the money paid him by Von Bork for his false espionage as Altamont (LAST).

The King of Bohemia sent him a gold snuff-box as a souvenir of the Irene Adler case, and the reigning family of Holland rewarded him with a remarkable brilliant ring (IDEN). Queen Victoria personally presented him with an emerald tie-pin (BRUC).

METHODS

"Art in the blood," said Sherlock Holmes, "is liable to take the strangest forms" (GREE).

He was quick to admit that his "curious gifts of instinct and observation" (VEIL) were based upon "a kind of intuition" (STUD—SIGN, THOR), and that even in college he had already formed into a system those habits of observation and inference which were to play so important a part in his life (GLOR); see also HOLMES, MYCROFT. It was his habit, he declared, to hide none of his methods (REIG), which he said were based upon a "mixture of imagination and reality" (THOR) and characterized as "but systematized common sense" (BLAN). There should be, he said, "no combination of events for which the wit of man cannot conceive an explanation" (VALL).

The three qualities necessary to the ideal detective, he insisted, were the power of observation, the power of deduction, and a wide range of exact knowledge (SIGN).

Observation. Holmes possessed "ex-

"You know my method. It is founded upon the observation of trifles."

traordinary powers" of observation (SCAN—CARD, IDEN, STUD), and his deductions were raised, said Watson, upon the solid basis of "minute and laborious" examinations of the evidence (ABBE). "You know my methods," he insisted (BLUE, BOSC, HOUN, SIGN, STOC); they were founded, he said, "upon the observation of trifles" (BOSC). See also LENS; MICROSCOPE.

"It has long been an axiom of mine that the little things are infinitely the most important" (IDEN). Even the most trivial facts could be of use, he maintained (VALL), and one must pay attention to details (BLAC), for "there is nothing so important as trifles" (TWIS) and "the gravest issues may depend upon the smallest things" (CREE). "The smallest point may be the most essential" (REDC). "I dare call nothing trivial when I reflect that some of my most classic cases have had the least promising commencement" (SIXN). "To a great mind, nothing is little" (STUD).

Evidence taken on the spot has a special value, he argued (RETI, STUD), and possessing as he did an "extraordinary gift for minutiæ" (SIGN) he was highly critical of others' efforts to apply his methods (BLAC). "You see, but you do not observe," he counselled (SCAN). "Never trust to general impressions . . . but concentrate yourself upon details" (IDEN). "There is nothing more deceptive than an obvious fact" (BOSC). "It is of the highest importance in the art of detection to be able to recognize, out of a number of facts, which are incidental and which are vital" (REIG—NAVA, PRIO). He declared that "nothing clears up a case so much as stating it to another person" (SILV), a technique he used often (CREE, CROO, THOR, TWIS), and was always ready to hear the facts of an experience repeated (BLAC, DANC, HOUN, REDH).

"I make a point of never having any prejudices, and of following docilely wherever fact may lead me," he said (REIG—ABBE, BOSC, NAVA), and approached each case with "an absolutely blank mind" (CARD). "I have no data," he would say (COPP, SIXN). "I presume nothing" (HOUN). "I imagine nothing" (VALL). "Data! data! data! I can't make bricks without clay" (COPP).

He would ponder a problem, Watson said, until he had solved it "or convinced himself that his data were insufficient" (TWIS). "I can discover facts, Watson, but I cannot change them" (THOR).

Deduction. "The more *outré* and grotesque an incident is," he said, "the more carefully it deserves to be examined, and the very point which appears to complicate a case is, when duly considered and scientifically handled, the one which is most likely to elucidate it" (HOUN). "It is a mistake to confound strangeness with mystery" (STUD). "As a rule, the more bizarre a thing is the less mysterious it proves to be" (REDH). "Singularity is almost invariably a clue" (BOSC). "It is only the colourless, uneventful case which is hopeless" (SHOS). "The most commonplace crime is often the most mysterious, because it presents no new or special features from which deductions may be drawn" (STUD—BOSC, REDH).

Having acquired his first-hand evidence and collected the other facts of the case, Watson said, Holmes preferred to withdraw to "seclusion and solitude" for "those hours of intense mental concentration during which he weighed every particle of evidence, constructed alternative theories, balanced one against the other, and made up his mind as to which points were essential and which immaterial" (HOUN).

"It is a capital mistake to theorize before you have all the evidence," he warned (STUD—SCAN, SECO, WIST). "Insensibly one begins to twist facts to suit theories, instead of theories to suit facts" (SCAN). "I never guess. It is a shocking habit—destructive to the logical faculty" (SIGN). "I never make exceptions. An exception disproves the rule" (SIGN).

A hypothesis nonetheless must cover all the facts, he said (SIGN), and then one must follow wherever it leads (BOSC). When several explanations present themselves "one tries test after test until one or other of them has a convincing amount of support" (BLAN). He maintained that there was a line of least resistance which would reconcile all the facts of a case and was the starting-point of every investigation (EMPT). "One forms provisional theories and waits for time or fuller knowledge to explode them. A bad habit . . . but human nature is weak" (SUSS). "One should always look for a possible alternative and provide against it. It is the first rule of criminal investigation" (BLAC). "It is impossible as I state it," he said of one set of facts, "and therefore I must in some respect have stated it wrong" (PRIO). "When a fact appears to be opposed to a long train of deductions, it invariably proves to be capable of bearing some other interpretation" (STUD). "It is an old maxim of mine," he said (BERY), that "when you have eliminated the impossible, whatever remains, however improbable, must be the truth" (SIGN—BERY, BLAN, BRUC).

He advocated the use of imagination

(RETI, SILV) and intuition (SIGN), and defended speculation as "the scientific use of the imagination" (HOUN). Imagine what might have happened, he suggested, and then act upon the supposition (SILV), and provided one had always a material basis upon which to start, such an exploration "into the region where we balance probabilities and choose the most likely" was permissible (HOUN). This often involved putting himself in the place of one whose motives or actions he wished to trace (EMPT, FINA, MUSG, RETI, SIGN); see PERSONAL EQUATION.

"Circumstantial evidence," he concluded, "is a very tricky thing. It may seem to point very straight to one thing, but if you shift your own point of view a little, you may find it pointing in an equally uncompromising manner to something entirely different" (BOSC). It could be, though, he agreed, "occasionally very convincing" (NOBL).

See DEDUCTION AND ANALYSIS; see also ANALYSIS; DEDUCTION; SYNTHESIS.

Knowledge. "Breadth of view," Holmes remarked, "is one of the essentials of our profession. The interplay of ideas and the oblique uses of knowledge are often of extraordinary interest" (VALL). His studies were said to be "eccentric," and he did in fact amass an amazing lot of out-of-the-way knowledge (STUD). "I am an omnivorous reader with a strangely retentive memory for trifles," he said (LION). "All knowledge comes useful to the detective" (VALL).

"The ideal reasoner would, when he had once been shown a single fact in all its bearings, deduce from it not only all the chain of events which led up to it but also all the results which would follow from it," he argued (FIVE—STUD). Ideal reasoning implied a possession of all knowledge, he conceded, but it was not impossible to possess all knowledge likely to be useful in one's work, "and this I have endeavoured in my case to do" (FIVE).

It was said he had "a passion for definite and exact knowledge" (STUD). "I hold a vast store of out-of-the-way knowledge without scientific system, but very available for the needs of my work. My mind is like a crowded BOX-ROOM with packets of all sorts stowed away therein—so many that I may well have but a vague perception of what was there" (LION). "It was one of the peculiarities of his proud, self contained nature," Watson wrote, "that though he docketed any fresh information very quickly and accurately in his brain, he seldom made any acknowledgment to the giver" (SUSS).

A man should keep his brain stocked with all the knowledge he was likely to use, Holmes maintained, and the rest he could keep handy in his library, "where he can get at it if he wants it" (FIVE). Among the works in his own library were his BRADSHAW (COPP, VALL), the *American Encyclopædia* (FIVE), Watson's MEDICAL DIRECTORY (HOUN), the "red-covered volume" in which he turned up Lord Robert St. Simon (NOBL), the "encyclopædia of reference" in which he sought the Duke of Holdernesse (PRIO), his CROCKFORD (RETI), two gazetteers (SCAN, SIGN), and no doubt the several "trustworthy books of reference" in which he found Professor Moriarty's salary (VALL). He also retained the back numbers of several newspapers (SIXN). See also COMMONPLACE BOOK.

Examples of the range of his professional knowledge include TOBACCO ashes (BOSC, SIGN, STUD), the shapes of ears (CARD), dogs (CREE, MISS, SIGN), CRYPTOGRAPHY (DANC, GLOR, REDC, VALL), some researches which had a "medico-criminal aspect" (DYIN), an exact knowledge of London (EMPT, REDH, SIGN), newspaper types (HOUN), perfumes (HOUN), the dating of documents (HOUN), the typewriter and its relation to crime (IDEN), bicycle tyres (PRIO), tattoos (REDH), FOOTSTEPS (SIGN), the influence of the trade upon the form of the hand (SIGN), and perhaps the names and trade-marks of the world's major gun-making firms (VALL). See also AGONY COLUMN; MONOGRAPH; also *Appearance and Condition* and *Character: Hobbies,* above.

See also ANATOMY; ART; ASTRONOMY; ATAVISM; BERTILLON SYSTEM; BIBLE; BOTANY; BRITISH LAW; CHEMISTRY; FINGERPRINT; GEOLOGY; HANDWRITING; LITERATURE; PHILOSOPHY; PHOTOGRAPHY; POISON; POLITICS.

Much of Holmes's success was due to his minute knowledge of the history of crime (HOUN, IDEN, NOBL, REDH, SIGN, STUD). His knowledge of "sensational literature," Watson observed early in their association, was "immense; he appears to know every detail of every horror perpetrated in the century" (STUD). Everything comes in circles, insisted Holmes, and the most practical thing a detective could do would be "to shut yourself up for three months and read twelve hours a day at the annals of crime" (VALL). "There is nothing new under the sun" (STUD). "The old wheel turns, and the same spoke comes up. It's all been done before, and will be again" (VALL). In addition he maintained many underworld contacts (ILLU), boasted that there was no one who knew the higher criminal world of London as well as he (FINA), and made it his business to follow the details of Continental crime (ILLU).

See also ABERDEEN; ANDERSON MURDERS; ANDOVER; DOLSKY; FOLKESTONE COURT; GRODNO; HAGUE, THE; HAMMERFORD WILL CASE; LEFEVRE; LETURIER; LONG ISLAND; MASON; MOLESEY; MORGAN; MORAN, COL. SEBASTIAN; MULLER; MUNICH; PALMER, WILLIAM; PEACE, CHARLES; PRITCHARD, EDWARD WILLIAM; RATCLIFF HIGHWAY MURDERS; RIGA; ST. LOUIS; SAMSON; SENEGAMBIA; VAN JANSEN; VON BISCHOFF; WAINWRIGHT; WILD, JONATHAN; also cases under BURGLARY; LARCENY; MURDER; ROBBERY; also *Untold Tales,* below.

Disguises. "You would have made an actor and a rare one," Athelney Jones told Holmes (SIGN). "The stage lost a fine actor" when he became a specialist in crime, Watson agreed; his expression, his manner, "his very soul seemed to vary with every fresh part that he assumed" (SCAN). He boasted that he had "the thoroughness of the true artist" (DYIN) and that "old Baron Dowson said the night before he was hanged that in my case what the law had gained the stage had lost" (MAZA).

"He had at least five small refuges in different parts of London, in which he was able to change his personality," Watson disclosed (BLAC). Among the rôles he assumed was that of a "common loafer" (BERY), an East End familiar known as Captain Basil (BLAC), a rakish young plumber named Escott (CHAS), an elderly, deformed bibliophile (EMPT), a venerable Italian priest (FINA), a French

"It was not merely that Holmes changed his costume. His expression, his manner, his very soul seemed to vary with every fresh part that he assumed. The stage lost a fine actor, even as science lost an acute reasoner, when he became a specialist in crime."

ouvrier (LADY), a workman looking for a job, also described as an "old sporting man" (MAZA), an old woman (MAZA), a "drunken-looking groom" (SCAN), an "amiable and simple-minded" Nonconformist clergyman (SCAN), a sailor (SIGN), an asthmatic old master mariner (SIGN), a doddering opium smoker (TWIS), and finally the Irish-American spy Altamont (LAST).

"It is the first quality of a criminal investigator that he should see through a disguise," he remarked (HOUN), but he failed to penetrate disguise of "Mrs. Sawyer" (STUD) or of Hugh Boone, whom he said he had observed often in the streets of the City (TWIS).

Failures and Errors. Blunders upon his part, Holmes said, were "a more common occurrence than anyone would think" (SILV). His long career naturally included some complete and unavoidable failures, Watson pointed out (FIVE, SOLI, THOR), while others remained only partially cleared up (FIVE). "You have seen me miss my mark," he reminded Watson (THOR). "I have been beaten four times—three times by men, and once by a woman," he said in 1887 (FIVE).

"So accustomed was I to his invariable success," Watson said of their relationship in 1888, "that the very possibility of his failing had ceased to enter into my head" (SCAN). Nonetheless two of his published cases were utter failures from a professional point of view (SCAN, YELL), and Holmes criticized himself often for his own mental slowness (ABBE, CREE, LION, THOR, TWIS).

He was nearly misled by false evidence in the Abbey Grange case (ABBE) and suspected the wrong man of the theft of the Bruce-Partington plans (BRUC). In the Baskerville case he erred in attempting to approach the mysterious hansom in Regent Street and nearly mismanaged the whole affair, he admitted, by holding back his hand at the conclusion (HOUN). He nearly erred fatally in his search for Lady Frances Carfax by failing to recognize a trivial but essential clue (LADY). His mistake in not entering the Silver Blaze case immediately was due to erroneous theories he had formed from the newspaper accounts (SILV), he had been unable to throw any light upon the theft of the black pearl of the Borgias (SIXN), and he blundered in not taking an earlier train in the matter of Violet Smith (SOLI).

He came to entirely wrong conclusions in several cases until new data was added by a personal examination of the scene (SHOS, SILV, SPEC), and he jumped to the wrong assumption in the murder of Eduardo Lucas (SECO), one of some half-dozen cases, Watson said, in which the truth was discovered even though Holmes erred (YELL); though in some editions this reference is not to "The Second Stain" but unaccountably to "The Musgrave Ritual."

Though Holmes always used the readiest and most direct means of getting results, Watson nonetheless remarked upon the likelihood of his falling into error "through the over-refinement of his logic—his preference for a subtle and bizarre explanation when a plainer and more commonplace one lay ready to his hand" (SIGN). Holmes agreed that "one drawback of an active mind is that one can always conceive alternative explanations" (THOR). "Perhaps, when a man has special knowledge and special powers like my own, it rather encourages him to seek a complex explanation when a simpler one is at hand" (ABBE).

Untold Tales

The Tarleton murders, the case of Vamberry the wine merchant, the adventure of the old Russian woman, and the singular affair of the aluminium crutch, as well as the case of Ricoletti of the club-foot and his abominable wife, all of which occurred before Holmes's acquaintance with Watson, were not all successes, but there were "some pretty little problems" among them (MUSG). The case of Mrs. Farintosh was concerned with an opal tiara (SPEC), and Mortimer Maberley had been one of his early clients (3GAB).

Shortly after his first meeting with Watson he advised Lestrade in a forgery case and received as clients a fashionably dressed young girl, a Jew peddler, a slipshod elderly woman, an old white-haired gentleman, and a railway porter (STUD). During the next few years he was associated with Lestrade in the "bogus laundry affair" (CARD), looked into the death of Victor Savage (DYIN), had the case of Colonel Warburton's madness introduced to his notice by Watson (ENGR), saved the good name, if not the life, of Wilson, the district messenger office manager (HOUN), easily found Mrs. Etherege's husband when the police had given him up for dead (IDEN), carried out a service for Lord Backwater (NOBL), had one or two encounters with John Clay (REDH), investigated the case of the woman at MARGATE (SECO), and enabled Mrs. Cecil Forrester to unravel a domestic complication (SIGN). He made use of a false alarm of fire in the Darlington substitution scandal and also in the Arnsworth castle business (SCAN). Athelney Jones remembered him from the Bishopgate jewel case (SIGN).

He managed a delicate case for the King of Scandinavia (FINA, NOBL) and saved Major Prendergast in the Tankerville Club scandal (FIVE) shortly before 1887. He was occupied with the problem of the Grosvenor

Square furniture van at the time of Hatty Doran's disappearance, and upon the morning of the St. Simon case he had letters from a fishmonger and a tide-waiter (NOBL). His immense exertions in the spring of 1887 were directed at the Netherland-Sumatra Company and the colossal schemes of Baron Maupertuis (REIG). Watson's own records for that busy year included the adventure of the Paradol Chamber, the AMATEUR MENDICANT SOCIETY, the loss of the British barque *Sophy Anderson,* the singular adventures of the Grice Patersons in the island of Uffa, and the CAMBERWELL POISONING CASE (FIVE). Holmes believed Col. Sebastian Moran to be at the bottom of the death of Mrs. Stewart, of Lauder, though nothing could be proved (EMPT). It was also in 1887 that the "terrible murderer" Bert Stevens wanted Holmes and Watson to get him off (NORW). In September the detective claimed to have been beaten four times—"three times by men and once by a woman" (FIVE).

He remarked in 1888 that the most winning woman he ever knew was hanged for poisoning three little children for their insurance-money (SIGN). He solved the Manor House case without his brother Mycroft's help (GREE) and was consulted by François le Villard in a case which presented some features of interest concerned with a will (SIGN). Twice toward the end of the 'eighties he had helped Alec MacDonald to attain successes (VALL).

He was preoccupied by the affair of the Vatican cameos in May 1888 (HOUN) and took a superficial interest in the Abbas Parva tragedy at a time some seven years or more prior to 1896 (VEIL). He claimed to be unable to go to Dartmoor in the Baskerville case because one of the most revered names in England was being besmirched by a blackmailer and only he could stop a disastrous scandal (HOUN), though this may have been a ruse. During November 1888 he exposed the atrocious conduct of Colonel Upwood in connection with the famous card scandal of the Nonpareil Club and defended the unfortunate Mme. Montpensier from the charge of murdering her stepdaughter Mlle. CARÈRE (HOUN).

From time to time after his wedding Watson heard accounts of Holmes's summons to Odessa in the case of the Trepoff murder, of his clearing up of the singular tragedy of the Atkinson brothers at Trincomalee, and of the mission which he accomplished so successfully for the reigning family of Holland (SCAN), this last a matter of such delicacy that he could not confide it even to Watson (IDEN). Holmes concluded the investigation of "a very commonplace little murder" and Watson recorded "The Adventure of the Tired Captain" in the July which immediately succeeded his marriage (NAVA). During 1890 Holmes was engaged in clearing up some small points in connection with the Dundas separation case and was referred an intricate matter from Marseilles (IDEN). He said that the case in which he had been of assistance to the French republic, together with his service to the King of Scandinavia, had left him in such a position that he might retire (FINA).

The histories of Morgan the poisoner, Merridew "of abominable memory," and MATTHEWS were to be found under *M* in Holmes's index of biographies (EMPT). The letter *S* of his commonplace book included mention of Arthur H. Staunton, the rising young forger, and Henry Staunton, whom he had helped to hang (MISS). The cases of Victor Lynch the forger, the venomous lizard or GILA, Vittoria the circus belle, VANDERBILT and the YEGGMAN, and Vigor the Hammersmith wonder were entered under *V* (SUSS).

In the months following Holmes's return from the Great Hiatus occurred the shocking affair of the Dutch steamship *Friesland* which nearly cost him and Watson their lives (NORW). They took Archie Stamford, the forger (SOLI), and locked up Colonel Carruthers (WIST). Watson's notes upon the year 1894 include the repulsive story of the red leech and the terrible death of Crosby the banker, an account of the Addleton tragedy and the singular contents of the ancient British barrow, the famous Smith-Mortimer succession case, and the tracking and arrest of HURET the BOULEVARD assassin (GOLD).

In April 1895 he was immersed in the very abstruse and complicated problem of the peculiar persecution to which John Vincent Harden, the well-known tobacco millionaire, had been subjected (SOLI). A curious and incongruous succession of cases engaged his attention in this "memorable year" of 1895, ranging from his famous investigation of the death of Cardinal Tosca at the express desire of the POPE, down to his arrest of Wilson, the notorious CANARY trainer (BLAC).

Brooks and Woodhouse were among fifty men Holmes said had good reason to take his life (BRUC). His intro-

duction to Dr. Moore AGAR had been a dramatic one (DEVI), and the dreadful business of the Abernetty family was first brought to his notice by the depth which the parsley had sunk into the butter upon a hot day (SIXN). The story of the *Matilda Briggs* was associated with the giant rat of Sumatra, a story for which the world is not yet prepared (SUSS). Stanley HOPKINS had called Holmes into seven cases by 1897 (ABBE), four of which remain untold. The detective was preoccupied with the case of the two Coptic patriarchs some time during the second half of 1898 (RETI).

He was able to do Sir James Saunders a professional service (BLAN), saved Count Von und Zu Grafenstein from murder by the Nihilist Klopman (LAST), saw to the hanging of old Baron Dowson (MAZA), arranged a "simple matter" for Fairdale Hobbs (REDC), and was consulted upon the theft of the black pearl of the Borgias but was unable to throw any light upon it (SIXN).

He could not possibly leave London while old Abrahams was in mortal terror of his life (LADY). He solved the ST. PANCRAS CASE and ran down a coiner by means of his microscope (SHOS) and was engaged upon the Conk-Singleton forgery case (SIXN). He interrupted the case of the Ferrers Documents to take up the Priory School investigation, at a time when the Abergavenny murder was coming up for trial (PRIO). In June 1902 he refused a knighthood offered him for services "which may some day be described" (3GAR), and he had a commission from the Sultan of TURKEY in January 1903 (BLAN).

He knew the details of Count Sylvius's rôle in the death of old Mrs. Harold, the life history of Miss Minnie Warrender, and the robbery in the train-de-luxe to the Riviera in 1893 (MAZA). He was aware of Sir James Damery's handling of the Hammerford Will case and of Baron Gruner's past crimes (ILLU) and had private knowledge of the killing of young Perkins outside the Holborn Bar (3GAB). See also *Methods: Knowledge,* above.

Not the least interesting among Holmes's problems, wrote Watson, were the complete failures, such as the case of James PHILLIMORE, the fate of the cutter ALICIA, and the remarkable story of Isadora PERSANO (THOR); see also *Methods: Failures and Errors,* above. Watson declared that if attempts to get at and destroy his notes were repeated, he would give to the public the whole story concerning the politician, the lighthouse, and the trained cormorant (VEIL).

*Holy Four: see SACRED COUNCIL OF FOUR.

Holy Land, or *Palestine,* a maritime region of the Turkish province of SYRIA, est. pop. 650,000. Dr. Shlessinger was said to be preparing a map of the Holy Land, with special reference to the kingdom of the Midianites (LADY). See the map of TURKEY.

Holy Peters: see PETERS, HENRY.

"Holy War, The," a famous allegorical tale of good and evil, written in 1682 by John Bunyan (1628–1688), but less successful than his better-known *Pilgrim's Progress.* In his disguise as an old bibliophile Holmes carried a volume entitled *The Holy War* (EMPT).

Holy Writ: see BIBLE.

Home Office, a department of the British Government, headed by a Cabinet minister, the *Secretary of State for Home Affairs,* who sees to the administration of internal matters. SCOTLAND YARD is under his supervision. The Home Secretary came to consult Holmes in the case of the Mazarin diamond (MAZA).

Homer: see POPE, ALEXANDER.

Hones, Johnny (d. 1847), a member of the Ferrier wagon party (STUD).

Honeydew tobacco, a kind of chewing tobacco prepared with molasses (CARD).

Honeysuckle, a common variety of climbing or standing shrub (YELL).

Honourable, in Great Britain, the title bestowed upon the younger sons of earls (EMPT) and the children of viscounts and barons (CHAS, LADY), and upon many persons occupying official places of trust and honour. The title *Right Honourable* is given to a number of dignitaries, including all Cabinet ministers (SECO). See also PEERAGE.

Honours list, the list of titles and dignities, with the names of those so honoured, conferred by the sovereign at certain times of the year, such as at the New Year and the monarch's birthday. Holmes declared that he did not have a fancy to see his name in the honours list (BRUC) and did in fact refuse a knighthood (3GAR).

Hood, John Bell (1831–1879), a Confederate general during the Civil War. Elias Openshaw fought under him (FIVE).

Hookah, an Eastern pipe of great size, the bowl of which is set upon an air-tight vessel partially filled with water. A small tube passes from the bowl down into the water, and the long, flexible smoking-tube is inserted in the side of the water-vessel. The smoke is thus made to pass through the water, being cooled and deprived of some noxious properties. Thaddeus Sholto smoked a hookah (SIGN).

Hookah.

Hook it, in English slang, to turn away or depart (SIGN).

Hooligan, any common rough or street-rowdy, especially one who is a member of an organized gang (REDC, SIXN).

Hope, a resident of St. Louis, and a close friend of John FERRIER. His son **Jefferson Hope,** betrothed to Ferrier's adopted daughter Lucy, attempted to help them escape from Utah and, failing, pledged vengeance upon their murderers, Enoch DREBBER and Joseph STANGERSON. Tracking them down in London after some twenty years, he took his revenge, but was decoyed to Holmes's residence and arrested (STUD). Holmes and Watson referred later to the Jefferson Hope murders (SIGN).

Hope, Trelawney: see TRELAWNEY HOPE.

Hope Town, a settlement in the Andaman Islands, on the slopes of Mount Harriet. Jonathan Small lived here

(SIGN). See the map of the ANDAMAN ISLANDS.

Hopkins, Ezekiah, the non-existent person created by John Clay, who was said to have made his fortune in America and founded the Red-Headed League in his will (REDH).

Hopkins, Stanley (b. 1865), a young Scotland Yard detective in whose career Holmes showed a very practical interest (GOLD). He was assigned to investigate the murders of Sir Eustace Brackenstall (ABBE), Peter Carey (BLAC), and Willoughby Smith (GOLD), and he advised Cyril Overton to consult Holmes (MISS).

Horace, properly **Quintus Horatius Flaccus** (65–8 B.C.), the greatest of Latin lyric poets. Thorneycroft Huxtable was the author of *Huxtable's Sidelights on Horace* (PRIO), and Holmes said there was as much sense in HAFIZ as in Horace, and as much knowledge of the world (IDEN). Watson quoted Horace's *First Satire: "Populus me sibilat, at mihi plaudo/Ipse domi simul ac nummos contemplor in arca"*—"People hiss at me, but I am satisfied with myself; I stay home and contemplate the money in my strongbox"—which he attributed to a "Roman miser" (STUD).

Horner, John, the London plumber who was wrongly arrested for stealing the blue carbuncle (BLUE).

Horse: see BAY; COB; TROTTER; see also CURB; OFF-FORELEG; LOOSE-BOX; also MIDDLE AGES (cloven horse-shoes); PONCHO; also CAB; CARRIAGE; FOUR-IN-HAND; also MEWS; SERVANT, subheaded *Domestic Servants: Stable Staff.*

See also COURSING; FOX HUNTING.

For cavalry terms see CALTROP; IMPERIAL YEOMANRY; TROOP.

For race-horses and racing terms see TURF, THE.

Horsham, a town in Sussex, pop. 9,446. Lamberley was south of Horsham (SUSS), where the Openshaws lived (FIVE).

Horsham slabs, the name given to sheets of a variety of sandstone quarried near Horsham in Sussex. An unusually hard sandstone which is capable of being split into thin slabs, it was formerly much used locally for building purposes. The roof of Cheeseman's was of Horsham slabs (SUSS).

Horsom, Dr., the physician who certified Rose Spender's death (LADY).

Hotel. The hotel is a comparatively modern development of the INN. A *commercial hotel* (VALL) caters principally to the needs of the commercial traveller; a *private hotel* (HOUN, MISS, STUD) is not licensed for the sale of spirits.

Jefferson Hope said he got by as a cab-driver once he had learned the locations of the principal hotels and stations (STUD). Trevor Bennett stayed at a London hotel (CREE), and Watson lived for a time at a private hotel in the Strand (STUD). Mr. Melas was an interpreter for wealthy visitors to London who stayed at the NORTHUMBERLAND AVENUE hotels (GREE), and Holmes was able to trace Francis Hay Moulton through a Northumberland Avenue hotel bill (NOBL). Watson remarked that the Hon. Philip Green looked as if he would be more at home in a country inn than in a fashionable hotel (LADY).

See also BENTLEY'S PRIVATE HOTEL; CHARING CROSS HOTEL; CLARIDGE'S HOTEL; DACRE HOTEL; GRAND HOTEL; GROSVENOR HOTEL; HALLIDAY'S PRIVATE HOTEL; HOTEL COSMOPOLITAN; LANGHAM HOTEL; MEXBOROUGH PRIVATE HOTEL; NORTHUMBERLAND HOTEL; ST. PANCRAS HOTEL.

Holmes and Watson took lunch at a Wallington hotel (CARD). John Hector McFarlane spent the night at the ANERLEY ARMS at Norwood (NORW). The main part of Leon Sterndale's baggage remained at his Plymouth hotel (DEVI), and Hall Pycroft stayed at a hotel in New Street in Birmingham (STOC). Holmes stayed in Coombe Tracey during the Baskerville case (HOUN).

See also BLACK SWAN HOTEL; BRAMBLETYE HOTEL; EAGLE COMMERCIAL; HEREFORD ARMS; RAILWAY ARMS; WESTVILLE ARMS.

Holmes and Watson argued in a Strasburg SALLE-À-MANGER (FINA), and Holmes visited Watson in his Montpellier hotel (LADY). See also ENGLISCHER HOF; HOTEL DULONG; HÔTEL DU LOUVRE; HOTEL ESCURIAL; HÔTEL NATIONAL.

*Hotel Cosmopolitan, the London hotel at which the Countess of Morcar was staying when the blue carbuncle was stolen (BLUE).

Hotel Directory: see DIRECTORY.

*Hotel Dulong, the hotel in Lyons where Watson found Holmes lying ill (REIG).

Hôtel du Louvre, properly **Grand Hôtel du Louvre,** one of the largest and best Paris hotels, located in the Rue de Rivoli opposite the Louvre Palace (BRUC).

*Hotel Escurial, a hotel at Madrid, at which Don Murillo and his secretary were assassinated (WIST).

The *Escorial,* often called in English the *Escurial,* is a remarkable building, constructed 1563–93 by the Spanish king Philip II, comprising at once a convent, a church, a palace, and a mausoleum. Striking in its size and grandeur, it stands upon a plain some thirty miles north-west of Madrid, near the village of Escorial, which possesses two hotels, the *Fonda de Miranda* and the *Fonda Nueva*.

Hôtel National, a hotel at Lausanne, from which Lady Frances Carfax disappeared (LADY).

Hotel servants. The servants at the Hôtel National remarked upon Lady Frances Carfax's baggage (LADY).

Clerk. Holmes spoke with the clerk at the Northumberland Hotel (HOUN), and a clerk at the Eagle Commercial remembered Ted Baldwin (VALL).

Waiter. James Ryder was the *upper-attendant,* that is, the head attendant in charge of those who wait upon guests, at the Hotel Cosmopolitan (BLUE). There was a waiter at the Hereford Arms (BOSC) and the Northumberland Hotel (HOUN). Peter Steiler the elder had been a waiter at the Grosvenor Hotel (FINA). Lady Frances Carfax's maid was engaged to a waiter at the Hôtel National (LADY). See also BOOTS.

Porter. Holmes dispatched young Cartwright to speak to the outside and hall porters of twenty-three hotels round Charing Cross (HOUN). A porter saw Godfrey Staunton leave Bentley's hotel (MISS), and a porter at the Eagle Commercial remembered Ted Baldwin (VALL).

Maid. A maid at the Northumberland Hotel may have been bribed to steal Sir Henry Baskerville's boots (HOUN), and a chambermaid at the Eagle Commercial also remembered Baldwin (VALL).

See also SERVANT.

*****Hotspur,** the brig which picked up the survivors of the *Gloria Scott* disaster (GLOR).

Hottentot, a peculiar, light-skinned race native to South Africa. They are nearly extinct, having been hunted and dispersed by the Boers. Dr. Mortimer and Sir Charles Baskerville spent "many a charming evening" discussing the comparative anatomy of the Bushman and the Hottentot (HOUN).

"Hound of the Baskervilles, The" (HOUN), a novel-length chronicle which appeared serially in the *Strand* magazine between August 1901 and April 1902 and was published in book form in the latter year. It concerns Holmes's investigation of Sir Charles Baskerville's death, the attempted murder of Sir Henry Baskerville, and their relationship to an old west-country legend. Watson dates the case as having occurred in 1889, but some authorities prefer a variety of years between 1886 and 1900.

Houndsditch, a street in the City. The non-existent Mrs. Sawyer claimed to live in DUNCAN STREET near Houndsditch (STUD). See the map of the CITY.

House, The, in the idiom of the City, the STOCK EXCHANGE (BLAC).

Housekeeper, a woman who manages the affairs of a household; especially, the woman who supervises the female servants of the household.

Holmes in his retirement had a housekeeper (LION). There was one at Stoke Moran (SPEC) and at Birlstone (VALL), and housekeepers were employed by the Tregennises (DEVI), Professor Coram (GOLD), Jonas Oldacre (NORW), Eduardo Lucas (SECO), Bartholomew Sholto (SIGN), and Bob Carruthers (SOLI). A woman who would appear to have been Irene Adler's housekeeper met

Holmes's party at the door of Briony Lodge (SCAN). Mrs. Saunders was caretaker for the building in which Nathan Garrideb had rooms (3GAR). Mrs. BARRYMORE was the housekeeper at Baskerville Hall (HOUN), and MARTHA was Von Bork's housekeeper (LAST). See also SERVANT.

Housemaid: see SERVANT.

House of Commons: see PARLIAMENT.

Houses of Parliament: see PARLIAMENT, HOUSES OF.

House-surgeon, a member of the resident surgical staff of a hospital. Dr. Mortimer had been a house-surgeon at Charing Cross Hospital (HOUN).

Howells, Rachel, the second housemaid at Hurlstone, recruited to assist in discovering the treasure of Charles II by her former fiancé BRUNTON, whom she trapped and left to die in the treasure crypt (MUSG).

***Howe Street,** a Bloomsbury street into which Great Orme Street was said to open (REDC).

Hudson, apparently a member of the Ku Klux Klan who outlined a platform of action to Elias Openshaw's local branch of the society (FIVE).

Hudson, a member of the *Gloria Scott*'s crew, who survived the destruction of the ship and attempted to blackmail fellow-survivors Beddoes and Trevor Senior. Holmes suspected that he was murdered by Beddoes (GLOR).

Hudson, Morse, the owner of a shop for the sale of pictures and statues in the Kennington Road (SIXN).

Hudson, Mrs., the landlady of Sherlock Holmes; see also BAKER STREET. Watson writes that she was fond of Holmes and stood in the deepest awe of him (DYIN). The doctor tried to ease her mind about Holmes's restlessness

(SIGN), and she hurried to him when she believed Holmes to be dying (DYIN). She was thrown into violent hysterics at his return from the Great Hiatus, later manipulating the bust in the trap set for Sebastian Moran (EMPT). Holmes wired to her to expect him and Watson (LADY). She inquired as to when he would be pleased to dine (MAZA), prepared an excellent breakfast (BLAC), and had it said of her that she had as good an idea of breakfast as a Scotchwoman (NAVA).

Watson remarked upon the landlady's "stately tread" (STUD) and her dismay at the arrival of the Baker Street Irregulars (SIGN, STUD). She informed Watson that Holmes had been out on the Irene Adler case since eight in the morning (SCAN); see TURNER, MRS.

When John Openshaw rang the bell, Holmes considered it likely that it was some crony of the landlady's (FIVE). She was awakened early in the morning by Helen Stoner and retorted upon Holmes (SPEC). She brought up John Garrideb's card (3GAR) and the telegram from Wilson Hargreave (DANC), and showed in the sailors inquiring for "Captain Basil" (BLAC), Mary Morstan (SIGN), Cecil Barker (VALL), and Gregson and Barnes (WIST). And for this, Watson said, Holmes's payments were "princely" (DYIN).

***Hudson Street,** the Aldershot street in which Henry Wood had lodgings (CROO).

Huguenots, the persecuted French Protestants of the sixteenth and seventeenth centuries, finally expelled from France in 1685. Charles Gorot was of Huguenot extraction (NAVA), and

Holmes attended a performance of "LES HUGUENOTS" (HOUN).

Hull down, so far away, as a ship, that the hull is invisible owing to the curvature of the earth's surface, while the masts and sails can still be seen. The *Gloria Scott* was hull down from her boat when she exploded (GLOR).

Hungary, a kingdom of AUSTRIA-HUNGARY (GREE, SUSS). The chief city is BUDA-PESTH; *see also* TRANSYLVANIA.

Hung-wu (d. 1398), a Chinese emperor, founder of the Ming dynasty. Watson read up on him as he prepared for his interview with Baron Gruner (ILLU).

Hunt (d. 1875), a Vermissa policeman who was murdered when he ventured to arrest a Scowrer (VALL).

Hunt, an association of huntsmen (HOUN); see FOX HUNTING.

Hunter, Ned, the stable-boy who was drugged in the theft of Silver Blaze (SILV).

Hunter, Violet, a governess whose adventures in the employ of Jephro RUCASTLE led to her appealing to Holmes (COPP).

Hunting-crop, a short, stout whip used by horsemen, having a crooked handle and a loop of leather at the end for securing it to the wrist. Sir Henry Baskerville armed himself with a hunting-crop (HOUN), Silas Brown carried one (SILV), and Dr. Grimesby Roylott shook his threateningly at Holmes (SPEC). Holmes's own favourite weapon was a loaded hunting-crop (SIXN), that is, one which has its handle weighted with iron, with which he struck the revolver from John Clay's hand (REDH), threatened James Windibank (IDEN), and smashed the last of the Napoleonic busts (SIXN).

Jack Woodley (SOLI), each of the Ferriers (STUD), and Ronder (VEIL) carried a RIDING-CROP.

Huret, the Boulevard assassin, the tracking and arrest of whom won for Holmes an autograph letter of thanks from the French President and the Order of the Legion of Honour (GOLD).

Hurlingham Club, a sporting club with extensive grounds in west London. Baron Gruner played polo here but was forced to resign his membership (ILLU). See the front endpaper map.

*Hurlstone, the Musgrave family estate in Western Sussex (MUSG).

Huxtable, Thorneycroft, the founder and principal of the Priory School, author of *Huxtable's Sidelights on Horace,* who summoned Holmes into the case of Lord Saltire's disappearance (PRIO).

Hyam, a victim of the Scowrers (VALL).

Hyams, the tailor of Jonas Oldacre (NORW).

Hyde Park, an extensive park in Westminster. It is the place in London perhaps most frequented by the fashionable world, who, during the Season, come here to ride, to drive, to walk, and to be seen. The Park is also a favourite rendezvous of organized crowds holding demonstrations. Hatty Doran was seen walking into Hyde Park in company with Flora Millar, and the police dragged the SERPENTINE for Hatty's body (NOBL). Irene Adler said she would drive out in the Park as usual after her wedding (SCAN). Sir Henry Baskerville went to look at the folk in "the park" (HOUN).

Watson strolled across the Park on his way from Kensington to PARK LANE (EMPT) and to Baker Street (REDH).

Hyde Park is the largest and most important of London's public parks.

Holmes and Watson took a walk in the Park upon the day of the Grant Munro case (YELL). See the map accompanying KENSINGTON.

Hydrocarbons, a series of chemical compounds consisting only of carbon and hydrogen. They are the simplest of the carbon compounds and are of considerable commercial importance. Holmes succeeded in "dissolving" a hydrocarbon (SIGN).

Hydrochloric acid, a colourless gas compounded of chlorine and hydrogen, having a suffocating odour. The "pungent cleanly" smell of hydrochloric acid told Watson that Holmes had spent the day engaged in chemical work (IDEN).

Hynes Hynes, a neighbour of Aloysius Garcia (WIST).

I

Ichneumon: see MONGOOSE.

Ichthyosis, also called *fish-skin disease* and *pseudo-leprosy,* in pathology, a congenital disease of the skin, in which it presents the whitened form of hard, dry scales. Godfrey Emsworth was found to have ichthyosis rather than leprosy (BLAN).

Idée fixe: see MONOMANIA.

Illinois, one of the central states of the United States, pop. 4,821,550. Little Lucy Ferrier was certain that God had made the country "down in Illinois" (STUD). See also CHICAGO; NAUVOO.

Illustrious Client, the euphemism used by Watson to refer to Sir James Damery's client, for whom Damery acted as intermediary with Holmes (ILLU). He is generally assumed to have been *Edward VII* (1841–1910), eldest son of Queen Victoria, and King of England 1901–10.

"Illustrious Client, The Adventure of the" (ILLU), a chronicle which appeared originally in the *Strand* magazine for February and March 1925 and *Collier's Weekly* of 8 November 1924 and was published in the 1927 collection entitled *The Case Book of Sherlock Holmes.* It concerns Holmes's efforts to prevent the marriage of Baron Adelbert Gruner to Violet de Merville, and Watson dates the case as having taken place in September 1902.

Imperial Envoy. Von Bork's cousin Heinrich was an Imperial Envoy (LAST), that is, a diplomatic agent acting in the personal interest of the German Emperor.

*Imperial Opera of Warsaw, the opera at which Irene Adler was prima donna (SCAN).

Imperial palace of Peking, the celebrated palace of the Chinese Emperors, located within the Forbidden City, where it is said the magnificent splendour of the rooms is not to be surpassed anywhere. Holmes doubted if there was a complete set of Ming pottery anywhere outside the Imperial palace of Peking (ILLU).

Imperial Theatre, a theatre in Westminster, opened in 1876 as part of the amusement emporium known as the *Royal Aquarium.* James Smith had been the orchestra conductor at the "old Imperial Theatre" (SOLI), by which is meant the period 1879–85. The theatre was closed 1885–1900 and was torn down in 1908. See the map of WHITEHALL.

Imperial Tokay: see TOKAY.

Imperial Yeomanry, the name given in 1901 to the volunteer mounted troops, formerly called the *Yeomanry*

Cavalry, organized in 1794 for home defense. Individuals and whole corps may volunteer for service abroad if called upon, and because of the decisive part played by cavalry in the South African War, some three thousand officers and men of the Imperial Yeomanry formed the nucleus of the British mounted forces against the Boers. Among these were James Dodd and Godfrey Emsworth (BLAN).

"I'm Sitting on the Stile, Mary," properly "The Lament of the Irish Emigrant," a popular ballad written in 1843 by the Scottish composer William R. Dempster (1808–1871), with words by Helen Selina Blackwood, Lady Dufferin (1807–1867), which begins with the line: "I'm sitting on the stile, Mary" (VALL).

In chief, in heraldry: see CHIEF.

Index: see COMMONPLACE BOOK.

India, or **The Indian Empire,** also called **British India** and **The Eastern Empire,** an extensive British possession of southern Asia, pop. 294,361,056.

India is administered separately from the rest of the BRITISH EMPIRE, and the official at the head of the government is the *Secretary of State for India, a*

The Indian Empire.

member of the British Cabinet. The executive officer is the *Viceroy,* formerly known as the GOVERNOR-GENERAL, who is appointed by the Crown and who has his residence in CALCUTTA, the capital. The three principal administrative divisions under the direct control of the British are *Bengal, Bombay,* and *Madras,* though Bengal has been subdivided into a number of regions, among them the NORTH-WEST PROVINCES and the PUNJAUB. India contains also nearly seven hundred native states which are controlled by their own rulers, subject to the sanction of the Viceroy; see RAJPOOTANA; see also RAJAH.

The British East India Company had established settlements in India as early as 1613; see COMPANY, THE. It was not until the break-up of the native Mogul Empire early in the eighteenth century, however, that extensive conquest of the sub-continent began, and the year 1757 is considered the date of the foundation of the Indian Empire. In 1857 the MUTINY occurred. As a result, the sovereignty of India and the powers of government hitherto vested in the East India Company were transferred to the British Crown, and in 1877 the Queen was proclaimed Empress of India.

Agriculture is the leading occupation of the country and engages the attention of a large part of the inhabitants; see INDIGO; PADDY-FIELD; TEA. Manufactures include textiles and metalwork; see BENARES. For the prevailing religions see BUDDHISM OF CEYLON; HINDU; MOHAMMEDAN; SIKHS. See also GANGES; HIMALAYA; KHYBER PASS; MAHRATTA; TERAI.

The Northumberland Fusiliers were stationed in India at the time Watson was attached to that regiment (STUD), and Watson claimed to have seen service here (CARD).† The events which led to the death of Colonel Barclay (CROO) and those surrounding the theft of the Agra treasure (SIGN) had their beginnings in India during the Mutiny. India was one of Mycroft Holmes's specialisms (BRUC), though Watson failed to interest Percy Phelps in the subject (NAVA). Colonel Sebastian Moran was said to have been the best heavy-game shot that the Eastern Empire had ever produced, and the story was told of how he crawled down a drain after a wounded tiger in the days before he made India too hot to hold him (EMPT). The rajah who owned

A Calcutta bazaar.

† This allusion is inserted in "The Resident Patient" in some editions.

A rural scene in Bengal.

the Agra treasure also was driven from India (SIGN). The letter bearing Elias Openshaw's death notice came from here (FIVE), and Dr. Grimesby Roylott had lived here (SPEC). There were parallel cases here to the murder of Bartholomew Sholto (SIGN), and the almanack article with which Holmes first attempted to decode Porlock's message dealt with the trade and resources of British India (VALL).

Daulat Ras was an Indian (3STU), and the Sholtos all hired Indian servants (SIGN). Grimesby Roylott smoked Indian cigars (SPEC), and Holmes spoke of the Indian LUNKAH (SIGN) and TRICHINOPOLY (SIGN, STUD); John Turner also was said to have smoked an "Indian" cigar (BOSC), but this may be an allusion to the DUTCH EAST INDIES. Eduardo Lucas was murdered with a curved dagger, one of a collection of Oriental arms possessed by the dead man (SECO), and Pondicherry Lodge was full of Indian curiosities (SIGN). Dr. Grimesby Roylott had a passion for Indian animals, and Holmes called Roylott's SWAMP ADDER "the deadliest snake in India" (SPEC).

The old soldier Holmes and his brother observed in Pall Mall had

served in India (GREE); see also INDIAN ARMY.

See also AGRA; ALLAHABAD; BENARES; BHURTEE; BOMBAY; CALCUTTA; CAWNPORE; DARJEELING; DELHI; LUCKNOW; MADRAS; MUTTRA; PESHAWUR; SHAHGUNGE; also ANDAMAN ISLANDS; NEPAUL; PONDICHERRY.

Indian Army, the military establishment of British India, distinct from the British Army. Historically the force developed as three separate armies— the Bengal, Madras, and Bombay armies—this triplicate organization growing naturally out of the original, separate settlements. By the time of the Indian Mutiny the total strength of the three armies amounted to 38,000 European troops and 348,000 Sepoys in the military employ of the East India Company.

The Mutiny, which affected only the Bengal Army, prompted a number of reforms, though three separate forces remained the basis of organization. In 1890 the armies in India numbered 73,000 British and 147,000 native troops. The European regiments having been assumed into the British Army, the Bengal, Madras, and Bombay armies now consist only of Sepoys, though their officers are still exclusively British. The three officer corps were unified under a single command in 1891 as the Indian Staff Corps, and in 1903 the Indian Staff Corps was renamed—in the first true use of the term—the *Indian Army*.

The name "John H. Watson, M.D., Late Indian Army" was painted upon the lid of Watson's dispatch-box (THOR), though his Army service was never with any of the Indian Army organizations.

Captain Morstan and Major Sholto had been officers in an Indian regi-

ment, the THIRTY-FOURTH BOMBAY IN-
FANTRY (SIGN). Colonel Sebastian
Moran had served in the FIRST
BENGALORE PIONEERS (EMPT) and
Major-General Stoner in the BENGAL
ARTILLERY (SPEC). The THIRD BEN-
GAL FUSILIERS and some members of
the GUIDES were at Agra during the
Mutiny (SIGN).

A number of BRITISH ARMY regiments are stationed at intervals in
India (CROO, SIGN, STUD). The
old soldier Holmes and his brother observed in Pall Mall had served in India
(GREE).

Indian Empire: See INDIA.

Indian Mutiny: see MUTINY, THE.

Indian Pete (d. 1847), a member of
the Ferrier wagon party (STUD).

Indians, American, or **Red Indians.**
A band of PAWNEE or BLACKFOOT
hunters occasionally traversed the
Great Alkali Plain, and the word
"Redskins" was on every lip as the
Mormons sighted the Ferriers; in later
years it was said that even the unemotional Indians relaxed their stoicism as
they marveled at the beauty of Lucy
Ferrier (STUD). Francis Hay Moulton was captured by the APACHE while
prospecting in New Mexico (NOBL),
and there were rumours in Utah of
murdered immigrants and rifled camps
in regions where Indians had never
been seen (STUD). Jefferson Hope
called himself a WASHOE hunter and
possessed a power of sustained vindic-
tiveness which he may have learned
from the Indians among whom he had
lived (STUD). Holmes's gazetteer said
the DIGGER Indians were among the
smallest races upon the earth (SIGN).

Holmes sometimes had the composure and utter immobility of counte-

nance of a Red Indian (CROO,
NAVA).

India-rubber, a word for rubber of
any kind (DANC, ENGR).

Indigo, a blue vegetable dye extracted from a plant which grows in
India. Abel White was an indigo-
planter (SIGN).

Ingle-nook, a corner by the fire.
Holmes discussed the Birlstone case
while seated in the ingle-nook of the
village inn (VALL).

In it, in English slang, to be on intimate terms with. Sam Merton, in
speaking of the wax bust of Holmes,
remarked that "Madame Tussaud's
ain't in it" (MAZA), implying that it
was much more lifelike and of better
quality than the waxwork to be found
at Madame Tussaud's.

Inn, a PUBLIC-HOUSE or tavern kept
for the lodging of such as may choose
to visit it.

Watson said that the Hon. Philip
Green looked as if he would be more at
home in a country inn than in a fashionable hotel (LADY). Holmes remarked that the titles of English country inns were too limited (LAST).

Holmes and Watson stayed at a
Cambridge inn opposite Leslie
Armstrong's house (MISS) and at the
inn of the village near Thor Place
(THOR), and offered to stay at the
local inn during their visit to the Priory
School (PRIO). Holmes stayed in
Coombe Tracey during the Baskerville
case (HOUN) and took tea at an inn
at Ripley (NAVA). His party
snatched a hurried breakfast at an inn
near Chatham (GOLD).

James Dodd spoke to the innkeeper
of the village near Tuxbury Old Park
about Godfrey Emsworth (BLAN).
"Elrige's" was not an inn (DANC).

Inquiries at the inns and lodgings round Yoxley Old Place were unproductive (GOLD). There were inns at Grimpen (HOUN), at the Leatherhead railway station (SPEC), and near Grant Munro's home (YELL).

See also ALPHA INN; BLUE ANCHOR; BULL; CHEQUERS; CROWN INN; FIGHTING COCK INN; GREEN DRAGON; RED BULL; also PUBLICAN. See also HOTEL.

Inner Temple: see TEMPLE, THE.

Innings, the time during which a player or team is in action during a cricket match. Hall Pycroft said that getting the position with Mawson & Williams' was his "innings" (STOC).

Inquisition, the name given to an ecclesiastical court in the Roman Catholic Church, officially known as the *Holy Office,* for the discovery and suppression of heresy. Not even the Inquisition of Seville was ever able to put a more formidable machinery in motion than the DANITES of Utah (STUD).

Insect. Young Master Rucastle showed remarkable talent in the capture of insects (COPP). Stapleton was an expert upon ENTOMOLOGY (HOUN); see also BEE; BLUEBOTTLE; LEPIDOPTERA.

In statu quo, a Latin phrase meaning *in the condition in which (it was before),* that is, in its original state (STUD).

Interlaken, a popular tourist town in the central part of Switzerland, pop. (1900) 2,962. Holmes and Watson made their way to Meiringen by way of Interlaken (FINA). See the map of SWITZERLAND.

International, in Rugby, a match between two of the teams representing England, Scotland, Ireland, or Wales, each team playing the other three once annually under the auspices of an International Board. Godfrey Staunton had played in five Internationals, and Cyril Overton said he had been first reserve for England against Wales (MISS).

In the sere and yellow: see SERE.

In the swim, in slang, to be on the inside or identified with the current of events, as in business or society (STOC).

Intimidation, in law, the wrongful use of violence or a threat of violence against any person with a view to compelling him to do or abstain from doing some act which he has a legal right to do or abstain from doing. The Spencer John gang specialized in assaults and intimidations (3GAB).

Iodoform, a yellow crystalline compound used an an antiseptic, possessing a very disagreeable odour. Holmes said that a man who smells of iodoform must be an active member of the medical profession (SCAN).

Ionides, the Alexandrian manufacturer of Professor Coram's cigarettes (GOLD).

Ireland, the more western of the two principal islands of the United Kingdom, pop. 4,458,775.

Baron Von Herling suggested that the impending Irish civil war had been created by the Germans (LAST) rather than the opposition of the northern Protestants to the Home Rule Bill —a claim perhaps disputed by the papers in Von Bork's safe marked "Ireland" and by Holmes's own experience there in the guise of the Irish-American Altamont (LAST). The Widow MacNamara was an Irishwoman (VALL). One of Susan Cushing's boarders had come from the north of Ireland (CARD), and Birdy Edwards emi-

Ireland.

grated to America from here when he was a very young man (VALL). Holmes said that the Royal Mallows was an Irish regiment (CROO). Sir James Damery possessed gray, frank "Irish" eyes (ILLU).

See also BELFAST; DUBLIN; MONAGHAN; SKIBBAREEN; WATERFORD.

Iris, the horse, belonging to the Duke of Balmoral, which finished a bad third in the Wessex Cup (SILV).

*Iron Dyke Company, a Vermissa mine-owning company, of which Chester Wilcox was chief foreman (VALL).

*Ironhill, a Gilmerton town or location (VALL).

Ironmaster, a manufacturer of iron (NAVA).

"Is Disease a Reversion?" the title of the essay with which Dr. Mortimer won the JACKSON PRIZE (HOUN).

Isle of Dogs, a region of Poplar, consisting of a large peninsula formed by a sudden bend in the Thames. It is separated from the rest of the borough

by the West India Docks, and is itself the site of several small docks. The *Aurora* was pursued round here (SIGN). See the front endpaper map.

Isle of Wight, an island off the coast of Hampshire, and an administrative county of England, pop. 82,418. By the time Holmes was certain that the *Lone Star* was the ship he sought, he said, she had left London and was not far from the Isle of Wight (FIVE). See the map of HAMPSHIRE.

Isonomy, a famous thoroughbred racing-horse, foaled in 1875. Owned by Frederick Gretton (1839–1882), a Staffordshire brewer, and trained by the well-known John Porter (1838–1922), he won seven major races between 1878 and 1880 for a total of some £120,000. Silver Blaze was from the Isonomy stock (SILV). In some editions the name is misprinted *Somomy.*

Italian Quarter, of London: see SAFFRON HILL.

Italy, a kingdom of southern Europe, pop. 32,965,504. The stolen naval treaty was between Britain and Italy (NAVA), and Douglas Maberley died here (3GAB). It was said that not even the secret societies of Italy could put a more formidable machinery in motion than the Danites of Utah (STUD).

Most of the principals of the Red Circle case (REDC) and the mystery of the Napoleonic busts (SIXN) were Italians, and Count Sylvius was half Italian (MAZA). Holmes disguised himself as an Italian priest to escape Professor Moriarty at Victoria Station (FINA). Annie Harrison was described as having large, dark "Italian" eyes (NAVA), and Jack McGinty was swarthy as an Italian (VALL). Holmes said that Josiah Amberley had the sort of mind one associated with the mediæval Italian nature rather than with the modern Briton (RETI).

Goldini's was an Italian restaurant (BRUC). Holmes seems to have had some familiarity with the Italian language (REDC) and stated that German music was more to his taste than Italian or French (REDH).

See also BARI; FLORENCE; MILANO; NAPLES; ROME. See the map of EUROPE.

Ivernian, relating to the supposed pre-Celtic population of Ireland. Dr. Mortimer said that Sir Charles Baskerville's head was half Gaelic, half Ivernian in its characteristics (HOUN).

Ivory. The box sent to Holmes by Culverton Smith was ivory (DYIN), as were the handles of John Straker's cataract knife (SILV) and the knife with which Willoughby Smith was killed (GOLD). An ivory letter-weight was stolen from old Acton (REIG), and the head of Lord Bellinger's umbrella was ivory (SECO). Lord Robert St. Simon showed Holmes an ivory miniature of Hatty Doran (NOBL).

Ivy. Lord Saltire made use of the ivy upon the walls of the Priory School to climb down from his room, as did Heidegger the German master (PRIO). Ivy also covered the front of the Abbey Grange (ABBE) and the south wall of Baskerville Hall (HOUN). There was WISTARIA upon the walls of Professor Presbury's house (CREE).

*Ivy Lane, a street in Brixton, where the Tangeys lived (NAVA).

*Ivy Plant, a public-house in Westminster, round the corner from Godolphin Street (SECO).

J

J pen, the designation given to a common type of broad-pointed, steel-nibbed desk pen (CARD, GREE).

Jack, a PIKE (SHOS).

Jack-in-office, in English slang, a public official who behaves in an arrogant or conceited manner (SIGN, SPEC).

Jack-knife, a large pocket-knife with blades which fold into the handle. Holmes kept his unanswered correspondence transfixed by a jack-knife into the centre of his wooden mantelpiece (MUSG).

Jackson, a doctor who looked after Watson's practice when he was away (CROO). Watson also refers to his "accommodating neighbour" (FINA, STOC) as *Anstruther* (BOSC).

Jackson, Thomas Jonathan (1824–1863), commonly known as *Stonewall Jackson,* Confederate general in the Civil War. Elias Openshaw fought in Jackson's army (FIVE).

Jackson Prize, properly **Jacksonian Prize,** an annual prize awarded by the Royal College of Surgeons for the best essay submitted upon an announced topic in practical surgery. Instituted in 1800 by *Col. Samuel Jackson,* a former surgical apprentice turned military officer, the £10 prize represents one of the oldest and best-respected competitions in English medicine. Dr. Mortimer had won the "Jackson Prize" for an essay in "Comparative Pathology" entitled "Is Disease a Reversion?" (HOUN).

*Jackson Prize for Comparative Pathology, a prize won by Dr. Mortimer (HOUN).

Jacobean, pertaining to JAMES I or his times (VALL, WIST).

Jacobs, the butler of Trelawney Hope (SECO).

*Jacobson's Yard, a boat-repair yard opposite the Tower, where Jonathan Small concealed the *Aurora* (SIGN).

James, a name apparently used by Mrs. Watson in speaking of her husband (TWIS), thereby creating much gleeful speculation among scholars.

James, the son of the Grimpen postmaster (HOUN).

James I (1566–1625), King of England and (as *James VI*) of Scotland. He succeeded to the English throne upon the death of Elizabeth in 1603. Birlstone Manor was built in the fourth year of his reign (VALL), and High Gable was described as a Jacobean structure (WIST).

James, Billy, a victim of the Scowrers (VALL).

James, Jack, an American citizen arrested as a German spy (LAST).

Japan, an island empire situated east of Asia, est. pop. 50,000,000. Trevor Senior had visited here (GLOR). There was a suit of Japanese armour in

Harold Latimer's house (GREE), Nathan Garrideb was the possessor of a Japanese vase (3GAR), and Trevor Senior owned a Japanese cabinet (GLOR). Holmes had a knowledge of BARITSU, "the Japanese system of wrestling" (EMPT). See also NARA.

Jarvey, in English slang, the driver of a cab or hired carriage (STUD).

Jaundice, a condition of the body in which the skin turns to a greenish-yellow colour (GLOR).

Jay, in English and American slang, a stupid person or simpleton. Abe Slaney admitted he had walked into Holmes's trap "like a jay" (DANC).

Jean Paul: see RICHTER.

Jenkins, the name of two brothers who fell victim to the Scowrers (VALL).

Jessamine, or *jasmine,* a plant cultivated for the delicate perfume-oil of its flowers. Beryl Stapleton wore a scent called *white jessamine* (HOUN).

Jet, a hard black fossil substance, susceptible of high polish, commercially wrought into toys, buttons, and personal ornaments of various kinds. Mary Sutherland's dress was decorated with little black jet ornaments (IDEN).

Jew. Holmes purchased his Stradivarius from a Jew pawnbroker in the Tottenham Court Road (CARD). One of Holmes's early clients was a gray-headed, seedy visitor, looking to Watson like a Jew peddler (STUD), and the biography of a Hebrew Rabbi was included in Holmes's index (SCAN). See also SHEENY.

See also MINORIES; OLD JEWRY; also LOMBARD STREET.

Jew, in opprobrious usage, a tight-fisted money-lender. Sir Robert Norberton said he was "in the hands of the Jews" (SHOS).

Jewels: see AGATE; AMETHYST; BERYL; CARBUNCLE; CAT'S-EYE; DIA-MOND; EMERALD; OPAL; RUBY; SAPPHIRE; TURQUOISE; see also AGRA TREASURE; BISHOPGATE; GROSS AND HANKEY'S; PEARL; WATER.

Jews' harp, a musical instrument of percussion consisting of a flexible metal tongue set in a small pear-shaped iron frame. One end is held to the player's mouth and pressed against his teeth; at the other end the tongue of the instrument passes out of the frame and terminates in a sharp bend at right angles so as to be struck with the hand or an elastic bow. Tones of different pitch are produced by altering the shape and size of the mouth-cavity, so as to reinforce the various

Jews' harp.

harmonics of the natural tone of the steel tongue, which is low in pitch. The instrument is capable of surprisingly sweet and elaborate effects. The garrotter Parker was said to be a remarkable performer upon the jews' harp (EMPT).

Jezail, a heavy long-barrelled musket, fired from a rest, manufactured and used by Asiatic natives. The term is applied to the weapon rather than to its ammunition. Watson was struck on the shoulder (STUD) or in the leg (SIGN) by a "Jezail bullet" at the battle of Maiwand, and some years later the wound still throbbed with a dull persistency (NOBL).

Jiddah, a town in Arabia, on the Red Sea, est. pop. 20,000. It is of importance mainly as the principal landing place of pilgrims to Mecca. Jon-

athan Small and Tonga were picked up
by a ship carrying pilgrims to Jiddah
(SIGN). See the map of TURKEY.

Jimmy. "Surely Jimmy will not
break his mother's heart," Holmes read
from the agony column of the *Daily
Gazette* (REDC).

Johannesburg, a city of the South
African Republic or, after the country's
conquest in the Boer War, the Transvaal Colony, pop. (1896) 48,330. The
city was built mostly by the foreigners
who came to the locality because of the
nearby gold-fields. Ralph Smith supposedly died here (SOLI). See the map
of SOUTH AFRICA.

John, the butler of Leslie Armstrong
(MISS).

John, the coachman of Irene Adler
(SCAN).

John, a coachman engaged by
Holmes during the St. Clair case
(TWIS).

John, Spencer: see SPENCER JOHN
GANG.

John Bull, the name used to signify
the personification of the English people (LAST).

Johnny, in English slang, a beginner
or novice. Hall Pycroft called himself a
"soft Johnny" (STOC).

John o' Groats, figuratively the
northern-most extremity of Great Britain, so called from the Dutchman who,
according to legend, built a house near
here in the fifteenth century. Holmes
said that a draghound would follow
aniseed "from here to John o' Groats"
(MISS).

Johnson, an Oxford Rugby player
(MISS).

Johnson, Shinwell, also known as
Porky Shinwell, a member of Holmes's
AGENCY, a former criminal who allied
himself to Holmes in the first years of
this century and provided information

from among the underworld (ILLU).

Johnson, Sidney (b. 1855), the senior clerk and draughtsman at Woolwich Arsenal (BRUC).

Johnson, Theophilus, a guest, with
his family, at the Northumberland Hotel (HOUN).

Johnston, one of the four principal
elders of the Mormons (STUD).

Joint, in American slang, a place of
meeting or resort for persons engaged
in evil and secret practices of any kind.
Old Patrick was boss of **The Joint** in
Chicago (DANC).

Jones, Athelney, the Scotland Yard
detective who was placed in charge of
the Sholto case (SIGN). *Athelney
Jones* may be a compound surname,
and *Peter Athelney-Jones* is conceivably a single person. The compound
surname is an upper-class affectation,
however, and Scotland Yard's policies
for advancement in rank require every
officer to begin at the very lowest level
of the uniform police, so discouraging
the would-be "gentleman detective."

Jones, Peter, the Scotland Yard inspector who participated in the vigil in
the City and Suburban Bank vault
(REDH).

José, the man-servant of Don Murillo (WIST).

Journal. Watson kept a journal in
which he recorded the incidents of the
Drebber case (STUD). See also DI-
ARY; NOTEBOOK; PORTFOLIO; SCRAP-
BOOK; YEAR-BOOK.

Journal de Genève, one of the more
important newspapers of Switzerland,
moderately liberal in politics, published
in French at Geneva. The story in the
Journal de Genève was one of three accounts of Professor Moriarty's death
which appeared in the public press
(FINA).

*"Journal of Psychology," a British

medical journal. Dr. Mortimer was the author of "Do We Progress?" for the journal (HOUN).

Jowaki campaign, one of two British military expeditions against the *Jowaki,* a Pathan clan living just east of the Afghan frontier, and to the south of Peshawur, in British India. Two separate punitive expeditions were mounted, in 1877 and 1877–78, in retaliation for Jowaki raids into British territory. The second of these was an invasion in force which completely pacified the tribe. Colonel Sebastian Moran had served in the Jowaki campaign (EMPT).

J.P.: see JUSTICE OF THE PEACE.

Jubilee, The, the name given to the national celebration in 1887 of the fiftieth year of Queen Victoria's reign, now more commonly called the *Golden Jubilee,* for the *Diamond Jubilee* was celebrated in similar fashion in 1897. Hilton Cubitt met his wife during "the Jubilee" (DANC), which might refer to either of these occasions.

The nation celebrated the fiftieth year of Queen Victoria's reign with the Jubilee of 1887.

Judge Lynch, the personification of lynch law. Old Morris suggested that the Scowrers might be tried by Judge Lynch should they become too repressive (VALL).

Juggernaut, the name given to an idol of the Indian god Krishna which is mounted upon a huge, sixteen-wheeled car in order that it might be conveyed from place to place near its temple upon the eastern coast. Holmes spoke of the Prussian Juggernaut upon the eve of the World War (LAST),† an allusion to the erroneous belief, once common among Europeans, that a part of the god's ritual involved the faithful's throwing themselves beneath the giant wagon's wheels.

Junk, salted meat carried aboard ships for long voyages (GLOR).

Junker (*yoong'ker*), a member of the aristocratic party in Prussia which controls the political principles and social ideas of the German Empire. Von Bork declared that no Junker was as bitter in his feelings toward England as an Irish-American (LAST).

Jupiter, the greatest of the Roman gods. Holmes compared Mycroft's coming to Baker Street with "Jupiter descending" (BRUC).

Justice of the peace, in England and the United States, a local magistrate appointed to preserve the peace, to try minor cases, and to perform other functions such as the legalizing of papers for record. In England they also preside at the QUARTER SESSIONS.

Enoch Drebber hurried before a justice of the peace in Cleveland, Ohio (STUD). Trevor Senior was a J.P. (GLOR), as were old Cunningham (REIG) and Mr. Hynes Hynes (WIST).

† This allusion appears only in the English magazine appearance of the case.

K

Kaiser, the title given to the King of Prussia in his office as president of the German Empire. The word means *Emperor,* and the office is hereditary in the male branch of the royal family of PRUSSIA. The Kaiser is heir not to a throne, but to an office, yet by the terms of the German constitution he may not be removed. His chief executive officer is the CHANCELLOR. His duties as Emperor are distinct from his responsibilities as King of Prussia. Von Bork was a devoted agent of the Kaiser (LAST), who in 1914 was *Wilhelm II* (1859–1941), Emperor 1888–1918.

Kansas, a central state of the United States, pop. (1905) 1,544,968. John Garrideb claimed to be from here (3GAR).

Keep, the inner-most and strongest structure, or central tower, of a mediæval castle. Holmes associated Reginald Musgrave with "all the venerable wreckage of a feudal keep" (MUSG).

Kemball, properly **Heber C. Kimball** (1801–1868), a prominent officer of the Mormon church (STUD) who was converted to the Latter-Day Saints in 1831. In 1847 he accompanied Brigham Young to Utah and shortly thereafter was made first counsellor to Young.

Kemp, Wilson, the accomplice to Harold Latimer (GREE).

Kennedy: see MORTON, CYRIL.

Kennington, a district in the north of Lambeth. Dr. Barnicot had his practice here (SIXN). See the front endpaper map.

Kennington Lane, correctly *Upper Kennington Lane* and *Lower Kennington Lane,* a thoroughfare in Lambeth, running eastward from Vauxhall Bridge. Holmes and Watson passed down Kennington Lane in pursuit of

Kaiser Wilhelm II.

Jonathan Small (SIGN). See Map IV of LONDON.

*Kennington Park Gate, a street or district of south London, where John Rance lived (STUD). *Kennington Park* lies just south and east of the OVAL, upon the eastern border of Lambeth; see Map IV of LONDON.

Kennington Road, a thoroughfare in Lambeth, extending south from the Westminster Bridge Road. Philip Green followed Annie Fraser up the Kennington Road (LADY). Morse Hudson's shop was here, as were Dr. Barnicot's residence and principal consulting-room (SIXN). See Map IV of LONDON.

Kensington, a western metropolitan borough of London, pop. 176,628. Once an exclusive suburb inhabited by members of court, Kensington has since had its historical connexions swept away by modern influences.

Watson at one time lived here (EMPT, NORW, REDH), as did Hugo Oberstein (BRUC), Horace Harker (SIXN), and Mr. Melville (WIST), and Harold Latimer claimed to live here (GREE). Lower Burke Street lay in the borderland between NOTTING HILL and the ancient region from which the borough takes its name (DYIN).

The "great church clock" which struck the quarters during the vigil at Caulfield Gardens (BRUC) is probably a reference to the bells of *St. Mary Abbot's,* the great parish church of Kensington, constructed 1869–81. See the front endpaper map and the map on the following page.

Kent, a south-eastern county of England, pop. 935,855. There are some industries in the north, round London and the Thames, but the majority of the county is under cultivation, and there are extensive forests.

Holmes in 1889 remarked that LEE was in Kent (TWIS), even though it was the year after passage of the act which transferred a portion of the ancient county to the new administrative county of London. J. G. Wood was attacked by *Cyanea capillata* when swimming off the coast of Kent (LION), and Jonathan Small said that India was as peaceful as Surrey or Kent just before the Mutiny (SIGN).

MARSHAM (ABBE) and YOXLEY OLD PLACE (GOLD) are scenes of Holmes's investigations in Kent. CANTERBURY (FINA) and TUNBRIDGE WELLS (VALL) too are here, and Birlstone lay in Sussex near the border of Kent (VALL). See also BECKENHAM; CHATHAM; GRAVESEND; MARGATE. See also DOWNS, THE; GOODWINS, THE. See the map of ENGLAND and the back endpaper map.

Kent, the surgeon who was retained to look after Godfrey Emsworth (BLAN).

Keswick, a London paperhanger (STUD).

K.G., the abbreviation for *Knight of the Garter,* a knight companion of the highest order of knighthood in Great Britain, instituted between 1344 and 1350 by Edward III. The Duke of Holdernesse was a K.G. (PRIO).

Khalifa, The (1846–1899), the name given to *Seyyid Abdullah ibn-Seyyid Mohammed,* ruler of the Sudan from 1885 until his death in battle against the British. Holmes claimed to have visited the Khalifa at KHARTOUM during the Great Hiatus (EMPT).

Khan, Abdullah, one of the FOUR (SIGN).

Khartoum, the capital of the Sudan, at the confluence of the White and

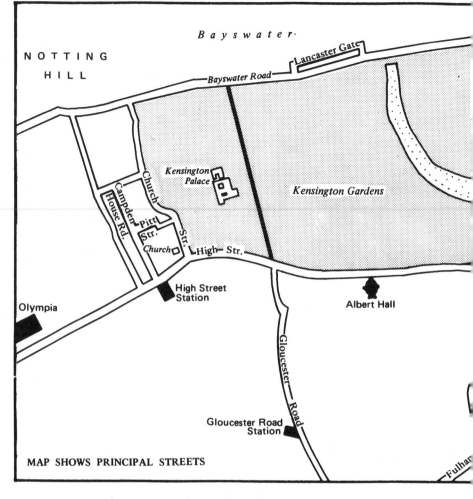

Kensington and Hyde Park.

Blue Nile, pop. (1907) 69,349. In 1885 it was taken by the Mahdi (1845–1885), the fanatical leader of the 1883–85 Sudanese insurrection, who massacred the entire British garrison, including its commander, General GORDON. In 1898 the city was recaptured by the British, who overthrew the Mahdi's successor, the KHALIFA. Holmes claimed to have visited Khartoum during the Great Hiatus (EMPT).

Khitmutgar (*kit'muht-gahr*), in India, the under-butler to the *khan-*

samah, or house-steward. Both Thaddeus and Bartholomew Sholto had a *khitmutgar* (SIGN), and Dr. Grimesby Roylott had been sentenced to a term of imprisonment for beating his native butler to death (SPEC).

Khyber Pass, the famous mountain pass in the north-east corner of Afghanistan, the chief gate between that country and India. Holmes referred to General de Merville as "De Merville of Khyber fame" (ILLU).

Kid. Holmes suggested that the

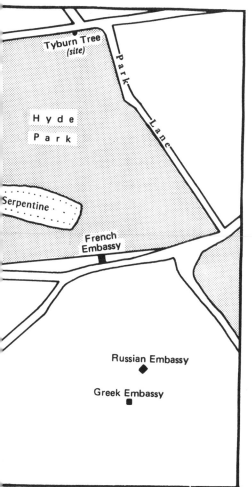

kidnapped Paul and Sophy Kratides, as well as Mr. Melas (GREE). Holmes did not take seriously his own suggestion to Lord Mount-James that Godfrey Staunton had been kidnapped (MISS), and Von Bork accused Holmes of kidnapping him (LAST). Lord Saltire had been abducted not for the purpose of levying ransom but to force the Duke of Holdernesse to leave his property to his illegitimate son (PRIO). Hugo Baskerville abducted the daughter of a yeoman (HOUN), and Jack Woodley and Williamson were convicted of abduction and assault (SOLI). Lady Frances Carfax (LADY) and Miss Burnet (WIST) were abducted, and it was believed

bones found at Wisteria Lodge were those of a lamb or a kid (WIST), and asked Sebastian Moran if he had never baited a tiger trap with a young kid (EMPT). Sir James Damery wore kid gloves (ILLU), and a black kid glove was found near Gorgiano's body (REDC).

Kidnapping, the act of forcibly carrying off a human being. *Abduction* is the particular act of leading away or carrying off a wife, child, or ward.

Harold Latimer and his accomplice

The most important of the gateways to India is the strongly guarded Khyber Pass, through which conquering armies for centuries have invaded the plains of Hindustan.

that Hatty Doran may have been (NOBL).

Kilburn, a region on the border between Middlesex and the London borough of Hampstead. James Ryder's friend Maudsley lived here (BLUE). See the front endpaper map.

Kimberley, a city of Cape Colony, centre of the South African diamond fields, pop. (1904) 34,331. Jack Woodley's reputation was known from Kimberley to Johannesburg (SOLI). See the map of SOUTH AFRICA.

King, Mrs., the cook at Ridling Thorpe Manor (DANC).

King Edward Street, a street in the City, north of St. Paul's. Duncan Ross, in his alias as William Morris, gave an address here (REDH). See Map I of LONDON.

King's College Hospital, a hospital in the City, founded in 1839 by King's College of the University of London. Dr. Percy Trevelyan occupied a minor position at the hospital while he devoted himself to research into nervous diseases (RESI). See Map II of LONDON.

King's Cross, an open area of central London, at the head of Gray's Inn Road. Mary Sutherland was to have been married at ST. SAVIOUR's church near here (IDEN). The adjoining **King's Cross Station** is the London terminus of the *Great Northern Railway,* and Holmes and Watson took a train for Cambridge here (MISS). See Map I of LONDON.

*King's Pyland, the Dartmoor training stable belonging to Colonel Ross (SILV).

Kingston-on-Thames, a pleasant residential town in the north of Surrey, situated upon the right bank of the Thames and forming one of the more exclusive suburbs of London, pop.

34,375. Baron Gruner lived near here (ILLU). See the back endpaper map.

Kirwin, William (d. 1887), the Cunninghams' coachman, who was murdered by his employers. His mother **Mrs. Kirwin,** who was always feebleminded, was made half-witted by the shock of her son's death (REIG).

K.K.K.: see KU KLUX KLAN.

Klein, the German sugar king. His widow **Isadora Klein,** of Pernambuco, became a notorious adventuress. Among her lovers was the late Douglas MABERLEY, whose novel about her she was determined to secure, and her efforts to do so prompted Maberley's mother to call upon Holmes (3GAB).

Klopman, the Nihilist from whom Holmes saved Von Bork's uncle (LAST).

Kneller, Sir Godfrey (1646–1723), a German-English portrait painter. One of the Baskerville family portraits was a Kneller (HOUN).

Knickerbockers, loosely-fitting knee-breeches, including the long stockings worn with them, worn by young boys and sportsmen. John Hopley Neligan was dressed in them (BLAC).

Knighthood, in Great Britain, a non-hereditary dignity conferred by the sovereign in recognition of personal merit or as a reward for services rendered to Crown or country. Knights have the right to the title *Sir* prefixed to the Christian name. Watson writes that Holmes refused a knighthood in June 1902 (3GAR) and had no interest in seeing his name upon the HONOURS LIST (BRUC). See also BARONET; C.B.; K.G.; LEGION OF HONOUR.

Knight's Place, a group of houses at the corner of the Wandsworth Road and Miles Street in south London (SIGN). See Map IV of LONDON.

Knock up, to arouse or get out of

bed by knocking at the door (ENGR, SIGN, SPEC).

Knocked up, exhausted with fatigue. Watson warned Holmes that he was knocking himself up in the Sholto case (SIGN).

Knox, Jack, an opponent of the Scowrers (VALL).

Kratides, Paul, a member of a wealthy Greek family who was tortured and murdered by Harold Latimer and Wilson Kemp, the abductors of his sister **Sophy Kratides,** in their effort to acquire the Kratides property. Sophy killed the two Englishmen in Buda-Pesth, but her fate is unknown (GREE).

Ku Klux Klan, a secret society founded in the southern part of the United States about 1866. The primary object of the society was social improvement, but its political purpose was to intimidate Negroes and those who favoured the government's reconstruction measures, and thus to prevent them from voting. Many outrages were committed by them, and in 1871 the government took active steps to break up the organization. The description found in Holmes's *American Encyclopædia* is almost wholly false (FIVE).

L

*Laburnum Vale, apparently a street or district of Chiswick, where Josiah Brown's home **Laburnum Villa** or **Laburnum Lodge** was located (SIXN). *Laburnum* is a name given to a number of small Alpine trees and other similar but unrelated plants.

*Lachine, the name of Colonel Barclay's villa at Aldershot (CROO). It is probably an Anglicization of the French *la Chine,* or "China."

Lady, in Great Britain, the proper title of any woman whose husband is a nobleman, or who is the daughter of a duke, marquis, or earl, though the title is given by courtesy also to the wives of baronets and knights. See PEERAGE.

Lady Day, the common name for 25 March, upon which the Feast of the Annunciation is celebrated. It is one of the QUARTER DAYS. Dr. Percy Trevelyan moved into his house on Lady Day (RESI), and the Wisteria Lodge case began in March shortly before quarter day (WIST).

"Lady Frances Carfax": see "DISAPPEARANCE OF LADY FRANCES CARFAX, THE."

*Lafter Hall, the residence of old Frankland (HOUN).

Lag, in underworld cant, to deliver into the hands of justice; to cause to be punished for a crime (MAZA, SIGN).

"La Jeune Fille à l'Agneau," painting: see GREUZE.

*Lake Saloon, the Chicago saloon where Jonas Pinto was shot (VALL).

Lal Chowdar: see CHOWDAR.

Lal Rao: see RAO.

Lama, a priest of that variety of Buddhism known as *Lamaism,* which dates from the seventh century and prevails chiefly in Tibet and Mongolia. In the priesthood there are two heads, in whom Buddha is supposed to be incarnate. These are the *Dalai Lama,* residing at Potala near Lhassa, and the *Panchen Lama,* often incorrectly called the "Teshai Lama" by Europeans, living at Shigatse. They are equal in rank and authority in name only, for the Dalai Lama is in reality much the more powerful, and he is the acknowledged head of the Buddhists not only in Tibet but throughout Mongolia and China.

Holmes claimed to have visited the "head Lama" of Tibet during the Great Hiatus (EMPT), but both the 13th Dalai Lama (1876–1933) and the 9th Panchen Lama (1882–1937) were sequestered youngsters undergoing instruction at the time, and the identity of whomever Holmes did visit remains a mystery. The misspelling *Llama* is common to many editions.

Lamb. Holmes suggested that the

bones found at Wisteria Lodge were those of a lamb or KID (WIST).

*Lamberley, a town in Sussex, where Robert Ferguson lived (SUSS).

Lambeth, a southern metropolitan borough of London, pop. 301,895. It is mostly of a residential and light manufacturing character, its inhabitants growing more affluent and less crowded as they reside farther to the south. The borough takes its name from the ancient region of Lambeth by the Thames, where old Sherman lived (SIGN). See the front endpaper map and Map IV of LONDON. See also BRIXTON; KENNINGTON; NORWOOD.

Lancashire, a north-western county of England, pop. 4,406,409. It is one of the principal manufacturing and shipping regions of the kingdom, the chief city and seaport being LIVERPOOL. The Duke of Holdernesse held mineral rights, granted by the Crown, here (PRIO).

Lancaster, James, a harpooner who came to be interviewed by "Captain Basil" (BLAC).

Lancaster Gate, a street of exclusive private residences lying immediately north of Hyde Park. Aloysius Doran took a house here (NOBL). See the map accompanying KENSINGTON.

Lance-corporal, a private performing the duties of a corporal, with temporary rank as such. Godfrey Emsworth had been a lance-corporal in the Imperial Yeomanry (BLAN).

"Lancet," an independently published British medical journal, begun in 1823. Dr. Mortimer was the author of "Some Freaks of Atavism" for the *Lancet* (HOUN), and Holmes wished to determine if Godfrey Emsworth's keeper was perhaps reading it (BLAN).

Landau, a two-seated carriage having the top in two parts, both of which are arranged to fold down behind the seats. Irene Adler kept a landau (SCAN), as did Colonel Ross (SILV).

Landau.

Lander, a Scowrer (VALL).

Langham Hotel, the most prestigious of London hotels, located in the West End. The King of Bohemia stayed at the Langham (SCAN), as did Captain Morstan (SIGN) and the Hon. Philip Green (LADY). See Map III of LONDON.

Langmere, a hamlet of southern Norfolk. Donnithorpe was said to be just north of here (GLOR).

Langur, a moderate-sized climbing monkey found throughout India. Lowenstein used a black-faced langur in preparing his rejuvenescent serum for Professor Presbury rather than an ANTHROPOID (CREE).

Lanner, the Scotland Yard inspector who investigated Blessington's apparent suicide (RESI).

Lantern: see BULL'S-EYE; DARK LANTERN; POCKET LANTERN; STABLE-LANTERN.

Lappet, a small flap or pendant decorating a hat or coat. Thaddeus Sholto wore lappets on his cap (SIGN).

Larbey, a beating victim of the Scowrers. His wife Mrs. Larbey was shot while nursing him (VALL).

Larceny, the misappropriation of the property of another without that person's consent. Commonly called *theft,* larceny is distinct from BURGLARY and ROBBERY.

Mary Holder stole the Beryl Coronet for her lover Sir George Burnwell (BERY), James Ryder and Catherine Cusack stole the Countess of Morcar's blue carbuncle (BLUE), and Joseph Harrison took the naval treaty (NAVA). The plans of the Bruce-Partington submarine were stolen from Woolwich Arsenal (BRUC), two mismatched boots were stolen from Sir Henry Baskerville (HOUN), a collection of worthless items was taken from old Acton's study (REIG), and the Agra treasure was stolen several times (SIGN). The black pearl of the Borgias had been stolen from the Prince of Colonna, and Lestrade characterized Beppo's attempts to recover it as nothing more than petty theft; and in fact Beppo had been in gaol for petty theft (SIXN).

John Clay was a well-known thief (REDH), and the butler Brunton was given notice for suspected theft (MUSG). Cash and securities were supposedly taken from Josiah Amberley's strong-room (RETI), and five attempts had been made to recover the photograph of Irene Adler and the King of Bohemia (SCAN). Holmes said that a thief or murderer could roam London unseen in the fog, and numerous petty thefts were indeed reported in the press (BRUC). He remarked too that petty thefts reported in the newspapers could often be traced back to Professor Moriarty (NORW).

Larch, a North American cone-bearing tree. The route from Utah passed among stands of larch (STUD).

Larkhall Lane, a street in Lambeth. Holmes's party crossed here on their way to meet Thaddeus Sholto (SIGN). See Map IV of LONDON.

La Rothière, Louis, an international agent, one of the few spies capable of playing such bold games as the thefts of the Trelawney Hope document (SECO) or the Bruce-Partington plans (BRUC).

La Scala, properly **Teatro alla Scala,** the great opera house of Milan. Irene Adler had sung here (SCAN).

Lascar, a native East Indian sailor. The keeper of the Bar of Gold was a Lascar (TWIS).

Lassus, Orlandus (d. 1594), or *Orlando Lasso,* originally *Roland Delattre,* the leading German composer of the sixteenth century. He composed over two thousand works, chiefly sacred, including between fifty and sixty masses, more than five hundred MOTETS, and hundreds more madrigals and songs. Holmes undertook a monograph upon the polyphonic motets of Lassus which was printed for private circulation and was said by some experts to be the last word upon the subject (BRUC).

Latimer, Harold, the kidnapper of Mr. MELAS, responsible too for the abduction of Sophy KRATIDES and the murder of her brother (GREE).

*****Latimer's,** an Oxford Street bootmaking firm (LADY).

Latin. The volume *De Jure inter Gentes* was published in Latin (STUD).

Latin characters, the common or block-letter method of printing, as opposed, for example, to the italic or Cyrillic. Holmes recognized that the word *"Rache,"* scrawled in blood near the body of Enoch Drebber, while printed somewhat after the German, or Gothic, fashion, had not been done by a German, who, he maintained, invariably prints in the Latin character (STUD).

Latin countries. Holmes said that it was well there was no fog in the Latin countries—"the countries of assassination" (BRUC). Watson called the Ferguson baby a wonderful mixture of the Saxon and the Latin (SUSS).

Latter-Day Saints: see MORMONS.

Lattice, work with open spaces formed by crossing, interlacing, or joining laths, bars, or rods of wood or metal. There were lattice-windows at Baskerville Hall and at Merripit House (HOUN). Hilton Soames's bedroom windows were lattice-paned (3STU).

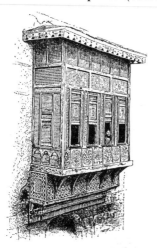

Lattice-window.

Laudanum, a brownish-red fluid, prepared from OPIUM and having the qualities of that drug, but in a milder degree. It is a frequent ingredient in patent medicines and is sometimes given to relieve colic and pains. Its use, however, is liable to be very injurious, and may lead to opium addiction. Isa Whitney first got the opium habit from drenching his tobacco with laudanum (TWIS).

Lauder, a town of central Scotland, pop. 719. Mrs. Stewart had lived here (EMPT).

Laurel, in common usage, any one of many diverse English garden plants (BRUC, CHAS, ILLU, NORW, REDH, SOLI, SPEC, VALL).

*Lauriston Gardens, a group of four houses off the Brixton Road, in one of which the body of Enoch Drebber was discovered (STUD).

Lausanne, a town in the west of Switzerland, near the Lake of Geneva, pop. (1900) 46,732. Lady Frances Carfax was last heard of from here (LADY).

Law: see BRITISH LAW.

Lawler, a Scowrer (VALL).

Lawyer: see BARRISTER; SOLICITOR.

Lay, a plan of action (HOUN).

Lead. The napoleons in the City and Suburban Bank vault were packed between layers of lead foil (REDH).

Leaded bourgeois type: see BOURGEOIS.

Leadenhall Street, a street in the City. Hosmer Angel said he was a cashier in a Leadenhall Street office, and Mary Sutherland addressed her letters to him at the Leadenhall Street Post Office (IDEN). See the map of the CITY.

Leader, a leading article in a newspaper, appearing as the expression of editorial opinion. Holmes said that the typeface of a *Times* leader was entirely distinctive (HOUN). Some of the London papers had leaders on the "Brixton Mystery" (STUD).

Leads (*ledz*), a flat roof covered with lead. Old Frankland's telescope stood on the flat leads of his house (HOUN).

League, a measure of length which varies in different countries. The English land league is three statute miles, and the nautical league is three equatorial miles, or 3.457875 statute miles. The French metric league is reckoned as equal to four kilometers, or 4,374 yards. The steamer *Norah Creina* was lost "some leagues" to the north of Oporto (RESI).

*League of Red-Headed Men: see RED-HEADED LEAGUE.

Leather: see MOROCCO; PATENT LEATHER; RUSSIAN LEATHER.

Leatherhead, a town in northern Surrey, pop. 4,694. Stoke Moran was twenty minutes' drive from here (SPEC). See the back endpaper map.

Lebanon, a city in Pennsylvania, pop. 17,628. Ezekiah Hopkins was said to have been from here (REDH).

Le Brun, a French "agent" who was beaten and crippled for life when he was inquiring into the affairs of Baron Gruner (ILLU).

Lecoq, the detective character created by Émile Gaboriau for a series of novels appearing 1866–69. While Watson admired the character, Holmes considered him a "miserable bungler" with nothing to recommend him save his energy (STUD).

Lee, a district in the northern part of Lewisham. Prior to the organization of the administrative county of LONDON it was a town of Kent. Neville St. Clair lived near here (TWIS), and John Scott Eccles was a resident (WIST). See the front endpaper map.

Lee, a Vermissa Valley mine-owner who was forced to sell out (VALL).

Lee, Robert E. (1807–1870), the commander-in-chief of the Confederate Army in the American Civil War (FIVE).

Leech: see RED LEECH.

Leeds Mercury, one of the most important of English provincial newspapers, established 1717 in the Yorkshire city of Leeds, and enjoying for many years a powerful moral and political influence in the North. Holmes confessed that when he was young he

once confused the type of the *Leeds Mercury* with the *Western Morning News* (HOUN).

Lee shore, in sailing, the shore toward which the wind is blowing (DEVI).

Lefevre, a man who escaped justice for a capital offense committed at Montpellier because there was no reliable test for blood stains (STUD).

Legation, an embassy (GREE, LAST).

Legion of Honour, a French order for the recognition of military and civil merit, instituted by Napoleon in 1802. The tracking and arrest of Huret, the Boulevard assassin, won for Holmes the Order of the Legion of Honour (GOLD).

Leicester (*les'ter*), the county-town of Leicestershire, pop. 211,579. The Birlstone murderer was reported from Leicester and nineteen other places (VALL).

Lemon. Watson gave Stanley Hopkins a "prescription" containing hot water and lemon (GOLD). See also FOUR OF GIN HOT.

Lens, or *magnifying glass.* Holmes's "lens" was an indispensable tool in his methods of crime detection. He made use of it to decipher the original inscription upon a palimpsest (GOLD), and Watson writes that a crack in one of his high-powered lenses would not be more disturbing to Holmes than a strong emotion within himself (SCAN). Mycroft Holmes declared that his *métier* was not to lie on his face with a lens to his eye (BRUC).

Holmes used his lens to study the tracks round the Boscombe Pool (BOSC), the laurel bush he found broken at Woolwich (BRUC), and the stone parapet of Thor Bridge (THOR). He examined the room in which Enoch Drebber was killed (STUD), the stairs at Pondicherry Lodge and the garret in which the Agra treasure had been hidden (SIGN), and one of the windows at Fairbanks (BERY). He examined the cracks between the stones of the floor in the City and Suburban Bank vault (REDH) and minutely studied Julia Stoner's bedroom, the hinges of her window-shutters, and the seat of one of Dr. Grimesby Roylott's chairs (SPEC).

Holmes offered James Windibank the use of his magnifying lens to observe the similarities in the typewritten letters from Windibank and from the missing Hosmer Angel (IDEN). He examined the cigar-ends found in Blessington's bedroom, and even without the lens, he said, it was easy to perceive by the scratches upon the key where pressure was applied to force the lock with a wire (RESI). He used his lens to study the Neligan notebook (BLAC), Henry Baker's hat (BLUE), the lamp in the room where Mortimer Tregennis died (DEVI), the scratch upon Professor Coram's bureau (GOLD), Dr. Mortimer's stick (HOUN), the marks upon Fitzroy McPherson's body (LION), the thumb-print at Deep Dene House (NORW), the rope used by Jonathan Small to climb into Bartholomew Sholto's chamber (SIGN), the blood-mark upon the Birlstone window-sill (VALL), and Watson's inherited watch (SIGN).

Leonardo (d. 1896), a circus strongman. The lover of Eugenia Ronder, he conspired with her to murder her husband but deserted her when she was attacked by the lion Sahara King. He was drowned in a bathing accident (VEIL).

Lepidoptera, the group of insects composed of moths and butterflies.

Stapleton's alias *Vandeleur* was given to a variety of moth which he was the first to describe, and he invited Watson to inspect his collection (HOUN). There were cases of butterflies and moths in Nathan Garrideb's flat (3GAR). Kitty Winter said that Baron Gruner collected women, and took "a pride in his collection, as some men collect moths or butterflies" (ILLU). See also CYCLOPIDES.

Leprosy. Godfrey Emsworth believed himself to have contracted leprosy at a South African leper hospital, but was in fact a victim of ichthyosis (BLAN). Part of Holmes's provisional theory of the Grant Munro problem was that Effie's first husband had possibly become a leper (YELL). Holmes remarked that Violet de Merville received him and Kitty Winter like "two rather leprous mendicants" (ILLU).

"Les Huguenots," an opera composed in 1836 by the German composer Giacomo Meyerbeer (1791–1864). Holmes had a box for a performance (HOUN).

Lesion, in pathology, any morbid change in the structure of an organ. The term is not restricted to anatomical changes, but may be applied to such as are revealed solely by a disturbance of function. A *nervous lesion* is one seated in or affecting some part of the nervous system. Dr. Percy Trevelyan was the author of a monograph upon obscure nervous lesions (RESI).

Lestrade, G., an inspector at Scotland Yard. Holmes called him the best of the professionals (HOUN), the "pick of a bad lot"—quick and energetic, but conventional (STUD), lacking in imagination (NORW), and normally out of his depth (SIGN). Nonetheless, Holmes said, Lestrade's "bulldog tenacity" had brought him to the top at Scotland Yard (CARD).

He professed a patronizing attitude toward Holmes's methods, yet he consulted Holmes in a number of cases, among them an early forgery case (STUD), the affair of the cardboard box (CARD), and the destruction of the Napoleonic busts (SIXN), and he and his rival Gregson together engaged Holmes in the Drebber murder (STUD). He was retained by those who believed in James McCarthy's innocence to investigate the Boscombe Valley tragedy in McCarthy's interest, and he in turn referred the case to Holmes (BOSC). Holmes refused to consult with him in finding the killers of Charles Augustus Milverton (CHAS).

He was assigned to investigate the deaths of Arthur Cadogan West (BRUC), Jonas Oldacre (NORW), and Eduardo Lucas (SECO) and was in charge of the St. Simon case (NOBL). He and Holmes had shared the "bogus laundry affair" (CARD), and he assisted Holmes in the taking of Sebastian Moran (EMPT). Holmes said that during the Great Hiatus he had investigated three murders in one year which he was unable to solve, but that he handled the Molesey Mystery fairly well (EMPT).

Holmes called Lestrade in for the end of the Baskerville case (HOUN) and consulted the Scotland Yarder in his search for Lady Frances Carfax (LADY). He helped Holmes locate Killer Evans in the Scotland Yard rogues' gallery in 1902 (3GAR), to complete some forty years with the C.I.D., having already put in twenty years in the early 1880s (STUD).

Lesurier, Madame, the proprietress

of a Bond Street milliner's where John Straker purchased his mistress's clothes (SILV).

Let in, in English slang, to cheat or to involve another in something undesirable. Cyril Overton felt that Godfrey Staunton must have had cause to "let in" his Rugby skipper (MISS), and the firm of Coxon & Woodhouse were "let in" through an unsuccessful business venture (STOC).

Leturier, a man who was murdered in Montpellier by the forcible administration of poison (STUD).

Leuk (*loik*), an ancient and very picturesque town in the south-west of Switzerland, built above the right bank of the Rhone, pop. (1900) 1,592. Holmes and Watson left the valley of the Rhone here (FINA).

Leverstoke, Lord, the father of a Priory School boy (PRIO).

Leverton, the Pinkerton detective who pursued Giuseppe Gorgiano from New York to London (REDC).

Lewes, the county-town of Sussex, pop. 11,249. Constable Anderson said he would "hear of it from Lewes" if he went wrong in the McPherson case (LION).

Lewis, Sir George. Sir James Damery negotiated with him over the Hammerford Will case (ILLU).

Lewisham, a south-eastern metropolitan borough of London, pop. 127,495. It is a favoured middle-class residential quarter, for the most part occupied by villas and semi-detached houses. Josiah Amberley lived here (RETI), and Stanley Hopkins spoke of the Randalls as "that Lewisham gang of burglars" (ABBE). See the front endpaper map. See also BLACKHEATH; LEE; SYDENHAM.

Lexington, Mrs., the housekeeper of

Jonas Oldacre, who conspired with her master to incriminate John Hector McFarlane (NORW).

Lhassa, the capital of Tibet, est. pop. 10,000. It is a great centre of Buddhism and is visited by thousands of pilgrims from China, Turkestan, and Nepaul. Late in the eighteenth century a law was established that no foreigner might enter the city, a prohibition which was not broken until it was entered by British forces in 1904. Holmes said that he visited Lhassa during the Great Hiatus (EMPT).

by the people by means of trust in the people.

Sir Charles Baskerville was a Liberal (HOUN). The *Standard,* in its editorial about the Drebber murder, commented upon the fact that lawless outrages of that sort usually occurred under a Liberal Administration; and the editorial in the *Daily News* observed that the Continental Governments were animated by despotism and hatred of Liberalism (STUD).

For Liberal newspapers see DAILY CHRONICLE; DAILY NEWS; DAILY TELE-

A view of Lhassa from the north, with the Himalayas beyond.

Libel, in law, the act of publishing malicious statements with the intent to expose persons or institutions to public hatred, contempt, or ridicule. The difference between libel and slander is that in the former case the defamation must be in writing or some other visible manner, while in the latter the offense is committed verbally. In calling Moriarty a criminal, Holmes said, Watson uttered libel in the eyes of the law (VALL).

Liberal Party, a British political party, opposed to the Conservatives. Broadly speaking, it stands for progressive legislation and advanced ethical ideas, claiming to represent government

GRAPH; ECHO; PALL MALL GAZETTE; STAR, THE.

Lichen. Lichen mottled the walls of Hatherley Farm (BOSC), the Stoke Moran manor house (SPEC), the wall round The Haven (RETI), and the roof of Cheeseman's (SUSS). Lichen studded the gate-pillars of Baskerville Hall (HOUN) and Charlington Hall (SOLI) and the court of St. Luke's College (3STU).

Lieder: see MENDELSSOHN-BARTHOLDY, FELIX.

Liége (*lyaij*), a town of Belgium, pop. (1900) 157,760. The volume *De Jure inter Gentes* was published here in 1642 (STUD), at which time the city was the capital of the ecclesiastical state known as the Bishopric of Liége.

Life interest, an interest in an estate which terminates with the life of the person to whom it belongs and may not be passed on at his death, the estate becoming instead subject to REVERSION. Lady Beatrice Falder held a life interest in Shoscombe Old Place (SHOS).

Life-preserver, a short stick with a weighted head, used as a weapon. Sir George Burnwell threatened Holmes (BERY) and Wilson Kemp threatened Mr. Melas (GREE) with a life-preserver, and Hugo Oberstein killed Cadogan West with one (BRUC).

Light Blue, a Cambridge 'Varsity athlete (MISS); see BLUE.

Lighter, a barge used in the loading and unloading of ships (SIGN); see the photographs on pp. 226 and 278.

Lighthouse. Folk who were in grief came to Mrs. Watson like birds to a lighthouse (TWIS). The elder Neligan was murdered two nights before the crew of the *Sea Unicorn* sighted the SHETLAND LIGHTS (BLAC). Watson's notes of Holmes's cases included that of "the politician, the lighthouse and the trained cormorant" (VEIL).

Lime, or *linden,* a common European ornamental tree. The drive leading to Trevor Senior's house was lime-lined (GLOR).

Lime-cream, a hair-cream scented with the fragrance of the aromatic flower of the common lime tree (BLUE).

Lime Street, a street in the City, lying between Leadenhall Street and Fenchurch Street. Von Seddar apparently lived here (MAZA). See the map of the CITY.

Lincoln, Abraham (1809–1865). Watson said that J. Neil Gibson gave

the impression of an Abraham Lincoln keyed to base uses instead of high ones (THOR).

Linder: see MAX LINDER AND CO.

Line, in coursing: see SWING TO THE LINE.

Lion. Eugenia Ronder was mutilated by a circus lion named Sahara King (VEIL). Dr. Leon Sterndale was a famous lion-hunter (DEVI), and Count Sylvius had shot lions in Algeria (MAZA).

"Lion's Mane, The Adventure of the" (LION), a chronicle which appeared originally in the *Strand* magazine for December 1926 and *Liberty* magazine of 27 November 1926 and was published in the collection entitled *The Case Book of Sherlock Holmes* the following year. It is written by Holmes himself and concerns his interest in the apparent assaults upon Fitzroy McPherson and Ian Murdoch during the summer of 1907, some years following his retirement from active practice.

Liquor: see BRANDY; CURAÇAO; GIN; RUM; WHISKY; see also WINE. See also PUBLIC-HOUSE.

List, a kind of cheap wool. The charwomen at the Foreign Office wore list slippers (NAVA).

Literature. During their early association Watson came to believe that Holmes knew nothing of contemporary literature; his list of Holmes's limits rated the detective's knowledge of literature as "nil," though his knowledge of what Watson termed "sensational literature" was described as "immense," for Holmes appeared to know "every detail of every horror perpetrated in the century" (STUD). Some years later Watson was to recall his evaluation with much humour (FIVE).

Lithotype. Holmes's monograph upon

the influence of the trade upon the form of the hand, he said, was illustrated by "lithotypes" of six different hands (SIGN). What he meant to say was *lithographs,* prints made by a process in which the image to be printed is first etched upon a piece of specially-prepared stone. A "lithotype" is actually a kind of STEREOTYPE reproduced by lithography.

Litmus-paper, a kind of paper sensitive to acids or to alkali, indispensable in chemical analyses (NAVA).

Little George Street, a short street in the borough of St. Pancras, lying just west of Euston Station. Halliday's Private Hotel was here (STUD). See Map I of LONDON.

*Little Purlington, a town in Essex, where Mr. Elman had his vicarage (RETI).

Little Russia, or the *Ukraine,* the name commonly given to a region of south Russia lying north of the Black Sea. Holmes said that an incident here in 1866 was analogous to the Baskerville case (HOUN). See the map of EUROPE.

*Little Ryder Street, the street in which Nathan Garrideb lived, described as a small offshoot from the Edgware Road, "within a stone-cast" of the old TYBURN TREE (3GAR), apparently located, therefore, in the south-eastern quarter of Paddington known as *Tyburnia.* Holmes refers to it once simply as *Ryder Street,* which is the name of a street near St. James's, Westminster, not in Tyburnia.

Liverpool, the second largest city and seaport of England, situated in Lancashire, pop. 684,958.

The Browners lived in Liverpool (CARD), where Count Sylvius planned to divert Holmes (MAZA)

and where a clue in the Priory School case came to naught (PRIO). The Birlstone murderer was reported from Liverpool and nineteen other places (VALL). Cunard liners sail from here (ILLU), and Drebber and Stangerson were planning to sail from Liverpool to New York but failed to take the express from London (STUD).

See also GRAND NATIONAL; NEW BRIGHTON.

Liverpool, Dublin, and London Steam Packet Company, the company for which James Browner worked as a steward (CARD).

Liverpool Street Station, a London railway station lying just north of the City boundary, London terminus of the *Great Eastern Railway.* Trains for Norfolk (DANC) and Little Purlington (RETI) departed from here. See Map I of LONDON and the map of London's RAILWAY STATIONS.

Living, in the Church of England, any ecclesiastical office by virtue of which the incumbent, usually a parish clergyman, has the right to enjoy certain church revenues on condition of discharging his services. The system of "pluralities" whereby the same incumbent might hold two or more livings has in the reign of Victoria been abridged so that no one may now hold two livings unless the churches associated with them are within three miles of each other and the annual value of one of them does not exceed £100, as in the case of J. C. Elman's receiving the living of *Mossmoor-cum-Little Purlington* as vicar of Little Purlington (RETI).

Llama: see LAMA.

Lloyd's, an association of merchants, shipowners, underwriters, and ship and insurance brokers, having its head-

At Lloyd's.

quarters in the Royal Exchange in London. Originally a gathering of merchants for business or gossip in a coffee-house kept by one *Edward Lloyd* (*fl. c.*1700) in the latter seventeenth century, this institution has gradually become one of the greatest organizations in the world in connexion with commerce. According to the 1871 act of incorporation, the main objects for which the society exists are the carrying out of the business of marine insurance; the protection of the interests of the members; and the collection, publication, and diffusion of intelligence and information with respect to shipping.

The annual "Lloyd's **Register of British and Foreign Shipping**" is published by an association of members of Lloyd's and contains the names of vessels, classifying them in accordance with their method of construction, age,

and state of repair. The registry offices occupy separate quarters in Fenchurch Street. Holmes found the *Lone Star* in Lloyd's registers (FIVE). See the map of the CITY.

Locus standi, a Latin phrase meaning *place of standing,* that is, one's recognized position. Holmes said that he and Watson's *locus standi* at the Copper Beeches was rather a questionable one (COPP), though in this sense it is not a legal term.

Lode, a deposit of ore. Jefferson Hope and his companions discovered some silver lodes in the Nevada Mountains (STUD).

Lodgekeeper, a servant who has charge of the entrance-gate to an estate and lives in a cottage or *lodge* nearby; a gatekeeper. There was a lodgekeeper at the Abbey Grange (ABBE), and a "keeper" opened the gates to Shoscombe Old Place (SHOS). Moran was the lodgekeeper for the Boscombe Valley Estate (BOSC). McMurdo was Bartholomew Sholto's "porter, or gatekeeper" (SIGN).

Lomax, the sub-librarian of the London Library, to whom Watson applied for a book about Chinese pottery (ILLU).

Lombard Street, a street in the City, running eastward from the Bank of England to Fenchurch Street. Among the busiest thoroughfares in London, it has been the most noted street in the City for banking and finance for more than five hundred years. It takes its name from the "Lombard" money-dealers from Genoa and Florence who in the fourteenth and fifteenth centuries took the place of the discredited and persecuted Jews as money-lenders. The stockbroking firm of Mawson & Williams' was here (STOC). See the map of the CITY.

Lomond, Duke of, the betrothed of Isadora Klein (3GAB). *Loch Lomond* is a well-known lake in west-central Scotland.

London, the largest city in the world, the capital of England and the British Empire, pop. 6,581,402. It is located in the south-eastern part of England on the river THAMES, which runs through the city from east to west and is navigable as far as the metropolis. London south of the river, which is the less important part of it, extends into the counties of SURREY and KENT, and in the north into MIDDLESEX and ESSEX.

The commercial and money-making parts of London are in the EAST END; here are the docks, the BANK OF ENGLAND, the STOCK EXCHANGE, the general post office, and many public buildings, besides the great ST. PAUL's cathedral. The WEST END, which is exclu-

The view from Whitehall to the Houses of Parliament.

sively associated with higher-class life, contains the Houses of Parliament, Westminster Abbey, the royal palaces, the Government offices round WHITEHALL, the BRITISH MUSEUM and other cultural and scientific institutions, and the residences of the aristocracy and wealthy citizens.

The administrative County of London, as it was politically organized in 1888, is about 16 miles long and 10′ miles wide, covering an area of 117 square miles and including 4,509,618 inhabitants; see the front endpaper map. Beyond these limits, however, is a wide area extending some 15 miles in every direction from CHARING CROSS, the official centre of the metropolis, and embracing about 700 square miles, which is almost exclusively devoted to suburbs supporting an additional population of more than two million; see the back endpaper map. The City of London proper is a separate municipality having an ancient and unique government of its own; see CITY, THE.

London is not a beautiful city, though it has many magnificent buildings and some fine streets. In the business portions the streets are narrow and crooked, and the fogs and smoke have rendered the buildings unattractive in appearance. East of the City proper lies

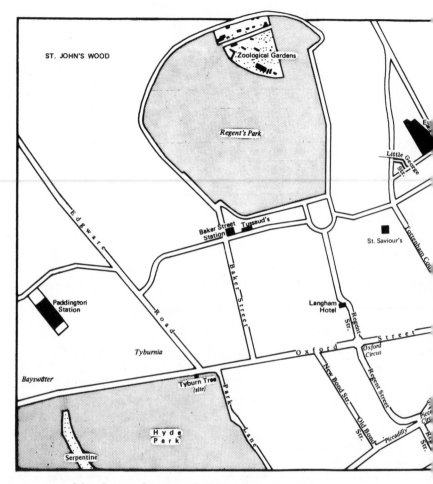

MAP I: *London from Paddington to the City.*

one of the most densely crowded and poorest regions on earth. In striking contrast are the homes of the lower middle classes to the north of the City, where hundreds of thousands dwell in comparative comfort, and the other thousands of luxurious homes of the wealthy middle class and the aristocracy far out to the west. South of the Thames poor quarters are to be found adjacent to the river over the whole distance from Lambeth to Greenwich, merging southward into better class residential districts. London has no well-defined manufacturing quarter.

Communication. Communication among the different parts of the city is effected by cabs, tramways, omnibus lines, and the steamboats which ply regularly along the Thames from its mouth as far as Oxford. Elaborate UNDERGROUND RAILWAY systems afford access to every district and join the great national and suburban RAILWAY

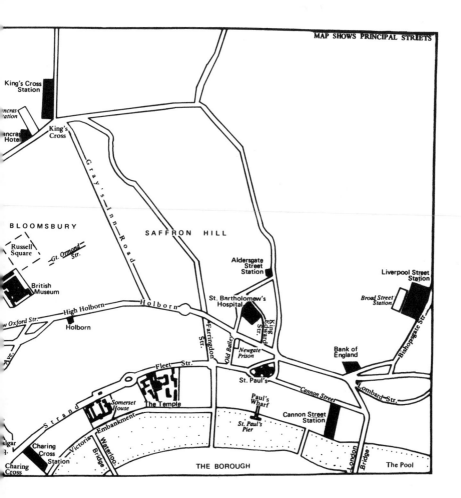

STATIONS of London. The river is spanned by a number of broad bridges, some of which have been constructed upon the sites of other structures erected hundreds of years ago, and all of which are so arranged as not to interfere with navigation.

Nearly five hundred newspapers of all sorts are published in London and its environs; see NEWSPAPER. Telephone service was given needed stimulation with the creation in 1901 of a second telephone exchange, operated by the Post Office in competition with the private National Telephone Company, while intercommunication between the two systems is provided for; see TELEPHONE. See also COMMISSIONNAIRE; DISTRICT MESSENGER; DIRECTORY.

The first systematic attempt to provide for the lighting of the streets after dark began with oil lamps in the City in 1736. Gaslights were introduced in

The West End is exclusively associated with the higher-class life of London. Park Lane, shown here, is the most prestigious thoroughfare in the metropolis.

1807 in Westminster, and service was effectively developed over the ensuing fifty years to include all of the metropolis; see GAS, ILLUMINATING. Electrification was begun during the 1870s and is proceeding rapidly.

Streets and Parks. Among the noted streets which run from east to west are Piccadilly, PALL MALL, the STRAND and its continuation FLEET STREET, OXFORD STREET and its continuations HIGH HOLBORN and HOLBORN. The EMBANKMENT extends along the north shore of the Thames north and east from the Houses of Parliament. Major thoroughfares extending northward are TOTTENHAM COURT ROAD, REGENT STREET, BOND STREET, EDGWARE ROAD, and BAKER STREET. Upon the Surrey shore the principal thoroughfares include the WATERLOO ROAD, WANDSWORTH ROAD, and BRIXTON ROAD.

HYDE PARK is the most fashionable of London's parks, which include Regent's Park and St. James's Park in the West End, Greenwich Park and BLACKHEATH in the south-east, HAMPSTEAD HEATH upon the north, and WANDSWORTH COMMON and the Kennington Oval (see OVAL, THE) in the south. Regent's Park contains the gardens of the Zoological Society, or the zoo. Provision is made for cricket, football, RUGBY, and other games in a number of the three dozen parks throughout the metropolis. Fashionable society takes its pastimes at the grounds of private clubs such as the Ranelagh, the HURLINGHAM, and PRINCE'S. See also TURF, THE.

Cultural Life. There are many music halls, theatres, concert halls, and opera houses presenting every variety of entertainment, among them ALBERT HALL, the ALLEGRO, COVENT GARDEN THEATRE, the CRITERION, HAYMARKET THEATRE, IMPERIAL THEATRE, LYCEUM THEATRE, ST. JAMES'S HALL, and WOOL-

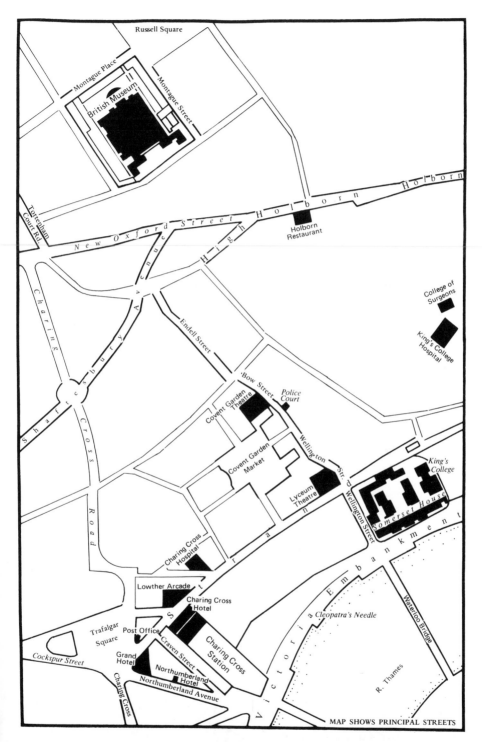

MAP II: *London from the British Museum to Charing Cross.*

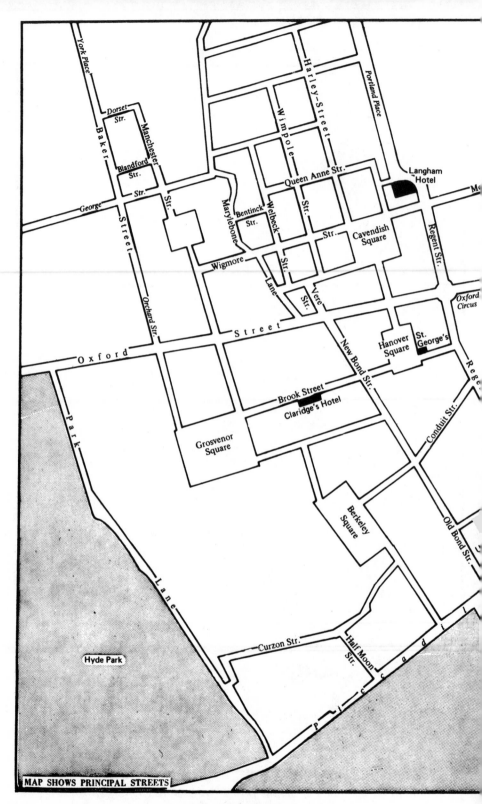

MAP III: *The West End.*

WICH THEATRE; see also CRYSTAL PAL-ACE; OLYMPIA; TUSSAUD'S. The principal CLUBS and picture-galleries are in and about Piccadilly and Pall Mall. See also COLLEGE OF SURGEONS; LONDON LIBRARY; also LONDON SEASON.

Public Buildings and Monuments. St. James's Palace, Buckingham Palace, and Kensington Palace are among the royal palaces which grace the city. The imposing Houses of Parliament stand upon the Thames in Westminster (see PARLIAMENT, HOUSES OF), and other noteworthy buildings are WESTMINSTER ABBEY, Somerset House (see DOCTORS' COMMONS), the TOWER OF LONDON, and the Inns of Court (see TEMPLE, THE). Notwithstanding its fogs and dirt, London is, taken as a whole, one of the healthiest cities in the world, and its public and charitable institutions are numerous; e.g., CHARING CROSS HOSPITAL; KING'S COLLEGE HOSPITAL; ST. BARTHOLOMEW'S HOSPITAL. Throughout the city are many monuments and statues; see DUKE OF YORK'S STEPS; TRAFALGAR SQUARE.

Commerce. The commerce of London is enormous. Besides that which is transacted over the railways from Southampton and Liverpool, and the internal commerce with the other cities of Great Britain, there is an immense tonnage from all parts of the world arriving at the extensive system of docks in the East End. That part of the Thames below London Bridge and the POOL is devoted almost exclusively to these docks, the most important being the WEST INDIA DOCKS, the Surrey Commercial Docks of ROTHERHITHE, and the BLACKWALL system, all round the ISLE OF DOGS; the Royal Victoria and Albert system (see ALBERT DOCK); and the newly built Tilbury Docks in Essex, opposite GRAVESEND, which the

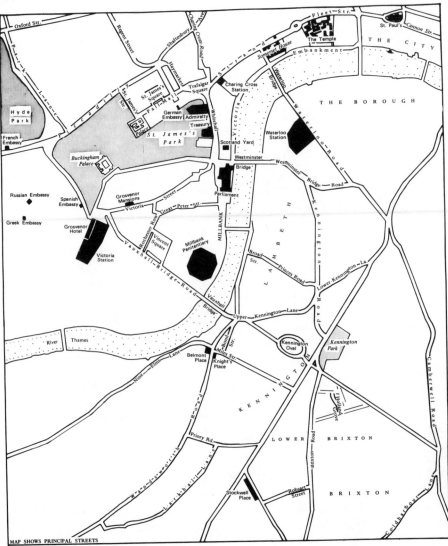

MAP IV: *Westminster and the Surrey Side.*

largest steamers now use. A consolidated *Port of London Authority* was brought into being in 1909. See also LLOYD'S.

The value of the imports received here is estimated at more than one-third that of all the United Kingdom, while the manufactures of London are almost limitless in number and variety.

Shops, bazaars, and markets abound everywhere, though the most attractive shops are in the West End round Regent Street and Oxford Street, and the wholesale markets are principally in the City; see COVENT GARDEN MARKET; see also LOWTHER ARCADE.

Government. Excluding the City, the County of London is divided into twenty-eight metropolitan boroughs, each governed by a mayor and a council; see BERMONDSEY; BOROUGH, THE (Southwark); CAMBERWELL; GREENWICH; HAMMERSMITH; HAMPSTEAD; KENSINGTON; LAMBETH; LEWISHAM; PADDINGTON; POPLAR; ST. PANCRAS; STEPNEY; WESTMINSTER; WOOLWICH. The Metropolitan Police, or SCOTLAND YARD, is not a municipal organization but is administered by the Government at Whitehall; see also MILLBANK PENITENTIARY; NEWGATE CALENDAR; PENTONVILLE PRISON; TYBURN TREE. The postal authorities divide Greater London into eight postal districts; see EAST LONDON; E.C. (*East Central*); N.W. (*North-West*); S.W. (*South-West*); W. (*West London*). See also BOARD SCHOOL; WORKHOUSE.

For London suburbs see BECKENHAM; CHISWICK; CROYDON; EAST HAM;

Postal map of London.

ESHER; HARROW-ON-THE-HILL; HARROW WEALD; KILBURN; KINGSTON-ON-THAMES; MARSHAM; NORBURY; NORWOOD; OXSHOTT; PENGE; PINNER; RICHMOND; WALLINGTON; WILLESDEN; WIMBLEDON.

See also the maps of BAKER STREET; CITY, THE; KENSINGTON; WHITEHALL; the endpaper maps; also the maps accompanying SCOTLAND YARD; RAILWAY STATIONS; UNDERGROUND RAILWAY.

The crowded streets of the City teem with all the peoples of the Empire. Note the overflowing London omnibuses at left and the costermongers with their barrows upon the right.

The Pool, the highest point of the Thames which may be reached by ocean-going vessels. The above view is westward, or up-river, with the Borough on the left and the City upon the right. The hazy dome of St. Paul's can be seen above the roof of Cannon Street Station. The nearest of the three bridges is London Bridge. Observe the clusters of lighters riding at anchor in mid-river. In the reverse perspective below, the Pool is spanned by the new Tower Bridge, and beyond sprawl Stepney, the Isle of Dogs, and the rest of the East End, with the line of the North Downs, twenty miles away in Kent, upon the horizon. In the fore-ground, left and centre, may be seen some of the more than 25,000 tenement "sweat-shops" which infest the City.

London, University of, an institution of higher learning in Westminster,

The University of London before its move in 1900 to more spacious quarters nearby.

chartered 1836. Until 1898 the university was not a teaching establishment but merely an examining board, granting degrees in arts, science, medicine, music, and law, to candidates wherever educated. Teaching functions were assumed in 1898. Watson took his degree of Doctor of Medicine here in 1878 (STUD), and Dr. Percy Trevelyan said that he was a London University man (RESI).

London Bridge, the oldest and most important of the bridges over the Thames, and until the late eighteenth century the only one. It connects the City with the Borough. The present structure was built of granite between 1825 and 1831, and carries some 22,000 vehicles and 110,000 pedestrians across the river daily. Upper Swandam Lane was said to be located just east of London Bridge; and it probably was the "broad balustraded bridge" across which Holmes and Watson drove (TWIS).

The large seagoing vessels have access to the Thames only as far as the POOL immediately below the bridge, and so upstream from here the riverbank is dotted with small piers and wharves, but not with any extensive system of docks. For miles below the bridge, however, as Holmes observed, there is a "perfect labyrinth" of landing-places in which the *Aurora* could hide (SIGN).

London Bridge Station, a railway

London Bridge, looking toward the City.

station in Bermondsey, the main terminus of the *London, Brighton and South Coast Railway,* and shared by the *South-Eastern and Chatham Railway.* Holmes and his party embarked for Woolwich (BRUC) and Beckenham (GREE) from here, and Watson arrived here from Blackheath (RETI). John Hector McFarlane took a train from Norwood to London Bridge Station, from which he was followed by the police to Baker Street (NORW). See the map accompanying RAILWAY STATIONS.

London Library, a circulating library for paying members, located in St. James's Square. Watson was probably a member and applied to Lomax, the sub-librarian, for a book about Chinese pottery (ILLU). See Map III of LONDON.

London Road. Watson writes that he and Holmes drove down the "London Road" from The Cedars (TWIS), almost certainly a reference to the *Lee High Road.*

London season, the months of May, June, and July, when Parliament is sitting, the aristocracy are at their town residences, and the world's great artists are performing in the metropolis. Lady Eva Brackwell was the most beautiful *débutante* of the season before her marriage (CHAS), and Hatty Doran had been brought to London for the season (NOBL).

London University: see LONDON, UNIVERSITY OF.

*Lone Star, the American barque, commanded by Captain James Calhoun, which apparently was lost in an Atlantic gale in September 1887 (FIVE).

*Long Down, a place on Dartmoor, where Dr. Mortimer excavated a neo-

lithic barrow (HOUN). *Longdown* is a hamlet south-east of Exeter, but it is thirty miles from Dartmoor.

Long Island, an island off New York, and belonging to it. Holmes called Leverton the hero of the "Long Island Cave mystery" (REDC), which may allude to Long Island itself, though there are no caves here.

Long vacation, the period from July to October during which an English university is formally closed (GLOR).

Loose-box, the enclosed part of a stable without stalls (MISS).

Lopez, the secretary of Don Murillo, who was murdered together with his master in Madrid. He was sometimes known by the aliases *Lucas* and *Rulli* (WIST).

Lord, a title of honour given in Great Britain to noblemen other than dukes, and as a courtesy to certain other persons; see PEERAGE. For names beginning thus, see the second element; e.g. for *Lord Saltire* see SALTIRE, LORD.

Lord-Lieutenant, the principal official of an English county, appointed by the Crown, who controls the appointment of justices of the peace and the issue of commissions in the local military organizations. The Duke of Holdernesse was Lord-Lieutenant of Hallamshire (PRIO).

*Lord Street, a street in Brixton, where Stanley Hopkins apparently lived (BLAC).

Lothario, a libertine in the play *The Fair Penitent,* written in 1703 by the English dramatist Nicholas Rowe (1674–1718). Holmes compared Ray Ernest with the character (RETI).

Louisiana, one of the southern states of the United States, pop. 1,381,625. The Ku Klux Klan had branches here (FIVE).

Louvre, hotel: see HÔTEL DU LOUVRE.

Love-gage, a love-pledge; a token of one's faith given to another (GOLD).

Love-lock, formerly a long and flowing lock of a man's hair, dressed separately and allowed to hang down in front of the shoulder. In some instances two were worn, one on each side. Love-locks were fashionable during the first half of the seventeenth century, and Hugo Baskerville was painted wearing them (HOUN).

Lowenstein, H., an obscure scientist, living in Prague, whose rejuvenescent serum Professor Presbury took (CREE).

Lower Brixton: see BRIXTON.

Lower Brixton Road: see BRIXTON ROAD.

*****Lower Burke Street,** the residential street, lying in the borderland between Notting Hill and Kensington, in which Culverton Smith lived (DYIN).

Lower Camberwell: see CAMBERWELL.

*****Lower Gill Moor,** the moor which lay to the north of the Priory School (PRIO).

*****Lower Grove Road,** the street in Reading in which Mr. Sandeford lived (SIXN).

Lower Norwood: see NORWOOD.

Lowlands, the low-lying part of Europe along the North Sea coast occupied by Belgium and the Netherlands (STUD).

Lowther Arcade, a London bazaar, located in the Strand. This emporium houses pleasant covered walks between rows of shops stocked with toys and other useful articles at moderate prices. Watson's route to Victoria Station lay through here (FINA). See Map II of LONDON.

Lucas: see LOPEZ.

Lucas, Eduardo, the international agent who blackmailed Lady Hilda Trelawney Hope into stealing a government document from her husband's dispatch-box. For years he had lived a double life as Eduardo Lucas in London and as *Henri Fournaye* in Paris, where he lived with his French wife. He was murdered by **Madame Fournaye,** who was apprehended by the Parisian police (SECO).

Lucca, Gennaro, an Italian living in New York, and an impressed member of the Red Circle. He and his wife **Emilia Lucca** fled to London to escape the society, and Gennaro there killed Giuseppe GORGIANO (REDC).

Lucerne, a city and highly popular tourist resort of central Switzerland, pop. (1900) 29,255. The non-existent consumptive Englishwoman was said to be journeying to Lucerne (FINA), and Douglas Maberley's trunks passed through here on their way to England (3GAB). See the map of SWITZERLAND.

Lucerne.

Lucknow, a city in India, pop. 264,000. It was besieged during the Mutiny and relieved by a British force which was itself besieged. A second relief force under Sir Colin CAMPBELL allowed the inhabitants to be evacuated (SIGN).

Lumbago, rheumatic pains affecting the muscles of the loins. Watson suggested that Professor Presbury's peculiar crouched posture was due to lumbago (CREE).

Lumber-room, a room for the storage of *lumber,* that is, household items, more or less bulky and cumbersome, set aside as of no present use or value. A lumber-room is commonly at the top of a house, under the eaves; an attic. One of the Baker Street lumber-rooms was used to file copies of old daily papers (SIXN), and Elias Openshaw kept the relics of his life in America in his (FIVE). Alexander Holder's bureau was opened with the key to the cupboard in his house's lumber-room (BERY).

Holmes considered a man's brain like an empty attic, and believed that only a fool took in "all the lumber of every sort" that he came across (STUD). "A man should keep his little brain attic stocked with all the furniture that he is likely to use," he said, "and the rest he can put away in the lumber-room of his library" (FIVE), a remark he directly contradicted later in life when he referred to his own mind as a crowded BOX-ROOM (LION).

Lunkah, a strong Indian cigar resembling a cheroot (SIGN).

Lurcher, a variety of hunting dog, best known in England, where it is much favoured by poachers. The species is said to be descended from the collie and the greyhound. TOBY was half spaniel and half lurcher (SIGN).

Luxembourg, the capital of the grand duchy of the same name, pop. (1905) of the city 20,984, of the duchy 246,455. Holmes and Watson made

their way into Switzerland by way of Luxembourg (FINA). See the map of EUROPE.

Lyceum Theatre, one of the chief London theatres, located in the Strand. Shakespearean pieces, comedies, and dramas are presented. The rendezvous with Thaddeus Sholto's servant took place outside the Lyceum (SIGN).

The old Lyceum Theatre, in Wellington Street, Strand, before it was rebuilt in 1904.

Lynch: see JUDGE LYNCH.

Lynch, Victor, a forger entered in Holmes's index (SUSS).

Lynx, the name given to various wild cats found throughout the world. It was said that Jefferson Hope's prairie training had given him the ears of a lynx (STUD).

*Lyon Place, the street in Camberwell in which Mary Sutherland lived with her mother and stepfather (IDEN).

Lyons, an artist who lived for some time upon Dartmoor. He married the daughter of old FRANKLAND and then deserted her. His wife **Laura Lyons** became the dupe of Stapleton in the murder of Sir Charles Baskerville (HOUN).

Lyons (*lee-oN'*), the third largest city of France, pop. 459,099. Watson received a telegram informing him that Holmes was lying ill here, and immediately hurried to his side (REIG).

M

M.A., the abbreviation for the degree *Master of Arts* (RETI).

Maberley, Mortimer, a man who once used Holmes's services in some "trifling matter." His widow **Mary Maberley** called upon Holmes in the affair of the Three Gables, which was found to be linked to the novel written by her son **Douglas Maberley** to expose Isadora Klein before his death by pneumonia while attaché at Rome (3GAB).

MacDonald, Alec, a Scotland Yard inspector. Originally from Aberdeen, he apparently joined the force during the 1880s and by 1914 had achieved national fame. He did not hesitate to consult Holmes in difficult cases, and he did so in the Birlstone affair (VALL).

Machiavelli, Niccolò (1469–1527), a distinguished Italian statesman and historian, best known for his book *The Prince.* His name was long synonymous with all that is tortuous and treacherous in state affairs. Holmes jokingly spoke of Watson's intellect as "Machiavellian" (VALL).

MacKinnon, the Scotland Yard inspector who was assigned to the Amberley case (RETI).

Mackintosh, an overcoat rendered waterproof by a solution of india-rubber, either applied on the surface or placed between two thicknesses of cloth (SILV). See also BURBERRY.

*Mackleton, a town in Hallamshire, near which the Priory School was located. Thorneycroft Huxtable took a train for London from **Mackleton Station,** where Holmes sent a number of telegrams (PRIO).

MacNamara, the widow who maintained a boarding-house on the outskirts of Vermissa (VALL).

Macphail, the coachman of Professor Presbury (CREE).

MacPherson, the constable on duty at the house of Eduardo Lucas, duped into allowing Lady Hilda Trelawney Hope the opportunity to retrieve the stolen document (SECO).

Madeira (*mah-deh'rah*), a Portuguese island in the Atlantic, about four hundred miles from the coast of Morocco, pop. (1900) 150,574. Holmes asked Mary Maberley if she would like to visit here (3GAB). See the map of AFRICA.

Madras (*mah-drahs'*), a city of south-eastern India, founded by the British in 1639, pop. 509,346. Jonathan Small spent time in prison here, where he suggested a boat could be found for an escape from the Andaman Islands (SIGN).

Madrid, the capital city of Spain, pop. (1900) 539,835. A letter from

Madrid was in Trelawney Hope's dispatch-box (SECO), and Don Murillo and his secretary were murdered here (WIST).

Mafia, according to Inspector Lestrade, a secret Italian political society. Pietro Venucci had been connected with them (SIXN).

Magnifique, a French word meaning *splendid* (SIGN).

Magnifying glass: see LENS.

Magnum opus, a Latin phrase meaning *great work;* a literary or artistic work on which one spends his best powers (GOLD, LAST).

Mahomet Singh, one of the FOUR (SIGN).

Mahratta, pertaining to the *Mahrattas,* a people occupying much of western and central India and speaking a common language. The first word of Porlock's message to Holmes, according to the wrong almanack, was "Mahratta" (VALL).

Maid: see SERVANT.

Mail-boat: see STEAM PACKET.

Maiwand, a village of Afghanistan, fifty miles north-west of Candahar, chiefly notable for the defeat inflicted here on 27 June 1880 upon a British force sent out from Candahar to stop and punish Ayub Khan, the insurrectionist brother of the emir of AFGHANISTAN. The Afghans, whose numbers have been estimated at from 9,000 to 25,000, outflanked the British, the artillery expended its ammunition, and the native portion of the brigade were forced back on the few British infantry. The British were completely routed and had to thank the apathy of the Afghans for escaping annihilation. Of the 2,476 British troops engaged, 934 were killed and 175 wounded or missing.

Watson, serving with the BERK-

SHIRES, was severely wounded at the fatal battle by a Jezail bullet and was saved only because his orderly Murray threw him across a packhorse and succeeded in bringing him safely to the British lines (STUD).

Make head, to resist successfully, or to advance in spite of. Holmes remarked that the Royal party "made head" in England even after the death of Charles I (MUSG).

Malay, the chief native race of the Malay peninsula and the East Indies. The keeper of the Bar of Gold was a Malay (TWIS). Jonathan Small and Tonga were picked up by a trader carrying Malay pilgrims from Singapore to Jiddah (SIGN). See also LASCAR.

Malplaquet (*mahl-plah-kay'*), a village of France, near the Belgian frontier, famous as the scene of an allied victory over the French in September 1709, the bloodiest battle of the War of the Spanish Succession of 1701–14. The Cunningham house bore the date of Malplaquet upon the lintel of the door (REIG).

Malthus, Thomas Robert (1766–1834), the great English political economist. The *Daily Telegraph* alluded airily to the principles of Malthus in its editorial about the Drebber murder (STUD).

Man-about-town, a man of the leisure class who frequents places of public or social resort; a fashionable idler (MAZA, TWIS).

Manaos (*mah-nah'ōs*), the principal city of northern Brazil, situated some eight hundred miles from the mouth of the Amazon, upon one of its largest tributaries, est. pop. (1908) 40,000. Located at the centre of the greatest rubber-producing region in the world, it is the largest and most important city of the South American interior. Maria

Pinto's father had been a government official here (THOR).

Manchester Street, a street in the West End, running parallel to Baker Street. Holmes led Watson down the street on their way to Camden House (EMPT). See Map III of LONDON.

Manders, a Scowrer (VALL).

Mangles: see ROSS AND MANGLES.

Mangrove, a genus of tropical, fruit-bearing tree. There were mangrove-trees in the Andaman Islands (SIGN).

Manor House case, a case Holmes solved shortly before the Melas affair (GREE).

Manorial law, a form of feudal law defining the political and economic relationships between the lord of a manor and the dependent population living in the farms and villages of the demesne. Based as it was on rights of land-tenure, manorial law still has limited application to certain landlord-tenant obligations in the present day. Old Frankland was learned in old manorial and COMMUNAL rights (HOUN).

Mansel, a Scowrer (VALL).

Man-servant: see VALET.

Manson, a Vermissa Valley iron-works-owner who was forced to sell out (VALL).

Mantle, a loose cloak having neither sleeves nor arm-holes (SECO, YELL).

"Man with the Twisted Lip, The" (TWIS), a chronicle which appeared originally in the *Strand* magazine for December 1891 and was published in the collection entitled *The Adventures of Sherlock Holmes* the following year. It concerns Holmes's investigation of the disappearance of Neville St. Clair, and Watson dates the case as having taken place in June 1889.

Watson observed that the case had been free of any legal crime (BLUE, COPP).

Map, or **chart.** Dr. Shlessinger was said to be preparing a map of the Holy Land, with special reference to the kingdom of the Midianites (LADY). The Ferrier wagon party became lost upon the Great Alkali Plain due to errors in compasses or maps (STUD). Holmes more than once made use of an ORDNANCE MAP (ENGR, HOUN, PRIO) and consulted his map of London (BRUC). A shilling map of London was found upon the body of Pietro Venucci (SIXN), and a cycle map of Sussex was discovered in the man Hargrave's hotel room (VALL).

The survivors of the *Gloria Scott* disaster had been given a chart (GLOR). There were maps and charts in Peter Carey's cabin (BLAC), and the captain of the *Gloria Scott* died with his head upon a chart of the Atlantic (GLOR).

Reginald Musgrave discovered Brunton in the Hurlstone library, comparing a map or chart of the grounds with the manuscript of the Musgrave Ritual (MUSG). A plan of the Agra fortress was found among Captain Morstan's papers (SIGN). Maps were drawn and charts prepared in which Salt Lake City was sketched out by the Mormons (STUD). Plans of Professor Coram's house (GOLD) and the Foreign Office (NAVA) and a sketch-map of the region round the Priory School (PRIO) assisted in an understanding of the details of the cases.

Mapleton: see CAPLETON.

Marbank: see WESTHOUSE & MARBANK.

Marchioness: see MARQUESS.

*Marcini's, a London restaurant where Holmes and Watson dined (HOUN).

Marconi. The naval codes Holmes claimed to have acquired for Von Bork included the Marconi (LAST), that is, the codes used in wireless telegraphy, which was developed 1895–1901 by *Guglielmo Marconi* (1874–1937).

Marengo, a village in the north of Italy which gives its name to a battle fought 14 June 1800 between the French, under Napoleon Bonaparte, and the Austrians. The Austrians were utterly defeated and Napoleon's supremacy firmly established as a result of the battle. Holmes put himself in the place of Napoleon's enemies when he compared the Brackenstall case with Marengo, "for it begins in defeat and ends in victory" (ABBE).

Mare's-tail, a plant resembling a horse's tail. Mare's-tails grew upon Dartmoor (HOUN).

Mare's-tail.

Margate (*mahr'g't*), a seaside resort in Kent, pop. 23,118. Holmes and Watson investigated a case at Margate in which Holmes suspected a woman because she maneuvered to have the light at her back, and the correct solution to the case seems to have stemmed

from her having no powder on her nose (SECO). The strong-man Leonardo was drowned while bathing here (VEIL).

Marines, a body of soldiers carried aboard naval vessels, first created in the British Army in 1755. Julia Stoner became engaged to a half-pay major of Marines (SPEC). Holmes was able to identify a retired sergeant of the ROYAL MARINE LIGHT INFANTRY by the man's manner and appearance (STUD). A detachment of soldiers accompanied the *Gloria Scott* upon her last voyage (GLOR).

Marker, Mrs., the housekeeper to Professor Coram (GOLD).

*****Market Square** a square in Vermissa, in which stood John McGinty's saloon (VALL).

Market Street, a street in the warehouse district of eastern Chicago. The Lake Saloon was here (VALL).

Marl, a kind of incoherent clay (LION).

*****Marley Creek,** a Gilmerton town or location (VALL).

Marquess (*mahr'kwess*), or *marquis,* in France, Great Britain, and other countries where corresponding titles exist, a nobleman whose rank is intermediate between that of a count, or earl, and a duke. Don Murillo posed as the Marquess of Montalva (WIST).

The wife or widow of a marquis is known as a **marchioness** (*mahr'shohness*) in English, a *marquise* in French; e.g., the Marquise de BRINVILLIERS (STUD).

Marseilles (*mahr-say'*), the principal commercial seaport of southern France, pop. 491,161. Save for one rather intricate matter referred to him from here, Holmes had no case of interest at the time of the Sutherland affair (IDEN).

*****Marsham,** a village or district in

Kent, not far from CHISLEHURST STATION, where the Abbey Grange was located (ABBE).

Martha, the housekeeper of Von Bork, in reality a counter-espionage agent working for Holmes (LAST).

Martin, Inspector, an official of the Norfolk constabulary, who was assigned to investigate the murder of Hilton Cubitt (DANC).

Martin, Lieutenant (d. 1855), the officer who was killed with his soldiers in the mutiny aboard the *Gloria Scott* (GLOR).

Martini-Henry rifle, a rifle adopted by the English Government for use by its armed forces, superseded in 1889. Holmes said he would rather face a Martini bullet than one of Tonga's poison darts (SIGN).

"Martyrdom of Man": see READE, WILLIAM WINWOOD.

Marvin, Teddy, a captain of the Vermissa Coal and Iron Police, formerly of Chicago, who worked in support of Birdy Edwards and the Pinkertons (VALL).

Marx, the proprietor of **Marx and Co.,** a London clothier's where Aloysius Garcia bought many of his clothes (WIST).

Mary, a servant of Elias Openshaw (FIVE).

Mary, the maid of Mary Maberley (3GAB).

Mary Jane, the Watsons' servant girl. She was incorrigibly careless, and Mrs. Watson gave her notice (SCAN).

Marylebone (*mair'ee-leh-bōn*) **Lane,** a winding street in London's West End, in the borough of St. Marylebone, opening into Oxford Street. Holmes was nearly run down by a van which dashed down Bentinck Street from Marylebone Lane (FINA). See Map III of LONDON.

Mason, the platelayer who found Cadogan West's body (BRUC).

Mason, a man who escaped justice at Bradford because there was no reliable test for blood stains (STUD).

Mason, John, the head trainer at the Shoscombe stables, who engaged Holmes over the strange behaviour of Sir Robert Norberton (SHOS).

Mason, Mrs., the nurse to the Ferguson baby (SUSS).

Mason, White: see WHITE MASON.

Masonic orders: see FREEMASONRY.

Master mariner, the captain of a merchant ship or fishing vessel (SIGN).

Mastiff, a large dog of the hound group. Holmes deduced that Dr. Mortimer's dog was smaller than a mastiff (HOUN). Jephro Rucastle owned such a dog (COPP), and Stapleton's giant hound appeared to be a combination of the mastiff and the bloodhound (HOUN).

Mastiff.

Matheson: see VENNER & MATHESON.

*Matilda Briggs, the name of a ship associated with the giant rat of Sumatra, a story for which the world is not yet prepared (SUSS).

Matthews, a man who knocked out Holmes's left canine tooth in the waiting-room at Charing Cross Station (EMPT).

Maudsley, a friend of James Ryder's who had a criminal record and whom Ryder intended to consult about disposing of the blue carbuncle (BLUE).

Maupertuis, Baron, the most accomplished swindler in Europe, whose "colossal schemes" baffled the police of three countries until he was finally outwitted by Holmes in the spring of 1887 (REIG).

Mauritius (*maw-rish′yus*), a British-owned island in the Indian Ocean, pop. 371,023, about 3,000 of whom are whites. Young Fowler received a government appointment here (COPP). See the map of AFRICA.

*Mawson & Williams', a London stockbroking firm. They hired Hall Pycroft as a clerk and did not suspect that one of the Beddington brothers had taken his place (STOC).

Maxillary curve, the curve of the jaw-bone (HOUN). See CRANIOLOGY.

*Max Linder and Co., a Vermissa firm which paid to be left alone by the Scowrers (VALL).

May Day, a steam packet with the Liverpool, Dublin, and London Steam Packet Company. James Browner was steward in her (CARD).

*Mayfield Place, a street in Peckham, where the non-existent Tom and Sally Dennis were said to have lodgings (STUD).

Maynooth, Earl of, governor in 1894 of one of the Australian colonies. His wife **Lady Maynooth** returned to England for a cataract operation, bringing with her their daughter **Hilda Adair** and their second son Ronald ADAIR

(EMPT). *Maynooth* is an Irish town a few miles from Dublin.

Mazarin stone, or the **Crown diamond,** a great yellow diamond stolen from Whitehall by Count Sylvius and recovered by Holmes (MAZA). It bore the name of *Cardinal Jules Mazarin* (1602–1661), an Italian-born French diplomat.

"Mazarin Stone, The Adventure of the" (MAZA), a chronicle which appeared originally in the *Strand* magazine for October 1921 and *Hearst's International* for November 1921 and was published in the collection entitled *The Case Book of Sherlock Holmes* in 1927. It concerns Holmes's efforts to recover the stolen Mazarin stone, and the case is commonly dated as occurring in 1903. The story is written in the third person and is based upon a one-act play entitled *The Crown Diamond: An Evening with Sherlock Holmes* by Sir Arthur Conan Doyle, which was performed in London during two weeks in 1921.

McCarthy, Charles, an English blackmailer who lived for years off the bounty of John TURNER, whose past he knew, and who finally killed him. His son **James McCarthy** was suspected of the crime but was cleared by Holmes and acquitted (BOSC).

McCauley, a man threatened by the Ku Klux Klan in 1869, who apparently fled the South. (FIVE).

McFarlane, a man who wooed the former fiancée of Jonas OLDACRE and ultimately married her, she becoming **Mrs. McFarlane.** Their son **John Hector McFarlane** (b. *c.*1868), a solicitor, was implicated in Oldacre's apparent murder on the basis of evidence falsified by Oldacre himself in an effort to revenge himself upon the young man's parents (NORW).

*McFarlane's, a carriage-building depot near the City, backing on to Jabez Wilson's pawnshop (REDH).

McGinty, John ("Jack") (d. 1875), the Vermissa saloon-owner and politician who was bodymaster of the SCOWRERS. He was hanged through the efforts of Birdy EDWARDS (VALL).

McGregor, Mrs. (d. 1847), a member of the Ferrier wagon party, who died when they became lost upon the Great Alkali Plain (STUD).

McLaren, Miles, a student at St. Luke's College and a contestant for the Fortescue Scholarship (3STU).

McMurdo, the former prizefighter and servant to Bartholomew Sholto whom Holmes had once boxed (SIGN).

McMurdo, John ("Jack"): see EDWARDS, BIRDY.

McPherson, Fitzroy (d. 1907), the science master at Stackhurst's coaching establishment, who was killed by *Cyanea capillata.* He had an uncle who was very old and said to be dying (LION).

McQuire's Camp, the prospecting settlement "near the Rocky Mountains" where Francis Hay Moulton and Hatty Doran met (NOBL).

M.D.: see DOCTOR.

Mecca, a city of Arabia. As the birthplace of Mohammed, it is the holiest city of the Moslem world, and at the time of the annual pilgrimage which was enjoined by Mohammed upon all his followers the population is increased from 50,000 to nearly 200,000. Jonathan Small and Tonga were picked up by a ship carrying pilgrims to JIDDAH (SIGN), and Holmes "looked in" at Mecca during the Great Hiatus (EMPT), an action which could have cost him his life had he been exposed as an unbeliever. See the map accompanying TURKEY.

Mediæval: see MIDDLE AGES.

Medical Directory, a published directory detailing the individuals enrolled upon the government's Medical Register of qualified practitioners. Watson turned up Dr. Mortimer in the Medical Directory (HOUN).

Medical officer of health, in England, a county official appointed to bear responsibility for enforcing the means of health within a given district. Established in 1875, the office must be filled by a qualified physician. Dr. Mortimer was medical officer for the Devonshire region composed of the parishes of Grimpen, Thorsley, and High Barrow (HOUN).

Medicine: see DOCTOR.

Mediterranean Sea. The stolen naval treaty foreshadowed British policy in the event of the French fleet gaining a complete ascendancy over that of Italy in the Mediterranean (NAVA). Baron Gruner met Violet de Merville on a Mediterranean yachting voyage (ILLU).

Meek, Sir Jasper, one of the best medical men in London, whom Watson wished to fetch for Holmes (DYIN).

Meet, a meeting of huntsmen for COURSING or FOX HUNTING (VALL).

Meiringen (*mī'ring-en*), a village and tourist centre of central Switzerland, pop. (1900) 3,077. It is built at a height of 1,968 feet, upon the floor of the Hasle Valley on the right bank of the Aar River. In October 1891 it was in great part destroyed by fire. Holmes and Watson spent a night here in their flight from Moriarty (FINA). See the map of SWITZERLAND. See also REICHENBACH FALLS; ROSENLAUI.

Melas, a linguist and interpreter for

London tourists and the law courts. An Englishman of Greek extraction, he was called upon to translate for Paul Kratides and his kidnappers, who later attempted to murder Melas himself after he had told his story to Holmes (GREE).

Melbourne, the capital of the Australian colony of Victoria, pop. 68,374. The Ballarat Gang robbed a gold shipment bound for here (BOSC).

Melon. Melon seeds were sometimes used as a warning sent to enemies of the Ku Klux Klan, according to the *American Encyclopædia* (FIVE).

Melville, a retired brewer who introduced Scott Eccles to Aloysius Garcia (WIST).

"Memoirs of Sherlock Holmes, The," the second collection of Sherlock Holmes cases, published in 1894 and containing, in order of their first English magazine appearances, the following: "Silver Blaze" (SILV), "The Cardboard Box" (CARD), "The Yellow Face" (YELL), "The Stockbroker's Clerk" (STOC), "The *Gloria Scott*" (GLOR), "The Musgrave Ritual" (MUSG), "The Reigate Squires" (REIG), "The Crooked Man" (CROO), "The Resident Patient" (RESI), "The Greek Interpreter" (GREE), "The Naval Treaty" (NAVA), and "The Final Problem" (FINA). "The Cardboard Box" is omitted from some editions.

Ménage, a household (SOLI).

Mendelssohn-Bartholdy, Felix (1809–1847), a distinguished German composer, born at Hamburg. His best-known works are the *Lieder ohne Wortes (Songs without Words)*. At Watson's request Holmes played some of Mendelssohn's Lieder on the violin (STUD).

Meningitis: see SPINAL MENINGITIS.

Meiringen.

Menzies (d. 1875), the engineer of the Crow Hill Mine, murdered by the Scowrers (VALL).

Mercer, a member of Holmes's AGENCY, his "general utility man who looks up routine business" such as the identity of Dorak (CREE).

Mercer (d. 1855), the second mate of the *Gloria Scott,* who was bribed to join the convicts' mutiny and was killed in the explosion which destroyed the ship (GLOR). In some editions the name is misprinted *Mereer.*

Mere, a lake, pond, or marsh (MUSG, THOR).

Meredith, George (1828–1909), an English poet and novelist. Holmes insisted upon discussing him rather than the Boscombe Valley case (BOSC).

Mereer: see MERCER.

Merivale, an official at Scotland Yard, who asked Holmes to look into the St. Pancras case (SHOS).

Merona: see MORONI.

Merridew, an entry "of abominable memory" in Holmes's commonplace book (EMPT).

Merrilow, Mrs., the landlady of Eugenia Ronder, who suggested Holmes as a confessor (VEIL).

*Merripit House, the Stapletons' Dartmoor residence (HOUN).

Merrow, Lord, an English peer, a letter from whom was in Trelawney Hope's dispatch-box (SECO). *Merrow* is a town immediately north-east of Guildford in Surrey.

Merryweather, a director of the City and Suburban Bank, present at the vigil in the branch bank vault (REDH).

Merton, Sam, the prizefighter who was accomplice to Count Sylvius (MAZA).

*Merton County, an agricultural county in the Gilmerton region of the United States, not far from Vermissa Valley (VALL).

Metals, in England, the rails of a railway (BRUC).

Métier, one's trade, profession, or craft (BOSC, BRUC).

Metropolitan Railway, the name of the principal UNDERGROUND railway company of London, which, together with the *Metropolitan District Railway,* forms the *Inner Circle,* itself often referred to as "the Metropolitan." BAKER STREET STATION is a Metropolitan station (BERY), and the body of Cadogan West was found by a Metropolitan line, upon which it had been carried from Kensington (BRUC).

Meunier, Oscar, the French sculptor who created the bust of Holmes used to trap Sebastian Moran (EMPT).

Mews, an alley or court in which stables are situated within a city or town. Holmes led Watson through a network of mews and stables on their way to Camden House (EMPT). There was a mews back of Halliday's Private Hotel (STUD), and the SERPENTINE MEWS lay behind Briony Lodge (SCAN).

*Mexborough Private Hotel, a hotel in Craven Street, where the Stapletons stayed while in London (HOUN).

Meyer, Adolph, an international agent, one of the few who would handle so big an affair as the Bruce-Partington theft (BRUC).

Meyers, a Toronto bootmaker (HOUN).

Mica. Lucy Ferrier was enchanted by the glittering fragments of mica found upon the Great Alkali Plain (STUD).

Michael, the Fergusons' stable-hand (SUSS).

Michaelmas, the feast of St. Michael the Archangel, falling on 29 September. It is one of the QUARTER DAYS. Hugo Baskerville died upon a Michaelmas (HOUN).

Michigan, a north-central state of the United States, pop. 2,420,982. John McMurdo had worked in the lumbercamps here (VALL).

Microscope. Nathan Garrideb possessed a powerful microscope (3GAR). Holmes considered microscopic examination of stains for identifying blood corpuscles to be clumsy and uncertain (STUD). He solved the St. Pancras case with the aid of his microscope, and said that Scotland Yard had begun to recognize its importance in the detection of crime (SHOS). Grit in a sensitive instrument, said Watson, or a crack in one of his high-powered lenses, would not be more disturbing to Holmes than a strong emotion within himself (SCAN). See also LENS.

Mid-Devon, or *Ashburton,* one of the eight parliamentary divisions of Devonshire. Sir Charles Baskerville had been mentioned as the probable Liberal candidate for Mid-Devon (HOUN).

Middle Ages, a term loosely applied to that period in European history which lies between the ancient and modern civilizations, the opening and closing dates of which vary widely according to different authorities.

Holmes exhibited a deep and continuing interest in the Middle Ages, making special studies of MIRACLE PLAYS (SIGN), a fifteenth-century PALIMPSEST (GOLD), EARLY ENGLISH CHARTERS (3STU), mediæval pottery (SIGN), and the music of the Middle Ages, notably that of LASSUS (BRUC). He remarked that Josiah Amberley had the sort of mind one associates with the mediæval Italian nature rather than with the modern Briton (RETI) and characterized the letter from Robert

Ferguson's solicitors as a mixture of the modern and the mediæval (SUSS). He said he had seen the ethereal otherworld beauty possessed by Violet de Merville upon the faces in the pictures of the old masters of the Middle Ages (ILLU).

St. Luke's College displayed some curious pieces of mediæval domestic architecture (3STU). Old Frankland was learned in old MANORIAL and COMMUNAL rights (HOUN). The horse-shoes which left cloven tracks were supposed to have belonged to "the marauding Barons of Holdernesse" in the Middle Ages (PRIO). Baron Von Herling declared that "honour" was a mediæval conception (LAST).

Middlesex, a south-eastern county of England, pop. 798,738. Part of the ancient county was transferred to London in 1888 and 1899, and the visible influence of London has spread over practically the whole county. Holmes and Watson drove from Middlesex through an angle of Surrey into Kent on their journey to The Cedars (TWIS). HARROW (SPEC) and PINNER (YELL) are in Middlesex; see also CHISWICK; KILBURN; WILLESDEN. See the back endpaper map.

Middlesex Corps, properly **Middlesex Hussars,** the regiment of IMPERIAL YEOMANRY in which James Dodd and Godfrey Emsworth served (BLAN).

Middleton, a Dartmoor resident against whom old Frankland won a judgement (HOUN).

Midianites, an Arabian tribe, represented in the Old Testament as the descendants of Midian, son of Abraham. They dwelt in the land of Moab, to the south-east of Canaan. Dr. Shlessinger was said to be preparing a monograph upon the kingdom of the Midianites (LADY).

*Midland Electric Company, the Coventry firm which employed Cyril Morton (SOLI).

Midlands, the inland-central part of England (STOC).

Milano, or *Milan,* a city of northern Italy, and the second city of that kingdom, pop. 491,460. Douglas Maberley's trunks passed through here on their way to England (3GAB).

Miles, Hon. Miss, a victim of Charles Augustus Milverton (CHAS).

Miles Street, a short street in Lambeth, opening into the Wandsworth Road. Holmes and Watson passed down here in pursuit of Jonathan Small (SIGN). See Map IV of LONDON.

Millar, Flora, the dancer who attempted to disrupt the wedding between Lord Robert St. Simon and Hatty Doran, and later was arrested on suspicion of murdering the bride (NOBL).

Millbank, the common name for that portion of the Westminster bank of the Thames which lies between the Houses of Parliament and Vauxhall Bridge. **Millbank Penitentiary,** a prison formerly located here, was taken down

Millbank Penitentiary, before its removal in 1893.

in 1893, and the site is now occupied partly by industrial buildings and partly by an art gallery. Mordecai Smith's landing-stage lay opposite Millbank, and Holmes and Watson landed near the penitentiary when they crossed the river by wherry (SIGN). See Map IV of LONDON.

*Miller Hill, an ill-kept public park in the centre of Vermissa (VALL).

Milman, a victim of the Scowrers (VALL).

Milner, Godfrey, a card-playing companion of Ronald Adair (EMPT).

Milverton, Charles Augustus, the man whom Holmes called "the worst man in London" and "the king of the blackmailers." He blackmailed Holmes's client Lady Eva Brackwell, prompting Holmes and Watson to burgle his home for the letters involved. There they witnessed Milverton's murder at the hands of a noblewoman whose life he had ruined (CHAS).

Mincing Lane, a street in the City, leading south from Fenchurch Street. It is the centre of wholesale trade with the colonies, and was the street in which the tea-brokers Ferguson & Muirhead were located (SUSS). See the map of the CITY.

Mine Constabulary, or **Mine Police:** see POLICE.

Ming, the Chinese dynasty founded in the middle of the fourteenth century by HUNG-WU and which fell to the Manchu invaders in 1642. Watson took to his appointment with Baron Gruner a blue egg-shell saucer of the Ming dynasty (ILLU). The Ming period saw much innovation in ceramics, the eggshell style being originated then, and the deep "Mohammedan" blue colour is also characteristically Ming, though the blue-and-white specimens are more prized by collectors than the "solid" blue examples such as that which Watson apparently had.

Minister: see CABINET.

Minories, The, an unattractive street in the eastern part of the City, extending from Houndsditch to the Tower, and the centre of the Jewish quarter. Straubenzee's workshop was here (MAZA). See the map of the CITY.

Miracle plays, a sort of dramatic entertainment common in the Middle Ages, in which the subjects were taken from the lives of saints and the miracles they wrought. Holmes spoke authoritatively on them (SIGN).

"Missing Three-Quarter, The Adventure of the" (MISS), a chronicle which appeared originally in the *Strand* magazine for August 1904 and *Collier's Weekly* of 26 November 1904 and was published in the collection entitled *The Return of Sherlock Holmes* the following year. It concerns the disappearance of Godfrey Staunton and Holmes's efforts to locate him. The case is commonly dated as having taken place in 1896, 1897, or 1898.

Mississippi River, the principal river of North America. The Mormons struggled from the Mississippi to the western slopes of the Rocky Mountains with an "unparalleled constancy" (STUD).

Missouri River, a great river of the United States, the principal tributary of the Mississippi. Little Lucy Ferrier was certain that God had made the Missouri (STUD).

Mitral valve, in anatomy, that valve in the heart between the left ventricle and the left auricle. Thaddeus Sholto expressed doubts about his (SIGN).

Mitton, John, the valet of Eduardo Lucas (SECO).

Mob cap, an old-fashioned cap, worn by women, with a bag-shaped or puffy crown, a broad band, and frills. Philip Green remembered Susan Dobney in her mob cap (LADY).

Mob cap.

Moffat, one of the WORTHINGDON BANK GANG (RESI).

Mohammedan, the name commonly but improperly applied by Christians to a follower of Islam. With the exception of Jonathan Small, Holmes believed the FOUR to be Hindus or Mohammedans, though in reality they were Sikhs (SIGN).

Moidore (*moy'dōr*), a gold coin formerly current in Portugal and common in England during the first half of the eighteenth century; later, in English use, the word survived as a name for the sum of twenty-seven shillings, which was approximately the value of the coin. Jonathan Small dreamed of returning home with his pockets full of "gold moidores" (SIGN).

Molesey, properly **East and West Molesey,** a town of northern Surrey, on the Thames, pop. 6,034. Holmes said that Lestrade had handled the "Molesey Mystery" fairly well in his absence (EMPT), possibly an allusion to this town. See the back endpaper map.

Monaghan, a northern county of Ireland, pop. 74,611. Birdy Edwards came originally from here (VALL).

Mongoose, the common name for a

carnivorous animal of the genus *Ichneumon,* native to Egypt and Asia, and domesticated in India to rid households of snakes and other vermin. The extreme quickness of its movements gives it its chief advantage over its prey. Henry Wood owned a mongoose named Teddy (CROO).

Mongoose, or ichneumon.

Monkey: see ANTHROPOID; BABOON; LANGUR.

Monograph, an account or description of a single thing or class of things, whether published as a book, article, or paper.

Holmes was the author of a number of monographs, all of them, he said, on technical subjects (SIGN). Among them were a special study of tobacco ashes (BOSC, STUD) entitled *Upon the Distinction Between the Ashes of the Various Tobaccos* (SIGN), a monograph upon the polyphonic motets of Lassus which was printed for private circulation and was said by some experts to be the last word upon the subject (BRUC), two short articles on ears in the *Anthropological Journal* (CARD), a "trifling" monograph upon the subject of secret writings in which he analyzed 160 separate ciphers (DANC) and one upon the dating of documents (HOUN), a contribution to the literature of tattoos (REDH), monographs upon the tracing of footsteps (SIGN) and upon the influence of the trade upon the form of the hand (SIGN), and "The Book of Life" (STUD).

François le Villard translated some of Holmes's works into French (SIGN). Holmes said he thought of writing monographs upon the uses of dogs in the work of the detective (CREE), malingering (DYIN), and the typewriter and its relation to crime (IDEN). His studies of the Chaldean roots of the Cornish language (DEVI) and Early English charters (3STU) may have resulted in monographs. He promised Watson that some day he would write his own accounts of his cases (ABBE), which he in fact did (BLAN, LION). In retirement he penned the *Practical Handbook of Bee Culture* (LAST) and proposed to devote his declining years to the composition of a textbook which would focus the whole art of detection into one volume (ABBE).

Sebastian Moran was the author of *Heavy Game of the Western Himalayas* and *Three Months in the Jungle* (EMPT), and Dr. Mortimer was the author of several medical essays, one of which won the JACKSON PRIZE (HOUN). Baron Gruner had written a book upon the subject of Chinese pottery (ILLU), and Dr. Shlessinger was said to be preparing a monograph upon the kingdom of the Midianites (LADY). Dr. Leslie Armstrong declared that his time would be better spent in the writing of a treatise than in conversing with Holmes (MISS). Dr. Percy Trevelyan's monograph upon obscure nervous lesions won the Bruce Pinkerton prize and medal (RESI), and Holmes's index contained the biography of a staff-commander who had written a monograph upon deep-sea fishes (SCAN). See also TRACT.

Monomania, the name for a form of insanity in which the mind of the patient is absorbed by one idea or impulse. Victor Hatherley thought that the girl Elise might be a monomaniac (ENGR). Lestrade believed that the destroyer of the Napoleonic busts was a monomaniac, and Watson remarked that there were no limits to the possibilities of the condition which the modern French psychologists called the *idée fixe* (SIXN).

Montague Place, a street running along the north side of the British Museum. Violet Hunter apparently lived here (COPP). See Map II of LONDON.

Montague Street, a street of central London, extending along the eastern side of the British Museum. Holmes had rooms here when he first began his practice as a consulting detective (MUSG). See Map II of LONDON.

Montalva, Marquess of: see MURILLO.

Montana, one of the north-western states of the United States, pop. 243,329. Francis Hay Moulton prospected here (NOBL).

Montgomery, the Scotland Yard inspector who took James Browner's statement (CARD).

Montmartre (*mōn-mahr'tr*), an administrative district of Paris, embracing the Arc de Triomphe, the Champs Élysées, and many other famous features of the city, pop. (1906) 258,174. Le Brun was beaten by Apaches here (ILLU).

Montpellier, a well-known city in the South of France, pop. (1906) 65,983. Lefevre committed his crimes at Montpellier, and Leturier was murdered here (STUD). Watson located Marie Devine at "Montpelier" (LADY), where Holmes conducted some re-searches into coal-tar derivatives during the Great Hiatus (EMPT).

Montpensier, Madame, a Frenchwoman whom Holmes defended against a charge of murder (HOUN).

Montrachet, a choice white Burgundy wine, which Holmes and Watson drank at lunch (VEIL).

Moon. Holmes maintained that if the earth travelled round the sun or round the moon it would not make a pennyworth of difference to him or his work (STUD).

Moor, a tract of open, untilled, and more or less elevated land, often overrun with heath. The area round Poldhu Bay was a country of rolling moors (DEVI), and the Peak country consists largely of moorland (PRIO). Baskerville Hall (HOUN) and King's Pyland (SILV) lay upon DARTMOOR, and the word "moor" in the anonymous note to Sir Henry Baskerville was printed in ink (HOUN). See also DOWN.

Moorhouse, a Cambridge Rugby player, trained as a half, whom Cyril Overton would have to substitute for Godfrey Staunton (MISS).

*Moorside Gardens, the London street, in the N.W. postal district, where Count Sylvius lived (MAZA).

*Moorville, the town in Kansas from which John Garrideb claimed to be (3GAR).

*Moosmoor: see MOSSMOOR-CUM-LITTLE PURLINGTON.

Moran, the lodgekeeper of the Boscombe Valley Estate. His daughter **Patience Moran** was a witness in the case of Charles McCarthy's death and told her mother **Mrs. Moran** about what she had seen (BOSC).

Moran, Sir Augustus, a former British minister to Persia (EMPT). His son **Colonel Sebastian Moran** (b. 1840), an Indian Army officer and renowned heavy-game hunter, was forced to leave India and went to London, where he was sought out as the chief of staff for Professor MORIARTY (EMPT) at a salary of £6,000 per annum (VALL). He witnessed Moriarty's death at Reichenbach Falls and attempted to kill Holmes there and in London some three years later, the latter attempt resulting in his arrest for the murder of Ronald Adair, who had threatened to end Moran's card-playing livelihood (EMPT). Nonetheless he escaped the gallows (ILLU) and was still living in 1914 (LAST).

Morcar, Countess of, a noblewoman of uncertain nationality, though *Morcar* is the name of a famous Saxon nobleman of the eleventh century. The stolen blue carbuncle belonged to her, and she offered a reward of £1,000 for its return (BLUE).

Morecroft: see EVANS, "KILLER."

Morgan, a poisoner entered in Holmes's commonplace book (EMPT).

Moriarty, Professor James (d. 1891), the Napoleon of crime. Endowed with a phenomenal mathematical faculty, he wrote a treatise upon the BINOMIAL THEOREM which won him the mathematical chair at a small English university (FINA), where no doubt he penned *The Dynamics of an Asteroid* (VALL). But "dark rumours" compelled him to resign and become an Army coach in London, where he became also the centre of organized English crime and the object of Sherlock Holmes's investigative energies, leading at last to a personal confrontation at Reichenbach Falls and the Professor's death (EMPT, FINA).

Holmes spoke often of Moriarty's genius (VALL) and criminal ability

Prof. James Moriarty.

(EMPT), and his horror at Moriarty's crimes, he said, was lost in admiration for his skill (FINA). His assessment of the Professor as his intellectual equal in life (FINA) led perhaps to a certain regret of Moriarty's death and the end of his greatest battle of wits (ILLU, LAST, MISS, NORW).

Moriarty had two brothers. His younger brother was a station-master in the West of England (VALL), and another brother was **Colonel James Moriarty,** whose letters to the press Watson characterized as an absolute perversion of the facts of the Professor's death (FINA). The possession of the name *James* by both the Professor (EMPT) and the Colonel (FINA) has led to the speculation that *James Moriarty* was a compound surname.

Morland, Sir James, a Dartmoor resident against whom old Frankland won a judgement (HOUN).

Mormons, the adherents of **The Church of Jesus Christ of Latter-Day Saints,** a religious organization founded by Joseph SMITH in 1830. Between 1823 and 1827, Smith claimed, he was visited several times by the angel MORONI, and in the latter year there were delivered into his hands the golden plates of the *Book of Mormon,* which miraculously he was able to translate from the language he called the "Reformed Egyptian." The *Book of Mormon* was first issued at PALMYRA, New York, in 1830 and contains the history of America from its settlement by a colony from the Tower of Babel to the beginning of the fifth century A.D. It is said to be an abridgement made by the fourth-century prophet *Mormon* and his son Moroni of other records which were in their hands, and is believed by the Latter-Day Saints to be of equal authority with the Jewish and Christian Scriptures and to form an indispensable supplement to them. The church is presided over by a president and two chief counsellors, and a subordinate Council of Twelve.

The new sect met with persecution from the start. They settled first at Kirtland, Ohio, then in Missouri, and, having made multitudes of zealous converts and their consequent expulsion from these places, at NAUVOO in Illinois. For a time the colony flourished, but it was not long before trouble again arose, and Joseph Smith and his brother Hyrum were shot to death by a mob in 1844.

Some time later, under a fresh revelation received by their new leader Brigham YOUNG, the Mormons emigrated to UTAH in 1847, where they have remained relatively undisturbed. In 1890 the practice of polygamy was abandoned, and in 1896 Utah was admitted to the Union. The church now claims 300,000 communicants in the United States and foreign fields, through strong anti-Mormon sentiments continue to persist in America and elsewhere (STUD).

See also DANITES; KEMBALL; SACRED COUNCIL OF FOUR; SCHISM; ZION.

Mormon Temple: see SALT LAKE CITY.

Morning Chronicle, one of the great daily newspapers of London. Begun in 1769, it was better known for its journalistic and literary excellence than for its commercial prosperity, and it ended in bankruptcy in 1862. The Red-Headed League's advertisement is supposed to have appeared in the *Morning Chronicle* for 27 April 1890 (REDH).

Morning Post, the oldest of the existing London papers, founded in 1772, strongly Conservative in its politics. Until 1881 it was the principal organ of the fashionable world; since that time it has become a more widely popular publication of great influence upon Conservative opinion. Watson first read of the impending marriage of Lord Robert St. Simon and Hatty Doran in the *Post* (NOBL). Paragraphs here announced the cancellation of the weddings between the Hon. Miss Miles and Colonel Dorking (CHAS) and between Baron Gruner and Violet de Merville (ILLU).

Morocco, a reddish leather made from goatskins and possessing a grained, embossed texture (BERY, BLUE, SIGN).

Moroni, in Mormon theology, the last of a long line of prophets whose writings constitute the *Book of Mormon.* In life he closed the ancient records of the Book and deposited them in the earth around the year A.D. 421. As a resurrected personage he appeared to Joseph Smith a number of times between 1823 and 1827 and revealed to Smith the location of the buried tablets (STUD). In some editions the name is misspelled *Merona.* See MORMONS.

Morphine, or **morphia.** Holmes apparently took morphine as well as cocaine upon occasion (SIGN). Holmes (ILLU), Professor Presbury (CREE), and Baron Gruner (ILLU) were treated with morphine, and Ian Murdoch shouted for morphia to ease his pain (LION).

Morphy, a professor at Camford University. His colleague Professor Presbury became engaged to his daughter **Alice Morphy** (CREE).

Morris, a Scowrer who was not sympathetic to the methods of the society. One of his young children was named *Fred* (VALL).

Morris, William: see ROSS, DUNCAN.

Morrison, Annie, a woman mentioned in the note from the Cunninghams to William Kirwin, though her role in the case is uncertain (REIG).

Morrison, Miss, a neighbour of the Barclays (CROO).

*Morrison, Morrison, and Dodd, a firm of London solicitors. Holmes seems to have been associated with them in the case of the *Matilda Briggs,* and they recommended him to their client Robert Ferguson (SUSS).

Morstan, Captain Arthur (d. 1878), an Indian Army officer. Assigned to the convict settlement in the Andaman Islands, he became associated with Jon-

athan SMALL, Major SHOLTO, and the AGRA TREASURE. Betrayed by Sholto, he went to London in search of the treasure but died there of a paroxysm (SIGN).

His daughter **Mary Morstan** (b. 1861) consulted Holmes about the mystery surrounding her father's death and so made the acquaintance in 1888 of Dr. Watson (SIGN), whom she married soon afterward (BOSC, STOC).

Mary Morstan.

The cause of her death between 1891 and 1894 (EMPT) is not known. See WATSON, JOHN H., subheaded *Marriages.*

Mortimer: see SMITH-MORTIMER.

Mortimer, the gardener to Professor Coram (GOLD).

Mortimer, James, a country physician. He and his wife lived at Grimpen, on Dartmoor. He was a friend of Sir Charles Baskerville's and introduced

Holmes to the Baskerville case (HOUN).

*Mortimer's, a tobacconist's near the City, backing on to Jabez Wilson's pawnshop (REDH).

Mortimer Street, a street in the West End, running between Regent Street and Goodge Street. Watson writes that his house backed on to Mortimer Street (FINA), a statement which is at variance with a practice in Paddington (ENGR, STOC) or in Kensington (EMPT, NORW, REDH). See WATSON, JOHN H., subheaded *Practices*. See Map III of LONDON.

Morton, the Scotland Yard inspector assigned to investigate the murder of Victor Savage (DYIN).

Morton, an Oxford Rugby player (MISS).

Morton, Cyril, the betrothed of Violet Smith, an electrical engineer who later became the senior partner of Morton and Kennedy, a well-known Westminster firm (SOLI).

*Morton & Waylight, the firm in the Tottenham Court Road for whom Mr. Warren was a timekeeper (REDC).

Moser, the well-known manager of the Hôtel National at Lausanne (LADY).

Moss. The parish church near Tredannick Wollas was overgrown with moss (DEVI). The ledge overlooking Reichenbach, upon which Holmes lay, was covered with it (EMPT), and moss topped the wall round The Haven (RETI).

*Mossmoor-cum-Little Purlington, the name given to the LIVING enjoyed by J. C. Elman (RETI), which presumably was composed of the revenues attached to the Essex parishes of Mossmoor and Little Purlington. In some editions the name is misspelled *Moosmoor*.

Moss rose: see ROSE.

Motet, a vocal composition in somewhat strict polyphonic style, having a Biblical or similar prose text, and intended to be sung in a church service. The earliest motets date from about 1300. The use of an instrumental accompaniment is usually limited and often avoided altogether. A polyphonic motet is one in which two or more voice-parts are simultaneously combined without losing their independent character, but with harmonious effect. The mediæval motet is by definition polyphonic, and differs from the modern motet in being much more limited in its scope.

Holmes undertook a monograph upon the polyphonic motets of LASSUS which was printed for private circulation and was said by some experts to be the last word upon the subject (BRUC).

Moth: see LEPIDOPTERA.

Moulton, Francis Hay, an American gold prospector and the secret husband of Hatty Doran (NOBL).

Mount Harriet, a mountain of Blair Island, in the Andamans, elevation 1,200 feet. Hope Town is on its slopes (SIGN).

Mount-James, Lord, the uncle of Godfrey Staunton (MISS).

Mounts Bay, an extensive bay of the English Channel, situated on the southern coast of Cornwall. The cottage which Holmes and Watson occupied looked down upon it (DEVI). See the map accompanying DEVONSHIRE and the engraving of POLDHU BAY.

Mouse. Young Master Rucastle showed remarkable talent in the capture of mice (COPP). Percy Phelps heard a sound in the night, he said, like that of a mouse gnawing a plank (NAVA).

Mousseline-de-soie, a thin and gauzy

muslin, sometimes embroidered (TWIS).

M.R.C.S.: see COLLEGE OF SURGEONS.

Mug, in English slang, a fool (LAST).

Muirhead: see FERGUSON, ROBERT.

Mule. Lucy Ferrier rode upon a mule in her escape from the Mormons (STUD).

Muller, a notorious criminal who escaped justice because there was no reliable test for blood stains (STUD).

Mullion, a division, typically of stone, between the panes of windows. The windows of Baskerville Hall were mullioned (HOUN). Holmes associated Reginald Musgrave with mullioned windows (MUSG).

Mullion.

Munich, the capital city of Bavaria, pop. (1900) 499,932. Holmes knew of an instance parallelling the St. Simon case which had occurred here in 1871 or 1872 (NOBL).

Munro, Colonel Spence, a former employer of Violet Hunter, for whom she was governess for five years (COPP). *Spence Munro* may be a compound surname.

Munro, Grant ("Jack"), a London hop merchant. He hired Holmes to investigate the mysterious behaviour of his wife **Effie Munro,** who was the widow of John HEBRON and mother of **Lucy Hebron** (YELL). *Grant Munro* may be a compound surname.

Murcher, Harry, the London constable who had the Holland Grove beat, brought to the murder scene by Constable Rance's alarm (STUD).

Murder, the act of unlawfully killing a human being with premeditated malice. See also ASSAULT AND BATTERY.

Holmes said that he had had to do with some fifty murders in his career (CHAS), and some five hundred cases of "capital importance" (HOUN). He investigated the murders of Sir Eustace Brackenstall (ABBE), Peter Carey (BLAC), Charles McCarthy (BOSC), Arthur Cadogan West (BRUC), Hilton Cubitt (DANC), Brenda and Mortimer Tregennis (DEVI), Victor Savage (DYIN), John Openshaw (FIVE), Willoughby Smith (GOLD), Heidegger the German master (PRIO), William Kirwin (REIG), Blessington (RESI), Eduardo Lucas (SECO), the policeman killed in the St. Pancras case (SHOS), Bartholomew Sholto (SIGN), Enoch Drebber and Joseph Stangerson (STUD), and Aloysius Garcia (WIST), as well as the Tarleton murders (MUSG), the Abergavenny murder (PRIO), the Trepoff murder at Odessa (SCAN), and a "very commonplace little murder" brought to his attention immediately before he entered the Phelps case (NAVA). Murder presumably was committed in the Camberwell poisoning case (FIVE).

His own cases reminded Holmes of the Anderson murders (HOUN) and the cases of Dolsky and Leturier (STUD). He declared that the most winning woman he ever knew was hanged for poisoning three little children for their insurance-money (SIGN), and he felt Moriarty's presence in a number of murders (FINA). John Clay was said to be a murderer (REDH), as was Bert Stevens (NORW), and Holmes called Baron Gruner a murderer who apparently killed someone in Prague and his wife at the Splügen Pass, in addition to being responsible for one or two others, according to Kitty Winter (ILLU). Holmes said that Morgan was a poisoner (EMPT), and that the thief or murderer could roam London unseen in the fog (BRUC). It was said that Giuseppe Gorgiano was at the bottom of fifty murders (REDC), Pietro Venucci was described as one of the greatest cut-throats of London (SIXN), and Huret was known as "the Boulevard assassin" (GOLD).

The elder Neligan was killed by Peter Carey (BLAC), Mary Browner and her lover Alec Fairbairn by Mary's husband James Browner (CARD), Charles Augustus Milverton by an unknown assassin (CHAS), and Ronald Adair by Colonel Sebastian Moran (EMPT). Lysander Stark apparently murdered Jeremiah Hayling and attempted to murder Victor Hatherley (ENGR). Harold Latimer and Wilson Kemp murdered Paul Kratides and were killed in turn by their victim's sister Sophy (GREE). Stapleton was responsible for the deaths of Sir Charles Baskerville and the convict Selden, and he attempted the murder of Sir Henry Baskerville (HOUN). Holy Peters and his accomplice planned and in fact attempted to murder Lady Frances Carfax (LADY), and Rachel Howells deliberately did not seek help to rescue Richard Brunton (MUSG). Giuseppe Gorgiano was killed when he

attempted to murder Gennaro Lucca, who had refused to kill his benefactor (REDC). Josiah Amberley suffocated his wife and her lover Ray Ernest with gas (RETI), Jonathan Small murdered a Pathan prison guard with his wooden leg (SIGN), and Pietro Venucci was killed by Beppo, who earlier had stabbed another man (SIXN). Holmes suggested murder in the abduction of Violet Smith, and Bob Carruthers attempted to kill Jack Woodley (SOLI). Dr. Grimesby Roylott murdered his Indian butler and his stepdaughter Julia Stoner, and attempted murder upon Julia's sister Helen (SPEC). Killer Evans had shot if not killed three men in the United States, as well as Rodger Prescott (3GAR). Ted Baldwin was killed attempting to murder John Douglas, who was acquitted at the Assizes (VALL), the showman Ronder was murdered by his wife and the strong-man Leonardo (VEIL), and Don Murillo was assassinated at Madrid (WIST).

Inspector Lestrade apparently investigated three murders in one year which he was unable to solve (EMPT). There had been two murders committed for the sake of the blue carbuncle (BLUE), and the Bar of Gold was known as the vilest murder-trap on the riverside (TWIS). Holmes believed that Mrs. Stewart was murdered (EMPT) and suspected that Beddoes had killed the sailor Hudson (GLOR).

The Ballarat Gang committed murder during a robbery (BOSC), as did the Worthingdon Bank Gang (RESI), the Four (SIGN), and Beddington (STOC). The Folkestone Court page was cold-bloodedly "pistolled," which may refer to shooting or to the use of the pistol as a club (HOUN).

Holmes said that the only punishment in Moriarty's code was death (VALL). The three Openshaws were murdered by the Ku Klux Klan, as apparently were one Paramore of St. Augustine and others (FIVE). Many murders were committed by the Danites in Utah, among them that of John Ferrier (STUD). The Mafia enforced its decrees by murder (SIXN), as did the Scowrers, who killed dozens of people (VALL). A police officer was killed by the Nihilists in Russia (GOLD), and Don Murillo murdered all possible rivals to his dictatorship in San Pedro (WIST). Mass murder was committed in the mutiny aboard the *Gloria Scott* (GLOR), and hundreds were slaughtered during the Indian Mutiny (SIGN).

The medical evidence showed conclusively that Colonel Barclay was not, after all, murdered (CROO). Holmes defended Mme. Montpensier from a charge of murder (HOUN). John Hector McFarlane was arrested for the murder of Jonas Oldacre, but Inspector Lestrade was able to say later that Oldacre himself might face a charge of attempted murder against McFarlane (NORW). John Straker was thought to have been murdered (SILV), Ian Murdoch was suspected of murdering Fitzroy McPherson (LION), Grace Dunbar was arrested for the murder of Maria Gibson (THOR), and Hugh Boone was arrested as Neville St. Clair's murderer (TWIS). John McMurdo claimed to have killed Jonas Pinto (VALL).

Holmes claimed there were fifty men who had good reason for taking his life (BRUC), and among those who tried it were Culverton Smith (DYIN), Sebastian Moran (EMPT), Professor Moriarty's agents (FINA) and the Professor himself at Reichenbach (EMPT, FINA), Count Sylvius (MAZA), the Cunninghams (REIG), and Killer Evans, who wounded Watson in the attempt (3GAR).

Murdoch, Ian, the mathematical coach at Stackhurst's coaching establishment. He was a suspect in Fitzroy McPherson's death until he was himself attacked by *Cyanea capillata* (LION).

Murdoch, James, a man mutilated by the Scowrers (VALL).

Murger, Henri (1822–1861), a French author. Watson sat up skipping over the pages of his *Vie de Bohème* (1848) waiting for Holmes to return (STUD).

Murillo, Don Juan, for many years the dictator of the Central American country of San Pedro, known as the *Tiger of San Pedro* for his cruelty, until he was deposed and fled to Europe. Under the name *Henderson* he lived in England until the death of a would-be assassin exposed his identity. Fleeing to Spain as the *Marquess of Montalva,* he was murdered in Madrid by his enemies. Apparently a widower, he had two adolescent daughters (WIST). Watson recalled the case of "the papers of ex-President Murillo" (NORW).

Murphy, a gipsy horse-dealer who heard Sir Charles Baskerville's death-cry (HOUN).

Murphy, a Chicago acquaintance of John McMurdo's (VALL).

Murphy, Major, the officer of Colonel Barclay's regiment who called Holmes into the case (CROO).

Murray, the orderly to Watson in the Afghan campaign. Wounded at the battle of Maiwand, Watson would have fallen into the hands of the murderous Ghazis had it not been for the devotion and courage shown by Murray, who threw him across a packhorse and succeeded in bringing him to safety (STUD).

Murray, a member of the Bagatelle Card Club, with whom Ronald Adair played upon the night of his death (EMPT).

Museum, The: see BRITISH MUSEUM.

Museum of the College of Surgeons: see COLLEGE OF SURGEONS.

Musgrave, one of the very oldest families of England, a cadet branch of which was established at Hurlstone in Western Sussex. **Sir Ralph Musgrave** was a prominent Cavalier and the closest companion of Charles II in his wanderings. It was a Musgrave who secreted the ancient Stuart crown of England at Hurlstone and left the **Musgrave Ritual** as a clue to its location. **Reginald Musgrave,** whose father died shortly after Reginald's graduation from the university where he had known Holmes, hired the detective to solve the disappearance of his butler and second housemaid, which led to a discovery of murder and the restoration of the priceless crown (MUSG).

"Musgrave Ritual, The" (MUSG), a chronicle which appeared originally in the *Strand* magazine for May 1893 and *Harper's Weekly* of 13 May 1893 and was published in the collection entitled *The Memoirs of Sherlock Holmes* the following year. It is the story of Holmes's third case after establishing himself as a consulting detective in London, that of the Musgrave family and the Musgrave Ritual. It is the only full account of a case handled by Holmes, as a professional, before his meeting with Watson, told in the form of a monologue in which he relates the details to Watson many years after the event. It has been variously dated as having taken place in 1878, 1879, and 1880; and even the time of the year is

disputed, opinions ranging from July to October.

The affair of the Musgrave Ritual, Watson said, was one of the half-dozen cases in which the truth was discovered even though Holmes erred (YELL), a rather incomprehensible statement in that he succeeded brilliantly in this matter; though in most editions this reference is to "the second stain."

Mute, a hired attendant at a funeral. The effect of Lord Mount-James's unkempt, black-clad appearance was to remind Watson of an undertaker's mute (MISS).

Mutiny, in law, any rebellion against constituted authority on the part of soldiers, naval personnel, or merchant seamen. The crew and transported convicts aboard the *Gloria Scott* mutinied under the leadership of Jack Prendergast (GLOR). The Sepoy Mutiny of 1857–58 was an important event in the history of India (CROO, SIGN); see MUTINY, THE.

Mutiny, The, or *Sepoy Rebellion,* the revolt of SEPOY troops in India against British authority 1857–58.

Caused primarily by an injudicious disregard of Hindu religious tenets by the East India Company which then ruled the country, several outbreaks among the Sepoys took place during March 1857, but the most formidable revolt was at Meerut, on 10 May, when the Sepoys rose and massacred the Europeans. They then fled to DELHI, where they were immediately joined by the native garrison, and another massacre took place. The revolt spread rapidly from the north-western provinces down to lower Bengal, though the Punjaub remained peaceful and the SIKHS continued loyal. Wherever the mutiny broke out, it was attended with savage excesses, as at CAWNPORE. By May 1858 order had been partially restored, and the Mutiny was at an end. As a result the powers of government were transferred to the Crown, and in 1877 Victoria was proclaimed Empress of India.

Colonel Barclay's regiment fought in the Mutiny (CROO), and the events surrounding the original theft of the Agra treasure occurred at this time (SIGN).

See also AGRA; LUCKNOW; SHAHGUNGE; also CAMPBELL, SIR COLIN; GREATHED, SIR EDWARD HARRIS; NEILL, JAMES GEORGE SMITH; also NANA SAHIB; PANDIES; also BRITISH ARMY; INDIAN ARMY.

Muttra, a city of India, located some thirty miles from Agra, pop. 60,042. Abel White's plantation was nearby (SIGN).

*Myrtles, The, the name of Harold Latimer's rented house in Beckenham (GREE). The *myrtle* is a common European shrub possessing white, sweet-scented flowers.

N

Nana Sahib (b. *c.*1820), a leader of the Indian Mutiny. His real name was *Dandhu Panth*. The heir of a Mahratta ruler, he was refused the succession by the British and opportunistically placed himself at the head of the mutineers upon the outbreak of the rebellion. He is infamous for his treachery at CAWN-PORE. Defeated by the British, he escaped into Nepaul, and all knowledge of him ceased (SIGN).

Naples, a seaport and the largest city of Italy, pop. 547,503. Pietro Venucci was from Naples (SIXN), and the Luccas were from POSILIPPO near here (REDC).

Napoleon, a French coin of the value of 20 francs, or about 9½s. There were 30,000 napoleons from the Bank of France in the vault of the City and Suburban Bank branch (REDH).

Napoleon I (1769–1821), the Emperor of the French 1804–15, renowned as one of the greatest military geniuses of all time. Holmes called Professor Moriarty "the Napoleon of crime" (FINA, VALL). The case of the black pearl of the Borgias began with the mysterious destruction of several plaster busts of Napoleon I (SIXN).

Nara, a town of Japan, est. pop. 32,000. It was the capital of Japan A.D. 709–84 and is celebrated for the specimens of applied art preserved for nearly twelve hundred years in a storehouse here known as the *Shoso-in*. Baron Gruner tested Watson's knowledge of Oriental art by asking how he associated the Emperor Shomu with the Shoso-in near Nara (ILLU).

Narbonne, a town on the southern coast of France, pop. (1906) 23,289. Watson received a note from Holmes dated from here (FINA).

Narcotic. In the first weeks of their association Watson said he might have suspected Holmes of being addicted to the use of some narcotic, had not the temperance and cleanliness of his whole life forbidden such a notion (STUD). See also COCAINE; MORPHINE; OPIUM.

Nark, in underworld cant, a police-spy; an informer (ILLU).

National Hotel: see HÔTEL NATIONAL.

Nauvoo, a city of Illinois, pop. 1,321. Commerce City was laid out on the site in 1834, but the first settlement of importance was made by the MORMONS in 1839, who named it Nauvoo. In 1844 its population was about 15,000 and a large Mormon temple had been built (STUD). Following the Mormon exodus to Utah the town declined steadily.

"Naval Treaty, The" (NAVA), a chronicle which appeared originally in the *Strand* magazine for October and

November 1893 and in *Harper's Weekly* of 14 and 21 October 1893 and was published in the collection entitled *The Memoirs of Sherlock Holmes* the following year. It concerns Holmes's efforts to locate government documents stolen from the Foreign Office in Whitehall. The case is variously dated as having taken place in 1887, 1888, and 1889.

Watson said that Holmes's interference in the matter had the unquestionable effect of preventing a serious international complication (FINA).

Navy: see ROYAL NAVY.

Neale, a Vermissa clothing outfitter (VALL).

Neanderthal, a celebrated prehistoric skull found in western Prussia in 1857. It is less human and more simian in character than any other known type. Nathan Garrideb possessed a skull labelled "Neanderthal" (3GAR).

Nebraska, a state in the west-central United States, pop. 1,068,539. It was supposedly the eastern limit of the Great Alkali Plain (STUD).

Ned, the uncle of Mary Sutherland, who left her £2,500 in New Zealand stock paying 4½ per cent (IDEN).

Negro, The, the name of a horse which ran in the Wessex Cup (SILV).

Negro race. The reason for Elias Openshaw's leaving the United States was his aversion to Negroes and his dislike of the Republican policy in extending the franchise to them, and the Ku Klux Klan was formed principally for the terrorizing of Negro voters (FIVE). Steve Dixie was a Negro (3GAB), as were John Hebron and, at least in appearance, his daughter Lucy (YELL). Dr. Mortimer claimed he could tell the skull of a Negro from that of an Esquimaux (HOUN). Aloysius Garcia's mulatto cook was a devotee of VOODOO, which prompted Holmes to consult Eckermann's *Voodooism and the Negroid Religions* (WIST).

See also BUSHMEN; HOTTENTOT.

Neill, James George Smith (1810–1857), a British soldier and Indian administrator. In command of the right wing in the advance from Cawnpore to Lucknow during the Indian Mutiny (CROO), he was shot and killed in the attack on Lucknow.

Neligan, J. H. (d. 1883), a Cornwall banker who fled England when his firm failed and was murdered for the securities he carried by Peter Carey. His son **John Hopley Neligan** (b. 1873) tracked down Carey and was arrested for his murder before Holmes found the guilty man (BLAC).

Nelson: see BRODERICK AND NELSON'S.

Neolithic, a division of the late "stone age." The remains of neolithic man were thick upon the moors of Devonshire (HOUN) and Cornwall (DEVI).

Nepaul, or **Nepal,** an independent state of India, in the Himalayas north of Bengal, est. pop. between 3,000,000 and 4,000,000. Henry Wood was taken here as a prisoner (CROO).

Neruda: see NORMAN-NÉRUDA, WILHELMINE.

Nervous lesion, a LESION affecting the nervous system (RESI).

Netherlands, The, or **Holland,** a kingdom of western Europe, pop. (1900) 5,104,137.

Holmes accomplished an important mission for the reigning family of Holland (SCAN) which was of such delicacy that he could not confide it even to Watson (IDEN). The King of the Netherlands 1849–90 was *William III* (1817–1890).

Count Sylvius and Sam Merton planned to flee to Holland (MAZA), and Holmes as Altamont declared his intention of escaping here (LAST). The *Friesland* was a Dutch ship (NORW), and Van Seddar was a Dutchman (MAZA). The lepers among whom Godfrey Emsworth found himself, he said, all spoke Dutch (BLAN), more likely *Taal,* the dialect common to South Africa.

See also AMSTERDAM; FLUSHING; HAGUE, THE; ROTTERDAM; UTRECHT.

Two of the Worthingdon Bank Gang smoked cigars imported by the Dutch from their East Indian colonies (RESI), and Holmes said that the Dutch knew more about the Sumatran disease from which he suffered than did the English (DYIN). See DUTCH EAST INDIES; SUMATRA.

*Netherland-Sumatra Company, the company involved in the colossal schemes of Baron Maupertuis (REIG).

*Nether Walsling, the house belonging to the Rev. Stone (WIST).

Netley, a village in Hampshire, site of the vast **Netley Hospital,** the principal military hospital in Great Britain. Here Watson went through the course prescribed for surgeons in the Army (STUD). See ARMY MEDICAL DEPARTMENT.

Nevada, one of the far-western states of the United States, pop. 42,335. John and Lucy Ferrier, led by Jefferson Hope, fled from Salt Lake City toward Nevada (STUD), which in 1860 was a part of the Territory of Utah.

*Nevada Mountains, a range in the vicinity of Salt Lake City, where Jefferson Hope and his companions discovered silver (STUD).

New Brighton, a town in the county of Cheshire, across the Mersey River from Liverpool. Formerly a fashionable sea-bathing resort, the quality of its visitors declined in the last decades of the nineteenth century. The town then was known chiefly for the long, narrow promenade known popularly as the *Ham and Egg Parade,* from which a view might be afforded of the shipping and docks of Liverpool, the Irish Sea,

Netley Hospital.

The "Ham and Egg Parade" at New Brighton, so called from the many eating houses and cheap refreshment-rooms lining it, acquired an unenviable reputation for the class of visitors attracted by the nearby side-shows and amusement-stalls, and was removed in 1905.

and the mountains of Wales. James Browner followed his wife and her lover to New Brighton and along the Parade (CARD).

Newcastle-upon-Tyne, an important river-port and manufacturing city in Northumberland, pop. 215,328. Theophilus Johnson was from here (HOUN).

New England, the far-north-eastern portion of the United States, comprising those states lying east of New York. Josiah Dunn was a New Englander (VALL).

New Forest, an extensive forest in Hampshire, lying to the south-west of Southampton and belonging largely to the Crown. Watson yearned to visit here (CARD).† See the map of HAMPSHIRE.

Newfoundland dog, a large black

† This allusion is inserted in "The Resident Patient" in many editions.

hunting dog with a bushy coat (CREE, SIGN).

Newgate Calendar, a publication first issued in 1773, listing the more notorious prisoners confined in London's famous *Newgate Prison* and setting forth sensational accounts of their lives and crimes. Holmes agreed that it was not part of Watson's profession to carry about a portable Newgate Calendar in his memory (3GAR).

Newhaven, a seaport in Sussex, pop. 6,772. Holmes and Watson left England here rather than at Dover (FINA).

New Jersey, one of the eastern states of the United States, pop. (1905) 2,144,143. Irene Adler was born here (SCAN).

Newmarket Heath, the principal racing-ground of England, located at the Suffolk town of *Newmarket,* pop. 10,688, where no fewer than eight

The notorious Newgate Prison, as it was before its demolition in 1902. Opened in 1782, it was the public place for execution in London from 1783, when they were moved here from Tyburn, until 1868, when public hangings were abolished. The prison was remodeled in 1858 and ended its days as a temporary house of detention for prisoners awaiting trial. Observe the Bayswater bus.

major race-meetings take place annually. Sir Robert Norberton horse-whipped Sam Brewer here (SHOS).

New Mexico, a territory in the south-western part of the United States, pop. 195,310. Francis Hay Moulton prospected here, where he apparently was captured by Apache Indians (NOBL).

New Orleans, a city in Louisiana, pop. 287,104. Samson committed his crimes here (STUD).

News: see DAILY NEWS; EVENING NEWS.

News-agent, a person who sells newspapers (SILV).

Newspaper. Holmes remarked that the press was a most valuable institution, "if you only know how to use it"

(SIXN). He claimed to read nothing but the criminal news and the AGONY COLUMN (NOBL) and took to cocaine when they were uninteresting (YELL).

It was Watson's opinion that police cases which were reported in the papers were bald and vulgar, and Holmes agreed that realism was wanting in the newspaper police report, where more stress was laid upon the platitudes of the magistrate than upon the details of the case (IDEN). Watson commented as well that newspaper references to a fresh clue seemed to be a STEREOTYPE form "whenever the police have made a blunder" (SIGN). J. Neil Gibson said that if Holmes were able to clear Grace Dunbar, every paper in England

and America would be booming him (THOR), and though the detective boasted that his name figured in no newspaper (SIGN), Watson writes that some of his cases did gain publicity through them (FIVE). He said too that the detection of newspaper types was one of the most elementary branches of knowledge to the special expert in crime (HOUN).

LONDON NEWSPAPERS

Holmes was a tireless reader of the daily newspapers (BLUE, BOSC, COPP, DANC, GOLD, NORW, SILV), which he filed in one of the Baker Street lumber-rooms (SIXN) and cut up for his COMMONPLACE BOOK. He spent a day seeking the *Lone Star* in "the files of old papers" (FIVE), presumably shipping papers he did not take himself. He complained that the papers were sterile (WIST) and contained nothing of criminal interest (BRUC), and that the sensational cases which once could be traced back to Professor Moriarty had gone out of them (NORW). He remarked that they always had questions to ask of Scotland Yard (RETI). He read of the theft of the blue carbuncle here (BLUE) and confessed that any theories he had formed about the Silver Blaze case from them were erroneous (SILV). He watched the London criminal news even during his sojourn in France (EMPT).

Watson commonly surrounded himself with a cloud of newspapers (CARD, FINA, NOBL), where he read of Lowenstein's work (CREE), the attack upon Holmes and the "sinister paragraphs" about his condition (ILLU), the wedding of Lord Robert St. Simon (NOBL), and the murders of John Openshaw (FIVE) and

Eduardo Lucas (SECO). He followed Holmes's career here (FINA, SCAN), and letters from Colonel James Moriarty which apparently were published in the English papers provided one of three press accounts of Professor Moriarty's death and prompted Watson to write "The Final Problem" (FINA). Holmes's explorations in Tibet under the name Sigerson seemingly were reported in the press, for Holmes thought Watson might have read of them (EMPT).

Lestrade spoke of the newspapers (SIXN), which reported Victor Hatherley's story (ENGR), the Worthingdon Bank Gang's release from prison (RESI), Captain Morstan's disappearance and the Sholto murder (SIGN), the "Brixton Mystery" (STUD), and Maria Gibson's death (THOR). Susan Cushing did not like having her name in the papers (CARD), where Holmes said Athelney Jones's view of the Sholto case would appear (SIGN). Vincent Spaulding came to Jabez Wilson in answer to an advertisement, and Wilson first learned of the Red-Headed League here (REDH). Grace Dunbar answered J. Neil Gibson's advertisement for a governess (THOR).

The London press had not had very full accounts of the Boscombe Valley case (BOSC), and only a most imperfect account of the Cornish Horror reached here (DEVI). Until his own telling of it, Watson writes, the Blessington case had never been dealt with in any public print (RESI). A good deal of the particulars of the so-called Park Lane Mystery were suppressed at the time of the police investigation (EMPT), and Holmes said that Sir James Damery had rather a reputation for arranging delicate matters which were to be kept out of the papers (ILLU). Mycroft Holmes said that the press would be furious if word of the Bruce-Partington theft came out (BRUC), and some rumours of the naval treaty had got into the public print (NAVA).

A small newspaper shop backed on to Jabez Wilson's pawnshop (REDH). Horace Harker was with the CENTRAL PRESS SYNDICATE (SIXN), Isadora Persano was a well-known journalist (THOR), and Neville St. Clair had worked as a reporter for a London evening newspaper (TWIS). It was said that Langdale Pike made a four-figure income by the paragraphs which he contributed to the "garbage papers" which cater for an inquisitive public (3GAB).

See also DAILY CHRONICLE; DAILY GAZETTE; DAILY NEWS; DAILY TELEGRAPH; ECHO; EVENING NEWS; EVENING STANDARD; GLOBE; MORNING POST; NORTH SURREY OBSERVER; PALL MALL GAZETTE; "PINK 'UN"; ST. JAMES'S GAZETTE; SPECTATOR; STANDARD; STAR; TIMES, THE; also FLEET STREET.

PROVINCIAL AND FOREIGN NEWSPAPERS

Provincial Press. Laura Lyons learned of the death of Sir Charles Baskerville in the paper (HOUN), and Watson read of the mulatto's capture (WIST). Holmes pointed out that Leon Sterndale could not have learned of the Tregennis tragedy in the Plymouth morning papers (DEVI). Watson read an account of the Boscombe Valley case from the "weekly county paper" (BOSC), any one of three or four Herefordshire papers with a county-wide distribution, all of which are weeklies. Holmes and Watson read of the Cambridge Rugby team's defeat in the local paper (MISS), possibly the *Cambridge Daily News,* the only daily of the four local organs. Killer Evans showed Holmes an advertisement from a Birmingham paper (3GAR), one of a dozen or more daily and weekly papers published in Birmingham and its suburbs, the most likely possibility being perhaps the *Aston and East Birmingham News.* See also DEVON COUNTY CHRONICLE; LEEDS MERCURY; WESTERN MORNING NEWS.

Foreign Press. Don Murillo's new identity had been a frequent subject for comment in the European press (WIST). Holmes and Watson read of Harold Latimer and Wilson Kemp's murders in a cutting from Buda-Pesth (GREE). See also JOURNAL DE GENÈVE; also REUTER'S.

American Press. Hatty Doran read of Francis Hay Moulton's death in a newspaper account (NOBL). Jefferson Hope got the idea of writing *"Rache"* in blood from the New York newspapers (STUD). J. Neil Gibson said that if Holmes were able to clear Grace Dunbar, every paper in America would be booming him (THOR). See also DAILY HERALD; NEW YORK PRESS.

*New Street, a street in Wallington, where Sarah Cushing lived (CARD).

New Street, one of the main streets of Birmingham, the principal business thoroughfare of the town. Hall Pycroft stayed in a hotel here (STOC). See the map of BIRMINGHAM.

Newton, Heath: see HEATH NEWTON.

New York, a city of the United States, next to London the largest city in the world, pop. 3,437,202.

The big companies moving into the Vermissa Valley were headquartered in New York and Philadelphia, and so were unafraid of the Scowrers (VALL). The Luccas went to live in BROOKLYN, from which they fled four years later to escape the Red Circle (REDC).

The Randalls were arrested at New York (ABBE), where Mlle. Carère was discovered alive and married (HOUN). Archie Swindon apparently fled here from the Scowrers, as Ettie Shafter wished to do (VALL).

Enoch Drebber and Joseph Stangerson were preparing to take ship for New York upon their deaths, which Jefferson Hope arranged to resemble political murders he had read of here (STUD). Von Bork said that Altamont could get a boat for here at Rotterdam (LAST).

New York Police Bureau, properly **New York Police Department.** Wilson Hargreave was an official (DANC).

New York Press, a morning Republican newspaper of New York City, established in 1887. Birdy Edwards was said to be posing as a reporter for the *New York Press* in 1875 (VALL).

New Zealand, a British colony in the South Pacific Ocean, pop. 815,862. Trevor Senior had been to New Zealand (GLOR), and Mary Sutherland's uncle Ned had lived here (IDEN).

New Zealand Consolidated, a stock listed on the London Stock Exchange (STOC). Mary Sutherland's uncle Ned left her some New Zealand stock (IDEN), which it would be pleasant to identify with this issue.

Niagara Falls, the great water-fall of the Niagara River, on the border between the United States and Canada. All Niagara, he said, seemed to be whizzing and buzzing in James Browner's ears (CARD). From a drop of water, Holmes maintained, a logi-

cian could infer the possibility of an Atlantic or a Niagara without having seen or heard of one or the other (STUD).

Nicholson, a family which fell victim to the Scowrers (VALL).

Nickel. Large masses of nickel and tin were discovered in an outhouse of Dr. Becher's home (ENGR).

Night-glass, a binocular telescope constructed so as to concentrate as much light as possible, and thus adapted for seeing objects at night (SIGN).

Nihilism (*nï'hil-izm*), the name applied around 1860 to a Russian revolutionary philosophy, its object being to destroy all forms of government, overturn all institutions, annihilate all class distinctions, and sweep away all traditions. A program of violence and arson 1874–81 ended with the assassination of Czar Alexander II, after which the Nihilists' doctrines have been similar to SOCIALISM and have been more peacefully promulgated. The name is now applied indiscriminately to Russian revolutionists, and, as a result of the violence associated with them, to the more intemperate factions within socialism and ANARCHISM.

Morse Hudson declared his belief that the smashing of the Napoleonic busts was a Nihilist plot (SIXN), and the murder of Don Murillo and his secretary in Madrid was ascribed to Nihilism (WIST). Professor Coram and his wife Anna had belonged to a Russian Nihilist organization (GOLD), and KLOPMAN was a Nihilist (LAST).

Nîmes (*neem*), a city of southern France, pop. (1906) 70,708. Watson received a note from Holmes dated from here (FINA).

Nine Elms Lane, a street in Lambeth, running from the Wandsworth

Road south-westerly alongside the Thames. Toby led Holmes and Watson down Nine Elms (SIGN). See Map IV of LONDON.

Nipper, in English slang, a boy or lad (BLUE).

Nitrate, in chemistry, a salt of nitric acid, much used in medicine, in agriculture, and in the manufacture of explosives. Enormous accumulations exist in Chile and Peru, and Robert Ferguson met his father-in-law in connexion with the importation of Peruvian nitrates (SUSS). The most valuable of these is **nitrate of silver,** which is used extensively in surgery because of its antiseptic and cauterant properties. Watson had the black mark of it upon his finger (SCAN).

Nitrite of amyl, in medicine, an amber-coloured, therapeutic liquid, generally inhaled and used in treating heart conditions and nervous disorders. Dr. Percy Trevelyan said he had obtained good results with it in the treatment of catalepsy (RESI).

Nitsky. Holmes as Altamont said that he had to pay an extra £100 for the naval codes or "it would have been nitsky" for him and Von Bork (LAST). It is probably a variant of *nixie,* an American slang word meaning *next to nothing.*

Nobility: see PEERAGE.

"Noble Bachelor, The Adventure of the" (NOBL), a chronicle which appeared originally in the *Strand* magazine for April 1892 and was published in the collection entitled *The Adventures of Sherlock Holmes* the same year. It concerns the disappearance of Hatty Doran shortly after her wedding to Lord Robert St. Simon. The case may be dated as having taken place between 1886 and 1888, and Watson places it in the month of October.

Holmes maintained that the matter had been outside the pale of the law (COPP).

Nom-de-plume, a writer's pseudonym (VALL).

Nonconformist, in England, one who is not a member of the Church of England. Holmes disguised himself as a Nonconformist clergyman in order to penetrate Briony Lodge (SCAN).

*Nonpareil Club, the club in which Holmes investigated a card scandal (HOUN).

*Norah Creina, the steamer lost with all hands and the surviving members of the Worthingdon Bank gang upon the Portuguese coast, some leagues north of Oporto (RESI).

Norberton, Sir Robert, a well-known eccentric and penniless baronet, who depended upon his sister Lady Beatrice FALDER for his livelihood. Deep in debt, he found himself in danger of absolute ruin upon his sister's death, which he attempted to conceal until exposed by Holmes (SHOS).

Norbury, a semi-rural suburb of London. Situated in Surrey, immediately south of the London county border, it consists of a number of country villas served by a railway station. Grant Munro lived here (YELL). See the back endpaper map.

Because of his failure in the Grant Munro case, Holmes suggested that if he should ever become over-confident in his powers Watson should whisper "Norbury" in his ear (YELL).

Norfolk, an eastern county of England, pop. 460,120. It is mostly under cultivation, and there is much pastureland. Hilton Cubitt (DANC) and Trevor Senior (GLOR) were Norfolk squires.

Norfolk jacket, a short coat without tails, worn by sportsmen (BLAC).

Norlett, an actor who impersonated Lady Beatrice Falder after her death. His wife **Carrie Norlett** was Lady Beatrice's maid under her maiden name *Carrie Evans* (SHOS).

Norman-Néruda (*nor'mahn-ner'oo-dah*), **Wilhelmine** (1839–1911), a celebrated European violinist. Born *Wilhelmine Néruda* in Austria, in 1864 she married Ludwig Norman (d. 1885), a Swedish musician. After 1864 she appeared regularly in England, especially at the concerts of Sir Charles HALLÉ, whom she married in 1888, after which she was known as *Lady Hallé.* Holmes declared that her attack and her bowing were splendid, and took time during the Drebber investigation to hear her play (STUD).

Wilhelmine Norman-Néruda.

Normans, the descendants of the Northmen who established themselves in northern France, hence called *Normandy,* in the eighth century, and who invaded and conquered Saxon England in 1066 under the leadership of William, Duke of Normandy, known to English history as William the Conqueror. Reginald Musgrave said that the magnificent oak tree at Hurlstone had in all probability been standing at the time of the Norman Conquest (MUSG). A long line of Norman Falders were buried in the Shoscombe crypt (SHOS).

North Africa. Sahara King was a North African lion (VEIL).

North America. The Great Alkali Plain occupied the central portion of the continent (STUD). See also CANADA; UNITED STATES.

North Camp, the northern half of the great Aldershot military camp, lying to the north of the town and divided from South Camp by a boat-canal. Colonel Barclay's villa was nearby (CROO).

North Carolina, one of the southeastern states of the United States, pop. 1,893,810. The Anderson murders occurred here (HOUN). The Ku Klux Klan had branches in the Carolinas (FIVE).

North Devon line, a line of the *London and South-Western Railway* which skirts the north and west of Dartmoor. Originally opened as the *North Devon Railway* in 1854, the line was purchased by the London and South-Western in 1865. Stapleton brought his hound to the moor by way of the North Devon line (HOUN).

North Downs, the name given to the treeless range of chalk hills extending from the north of Hampshire through Surrey into Kent. The wood round

Birlstone thinned away until it reached the northern chalk downs (VALL). See the back endpaper map. See also SOUTH DOWNS.

Northern Wei dynasty: see WEI.

*North Surrey Observer, the bi-weekly newspaper in which Holmes and Watson read an account of the Amberley case (RETI).

Northumberland, the northern-most county of England, pop. 603,498. The Harrisons were from here (NAVA).

Northumberland Avenue, a thoroughfare in Westminster, running between Charing Cross and the Embankment and renowned for the splendour of its buildings. Three large, handsomely furnished hotels, the *Hotel Métropole,* the *Hotel Victoria,* and the GRAND HOTEL, were erected here after the street was laid out in 1874. Mr. Melas was an interpreter for wealthy visitors to London who stayed at the Northumberland Avenue hotels (GREE), and Francis Hay Moulton resided for a time here (NOBL). Holmes and Watson patronized the TURKISH BATH establishment here (ILLU). See Map II of LONDON and the map of WHITEHALL.

Northumberland Fusiliers: see FIFTH NORTHUMBERLAND FUSILIERS.

Northumberland Hotel, a small hotel situated just east of Charing Cross. Sir Henry Baskerville stayed here while in London (HOUN). See Map II of LONDON and the map of WHITEHALL.

North Walsham, a town in Norfolk, pop. 3,981. Ridling Thorpe Manor was nearby (DANC).

North-west Provinces, a great political division of British India, pop. (1872) 30,781,204. Created in 1835, it was enlarged in 1877 and renamed the *United Provinces* in 1902. ALLAHABAD

The view down Northumberland Avenue to Charing Cross and Trafalgar Square.

is the capital. Muttra was in the Northwest Provinces, near the border with Rajputana (SIGN).

Norton, Godfrey, a London lawyer, residing at the Inner Temple, who married Irene ADLER and fled London with her (SCAN).

Norway, a country in the north of Europe, pop. (1900) 2,221,477. Between 1814 and 1905 it was united with Sweden; see SCANDINAVIA, KING OF. Holmes posed as a Norwegian during his travels in Tibet (EMPT). The elder Neligan was on his way to Norway when he was killed, and Holmes and Watson followed up the Peter Carey case here (BLAC).

Norwich (*nor'ij*), the county-town of Norfolk, pop. 111,733. Abe Slaney was taken here for trial (DANC).

Norwood, a district lying partly in Surrey and partly in the London borough of Lambeth, consisting principally of villa residences and detached houses inhabited by the better classes. The district is divided into three general groups called **Lower Norwood, Upper Norwood** and *South Norwood,* each more southerly than the one before. Jonas Oldacre lived in Lower Norwood (NORW), and Pondicherry Lodge was in Upper Norwood (SIGN).

Athelney Jones happened to be at the **Norwood Police Station,** actually the *South Norwood Police Station,* when the first alarm was brought in the Sholto case (SIGN). See the front endpaper map.

"Norwood Builder, The Adventure of the" (NORW), a chronicle which appeared originally in the *Strand* magazine for November 1903 and *Collier's Weekly* of 31 October 1903 and was published in the 1905 collection enti-

tled *The Return of Sherlock Holmes.* It concerns Holmes's investigation of the apparent murder of Jonas Oldacre by John Hector McFarlane. Watson dates the case as having occurred in an August "some months" after Holmes's return from the Great Hiatus, which would suggest either 1894 or 1895.

Notebook. A blood-stained notebook was a vital clue in the Peter Carey murder (BLAC). Watson took his account of Jefferson Hope's confession from Lestrade's notebook (STUD).

Holmes kept the details of Count Sylvius's life and crimes in a fat notebook (MAZA), jotted down some memoranda on the Priory School case (PRIO), and carried the bill from Dr. Leslie Armstrong here (MISS). The Emsworth case was recorded in his notebook (BLAN), and he turned up the quotation from Eckermann's *Voodooism and the Negroid Religions* here (WIST); these may be allusions to his CASE-BOOK, to his COMMONPLACE BOOK, to his DIARY, or to yet another of his many self-compiled volumes.

Holmes remarked that the case of the dancing men had resulted in something unusual for Watson's notebook (DANC), and the doctor refers to his notebook of cases for the year 1895 (SOLI); see also DIARY; JOURNAL; PORTFOLIO; SCRAPBOOK; YEAR-BOOK.

Nottingham, the county-town of Nottinghamshire, pop. 239,743. The Birlstone murderer was reported from here and nineteen other places (VALL).

Notting Hill, a residential district in Kensington. Selden was known as "the Notting Hill murderer" (HOUN). Louis La Rothière lived here (BRUC), and Lower Burke Street lay in the borderland between Notting Hill and the ancient region of Kensington (DYIN). Watson writes that Inspector Gregson treated Emilia Lucca "with as little sentiment as if she were a Notting Hill hooligan" (REDC), a singular statement in that Notting Hill is known for its respectability rather than for its hooligans; SAFFRON HILL is probably meant. See the front endpaper map.

Nous verrons, a French phrase meaning *we shall see* (BOSC).

Nouveaux riches, a French phrase meaning *newly rich;* hence, those who recently have acquired wealth (HOUN).

Nova Scotia, an eastern province of Canada, pop. 459,574. Col. Spence Munro received an appointment here (COPP).

Nullah, in India, the dry bed of a water-course. Jonathan Small found Mrs. Dawson's body in a nullah (SIGN), and Henry Wood's escape-route from Bhurtee lay down a dried-up water-course (CROO).

Nurse: see SERVANT, subheaded *Commercial and Public Servants.*

Nurse-girl: see SERVANT, subheaded *Domestic Servants: Household Staff.*

N.W. (*North-West*), the designation given to the London postal district which lies to the north and west of Regent's Park (MAZA). See the postal map of LONDON.

O

Oak. An oak figured prominently in the Musgrave Ritual (MUSG). Charlington Hall was surrounded by ancient oak trees (SOLI), and the avenues to the Cunninghams' estate (REIG) and to Birlstone Manor (VALL) passed through stands of oak. The Dartmoor countryside was dense with SCRUB OAK (HOUN). A sprig of oak leaves was supposedly used as a warning sent to enemies of the Ku Klux Klan (FIVE).

The barometer stolen from old Acton's house was oaken (REIG). Arthur Charpentier's walking-stick was described as a "stout oak cudgel" (STUD), as was Holmes's stick in his disguise as an asthmatic old sailor (SIGN), and the sticks belonging to James Browner (CARD) and John Hector McFarlane (NORW) were of oak.

Oak was used in the construction and decoration of the Abbey Grange (ABBE), Ridling Thorpe Manor (DANC), Baskerville Hall (HOUN), Stoke Moran (SPEC), Cheeseman's (SUSS), and St. Luke's College (3STU), and of the houses occupied by Dr. Becher (ENGR), Trevor Senior (GLOR), and Von Bork (LAST).

Oakington, a village to the north of Cambridge, where Holmes sought Godfrey Staunton (MISS). See the map of the vicinity of CAMBRIDGE.

Oakshott, Maggie, the married sister of James Ryder who raised eggs and poultry in the Brixton Road (BLUE).

Oakshott, Sir Leslie, the famous surgeon who attended Holmes after he was attacked in Regent Street (ILLU).

Oberstein, Hugo, one of the few spies capable of playing so bold a game as the theft of the Trelawney Hope document (SECO). It was he who instigated the theft of the Bruce-Partington plans and murdered Arthur Cadogan West (BRUC).

Obliquity of the ecliptic: see ECLIPTIC.

Occipital bone, the bone constituting the back of the skull (BOSC). See the illustration accompanying CRANIOLOGY.

Odd, being of a pair or series of which the rest is missing (CARD, REIG).

Odessa, a Russian seaport on the Black Sea, pop. (1900) 499,673. The Dolsky case took place here (STUD), and Holmes was summoned to Odessa in the case of the Trepoff murder (SCAN).

*Odley's, a house in Sussex (SUSS).

Off colour, in English slang, indisposed or out of sorts (TWIS).

Off foreleg, the right-hand foreleg of a draught animal, so called from the driver's position on the left, the left-hand side becoming the *near,* the right-hand side the *off* side of a horse or pair. These terms are applied at times to any horse, whether or not it is used to pull a vehicle. Silver Blaze's was mottled in colour (SILV), and Jefferson Hope's cab-horse had a new shoes on its off foreleg (STUD).

Official Registry. Holmes said he had wired to get John Clayton's name and address from the "Official Registry" (HOUN), presumably the registration files of Scotland Yard's Public Carriage Office, which is charged with the licensing of cabs and drivers in London.

Ohio, a mid-western state of the United States, pop. 4,157,545. Enoch Drebber and Joseph Stangerson resided for some years in Cleveland (STUD).

Oldacre, Jonas (b. *c.*1843), a successful builder who was rejected as a husband in prospective by the woman who was to become the mother of John Hector McFarlane. Years later, his finances in a bad way, he falsified evidence of his own murder by McFarlane as part of a scheme to cheat his creditors and at the same time revenge himself upon the McFarlanes (NORW).

Old Deer Park, an extensive park at Richmond, distinct from the much larger *Richmond Park,* site of the famous Kew botanical gardens and observatory, and of the playing-field of the Richmond Rugby club. Watson and Robert Ferguson had played one another here (SUSS).

Old gold, aged gold which has taken on the colour of a dulled golden yellow with a brownish tinge (IDEN).

Old Jewry, a short street in the City, lying just west of the Bank of England. It derives its name from the synagogue which stood here prior to the expulsion of the Jews from England in 1291.

Robert Ferguson's solicitors were located here (SUSS). See the map of the CITY.

Oldmore, a former mayor of Gloucester. His wife, or possibly his widow, **Mrs. Oldmore,** was a guest at the Northumberland Hotel (HOUN).

Olympia, The, a huge amphitheatre in the West End. It holds 10,000 people and is used for spectacular performances, sporting shows, and military tournaments. Von Bork had raced his four-in-hand here (LAST). See the map accompanying KENSINGTON.

*One Hundred and Seventeenth Foot: see ROYAL MUNSTERS.

"On the Banks of Allan Water," a traditional Scottish air with words by the English writer and dramatist Matthew Gregory Lewis (1775–1818). John McMurdo sang the song. (VALL).

On the cross: see CROSS.

Onyx. There was a great variety of onyxes in the Agra treasure (SIGN).

Opal. The case of Mrs. Farintosh had concerned an opal tiara (SPEC).

Openshaw, an Anglo-American family residing originally at Coventry, later near Horsham. **Colonel Elias Openshaw** (d. 1883), formerly a member of the KU KLUX KLAN, was murdered by them for documents concerning the society many years after his return from the United States to England, though the coroner's verdict was suicide. His brother **Joseph Openshaw** (d. 1885), unable to provide the documents demanded by the mysterious "K.K.K." because Elias had burned them, apparently met with a fatal riding accident. Joseph's son **John Openshaw** (1865–87) received the same message which had been sent to his father and consulted Holmes, but he was murdered on his way home from Baker

Street. Holmes vowed vengeance upon the murderer, Captain CALHOUN (FIVE).

Opera: see ADLER, IRENE; COVENT GARDEN THEATRE; DE RESZKES; HOFFMANN BARCAROLLE; IMPERIAL OPERA OF WARSAW; LA SCALA; "LES HUGUENOTS"; WAGNER.

Opium, the dried juice of a species of poppy. It is one of the most powerful of narcotics and one of the most important of medicines. Opium is an ingredient in various patent medicines and remedies such as LAUDANUM, MORPHINE, and PAREGORIC.

Watson rated Holmes's knowledge of botany as "variable," but said that he was "well up in belladonna, opium, and poisons generally" (STUD).

Isa Whitney became addicted to opium after reading some of the works of DE QUINCEY; and when Watson went to retrieve him from the BAR OF GOLD, he met Holmes, who assured the doctor that he had not added opium-smoking to his cocaine injections (TWIS). Jonathan Small said that the Sepoy mutineers besieging Agra were drunk with opium and bhang (SIGN).

Ned Hunter was drugged with opium (SILV), as was Miss Burnet (WIST), and Ian Murdoch shouted for opium to ease his pain (LION).

Opium pipe, a pipe with a very small bowl, often of metal, and a long stem, adapted to the smoking of the drug (TWIS).

Oporto, a city and seaport of Portugal, pop. (1900) 167,955. The steamer *Norah Creina* was lost with all hands some leagues north of here (RESI).

Orange. According to the *American Encyclopædia,* orange pips were sometimes used by the Ku Klux Klan as a notice to its enemies of impending death; such pips were sent to each of the three members of the Openshaw family, and by Holmes to Captain Calhoun (FIVE).

Orchid. Orchids grew upon Dartmoor (HOUN).

Ordeal, a form of trial to determine guilt or innocence, still practised in parts of the East and by various savage tribes, which consists of testing the effect of fire, water, poison, and the like upon the accused. If he comes through the test signifiantly unaffected, he usually is considered innocent; if harmed or injured, guilty. Ordeal by poison is common in West Africa, and the devil's-foot powder was used there as an ordeal poison (DEVI).

*Order, The: see BROTHERHOOD.

Order of the Legion of Honour: see LEGION OF HONOUR.

Orderly, in the Army, a private soldier or non-commissioned officer who attends upon a superior officer to carry orders or messages. MURRAY was Watson's orderly (STUD).

Ordnance map, a map of a portion of Great Britain, prepared by the *Ordnance Survey,* a periodic government survey of the kingdom. The scale used for Ordnance maps of counties is that of six inches to the mile. Inspector Bradstreet used an ordnance map of the country round Eyford (ENGR). Holmes sent for an Ordnance map of Dartmoor (HOUN) and obtained one of the neighbourhood round the Priory School (PRIO).

Organic chemistry: see CHEMISTRY.

*"Origin of Tree Worship, The," the name of a book Holmes carried in his disguise as an old bibliophile (EMPT).

Ormstein, the name of the Royal House of the King of Bohemia (SCAN).

Orontes (*ō-ron'teez*), a Britsh troopship. Watson returned to England from India aboard her (STUD).

Ostler, a stable-hand (SCAN); see SERVANT.

"Out of Doors": see WOOD, J. G.

Outré, a French word meaning *excessive;* hence, extravagantly peculiar or passing the bounds of what is proper or conventional (BOSC, HOUN, IDEN, STOC, STUD).

Ouvrier, a French word meaning *workman* or *labourer.* Holmes disguised himself as a French *ouvrier* in Montpellier (LADY).

Oval, The, properly **Kennington Oval,** a cricket ground in south London, near Vauxhall Bridge. Holmes and Watson passed nearby in pursuit of Jonathan Small (SIGN). See Map IV of LONDON.

Overton, Cyril, captain of the Cambridge Rugby team, who called upon Holmes to find the missing Godfrey Staunton (MISS).

Owl. The Danites used the cry of an owl as a recognition sign (STUD).

Oxfordshire, an inland county of England, pop. 181,120. The county-town is *Oxford,* site of the University. Eyford was in Berkshire near the borders of Oxfordshire (ENGR).

Oxford Street, one of the principal streets of London, running from Holborn into the West End. The eastern end of this imposing artery contains a number of the most important shops in London, and presents a scene of immense traffic and activity, while the western part, with the adjoining streets and squares, comprises many aristocratic residences. See Maps I and III of LONDON.

Holmes and Watson often crossed or passed down Oxford Street on their way to and from their Baker Street rooms (BLUE, CHAS, REDH, RESI), and followed Sir Henry Baskerville and Dr. Mortimer down here toward their

Oxford Street is the main thoroughfare between the West End and the City.

hotel (HOUN). Stanley Hopkins arrived at Baker Street in a cab which came up from the Oxford Street end (GOLD), and Holmes and Watson took a cab to Hampstead from here (CHAS). The Adair house was at the Oxford Street end of Park Lane (EMPT).

Holmes was attacked on his way to do business in Oxford Street (FINA), where Bradley's tobacco-shop (HOUN), Latimer's boot-shop (LADY), and Holmes's branch of the Capital and Counties Bank (PRIO) were located.

Mr. Melas said that Harold Latimer took him into Oxford Street from Shaftesbury Avenue (GREE), thus actually referring to *New Oxford Street,* that part of the thoroughfare between Oxford Street proper and High Holborn.

Oxford University, the oldest and most famous English university, located in the city of Oxford, on the Thames fifty-five miles above London. Probably established in the twelfth century, the University is a federation of twenty-one colleges for men and four for women. The curriculum embraces nearly all branches of knowledge, and degrees are conferred by the University and not by the individual colleges.

Colonel Sebastian Moran (EMPT) and John Clay (REDH) were educated here. Without Godfrey Staunton, the Cambridge 'Varsity was defeated by Oxford's Rugby team (MISS). The university which Holmes attended (GLOR, MUSG), the one at which he pursued his researches into Early English charters (3STU), and the one thinly disguised by Watson as "Camford" (CREE) might be either Oxford or Cambridge.

Oxford.

Oxshott, a residential district of north-western Surrey. Wisteria Lodge was between here and Esher (WIST). See the back endpaper map.

Oxshott Common, the name apparently given by Watson to the combined *Esher Common* and *Oxshott Heath,* two adjoining commons lying between Esher and Oxshott, where Aloysius Garcia's body was found (WIST).

*Oxshott Towers, the house belonging to Sir George Folliott (WIST).

Oyster. Holmes served oysters to Watson and Athelney Jones (SIGN).

In his illness he feigned to wonder why the whole bed of the ocean was not one solid mass of oysters, so prolific the creatures seemed (DYIN).

P

Pacific slope, properly that part of the United States between the Sierra Nevada and the Pacific Ocean. Aloysius Doran was said to be the richest man here (NOBL). The term apparently refers also to that part of the United States west of the continental divide of the Rocky Mountains, including Utah, for it was said too that Lucy Ferrier was as fair a specimen of American girlhood as could be found "in the whole Pacific slope" (STUD).

Packet: see STEAM PACKET.

Paddington, a north-western metropolitan borough of London, pop. 143,976. It is mainly residential. Watson bought a practice here (STOC). See the front endpaper map.

Paddington Station, a railway station in Paddington, London terminus

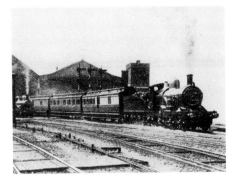

An express train of the Great Western Railway speeds toward Cornwall.

of the *Great Western Railway.* Watson happened to live no very great distance from here and got a few patients from among the officials, one of whom brought Victor Hatherley to his consulting-room (ENGR). Sir Henry Baskerville and his party took a train from Paddington for Dartmoor (HOUN), and Holmes and Watson left for the Boscombe Valley (BOSC) and for Exeter (SILV) here. See Map I of LONDON.

Paddy-field, a rice-field (SIGN).

Paganini, Niccolò (1782–1840), a celebrated Italian violinist, generally considered to be the greatest master of violin technique who ever lived. Holmes told Watson "anecdote after anecdote of that extraordinary man" (CARD).

Page, a household or professional servant, almost invariably a young boy, whose primary duty is to answer the door and show callers in to the proprietor.

Alexander Holder employed a page (BERY), and there was one at Westaway's agency for governesses (COPP). The page at Folkestone Court was "pistolled" in cold blood (HOUN). Dr. Percy Trevelyan's page, who was in league with the Worthingdon Bank Gang, fled and was captured by Scotland Yard, but the proceedings against him broke down for want of evidence (RESI).

There was a succession of pages at Baker Street (IDEN, NAVA, NOBL, WIST, YELL), at least two of whom seem to have been named BILLY (MAZA, THOR, VALL).

Painter, the rope attached to the bow of a boat which is used to tie it to another object (GLOR).

Paisley shawl, a kind of imitation cashmere shawl, so called from the Scottish town where it was originally manufactured (NAVA).

Palace, The: see CRYSTAL PALACE.

Palimpsest, a manuscript prepared by erasure for being written upon again, especially a parchment so prepared by washing or scraping. This custom was brought about by the costliness of writing materials and was practised extensively in the monasteries, especially from the seventh to the thirteenth centuries. The parchments which have been scraped are indecipherable, but those which have been washed have often been revived by chemical processes. Fragments of the *Iliad* and extensive portions of many Greek and Roman manuscripts have been recovered by these means.

Holmes deciphered the remains of the original inscription upon a palimpsest, which appeared to him to be nothing more exciting than an abbey's accounts dating from the second half of the fifteenth century (GOLD).

Palladio, Andrea (1518–1580), an Italian architect of the Renaissance. The Abbey Grange was pillared in front after the fashion of Palladio (ABBE), in which the ancient Roman style is employed rather as a decorative feature than as a constructive element, and is applied without regard to classic precedent.

Pallet bed, a bed, often of straw, made up upon the floor (COPP).

Pall Mall (*pel-mel*), a major street in Westminster. It is the centre of London club-life, most of the more prestigious clubs, among them the BALDWIN CLUB, the CARLTON CLUB, and the DIOGENES CLUB, being located here. The offices of the Adelaide-Southampton steamship line stood "at the end of Pall Mall" (ABBE), and Charlington Hall was let by a firm of house agents here (SOLI). Mycroft Holmes lodged in Pall Mall, opposite the Diogenes (BRUC, FINA, GREE). See Map III of LONDON.

Pall Mall Gazette, a London evening newspaper, founded in 1865. Originally independent and non-political, it became Liberal in 1880 and Conservative in 1892 with successive changes of ownership which have altered too the price, size, and style of the journal. Holmes advertised here for Henry Baker (BLUE).

Palmer, an English manufacturer of bicycle tyres (PRIO).

Palmer, William (1824–1856), an infamous British poisoner. An M.R.C.S. who had studied at St. Bartholomew's Hospital, he was hanged for the poisoning of his wife, his brother, and an associate for their insurance-money. Holmes said he had been at the head of the medical profession (SPEC).

Palmyra, a village of New York, pop. 1,937. It was here that Joseph Smith received the golden tablets of the *Book of Mormon* (STUD) and the first copies were published.

*Palmyra, the ship aboard which John and Ivy Douglas set out for South Africa, and from which Douglas was lost overboard (VALL).

Panama hat, a wide-brimmed hat

plaited from the young leaves of a South American tree, or a hat in imitation of this (DANC).

Pandies, a colloquial name given to the Sepoys who took part in the Indian Mutiny (SIGN), from *Pande,* a common high-caste Hindu surname.

Pannikin, a metal drinking-cup (HOUN).

Parade, The: see NEW BRIGHTON.

*Paradol Chamber, a place which figured in an investigation Holmes carried out in 1887 (FIVE).

Paramore (d. 1869), apparently a victim of the Ku Klux Klan (FIVE).

Paregoric, a tincture of opium flavoured with aromatics, used to relieve pain (3GAB).

Parietal bone, one of the two bones, left and right, which form the top and sides of the skull. The posterior third of Charles McCarthy's left parietal bone had been shattered (BOSC). Dr. Mortimer wished to run his finger along Holmes's **parietal fissure** (HOUN), by which he probably meant the *interparietal suture,* the line running down the centre of the skull from front to back and which separates the two parietal bones at the top of the head. See the illustration accompanying CRANIOLOGY.

Paris, the capital and largest city of France, pop. 2,660,559.

Eduardo Lucas, under the name Henri Fournaye, maintained a wife and a small villa in Paris, and while the Parisian police made the important discoveries in Lucas's murder (SECO), it was Holmes who demonstrated the true facts of the case to them (NAVA). The Hôtel du Louvre is in Paris (BRUC), to which Jefferson Hope pursued Drebber and Stangerson (STUD), and where an attempt had

been made upon Don Murillo's life (WIST).

Hall Pycroft was to manage the Paris depot of the Franco-Midland Hardware Company (STOC). Mr. and Mrs. Francis Hay Moulton were planning to leave for here (NOBL), and Holmes and Watson booked their luggage to Paris, where Moriarty would locate it (FINA).

See also BOULEVARDS; MONTMARTRE.

Paris, plaster of: see PLASTER OF PARIS.

Parish, a civil division of an English county for the purposes of local self-government, such as the care of the poor, education, and sanitation (ENGR, HOUN, ILLU, REIG, VEIL). See also SQUIRE; TOWNSHIP.

The civil parish is generally conterminous with the Church of England ecclesiastical parish (DANC, DEVI, SPEC) from which it originated. A **parish vestry** is a meeting of the inhabitants or ratepayers of an ecclesiastical parish, or their elected representatives, for the dispatch of official business, such as the maintenance of church property and assistance to the poor (HOUN). See also PARSONAGE; VICAR.

Park, The: see HYDE PARK.

Parker, the vicar of Hilton Cubitt's parish in Norfolk (DANC).

Parker, the sentinel posted by Sebastian Moran to watch the Baker Street rooms (EMPT).

Parker, the manager of Coxon & Woodhouse (STOC).

Parkhurst Prison, a prison upon the Isle of Wight, where Shinwell Johnson had served two terms (ILLU).

Park-keeper: see SERVANT.

Park Lane, a street in Westminster, forming the eastern boundary of Hyde Park and extending from Oxford Street to Piccadilly. The fine mansions which occupy the street are unparallelled in their magnificence. The Adairs lived here (EMPT). See Map III of LON-DON and the photograph on p. 220.

Parliament. Parliament had *risen* (CARD),† that is, had completed its

Reginald Musgrave said he was "member for my district" (MUSG), by which he presumably meant that he was one of the two Members of Parliament elected at large to represent the parliamentary division of Western Sus-

In the House of Commons.

deliberations for the legislative season, an event which generally occurs late in August.

Sir William Baskerville had served in the House of Commons (HOUN).

† This allusion is inserted in "The Resident Patient" in some editions.

sex as it was constituted 1832–85. Sir Charles Baskerville had been mentioned as a probable Liberal candidate for MID-DEVON (HOUN).

See also CABINET; CHAIRMAN OF COMMITTEES; ESTIMATES; also CONSERVATIVE PARTY; LIBERAL PARTY. See also LONDON SEASON.

The Houses of Parliament as seen from the Thames. The three towers are, from left, the Victoria Tower, the Middle Tower, and the Clock Tower in which Big Ben hangs.

Parliament, Houses of, or *New Palace of Westminster,* the imposing structure overlooking the Thames, built 1840–57 to replace the former meeting-place of the House of Commons. The huge building contains the House of Lords and the House of Commons, as well as eleven quadrangles and over eleven hundred richly decorated apartments. Its three towers are the northern *Clock Tower* which houses BIG BEN, the *Middle Tower,* and the southern-most *Victoria Tower,* which is the largest of the three.

Holmes and Watson passed the Houses of Parliament on their way to Poultney Square (LADY), and Watson writes that Godolphin Street lay "almost in the shadow" of the great tower (SECO), that is, the Victoria Tower.

Parr, Lucy, the second waiting-maid to Alexander Holder (BERY).

Parsley, sunk into butter: see ABERNETTY.

Parsonage, the mansion or dwelling-house of a parson, provided by the parish (SPEC).

Parthian shot, a concluding retort, in allusion to the manner of fighting of the ancient *Parthians,* a Persian race famous for their skill at firing arrows from horseback even in retreat (STUD).

Partie carrée, a French phrase meaning a *party of four,* commonly in reference to two couples (REDH).

Partington: see BRUCE-PARTINGTON.

Partridge. Holmes and Watson lunched upon cold partridge (VEIL).

Parva: see ABBAS PARVA.

Pâté-de-foie-gras pie, a pie or pasty made of fat goose livers (NOBL).

Patent leather, a heavy, specially tanned leather having a finely varnished surface. The special varnish, consisting chiefly of linseed-oil and colouring materials, is applied in coats with intermediate drying and smoothing between applications in a manner which was once protected by patent. Sir Henry Baskerville wore patent-leather boots (HOUN), as did Lord Robert St. Simon (NOBL) and Enoch Drebber (STUD), and Watson wore patent-leather slippers (STOC).

Paterson: see GRICE PATERSON.

Pathan (*pah-thahn'*), a member of one of the native tribes of Afghanistan. The guard Jonathan Small killed in the Andamans was a Pathan (SIGN). See also JOWAKI.

Pathology, the science treating of the nature, origin, and progress of disease. Holmes spoke of the Presbury case "with the air of a pathologist who presents a rare specimen" (CREE), and said there were many pathological possibilities in the East (DYIN). Dr. Mortimer was a corresponding member of the Swedish Pathological Society (HOUN), Dr. Percy Trevelyan excited considerable interest by his research into the pathology of catalepsy (RESI), and Watson plunged into the latest treatise upon the subject (SIGN).

The science of **comparative pathology** treats of the comparison of diseases, causes, and treatments. Dr. Mortimer was a winner of the JACKSON PRIZE for comparative pathology (HOUN).

See also AGUE; ANEURISM; BLACK FORMOSA CORRUPTION; BRAIN FEVER; CATALEPSY; CATARACT; CLUBFOOT; CONSUMPTION; DIABETES; DIPHTHERIA; DROPSY; DYSPNOEA; EPILEPSY; ERYSIPELAS; HACK; HECTIC; ICHTHYOSIS; JAUNDICE; LEPROSY; LESION; LUMBAGO; NERVOUS LESION; PNEUMONIA; RHEUMATIC FEVER; RHEUMATISM; RIGOR MORTIS; RISUS SARDONICUS; ST. VITUS'S DANCE; SPINAL MENINGITIS; TETANUS; TYPHOID FEVER; YELLOW FEVER; also ATAVISM; BRUISE.

Patrick, a Chicago gang-leader and deviser of the "dancing men" cipher. His daughter Elsie married Hilton CUBITT (DANC).

Patterson, the Scotland Yard inspector apparently in charge of gathering up the Moriarty organization (FINA).

Pattins, Hugh, a harpooner who came to be interviewed by "Captain Basil" (BLAC).

Paul's Wharf, a lane in the City, leading to *St. Paul's Pier* on the Thames. Watson writes that the back of the Bar of Gold was near Paul's Wharf (TWIS), but the lane is far to the west of London Bridge, while Watson locates the Bar of Gold itself east of the bridge. See Map I of LONDON.

Pawnee, formerly a large tribe of American Indians living in what is now the states of Nebraska and Kansas, whence they often went south and west on expeditions across the plains (STUD).

P.C., the abbreviation for *Privy Councilor,* a member of the principal body of advisers to the English sovereign. The Privy Council's political importance has been superseded by the CABINET, whose ministers belong to it. The Duke of Holdernesse was a privy councilor (PRIO).

Peace, Charles (1832–1879), a celebrated murderer who became a national sensation through his daring burglaries and ingenious talent for disguise. He was hanged for the murder of a rival in love. Holmes remarked that he had been a violin virtuoso (ILLU), perhaps a sarcastic allusion to the fact that Peace as a young man appeared on the stage as "the modern Paganini," playing a violin with one string.

Peach, in underworld cant, to betray one's accomplices; to turn informer. Holmes said that Ikey Sanders had "peached" (MAZA). See also SPLIT.

Pea-jacket, a heavy coat originally worn by seamen. Lestrade (NOBL) and John McMurdo (VALL) wore them. A pea-jacket formed part of Holmes's disguise as a sailor (SIGN), and he wore one to the vigil in the City and Suburban Bank vault (REDH).

Peak country, the hilly district in the north-west of the English Midlands. *The Peak* itself, in the northern part of the district, consists mainly of a series of bleak moorland hills. The Priory School was situated in the Peak country (PRIO), which was included within the ancient county of HALLAMSHIRE. See the map of ENGLAND.

Peaky, thin and sickly-looking; peaked. Thaddeus Sholto had a "peaky" face (SIGN).

Pearl. There were nearly three hundred pearls in the Agra treasure, twelve of which were set in a gold coronet, and six of these were sent to Mary Morstan by the Sholtos (SIGN). Holmes was instrumental in recovering the black pearl of the Borgias (SIXN). Sir James Damery wore a pearl pin in his cravat (ILLU).

Peat, partly decomposed vegetable matter, occurring in damp or swampy regions, of considerable importance in certain localities as fuel. It is generally cut in chunks from the surface of the soil with which it is mixed. Holmes and Watson dispatched a peat-cutter to report finding Heidegger's body (PRIO). Grimpen Mire was flanked by firm, peaty soil (HOUN).

Peckham, a region of Camberwell. The non-existent Tom and Sally Den-nis were said to live here (STUD). See the front endpaper map.

Peerage, in Great Britain, the rank of dignity of a *peer,* a holder of the the title of one of the five degrees of hereditary nobility—*duke, marquis, earl, viscount,* or *baron.*

Duke. In strict usage a duke is never styled *Lord,* but is referred to by his full and proper title—e.g., the *Duke of Belminster* (SECO), the *Duke of Holdernesse* (PRIO), the *Duke of Lomond* (3GAB)—though in more casual use a duke occasionally is so called, as in Watson's allusion to the *Duke of Balmoral* (NOBL, SILV) as *Lord Balmoral* (EMPT). A duke is addressed "Your Grace." The wife of a duke is a *duchess;* e.g., the *Duchess of Balmoral* (NOBL), the *Duchess of Holdernesse* (PRIO).

Marquises, earls, and viscounts generally are styled *Lord* in other than strict ceremonial usage, and are addressed "my lord" or "Your Lordship."

Earl. The earl corresponds to the title *count* in other countries; e.g., the Earls of Blackwater (PRIO), Dovercourt (CHAS), Maynooth (EMPT), and Rufton (LADY). The wife or widow of an earl is a *countess;* e.g., the *Countess of Morcar* (BLUE) and the *Countess d'Albert* (CHAS), assuming them to be English countesses and not Continental ones. A countess is styled *Lady;* e.g., *Lady Maynooth* (EMPT).

Baron. A baron is always styled *Lord* in the British peerage; e.g., Baron Dowson (MAZA) is properly called *Lord Dowson,* assuming him to be English.

The ranks of Lords Backwater (NOBL, SILV), Bellinger (SECO), Cantlemere (MAZA), Flowers (SECO), Harringby (WIST), Holdhurst (NAVA), Leverstoke (PRIO), Merrow (SECO), Mount-James (MISS), Singleford (SILV), and Southerton (COPP) are not apparent.

For ranks of Continental nobility see BARON; COUNT; GRAND DUKE; MARQUESS; PRINCE.

Inferior titles. When a nobleman possesses more than one title, he is known by that which carries the highest rank; thus the Duke of Holdernesse was also *Baron Beverley,* the *Earl of Carston,* and *Marquis Saltire* (PRIO).

Courtesy titles. A courtesy title is one to which a person has no valid claim but which is assumed or given by popular consent. When a nobleman has more than one title, it is usual for his eldest son to assume the highest-ranking of his inferior titles; thus the Duke of Holdernesse's son Arthur was called *Lord Saltire* (PRIO). The younger sons of dukes and marquises have the appellation *Lord* prefixed to their Christian names; so the younger sons of the Duke of Balmoral were called *Lord Robert St. Simon* and *Lord Eustace St. Simon* (NOBL), though in some editions Lord Robert's signature upon his letter to Holmes appears merely as "St. Simon," which is improper, and though he is repeatedly referred to as "Lord St. Simon," which is equally in error.

The courtesy title *Honourable* is applied to the younger sons of earls and the children of viscounts and barons; thus the *Hon. Ronald Adair* was a son of the Earl of Maynooth (EMPT), the *Hon. Miss Miles* (CHAS) was the daughter of a viscount or baron, and Admiral Green, father of the *Hon. Philip Green* (LADY), was created an earl, viscount, or baron.

Women. Women may serve as peeresses in their own right only in very limited circumstances. The appellation *Lady* is given to a woman whose husband is a nobleman or whose father is a duke, marquis, or earl; it is also the courtesy title of the wives of baronets and knights. *Lady Frances Carfax* was the daughter of an earl (LADY), as was Hilda Adair (EMPT), who properly would be called *Lady Hilda Adair. Lady Hilda Trelawney Hope* was so called not because she was the wife of a Cabinet minister but because she was the daughter of a duke (SECO), as was *Lady Clara St. Simon* (NOBL). *Lady Eva Brackwell* was the daughter of a duke, marquis, or earl (CHAS). As the wife of Lord Robert St. Simon, Hatty Doran would have been *Lady Robert St. Simon* (NOBL), and *Lady Mary Brackenstall* (ABBE) and *Lady Beatrice Falder* (SHOS) were the wives of baronets. The relationships of *Lady Alicia Whittington* (NOBL) are unclear.

See also BARONET; KNIGHTHOOD.

Peine forte et dure, a French phrase meaning, literally, *intense and severe punishment.* Often called *pressing* in English, the term refers to the barbarous torture formerly inflicted upon those who, being arraigned of felony, refused to plead and stood mute. It was inflicted by putting increasingly heavy weights on the prostrate body of the prisoner until he pleaded or died. Watson was convinced that no *peine forte et dure* would ever force Cecil Barker to speak against his will (VALL).

Peking, the capital of the Chinese Empire, est. pop. 1,300,000. Holmes doubted if there was a complete set of Ming pottery outside the IMPERIAL PALACE of Peking (ILLU).

Pelties, properly **peltry,** a pelt or furskin, or several pelts together. The Indians journeyed into Salt Lake City with their "pelties" (STUD). This reference appears as *pelties, peltries,* or *peltry* in various editions.

Penang lawyer, a walking-stick, usually with a bulbous head, made of palm-wood and imported from *Penang,* a British-owned island off the west coast of Malaya, or from Singapore. Dr. Mortimer (HOUN) and Fitzroy Simpson (SILV) each carried a "Penang lawyer." See WALKING-STICK.

Pence, the plural of PENNY.

Penge, an urban district of Kent, suburban to London, pop. 22,465. Susan Cushing had once lived here (CARD). See the front endpaper map.

Pennsylvania, an eastern state of the United States, pop. 6,302,115. The late Ezekiah Hopkins was supposedly from LEBANON, Pennsylvania (REDH). See also PHILADELPHIA.

*Pennsylvania Small Arms Company, the "well-known American firm" which manufactured the shot-gun used in the Birlstone tragedy (VALL).

Penny, an English money of account and the oldest British coin-denomination still in use. It is equivalent to four farthings, one-twelfth of one shilling, and one two-hundred-fortieth of a pound sterling. It is equal to two cents in United States money. Its abbreviation is *d.,* having been derived from the Roman *denarius.* It is called a *copper* in slang after the metal from which it originally was minted, though since 1860 it has been of bronze.

Pension, a French word meaning *boarding-house* (LADY).

Pentonville Prison, a prison in north London, dating from 1842. James Ryder's friend Maudsley had served time here (BLUE). See the front endpaper map.

Perfume. Holmes said that cases had depended upon the prompt recognition of perfumes, and that it was necessary for the criminal expert to be able to distinguish them (HOUN).

Perkins, the groom at Baskerville Hall (HOUN).

Perkins, a young man who was killed, presumably by Steve Dixie, outside the Holborn Bar (3GAB).

Pernambuco (*per-nahm-boo'kō*), a seaport of Brazil, and the third largest city in the country, est. pop. (1900) 120,000. Isadora Klein's family had been leaders here for generations (3GAB).

Persano, Isadora, the well-known journalist and duellist, who was found stark mad with a match-box in front of him which contained a remarkable worm said to be unknown to science (THOR).

Pershore (*per'shore*), a town in Worcestershire, pop. 3,348. Jonathan Small was born near here (SIGN).

Persia, a kingdom of south-western Asia, est. pop. over 9,000,000. During the Great Hiatus, Holmes passed through Persia, where, no doubt coincidentally, Colonel Sebastian Moran's father had once been the British minister (EMPT). Holmes quoted a Persian saying which he attributed to HAFIZ: "There in danger for him who taketh the tiger cub, and danger also for whoso snatches a delusion from a woman" (IDEN).

Persian slipper, a soft, heel-less leather slipper made in Persia. Holmes kept his tobacco in the toe-end of a Persian slipper (EMPT, ILLU, MUSG, NAVA). Dr. Grimesby Roylott wore TURKISH SLIPPERS (SPEC).

Personal equation, the tendency to error peculiar to a given observer or reasoner for which it is possible to make an approximate allowance. Holmes made use of the conception of the personal equation when putting himself in the place of one whose actions or motives he was endeavouring to trace (MUSG).

Peru, a republic of South America, est. pop. 3,500,000. Robert Ferguson's wife was the daughter of a Peruvian merchant (SUSS).

Peshawur (*peh'shoo-uhr*), or *Peshawar,* a town in India, capital of the north-western possessions here. Watson was removed to the base hospital here following the battle of Maiwand (STUD).

Peter (b. 1878), the groom of Bob Carruthers, struck down by Jack Woodley (SOLI).

Peters, Henry ("Holy"), the Australian criminal who, as *Dr. Schlessinger,* gained the confidence of Lady Frances Carfax, and attempted to murder her for her jewellery. He and his accomplice Annie FRASER avoided capture (LADY).

Petersfield, a town in Hampshire, pop. 3,265. Lord Backwater owned an estate near here (NOBL). See the map of HAMPSHIRE.

Peterson, the London commissionaire who rescued Henry Baker's hat and goose. His wife discovered the blue carbuncle in the bird's crop (BLUE).

Petrarch, or *Francesco Petrarca* (1304–1374), an Italian poet and scholar. Holmes read a pocket edition of his works on the train to Boscombe Valley (BOSC).

Petrel: see STORMY PETREL.

Pheasant, an English game-bird. There were pheasant preserves upon the Thor Place estate (THOR). A hen pheasant figured in the coded message sent by Beddoes to Trevor Senior (GLOR), and pheasant was served at Holmes's cold supper for Mr. and Mrs. Francis Hay Moulton (NOBL).

Pheasant months, the months of October through January, during which the shooting of pheasant is legal in Great Britain (MUSG).

Phelps, Percy, a clerk employed at the Foreign Office. During the time it was entrusted to him, the secret naval treaty was stolen, and he appealed to Holmes to recover it (NAVA).

Philadelphia, the chief city of Pennsylvania, pop. 1,293,679. The big companies moving into the Vermissa Valley were headquartered in New York or Philadelphia, and so were unafraid of the Scowrers (VALL). Jephro Rucastle claimed his daughter was in Philadelphia (COPP). Old Morris joined the Scowrers here, to which Ettie Shafter wished to flee (VALL).

Phillimore, James. Among the unfinished tales in Watson's files was that of Mr. James Phillimore, who, stepping back into his own house to get his umbrella, was never more seen in this world (THOR).

Philosophy, the science which deals with speculation upon the final reality of things and upon the validity of the general concepts and principles underlying all branches of scientific knowledge.

During their early association Watson came to believe that Holmes knew nothing of contemporary philosophy, and his list of Holmes's limits rated the detective's knowledge of philosophy as "nil" (STUD), though some years later he recalled his evaluation with much humour (FIVE). Holmes spoke of Professor Moriarty as a philosopher of crime (FINA), and Sebastian Moran was described as having the brow of a philosopher (EMPT). Holmes spoke of Professor Presbury as a philosopher (CREE) in the sense of a *natural philosopher,* that is, a scientist, and Watson referred to Holmes's "philosophical instruments" (STUD). Holmes in retirement divided his time between philosophy and agriculture (PREF); see HOLMES, SHERLOCK, subheaded *Character: Philosophy and Religion.*

Phoenicians, the name applied to the ancient Semitic inhabitants of coastal Syria to the north of Palestine, known for their contributions to the art of writing, for their skills in mining, and for their extensive commercial and trading enterprises, which made them the carriers of merchandise from as far away as England. The Phoenicians were seldom wholly independent of their invariably stronger neighbours, and during much of the sixth century B.C. were subject to CHALDEA, but the country maintained its commercial supremacy until the time of Alexander the Great. Holmes had conceived the idea that the ancient Cornish language was akin to the Chaldean, and had derived largely from the Phoenician traders in tin (DEVI).

Phosphorus. Stapleton's hound had been treated with a "cunning preparation" of phosphorus (HOUN).

Photography. Photography was the supposed hobby of Vincent Spaulding (REDH) and Jephro Rucastle (COPP). Holmes rather unaccountably claimed that it was one of his methods (LION).

Physiology, that branch of science which deals with the functions, properties, changes, and actions of the living body. Professor Presbury was a physiologist (CREE).

Pickpocket. Holmes said that Moriarty stood at the head of the criminal chain which ended with the minor criminals such as the pickpocket (VALL).

Pickwick, Samuel, the genial hero of

Dickens's *Pickwick Papers* (1837), whom Watson said Charles Augustus Milverton resembled (CHAS).

Pierrot, the name signed by Hugo Oberstein to the messages in the *Daily Telegraph* (BRUC).

Pig. Holmes found himself unable to transfix a dead pig with a single blow from a whaling harpoon (BLAC).

Pigs'-bristles, the stiff, coarse hairs of the domestic pig, extensively used for the manufacture of brushes. The appearance of the word "pigs'-bristles" in the message from Porlock convinced Holmes that he was keying the code to the wrong book (VALL).

Pike, a common fresh-water game-fish (SHOS).

Pike, Langdale, the name used by a London gossip-monger and newspaper writer, whom Holmes consulted (3GAB). The name is obviously a pseudonym, probably the one with which he signed his columns, a common practice among society writers. The *Langdale Pikes* are in fact a pair of scenic hills in Westmorland.

Pince-nez (*pans'nay*), eyeglasses which are lacking ear-pieces and are kept in place on the nose by a spring. John Openshaw wore a pince-nez (FIVE), and Holmes deduced that Mary Sutherland wore one from the dint at either side of her nose (IDEN). Professor Coram's wife Anna wore a golden pince-nez which became a valuable clue in the Willoughby Smith murder (GOLD).

*Pinchen Lane, a street in Lambeth, near the Thames, where old Sherman lived (SIGN).

Pine. Lucy Ferrier grew up among the pines of Utah (STUD). Half-grown pines grew round the Three Gables (3GAB). See also SCOTCH FIR.

Pinfire revolver, a breech-loading revolver which fires a cartridge, invented in 1836, consisting of a paper body and a metal base into which a percussion-cap is placed at the time of loading. An old-fashioned pinfire revolver was found at Wisteria Lodge (WIST).

Pinkerton, Allan (1819–1884), a Scottish-American detective, founder of the **Pinkerton National Detective Agency.** The agency is famous for its exploits on behalf of the North in the Civil War and its questionable practices in the handling of labour disputes. LEVERTON (REDC) and Birdy EDWARDS (VALL) were both Pinkerton detectives.

Pinkerton, Bruce: see BRUCE PINKERTON PRIZE.

"Pink 'Un," the popular name given to *The Sporting Times,* a weekly racing paper, established in 1865, which receives its nickname from being printed on pink paper. The paper's popularity rests less on its reporting of sports news than upon its attention to the personalities associated with the sporting world, and it is considered to be perhaps the least reputable member of the established sporting press. Holmes said that a man with the "Pink 'Un" in his pocket could always be drawn by a bet (BLUE).

Pinna, that part of the outer ear which projects from the head (CARD).

Pinner: see BEDDINGTON.

Pinner, a village in Middlesex. Grant Munro met his wife when she was living with her aunt here (YELL). See the back endpaper map.

Pinto, a Brazilian government official, whose daughter Maria married J. Neil GIBSON (THOR).

Pinto, Jonas (d. 1874), a Chicago criminal said to be engaged in passing counterfeit money, and for whose murder John McMurdo claimed responsibility (VALL).

Pip, the kernel or seed of a fruit (FIVE).

Pipe. Watson writes that he became an institution in Holmes's life like the "old black pipe" (CREE), an allusion to the "old and oily" (IDEN) black clay pipe (BLUE, COPP, HOUN, REDH) which was his favourite counsellor (IDEN), probably identifiable also as his "meditative" pipe (SOLI), as "the unsavoury pipe which was the companion of his deepest meditations" (VALL), and as the one used as an accessory in his disguise as Escott the plumber (CHAS). He also smoked a brier upon occasion (SIGN, TWIS), possibly one with an amber stem (PRIO), but his cherrywood was wont to replace the clay when his mood was disputatious rather than meditative (COPP). A litter of pipes was scattered over the mantelpiece in his bedroom (DYIN), and others were kept in the coal-scuttle (MAZA). His before-breakfast pipe was composed of "all the plugs and dottles left from his smokes of the day before, all carefully dried and collected on the corner of the mantelpiece" (ENGR). The nature of his after-breakfast pipe (THOR) is unrecorded.

John Straker smoked an A.D.P. PIPE (SILV), and Watson at the Bar of Gold refused the offer of an OPIUM PIPE (TWIS). Holmes was able to tell a great deal about Grant Munro from his pipe, remarking that "nothing has more individuality, save perhaps watches and bootlaces" (YELL). Thaddeus Sholto affected to smoke a HOOKAH (SIGN). See also TOBACCO.

Pipette, a small tube used to withdraw and transfer fluids or gases from one vessel to another (NAVA, STUD).

Pit, in commerce: see WHEAT PIT.

Pitch upon, to fix or decide upon. Paul Kratides's kidnappers "pitched upon" Mr. Melas as their interpreter (GREE).

Pitt, William (1759–1806), the Prime Minister of Britain 1783–1801 and 1804–6. Sir William Baskerville served under him in the House of Commons (HOUN).

Pitt Street, a short street in Kensington, between Campden House Road and Church Street. Horace Harker lived here (SIXN). See the map of KENSINGTON.

Place-kick, in Rugby, a kick made while the ball is stationary on the ground (MISS).

Plane tree, a variety of tree related to the maple (THOR).

Plantagenet (*plan-taj′eh-net*), the surname borne by the fourteen kings, from Henry II to Richard III, who occupied the English throne 1154–1485. In 1399 the family was divided into the branches of Lancaster and York, and from their union in 1485 sprang the House of Tudor. The St. Simon family were direct descendants of the Plantagenets and inherited Tudor blood on the distaff side (NOBL).

Plaster of Paris, a quick-setting plaster which at the moment of setting expands in bulk, making it a valuable material for filling cavities where other earths would shrink. Holmes's monograph upon the tracing of footsteps included some remarks upon the uses of plaster of Paris as a preserver of impresses (SIGN).

Plate, gold or silver dishes and utensils used at table or in the home (ABBE, BERY, MISS, NAVA).

Plate, a cup or flagon or other article of gold or silver awarded to the winner in a contest, as to the owner of the winning horse in a race. Silver Blaze won the Wessex Plate (SILV).

Plate, a sheet of metal which forms part of the structure of a ship. The *May Day* turned back to Liverpool because a loose hogshead *started,* that is, dislocated, a plate, presumably in the ship's hull (CARD).

Platelayer, a railway workman employed in laying rails (BRUC).

Plover, a common wading-bird. Holmes said that the plover and the curlew were the only inhabitants of Lower Gill Moor (PRIO).

Violet Hunter's face was freckled "like a plover's egg" (COPP). The distinctive olive-coloured egg of the green plover, or lapwing, marked with irregular black spots and nearly pointed at the small end, is much sought after by epicures.

Plumber, originally, one who worked in lead; in modern times, one who fits pipes and other apparatus for the conveyance of gas and water. John Horner was a plumber (BLUE), as Mary Sutherland's father had been (IDEN), and Holmes posed as a plumber in his wooing of Charles Augustus Milverton's housemaid (CHAS). Watson used a plumber's SMOKE ROCKET to create the appearance of fire at Briony Lodge (SCAN). Some work had been done on the gas in Watson's house (CROO), and Joseph Harrison hid the naval treaty in a floor-recess made for plumbers to get at the gas-pipes (NAVA). See GAS; GASFITTER.

Plumstead Marshes, an uninhabited, marshy lowland in the north-eastern part of Woolwich, bordering the Thames. The *Aurora* ran aground here (SIGN). See the front endpaper map.

Plunger, in sporting slang, a reckless

bettor; a dashing or venturesome gambler or speculator (SHOS).

Plush, a cloth of silk or cotton, and sometimes of wool, having a soft, velvety nap (IDEN, ILLU).

Plymouth, a historic seaport in Devonshire, pop. 107,636. The decorators and furnishers of Baskerville Hall's remodelling were from here (HOUN). Holmes suggested that he had met Mrs. Straker at Plymouth (SILV), and Leon Sterndale received word of Brenda Tregennis's death here (DEVI).

Pneumonia. Douglas Maberley died of pneumonia (3GAB).

Poacher, one who intrudes upon the preserves of another for the purpose of stealing or killing game. Trevor Senior helped break up a gang of poachers (GLOR). Watson suggested that it was a poaching case the Devon constabulary could not solve (HOUN).

Pocket lantern, a lantern of the same or similar design as the DARK LANTERN, made small enough to carry unlit upon the person. Holmes made notes by the light of his pocket lantern as his party drove to the Lyceum Theatre (SIGN), and he examined with it the footprints outside Wisteria Lodge (WIST).

Poe, Edgar Allan (1809–1849), an American poet and story writer. He is considered the father of the modern detective story by virtue of his stories about C. Auguste DUPIN—"The Murders in the Rue Morgue" (1841), "The Mystery of Marie Rogêt" (1842), and "The Purloined Letter" (1845). Holmes had no great respect for Poe's detective creation (STUD), but later he told Watson that he too, like Dupin in one of Poe's sketches ("The Murders in the Rue Morgue"), was in the habit of following the un-

Edgar Allan Poe.

spoken thoughts of those about him (CARD).†

Points, the switches or moveable railway tracks at a junction or station (BRUC, FINA, NORW).

Poison, any substance which, introduced into the body, produces dangerous or deadly effects.

Watson observed that Holmes was "well up" in his knowledge of BELLADONNA, OPIUM, and poisons generally, and Holmes confessed that he dabbled with them a good deal (STUD). Watson called him a "self-poisoner" by COCAINE and TOBACCO (FIVE), and characterized opium as such (TWIS). Young Stamford declared that Holmes would give a friend a pinch of ALKALOID just to observe its effects (STUD).

The Tregennis family were all poisoned with DEVIL'S-FOOT ROOT

† This allusion is inserted in "The Resident Patient" in many editions.

(DEVI), and Paul Kratides died of charcoal poisoning (GREE). Bartholomew Sholto was killed with a substance resembling STRYCHNINE (SIGN), Enoch Drebber with an alkaloid extracted from a South American arrow poison (STUD). Holmes investigated the Camberwell poisoning case (FIVE) and remarked that the most winning woman he ever knew was hanged for poisoning three little children for their insurance-money (SIGN). He said that the forcible administration of poison was by no means a new thing in criminal annals (STUD).

Morgan was known as a poisoner (EMPT). Julia Stoner's body was examined for poison, but without effect (SPEC), and Holmes suspected Holy Peters would use it to kill Lady Frances Carfax (LADY); see CHLOROFORM. The *Daily Telegraph* alluded airily to AQUA TOFANA in its editorial about the Drebber affair (STUD).

The woman Anna committed suicide by poison (GOLD), and Josiah Amberley attempted it (RETI). Holmes remarked that the rejuvenescent serum Professor Presbury was taking had "a passing but highly poisonous effect" (CREE). Inspector Gregory said that Ned Hunter had been poisoned (SILV), meaning that the boy had been drugged with opium, for in all likelihood there was no intent to do permanent harm.

Culverton Smith attempted to kill Holmes by bacterial poisoning (DYIN). Young Jack Ferguson poisoned his infant half-brother, though not fatally, for the baby's mother sucked out the poison in imitation of the legend of *Eleanor of Castile* (d. 1290), wife of Edward I, who sucked a wound in her husband's arm to draw

poison from it (SUSS); see CURARE. Eugenia Ronder sent Holmes a bottle of PRUSSIC ACID as a pledge not to take her own life (VEIL).

Poldhu Bay, properly **Poldhu Cove,** more commonly called *Mullion Cove,* an inlet upon the eastern side of Mounts Bay. Holmes and Watson's vacation in Cornwall found them in a small cottage near "Poldhu Bay" (DEVI).

The view across Mounts Bay from Poldhu Cove.

*Poldhu Cottage, the name given to the cottage where Holmes and Watson stayed (DEVI).

Police. By the nature of his profession, Holmes was brought often into contact with the police organizations of the world. The force with which he worked most often and most closely was of course SCOTLAND YARD, but he had extensive dealings with many others.

Holmes worked in co-operation with the county constabulary of *Berkshire* (ENGR, VEIL) and independently of that of *Cornwall* (DEVI). While old Frankland said that the *Devon* constabulary was in a scandalous state

(HOUN), Holmes had no difficulties with them (SILV.) The *Hallamshire* police were unable to solve the disappearance of Lord Saltire (PRIO). Holmes was called upon to supplement the efforts of the *Hampshire* police (CROO), who had Grace Dunbar in custody (THOR) and investigated Beddoes's disappearance (GLOR), and James McCarthy was arrested in *Herefordshire* (BOSC). Scotland Yard was called to *Kent* by the local force (GOLD). Holmes assisted the *Norfolk* constabulary (DANC) and worked with (REIG, WIST) and called upon (SOLI) the *Surrey* police. Scotland Yard was called to *Sussex* (BLAC), John Openshaw applied to the local police here (FIVE), and Holmes dealt with representatives of the Sussex constabulary (LION, MUSG, VALL).

The London CITY POLICE arrested Beddington (STOC). Holmes said he had given serious trouble to the constabulary at SKIBBAREEN (LAST), an allusion to the *Royal Irish Constabulary,* the semi-military force which polices the whole of Ireland excepting the city of Dublin. Gilchrist accepted a commission in the RHODESIAN POLICE (3STU).

Captain Marvin had served with the Chicago force (VALL). Holmes wired for information to the police at Liverpool (CARD), New York (DANC), and Cleveland (STUD). In the case of Baron Maupertuis, he succeeded where the police of three countries had failed (REIG). He demonstrated the true facts of the case of the second stain to the Paris police (NAVA), who in fact made the first important discoveries in the affair (SECO), and he may have associated with a representative of the Dantzig police (NAVA). Lestrade wired to the police at Liverpool

(STUD). A police officer was killed by the Nihilists in Russia (GOLD). The railway and colliery companies of Vermissa Valley raised their own private *Coal and Iron Police,* or *Mine Constabulary,* to supplement the civil police, who were helpless against the Scowrers (VALL).

See also CHIEF CONSTABLE; CONSTABLE; CONSULTING DETECTIVE; PRIVATE DETECTIVE.

Police-constable: see CONSTABLE.

Police-court, a court for the trial of offenders brought up on charges preferred by the police (BOSC, BRUC, COPP, ILLU, NAVA, SPEC, THOR). The more serious cases requiring trial by jury are referred at the police trial to the ASSIZES (BLUE, VALL). Holmes remarked that realism was wanting in the newspaper police report, where more stress was laid upon the platitudes of the magistrate, he said, than upon the details of the case (IDEN). Holmes and Watson hurried to the BOW STREET police-court to examine Hugh Boone (TWIS).

Policeman: see CONSTABLE.

"Police News of the Past," the paper young Stamford laughingly suggested Holmes might start (STUD).

Police trial: see POLICE-COURT.

Politics. During their early association Watson came to believe that Holmes knew next to nothing of contemporary politics, and his list of Holmes's limits rated the detective's knowledge of the subject as "feeble" (STUD). Some years later he recalled this evaluation with some humour (FIVE).

The question of the Netherland-Sumatra Company and the colossal schemes of Baron Maupertuis was intimately concerned with politics and finance (REIG). Eduardo Lucas was on intimate terms with the leading politicians of several countries (SECO). Percy Phelps was convinced that the theft of the naval treaty was part of a larger "political intrigue" (NAVA). There was complete confidence between Trelawney Hope and his wife on all matters save this, for Lady Hilda was unable to understand the consequences of political acts (SECO). Elias Openshaw was strongly concerned with American politics (FIVE), and Killer Evans was released from an American penitentiary through political influence (3GAR). Politics was believed to have been the motive for Enoch Drebber's murder (STUD).

Watson's notes of Holmes's cases contained many an official scandal of the late Victorian era, including that of "the politician, the lighthouse and the trained cormorant" (VEIL).

Pollard, a tree which has had its top branches cropped nearly to the trunk, and thus caused to form a dense head of spreading branches. Birlstone's village street was lined with pollarded elms (VALL).

Pollock, Constable, a member of the City Police, who helped arrest Beddington (STOC).

Polyphonic motet: see MOTET.

Pompey, the draghound Holmes used to track Leslie Armstrong (MISS).

Poncho, the mustang belonging to Lucy Ferrier (STUD).

Pondicherry, a town on the eastern coast of India, capital of the French possessions there, pop. 174,456. The letter bearing Elias Openshaw's death notice was postmarked here (FIVE).

*Pondicherry Lodge, the Upper Norwood home of Major Sholto and later his son Bartholomew (SIGN).

Pool, The, that portion of the Thames immediately below London Bridge and extending as far as the western end of the West India Docks. This is as far upriver as the largest seagoing vessels may travel. The *Aurora* was pursued through the Pool (SIGN). See the front endpaper map and the photographs on p. 226.

Poop, the stern or aftermost part of a ship, traditionally the province of the ship's officers. James Browner said that Alec Fairbairn once must have known more of the poop than the FORECASTLE (CARD).

The soldiers aboard the *Gloria Scott* fired through the skylight into the saloon from the poop (GLOR), that is, from the *poop-deck,* a deck above the ordinary deck in the after-part of a sailing-ship, usually over the captain's quarters or the main cabin.

Pope, the head of the ROMAN CATHOLIC CHURCH. The Pope 1878–1903 was *Leo XIII* (1810–1903), noted for his learning and statesmanlike qualities. Holmes was involved with the case of the Vatican cameos (HOUN) and investigated the sudden death of Cardinal Tosca (BLAC) in the service of the Pope.

Pope, Alexander (1688–1744), the celebrated English poet. During 1713–26 he was engaged on a poetical translation of Homer's works, the *Iliad* (1720) and the *Odyssey* (1725–26). A copy of Pope's *Homer* was stolen from old Acton (REIG).

Pope's Court, a narrow lane in the City, branching off from Fleet Street, where the offices of the Red-Headed League were located (REDH).

*Popham House, the name of John Scott Eccles's home at Lee (WIST).

Poplar, an eastern metropolitan borough of London, pop. 168,822. It is a district of narrow, squalid streets and mean houses inhabited by a poor and densely crowded population, including as it does the WEST INDIA DOCKS, the ISLE OF DOGS, and BLACKWALL. The borough takes its name from an ancient region north of the Docks. Holmes sent Athelney Jones a wire from here (SIGN).

Porcelain: see CERAMICS.

Porky Shinwell: see JOHNSON, SHINWELL.

Porlock, Fred, the assumed name of a member of Moriarty's criminal organization. He served as an informer to Holmes and sent a coded warning about the planned murder of John Douglas. Holmes made no effort to discover his true identity (VALL).

Port, a very strong, full-flavoured wine, originally produced in the north of Portugal and taking its name from OPORTO, the place of shipment (CREE, GLOR, SIGN).

Portalis, properly **Pourtalès Gallery of Art,** a private Paris gallery established in the home of *James-Alexandre, Comte de Pourtalès-Gorgier* (1776–1855). The collection was sold at auction in 1865, according to the terms of his will, which directed that it should be liquidated for the benefit of his heirs ten years following his death. Holmes quoted the price demanded by a GREUZE at "the Portalis sale" of 1865 (VALL), confusing *Pourtalès* with the better-known *Portalis,* the name of a distinguished family of French jurists.

Port Blair, the chief settlement of the Andaman Islands, first occupied in 1789 and refounded in 1856. Holmes's gazetteer made mention of it (SIGN).

Porter, one who is employed as a gatekeeper (SIGN).

Porter: see HOTEL SERVANTS; RAILWAY SERVANTS.

Porter, Mrs., the cook and house-keeper to the Tregennises (DEVI).

Portfolio. Watson writes of his portfolio of Holmes's cases (PREF). See also DIARY; JOURNAL; NOTEBOOK; SCRAPBOOK; YEAR-BOOK.

Portière, a door-curtain. A portière in Charles Augustus Milverton's study showed the entrance to his bedroom (CHAS).

Portland Prison, a convict-prison upon the peninsula known as *Portland Island,* on the south coast of England. Some sixteen hundred convicts are kept here, who work the nearby stone-quarries. Jack James was sentenced here (LAST).

Portsdown Hill, a hill in southern Hampshire, overlooking the Solent. Major Freebody commanded one of the forts here (FIVE).

Portsmouth, a seaport in Hampshire and the chief naval station of England, pop. 188,133. The harbour is extensively fortified.

Watson landed at Portsmouth when invalided home from Afghanistan (STUD). Von Bork possessed papers in his safe detailing the Portsmouth forts (LAST). Altamont's telegram to Von Bork was from here, and the spy Steiner was arrested here (LAST). Holmes and Watson took a Portsmouth train from Woking (NAVA), that is, a train passing through Woking on its way from Portsmouth to London.

See also FRATTON; SOUTHSEA.

Portugal, a south-western kingdom of Europe, pop. (1900) 5,423,132. The steamer *Norah Creina* was lost upon the Portuguese coast some leagues north of Oporto (RESI).

Posilippo, a suburban district of Naples. The Luccas and Giuseppe Gorgiano were from here (REDC).

Post, newspaper: see MORNING POST.

Post Office Savings Bank, a banking

system established in Britain in 1861 and operated by the Post Office department to encourage saving among the lower classes. Holmes remarked that when people buried treasure in the modern world they did so in a Post Office bank (3GAB).

Pott, Evans, a Scowrer official who held authority even over John McGinty (VALL).

*****Potter's Terrace,** the street in Hampstead where Hall Pycroft lived (STOC).

*****Poultney Square,** the square in Brixton where Holy Peters lived and Lady Frances Carfax was kept prisoner (LADY).

Pound sterling, the highest monetary denomination used in British money accounts, so called from originally being equal to a quantity of silver weighing one pound, and now equal to 20 shillings and to 240 pence. It is strictly a money of account, the coin representing it being the SOVEREIGN. It is equivalent to $4.8665 in United States money; to 25.175 French francs, Italian lire, or Spanish pesetas; to 20.412 German marks; to 9.43 Russian rubles; and to 18.0278 Danish, Swedish, or Norwegian crowns. The pound-shilling-penny system of moneys has been in use in England since the twelfth century. The symbol £ was derived from *libra,* the Latin word for *pound.*

"Practical Handbook of Bee Culture, with some Observations upon the Segregation of the Queen," the book written by Holmes in retirement, which he called "the fruit of pensive nights and laborious days" (LAST).

Prague, the chief city of Bohemia, pop. (1900) 204,498. The King of Bohemia journeyed to London from Prague expressly to engage Holmes (SCAN). Professor Presbury made a

secret journey to Lowenstein in Prague (CREE), and Baron Gruner seems narrowly to have escaped conviction here for an apparent murder (ILLU).

Prehistoric man: see BARROW; CAIRN; CELTS (people); CELTS (implements); CROMAGNON; HEIDELBERG MAN; IVERNIAN; NEANDERTHAL; NEOLITHIC; TIN; WIGWAM.

Premier: see PRIME MINISTER.

Prendergast, Jack (d. 1855), the leader of the convicts' mutiny aboard the *Gloria Scott,* killed in the explosion which destroyed the ship (GLOR).

Prendergast, Major, he whom Holmes helped clear of a charge of cheating at cards in the Tankerville Club scandal, and who later recommended Holmes to John Openshaw (FIVE).

Preparatory school, a school in which pupils are prepared to enter college. The Priory School was said to be the best and most select preparatory school in England (PRIO).

Presbury (b. 1842), the Camford professor whose experiments with the Lowenstein rejuvenescent serum resulted in his singular, ape-like behaviour. His daughter **Edith Presbury** was engaged to the Professor's secretary Trevor Bennett (CREE).

Prescott, Rodger (d. 1895), alias *Waldron,* a counterfeiter who was shot by Killer Evans, and whose bank-note plates Evans sought (3GAR).

Preserve, piece of land set aside for the breeding and preservation of small game. Reginald Musgrave said that he preserved (MUSG). The Copper Beeches was located in the preserves of Lord Southerton (COPP), Trevor Senior shot over Beddoes's preserves (GLOR), and there were pheasant preserves at Thor Place (THOR). Old Frankland won a trespass case against

Sir John Morland for shooting in his own WARREN (HOUN), and there was a rabbit-warren near Boscombe Pool (BOSC). See also GAMEKEEPER.

Press, an upright cupboard; specifically, a bookcase (REDH).

Press, newspaper: see NEW YORK PRESS.

Press, The, institution: see NEWSPAPER.

Pretoria, a city of the Transvaal, formerly the capital of the South African Republic, pop. (1904) 36,839. Godfrey Emsworth was wounded at Diamond Hill near here during the Boer War (BLAN). See the map of SOUTH AFRICA.

Price, the alias Watson used in his interview with Harry Pinner (STOC).

Prime Minister, or **Premier,** in Great Britain, the leader of the majority party in Parliament and head of the CABINET.

Lord Bellinger was twice Prime Minister (SECO), and Lord Holdhurst was a future Premier (NAVA). The Prime Minister himself came to Baker Street to consult Holmes in the case of the Mazarin diamond (MAZA). Colonel Sebastian Moran's salary from Professor Moriarty was more than the Prime Minister received (VALL).

Holmes apparently blamed the American Revolution upon the blundering of *Lord North* (1732–1792), who was Minister under George III (NOBL).

Mycroft Holmes said in November 1895 that he had never seen the Prime Minister so upset as he was over the theft of the Bruce-Partington plans (BRUC), the Premier 1895–1902 being *Lord Salisbury* (1830–1903), a Conservative. Holmes said that he was visited upon the Sussex Downs and asked to take on his counter-espionage assignment by the Premier himself

(LAST), who 1908–16 was *Herbert Asquith* (1852–1928), a Liberal.

Prince, in some countries upon the Continent, a title of nobility superior to a duke (SIXN). A **princess** is the consort of a prince (SIXN) or the courtesy title given to the daughter of a sovereign (SCAN).

Prince's Skating Cub, properly **Prince's Club,** a sporting club located at the south side of Hyde Park and devoted to rackets and court tennis. "Prince's Skating Club" was mentioned in the agony column of the *Daily Gazette* (REDC), but there are no provisions for any sort of skating at Prince's.

Prince's Street, properly **Princes Road,** a street in Lambeth, running from Kennington Road to the Thames. The western end is called BROAD STREET. Holmes and Watson passed down here in pursuit of Jonathan Small (SIGN). See Map IV of LONDON.

Princetown Prison, or **Dartmoor Prison,** a convict prison near the town of *Princetown,* on Dartmoor. Originally erected in 1809 for the accommodation of French prisoners of war, it was rebuilt and adapted to its present purpose in 1850. The convict Selden escaped from Princetown, which was said to be fourteen miles from Baskerville Hall (HOUN), and Jonathan Small expected to be sentenced to Dartmoor (SIGN).

In Princetown Prison.

Pringle, Mrs., the elderly housekeeper of Eduardo Lucas (SECO).

Priory Road, a short street in Lambeth, opening into the Wandsworth Road. Holmes's party passed along here on their way to meet Thaddeus Sholto (SIGN). See Map IV of LONDON.

*Priory School, the most select preparatory school in England, located near Mackleton in Hallamshire, from which Lord Saltire was abducted (PRIO). Holmes later referred to it as the *Abbey School* (BLAN).

"Priory School, The Adventure of the" (PRIO), a chronicle which appeared originally in the *Strand* magazine for February 1904 and *Collier's Weekly* of 30 January 1904 and was published in the collection entitled *The Return of Sherlock Holmes* the following year. It concerns the disappearance from the Priory School of Lord Saltire, son of the powerful Duke of Holdernesse. The case may be dated as having occurred in May of 1901, 1902, or 1903, the year 1901 being most favoured by commentators.

Many years after its first publication, Holmes mentioned "the case which my friend Watson has described as that of the Abbey School, in which the Duke of Greyminster was so deeply involved" (BLAN), an allusion which can be only to this case. Watson says that save in this case, Holmes seldom claimed a large reward for his services (BLAC).

Pritchard, Edward William (1825–1865), an English surgeon who purchased his M.D. in Germany and was hanged in Glasgow for the poisoning of his wife and mother-in-law. Holmes said he had been at the head of the medical profession (SPEC).

Private detective. Holmes said that there were many private detectives, but that he was the only CONSULTING DE-TECTIVE (STUD). He dealt with his friend and rival BARKER (RETI) and with the PINKERTON detectives (REDC), and said that many of his clients were referred to him by private inquiry agencies (STUD). He set other agencies at work in the Sholto case to find the *Aurora* (SIGN). LE BRUN may have been a private detective (ILLU), as possibly were Fritz VON WALDBAUM (NAVA) and François le VILLARD (SIGN). Professor Coram's wife Anna engaged an agent from a private detective firm to enter Yoxley Old Place posing as Coram's secretary (GOLD). John Scott Eccles declared that private detectives were a class with whom he had no sympathy (WIST).

Private hotel, a hotel not licensed for the sale of wine, spirits, or beer; e.g., MEXBOROUGH PRIVATE HOTEL (HOUN); BENTLEY's private hotel (MISS); HALLIDAY'S PRIVATE HOTEL (STUD). Watson stayed at a private hotel in the Strand before his meeting with Holmes (STUD).

Privet, a variety of European shrub much used for hedges (NORW).

"Problem of Thor Bridge, The" (THOR), a chronicle which appeared originally in the *Strand* magazine and *Hearst's International* for February and March 1922 and was published in the collection entitled *The Case Book of Sherlock Holmes* in 1927. It concerns Holmes's investigation of the supposed murder of Maria Gibson by Grace Dunbar. The case is commonly dated as having occurred in October of 1900 or 1901.

Prognathous, in anatomy, characterized by having protrusive jaws. Watson described Enoch Drebber's jaw as prognathous and ape-like (STUD).

Proosia: see PRUSSIA.

Prophet, The, among Mormons, a

title of honour given to both Joseph Smith and Brigham Young (STUD).

Prosper, Francis, the one-legged sweetheart of Lucy Parr (BERY).

Prussia, a kingdom of Europe, the largest state of the German Empire, pop. (1900) 34,472,509. Von Bork was a Prussian (LAST), and Holmes referred to the FRANCO-PRUSSIAN WAR (NOBL).

Mr. Breckinridge told James Ryder that he could ask the "King of Proosia" about his geese (BLUE). *Wilhelm I* (1797–1888) succeeded to the Prussian throne in 1861 and was proclaimed KAISER of the German Empire in 1871; he was succeeded by his son *Frederick III* (1831–1888) and his grandson *Wilhelm II* (1859–1941), who abdicated in 1918. Breckinridge's remark might allude to either Wilhelm, depending upon the date assigned to the case.

Prussic acid, one of the strongest poisons known, appearing as a colourless liquid having an odour of almonds (VEIL).

Pseudo-leprosy: see ICHTHYOSIS.

Psychology: see ALIENIST; ATAVISM; BRAIN FEVER; BROADMOOR ASYLUM; DOCTOR; HARLEY STREET; "JOURNAL OF PSYCHOLOGY"; MONOMANIA.

Pub, a public-house (SOLI).

Publican, the keeper of a public-house or inn (PRIO).

Public-house, or **pub,** a tavern (BLAC, BLUE, SIGN, SOLI). A public-house differs from an INN by having no provisions for lodgers.

Enoch Drebber frequented one or two "liquor shops" and a "gin palace" the night he was murdered (STUD). The Bar of Gold was situated next a "gin shop" (TWIS). See also IVY PLANT; WHITE EAGLE; WHITE HART.

See also ALEHOUSE.

Pugilist, the name of a horse which ran in the Wessex Cup (SILV).

Pulling jockey, in horse-racing, a jockey who deliberately checks or holds back a horse in order to keep it from winning (SILV).

Pullman car, a railway parlour- or sleeping-car, built and operated by the company bearing the name of its inventor and promoter, *George M. Pullman* (1831–1897). Holmes and his party returned from Winchester in a Pullman car (SILV). See also TRAIN-DE-LUXE.

Punjaub, or **Punjab,** a province of British India, pop. 24,754,737. While the SIKHS form less than 10 per cent of the population, they have been the dominant element since late in the eighteenth century and ruled the region until the British conquest of 1849, and for this reason Jonathan Small alluded to the Sikhs as **Punjaubees** (SIGN). Henry Wood settled in the Punjab (CROO). See the map of INDIA.

Punt, any flat-bottomed, square-ended, mastless boat, of whatever size, whether used in fishing, ferrying, or lighterage (SIGN).

Punt, in Rugby, to kick the ball when it is dropped from the hands and before it reaches the ground; a drop-kick. Cyril Overton said that a player who could not punt or DROP was not worth a place on the team for speed alone (MISS).

*Purdey Place, the house belonging to Mr. Hynes Hynes (WIST).

Put up, in hunting, to cause game to rise from cover. Holmes said that the agony column was his "favourite covert for putting up a bird" (3GAR).

Pycroft, Hall, the stockbroker's clerk whose remarkable experience brought Holmes into the Beddington case (STOC).

Q

Quarter, that part of a ship or boat's side between the midpoint and the stern. The *Gloria Scott* was off her boat's starboard quarter when she blew up (GLOR).

Quarter days, the days that begin each quarter of the year. They are LADY DAY (25 March), Midsummer Day (24 June), MICHAELMAS (29 September), and Christmas Day (25 December). These are the usual landlords' and tenants' times for entering or quitting lands or houses and for paying rent. The Wisteria Lodge case began in March shortly before quarter day (WIST), and Dr. Percy Trevelyan moved into his house in Brook Street on Lady Day (RESI).

Quarter Sessions, in England, courts of limited criminal and civil jurisdiction held quarterly in rural areas by the justices of the peace. John Douglas was said to have been acquitted at the Quarter Sessions (VALL), though in most editions this reference is more properly to the ASSIZES.

Queen Anne, in architecture, an unpretending and simple style, making extensive use of brick as the principal material, characteristic of the reign of *Queen Anne* (1665–1714), who occupied the English throne 1702–14. Watson described the Cunningham residence as a fine old Queen Anne house (REIG), and Holmes asked if Nathan Garrideb's house was Queen Anne or GEORGIAN (3GAR).

Queen Anne Street, a street in the West End, in the vicinity of HARLEY STREET and possessing nearly the same professional standing as the residence of physicians. Watson had rooms here in 1902 (ILLU). See Map III of LONDON.

Queen's Bench: see COURT OF QUEEN'S BENCH.

Queen's shilling: see SHILLING.

Queer, in English and American slang, counterfeit money (VALL). See SHOVE THE QUEER.

Queer Street, an imaginary place where persons in financial or other difficulties, and flighty, uncertain, and "shady" characters generally, are feigned to live. Lestrade told Constable MacPherson that he was lucky no harm had been done by the constable's blunder, or MacPherson would have found himself in Queer Street (SECO). Watson said that Sir Robert Norberton was "so far down Queer Street that he may never find his way back again" (SHOS).

Quid, in British slang, a sovereign or a pound sterling (MAZA).

Quinsy, an inflammation of the membranes of the tonsils, often followed by the formation of ulcers which are difficult to heal. Hosmer Angel attributed his hesitating, whispering fashion of speech to quinsy and swollen glands when he was young (IDEN).

R

Rabbi, a title of honour among the Hebrews, now applied to regularly appointed teachers of Talmudic Judaism. The biography of a Hebrew Rabbi was included in Holmes's index (SCAN).

Rabbit. There was a rabbit-warren near Boscombe Pool (BOSC). A stuffed rabbit could be seen in old Sherman's window (SIGN), and Holmes suggested that rabbits had been burned in Jonas Oldacre's wood-pile to produce the organic remains found there (NORW). Thaddeus Sholto wore a rabbit-skin cap (SIGN).

"Rache," the German word for *revenge,* scrawled in blood upon the wall at Lauriston Gardens (STUD).

Racing: see TURF, THE.

Radix pedis diaboli: see DEVIL'S-FOOT ROOT.

Rae, Andrew (d. 1875), a co-owner of the Merton County coaling firm of **Rae and Sturmash** who was murdered by the Scowrers (VALL).

*Ragged Shaw, the name given to a grove of trees lying north of the Priory School (PRIO).

Railway. Helen Stoner's mother was killed in a railway accident (SPEC), and Beddington stole nearly £100,000 in American railway bonds (STOC). Holmes pointed out that Jonas Oldacre's will had been written in a train moving upon a suburban line (NORW). Moriarty engaged a SPECIAL in his pursuit of Holmes (FINA).

See also AYRSHIRES; CANADIAN PACIFIC RAILWAY; EASTERN RAILWAY LINE; NORTH DEVON LINE; STATE AND MERTON COUNTY RAILROAD COMPANY; UNDERGROUND RAILWAY.

See also BRADSHAW'S RAILWAY GUIDE; METALS; PLATELAYER; POINTS; PULLMAN CAR; STATION-MASTER; TRAIN-DE-LUXE; TRAMWAY; also RAILWAY STATIONS.

*Railway Arms, the hotel at Little Purlington where Watson and Josiah Amberley spent the night (RETI).

Railway servants. One of Holmes's early clients was a railway porter (STUD). He argued with a porter in his disguise as an Italian priest (FINA). There was a porter at Eyford station (ENGR) and others at the Dartmoor wayside station near Baskerville Hall (HOUN), and Mr. Melas was assisted by one (GREE).

Mycroft Holmes said that to cross-question railway guards was not his *métier* (BRUC). Watson had befriended a Paddington railway guard, who brought Victor Hatherley to him (ENGR).

See also STATION-MASTER.

Railway stations, of London. Jefferson Hope said he got by as a cab-driver once he had learned the locations of the principal hotels and stations (STUD). The major national termini are CANNON STREET STATION (TWIS), CHARING CROSS STATION (ABBE,

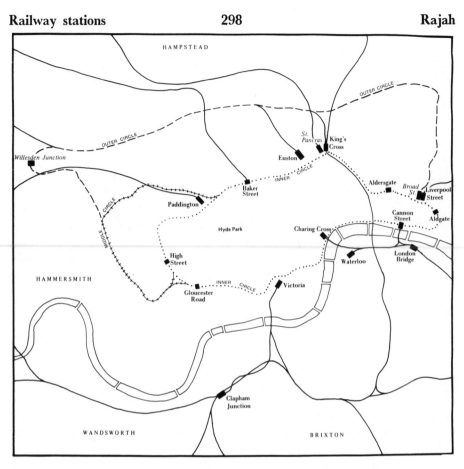

The principal railway termini of London.

EMPT, GOLD, ILLU, SCAN, SECO), EUSTON STATION (BLAN, PRID, STUD), CLAPHAM JUNCTION (GREE, NAVA, SILV), KING'S CROSS STATION (MISS), LIVERPOOL STREET STATION (DANC, RETI), LONDON BRIDGE STATION (BRUC, NORW, RETI), PADDINGTON STATION (BOSC, ENGR, HOUN, SILV), VICTORIA STATION (FINA, GREE, SILV, SUSS, VALL), and WATERLOO STATION (CROO, FIVE, HOUN, NAVA, SPEC). These stations also serve trains run by the principal railway companies and others to some six hundred local and suburban stations in and about Greater London, among them BAKER STREET STATION (BERY), BLACKHEATH STATION (RETI), CHISLEHURST STATION (ABBE), WEALD STATION (3GAB), WILLESDEN JUNCTION (BRUC), and WOOLWICH STATION (BRUC). See also UNDERGROUND RAILWAY.

Railway stations, provincial: see EYFORD STATION; MACKLETON STATION; SHOSCOMBE STATION.

Raj, a Hindi word meaning *rule* or *dominion* (SIGN).

Rajah, in India, a Hindu prince ruling a territory. The power of nearly all the rajahs is now subordinate to that of British officials resident at their courts. Those who retain some degree of actual

London is served by no fewer than seventeen major railway termini, at which passengers arrive from every corner of the kingdom, in addition to the dozens of goods depôts and hundreds of suburban and Underground stations throughout the metropolis. Pictured here is King's Cross Station.

sovereignty are commonly distinguished by the title *maharajah*. The Agra treasure belonged to a northern rajah (SIGN).

Rajpootana, or *Rajputana,* the name given collectively to some twenty native states, under British protection, situated in the north-western part of India, pop. 9,723,301. Achmet had crossed Rajpootana to reach Agra (SIGN). See the map of INDIA.

Ralph, the butler of Tuxbury Old Hall. His wife had been Godfrey Emsworth's nurse (BLAN).

Ramp, to leap or spring up. Holmes as Altamont said that within a week "John Bull will be on his hind legs and fair ramping" (LAST); see also RAMP-ANT.

Rampant, in heraldry, denoting a lion or other beast of prey shown rising with both fore-feet elevated and the head seen sidewise (VALL).

Rance, John, the London constable who found the body of Enoch Drebber and failed to recognize Jefferson Hope as the murderer (STUD).

Randall, the name of a gang of burglars, a father and two sons, who were blamed for the Brackenstall murder but were arrested in New York the same day (ABBE).

Rao, Lal, the Indian butler of Bartholomew Sholto, in league with Jonathan Small (SIGN).

Raphael Santi (1483–1520), one of the greatest painters of the Italian Renaissance. Holmes humorously asked Mary Maberley if she had a Raphael (3GAB).

Ras, Daulat, a student at St. Luke's College and a contestant for the Fortescue Scholarship (3STU).

Rasher, a slice of meat, especially of bacon, intended for frying or broiling (ENGR).

Rasper, the name of a horse which ran in the Wessex Cup (SILV).

Rat. James McCarthy believed his father to have made a dying allusion to a rat (BOSC). Holmes was involved in the case of the *Matilda Briggs,* a ship associated with the giant rat of Sumatra, a story for which the world is not yet prepared (SUSS).

Ratcliff Highway, a thoroughfare in the south of Stepney, of such extremely sinister repute that it has since been renamed *St. George's Street.* The Sumner shipping agency was located here (BLAC). In its editorial about the Drebber murder, the *Daily Telegraph* alluded airily to the **Ratcliff Highway murders** (STUD), a series of seven brutal murders committed in and around the Ratcliff Highway in December 1812 by a former seaman named John Williams.

Raven. Watson heard a pair of ravens upon Dartmoor (HOUN). Holmes said that Selden's body could not be left on the moor for the foxes and the ravens (HOUN).

Read, to study a subject through the books written about it. Holmes did not appear to be pursuing any particular course of reading in his first weeks with Watson (STUD).

Reade, William Winwood (1839–1875), an English writer and African traveller. His works display much ethnological knowledge combined with a strong anti-theological bias. His *Martyrdom of Man* (1872) is an elaborate and learned impeachment of Christianity from a historical and ethnological point of view. Holmes recommended the *Martyrdom of Man* to Watson as one of the most remarkable books ever penned and paraphrased a passage from it (SIGN).

Reading (*red'ing*), the county-town of Berkshire, pop. 72,217. It is a manufacturing town and an important railway junction. Holmes busied himself with the newspapers he had brought with him until their train was past Reading (BOSC, SILV). Eyford was located within seven miles of Reading (ENGR). Mr. Sandeford lived here (SIXN), and Mr. Armitage resided at Crane Water nearby (SPEC).

Reagent, in chemistry, a substance used to effect chemical change in another substance for the purpose of identifying its component parts. Holmes believed he had discovered a reagent which was precipitated by hæmoglobin and by nothing else (STUD).

Rear-admiral, the third degree of admiralty rank, after *admiral* and *vice-admiral.* A Baskerville ancestor had been a rear-admiral (HOUN).

Recherché, a French word meaning *sought after;* hence, rare or otherwise out of the common (MUSG).

Rectified spirits, alcohol from which the impurities have been removed. Holmes said that carbolic or rectified spirits would be the preservatives which

Winwood Reade.

would suggest themselves to the medical mind (CARD).

*Red Bull, an inn upon the road to the west of the Priory School (PRIO).

*Red Circle, the Italian political society, allied to the old CARBONARI, from which the Luccas fled (REDC).

"Red Circle, The Adventure of the" (REDC), a chronicle which appeared originally in the *Strand* magazine for March and April 1911 and the U.S. edition of the *Strand* for April and May 1911 and was published in the 1917 collection entitled *His Last Bow.* It concerns Holmes's interest in the adventures of Gennaro and Emilia Lucca, whom he was too late to assist in their flight from the Red Circle. Estimates of the case's date have spanned the whole of Holmes's career, from 1881 to 1902, though most authorities place it after 1893.

*Red-Headed League, the non-existent benevolent organization concocted by John Clay to dupe Jabez Wilson away from his pawnshop (REDH).

"Red-Headed League, The" (REDH), a chronicle which appeared originally in the *Strand* magazine for August 1891 and was published in the collection entitled *The Adventures of Sherlock Holmes* the following year. It concerns the strange events which befell Jabez Wilson in his association with the Red-Headed League, and the taking of John Clay. Watson dates the case as having taken place in October 1890, but scholarly opinion is divided among 1887, 1888, 1889, and 1890. Holmes alluded later to the case (WIST).

Red Indians: see INDIANS, AMERICAN.

Red King, the name given to *William II Rufus* (*c.*1056–1100), the son of William the Conqueror and King of England 1087–1100. He granted Birlstone to Hugo de Capus (VALL).

Red lamp, the night-time sign of a doctor's consulting-room (SIXN).

Red leech. Holmes handled the repulsive case of the red leech and the terrible death of Crosby the banker in 1894 (GOLD).

Red republican, a radical or revolutionary republican, usually antimonarchical in philosophy, so called from the more fanatical leaders of the bloody French Revolution. Morse Hudson declared that his bust of Napoleon had been smashed by "red republicans" (SIXN).

Redruth, a town of Cornwall, a chief centre of the tin-mining industry, pop. 10,451. The Tregennis family had been mine-owners here (DEVI).

Reefer jacket, a kind of short coat in fashion 1888–90 patterned after the heavy, close-fitting jacket commonly worn by sailors and fishermen. Ted Baldwin wore one in England (VALL).

Regency, that period in English history 1810–20 during which the insanity of George III necessitated his son, the future George IV, governing as Regent. The era was characterized by a flourishing intellectual life and a dissolute moral atmosphere. The Roylott family ruin was completed by a gambler in the days of the Regency (SPEC). A Baskerville ancestor was a Regency buck (HOUN), and Watson said that Sir Robert Norberton should have been such a man (SHOS).

Regent Circus, the name given to either of two circuses in Westminster, popularly known as *Oxford Circus* and *Piccadilly Circus.* Oxford Circus is located at the intersection of Oxford Street and Regent Street, Piccadilly Circus at the crossing of Regent Street

Regent Street is one of the West End's busiest thoroughfares.

and Piccadilly. Holmes and Watson walked toward "Regent Circus" to meet Mycroft Holmes (GREE) and down Oxford Street toward a "Regent Circus" which is surely Oxford Circus to view the photograph of Charles Augustus Milverton's assassin (CHAS). See Map III of LONDON.

Regent Street, one of London's finest streets, extending from north of Oxford Street to the south of Piccadilly, and containing many of the city's handsomest shops. Holmes and Watson saw the disguised Stapleton here (HOUN), where Holmes was attacked by Baron Gruner's roughs (ILLU). John Turner met Charles McCarthy in Regent Street (BOSC). The establishment of Gross and Hankey was located here (SCAN). See Map III of LONDON.

Regina, a Latin word meaning *queen;* in Great Britain, an appellation given to the reigning queen as a per-

sonification of the state. Old Frankland said that the case of *Frankland* v. *Regina* would bring the state of the Devon constabulary before the public (HOUN). See also V.R.

Registration agent, one who assists in making up lists of eligible voters for official review. Holmes posed as one when he spoke with Henry Wood's landlady (CROO).

Registry office, or *district registry,* in England, an office in a provincial town for the transaction and recording of legal documents, in order to avoid the necessity of taking them to the central offices in London. Registrars may exercise limited judicial authority, including the performance of civil marriages. James McCarthy and his barmaid-wife were married at a registry office in Bristol (BOSC), Hilton and Elsie Cubitt presumably somewhere near London (DANC).

Reichenbach Falls.

Reichenbach Falls, a celebrated series of falls of the River Reichenbach, a tributary of the Aar, in central Switzerland. The lower fall is some ten minutes' walk from Meiringen, and the impressive central or *Kessel Fall* is fifteen minutes higher. A walk of thirty minutes more reaches the upper fall, with its beautiful jets; a narrow footpath leads to a footbridge which affords a view of the fall from above, and thence toward Rosenlaui. The death-struggle between Holmes and Moriarty took place on a ledge overlooking Reichenbach Falls (FINA, EMPT). See the map of SWITZERLAND.

Reigate, a town in Surrey, pop. 25,993. Holmes and Watson were invited to Colonel Hayter's home near here, where Holmes was introduced to the case of William Kirwin's murder (REIG).

"Reigate Puzzle": see "REIGATE SQUIRES, THE."

"Reigate Squires, The" (REIG), a chronicle which appeared originally in the *Strand* magazine for June 1893 and as **"The Reigate Puzzle"** in *Harper's Weekly* of 17 June 1893 and was published in the collection entitled *The Memoirs of Sherlock Holmes* the following year. It concerns Holmes's investigation of the murder of William Kirwin by his employers the Cunninghams. Watson dates the case as having taken place in April 1887.

Reilly, a lawyer hired by the Scowrers (VALL).

Reilly, a Scowrer (VALL).

Remand, in law, to send a prisoner back to the court of original jurisdiction upon refusal by a higher court of his application to be released due to a lack of evidence (TWIS, WIST).

Remington, an American brand of typewriter manufactured by the well-known gun-making firm of *E. Remington & Sons* of New York. Laura Lyons possessed such a machine (HOUN).

"Reminiscences," an unpublished work apparently penned by Watson prior to his publication of *A Study in Scarlet,* which is represented as a "reprint" from these "reminiscences" (STUD).

Republican Party, a political party of the United States, organized in 1856 on the basis of opposition to the growth of slavery. The reason for Elias Openshaw's leaving the United States was his aversion to Negroes and his dislike of the Republican policy in extending the franchise to them (FIVE).

Reserve, in Rugby, an additional player kept in readiness to take the place of another, prior to the start of a match, if required. Stevenson was first reserve for Cambridge, and Cyril Overton had been first reserve for the English team in the International against Wales (MISS).

"Resident Patient, The" (RESI), a chronicle which appeared originally in the *Strand* magazine for August 1893 and *Harper's Weekly* of 12 August 1893 and was published in the collection entitled *The Memoirs of Sherlock Holmes* the following year. It concerns the murder of Mr. Blessington, the resident patient of Dr. Percy Trevelyan, at the hands of the Worthingdon Bank Gang. The case has been dated as having occurred in the years between 1881 and 1887, and Watson places it in the month of October, although through the loss of some memoranda upon the matter, he writes, he cannot be certain of the exact date.† The famous "mind-reading" incident which in many editions opens this tale properly belongs to "The Cardboard Box."

"Retired Colourman, The Adventure of the" (RETI), a chronicle which appeared originally in the *Strand* magazine for January 1927 and *Liberty* magazine of 18 December 1926 and was published in the 1927 collection entitled *The Case Book of Sherlock Holmes*. It concerns Holmes's investigation of the disappearance of Mrs. Amberley. The case is commonly dated as having occurred in 1898.

Retort, a glass vessel used in chemistry (COPP, NAVA, SIGN, STUD).

"Return of Sherlock Holmes, The," the third collection of Sherlock Holmes cases, published in 1905 and containing, in order of their first English magazine appearances, the following: "The Adventure of the Empty House"

† This passage appeared in the original magazine and book publications of "The Resident Patient" but was omitted from the American omnibus and subsequent editions.

(EMPT), "The Adventure of the Norwood Builder" (NORW), "The Adventure of the Dancing Men" (DANC), "The Adventure of the Solitary Cyclist" (SOLI), "The Adventure of the Priory School" (PRIO), "The Adventure of Black Peter" (BLAC), "The Adventure of Charles Augustus Milverton" (CHAS), "The Adventure of the Six Napoleons" (SIXN), "The Adventure of the Three Students" (3STU), "The Adventure of the Golden Pince-Nez" (GOLD), "The Adventure of the Missing Three-Quarter" (MISS), "The Adventure of the Abbey Grange" (ABBE), and "The Adventure of the Second Stain" (SECO).

Reuter's (*roi'ter*) **Telegraph Agency,** an agency for the collection and transmission of news, developed by P. J. *von Reuter* (1816–1899) in the decade 1850–60 and later, and now extending over nearly the entire world. The Reuter's dispatch in the English papers was one of three accounts of Professor Moriarty's death which appeared in the public press (FINA).

Reversion, in heredity: see ATAVISM.

Reversion, in law, a right to property which remains after an interest in that property, granted by the owner to another, has ceased. Victor Savage was murdered because he stood between his uncle and a reversion (DYIN). Shoscombe Old Place reverted to the brother of the late Sir James Falder upon the death of Sir James's widow, Lady Beatrice (SHOS).

Reynolds, Sir Joshua (1723–1792), an English portrait painter, born in Devonshire. He was the most popular portraitist of his day and was principal portrait painter to George III. One of the Baskerville family portraits was a Reynolds (HOUN).

Rheumatic fever, an acute constitutional disease, characterized by fever, sweating, and occasional delirium, and frequently leaving permanent cardiac lesions (LION).

Rheumatism. Holmes was somewhat crippled by occasional attacks of rheumatism during his retirement years (PREF). Watson complained of feeling "rheumatic and old" (LADY).

Rhine River, one of the principal rivers of western Europe. The spa of Baden is near here (LADY).

Rhodesia, a British possession in South Africa, administered by the British South Africa Company, est. pop. 946,000, of which not more than 16,000 are Europeans and Asiatics. Young Gilchrist accepted a commission in the **Rhodesian Police** (3STU), officially known as the *British South African Police,* the 900-man military establishment of the colony.

Rhododendron. Holmes hid in a rhododendron bush at Briarbrae (NAVA), near Woking, which is known for its rhododendrons.

Rhone, a river of Europe which rises in the south of Switzerland, enters France through Lake Geneva, and flows into the Mediterranean. Holmes and Watson travelled in Switzerland up the valley of the Rhone to Leuk (FINA).

Ribston-pippin, a variety of winter apple. Watson described James Lancaster as a little ribston-pippin of a man (BLAC).

Richards, Dr., the physician who attended upon the Tregennis family (DEVI).

Richmond, a city of Surrey, pop. 31,672. It lies on the right bank of the Thames and has grown into a residential suburb of London. The *Aurora* was sought as far up the Thames as Richmond (SIGN), and the Birlstone murderer was reported from here and nineteen other places (VALL). Robert Ferguson had played three-quarter for the Richmond Rugby club (SUSS); see also OLD DEER PARK. See the back endpaper map.

Richter, Johann Paul Friedrich (1763–1825), commonly called **Jean Paul,** a German author, best known as a writer of romances and humorous works, as well as sound philosophical treatises. Watson said he was fairly well up in his Jean Paul, having worked back to him through Carlyle, who was much influenced by him, and Holmes maintained that there was much food for thought in Richter (SIGN).

Ricoletti, a club-footed man who, with his abominable wife, figured in a case in which Holmes was involved before his meeting with Watson (MUSG).

Riding-crop, or **riding-whip,** a HUNTING-CROP (SOLI, STUD, VEIL).

*Ridling Thorpe Manor, the Norfolk estate of Hilton Cubitt (DANC). This name appears as *Ridling Manor* or *Riding Thorp Manor* in various editions.

Riga, a seaport of Russia, located on the Baltic Sea, pop. (1897) 282,943. A case in Riga in 1857, Holmes said, was parallel to the one referred to him by François le Villard (SIGN).

Rigor mortis, the characteristic stiffening of the body caused by the contraction of the muscles after death. Bartholomew Sholto's muscular contraction far exceeded the usual *rigor mortis* (SIGN).

Rio Grande, the river which forms the boundary between Mexico and Texas. The *Rio Grande* which was said to lie at the right of the "Sierra Blanco" (STUD) is clearly fictitious.

Ripley, a village near Woking, in Surrey, where Holmes took tea at an inn (NAVA). See the back endpaper map.

Risus sardonicus, or **Hippocratic smile,** a spasmodic grin exhibited during TETANUS. A *risus sardonicus* was frozen upon the face of Bartholomew Sholto's body (SIGN).

River police, or **water police,** properly the **Thames Division,** one of the twenty-two administrative divisions of the Metropolitan Police. It is the oldest

robbery of the train-de-luxe to the Riviera (MAZA).

Robbery, in law, the forcible taking away of another's property from his person or from under his personal protection by violence or intimidation. By extension, the word is often commonly applied to any BURGLARY or LARCENY in which very large amounts are involved.

There had been several robberies for the sake of the blue carbuncle (BLUE). The Worthingdon Bank Gang committed robbery (RESI), as did Beddington (STOC). John Horner

A Scotland Yard police launch.

of the police branches now incorporated within Scotland Yard, having been established in 1798, and includes within its area of patrol the whole of the River Thames from just below Kingston to Barking. The river police helped Lestrade in the arrest of James Browner (CARD) and assisted in recovering John Openshaw's body (FIVE). A police launch was used to pursue the *Aurora* (SIGN).

Riviera, that part of the French and Italian coastline lying between the Alps and the Mediterranean, celebrated for its scenery and popular as a vacation site. Holmes asked Mary Maberley if she would like to visit here (3GAB) and knew of Count Sylvius's part in the

had a previous conviction for robbery (BLUE), old Turner had been a BUSHRANGER in Australia (BOSC), and Sir Henry Baskerville was afraid that Selden might "hold someone up" (HOUN). Holmes knew of Count Sylvius's part in the robbery of the train-de-luxe to the Riviera (MAZA) and felt Moriarty's presence in a number of robberies (FINA). Parker was a GARROTTER by trade (EMPT).

Dr. Grimesby Roylott beat his native butler to death in a fit of anger caused by some robberies in the house (SPEC). The attempted theft of the Beryl Coronet was referred to as a robbery (BERY), as were the taking of the Countess of Morcar's blue carbuncle (BLUE) and the bogus theft of securities from Josiah Amberley (RETI).

There was no reason to suspect robbery in the Peter Carey murder, though some securities were taken (BLAC). No robbery was committed in the Willoughby Smith murder, though Holmes said that such had been Anna's purpose in coming to Yoxley Old Place (GOLD). Robbery was not the motive in the murders of Cadogan West (BRUC), Joseph Openshaw (FIVE), Eduardo Lucas (SECO), Enoch Drebber and Joseph Stangerson (STUD), and Aloysius Garcia (WIST).

Roberts, Frederick Sleigh, Earl Roberts (1832–1914), a celebrated British general. He was distinguished in the Afghan War of 1878–80 (see AFGHANISTAN) and commanded at CHARASIAB and at CABUL. He was commander-in-chief in South Africa 1899–1900 during the SOUTH AFRICAN WAR, and commander-in-chief of the British Army 1900–4.

Holmes declared that the prospect of an interview with Lord Roberts would not have excited greater wonder and pleasure in a raw subaltern than was reflected upon the face of Mr. Kent at the mention of Sir James Saunders (BLAN).

Robert Street, since 1880 called **Robsart Street**, a short street in south London, opening into the Brixton Road. Holmes's party passed through "Robert Street" on their way to meet Thaddeus Sholto (SIGN). See Map IV of LONDON.

Robespierre, Maximilien Marie Isidore (1758–1794), a French revolutionist. His radical policies were opposed by DANTON, whom he caused to be executed, but shortly thereafter his own supporters deserted him and he too was guillotined. Evans Pott was compared with him (VALL).

Robinson, John, the alias attempted by James RYDER (BLUE).

Rochester Row, a street in the southern part of Westminster, opening into the Vauxhall Bridge Road. Holmes's party passed along here on their way to meet Thaddeus Sholto (SIGN). See Map IV of LONDON.

Rocket: see SMOKE ROCKET.

*Rock of Gibraltar, the ship in which Mary Fraser travelled to England, and of which Jack Croker was first officer (ABBE).

Rocky Mountains, the name generally applied to the largest mountain system of North America (NOBL, STUD).

Rodney, George Brydges, Baron Rodney (1718–1792), a noted English admiral. He gained a significant victory over the French in the West Indies in 1782. Rear-Admiral Baskerville served under him (HOUN).

Roman Catholic Church. Mrs. Barclay was a Catholic (CROO), and old Morris was excommunicated from the Church for being a Scowrer (VALL). Robert Ferguson's wife was no doubt a Catholic, for her "alien religion" caused a separation of interests and feelings between her and her husband (SUSS). Pietro Venucci had "some Catholic emblem" round his neck (SIXN). Holmes disguised himself as an Italian priest at Victoria Station (FINA). See also POPE.

Roman miser: see HORACE.

Rome, the capital of Italy, pop. 462,743. Douglas Maberley was an attaché at Rome, where he died (3GAB), and Don Murillo had stayed here for a time (WIST). Harry Pinner reminded Hall Pycroft that "Rome was not built in a day" (STOC). See also VATICAN.

Ronder (d. *c*.1889), a circus-owner, one of the greatest showmen of his day. A bully, profligate, and coward, he was murdered by his wife **Eugenia Ronder** and her lover, but in the incident she was attacked and mutilated by a maddened circus lion. Some seven years later Holmes persuaded her not to commit suicide (VEIL).

Rosa, Salvator (1615–1673), an Italian artist, especially known as a painter of wild and romantic landscapes. There was some doubt as to the genuineness of Thaddeus Sholto's (SIGN).

Rose. Victor Hatherley fainted among the rose-bushes (ENGR).

Holmes pretended to admire a **moss rose** (NAVA), a popular class of rose having large, globular flowers with broad pink petals, of which many hybrid varieties are bred.

The **sulphur rose** is a variety of yellow rose, native to western Asia, introduced into Europe in the seventeenth century. Watson wrote that Laura Lyons's cheeks were of "the dainty pink which lurks at the heart of the sulphur rose" (HOUN).

Rosenlaui Bad, a hamlet in the central part of Switzerland, on the right bank of the River Reichenbach. While it is just three miles from Meiringen, it is more than two thousand feet higher in elevation and the walk from Meiringen requires at least three hours via the Reichenbach Falls. Holmes and Watson set off for here from Meiringen (FINA).

Ross, a town in Herefordshire, pop. 3,303. Boscombe Valley was said to be not far from here (BOSC).

Ross, Colonel, the owner of Silver Blaze, who asked Holmes to enter the case (SILV).

Ross, Duncan, one of the aliases assumed by an accomplice of John Clay when posing as a pensioner of the Red-Headed League. His real name apparently was *Archie,* and another alias was *William Morris* (REDH).

*Ross and Mangles, a firm of animal dealers in the Fulham Road, from whom Stapleton bought his giant hound (HOUN).

Rosyth, an important naval base in Scotland, located upon the northern shore of the Firth of Forth a few miles to the west of Edinburgh. One of the pigeon-holes in Von Bork's safe was so

In Herefordshire, near Ross.

marked (LAST). In some editions the name appears as *Rosythe*.

Rotherhithe, a region of Bermondsey, comprising most of the extensive Surrey side dock system known as the *Surrey Commercial Docks,* a busy manufacturing district inhabited chiefly by sailors, dockworkers, and watermen. Holmes had been working on a case here before falling ill (DYIN). See the front endpaper map.

Rotterdam, the chief commercial port of the Netherlands, pop. (1900) 318,507. John Turner smoked an Indian cigar of the variety which were rolled in Rotterdam (BOSC). Von Bork said that Altamont could get a boat from here to New York (LAST).

Round, to turn upon or against. Williamson warned Bob Carruthers not to round on his pals (SOLI).

Roundhay, the vicar of the parish round Tredannick Wollas (DEVI).

Roy, the wolf-hound belonging to Professor Presbury (CREE).

Royal Artillery, a regiment of the British Army, dating from 1722 and organized for the carrying out of artillery duties. The old soldier Holmes and his brother observed in Pall Mall had served here (GREE).

Royal cream paper: see CREAM-LAID PAPER.

Royal Duke: see DUKE.

*Royal Mallows, the distinguished British Army regiment commanded by Colonel James Barclay (CROO). In some editions this appears as ROYAL MUNSTERS.

Royal Marine Light Infantry, a regiment of MARINES (STUD).

Royal Munsters, properly **Royal Munster Fusiliers,** a regiment of the British Army, consisting of the 101st and 104th Regiments of Foot, which were amalgamated in 1881 as the first and second battalions of the Royal Munsters. The 101st was raised in 1758 as the Bengal European Regiment of the Bengal Army and was known at the time of the Mutiny as the 1st Bengal European Fusiliers. In 1861 it was assumed into the British Army as the 101st Royal Bengal Fusiliers, and in 1881 it was combined with the 104th, whose regimental history is nearly identical.

The first battalion of the Royal Munsters, which Holmes called "the old 117th," was stationed at Aldershot under the command of Colonel James Barclay (CROO), though it must be noted that despite its name the Royal Munsters was not an Irish regiment, did not serve in the Crimea, was not besieged during the Mutiny, and never carried the number 117. In some editions the name appears as *Royal Mallows*.

Royal Navy. Arthur Charpentier was a sub-lieutenant in Her Majesty's Navy (STUD). A Baskerville ancestor had served under Admiral RODNEY (HOUN), and Holmes's index contained the biography of a STAFF-COMMANDER who had written a monograph upon deep-sea fishes (SCAN). Design and construction of the Bruce-Partington submarine was the responsibility of the Navy (BRUC). Holmes as Altamont claimed to have acquired the new naval codes for Von Bork (LAST). The Navy was one of Mycroft Holmes's specialisms (BRUC), and Holmes spoke authoritatively upon the warships of the future (SIGN).

See also ADMIRALTY; CHIEF CONSTRUCTOR; HARWICH; MARCONI; MARINES; ORONTES; PORTSMOUTH; REAR-ADMIRAL; ROSYTH; SUB-LIEUTENANT; SUBMARINE.

Roylott, one of the oldest families in

England, and at one time one of the richest. In the eighteenth century, however, four successive heirs to STOKE MORAN were of a dissolute and wasteful disposition, and the family ruin was completed by a gambler in the days of the Regency. The last squire dragged out his existence as an aristocratic pauper. His only son **Grimesby Roylott** (d. 1883) established a medical practice at Calcutta, where he married Mrs. STONER, and after her death in 1875 returned to Stoke Moran with his two stepdaughters Julia and Helen Stoner. His murder of Julia by means of a poisonous SWAMP ADDER led Helen to engage Holmes, who occasioned Roylott's death when he caused the snake to turn upon the doctor (SPEC).

Rt. Hon., the abbreviation for *Right Honourable,* the title bestowed upon a number of dignitaries in Britain, including all Cabinet ministers (SECO); see HONOURABLE.

Rubber: see WHIST.

Ruby. There were 170 rubies in the Agra treasure (SIGN). A gold pin in the form of a bulldog's head with rubies as eyes was found upon the body of Enoch Drebber (STUD).

Rucastle, Jephro, a country gentleman residing with his second wife **Mrs. Rucastle** at the Copper Beeches in Hampshire. His daughter **Alice Rucastle,** by his first wife, he kept imprisoned in the house to prevent her marriage, which would deprive him of the use of her inheritance. He hired Violet Hunter to be governess to his young son **Edward Rucastle,** the child of his second marriage, and she unwittingly impersonated Alice until Holmes revealed the truth (COPP).

Rudge-Whitworth, a brand of bicycle. Ted Baldwin's machine was one (VALL).

*Rue Austerlitz, a street in Paris, in which Eduardo Lucas, in his alias as Henri Fournaye, owned a small villa (SECO).

*Rue de Trajan, the street in Montpellier where Marie Devine lived (LADY).

Rufton, Earl of, the father of Lady Frances Carfax (LADY).

Rugby, a form of football, devised accidentally at Rugby College in 1823, which permits the option of carrying the ball in the arms. This option is the chief distinction between the rules of the Rugby Football Union and the kicking or "soccer" game of the Football Association. The season is from September to April, and since 1895 the game has gained much attention in London, though Association football remains the more popular. The Oxford and Cambridge matches are held at the Queen's Club in Kensington.

The number 31 had been Watson's "old school number" (RETI), perhaps his Rugby number. Watson at one time had played for BLACKHEATH, and Bob Ferguson for Richmond (SUSS). Gilchrist was a Rugby player (3STU). Without Godfrey Staunton, the Cambridge team lost its match with Oxford (MISS).

For specific Rugby terms see BACK; DRIBBLE; DROP; GOAL; HACK; HALF-BACK; INTERNATIONAL; PLACE-KICK; PUNT; RESERVE; SCRUM; TACKLE; THREE-QUARTER; TOUCH LINE; TRY; TWENTY-FIVE LINE; WING.

Rugger, in English slang, Rugby football (MISS).

Rule of three, in mathematics, the method of finding the fourth term of a proportion when three are known. The numbers being so arranged that the first is to the second as the third is to the fourth, which last is the term required to be found, then it is found by multiplying the second and third terms and dividing the product by the first. Holmes jocularly compared his own reasoning to the rule of three (SIGN).

Rulli: see LOPEZ.

Rum. Peter Carey and Patrick Cairns drank rum together (BLAC).

Rum, in English slang, queer or odd (SIGN).

Rupee, the standard silver coin of British India, the sterling value of which varies between one and two shillings, or between thirty and fifty cents (CROO, SIGN).

*Ruritania, a liner of the CUNARD LINE, in which Baron Gruner planned to leave England (ILLU).

Rush. Rushes grew in Grimpen Mire (HOUN).

Russell, William Clark (1844–1911), an American novelist, the writer of many nautical tales. Watson was deep in one of his "fine sea stories" when John Openshaw arrived at Baker Street (FIVE).

Russell Square, a square in central London, adjacent to the British Museum. Hilton Cubitt met his wife at a boarding-house here (DANC). See Map I of LONDON.

Russia, or *The Russian Empire,* next to Great Britain the largest empire in the world, est. pop. (1897) 130,000,-000.

A note on the Russo-German grain taxes was in Trelawney Hope's dispatch-box (SECO). John McGinty compared the police practices in Vermissa to those of Russia (VALL).

Holmes participated in the adventure of the old Russian woman before his meeting with Watson (MUSG), and Professor Coram and his wife

Anna were Russians who had once belonged to a Nihilist organization (GOLD). Two of the Worthingdon Bank Gang posed as a Russian count and his son (RESI). Holmes declared that a Russian could not have written the note received from the King of Bohemia (SCAN).

The **Russian Embassy** is in Belgrave Square, Westminster. Holmes and Watson delivered here the papers which would assure the release of Alexis (GOLD), and it was said that the Russian Embassy would pay an immense sum for the stolen naval treaty (NAVA).

See also GRODNO; ODESSA; RIGA; ST. PETERSBURG; WARSAW; also CRIMEA; FINN; LITTLE RUSSIA; SIBERIA. See also NIHILISM; TRIPLE ALLIANCE.

Russian leather, a fine, brownish-red leather prepared by very careful willow-bark tanning, dyeing with sandalwood, and soaking in birch-oil. A Russian leather card-case was found upon the body of Enoch Drebber (STUD).

Rutland Island, one of the smaller of the principal Andaman Islands, lying off the southern end of Blair Island. Holmes's gazetteer mentioned Rutland Island, which figured in Jonathan Small's first aborted escape plans (SIGN). See the map of the ANDAMAN ISLANDS.

Ryder, James ("Jem"), the upper-attendant at the Hotel Cosmopolitan, who with Catherine Cusack stole the Countess of Morcar's blue carbuncle, lost it, and confessed when found by Holmes, though he was not denounced to the police (BLUE).

*Ryder Street: see LITTLE RYDER STREET.

S

S. Holmes said that the alternative use of the long and short *S* in the Baskerville manuscript had enabled him to date it (HOUN).

S, the symbol for SHILLING.

Sable, in heraldry, the colour black (NOBL); see HERALDRY.

*Sacred Council of Four, the ruling body of the MORMONS (STUD).

Saffron Hill, a region of central London bordering upon the western part of the City. It is inhabited largely by foreigners, mostly Italians, and is part of the *Italian Quarter* of London. Inspector Hill made a specialty of Saffron Hill and the Italian quarter (SIXN). See also NOTTING HILL. See Map I of LONDON.

Sahara King, the name of the circus lion which mutilated Eugenia Ronder (VEIL).

Sahib (*sah'ib*), a term of respect used by the natives of India and Persia in addressing or speaking of Europeans (SIGN); also occasionally used as a specific title, meaning *master* or *lord,* among both Hindus and Moslems; e.g., NANA SAHIB (SIGN).

Sailing: see SHIP.

St. Augustine, a city of Florida, pop. 4,272. Three men apparently were threatened by the Ku Klux Klan here in March 1869 (FIVE).

St. Bartholomew's Hospital, popularly known as **Barts** or **Bart's,** a great London hospital, affiliated with the

The chemical laboratory, one of several at "Bart's," was constructed in 1870.

The main entrance to St. Bartholomew's Hospital. The façade shown here and the other buildings visible behind it date from early in the eighteenth century.

University of London, of which it is one of the medical schools. It is the oldest benevolent institution in the metropolis, having been founded in 1123, and still stands upon its original site in the north-western part of the City, though it has been rebuilt and added to many times over the centuries. Its vast complex includes many research laboratories, classrooms, libraries, and a museum in addition to the wards. See Map I of LONDON.

Young Stamford had been Watson's dresser here, and it was in the chemical laboratory that the historic meeting between Holmes and Watson took place (STUD).

St. Clair, Neville (b. 1852), the professional mendicant who, in his disguise as *Hugh Boone,* was arrested as his own murderer. His wife **Mrs. St. Clair** engaged Holmes to investigate (TWIS).

*St. George, Guild of: see GUILD OF ST. GEORGE.

St. George's, a London church of considerable social standing, located in Hanover Square. Lord Robert St. Simon and Hatty Doran were married here (NOBL). See Map III of LONDON.

*St. George's, Theological College of, the institution of which Elias Whitney, D.D., was Principal (TWIS).

St. Helena, an island in the south Atlantic, twelve hundred miles west of the African coast, pop. 9,850. It belongs to Great Britain and is celebrated as the place of Napoleon's exile 1816–21. John Douglas was lost at sea in a gale nearby (VALL). See the map of AFRICA.

St. Ives, a charming fishing-town on the northern coast of Cornwall, pop. 6,699. Mrs. Porter's family lived here (DEVI).

St. James's Gazette, an intellectual Tory newspaper, founded in 1880 and conspicuous for its literary character. An evening paper, in 1905 it was amalgamated with the *Evening Standard.*

Holmes advertised for Henry Baker here (BLUE).

St. James's Hall, a great concert hall in Westminster, used for concerts, balls, and public meetings. Opened in 1858, it was demolished in 1905. A new edifice, erected in 1907, now bears the name. Holmes interrupted his investigation of the Red-Headed League to hear Sarasate play here (REDH). See Map III of LONDON.

St. James's Square, a square in Westminster, off Pall Mall, containing a number of aristocratic residences as well as the LONDON LIBRARY (ILLU). See Map III of LONDON.

St. James's Street, a street in Westminster, extending from Piccadilly to Pall Mall, and the site of many of London's clubs. Watson writes that Langdale Pike spent his waking hours in a St. James's Street club (3GAB). Holmes and Watson entered Pall Mall at "the St. James's end" on their way to visit Mycroft Holmes (GREE). See Map III of LONDON.

St. John's Wood, a residential district in the north-west of London, bordering on Regent's Park. Irene Adler's home was here (SCAN). See the front endpaper map.

St. Louis, a city in Missouri, pop. 575,238. Jefferson Hope's family was from here (STUD). A case in St. Louis in 1871 was parallel to the one referred to Holmes by François le Villard (SIGN).

*St. Luke's, the name given to the university college where Hilton Soames taught. In writing of the case Watson deliberately avoids giving any details which would help the reader identify the college involved (3STU).

*St. Monica, the church in the Edgware Road where Godfrey Norton and Irene Adler were married (SCAN).

*St. Oliver's, the Yorkshire private school kept by the Stapletons (HOUN).

St. Pancras, a northern metropolitan borough of London, almost wholly residential in character, pop. 235,317. Holmes was consulted in the *St. Pancras case,* which involved a picture-frame maker who was accused of killing a policeman (SHOS).

St. Pancras Hotel, properly the **Midland Grand Hotel,** a hotel in central London, owned by the Midland Railway, proprietors of *St. Pancras Station,* which it adjoins. Hosmer Angel and Mary Sutherland's wedding breakfast was to take place here (IDEN). See Map I of LONDON.

St. Pancras Station and Hotel.

St. Paul's, the great cathedral of the City of London, the most magnificent

St. Paul's as viewed from the river.

of London's buildings. Completed in 1710 by Sir Christopher Wren, it is the third largest church in Christendom, surpassed only by St. Peter's in Rome and the Cathedral of Milan. King Edward Street is nearby (REDH), and Watson noted the last rays of the sun upon the summit of the dome as the police launch passed the City (SIGN). See Map I of LONDON.

St. Petersburg, the capital of the Russian Empire, situated upon the Gulf of Finland, pop. (1902) 1,487,720. Jefferson Hope pursued Drebber and Stangerson to St. Petersburg, and from here to Paris (STUD).

St. Saviour's, a parish church of central London, lying in the southern-most part of St. Pancras, just west of the Tottenham Court Road. Its poor, working-class congregation numbers some 5,000 souls. Mary Sutherland was to have been married, she said, at "St. Saviour's, near King's Cross" (IDEN), to distinguish between it and the historic church of the same name in the Borough. See Map I of LONDON.

St. Simon, Lady Clara: see BALMORAL, DUKE OF.

St. Simon, Lord Eustace: see BALMORAL, DUKE OF.

St. Simon, Lord Robert Walsingham de Vere (b. 1846), the second son of the Duke of Balmoral. Immediately after his wedding to Hatty DORAN, the bride vanished, and he engaged both Scotland Yard and Holmes to find her (NOBL).

St. Vitus's dance, the popular name for *chorea,* a nervous disease in which the muscles of the body are thrown into involuntary and irregular motions. Old Farquhar suffered from such an affliction (STOC), and Wilson Kemp

twitched like a man with St. Vitus's dance (GREE).

Salle-à-manger, a French term meaning *dining-room.* Holmes and Watson argued in a Strasburg salle-à-manger (FINA), presumably in their hotel.

Saltire, Lord, an inferior title held by the Duke of HOLDERNESSE; the courtesy title of the Duke's son and heir (PRIO).

Salt Lake City, the capital of Utah, pop. 53,531. Founded in 1847 by the MORMONS under Brigham YOUNG (STUD) as the *City of the Great Salt Lake,* it was given its present name in 1868.

The city is regularly laid out and centres about Mormon Square, or the Temple Block, which covers an area of some ten acres and includes the Tabernacle, the Mormon Temple, the Assembly Hall, and formerly the ÉNDOWMENT HOUSE. The Temple is the most prominent structure in the city, built 1853–93 of Utah granite and surmounted by three lofty towers at each end. The highest spire supports a figure of the Mormon angel MORONI.

Salt Lake City has been the headquarters of the Mormon Church since the city's founding. It prospered upon the route to the California gold-fields, and after the discovery of gold and silver in its immediate vicinity, non-Mormons began to invade the region and settle in the city. Only about two-thirds of the population now are Mormons. See also UTAH.

*Salt Lake Mountains, a range in Utah, where Jefferson Hope claimed to have contracted his aortic aneurism (STUD).

Samson, a man who escaped justice for a capital offense committed in New

A view of the Temple Block, Salt Lake City, in 1867. The dome of the completed Tabernacle looms above the Temple's rising foundations.

Orleans because there was no reliable test for blood stains (STUD).

Samuel, the name given to two books in the Christian and one book in the Hebrew canon of the Old Testament. Their history relates the events from the close of David's reign to the destruction of the Jerusalem Temple, and includes (*II Sam.* 11) the story of David and Bathsheba (CROO).

Sand, George (1804–1876), the pen name of the celebrated French novelist *Armandine Lucile Aurore, Baroness Dudevant.* Holmes quoted from a letter to her from Gustave FLAUBERT (REDH).

Sandeford, the purchaser of one of the Napoleonic busts, who sold the statue to Holmes (SIXN).

Sanders, Ikey, the gem-cutter who refused to cut the Mazarin diamond (MAZA).

San Francisco, the chief city of California, pop. 342,782. Aloysius Doran retired to San Francisco, his daughter Hatty was secretly married here, and here she first met Lord Robert St. Simon (NOBL).

Sanger, John (1816–1889), called *"Lord John" Sanger,* an English showman, the most successful of the British circus-proprietors. Ronder's fame rivalled that of Wombwell and Sanger (VEIL).

San Paulo, properly **São Paulo,** the second largest city of Brazil, pop. (1900) 2,282,279. "San Paulo" was a heading in the Neligan notebook (BLAC).

*San Pedro, apparently a Central American country ruled for some years by Don Murillo, who was known as the *Tiger of San Pedro* (WIST).

San Remo a seaport and resort town of northern Italy, pop. 17,114. The

Franco-Midland Hardware Company supposedly had a branch here (STOC).

Sapper, a soldier employed in the building of fortifications and field-works (GREE).

Sapphire. There were 210 sapphires in the Agra treasure (SIGN).

Sarasate y Navascués, Pablo Martín Melitón (1844–1908), a noted Spanish violinist and composer. Holmes interrupted his investigation of the Red-Headed League to hear Sarasate play at St. James's Hall (REDH).

Saunders, the housemaid at Ridling Thorpe Manor (DANC).

Saunders, Mrs., the caretaker for the building in which Nathan Garrideb had rooms (3GAR).

Saunders, Sir James, the specialist in dermatology whom Holmes asked to examine Godfrey Emsworth (BLAN).

Savage, Victor, the nephew of Culverton Smith, murdered by him for a reversion (DYIN).

Savannah, a city and seaport of Georgia, est. pop. (1905) 70,000. The *Lone Star* was registered here (FIVE).

Sawyer, Mrs., the identity assumed by Jefferson Hope's accomplice in order to retrieve Hope's ring from Holmes (STUD).

*****Saxe-Coburg Square,** a square near the City, not far from Aldersgate Station and the Strand, where Jabez Wilson's pawnshop was located (REDH).

Saxe-Meningen, properly **Saxe-Meiningen,** a duchy of south-central Germany, one of the states of the German Empire, pop. (1895) 232,818. The royal family of Scandinavia was said to be of the house of "Saxe-Meningen" (SCAN).

Saxons, a Teutonic race that in the fifth century crossed from the Continent and laid the foundations of the Saxon kingdoms in Britain. Watson wrote that the impenetrable WEALD once held the Saxon invaders at bay (BLAC). The Roylott family was one of the oldest Saxon families in England (SPEC), and one of the graves in the Shoscombe crypt appeared to be Saxon (SHOS). Watson called the Ferguson baby a wonderful mixture of the Saxon and the Latin (SUSS). See also ANGLO-SAXON.

Scabby, afflicted with scabies; mangy. John McGinty called old Morris a scabby sheep in the Scowrer's fold (VALL).

"Scandal in Bohemia, A" (SCAN), a chronicle which appeared originally in the *Strand* magazine for July 1891 and was published in the collection entitled *The Adventures of Sherlock Holmes* the following year. It concerns Holmes's engagement by the King of Bohemia to recover a compromising photograph from the King's former mistress, Irene Adler, and is distinguished as the first of the short tales as well as the first to appear in the *Strand*. Watson dates the case as having taken place in March 1888, but other opinions include 1887 and 1889.

A gold snuff-box, given the detective by the King, served as a souvenir of the case, the only one at the time of publication in which Watson had known Holmes to fail (IDEN), though the affair had been free of legal crime (BLUE, COPP).

Scandinavia, King of, a monarch for whom Holmes managed a delicate and confidential case (FINA, NOBL). The King of the united SWEDEN and NORWAY during 1872–1905 was *Oscar II* (1829–1907); from 1905 he was King of Sweden only, Norway having become independent. The King of Bohemia was engaged to marry **Clotilde**

Lothman von Saxe-Meningen, the fictional second daughter of the "King of Scandinavia" (SCAN).

Scanlan, Mike, a Scowrer and friend of John McMurdo's (VALL).

Schism, Mormon. A schism among the Mormons between 1860 and 1865 had been the immediate cause of Drebber and Stangerson's leaving Utah (STUD). The *Morrisite* movement of 1862 involved not only a religious schism but a brief armed rebellion against the civil authority of the Utah Territory. A mission to Utah 1863–64 converted a few people to the *Reorganized Church of Latter-Day Saints,* a group which had remained at Nauvoo under a son of Joseph Smith and which rejected polygamy.

Schoenbrunn Palace, the magnificent summer residence of the Emperor of Austria, located in the south-western part of Vienna and constructed throughout the first half of the eighteenth century. Von Bork's Tokay was said to be from Franz Joseph's special cellar here (LAST).

Scorbutic, pertaining to *scurvy,* a disease usually presenting swollen, easily bleeding gums, hæmorrhages beneath the skin, rheumatoid pains, anemia, and prostration. It usually develops in those employing an unvaried diet, especially one from which vegetables are excluded. Watson described Shinwell Johnson as scorbutic (ILLU), not unusual for one who has spent long periods in prison.

Scotch bonnet, a brimless, closely woven, and seamless woollen cap (BLUE).

Scotch fir, or *Scotch pine,* the name given to a variety of European pine tree (YELL).

Scotland, the political division occupying the northern part of Great Brit-

Scotland.

ain, co-ordinate in its rights and privileges with England, pop. 4,472,103.

The *Sea Unicorn* sailed out of Scotland (BLAC), and Peter Jones said that John Clay would crack a crib here one week and be raising money to build an orphanage in Cornwall the next (REDH). Inspector MacDonald was a Scotsman (VALL), as was Menzies (VALL), and Lucy Hebron's nurse was a Scotchwoman (YELL). Holmes said that Mrs. Hudson had as good an idea of breakfast as a Scotchwoman (NAVA).

See also ABERDEEN; CARSTAIRS; DUNDEE; EDINBURGH; JOHN O' GROATS; LAUDER; ROSYTH; SHETLAND LIGHTS.

Scotland Yard, the popular name given to the *Metropolitan Police* force of London, and, more specifically, to its *Criminal Investigation Department* (C.I.D.). See also CONSTABLE; POLICE.

The Metropolitan Police were created in 1829, and the force is under the control of the HOME OFFICE. The police of metropolitan London, then, are the responsibility of Parliament, and not of the County of London authorities, and are the only law enforcement body in the kingdom not subject to direct local control. The City has its own independent force; see CITY POLICE.

The headquarters of the Metropolitan Police originally occupied a building in a part of Westminster known as *Scotland Yard,* now called *Great Scotland Yard,* because the place had once been the site of a palace where, in Saxon times and later, the Kings of Scotland resided when they visited London. A terrorist bombing on the night of 30 May 1884 nearly destroyed the C.I.D. offices and demolished a nearby pub, many persons being hurt. When the police moved in 1890 to newly built quarters on the Victoria Embankment, the new building was officially named *New Scotland Yard.* Constructed upon the foundations of an opera house that was never completed, New Scotland Yard is an imposing structure built of granite quarried and dressed by Dartmoor convicts. See the map of WHITEHALL.

The Metropolitan Police District, within which Scotland Yard has jurisdiction, is nearly seven hundred square miles in extent and reached its present limits in 1840; see the back endpaper map. The district embraces portions of the counties of Essex, Hertford, Kent, and Surrey, and the whole of London and Middlesex. It is divided into twenty-two administrative divisions, excluding the City, which are very generally apportioned by population, the exception being the *Thames Division,* or

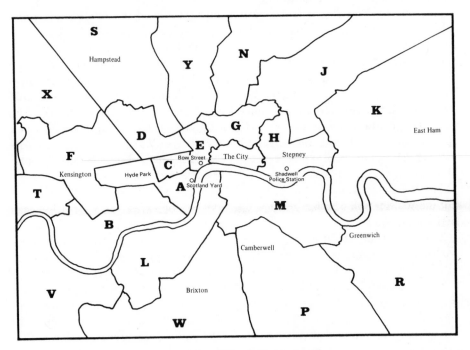

Scotland Yard divisions.

The Metropolitan Police were headquartered in Great Scotland Yard until 1890.

RIVER POLICE. See B DIVISION; H DIVI-SION; see also BOW STREET; NORWOOD POLICE STATION; SHADWELL POLICE STATION. The force's reported strength in 1893 was about 15,200.

THE C.I.D.

The Detective Department of the Metropolitan Police came into being in 1842 in imitation of a number of Continental systems. It was piteously small at first—there were only two detectives in 1842, only fifteen in 1868—and had overlapping duties with the uniformed force. Reorganization came in 1878; the detective and the constable were clearly separated, and the Detective Department was renamed the Criminal Investigation Department. Thereafter the C.I.D. expanded rapidly and gained in expertise. The events of the turbulent 1880s, followed as they were by the relatively crime-free 1890s, in-

creased its acceptance and its popularity with the residents of the metropolis.

Plain-clothes detectives are distributed throughout the divisions (BLUE, ILLU, RESI, 3GAB) as well as assigned to the central office at Scotland Yard. The headquarters staff investigate cases of an imperial or national character (BERY, BRUC, MAZA, NAVA); and cases in which inquiries may have to be pursued in several districts (FINA, GREE, LADY, NOBL, SIXN, 3GAR, TWIS) or otherwise can best be handled by them (EMPT, ENGR, REDH), including those referred from provincial forces (WIST) or foreign ones (REDC); and often those involving special investigative expertise, such as murder cases (ABBE, CARD, CHAS, DYIN, NORW, RETI, SECO, SHOS, SIGN, STUD). The *Special Branch*, established in 1886 to deal with the dynamite outrages of the Irish nationalists, now is primarily devoted to the protection of royalty, Government officials, and foreign dignitaries, and, during the World War, to counter-espionage. See also CHIEF; OFFICIAL REGISTRY. The *Standard* argued in favour of the continued decentralization of the Scotland Yard detectives (SIGN).

While Holmes never professed a great deal of respect for the Yard's detectives or their methods, he was sought out by them in his capacity as a CONSULTING DETECTIVE and had dealings with many, among them Barton (TWIS), BRADSTREET (BLUE, ENGR, TWIS), Brown and his unnamed partner (SIGN), Forbes (NAVA), GREGORY (SILV), Gregson (GREE, REDC, STUD, WIST), Hill (SIXN), HOPKINS (ABBE, BLAC, GOLD), Athelney JONES (SIGN), Peter Jones (REDH), Lanner (RESI), LESTRADE (BOSC, BRUC, CARD, CHAS, EMPT, HOUN, LADY, NOBL, NORW, SECO, SIXN, STUD, 3GAR), MACDONALD (VALL), MacKinnon (RETI), Merivale (SHOS), Montgomery (CARD), Morton (DYIN), Patterson (FINA), Youghal (MAZA), and others (BERY, ILLU, SIGN, STUD, 3GAB). A policewoman followed Mrs. Tangey (NAVA).

Holmes liked to keep in touch with all that was going on at headquarters (SIXN), though he complained that the lack of challenging crime to detect left at most "some bungling villainy even a Scotland Yard official can see through" (STUD) and said that he was not retained by the police to supply their deficiencies (BLUE). He later mellowed in his attitudes and remarked that while there might be an occasional want of imaginative intuition at Scotland Yard, they led the world for thoroughness and method (3GAR).

Dr. Grimesby Roylott called Holmes a "Scotland Yard jack-in-office," which the detective interpreted as a considerable insult (SPEC). When "Mrs. Sawyer" eluded him, he said he wouldn't have the Scotland Yarders know it for the world (STUD), and in retirement he joked that *Cyanea capillata* "very nearly avenged Scotland Yard" (LION). Lestrade asserted that the police at the Yard were very proud of Holmes, and not at all jealous of his successes (SIXN).

The Yard was not informed of the theft of the Trelawney Hope document for fear that the news would become public (SECO). Watson suspected one of the crowd in Park Lane of being a plain-clothes detective (EMPT). Every man James Ryder met, he said, seemed to be a policeman or detective (BLUE).

While the C.I.D. has no jurisdiction beyond the Metropolitan Police District, upon occasion it may be called upon by the CHIEF CONSTABLE of provincial forces who wish to avail themselves of the Yard's experience and resources in the investigation of certain cases. Such instances are rare and usually involve murder (BLAC, DANC, GOLD, SILV, VALL). Sergeant Coventry of the Hampshire constabulary said that if Scotland Yard was called into a provincial case, then the local constabulary lost all credit for success and might be blamed for failure (THOR).

The Metropolitan Police Act of 1839 permits the hiring of official police personnel by private firms or individuals, for private purposes, provided the entire cost of the policeman's maintenance is borne. Thus Lestrade was

New Scotland Yard as viewed from the Thames. The wharf in the fore-ground is Westminster Pier.

hired by the friends of James McCarthy to investigate the Boscombe Valley murder in McCarthy's interest (BOSC), and he may also have been retained by Holmes himself for the conclusion of the Baskerville case (HOUN). Two policemen hired by Lord Robert St. Simon, apparently posing as footmen, ejected Flora Millar from Aloysius Doran's residence (NOBL).

The famous **Scotland Yard Museum** of criminal relics, also called the *Black Museum,* is maintained at New Scotland Yard and is open to the public. Here items relating to the C.I.D.'s cases are kept on display. Holmes remarked that Von Herder's infamous air-gun would finally embellish the museum (EMPT).

Scott, James H., bodymaster of Lodge 29, Chicago, of the Ancient Order of Freemen (VALL).

Scott Eccles, John, the man chosen by Aloysius Garcia to unwittingly provide an alibi for Garcia's murder of Don Murillo. Suspected in Garcia's own death, he engaged Holmes to investigate (WIST).

*Scowrers, The, the local name for the members of Lodge 341 of the *Ancient Order of Freemen* in Vermissa Valley. Elsewhere a benevolent fraternal order, the Freemen of Vermissa turned the lodge organization to their advantage in fighting what they considered the repressive practices of the railways and colliery companies in the coal and iron country of the United States. They were suppressed in 1875 through the efforts of Birdy Edwards and the Pinkertons (VALL). In some editions the name also appears as the *Eminent Order of Freemen.*

"Scowrers, The": see "VALLEY OF FEAR, THE."

Scrapbook. Watson kept a scrapbook about Holmes's career, in which are numerous clippings and extracts upon the Drebber case (STUD). See also DIARY; JOURNAL; NOTEBOOK; PORTFO-LIO; YEAR-BOOK.

Holmes's own scrapbooks (EMPT, REDC, 3STU) would seem to be identifiable with his COMMONPLACE BOOK.

Scratch, in racing, the start or time of starting of a race. When Holmes told Jabez Wilson to "go at scratch" (REDH), he meant for him to tell his story from the beginning.

Screw, in English slang, wages or salary (STOC).

Screw loose, in English slang, something wrong or improper, as in an undertaking. Mordecai Smith, said Jonathan Small, knew that "there was some screw loose" in Small's business, but he was not an accomplice (SIGN).

Scrip, in commerce, an interim or provisional document or certificate to be exchanged for a more formal certificate when certain payments have been made or conditions complied with, as with stocks or bonds (NORW, STOC).

Scrub oak, stunted oak trees (HOUN).

Scrum, properly **scrummage,** in Rugby, the scrimmage, or the formation of forwards as they attempt to get possession of the ball for their own team (MISS).

Scullery-maid, a maid of the lowest rank in a household, who performs the most menial tasks of the kitchen (HOUN, SOLI); see SERVANT.

Scylla and Charybdis (*sil'uh* and *kah-rib'dis*), in classical mythology, twin sea monsters between which mariners often had to pass; thus, twin perils, neither of which can be avoided

without danger from the other (RESI).

Seal. Peter Carey was a former sealer (BLAC). John Straker carried a sealskin tobacco pouch (SILV), and such a pouch was a clue in the Carey murder (BLAC).

Season, The: see LONDON SEASON.

*Sea Unicorn, the steam-sealer which Peter Carey captained in 1883–84 (BLAC).

Second Afghan War: see AFGHAN-ISTAN.

"Second Stain, The Adventure of the" (SECO), a chronicle which appeared originally in the *Strand* magazine for December 1904 and *Collier's Weekly* of 28 January 1905 and was published in the 1905 collection entitled *The Return of Sherlock Holmes*. It concerns the theft of a confidential document from the home of the Rt. Hon. Trelawney Hope and the death of Eduardo Lucas, the suspected thief. Watson has deliberately obscured the date of the case, saying that it took place "in a year, and even in a decade, that shall be nameless," and opinions as to the true date range from 1886 to 1894.

Elsewhere, however, Watson states that the adventure occurred in the July immediately succeeding his marriage, but that it would be impossible to make the case public before the turn of the century, and mentions details which were not revealed in the final appearance of the tale (NAVA).

The affair of the second stain was said to be one of the half-dozen cases in which the truth was discovered even though Holmes erred (YELL); in some editions this reference is to "The Musgrave Ritual."

Secretary. Secretaries were employed by Charles Augustus Milverton

(CHAS), J. Neil Gibson (THOR), and Don Murillo (WIST), and Professor Coram hired a succession of them, one of whom was a spy for the Brotherhood, another Willoughby Smith (GOLD). Trevor Bennett acted as secretary to Professor Presbury (CREE), James Wilder to the Duke of Holdernesse (PRIO), and Joseph Stangerson to Enoch Drebber (STUD). "Ferguson" was introduced as Lysander Stark's secretary (ENGR).

Secretary of State: see CABINET.

Secret societies: see BROTHERHOOD, THE; CARBONARI; DANITES; KU KLUX KLAN; MAFIA; RED CIRCLE; SCOWRERS; VEHMGERICHT; see also BUFFALO (city); TURKEY.

Secret writing: see CRYPTOGRAPHY.

Securities: see STOCKS.

Selden (d. 1889), the infamous Notting Hill murderer, sentenced to Princetown Prison. He was the brother of Mrs. BARRYMORE and so was able with her help to remain at liberty upon the moor until he was killed fleeing from Stapleton's hound (HOUN).

Senegambia, a region of western Africa belonging to France. Its particular boundaries and form of colonial administration often have been altered during the expansion of French influence in the area, but in general Senegambia extends from the Gambia River on the south to the Sahara upon the north and westward to the country of the Niger. It takes its name from the Senegal and Gambia rivers which lie within its boundaries, and it should be considered in geographical rather than political terms. Cases in India and Senegambia were parallel to the murder of Bartholomew Sholto (SIGN). See the map of AFRICA.

Sepoy, the name given to a native British Indian soldier. The Sepoys form an important part of the Army in India, and number in all some 140,000. The theft of the Agra treasure occurred during the Sepoy MUTINY of 1857–58 (SIGN), at a time when they numbered 348,000.

Sere, dry and withered, said especially of vegetation. Holmes remarked that a man who could stride four and a half feet without effort was not *in the sere and yellow* (STUD).

Sergeant, of police: see CONSTABLE.

Sergius: see CORAM.

Serpentine, The, a large artificial

The view over the Serpentine.

lake in Hyde Park. Hatty Doran's wedding-clothes were found floating here, and Lestrade had it dragged for her body (NOBL).

*Serpentine Avenue, the street in St. John's Wood in which Irene Adler lived. Holmes learned much about her from the ostlers working in Serpentine Mews, which lay behind Briony Lodge (SCAN).

Serum of Anthropoid: see ANTHRO-POID.

Servant, one who owes his services to another for a limited period but cannot bind his employer by contract. Servants in general may be classed as *domestic servants, professional* or *commercial servants,* and *public servants.*

DOMESTIC SERVANTS

Servants were employed by the Brackenstalls (ABBE), the Cunninghams (REIG), and Mrs. Cecil Forrester (SIGN). Charles Augustus Milverton kept a large number of servants (CHAS), and there was a small staff at Charlington Hall (SOLI). Birlstone Manor had a staff of eight (VALL). John Ferrier's servants slept in an outhouse (STUD). Elias Openshaw made his nephew John his representative among the servants (FIVE), and Madame Fournaye's servants reported her to the police as insane (SECO). Charles Augustus Milverton received many of his blackmailing wares from treacherous servants (CHAS). Holmes considered it suggestive that there were so few servants at Tuxbury Old Park (BLAN), it struck Dr. Horsom as remarkable that the Schlessingers should have no servants (LADY), and no servants would remain with Dr. Grimesby Roylott (SPEC). Joseph Harrison used the servants' door at Briarbrae (NAVA).

Charles McCarthy employed a serving-man (BOSC). WILLIAMS was servant to Thaddeus Sholto, MCMURDO to Bartholomew Sholto (SIGN). Mr. and Mrs. TOLLER were the Rucastles' servants (COPP). The Stauntons had one servant (MISS), as did Chester Wilcox (VALL).

Major Sholto brought a staff of Indian servants to London (SIGN), and James Barclay betrayed Henry Wood by means of a native servant (CROO).

HOUSEHOLD STAFF. In the larger households the servants are under the general direction of the BUTLER.

John Turner kept at least a half-dozen household servants (BOSC), and Don Murillo kept a "houseful" of servants at High Gable in addition to the outside staff (WIST). The Musgrave estate at Hurlstone employed thirteen servants—eight maids, a cook, a butler, two footmen, and a boy—in addition to the garden and stable staffs (MUSG). Von Bork sent his household on to Germany ahead of him (LAST). Holmes sarcastically remarked that J. Neil Gibson seemed to have "a nice loyal household" (THOR). BARRYMORE was the son of Baskerville Hall's old caretaker, and Sir Henry Baskerville sought new servants to replace Barrymore and his wife (HOUN).

The Tregennis family was said to have a housekeeper and a young girl to look after their wants, though a boy was found to go for the doctor (DEVI). Peter Carey kept two female servants (BLAC), Jabez Wilson employed a girl of fourteen to cook and clean (REDH), Mary Maberley employed Susan STOCKDALE and a girl (3GAB), and the Warrens kept a girl (REDC). Watson had servants (CROO). Charles Augustus Milverton's assassin posed as a servant of the

Countess d'Albert (CHAS), and Mortimer Tregennis's body was discovered by his servant or by Mr. Roundhay's (DEVI). The Amberleys had one woman servant who came in by the day (RETI).

Maid. Trevor Senior had maids (GLOR), and Dr. Percy Trevelyan employed a maid or maids (RESI). Enoch Drebber's manners toward Madame Charpentier's maid-servants was "disgustingly free and familiar" (STUD). Holmes remarked that Don Murillo kept a "houseful" of maid-servants (WIST). Reginald Musgrave employed eight maids (MUSG), Alexander Holder four (BERY), and the Fergusons two (SUSS). Servant-maids were among the crowd outside Briony Lodge (SCAN).

A single maid was employed by Charles McCarthy (BOSC), the Barclays (CROO), Hilton Cubitt (DANC), Lady Maynooth (EMPT), Professor Coram (GOLD), Laura Lyons (HOUN), the Stapletons (HOUN), Irene Adler (SCAN), the Trelawney Hopes (SECO), John Straker (SILV), and Grant Munro (YELL). Susan Cushing had a serving-girl (CARD). AGATHA was maid to Charles Augustus Milverton (CHAS). There was a maid at Baker Street (BRUC, FIVE, STUD), and Watson employed a maid (BOSC, ENGR, EMPT) who at one time was named MARY JANE (SCAN).

Catherine Cusack was WAITING-MAID to the Countess of Morcar (BLUE), and Alexander Holder referred to Lucy Parr as his "second waiting-maid" (BERY). There was a SCULLERY-MAID at Baskerville Hall (HOUN). Lady Frances Carfax travelled with a maid (LADY), as did Mrs. Oldmore (HOUN). Carrie NORLETT was a maid

at Shoscombe Old Place (SHOS). Lady Brackenstall's maid was Theresa WRIGHT (ABBE). Hatty Doran's confidential maid was named Alice (NOBL), and Dolores was Mrs. Ferguson's personal maid (SUSS).

Cook. Jabez Wilson employed a girl of fourteen to cook and clean (REDH). There was a cook at Ridling Thorpe Manor (DANC), at Hurlstone (MUSG), and at Baker Street (THOR). The Barclays (CROO), Trevor Senior (GLOR), and Dr. Percy Trevelyan (RESI) employed a cook, and Aloysius Garcia kept a half-breed cook whose voodoo rituals added to the grotesque nature of the Wisteria Lodge case (WIST).

Nurse. Theresa Wright was the former nurse of Lady Mary Brackenstall (ABBE), and the wife of Ralph the butler had been Godfrey Emsworth's (BLAN). The Scotchwoman who had been servant to John and Effie Hebron became nurse to little Lucy (YELL). The Fergusons employed one for their infant (SUSS). A nurse-girl was among the crowd outside Briony Lodge (SCAN). Annie Fraser claimed old Rose Spender as her former nurse (LADY).

See also BUTLER; CHARWOMAN; FOOTMAN; GOVERNESS; HOUSEKEEPER; PAGE; SECRETARY; VALET.

GARDEN STAFF. There was a garden staff at Hurlstone (MUSG), and Professor Coram employed a gardener (GOLD). Watson was nearly caught by Charles Augustus Milverton's under-gardener (CHAS). The sailor Hudson was promoted to butler when the position of gardener did not suit him (GLOR). See also GAMEKEEPER; LODGEKEEPER.

STABLE STAFF. The terms *groom, ostler,* and *stable-hand* are synonymous.

Groom. Holmes posed as an out-of-work groom to learn about Irene Adler from the inhabitants of Serpentine Mews (SCAN). There was a groom at Ridling Thorpe Manor (DANC), Baskerville Hall (HOUN), Hurlstone (MUSG), Briarbrae (NAVA), and at Capleton (SILV). Alexander Holder (BERY) and Bob Carruthers (SOLI) had a groom. Charles McCarthy's serving-man acted as groom (BOSC), and Hugo Baskerville ordered his grooms to saddle his horse and unkennel the dogs (HOUN). The grooms and other employees of Ronder's circus responded to Eugenia Ronder's screams (VEIL).

Ostler. Holmes learned a great deal about Irene Adler from the ostlers of Serpentine Mews, and others were among the crowd outside Briony Lodge (SCAN). The Fergusons employed a stable-hand (SUSS).

Stable-boy. Dr. Grimesby Roylott employed a stable-boy who drove his trap (SPEC), and three lads worked under John Straker (SILV). There was a stable-boy at Ridling Thorpe Manor (DANC), and Neville St. Clair employed a stable-boy (TWIS). Watson said that John Mason wore the firm, austere expression of a man used to controlling boys (SHOS).

Coachman. Coachmen were employed by Professor Presbury (CREE), the Barclays (CROO), Sir James Damery (ILLU), Dr. Percy Trevelyan (RESI), and Irene Adler (SCAN). The Brackenstalls employed a driver (ABBE), and Harold Latimer kept a coachman and his wife as servants (GREE). Lysander Stark probably kept a coachman (ENGR), and there was one at Shoscombe Old Place (SHOS). Leslie Armstrong's coachman could not be approached (MISS). The groom at Baskerville Hall acted as coachman (HOUN). Reuben Hays had once been the Duke of Holdernesse's coachman (PRIO), and William Kirwin was the Cunninghams' (REIG). See also CHAUFFEUR.

COMMERCIAL AND PUBLIC SERVANTS

Professional and Commercial Servants. When Lord Saltire was found to be missing, a complete roll was taken of the Priory School's boys, masters, and servants (PRIO). The grooms and other employees of Ronder's circus responded to Eugenia Ronder's screams (VEIL). Watson's boots had been done up by the boy at the Turkish bath (LADY). Holder and Stevenson's bank employed a cashier (BERY). Morse Hudson and Mr. Harding each employed a shop assistant (SIXN), as Jabez Wilson employed Vincent Spaulding (REDH). There was a trustworthy watchman at the Woolwich submarine office (BRUC), and the watchman at Mawson & Williams' was murdered by Beddington (STOC), as Tobin was by the Worthingdon Bank Gang (RESI). The Diogenes Club employed a waiter (GREE), and Mrs. Tangey was a CHARWOMAN at the Foreign Office (NAVA).

Tom Dennis was said to be a steward in a Union boat (STUD), James Browner in the *May Day* (CARD). A nurse was employed to sit up with Rachel Howells (MUSG) and to look after Percy Phelps at night (NAVA).

See also BILLIARD-MARKER; BOOTS; CLERK; COMMISSIONNAIRE; HOTEL SERVANTS; MUTE; PAGE; RAILWAY SERVANTS; TIME-KEEPER.

Public Servants. Hatty Doran's wedding-dress was found in Hyde Park by a park-keeper (NOBL). See also CLERK; CONSTABLE; POLICE.

Serving-girl, a maid (CARD); see SERVANT.

Serving-man, a SERVANT (BOSC).

Severn, the second largest river in England, flowing into the Bristol Channel (BOSC).

Seville, a city of Spain, pop. (1900) 148,315. It is associated historically with the notorious Spanish INQUISITION (STUD).

Shadwell, a very poor docking region in the south of Stepney. James Browner's statement was taken at the **Shadwell Police Station** here (CARD).

Shafter, Jacob, the owner of a boarding-house in Vermissa. Birdy EDWARDS married his daughter Ettie (VALL).

Shaftesbury Avenue, a thoroughfare of central London which extends in a somewhat winding fashion from Piccadilly to New Oxford Street. Opened in 1886, it is a street appealing to shoppers and theatre-goers. Harold Latimer took Mr. Melas up here (GREE). See Maps I and II of LONDON.

Shag, a strong, coarsely cut tobacco. Holmes received two fills of shag for helping the Serpentine Mews ostlers in their work (SCAN). He ordered a pound of shag from Bradley, Watson's tobacconist (HOUN), consumed an ounce during the night at The Cedars (TWIS), and charged and recharged his pipe with "the strongest black tobacco" while waiting for news of Silver Blaze (SILV). Watson writes that he became an institution in Holmes's life like the shag tobacco and others (CREE).

Shahgunge, or *Shahganj,* a western suburb of Agra. A battle fought near here on 5 July 1857, between the defenders of Agra and the Sepoy mutineers who were then approaching to besiege the city, resulted in a retreat by the Europeans. Jonathan Small fought in the engagement (SIGN).

Shakedown, a temporary bed, originally made by shaking down or spreading hay, rushes, or the like, now extended in meaning to include quilts or mattresses, with coverings, laid upon a floor (ENGR).

Shakepeare, William (1564–1616), the greatest of English poet-dramatists. Holmes humorously asked Mary Maberley if she had a FIRST FOLIO (3GAB).

Holmes twice misquoted from his *Twelfth Night,* Act II, Scene 3: "Journeys end in lovers meeting" (EMPT, REDC), which he attributed to "the old play" (EMPT), and correctly quoted *King Henry VI, Part II,* Act III, Scene 2: "Thrice is he armed that hath his quarrel just" (LADY). A number of remarks can be attributed to or would appear to be inspired by Shakespeare, but not with absolute certainty.

Shares: see STOCKS.

Shark. Holmes's gazetteer alluded to sharks round the Andaman Islands (SIGN).

Shaw, a small wood or grove; e.g., the RAGGED SHAW (PRIO).

Sheeny, in vulgar slang, a Jew (STOC).

Sheep. Sheep grazed upon Lower Gill Moor (PRIO), and three of those at King's Pyland had gone lame (SILV).

Sheets, or *stern-sheets,* the after-most seat in a boat, located usually in the very stern, where the officer in command of the boat sits to work the tiller (GLOR).

Shepherd's check, a plaid design in small checkers of black and white (MUSG, REDH).

*Sheridan Street, the street in Vermissa where Jacob Shafter's boarding-house was located (VALL).

Sherman, an old bird-stuffer who loaned Toby to Holmes and Watson (SIGN). He is notable as the only person other than Mycroft Holmes to refer to Sherlock by his Christian name.

Sherpur, a fortified plain outside Cabul, the scene of a British victory in the Second Afghan War. The British were encamped within the walls of Sherpur while they awaited reinforcements. The engagement occurred on 23 December 1879 when the Afghans came out to do battle and were driven back inside the city. The assault upon Cabul followed some days later. Colonel Sebastian Moran fought here (EMPT).

Sherry, the name given in English to a naturally dry, fortified wine originally made in the south-west of Spain, and now applied to its many imitations as well (GLOR, NOBL).

Shetland lights. The elder Neligan was murdered two nights before the crew of the *Sea Unicorn* sighted "the Shetland lights" (BLAC), an allusion to the numerous lighthouses which dot the *Shetland Islands,* the most northerly of the British Isles, as warning lights and aids to navigation.

Shikari (*shih-kahr'ee*) a Hindi word meaning *hunter.* Holmes called Sebastian Moran an "old shikari" (EMPT).

Shilling, an English silver coin, equal in value to twelve pence, or one-twentieth of a pound sterling, and approximately equal to twenty-four American cents. Its symbol is *s.*

In slang the shilling is called a *bob* (SIGN).

The British camp at Sherpur in December 1879, before the taking of Cabul.

It was at one time the custom of British Army recruiting-officers to present a shilling to each new enlistee, a practice discontinued in 1879. Hence *to take the Queen's shilling* means to join the Army (SIGN).

Shingle, a kind of coarse sand, generally considered in reference to the seashore. Watson yearned for the shingles of Southsea (CARD),† and there was shingle upon the beach near Holmes's retirement villa (LION).

Shin out, in English slang, to clear off or run away. John Ferrier said that he and Lucy had best "shin out" of Utah (STUD), thus making use of a distinctly English colloquialism in the midst of the American West.

Ship: see BARQUE; BRIG; CLIPPER; CUTTER; STEAM PACKET; YAWL; see also BOAT.

For particular ships see ALICIA; BASS ROCK; CONQUEROR; ESMERALDA; FRIESLAND; GLORIA SCOTT; HOTSPUR; LONE STAR; MATILDA BRIGGS; MAY DAY; NORAH CREINA; ORONTES; PALMYRA; ROCK OF GIBRALTAR; RURITANIA; SEA UNICORN; SOPHY ANDERSON.

For steamship companies see ABERDEEN SHIPPING COMPANY; ADELAIDE-SOUTHAMPTON COMPANY; CUNARD LINE; GUION STEAMSHIP COMPANY; LIVERPOOL, DUBLIN, AND LONDON STEAM PACKET COMPANY; UNION BOAT.

For other nautical terms see ABACK; AFTER-HOLD; BEAT; CLEAR; FORECASTLE; HARNESS-CASK; HELM; HULL DOWN; JUNK; LEAGUE; LEE SHORE; MASTER MARINER; PAINTER; POOP; QUARTER; SHEETS; SQUARE; STAND OUT; TACK; TRAMP; 'TWEEN DECKS; see also PEA-JACKET; REEFER JACKET; SLOP SHOP; also SHIP'S.

See also RUSSELL, WILLIAM CLARK.

† This allusion is inserted in "The Resident Patient" in many editions.

See also ADMIRALTY; ROYAL NAVY; also LLOYD'S; also GRAVESEND; THAMES; LONDON, subheaded *Commerce.*

*Shipley's Yard, the cab-yard out of which John Clayton worked (HOUN).

Ship's, the name given in English to *Schippers Tabak Special,* a strong tobacco blend manufactured in the Netherlands and much favoured by sailors. Watson professed to smoke "ship's" at his first meeting with Holmes (STUD), and there was half an ounce of "strong ship's tobacco" in the tobacco-pouch left in Peter Carey's cabin (BLAC).

Shlessinger: see PETERS, HENRY.

Sholto, Major John (d. 1882), an Indian Army officer, involved in the theft of the Agra treasure and the betrayal of Captain MORSTAN and Jonathan SMALL. The treasure remained hidden at his death, and his twin sons **Bartholomew Sholto** (1858–88) and **Thaddeus Sholto** (b. 1858) searched for it for six years, after which time Bartholomew was murdered by TONGA and the treasure was lost (SIGN). Peter Jones recalled the Sholto murder (REDH), and Holmes believed that John Openshaw was in greater danger than had been the Sholtos (FIVE).

Shomu (d. 748), the Emperor of Japan 724–48, famous for his Buddhist religious mania and lavishly expensive ceremonials. Baron Gruner tested Watson by asking him how he associated the Emperor Shomu with the Shoso-in near NARA (ILLU), Shomu's chosen capital city.

Shooting, the right, purchased or conferred, to kill game with fire-arms, and the defined tract of ground over which this permission applies. Holmes found excellent wild-duck shooting in the Broads near Donnithorpe, and

Trevor Senior was invited each autumn to shoot over the preserves of his friend Beddoes (GLOR). Old Frankland won a trespass case against Sir John Morland for shooting in his own warren (HOUN). Cecil Barker did not shoot (VALL). See also COVERT; GRASS; PHEASANT MONTHS; PRESERVE; PUT UP.

*Shosombe Old Place, also called *Shoscombe Hall,* the Berkshire residence of Sir Robert Norberton and his sister Lady Beatrice Falder. It lay in the centre of **Shoscombe Park** and was the site of the famous Shoscombe stud and training quarters. Pike were to be found in the Hall lake. The halt-on-demand **Shoscombe Station** was nearby (SHOS).

"Shoscombe Old Place, The Adventure of" (SHOS), a chronicle which appeared originally in the *Strand* magazine for April 1927 and *Liberty* magazine of 5 March 1927 and was published in the collection entitled *The Case Book of Sherlock Holmes* later that year. It concerns Holmes's investigation of the strange behaviour of both Sir Robert Norberton and his sister Lady Beatrice Falder. The case is variously dated as having occurred between 1882 and 1902, though the preponderance of authoritative opinion agrees upon the latter year. The tale has the distinction of being the last Sherlock Holmes case published.

Shoscombe Prince, the thoroughbred racing-horse owned by Sir Robert Norberton which won £80,000 at the Derby (SHOS).

Shoscombe spaniels, an exclusive variety of spaniel bred by Lady Beatrice Falder, one of which helped Holmes unravel the Shoscombe case (SHOS).

*Shoscombe Station: see SHOSCOMBE OLD PLACE.

Shoso-in: see NARA.

Shot-gun. John Douglas was believed to have been killed with a sawn-off shot-gun (VALL).

Shove the queer, in English and American slang, to pass counterfeit money (VALL).

Shuman, a Vermissa Valley ironworks-owner who was forced to sell out (VALL).

Siam, a kingdom of south-eastern Asia, est. pop. between 5,000,000 and 10,000,000. Mycroft Holmes was concerned about the state of Siam in November 1895 (BRUC), most likely an allusion to the Anglo-French dispute of 1893–96 over the French desire to absorb the country into their Indo-Chinese possessions, a question finally settled to Siam's advantage in January 1896.

Siberia. Professor Coram's wife and revolutionist companions were sentenced to Siberia (GOLD).

Sideboard, a large and elaborate dining-room side-table, usually containing one or more cupboards, several drawers, and a number of shelves, in addition to a broad top which is of a convenient height for receiving articles in immediate use in the service of the table. Sideboards often form an important part of the decoration of the dining-room. There was a sideboard at the Abbey Grange (ABBE) and in the Baker Street sitting-room (BERY, BLUE, FIVE, IDEN, NOBL, VEIL).

*Sierra Blanco. John Ferrier surveyed the Great Alkali Plain from the northern slope of "the Sierra Blanco" (STUD). *Sierra Blanca* is the name of an isolated mountain peak in New Mexico and a short range in Colorado, neither of which is near the trail taken by the Mormons in their trek to Utah.

Sierra Leone, a British colony upon

the west coast of Africa, pop. 76,655. The survivors of the *Gloria Scott* disaster decided it would be best to pull for here (GLOR).

Sierra Nevada, a mountain range in California (STUD).

Sigerson, the name assumed by Holmes during his travels in Tibet (EMPT).

Sign of the four: see FOUR, THE.

"Sign of the Four, The," or **"The Sign of Four"** (SIGN), originally subtitled *"The Problem of the Sholtos,"* a novel-length chronicle which appeared originally in *Lippincott's* magazine for February 1890 and was published in book form the same year. It concerns Holmes's investigation of the murder of Bartholomew Sholto and his search for Jonathan Small and the Agra treasure. It tells too the story of Watson's romance with Mary Morstan. Internal evidence dates the case as having taken place in 1888, though some authorities prefer 1887, and the month is very much in dispute.

Holmes alluded to the case (CARD, STOC). Watson recalled the case (GOLD), which he naturally associated with his "wooing" (SCAN), and when he looked back to this weird business, he said, he felt that it would be a strange tangle which Holmes could not unravel (IDEN). He expressed the opinion that it was a more fantastic case than that of the Openshaws (FIVE). Peter Jones observed that Holmes was more nearly correct than the official force in this business (REDH).

Sikhs, an Indian religious sect who worship one invisible God. They number some 2,000,000 in India, more than half of whom live in the Punjaub, where once they were the ruling class, which doubtless accounts for Jonathan Small's referring to them as *Punjaubees*

(SIGN). There was a company of them at Bhurtee (CROO), and three of the FOUR were said to be Sikhs (SIGN).

Silver. Jefferson Hope had been a silver explorer, and with some companions discovered some lodes in the Nevada Mountains (STUD). Lysander Stark's gang used an AMALGAM to take the place of silver in their counterfeit half-crowns (ENGR).

Silver Blaze, the racing-horse, of ISONOMY stock, which killed his trainer John Straker when Straker attempted to lame him and won the Wessex Cup for his owner Colonel Ross (SILV).

"Silver Blaze" (SILV), a chronicle which appeared originally in the *Strand* magazine for December 1892 and *Harper's Weekly* of 25 February 1893 and was published in the 1894 collection entitled *The Memoirs of Sherlock Holmes*. It concerns Holmes's investigation of the death of John Straker and the disappearance of Silver Blaze, and is dated as having taken place in various years between 1881 and 1891.

Silver nitrate: see NITRATE.

*Silvester's, the London banking firm with whom Lady Frances Carfax had her account (LADY).

Simpson (d. 1900), called *Baldy Simpson,* a companion of Godfrey Emsworth who was killed at Diamond Hill (BLAN).

Simpson, the Baker Street Irregular who watched over Henry Wood (CROO).

Simpson, Fitzroy, the London bookmaker who was suspected of John Straker's murder (SILV).

Simpson's Dining Rooms, a well-known restaurant in the Strand. Holmes wanted something nutritious at Simpson's after the taking of Culverton

Smith (DYIN), and Watson met him here twice during the Gruner case (ILLU).

Sinclair, Admiral, the officer with whom Sir James Walter dined the night the Bruce-Partington plans were stolen (BRUC).

Singapore, a British colony, consisting chiefly of the island and city of Singapore, lying between Malaya and Sumatra, pop. (1900) 193,089. Jonathan Small and Tonga were picked up by a ship carrying Moslem pilgrims from Singapore to Jiddah (SIGN).

Singh, Mahomet, one of the FOUR (SIGN).

Singleford, Lord, the owner of Rasper (SILV).

Singlestick, a wooden cudgel for use with one hand, about a yard in length and fitted with a guard for the hand, used for training in the art of the sabre or cutlass. Singlestick play has become a sport in itself. Watson described Holmes as an expert (STUD) whose ability served him when he was attacked by roughs in Regent Street (ILLU).

Singleton: see CONK-SINGLETON.

"Singular Experience of Mr. John Scott Eccles, The": see "WISTERIA LODGE, THE ADVENTURE OF."

Sir Colin: see CAMPBELL, SIR COLIN.

"Six Napoleons, The Adventure of the" (SIXN), a chronicle which appeared originally in the *Strand* magazine for May 1904 and *Collier's Weekly* of 30 April 1904 and was published in the collection entitled *The Return of Sherlock Holmes* the following year. It concerns Holmes's investigation of the mysterious destruction of a number of plaster busts representing the Emperor Napoleon. The case is commonly dated as having occurred in the year 1900.

Sixpence, an English silver coin, equal in value to six bronze pence, or one-half of a shilling.

Skibbareen, a town on the south coast of Ireland, pop. 3,208. Holmes said that as Altamont he had given serious trouble to the constabulary here (LAST).

Skiff, any oar-driven boat (SIGN).

Skull: see CRANIOLOGY.

Slabs, in roofing: see HORSHAM SLABS. See also LEADS.

Slaney, Abe, "the most dangerous crook in Chicago" and the murderer of Hilton CUBITT (DANC).

Slater, one whose occupation is the roofing of buildings with slate. One of Holmes's monographs dealt with the hands of slaters (SIGN).

Slater, the stonemason who saw Patrick Cairns in Peter Carey's cabin (BLAC).

Slavonians, an Aryan people occupying eastern Europe and embracing the Bulgarians, Serbians, Russians, Czechs, and Poles, among others. Holmes imagined that "Dorak" was a Slavonic name (CREE).

Sleepy Hollow, the name of the rustic setting of Washington Irving's *The Legend of Sleepy Hollow* (1820), used by Holmes to denote the Midlands country villages (MISS).

Sleuth-hound, a variety of BLOOD-HOUND. Watson mentioned them as an example of dogs used in detective work (CREE).

Sloane, Sir Hans (1660–1753), a celebrated British physician, traveller, and naturalist, and founder of the British Museum. With the $5,000,000 due him from the Garrideb estate, Nathan Garrideb said, he would be the Hans Sloane of his age (3GAR).

Slop shop, a shop where *slops,* or ready-made clothes, are sold (TWIS).

Slow-worm, a harmless, legless,

snake-like lizard, also called *blindworm* or *glass-snake*. Old Sherman kept one as a catcher of insects (SIGN).

Small, Jonathan (b. *c.*1838), the former soldier and plantation overseer whose criminal career began during the Indian Mutiny when he joined with three Sikhs for murder and the theft of the AGRA TREASURE. They were captured and sentenced to servitude in the Andaman Islands, but Small escaped, apparently in 1881 or early 1882, and sought the treasure, now in the hands of Major SHOLTO, in the name of the FOUR. After his confederate TONGA killed Sholto's son, Small was hunted and taken by Holmes (SIGN).

Smasher, in underworld cant, a passer of counterfeit coins (REDH).

Smith, Culverton: see CULVERTON SMITH.

Smith, James, the former orchestra conductor at the Imperial Theatre, who died before December 1894, leaving a widow and a daughter, **Violet Smith**. His brother **Ralph Smith** (d. 1895) went to Africa about 1870, where he died leaving no will, the heir to his fortune being his brother James's daughter Violet. His acquaintances Bob CARRUTHERS and Jack WOODLEY arranged for Woodley to woo and marry Violet before her uncle's death, and so to acquire the money, but their plans were frustrated by dissension and by Violet's own suspicions, which led her to seek Holmes's assistance (SOLI).

Smith, Joseph, Jr. (1805–1844), the founder of the Mormon Church. He was shot to death by a mob in Illinois and was succeeded in the leadership of the church by Brigham YOUNG (STUD). See MORMONS.

Smith, Mordecai, the London boat-owner whose steam launch the *Aurora* was hired by Jonathan Small. Holmes

spoke to his wife **Mrs. Smith** and their son **Jack Smith** (b. 1882), while the eldest son **Jim Smith** was away with his father on the launch (SIGN).

Smith, Violet: see SMITH, JAMES.

Smith, Willoughby (d. 1894), the secretary of Professor Coram, mistakenly murdered by the Professor's wife Anna (GOLD).

Smith and Wesson, the well-known American gunmaking firm of Springfield, Massachusetts. Birdy Edwards owned a Smith and Wesson revolver (VALL).

Smith-Mortimer succession case, a case handled by Holmes in 1894 (GOLD).

*Smith's Wharf, the landing-stage belonging to Mordecai Smith, located at the foot of Broad Street in Lambeth (SIGN).

Smithy, the workplace of a smith, particularly a BLACKSMITH (PRIO).

Smoke rocket, in plumbing, a device for testing the tightness of house-drains and gas-pipes by generating smoke within them (SCAN).

Smoking-cap, a light, ornamented cap without a visor (DYIN).

Smoking concert, a concert, often for men only, at which smoking is permitted (VALL).

Snackle. Jefferson Hope remarked that he was "neatly snackled" by Holmes (STUD). The word is probably a distortion of *snabbled* or *snaffled,* both of which, in underworld cant, mean "taken" or "arrested."

Snake. Dr. Grimesby Roylott committed murder through the agency of a SWAMP ADDER (SPEC). Henry Wood called his mongoose Teddy a "snake-catcher" (CROO). The box sent Holmes by Culverton Smith contained a poisoned spring like a viper's tooth (DYIN). Charles Augustus Milverton impressed Holmes in the same way the serpents in the Zoo did (CHAS), and John Openshaw confessed he felt like a rabbit being approached by a snake (FIVE). See also COBRA; VIPER; also SLOW-WORM.

Snake-ring, a ring having the form of a twisted snake. The King of Bohemia offered Holmes an emerald snakering as a reward for his services (SCAN). John Douglas wore one (VALL).

Snib, to fasten a window by means of a *snib,* or window-catch. Bartholomew Sholto's chamber window was snibbed on the inside (SIGN).

Snuff, a powdered preparation of tobacco, inhaled through the nose. Mycroft Holmes took snuff (GREE), as did Jabez Wilson (REDH). Holmes offered Watson a pinch from a gold snuff-box, with a great amethyst in the centre of the lid, given him in gratitude by the King of Bohemia (IDEN). Watson said that the devil's-foot powder resembled snuff (DEVI).

Soames, Hilton, tutor and lecturer in Greek at the College of St. Luke's who asked Holmes to investigate when examination papers for the Fortescue Scholarship were tampered with (3STU).

Soames, Sir Cathcart, the father of one of the Priory School boys (PRIO).

Socialism, the name given to a theory which has for its object the reform of society on the principle of cooperation, instead of the principle of competition by which society is now largely controlled. While Socialism and ANARCHISM have in view the same end —the improvement of society—they seek this end through directly opposite means, although they are often confused in the public mind. Anarchism seeks general equality among men and

the largest freedom of the individual by abolishing all systems of law and government. Socialism, on the other hand, seeks the same end by increasing the powers of the state and making government paternal. See also NIHILISM; RED REPUBLICAN.

Holmes was correct in believing that the word *"Rache"* scrawled in blood near the body of Enoch Drebber was a blind to put the police upon a wrong track by suggesting Socialism and secret societies; and the *Daily Telegraph,* in its coverage of the Drebber murder, remarked that the Socialists had many branches in America, and that the deceased had no doubt infringed their unwritten laws and been tracked down by them (STUD).

Soft, in English slang, foolish or weak-minded. Hall Pycroft called himself a "soft Johnny" (STOC).

Solar System. Holmes professed to know nothing of the Copernican theory of the Solar System (STUD), but he demonstrated a knowledge of ASTRONOMY upon several occasions.

Solatium, the sum of money paid, over and above actual damages, to the injured party in a libel or slander suit, as a solice for wounded feelings. Holmes said that Moriarty would have Watson's pension as a solatium should he call Moriarty a criminal (VALL). It is not a legal term in England.

Solent, The, a strait of the English Channel between the mainland of Hampshire and the Isle of Wight. Holmes remarked that it would brighten his declining years to see a German cruiser navigating the Solent according to the mine-field plans he had furnished to Von Bork (LAST). See the map of HAMPSHIRE.

Solicitor, in England, a lawyer who generally sees to routine legal business and who acts as the go-between with the BARRISTER and his client.

John Hector McFarlane was a solicitor (NORW), and "William Morris" posed as one (REDH). The Cunninghams sought a paper which was in the strong-box of old Acton's solicitors (REIG).

Fordham "the Horsham lawyer" (FIVE) and Mrs. Maberley's lawyer Sutro (3GAB) were almost certainly solicitors. Morrison, Morrison, and Dodd was a law firm (SUSS). Holmes inquired if Theophilus Johnson were not a lawyer (HOUN). Carruthers and Woodley contacted Violet Smith and her mother through a lawyer (SOLI). Holmes supposed William Whyte had been "some pragmatical seventeenth-century lawyer" (STUD).

Augusto Barelli had been an Italian lawyer (REDC), Reilly an American one (VALL), and John Garrideb was supposedly an American counsellor at law (3GAR).

"Solitary Cyclist, The Adventure of the" (SOLI), a chronicle which appeared originally in the *Strand* magazine for January 1904 and *Collier's Weekly* of 26 December 1903 and was published in the 1905 collection entitled *The Return of Sherlock Holmes*. It concerns Holmes's interest in the strange appearance of "the solitary cyclist of Charlington" each week upon the road travelled by Violet Smith, and the unexpected tragedy which resulted. Watson dates the case as having occurred in April 1895.

Solomon (tenth century B.C.), the son of David by Bathsheba, and his successor as King of Israel, renowned for his wisdom. John McGinty said the dispute between Lander and Egan required a Solomon in judgement (VALL).

"Some Freaks of Atavism," the title of an article Dr. Mortimer wrote for the *Lancet* (HOUN).

Somerton, Dr., the Andaman prison surgeon (SIGN).

Somomy: see ISONOMY.

*****Sophy Anderson,** the British barque whose loss Holmes investigated in 1887 (FIVE).

Sotheby's (*suth'uh-bee*), a London auction-house. Nathan Garrideb said he occasionally drove to sales at Sotheby's or Christie's (3GAR), and Watson was to suggest them as the appraisers of his Ming saucer (ILLU).

South Africa, in common usage prior to the Boer War, a general term referring to the Boer republics and to the British possessions in southern Africa. These included the colonies of *Cape of Good Hope, Natal, Bechuanaland,* and *Rhodesia;* and the *Orange Free State* and the *South African Republic,* or *Transvaal.* The discovery of gold in the southern Transvaal in 1885 drew increasing numbers of foreigners to the region until the strained relations between the Boers and the British resulted in the outbreak of the SOUTH AFRICAN WAR in 1899.

Baron Gruner's house had been built by a South African gold king in the days of the great boom (ILLU), and Philip Green made his money in South Africa (LADY). Ralph Smith too made his fortune in the gold-fields, and both Carruthers and Woodley came from here (SOLI). Although Sir Charles Baskerville had made his fortune in South African speculation (HOUN), and while Bob Carruthers was "deeply interested" in South African gold securities (SOLI), Watson did not propose to invest in such securities (DANC).

John and Ivy Douglas sailed for

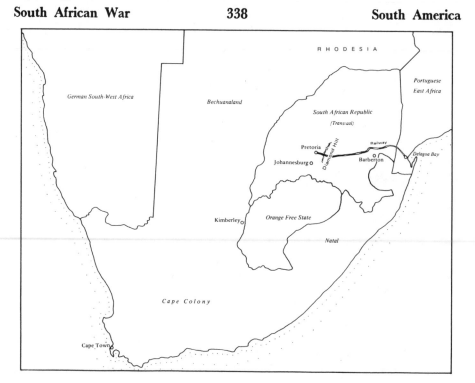

South Africa.

Cape Town aboard the *Palmyra* (VALL). Young Gilchrist accepted a commission in the Rhodesian police and left for South Africa at once (3STU). James Dodd and Godfrey Emsworth served here together in the Boer War (BLAN).

See RHODESIA; see also BARBERTON; BUFFELSSPRUIT; CAPE TOWN; DIAMOND HILL; JOHANNESBURG; KIMBERLEY; PRETORIA.

South African War, or The Boer War, the struggle which took place 1899–1902 in South Africa between Great Britain on the one hand and the South African Republic and the Orange Free State on the other. The war resulted in a hard-won victory for the British. The Boer republics were transformed into the Transvaal and Orange River colonies, which were united in 1910 with Natal and Cape Colony into the *Union of South Africa.*

Watson writes that the Garrideb case took place in June 1902, shortly after the end of the war (3GAR), which was concluded in May, and Holmes himself writes that the Emsworth case occurred in January 1903, "just after" the conclusion of the war, in which James Dodd and Godfrey Emsworth had served together (BLAN).

South America. James Browner gave up his berth in a ship to South America (CARD). Rodger Baskerville went to South America, from which Holmes suggested Stapleton might have claimed the Baskerville estate, and Barrymore was making preparations for Selden's escape here (HOUN). The Shlessingers supposedly had been missionaries here (LADY), and Watson

South America.

guessed that Tonga might be a South American (SIGN). The Neligan notebook listed a number of South American stocks (BLAC). A collection of South American utensils and weapons hung upon the walls at Cheeseman's (SUSS). Jefferson Hope murdered Enoch Drebber (STUD) and young Jack Ferguson attempted to kill his infant half-brother (SUSS) with a South American arrow poison.

See also ARGENTINE; AMAZON; BRAZIL; CENTRAL AMERICA; COSTA RICA; PERU; SAN PEDRO; SPANISH AMERICA; TIERRA DEL FUEGO; VENEZUELA.

Southampton, a major seaport city of Hampshire, pop. 104,824. Captain Croker's new ship was due to depart Southampton (ABBE), at which Sir Henry Baskerville arrived from Canada (HOUN). Godfrey Emsworth wrote to James Dodd from here (BLAN), Mr. Fowler and Alice Rucastle were

married here (COPP), and the Birlstone murderer was reported from Southampton and nineteen other places (VALL).

South Australia, formerly a British colony of Australia, since 1901 a state of the Australian Commonwealth, pop. 362,604. The capital is ADELAIDE. Lady Brackenstall was brought up here (ABBE).

South Brixton: see BRIXTON.

South Carolina, a south-eastern state of the United States, pop. 1,340,316. The Ku Klux Klan had branches in the Carolinas (FIVE).

South Downs, or **Sussex Downs,** the name given to the treeless upland extending from the centre of Hampshire across the length of Sussex. Holmes retired to the southern slope of the Downs (LAST, LION, PREF, SECO). See the maps of HAMPSHIRE and SUSSEX. See also NORTH DOWNS.

Southerton, Lord. The Copper Beaches was located in the midst of his preserves (COPP).

South London: see SURREY SIDE.

Southsea, a popular seaside resort and eastern suburb of Portsmouth. Watson yearned to visit here (CARD).†

Sovereign, an English gold coin, the standard of the coinage, of the value of one pound sterling (BLUE, GREE, LADY, PRIO, REDH, SCAN, SILV). The HALF-SOVEREIGN is also a current coin. See POUND. See also QUID; THICK 'UN.

Spain, a south-western kingdom of Europe, pop. (1900) 18,618,086.

Aloysius Garcia was of Spanish descent (WIST), Isadora Klein was of

† This allusion is inserted in "The Resident Patient" in many editions.

pure Spanish blood (3GAB), and Holmes spoke of Beryl Stapleton's Spanish blood (HOUN).

Spain's colonial possessions consist of a number of sparsely populated territories in Africa and, until 1898, Cuba and Puerto Rico in the Caribbean and the Philippines in Asia. Holmes said that "Antonio" was a common name in all "Spanish countries" (HOUN), by which he apparently meant Spain and her colonies.

Lady Francis Carfax inherited some "very remarkable" Spanish jewellery, for which she was abducted by Holy Peters (LADY), and some novels in the Spanish language were found at Wisteria Lodge (WIST).

The **Spanish Embassy** in London is in Westminster, not far from Victoria Station. John Scott Eccles inquired here about Aloysius Garcia (WIST).

See also BARCELONA: MADRID; SEVILLE.

Spaniel. Dr. Mortimer's dog, killed by Stapleton's hound, was a curly-haired spaniel (HOUN), and the Fergusons' dog Carlo was a spaniel (SUSS). Lady Beatrice Falder bred the SHOSCOMBE SPANIELS (SHOS). Old Sherman's dog Toby was half spaniel and half lurcher (SIGN).

Spanish America. Holmes said that "Antonio" was a common name in all Spanish-American countries (HOUN). See also CENTRAL AMERICA; SOUTH AMERICA.

Spanish countries: see SPAIN.

Spanish Embassy: see SPAIN.

Spanish language: see SPAIN.

Spartan, characterized by simplicity and frugality, reminiscent of the manner of living associated with the ancient inhabitants of Sparta. Watson thought the inhabitant of the neolithic burrow must be of Spartan habits (HOUN).

Spaulding, Vincent: see CLAY, JOHN.

Special, a railway-train hired privately for a special occasion. Moriarty engaged a special in his pursuit of Holmes (FINA).

Speckled band: see SWAMP ADDER.

"Speckled Band, The Adventure of the" (SPEC), a chronicle which appeared originally in the *Strand* magazine for February 1892 and was published in the collection entitled *The Adventures of Sherlock Holmes* late in the same year. It is the story of Helen Stoner and the attempt upon her life by her stepfather Dr. Grimesby Roylott. Watson dates the case as having taken place early in April 1883.

While waiting for Joseph Harrison to appear, Holmes recalled the vigil spent during this case (NAVA).

Spectator, a London weekly newspaper, one of the most influential and respected of the English press. Since 1886 it has espoused the cause of the Unionist party, which opposes self-government for Ireland. James Dodd said that the paper Dr. Kent was reading might have been the *Spectator* (BLAN).

Spencer John gang, the criminal gang to which Barney Stockdale and Steve Dixie belonged (3GAB).

Spender, Rose, the name of the workhouse crone claimed by Annie Fraser as her old nurse (LADY).

Spinal meningitis, an infectious disease, often fatal, producing inflammation of the membranes of the spinal cord. The veterinarian believed Carlo's affliction to be spinal meningitis (SUSS).

Spirit-lamp, an alcohol-burning lamp adapted for the heating of liquids (GOLD, NAVA).

Spirits of wine, alcohol (SILV).

Spit, in vulgar slang, an image or likeness. Sam Merton said that Tavernier's bust of Holmes was "the living spit of him" (MAZA).

Split, in English and American underworld cant, to inform upon one's accomplices. John McMurdo claimed to have killed Jonas Pinto because he threatened to split (VALL), and Ikey Sanders split on Count Sylvius and Sam Merton (MAZA).

Splügen (*sploo'gen*) **Pass,** a mountain pass through the Alps, altitude 6,945 feet. It forms part of the boundary between Switzerland and Italy. Holmes said that Baron Gruner had killed his wife here (ILLU). See the map of SWITZERLAND.

Spoon-bait, a spoon-shaped metallic lure used in trolling for certain kinds of fish (SHOS).

Spoor, the track of an animal (LION); see FOOTSTEP.

Spruit (*sproo'eet*), in South African Dutch, a small stream or water-course, usually almost or altogether dry except in the wet season; e.g., BUFFELSSPRUIT (BLAN).

Spud, a small spade (WIST).

Square, in sailing, horizontal and at right angles to the keel. The crew of the *Gloria Scott* brought the fore-yard square again after the mutiny (GLOR) for the purpose of keeping the ship before the wind.

Squire, in England, the courtesy title of the chief landed proprietor, usually the lord of the manor, in a parish. In some parts of the country it is not uncommon for the title to be given to the other landowners as well.

Hilton Cubitt (DANC) and Trevor Senior (GLOR) were Norfolk squires. Old Cunningham was squire at Reigate (REIG), and the Musgraves had been squires at Hurlstone since the sixteenth century (MUSG). The last Roylott squire of Stoke Moran dragged out his existence as an aristocratic pauper (SPEC). Lady Eva Brackwell was blackmailed with several imprudent letters she once wrote to an impecunious young country squire (CHAS). Von Bork was spoken of as a squire (LAST). Hugo Baskerville entertained the local squires the night of his death (HOUN).

Holmes remarked that his ancestors were country squires "who appear to have led much the same life as is natural to their class" (GREE).

Stable-boy: see SERVANT.

Stable-lantern, a large, sturdily constructed lantern (SHOS).

Stackhurst, Harold, the English educator and proprietor of a coaching establishment in Sussex who became Holmes's most intimate friend in the detective's retirement (LION).

Staff-commander, the second grade in the navigating branch of the British Navy. Holmes's index contained the biography of a staff-commander who had written a monograph upon deep sea fishes (SCAN).

Stag. There were stags' heads upon the walls at Baskerville Hall (HOUN).

Staghound, a variety of foxhound. Holmes, Gregson, and Lestrade sprang upon Jefferson Hope like "so many staghounds" (STUD).

*Stagville, a town at the foot of the Gilmerton Mountains, connected by rail with Vermissa Valley (VALL).

Stair-rod, a rod or strip of thin metal used to hold a stair-carpet in place. It is secured across the width of the step by rings or staples at either end, through which it is slipped. The stair-rods at Mrs. Cecil Forrester's home made a unique impression upon Watson (SIGN).

*Stake Royal, a Gilmerton town, or a mine owned by William Hales (VALL).

Stamford, the acquaintance of Holmes and Watson who was responsible for their meeting (STUD).

Stamford, Archie, a forger whom Holmes and Watson arrested in Surrey (SOLI).

Stamford's, properly **Stanford's Geological Establishment,** a maker and seller of maps, sole London agent for the sale of Ordnance Survey maps. Holmes sent to "Stamford's" for the Ordnance map of Dartmoor (HOUN).

Standard, The, a London newspaper of Conservative opinion. It is a morning paper, of much popularity, numbering among its staff many persons whose names are distinguished in letters as well as in journalism. In its editorial about the Drebber murder, the *Standard* commented upon the fact that lawless outrages of the sort usually occurred under a Liberal administration (STUD). Watson read two accounts of the Sholto murder in the *Standard,* in which Holmes advertised for the *Aurora* (SIGN). An evening edition called the EVENING STANDARD is also published.

Standard lamp, a hand-lamp with a tall *standard,* or stem (DEVI).

Stand out, in sailing, to steer clear by remaining in open water. Watson writes that the wise mariner "stands far out" from Mounts Bay (DEVI).

Stanger, James, the editor of the Vermissa *Daily Herald,* who was beaten by the Scowrers (VALL).

Stangerson, one of the four principal elders of the MORMONS. His son **Joseph Stangerson** (b. 1835) murdered John Ferrier and, some years later, fled Utah with Enoch Drebber, whose sec-

retary he became, and ultimately was stabbed to death in London by Jefferson HOPE (STUD).

Staphouse, a family murdered in an explosion set by the Scowrers (VALL).

Staples, the butler of Culverton Smith (DYIN).

Stapleton, Jack (d. 1889), an English schoolmaster, entomologist, and murderer. His real name was *Rodger Baskerville,* and he was the son of that Rodger Baskerville who was the youngest brother of Sir Charles Baskerville. Under the name *Vandeleur* he headed a school in Yorkshire and made a reputation in ENTOMOLOGY. As *Stapleton* he murdered Sir Charles Baskerville and attempted to kill Sir Henry Baskerville, using his giant hound, in an effort to obtain for himself the Baskerville fortune. He was exposed by Holmes and presumed lost in Grimpen Mire. His wife **Beryl Stapleton,** the former *Beryl Garçia,* was cruelly used by him (HOUN).

Star, The, a Liberal evening newspaper, established in London in 1888 and acquired by the *Daily News* in 1909. Holmes advertised for Henry Baker here (BLUE).

Stark, Colonel Lysander, the name assumed while in England by the German counterfeiter who seems to have murdered Jeremiah Hayling and attempted to kill Victor Hatherley. His real name appears to have been *Fritz* (ENGR).

Starr, Dr. Lysander, the fictional correspondent whom Holmes said was major of Topeka in 1890 (3GAR).

Stars and Stripes, the familiar name given to the flag of the United States. Holmes declared himself to be one of those who believed that succeeding generations would some day be citizens of the same world-wide country under a flag which would be a quartering of the Union Jack with the Stars and Stripes (NOBL). The Vermissa *Daily Herald* alluded passionately to "the starry flag of freedom" (VALL).

Start a plate: see PLATE.

*State and Merton County Railroad Company, the large and expanding company which was buying up much property in Vermissa Valley and was probably one of the five companies which joined to fight the Scowrers (VALL).

Station, in Australia, a stock-farm or ranch (BOSC).

Station-master, the official in charge of a railway station (BLAN, DANC, ENGR, HOUN). Professor Moriarty's younger brother was a station-master in the west of England (VALL).

Staunton, Arthur H., the rising young forger entered in Holmes's commonplace book (MISS).

Staunton, Godfrey, a student at Cambridge and a member of the university's Rugby team. His wife, whom he had married secretly, suffered from a virulent form of consumption, and her condition prompted him to desert his team without explanation two nights before an important match, summoned as he was by the girl's father, whose wife once had been Staunton's landlady. The disappearance resulted in Holmes's being called to investigate (MISS).

Staunton, Henry, a man whom Holmes "helped to hang" (MISS).

Steam packet, a steam-propelled mail-boat, usually with provision for passengers and cargo. The *Conqueror* and *May Day* were boats of the *Liverpool, Dublin, and London Steam Packet Company* (CARD). The letters to the Openshaws apparently came to England in a steam-driven mail-boat

(FIVE), and the non-existent Tom Dennis was supposedly a steward in a UNION BOAT (STUD).

Steele: see HOLLOWAY AND STEELE.

Steiler, Peter, the keeper of the Englischer Hof at Meiringen (FINA). The fact that Watson calls him *the elder* implies a Peter Steiler the younger of some importance, but his identity is nowhere apparent.

Steiner, one of Von Bork's spies, arrested in Portsmouth the night before Von Bork himself was taken (LAST).

Stendals, members of a family murdered by the Scowrers (VALL).

Stephens, the butler of Shoscombe Old Place (SHOS).

Stepney, an eastern metropolitan borough of London, pop. 298,600. It forms part of the East End and possesses the squalid streets and mean houses typical of the poorest class of inhabitants. Gelder & Co. was here (SIXN). See the front endpaper map.

Stereotype, in printing, a plate made from a mold of set type. Stereotyping permits repeated printing of items without the resetting of type, such as advertisements and headings which are printed in various publications or repeated in successive editions. Watson opined that newspaper references to a fresh clue seemed to be "a stereotyped form whenever the police have made a blunder" (SIGN). Holmes's monograph upon hands was illustrated with LITHOTYPE drawings (SIGN).

Sterndale, Leon, the famous lion-hunter and African explorer who brought the deadly DEVIL'S-FOOT ROOT to England and used it to murder Mortimer Tregennis in revenge for Brenda Tregennis's death. The laws of England prevented him from divorcing his estranged wife (DEVI).

Stethoscope. Watson carried his stethoscope in his top hat (SCAN).

Stevens, Bert, the "terrible murderer" with whom Holmes and Watson were concerned in 1887 (NORW).

Stevenson, a Cambridge Rugby player whom Cyril Overton might substitute for Godfrey Staunton (MISS).

Stevenson: see HOLDER, ALEXANDER.

Steward: see SERVANT.

Stewart, Jane, the housemaid at Lachine (CROO).

Stewart, Mrs. (d. 1887), a woman whom Holmes believed was murdered by Sebastian Moran (EMPT).

Stick: see WALKING-STICK.

Stimson, a London undertaker, proprietor of **Stimson & Co.** in the Kennington Road. His wife **Mrs. Stimson** gave the vital clue in the Carfax case (LADY).

Stoat, or ermine, a variety of WEASEL. Holmes said that the footprints he found outside Lachine seemed to belong to an animal of the weasel or stoat tribe (CROO), and Watson mistook a badger for a stoat at old Sherman's (SIGN).

Stoat or ermine.

Stock. Jack Prendergast said that his partner Wilson was "true as a stock to a barrel" (GLOR), alluding to the necessity of the stock and barrel of a rifle to be properly aligned in order to aim the weapon accurately.

Stockbroker, one who, for a commission, attends to the purchase and sale of stocks or shares and other securities in behalf of clients. On the London STOCK EXCHANGE brokers may not deal directly with one another but must treat with yet another class of operators called *stock-jobbers.*

James Dodd was a stockbroker (BLAN), and Coxon & Woodhouse and Mawson & Williams' were stockbrokers' firms (STOC). Stanley Hopkins sought a broker with the initials J.H.N. (BLAC), and Holmes thought at first that "Mr. Cornelius" might be a broker (NORW).

"Stockbroker's Clerk, The" (STOC), a chronicle which appeared originally in the *Strand* magazine for March 1893 and in *Harper's Weekly* of 11 March 1893 and was published in the collection entitled *The Memoirs of Sherlock Holmes* the following year. It concerns Holmes's interest in the unusual employment of Hall Pycroft, and the case is usually dated as having taken place in 1888 or 1889, as Watson states that it occurred shortly after his marriage to Mary Morstan.

Stockdale, Barney, a member of the Spencer John gang and Steve Dixie's "boss," hired by Isadora Klein to intimidate Holmes. His wife **Susan Stockdale** gained employment with Mary Maberley and acted as a spy within the Three Gables in the plot to retrieve Douglas Maberley's novel (3GAB).

Stock Exchange, the association of London stockbrokers and stock-jobbers, incorporated in 1773. The Stock Exchange building, familiarly known in the City as *The House,* is located just east of the Bank of England; see the map of the CITY. Members of the Exchange are not permitted to advertise, and stockbrokers who do so are the "outside brokers" who do not adhere to

At the Stock Exchange.

the stringent rules of professional conduct imposed upon members of the House.

Colonel Valentine Walter lost his money in the Stock Exchange (BRUC). Coxon & Woodhouse and Mawson & Williams' were both stockbroking firms, and Hall Pycroft said he read the Stock Exchange list every morning (STOC). The Neligan notebook appeared to contain lists of Stock Exchange securities, and Stanley Hopkins had examined the old Exchange lists for a broker within or outside the House whose initials were J.H.N. (BLAC).

Stocks. Mary Sutherland's uncle left her some stocks (IDEN). Watson did not propose to invest in South African securities (DANC), even though Sir

Charles Baskerville made large sums in such speculation (HOUN) and Bob Carruthers professed interest in South African gold shares (SOLI). Joseph Harrison lost his money in stocks (NAVA). The Beddingtons attempted a stock robbery (STOC), and some of Josiah Amberley's securities were supposedly carried off by his wife and her lover (RETI). The Neligan notebook appeared to contain lists of securities (BLAC), and Watson suggested that share certificates were in Professor Presbury's carved German box (CREE). Jonas Oldacre owned some SCRIP (NORW).

Stockwell Place, a long block of houses in south London. Holmes's party passed by here on their way to meet Thaddeus Sholto (SIGN). See Map IV of LONDON.

Stoep (*stoop*), in South African Dutch, a raised verandah running along the front and sometimes round the sides of a house (BLAN).

***Stoke Moran,** a village and former landed estate of north-western Surrey. In the **Stoke Moran Manor House,** ancestral seat of the ROYLOTT family, Dr. Grimesby Roylott murdered Julia Stoner, attempted to kill her twin sister Helen, and met his own death (SPEC).

Stone, Rev. Joshua, a neighbour of Aloysius Garcia (WIST).

Stoner, Major-General, an officer of the Bengal Artillery who died between 1850 and 1853. His widow **Mrs. Stoner** (d. 1875), whose maiden name was WESTPHAIL, married Dr. Grimesby ROYLOTT shortly before her own death in a railway accident. Her daughters **Julia Stoner** (1851–81) and **Helen Stoner** (1851–?1891), were brought up by Dr. Roylott at his Stoke Moran estate. Julia was murdered by her stepfather for her inheritance, and when he

attempted the same crime upon Helen she engaged Holmes, who prevented the murder and freed her to marry Percy ARMITAGE (SPEC).

Stoper, Miss, the manageress of Westaway's agency for governesses (COPP).

Stormy petrel, a common oceanic bird thought by sailors to foretell the approach of a storm. Holmes called himself (REIG) and Watson a stormy petrel of crime (NAVA).

Stradivarius, Antonio (1649–1737), a celebrated Italian violin maker. Holmes's own violin was a Stradivarius (CARD), and he was an expert upon them (STUD, SIGN).

Straker, John, the trainer at Colonel Ross's racing stables. He kept a "dashing" mistress and under the name *William Darbyshire*—in some editions *Derbyshire*—ran up such bills that he found it necessary to gain money by fixing a race. In his efforts to lame SILVER BLAZE he was kicked to death by the horse. His wife **Mrs. Straker** appears to have known nothing of the other woman (SILV).

Strand, the great artery between the City and the West End, one of the busiest and most important thoroughfares in London. It contains many of the handsomest shops, theatres, and restaurants in the metropolis, and presents a most variegated appearance, though recent widenings have shorn the street of much of its former picturesqueness.

Before his meeting with Holmes, Watson stayed for a time at a private hotel in the Strand (STUD), where the Lowther Arcade (FINA), Simpson's restaurant (ILLU), the American Exchange (STUD), and the shop where Sir Henry Baskerville bought his missing new boot (HOUN) were located. Cyril Overton's telegram carried

The view eastward, toward the City, along the Strand. The block at left houses the Strand telegraph office as well as the Lowther Arcade. The iron gate to the right stands before the Charing Cross Hotel and Station.

a Strand postmark (MISS). Holmes's party approached the Lyceum Theatre along the Strand (SIGN), near which was located Bentley's private hotel (MISS), and to which Holmes asked John Clay directions from Saxe-Coburg Square (REDH). Holmes and Watson took a stroll through London one night, watching the kaleidoscope of life as it ebbed and flowed through Fleet Street and the Strand (RESI).

Strasburg, or **Strasbourg,** also spelled *Strassburg,* a city of south-western Germany, pop. 151,041. Holmes received word of Moriarty's escape here (FINA).

Straubenzee, the maker of Count Sylvius's air-gun (MAZA).

Strauss, Herman, an opponent of the Scowrers (VALL).

Streatham (*streth'm*), a large residential district in the south-west of London. Alexander Holder lived here

(BERY), which Holmes and Watson traversed in pursuit of Jonathan Small (SIGN).

Street Arab, a neglected or abandoned boy or girl of the streets (SIGN, STUD); see BAKER STREET IRREGULARS.

Stroke: see APOPLEXY.

Stroud Valley, a narrow and picturesque valley in western England. The train to Herefordshire passed through here (BOSC).

Strychnine, an intensely poisonous vegetable alkaloid. The symptoms of strychnine poisoning are difficulty in breathing followed by convulsions in which the body becomes rigid. In very small doses it is a valuable tonic. In his agitation Watson confused the dosages of castor-oil and strychnine, but later he suggested that Bartholomew Sholto's death had been caused by some strychnine-like substance (SIGN).

Stuart, the royal family of Scotland 1371–1714 and of England 1603–1714 (MUSG); see JAMES I; CHARLES.

Student lamp, a portable lamp which may be raised and lowered at pleasure on its upright standard (CHAS).

"Study in Scarlet, A" (STUD), a novel-length chronicle which appeared in *Beeton's Christmas Annual* for 1887 and was published in book form the following year. It is in two parts, Part I being a reprint from Watson's "REMINISCENCES," briefly describing his Army experiences and dealing at length with his meeting and first case with Sherlock Holmes, that of the murders of Enoch Drebber and Joseph Stangerson by Jefferson Hope. It is dated as having taken place in the month of March, the year being variously identified between 1878 and 1886, though 1881 is most commonly accepted.

Part II, entitled "The Country of the Saints," is a retrospection, written in the third person, concerned with the Mormons of Utah and the origins of Hope's motive for revenge, and takes place during the years 1847–60. Its depiction of Mormon history and customs is so inaccurate as to be considered pure fiction; see DOYLE, SIR ARTHUR CONAN. The last two chapters are a return to Watson's narrative for Hope's confession and Holmes's explanation of his solution.

A Study in Scarlet has the distinction of being the first published chronicle of Sherlock Holmes as well as the story of the beginning of the Holmes-Watson partnership. Its title was suggested by Holmes's own comment that the case was a "study in scarlet"—"the scarlet thread of murder running through the colourless skein of life."

Both Holmes (BOSC, CARD, MUSG) and Watson (FINA, MUSG) recalled the case, and Holmes chided Watson over his telling of the story (SIGN). The Baker Street lodgings were always associated in Watson's mind with these dark incidents (SCAN), and when he looked back to the extraordinary circumstances connected with this case, he felt it would be a strange tangle indeed which Holmes could not unravel (IDEN); yet he purported to believe that, while the case demonstrated the value of Holmes's peculiar methods of investigation, the facts described were so commonplace that he barely felt justified in laying them before the public (RESI).

Sturmash, presumably a Merton County colliery-owner (VALL).

*Stylestown, a town in the Gilmerton district (VALL).

Subaltern, in the British Army, a junior officer below the rank of captain (BLAN).

Subclavian artery, the principal artery of the root of the neck, situated under the clavicle. Watson's subclavian artery was grazed at the battle of Maiwand (STUD).

Sub-lieutenant, the rank just below that of lieutenant. Arthur Charpentier held the rank in the Navy (STUD).

Submarine. The plans of the secret Bruce-Partington submarine were stolen from the Woolwich Arsenal, and the scandal apparently killed Sir James Walter, head of the Submarine Department of the Admiralty (BRUC). Baron Von Herling declared that the British were unprepared for submarine attack (LAST).

Sudbury, a student at Stackhurst's coaching establishment (LION).

Suez Canal. The *Rock of Gibraltar* was somewhere to the south of here (ABBE).

Suicide, the intentional killing of one's self. An unsuccessful attempt at suicide is a crime.

Inspector Lanner said that suicides are most common at five o'clock in the morning (RESI). There had been a suicide for the sake of the blue carbuncle (BLUE). Professor Coram's wife Anna took poison (GOLD), and Maria Gibson killed herself in such a way as to fasten a charge of murder upon Grace Dunbar (THOR). A mere suicide, Holmes said, would not have caused Stanley Hopkins to send for him (ABBE). The murders of Elias Openshaw (FIVE) and Blessington (RESI) were made to appear as such.

Holmes wondered if Sir James Walter had killed himself (BRUC), and it was suggested that Mortimer Tregennis (DEVI) and Willoughby Smith (GOLD) had committed suicide. It was attempted by Elsie Cubitt (DANC), Josiah Amberley (RETI), and Harry Pinner (STOC), and Neville St. Clair could not be charged, in Inspector Bradstreet's opinion, unless a case of attempted suicide could be made (TWIS). Jefferson Hope attempted to throw himself through the window of the Baker Street rooms, but after his rage subsided he assured his captors that they need not worry about his killing himself (STUD). Suicide was quickly ruled out in Enoch Drebber's death (STUD) and the Birlstone tragedy (VALL). Alexander Holder feared that his niece might commit suicide (BERY). Holmes persuaded Eugenia Ronder not to take her own life (VEIL).

Sulphur rose: see ROSE.

Sultan: see TURKEY.

Sumatra, a large island of the Dutch East Indies, est. pop. 3,500,000. Culverton Smith was a well-known planter

here (DYIN), and Holmes investigated the case of the Netherland-Sumatra Company (REIG). He claimed to suffer from a coolie disease from Sumatra (DYIN), and his gazetteer stated that the Andaman Islands were situated to the north of here (SIGN). Holmes was involved with the case of the giant rat of Sumatra, a story for which the world is not yet prepared (SUSS).

Sumner, the shipping agent in the Ratcliff Highway who assisted Holmes in finding Patrick Cairns (BLAC).

Sun. Holmes maintained that if the earth travelled round the sun or round the moon it would not make a pennyworth of difference to him or his work (STUD), and years later Watson recalled this indifference (HOUN).

Sung, a Chinese dynasty which occupied the throne from the tenth to the thirteenth centuries and was finally overcome by the Mongols. The ceramics of the period have much merit. Watson read up on the Sung in preparing for his interview with Baron Gruner (ILLU).

Sup, a small mouthful of liquid; a sip. Jefferson Hope said he had had no time for "bit or sup" (STUD), a common expression meaning *food or drink.*

Supra-orbital, situated over or above the orbit of the eye. Dr. Mortimer said that he had not expected such supraorbital development as he saw in Holmes's skull (HOUN), and Moriarty remarked that Holmes had less frontal development than he expected (FINA). Mortimer assured Holmes that the supra-orbital crest in a Negro would differ from that of an Esquimaux (HOUN). Reginald Musgrave said that Brunton had a "splendid forehead" (MUSG), Sebastian Moran was described as having the brow of a philosopher (EMPT), and Watson wrote that Inspector Mac-Donald's "great cranium" spoke clearly of his keen intelligence (VALL). Holmes too believed that a large brain "must have something in it" (BLUE).

Surd, in mathematics, the irrational root of a rational number. The square-root of 2, for example, is inexpressible as an ordinary fraction and is therefore an *irrational* number, and is thus a surd. The term is also used simply to denote any irrational number. Holmes said that Ian Murdoch seemed to live in some high, abstract region of surds and conic sections (LION).

Surgeon: see DOCTOR; see also COL-LEGE OF SURGEONS.

Surrey, a south-eastern county of England, pop. 675,774. It has become practically a great residential district for those who must live in the neighbourhood of London, and the important manufactures are chiefly confined to the metropolis and its immediate environs. GUILDFORD is the county-town.

Holmes and Watson drove in 1889 from Middlesex through an angle of Surrey into Kent on their journey to The Cedars (TWIS), though the county of London had been created a year earlier, at which time part of the ancient county of Surrey was transferred administratively to London. Jonathan Small said that India was as peaceful as Surrey or Kent just before the Mutiny (SIGN).

WOKING (NAVA), REIGATE (REIG), FARNHAM (SOLI), STOKE MORAN (SPEC), and ESHER and OXSHOTT (WIST) are scenes of Holmes's investigations in Surrey.

See the back endpaper map. See also CROYDON; KINGSTON; LEATHERHEAD; RICHMOND.

Surrey Side, The, or **South London,** that part of the metropolis south of the Thames (RETI, SIGN, SIXN, TWIS). See LONDON.

Susan: see STOCKDALE.

Sussex, a southern county of England, pop. 605,202. The salient physical

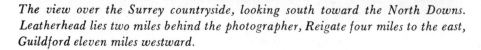

The view over the Surrey countryside, looking south toward the North Downs. Leatherhead lies two miles behind the photographer, Reigate four miles to the east, Guildford eleven miles westward.

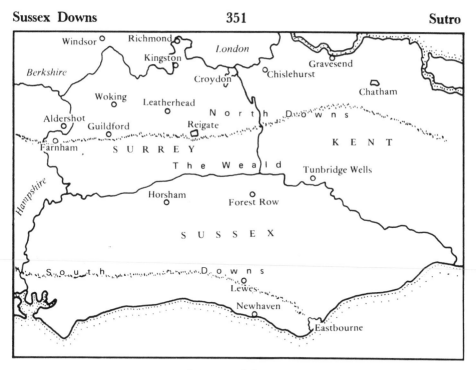

Surrey and Sussex.

feature is the hill range called the SOUTH DOWNS. The county is mostly agricultural. Manufacturing is meagre, but there are extensive fisheries. It is divided into *Eastern Sussex* and *Western Sussex,* each of which is an administrative county.

Holmes retired to Sussex (SECO), to a villa upon the southern slope of the Downs, commanding a view of the Channel (LION).

FOREST ROW (BLAC), HURLSTONE in Western Sussex (MUSG), LAMBERLEY (SUSS), and Birlstone (VALL) are scenes of Holmes's investigations in Sussex, and HORSHAM is also here (FIVE, SUSS). See also EASTBOURNE; LEWES; NEWHAVEN.

Sussex Downs: see SOUTH DOWNS.

"Sussex Vampire, The Adventure of the" (SUSS), a chronicle which appeared originally in the *Strand* magazine and *Hearst's International* for Jan-

uary 1924 and was published in the collection entitled *The Case Book of Sherlock Holmes* in 1927. It concerns Holmes's investigation of the circumstances which led Robert Ferguson to suspect that his wife was practising vampirism. The case is most commonly dated as having taken place in 1896 or 1897.

Sutherland, the Tottenham Court Road plumber whose widow married James WINDIBANK. His daughter **Mary Sutherland** consulted Holmes when her affianced Hosmer Angel vanished upon their wedding day (IDEN).

Watson observed that the case had been entirely free of any legal crime (BLUE), and Holmes mentioned that the Mary Sutherland case took place a few days before the affair of the Red-Headed League (REDH).

Sutro, the lawyer representing Mary Maberley (3GAB).

Sutton: see BLESSINGTON.

S.W. (*South-West*), the designation given to the postal district which embraces London on both sides of the Thames south of Hyde Park and west of Vauxhall Bridge (SIGN). See the postal map of LONDON.

Swag, in underworld cant, the booty of a robbery or theft (BOSC, MAZA), so called from the former slang meaning of property of any sort.

Swain, John, a man threatened by the Ku Klux Klan in 1869, who apparently fled the United States (FIVE).

Swamp adder, the snake used by Dr. Grimesby Roylott to murder his stepdaughter Julia Stoner, and which ultimately caused his own death. Holmes called it "the deadliest snake in India," and its brownish speckles prompted Julia's dying allusion to a "speckled band" (SPEC). There is no snake known as a "swamp adder," and the serpent as described fits no known species, Indian or otherwise. See also VIPER.

Swan and Edison, properly **Edison and Swan United Electric Light Company,** an English manufacturer of electric light apparatus. Sir Henry Baskerville declared he would have Baskerville Hall fitted with electric lamps, with a 1,000-candle power "Swan and Edison" right in front of the hall door (HOUN).

*Swandam Lane: see UPPER SWANDAM LANE.

Sweating, the practice, particularly in the tailoring and tobacco trades, of employing men, women, and children to make up goods in their own homes, or in tenement rooms called *sweatshops,* for scant pay; see the bottom photograph on p. 226. Jephro Rucastle declared that Violet Hunter's former salary of £4 per month was "rank sweating" (COPP).

Sweden, a kingdom of northern Europe, pop. (1900) 5,136,441. Until 1905 it was united with Norway. In some editions Jacob Shafter and his daughter Ettie are said to be Swedish (VALL). See also SCANDINAVIA, KING OF.

*Swedish Pathological Society, a society of which Dr. Mortimer was a corresponding member (HOUN).

Swim: see IN THE SWIM.

Swindon, an important railway town in the south-west of England, pop. 45,006. The train to Herefordshire stopped here for lunch (BOSC).

Swindon, Archie, a Vermissa mineowner who was driven out by the Scowrers (VALL).

Swing. Discovering the trap in the vault of the City and Suburban Bank, John Clay told his accomplice: "I'll swing for it" (REDH). He was perhaps alluding to the gallows, for he was a known murderer; or he was perhaps using the word in the slang sense of *to manage,* that is, to escape on his own.

Swing to the line, in coursing, to cause hounds to cast about, usually on leash, in search of the scent they are to follow, before they are loosed upon the *line,* or track, of the scent (HOUN).

Switzerland, a republic of central Europe, pop. (1900) 3,315,443. Holmes and Watson fled into Switzerland, where the final events of the Moriarty case took place (EMPT, FINA).

See also BASLE; DAVOS PLATZ; GENEVA; INTERLAKEN; LAUSANNE; LUCERNE; MEIRINGEN; ROSENLAUI; also DAUBENSEE; GEMMI PASS; REICHENBACH FALLS; SPLÜGEN PASS.

Sydenham (*sid'n-um*), a large residential district in the south of London.

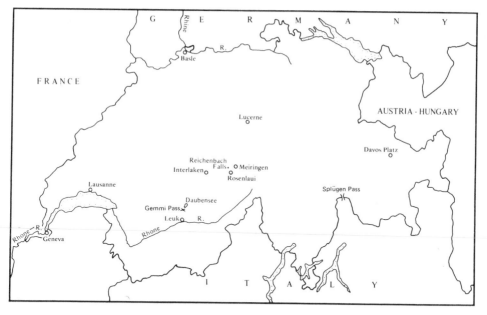

Switzerland.

The CRYSTAL PALACE is here. The Randalls had done a job at Sydenham, where Jack Croker lived (ABBE), and Jonas Oldacre lived near here (NORW). See the front endpaper map.

Sydenham Road, a thoroughfare of south London. DEEP DENE HOUSE was "at the Sydenham end of the road of that name" (NORW). See the front endpaper map.

Sydney, the capital of New South Wales and the chief naval station of Australia, pop. 112,137. The *Hotspur* delivered the survivors of the *Gloria Scott* disaster here (GLOR).

Sylvius, Count Negretto, the famous game-shot, sportsman, and man-about-town who stole the Mazarin diamond (MAZA).

Synthesis, a process of DEDUCTION which advances in a direct manner from principles established or assumed, and propositions already proved, to the conclusion; the opposite of ANALYSIS.

Holmes was pleased that Watson had chosen to chronicle those incidents which gave room for deduction and logical synthesis (COPP), but he maintained that there were fifty people who could reason synthetically for one who could reason analytically (STUD). See DEDUCTION AND ANALYSIS.

Syracuse, an ancient city upon the eastern coast of the island of Sicily, founded 734 B.C. and captured by the Romans in 212 B.C. At one time it was the most important city of the western Græcian world and had over 500,000 inhabitants. Nathan Garrideb valued a Syracusan coin in his possession (3GAR).

Syria, that portion of Asiatic Turkey lying south of Asia Minor and north of Arabia. Professor Coram said that his analysis of the documents found in the Coptic monasteries of Syria and Egypt would cut deep at the very foundations of revealed religion (GOLD). See the map of TURKEY. See also HOLY LAND.

T

Tack, to change the course of a sailing-ship by turning her bow toward the wind and bracing the yards so that she shall sail at a course obliquely against the wind. The sheltered Mounts Bay treacherously invited storm-tossed craft to tack into it for rest and protection (DEVI). See also BEAT.

Tackle, in Rugby, to seize and stop an opponent who has possession of the ball. In Association football the tackler may obstruct, but may not seize, an opposing player. It was said there was no one to touch Godfrey Staunton at passing, tackling, or dribbling (MISS).

Tag, the metalled end of a strap. Irene Adler's coachman had been compelled to hurry so in putting the horse to the landau that "all the tags of his harness were sticking out of the buckles" (SCAN).

Talc, in popular or commercial use, the name loosely applied to *Muscovy glass,* a glass-like material manufactured from mica and commonly used in lamps and lanterns. Its naturally "smokey" appearance masks carbon deposits left by the burning oil. The smoke-guard which covered the top of the chimney on Mortimer Tregennis's lamp was made of talc (DEVI).

Tan, crushed tree-bark (3STU).

Tang, or *T'ang,* a Chinese dynasty reigning A.D. 618–907. Baron Gruner owned a Tang vase dating from the seventh century (ILLU), it being pottery rather than ceramic, for no specimen of the primitive Tang porcelain survives.

Tangey, the commissionaire at the Foreign Office. His wife **Mrs. Tangey** was a charwoman here, suspected for a time of taking the naval treaty, and their eldest daughter lived with them (NAVA).

Tang-ying (*fl.* 1736–49), the famous director of the imperial Chinese porcelain kilns in the eighteenth century. Watson read up on him in preparing for his interview with Baron Gruner (ILLU).

*Tankerville Club, a London club of which Colonel Sebastian Moran was a member (EMPT), as was Major Prendergast, whom Homes cleared of an accusation of cheating at cards in the *Tankerville Club Scandal* (FIVE).

Tanner, in English slang, a SIXPENCE (SIGN).

Tantalus, a stand containing usually three cut-glass decanters which, though apparently free, cannot be removed until the bar which engages the stoppers is raised. There was a tantalus containing brandy and whisky in Peter Carey's cabin (BLAC).

Tapanuli fever, a disease Watson confessed he had never heard of

(DYIN). *Tapanuli* is a region of north-western Sumatra.

Taper, a small, slender candle (SIGN).

Tar: see COAL-TAR.

Tarleton murders, a case Holmes investigated before his meeting with Watson (MUSG).

Tarlton, Susan, the maid to Professor Coram (GOLD).

Tattoo. Trevor Senior had the initials "J.A." tattooed in the bend of his elbow, which he had attempted unsuccessfully to obliterate (GLOR). Jabez Wilson had a fish tattooed immediately above his right wrist in a delicate pink which Holmes said was "quite peculiar to China" (REDH), and Holmes noticed a large blue anchor tattooed upon the back of the retired sergeant of Marines's hand (STUD). Holmes had made a "small study" of tattoo marks and wrote a monograph upon the subject (REDH).

Tavernier, the modeller of the bust Holmes used in the Mazarin diamond case (MAZA).

Tavistock, a town in Devonshire, on the western border of Dartmoor, pop. 4,728; see BOSS. King's Pyland lay two miles east of here (SILV).

Tea. The *Gloria Scott* was built originally for the Chinese coastal tea trade (GLOR), and the firm of Ferguson & Muirhead were tea-brokers (SUSS). After his father's death, Victor Trevor entered the tea-planting business in the Terai (GLOR).

Tea, in England, an afternoon meal, held about four or five o'clock, generally consisting of bread and butter or cake served with tea (CARD, DEVI, GREE, ILLU, NAVA, 3STU, VALL, YELL). A **high tea** is a more substantial single-course meal usually including hot meats (VALL). Mrs. Maberley

possessed a Crown Derby tea-set (3GAB).

Teddy, the mongoose belonging to Henry Wood (CROO).

Telegraph. Watson remarks that Holmes had never been known to write where a telegram would serve (DEVI).

Telegraph, newspaper: see DAILY TELEGRAPH.

Telephone. Holmes used the telephone at Baker Street in his investigations of the De Merville (ILLU), Amberley (RETI), and Garrideb (3GAR) cases. Athelney Jones offered to telephone Scotland Yard (SIGN), which Watson apparently did do (3GAR), and there was a telephone upon the wall at the Bow Street police court (TWIS). Colonel Emsworth ordered his butler to telephone the police (BLAN). Watson turned up the name of Nathan Garrideb in the telephone directory (3GAR).

A terraced tea plantation in the Terai.

The Temple as viewed from its gardens.

Temple, Mormon: see SALT LAKE CITY.

Temple, The, the name given to a collection of buildings, lying between the Strand and the Victoria Embankment, upon the border between Westminster and the City, so called from the *Knights Templars* who first built upon the site in 1185. The area since 1346 has been occupied by teachers and students of the law and since 1609 by two legal corporations known as the *Inner Temple* and the *Middle Temple.* These are two of the four great *Inns of Court,* incorporations for the study of law possessing the exclusive privilege of calling barristers to the Bar; see BARRISTER.

The **Inner Temple** is so called from its position within the precincts of the City, the former Outer Temple, which has long since ceased to exist, having been beyond the City boundary, and the Middle Temple derives its name from its situation between the two. The stately buildings, constructed over several centuries and flanked by their famous gardens, include the ancient Temple Church, meeting and dining halls, libraries, and offices and living quarters for barristers and law students. Godfrey Norton had chambers at the Inner Temple (SCAN). See Map I of LONDON.

Tendo Achillis, the tendon of the heel (SIGN).

Tennessee, one of the south-central states of the United States, pop. 2,020,616. The Ku Klux Klan had branches here (FIVE).

Tennis lawn, a closely cropped, well-tended lawn upon which the game of lawn-tennis is played, or a lawn resembling one used for this purpose (DANC); see also CROQUET LAWN.

Terai, the name given to the strip of

jungle-land lying along the foot of the Himalayan range in Nepaul and northern India. Victor Trevor became a tea planter here (GLOR). See the map of INDIA and the photograph on p. 355.

Terrier. Mrs. Hudson owned an aging terrier which Holmes put out of its pain with poison (STUD). Holmes deduced that Dr. Mortimer's dog was larger than a terrier (HOUN). Victor Trevor owned a BULL-TERRIER (GLOR), and Fitzroy McPherson's dog was an AIREDALE (LION).

Tetanus, a spasmodic contraction of the muscles. Bartholomew Sholto's death was caused by a substance which produced tetanus (SIGN).

Tête-à-tête, a French expression meaning, literally, *head-to-head*, that is, face-to-face; private, intimate, or confidential, as between two persons (HOUN, WIST).

Teutonic, pertaining to the Germans (SIXN).

Texas, one of the south-central states of the United States, known as the *Lone Star State,* pop. 3,048,710. Watson noted that the barque *Lone Star* was named after Texas (FIVE).

Thames (*temz*), the most impor-tant, though not the largest, river in Great Britain. It rises in south-central England, flows south-easterly, and enters the North Sea through a broad estuary. LONDON is situated upon both banks of the Thames some sixty miles from its mouth, and the river is navigable for ocean steamers as far as the metropolis. Within the county of London it is spanned by twenty road, pedestrian, and railway bridges.

Holmes's agents sought the *Aurora* up and down the Thames, and the RIVER POLICE launch chased her at top speed from the Tower of London to Barking Level (SIGN), and Watson ever associated the reaches and marshes of the river with the pursuit (GOLD). The *May Day* was due here (CARD), from which the body of John Openshaw was recovered (FIVE). The Bar of Gold overlooked the Thames, into which were thrown the bodies of men murdered there, and Holmes feared Neville St. Clair had met the same fate since some of his clothes were found in the river (TWIS).

The lawns of Sir James Walter's house at Woolwich stretched down to the Thames (BRUC), and Dr. Bar-

A view over the Thames between London and Gravesend.

nicot had one of the largest practices upon the south side (SIXN). Holmes had been working on a case near the river before falling ill (DYIN), and Godolphin Street lay between the river and Westminster Abbey (SECO).

See also ALBERT DOCK; DEPTFORD REACH; PLUMSTEAD MARSHES; POOL, THE; WEST INDIA DOCKS; WESTMINSTER STAIRS. See also HAMMERSMITH BRIDGE; LONDON BRIDGE; VAUXHALL BRIDGE; WATERLOO BRIDGE; WESTMINSTER BRIDGE.

See also BARKING LEVEL; BLACKWALL; ISLE OF DOGS; MILLBANK; POPLAR; ROTHERHITHE; SHADWELL; WOOLWICH; also SURREY SIDE. See also GRAVESEND.

Theft: see LARCENY.

Theological College: see ST. GEORGE'S, THEOLOGICAL COLLEGE OF.

Thick 'un, in English slang, a SOVEREIGN; thus, something of the value of a sovereign; a job well done. Sam Merton said of Holmes that he would "do him down a thick 'un" (MAZA), that is, thrash him well.

Third Bengal Fusiliers, properly the **Third Bengal European Regiment,** a regiment of the Bengal Army in India, created 1854. It was stationed at Agra during the Mutiny and consisted of untried European volunteers. Jonathan Small called it the "3rd Bengal Fusiliers" (SIGN).

Third Buffs, properly the **Third East Kent Regiment of Foot,** an infantry regiment of the British Army, dating from 1665 and titled *The Buffs.* Jonathan Small said he joined the "Third Buffs" as it was starting for India (SIGN), though the regiment has not been stationed in India since 1843.

*Thirty-Fourth Bombay Infantry, the regiment of the Bombay Army in

India of which Major Sholto and Captain Morstan were officers (SIGN).

*Thor Bridge: see THOR PLACE.

"Thor Bridge": see "PROBLEM OF THOR BRIDGE, THE."

Thoreau, Henry David (1817–1862), the American naturalist and essayist. Holmes repeated his view of circumstantial evidence, calling it "occasionally very convincing, as when you find a trout in the milk, to quote Thoreau's example" (NOBL).

*Thor Mere: see THOR PLACE.

Thorn. Thorn-bushes grew upon Dartmoor (HOUN).

Thorpe, or **thorp,** a group of houses standing together in the country; a hamlet or village; used chiefly in place-names; e.g., DONNITHORPE (GLOR); RIDLING THORPE MANOR (DANC).

*Thor Place, the Hampshire estate of J. Neil Gibson. Maria Gibson was killed at the mouth of **Thor Bridge,** which spans **Thor Mere** upon the grounds (THOR).

*Thorsley, a parish in Devonshire, of which Dr. Mortimer was medical officer (HOUN).

Threadneedle Street, a street in the City, upon which the Bank of England fronts. The banking firm of Holder & Stevenson was located here (BERY), and Hugh Boone was said to be a familiar figure on Threadneedle Street (TWIS). See the map of the CITY and the bottom photograph on p. 75.

Three, rule of: see RULE OF THREE.

*Three Gables, The, the Harrow Weald villa belonging to Mary Maberley (3GAB).

"Three Gables, The Adventure of the" (3GAB), a chronicle which appeared originally in the *Strand* magazine for October 1926 and *Liberty* magazine of 18 September 1926 and was published in the collection entitled *The Case Book of Sherlock Holmes* the following year. It concerns Holmes's interest in the efforts of Isadora Klein and her hired ruffians to secure possession of the unpublished novel written by Douglas Maberley. The case is commonly dated as having occurred in 1896, 1902, or 1903.

"Three Garridebs, The Adventure of the" (3GAR), a chronicle which appeared originally in the *Strand* magazine for January 1925 and *Collier's Weekly* of 25 October 1924 and was published in the 1927 collection entitled *The Case Book of Sherlock Holmes*. It concerns Holmes's association with the remarkable story told by Killer Evans to lure Nathan Garrideb from his rooms. Watson dates the case as having occurred in June 1902.

*"Three Months in the Jungle," a book written by Colonel Sebastian Moran, published in 1884 (EMPT).

Threepence (*thrip'nce*), or *three-penny,* an English silver coin of the value of three pence; the sum or amount of three pence (RESI).

Three-quarter, in Rugby, one of four players on each team who are positioned behind the line of rushers, their duties being to run the ball and to kick and pass it to other members of their own side. Godfrey Staunton was the crack right-wing three-quarter of the Cambridge 'Varsity (MISS), and Robert Ferguson had played three-quarter for Richmond (SUSS). See also BACK.

"Three Students, The Adventure of the" (3STU), a chronicle which appeared originally in the *Strand* magazine for June 1904 and *Collier's Weekly* of 24 September 1904 and was published in the collection entitled *The*

Return of Sherlock Holmes the following year. It concerns Holmes's investigation of cheating in an examination by one of three students living at St. Luke's College. Watson dates the case as having taken place in 1895.

Throgmorton Street, a busy financial street in the City, lying north of the Stock Exchange. James Dodd had his office here (BLAN). See the map of the CITY.

Throw-back, an example of ATAVISM (HOUN).

Thucydides (*thoo-sid'ih-deez*) (c. 470–400 B.C.), the greatest of ancient Greek historians. His history of the Peloponnesian War, in eight books, is incomplete. The first examination in the Fortescue Scholarship competition consisted of translating half a chapter of Thucydides (3STU).

Thurston, a man with whom Watson played billiards (DANC). The London billiard-table manufacturer *Thurston & Co.* maintains a public billiard-room in the Strand.

Thyme, a small aromatic plant of the mint family. Holmes spoke of the South Downs as "thyme-scented" (LION).

Tibet, an extensive region of south-central Asia, lying between India and China, est. pop. 2,000,000 to 3,000,000. The entire region consists of a series of elevated plains or mountainous plateaus varying in altitude from 8,000 to 17,000 feet, and some of the peaks in the surrounding ranges such as the HIMALAYA mountains attain altitudes of more than 25,000 feet. LHASSA is the religious and political capital and chief city.

Tibet is the seat of a branch of Buddhism known as *Lamaism;* see LAMA. While the religious and civil affairs are

The palace of the Dalai Lama near Lhassa.

in the hands of two lamas, the *Dalai Lama* and the *Panchen Lama,* the government is controlled in its foreign relations by Chinese agents.

Holmes claimed to have travelled for two years in Tibet during the Great Hiatus, visiting Lhassa and spending some days with the "head Lama" (EMPT).

Tide-waiter, a custom-house officer who awaits the arrival of ships and sees to it that while in port the customs regulations and revenue laws are observed (NOBL).

Tierra del Fuego, a group of islands situated off the southern extremity of South America, belonging to Chile and Argentina. The native inhabitants, or **Tierra del Fuegians,** do not exceed 1,000 in number and are considered by some authorities to be the lowest on earth in the scale of human achievement. Holmes's gazetteer stated that the Tierra del Fuegians were exceedingly small in stature (SIGN).

Tiger. Watson supposedly had an amusing adventure with a tiger cub while in Afghanistan (SIGN). Colonel Sebastian Moran's bag of tigers was unrivalled, and the story was told in India of how he crawled down a drain after a wounded man-eater (EMPT). There was a tiger-skin hearthrug in the dining-room of the Abbey Grange (ABBE), and two great tiger-skins lay upon the floor of Thaddeus Sholto's apartment (SIGN). Holmes quoted a Persian saying: "There is danger for him who taketh the tiger cub, and danger also for whoso snatches a delusion from a woman" (IDEN).

Tiger of San Pedro: see MURILLO.

"Tiger of San Pedro, The": see "WISTERIA LODGE, THE ADVENTURE OF."

Timekeeper, one who notes and records the number of hours of work done by each of a number of workmen (REDC).

Times, The, the great daily newspaper of London. Begun in 1788, it has always claimed to be a national rather than a party organ, though in recent years it has taken on a more Conservative tone. *The Times* has long stood in a class by itself among newspapers, owing to its abundance of trustworthy news and its high literary standard.

Holmes looked over *The Times*

(ENGR, MISS), in which he read of the Countess of Morcar's blue carbuncle (BLUE) and found Major Sholto's death notice (SIGN). The mysterious warning letter to Sir Henry Baskerville was constructed from a page of *The Times* (HOUN). The Sholtos advertised here for Mary Morstan (SIGN) and Woodley and Carruthers for Violet Smith (SOLI), and Baron Von Herling said that the special German war tax should have revealed to the English the German intentions as clearly as an advertisement upon the front page of *The Times* (LAST).

Tin. Large masses of nickel and tin were discovered in an outhouse of Dr. Becher's home (ENGR).

Stapleton said that neolithic man mined tin upon Dartmoor, and it was at an old tin mine in the heart of Grimpen Mire that he concealed his giant hound (HOUN). Inspector Gregory said that Silver Blaze might lie at the bottom of an old Dartmoor mine (SILV), perhaps a tin mine.

Cornwall too is noted for its tin mines, which have been worked continually since pre-historic times, and Holmes had conceived the idea that the ancient Cornish language had derived from the Phoenician traders in tin (DEVI).

See also BRONZE.

Tinker, an itinerant mender of household utensils. Tinkers usually have been regarded as the lowest order of craftsmen and are traditionally the very type of the unwashed and intemperate lower class (ILLU, TWIS).

"Tired Captain, The Adventure of the," a case in Watson's notes which apparently remains untold (NAVA).

Tobacco. Holmes was a chronically heavy smoker (DEVI, HOUN, REDH, SECO, TWIS) whom Watson called a "self-poisoner by cocaine and tobacco" (FIVE), particularly SHAG (CREE, HOUN, SCAN, TWIS), which he kept in the toe-end of a Persian slipper (EMPT, ILLU, MUSG, NAVA), in the coal-scuttle (MAZA), and in the tobacco-pouches which littered the mantelpiece of his bedroom (DYIN). His before-breakfast pipe was composed of "all the plugs and dottles left from his smokes of the day before, all carefully dried and collected on the corner of the mantelpiece" (ENGR). He had made a special study of cigar ashes and believed he could distinguish at a glance the ash of any known brand of cigar or of tobacco (STUD), and he was the author of a monograph upon the subject (BOSC, STUD) entitled *Upon the Distinction Between the Ashes of the Various Tobaccos* (SIGN).

Isa Whitney first acquired the opium habit from drenching his tobacco with laudanum (TWIS). Thaddeus Sholto smoked Eastern tobacco in his hookah (SIGN). A sealskin tobacco-pouch was a clue in the Peter Carey murder (BLAC). The flap of the letter from Neville St. Clair to his wife had been gummed by someone who had been chewing tobacco (TWIS).

Watson's tobacconist was named Bradley, and Holmes patronized him as well (HOUN). Ionides was Professor Coram's cigarette-maker (GOLD), and a tobacconist's shop backed onto Jabez Wilson's pawnshop (REDH). John Vincent Harden was a well-known tobacco millionaire (SOLI).

Watson smoked SHIP's tobacco (STUD), but later favoured an ARCADIA mixture (CROO). John Straker smoked CAVENDISH (SILV). Holmes recognized Grant Munro's tobacco as GROSVENOR mixture (YELL) and compared the BIRD'S-EYE cut with the TRICHINOPOLY (SIGN). The cardboard box sent to Susan Cushing had once held HONEYDEW tobacco (CARD).

See also CIGAR; CIGARETTE; PIPE; SNUFF.

Tobin (d. 1875), the caretaker of the Worthingdon bank, murdered in the course of a robbery (RESI).

Toby, the dog belonging to old Sherman, loaned to Holmes in order to track the murders of Bartholomew Sholto (SIGN).

Todman, a Vermissa Valley mine-owner who was forced to sell out (VALL).

Toff, a dandy or swell. John Clayton said his fare was dressed like a toff (HOUN).

Tokay, a rich, heavy wine, somewhat sweet in taste and very aromatic, produced in northern Hungary. Thaddeus Sholto offered Mary Morstan a glass (SIGN). Holmes and Watson enjoyed the Tokay at Von Bork's house, which was said to be *Imperial Tokay* from Franz Joseph's special cellar at the Schoenbrunn Palace (LAST).

Toller, the groom to Jephro Rucastle. His wife **Mrs. Toller** was Rucastle's housekeeper (COPP).

Tonga (d. 1888), an Andaman Islander, the murderer of Bartholomew Sholto. He helped Jonathan Small escape from the Andamans and accompanied him to London, where he was shot by Holmes and Watson (SIGN), who ever associated the Thames with him (GOLD). Tonga is the only human being at whom Holmes ever fired a shot.

Took up, that is, *taken up,* engaged or preoccupied (STUD).

Topeka, the capital city of Kansas,

pop. (1905) 37,641. John Garrideb claimed to be from here (3GAR).

Tor, a hill or rocky eminence. The word is especially applied to the rugged and fantastic piles of granite conspicuous on Dartmoor (HOUN). See the photograph of DARTMOOR.

Toronto, a city of Canada, pop. (1891) 181,220. Sir Henry Baskerville had been here (HOUN).

*Torquay Terrace, a block of buildings in Camberwell, where Charpentier's Boarding Establishment was located (STUD).

*Torrington Lodge, the Blackheath residence of John Hector McFarlane and his parents (NORW).

Tosca, Cardinal (d. 1895), the Roman Catholic prelate whose sudden death Holmes investigated (BLAC).

Tottenham Court Road, a thoroughfare of central London, extending northward from Oxford Street. Mary Sutherland's father had been a plumber here (IDEN), where the firm of Morton & Waylight's was located (REDC) and where Henry Baker was attacked by street roughs (BLUE). Holmes had purchased his Stradivarius from a pawnbroker in Tottenham Court Road (CARD). See Maps I and III of LONDON.

Touch line, in Rugby, the boundary line on either side of the playing field, extending from goal-line to goal-line (MISS).

Tour-de-force, a feat of strength, power, or skill (CARD,† SIGN).

Tout, in horse-racing, a person who clandestinely watches the trials of race-horses at their training quarters and for a fee gives information for betting pur-

† This allusion is inserted in "The Resident Patient" in many editions.

poses; in more general use, one who solicits custom, as for an inn or shop. John Mason said that Sir Robert Norberton had been too clever for the touts (SHOS), and Ned Hunter thought Fitzroy Simpson to be one (SILV). A railway guard whom Watson had once treated became, he said, the "trusty tout" of his medical abilities (ENGR).

Tower of London, the ancient fortress and state-prison at the eastern extremity of the City. Situated on the Thames, the Tower is an irregular mass of buildings erected at various periods between 1078 and 1845 and is said to be historically the most interesting spot in England. It is now chiefly used as an arsenal and as a repository for the Crown Jewels. The police launch intercepted the *Aurora* opposite the Tower (SIGN). See the map of the CITY.

Township, in England, a local district within a parish, or the inhabitants of that district, usually centred about a village which is not the principal town of the parish. John Douglas said he recognized Ted Baldwin "in the township" (VALL) in referring to Tunbridge Wells, an improper use of the term, though it would be correct if he were alluding instead to the village of Birlstone.

In most states of the United States a township is a subdivision of a county (VALL).

Tract, a short printed treatise or discourse upon a topic of practical religion, usually in the form of a small pamphlet (GLOR).

Trafalgar Square, a square in Westminster, located at the Charing Cross end of the Strand. The famed Nelson

The central keep of the Tower of London was built by William the Conqueror in 1078, the inner wall with its thirteen towers by his son William Rufus, the "Red King." The moat was added by Richard I and the outer wall by Henry III.

Trafalgar Square, with the entrance to the Strand upon the right.

Column is here, as well as two fountains and a number of statues. Stapleton hailed John Clayton's cab here (HOUN), and when Holmes learned that Lestrade was having the Serpentine dragged for the body of Hatty Doran, he laughingly asked if the basin of the Trafalgar Square fountain was being dragged too, because there was as good a chance of finding the body in the one as in the other (NOBL). See Map II of LONDON.

"Tragedy of Birlstone, The": see "VALLEY OF FEAR, THE."

Trailed herring: see DRAGHOUND.

Train-de-luxe, in France, a railway train composed of first-class or PULLMAN carriages (MAZA).

Tramp, a cargo ship which runs upon no regular route or schedule. The sailor Hudson declared he was "just off a two-yearer in an eight-knot tramp" (GLOR), that is, two years' service aboard a tramp capable of a top speed of eight knots.

Tramway, a railway laid in the streets of a city or town, especially for the transportation of passengers, and which uses horses, cable, or electricity as the locomotive means. A number of tramway companies are in operation throughout London, almost all of which are now electrified. Holmes declared that Mycroft's coming round to Baker Street was like meeting a tramcar coming down a country lane (BRUC). See the photograph accompanying WESTMINSTER BRIDGE.

Transportation, in law, the removal, for a specified term, of a convict to a penal settlement in another country. In England the practice of transportation was fully abolished in 1868. Trevor Senior was transported to Australia aboard the *Gloria Scott* in 1855 (GLOR).

Transylvania, a former principality, now an administrative district, occupying the extreme eastern portion of Hungary, pop. (1900) 2,456,838. "Vampires in Transylvania" was an entry in Holmes's index (SUSS).

Trap, the name generally given to any two-wheeled, open pleasure carriage of whatever construction. It most commonly has two seats, which may be placed back-to-back or both facing front. The word is often used especially in referring to a DOG-CART.

Colonel Emsworth (BLAN), Charles McCarthy (BOSC), the Cunninghams (REIG), and Dr. Grimesby Roylott (SPEC) kept traps, and Holmes and Watson drove in a hired trap to the Copper Beeches (COPP), Yoxley Old Place (GOLD), Stoke Moran (SPEC), and Thor Place (THOR). John Scott Eccles drove to Wisteria Lodge in an apparently hired trap (WIST). The dog-carts belonging to Reuben Hays (PRIO), Bob Carruthers (SOLI), and Neville St. Clair (TWIS) were also called traps, as was Sir Henry Baskerville's WAGONETTE (HOUN).

Treasury, the department of government which has control over the collection, management, and expenditure of the public revenue.

In the British Government the Treasury is directed by a Cabinet minister, the *First Lord of the Treasury,* who usually is the Prime Minister himself. The Premier's official residence in Downing Street is in fact in the Treasury building. With all the British Treasury behind him, Holmes declared, he would attempt to buy back the stolen Trelawney Hope document (SECO). See the map of WHITEHALL.

The United States Treasury occupies a building which lies immediately east of the White House in Washington. Birdy Edwards said he would not spend

A country trap.

another three months among the Scowrers if he were set loose in the Treasury at Washington for it (VALL).

*Tredannick Wartha, the house near Poldhu in which the Tregennis family lived (DEVI).

Tredannick Wollas, properly **Predannack Wollas,** a hamlet in Cornwall, some six miles south of Helston, est. pop. 200. It was in and about "the hamlet of Tredannick Wollas" that the events of the Cornish Horror occurred (DEVI).

Tree worship, worship or religious veneration paid to trees by primitive races of men, from the belief that they were the fixed abode or a favourite resort of spirits capable of influencing human destiny. Many different kinds of trees have been specific objects of worship, but the oak has been particularly favoured, as among the Druids. In Greek mythology some special tree was in many cases sacred to an individual deity. Tree worship was practiced by the early Buddhists, as among many other pagan peoples, and it existed throughout Europe before the introduction of Christianity. The Old Testament has many indications of its existence among the people surrounding the Jews, and of lapses into the practice of it by the Jews themselves. In his disguise as an old bibliophile Holmes carried a volume entitled *The Origin of Tree Worship* (EMPT).

Tregellis, the head gamekeeper at Hurlstone. His daughter **Janet Tregellis** was in love with Richard Brunton (MUSG).

Tregennis, a family of Cornwall tin-mine owners who sold out in the 1890s to a larger mining company. After some years of disputing the division of the money, **Mortimer Tregennis**

(d. 1897) took it upon himself to poison with DEVIL'S-FOOT ROOT his brothers **George Tregennis** and **Owen Tregennis,** who were driven mad by the effect of the drug, and his sister **Brenda Tregennis** (d. 1897), who died of it. Mortimer was himself killed in the same manner by Brenda's lover Leon STERNDALE (DEVI).

Trelawney Hope, the Secretary for European Affairs in the second ministry of Lord Bellinger. A document of international importance was stolen from his home, and Holmes was called up to recover it. His wife **Lady Hilda Trelawney Hope** was found to be the thief, who had delivered the document to Eduardo LUCAS under threat of blackmail and who was shielded by Holmes upon recovery of the paper (SECO).

Trencher, a wooden plate or platter. Flagons and trenchers flew before Hugo Baskerville as he sprang atop the banquet-table (HOUN).

Trepoff murder, the case Holmes investigated in Odessia about 1888 (SCAN).

Trevelyan, Dr. Percy, the London physician who introduced Holmes to the Brook Street mystery (RESI).

Trevor, known as **Trevor Senior** (b. 1832), a Norfolk squire. His real name was *James Armitage,* and as a young man he was transported aboard the barque *Gloria Scott* for embezzlement and survived the destruction of that ship, reaching Australia a free man. He prospered in the gold-fields and after ten years returned to England, where he was blackmailed by the sailor HUDSON and died of apoplexy when betrayed to the authorities. It was Trevor who first suggested to the youthful Sherlock Holmes that he might become a detective. His son **Vic-**

tor Trevor was a student at Holmes's university and introduced the future detective to his father (GLOR).

Trichinopoly (*trich-ih-nah'puhl-ee*), a cigar made of the dark tobacco grown near the city of that name in southern India. Jefferson Hope smoked such a cigar, which Holmes was able to identify from its dark, flakey ash (STUD). Holmes maintained that to the trained eye "there is as much difference between the black ash of a Trichinopoly and the white fluff of bird's-eye as there is between a cabbage and a potato" (SIGN).

Trigonometry, that branch of mathematics which treats of the measurement of triangles and of the relations between their parts. Reginald Musgrave's childhood exercises in trigonometry were responsible for his remembering the height of an old elm on the Hurlstone estate which since had been cut down (MUSG).

Trim, to beat or thrash another (3GAB).

Trincomalee (*tring-kō-muh-lee'*), a town of Ceylon, situated upon a magnificent natural harbour, pop. 11,295. Holmes cleared up the singular tragedy of the Atkinson brothers at Trincomalee (SCAN).

Trinity College, a college of Cambridge University, founded by Henry VIII in 1546. It is the largest college in England, having some 190 undergraduates. The long list of its famous members includes the names of Newton, Bacon, Dryden, Macaulay, Byron, Thackeray, and Tennyson. Cyril Overton was a member, as was Pompey's owner Jeremy Dixon (MISS).

Triple Alliance, a league formed in 1883 for mutual defense among Germany, Austria-Hungary, and Italy. The stolen naval treaty defined the British position toward the Triple Alliance (NAVA). Lord Bellinger spoke of the "double league" which made a balance of military power in Europe (SECO), an allusion to the Triple Alliance upon the one hand and perhaps the alliance between France and Russia, dating from 1891–94, upon the other.

Troop, a body of cavalry about one hundred strong and commanded by a captain. There were two troops of horse at Agra (SIGN). A **trooper** is a cavalry soldier (BOSC).

Trotter, a trotting-horse (VALL).

Trout. Holmes and Watson caught some trout in the Shoscombe millstream (SHOS). Holmes quoted Thoreau's example of finding a trout in the milk to demonstrate the occasionally convincing nature of circumstantial evidence (NOBL).

Trumpington, a village to the south of Cambridge, near which Godfrey Staunton's cottage was located (MISS). See the map of the vicinity of CAMBRIDGE.

Try, in Rugby (1908 rules), the running of the ball into the opposing team's in-goal area and touching it to the ground for a score of three points. A successful try then entitles the team to attempt a *goal,* a kick over the goalposts, for two additional points. Without Godfrey Staunton, the Cambridge team lost to Oxford by a goal and two tries (MISS).

Tudor, the family name of the English royal line which reigned 1485–1603, beginning with Henry VII and ending with Elizabeth. The St. Simons inherited Plantagenet blood by direct descent and Tudor on the distaff side (NOBL).

The name **Tudor architecture** is given to the building style of the period, representing the latest of the English mediæval or Gothic style and characterized by flat arches and shallow moldings. The house at Thor Place was half Tudor and half Georgian (THOR), and Watson described Charlington Hall (SOLI) and Cheeseman's (SUSS) as possessing "Tudor chimneys," suggesting that these old houses were built during that period. Tuxbury Old Hall was built upon an ELIZABETHAN foundation (BLAN), and Holdernesse Hall was Elizabethan (PRIO).

Tunbridge Wells, an inland resort city of Kent, pop. 33,373. Patrick Cairns took a train for London from here (BLAC), which was ten or twelve miles east of Birlstone (VALL).

Turf, The, the race-course; hence, the occupation or profession of racing horses.

The Shoscombe case was intimately connected with the Turf (SHOS), as was the Silver Blaze affair (SILV). Holmes stated that amateur sport was not free from outside betting among the public, and that it might be worth someone's while to get at a Rugby player as the ruffians of the Turf get at a race-horse (MISS). The McCarthys were fond of racing (BOSC), and Arthur Holder had squandered money on the Turf (BERY), where Sir Jabez Gilchrist ruined himself (3STU). Watson said that he paid for his knowledge of the Turf with "about half" of his wound pension (SHOS).

For race-meetings see DERBY, THE; GRAND NATIONAL; NEWMARKET HEATH; WESSEX CUP.

For racing stables see CAPLETON; KING'S PYLAND. For horses see BAYARD; DESBOROUGH; IRIS; NEGRO, THE; PUGILIST; RASPER; SHOSCOMBE PRINCE; SILVER BLAZE; see also ISONOMY.

See also CUP; DARK HORSE; FURLONG; "PINK 'UN"; PLATE; SCRATCH; TOUT.

Turkey, or *The Ottoman Empire,* a country occupying portions of southeastern Europe, western Asia, parts of northern Africa, and several islands in the eastern Mediterranean, est. pop. 24,500,000.

Holmes in January 1903 had a commission from the Sultan of Turkey which, he said, called for immediate action, as political consequences of the gravest kind might arise from its neglect (BLAN).

The Sultan in 1903 was *Abdul-Hamid II* (1842–1918), who reigned 1876–1909, a cruel and repressive despot who was deposed in 1909 by the revolutionary Young Turk movement. The only Turkish political event of any international note at the time was the conclusion of the revolt of 1902–3 in the European province of Macedonia. In February 1903 a joint Russian-Austrian plan for administrative reform in Macedonia was prepared, agreed to by the other major Europeans powers, and imposed upon Turkey. The Macedonian revolutionaries were allied with the Young Turks, many of whom were in exile in England.

See also EGYPT; HOLY LAND; SYRIA; also MECCA.

Turkish bath, a kind of bath introduced from the East, in which the subject, after having undergone copious perspiration in a heated room, is subjected to various processes such as soaping, washing, and massaging, and ultimately proceeds to an outer apartment called a *drying-room* where he is placed on a couch to cool. Watson confessed a fondness for the Turkish bath (LADY) which Holmes later shared (ILLU), they patronizing the

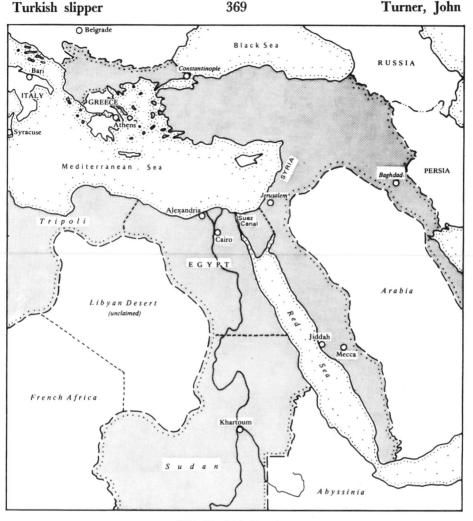

The Turkish Empire.

Northumberland Avenue establishment (ILLU) known as the *Charing Cross Baths* or *Nevill's.*

Turkish slipper, a slipper similar to the PERSIAN SLIPPER but made in Turkey (SPEC).

Turn, a short walk which ends in a return to one's starting-point. Holmes remarked that he had had "one or two little turns," that is, encounters, with John Clay (REDH).

Turn, a particular form or style.

Holmes remarked, perhaps only half-jokingly, that Watson had a "strong, natural turn" for burglary (CHAS). Robert Ferguson had a fine turn of speed as a Rugby player (SUSS).

Turner, John, an English squire, formerly an Australian bushranger known as *Black Jack of Ballarat.* After settling in England he was blackmailed by Charles McCarthy, a former victim, whom he finally killed. His daughter **Alice Turner** married McCarthy's son

James after her father's death (BOSC).

Turner, Mrs., a woman whose rôle in the Baker Street household in 1888 is very uncertain (SCAN).

Turning chair, a chair made to rotate upon its base (CHAS).

*Turpey Street, a street in the Borough, where John Clayton lived (HOUN).

Turquoise. There was a great variety of turquoises in the Agra treasure (SIGN).

Tuson, Sergeant, a member of the City Police, who arrested Beddington (STOC).

Tussaud's (*too-sō'*), or **Madame Tussaud's,** a collection of waxworks representing notable persons and various curiosities, located in London just east of Baker Street Station. It was established in 1802 by *Madame Marie Grosholtz Tussaud* (d. 1850), a Swiss who learned the modelling craft in Paris. Sam Merton exclaimed that Madame Tussaud's could not match the bust of Holmes he saw at Baker Street (MAZA). See Map I of LONDON.

Tutor, a private teacher. Fraser helped the Stapletons establish St. Oliver's school (HOUN), and Reginald Musgrave's childhood tutor was responsible for his knowing the former height of a sawn elm upon the Hurlstone estate (MUSG). See also COACH.

Tutor, in an English university, an officer who is specially entrusted with the care of the undergraduates of his college. Hilton Soames was tutor of St. Luke's College (3STU).

*Tuxbury Old Park, the Bedfordshire estate of Colonel Emsworth, and site of **Tuxbury Old Hall** (BLAN).

Tweed: see HARRIS TWEED; HEATHER TWEED.

'Tween decks, any of the decks of a ship except the upper one; the whole space between the upper and lower decks (GLOR).

Twenty-five line, in Rugby, the line drawn across the playing field twenty-five yards from each goal (MISS).

"Twisted Lip": see "MAN WITH THE TWISTED LIP, THE."

Twopence (*tup'nce*), an English silver coin of the value of two pence (IDEN, SCAN).

221b Baker Street: see BAKER STREET.

Two-yearer: see TRAMP.

Tyburn Tree, the name given to a gallows which once stood at the intersection of Oxford Street and the Edgware Road. The scene of countless executions, it was finally removed in 1759, after which time all executions took place at Newgate Prison. Watson writes that Little Ryder Street lay "within a stone-cast" of the old Tyburn Tree "of evil memory" (3GAR) in that region north of Hyde Park known as *Tyburnia*. See Map I of LONDON.

Typewriter. Holmes declared that a typewriter has quite as much individuality as a man's handwriting, and he thought of writing a monograph upon the typewriter and its relation to crime (IDEN). Mary Sutherland earned a living as a typewritist (IDEN), Laura Lyons had such a business (HOUN), and Lady Hilda Trelawney Hope entered the Lucas house pretending to answer an advertisement about typewriting (SECO). Holmes said he nearly fell into the error of mistaking Violet Smith's spatulate finger-ends, the result of piano playing, for those of a typewritist (SOLI). Typewriter characteristics confirmed Holmes's theory of the Sutherland case (IDEN).

Typhoid fever, or **enteric fever,** a serious, bacillus-related disease spread by contamination of food and water. Watson termed it "that curse of our Indian possessions" and was struck down by it (STUD). Ettie Edwards died of typhoid (VALL), as did a tenant of Lauriston Gardens (STUD).

U

Ubanghi country, that part of Central Africa which is drained by the *Ubanghi River,* the northern-most tributary of the Congo. The Ubanghi forms the boundary between the French and Belgian possessions in the Congo. Leon Sterndale said that he obtained his specimen of the devil's-foot root poison here (DEVI). See the map of AFRICA.

*Uffa, the mysterious island where the Grice Patersons experienced their singular adventures (FIVE).

Ulster, a type of long, loose overcoat,

On the London Underground.

reaching very nearly to the feet and sometimes girded with a belt. It often has a hood or cape and is worn as a travelling-cloak. Hatty Doran donned an ulster (NOBL). Holmes wore one (BLUE, STUD), as did Watson (BLUE, SCAN).

Uncle Sam, the name given to the figure personifying the American people (LAST, VALL).

Underground railway, a railway in a tunnel excavated for the purpose of placing the roadbed below the level of the street. London was the first city to adopt underground railways with the opening of the METROPOLITAN RAILWAY in 1863. This line together with the

Metropolitan District Railway forms an irregular oval, known as the *Inner Circle,* round the whole of the inner part of London. For the most part they run through tunnels, but also through cuttings between high walls. The *Middle Circle* is a westward extension of the Inner Circle.

Several other railway companies run suburban trains in connexion with the two Metropolitan lines. The *Outer Circle,* the most extensive of these suburban systems, reaches out in a wide curve from Kensington, passes through the north-western suburb of Willesden, and loops round from the north to the City. Most of the national railway ter-

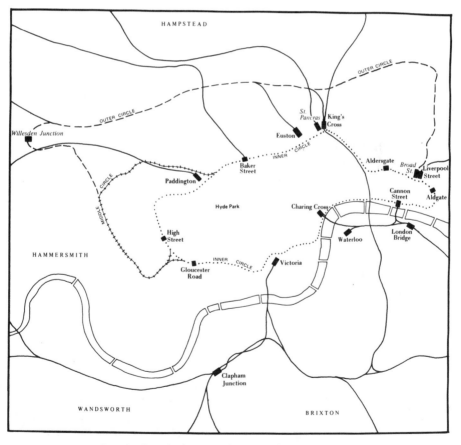

London's principal Underground railway lines.

mini also have adjoining Underground stations.

Watson declared that he would like to see the author of "The Book of Life" clapped down in a third-class carriage on the Underground and asked to give the trades of all his fellow-passengers (STUD). Holmes and Watson took the Underground to ALDERSGATE STATION on their way to Saxe-Coburg Square (REDH), and Alexander Holder rode the Metropolitan to BAKER STREET STATION (BERY). See also GLOUCESTER ROAD STATION; HIGH STREET STATION.

The body of Cadogan West was placed upon the roof of an Underground carriage which was stopped at the Kensington intersection of the Inner and Middle Circles, was carried round the Inner Circle, and was at last jolted off by the motion of the train travelling over points near ALDGATE STATION (BRUC); from the information given it is most likely, though not certain, that the train ran in a clockwise direction from Kensington to Aldgate, and that the dead man was found upon the north side of the station.

See also RAILWAY STATIONS.

Underwood, John, the London hatter through whose establishment, **John Underwood and Sons,** Enoch Drebber was traced (STUD).

Union boat, the popular name given to any of the ships of the *Union Steamship Company,* which carried mail and some passengers between England and the Continent and South Africa 1853–1900. The non-existent Tom Dennis was said to be a steward aboard a Union boat (STUD).

*Union House, the name of John McGinty's saloon (VALL).

Union Jack, the national ensign of the United Kingdom of Great Britain and Ireland. Holmes declared himself to be one of those who believed that succeeding generations some day would be citizens of the same world-wide country under a flag which would be a quartering of the Union Jack with the Stars and Stripes (NOBL).

United States, the republic occupying the central portion of North America, pop. 75,994,575. The capital is WASHINGTON.

J. Neil Gibson had been a Senator for some western state (THOR). Beddington stole nearly £100,000 in American railway bonds (STOC). One of the London society papers protested humorously against American girls marrying into the British noble houses (NOBL), and Holmes said that "paying for brains" was "the American business principle" (VALL). Many of Holmes's cases had major American connexions (DANC, FIVE, LAST, NOBL, REDC, STUD, 3GAR, VALL, YELL), and others lesser ones (ABBE, HOUN, ILLU, REDH). See also "STUDY IN SCARLET"; "VALLEY OF FEAR."

See also ARIZONA; CALIFORNIA; FLORIDA; GEORGIA; ILLINOIS; KANSAS; LOUISIANA; MICHIGAN; MONTANA; NEBRASKA; NEVADA; NEW JERSEY; NEW MEXICO; NORTH CAROLINA; OHIO; PENNSYLVANIA; SOUTH CAROLINA; TENNESSEE; TEXAS; UTAH.

See also ARKANSAS RIVER; COLORADO RIVER; MISSISSIPPI RIVER; MISSOURI RIVER; NIAGARA FALLS; RIO GRANDE; ROCKY MOUNTAINS; SIERRA NEVADA; VERMISSA VALLEY; YELLOWSTONE RIVER.

University of London: see LONDON, UNIVERSITY OF.

"Upon the Distinction Between the Ashes of the Various Tobaccos," the monograph written by Holmes as the

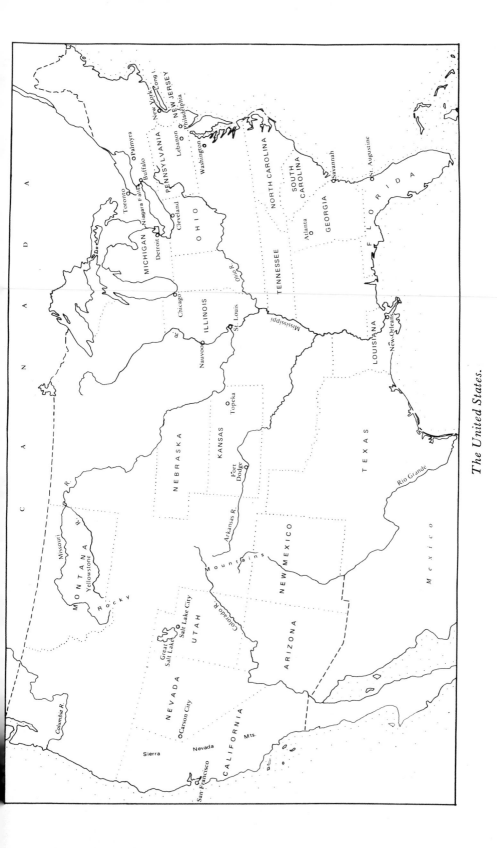

The United States.

result of a special study of tobacco ashes (BOSC, STUD). In it he enumerated 140 forms of cigar, cigarette, and pipe tobacco, with coloured plates illustrating the difference in the ash (SIGN).

Upper-attendant: see HOTEL SERVANTS.

Upper Norwood: see NORWOOD.

Upper Seymour Street: see WIGMORE STREET.

*Upper Swandam Lane, an alley in the east of the City, near London Bridge, in which the Bar of Gold was located (TWIS).

Uppingham School, a preparatory school at *Uppingham* in the eastern Midlands, founded 1584. Willoughby Smith had attended here (GOLD).

Upwood, Colonel, he whose atrocious conduct in the card scandal of the Nonpareil Club Holmes exposed (HOUN).

Uriah, in the Bible (*II Sam.* 11), an officer in the army of David, whose death in battle was arranged so that David might marry his wife Bathsheba. Holmes alluded to the story (CROO).

Utah, one of the Rocky Mountain states of the United States, pop. 276,749. Its history begins with the coming of the MORMONS and the founding of SALT LAKE CITY in 1847 (STUD). The Territory of Utah was organized in 1850 and substantially reduced in area with the admission of NEVADA as a state in 1864. Conflict between the Mormon residents and the United States Government continued until Utah's admission in 1896.

See also CARSON CITY; EAGLE CAÑON; GREAT SALT LAKE; NEVADA MOUNTAINS; SALT LAKE MOUNTAINS; WASATCH MOUNTAINS; WASHOE.

The Territory of Utah, 1860.

Utrecht (*yoo′trekt*), a city of the Netherlands, pop. (1900) 102,085. Van Jansen met his death here (STUD).

V

Valet, a man-servant performing duties chiefly relating to the person of his master. Valets were employed by Hugo Oberstein (BRUC), Trelawney Hope (SECO), Eduardo Lucas (SECO), and Don Murillo (WIST). Holmes was able to bribe Sir George Burnwell's valet (BERY). Don Murillo had a confidential man-servant (WIST), as did the Stapletons (HOUN) and Aloysius Garcia (WIST). BANNISTER was Hilton Soames's servant (3STU).

Valetudinarian, a person of an infirm or sickly constitution. Thaddeus Sholto declared he was compelled to be a valetudinarian (SIGN).

"Valley of Fear, The" (VALL), a novel-length chronicle which appeared serially in the *Strand* magazine between September 1914 and May 1915 and was published in book form in the latter year. It is in two parts. Part I, entitled "The Tragedy of Birlstone," concerns Holmes's investigation of the alleged murder of John Douglas of Birlstone Manor House. Watson places the case as having occurred in January at the end of the 1880s, and it is dated in various years between 1887 and 1900, though 1888 is most commonly accepted.

Part II, entitled "The Scowrers," is a retrospection, written in the third person, concerned with the Scowrers of Vermissa Valley, U.S.A., and their mass arrest by the Pinkertons after infiltration by Birdy Edwards. It takes place in 1875. A short epilogue returns to Watson's narrative.

Valley of the Rhone: see RHONE.

Vamberry, a wine merchant with whom Holmes had some professional contact before his partnership with Watson (MUSG).

Van Deher, a Vermissa Valley ironworks-owner who was forced to sell out (VALL).

Vandeleur: see STAPLETON.

Vanderbilt. The case of "Vanderbilt and the Yeggman" was entered in Holmes's index (SUSS). *Vanderbilt* is the name of a prominent family of American capitalists and railroad financiers.

Van Jansen, a man whose death in Utrecht in 1834 presented attendant circumstances similar to those of Enoch Drebber (STUD).

Van Seddar, apparently a courier of Count Sylvius, who was to take the Mazarin stone to Amsterdam (MAZA).

Van Shorst, a victim of the Scowrers (VALL).

Vatican, a palace in Rome, the residence of the Pope. Holmes was concerned with the case of the Vatican cameos (HOUN).

Vauxhall Bridge, a road bridge spanning the Thames between Westminster and Lambeth, built in 1816, enlarged in 1896, and rebuilt in 1906. Holmes's party crossed Vauxhall Bridge on their way to meet Thaddeus Sholto, and Watson was landed here from the police launch (SIGN). See Map IV of LONDON.

Vauxhall Bridge as it was originally built in 1816.

Vauxhall Bridge Road, a thoroughfare in Westminster, extending from Victoria Station to Vauxhall Bridge (SIGN). See Map IV of LONDON.

V.C., the abbreviation for *Victoria Cross,* a military decoration founded by Queen Victoria in 1856 and awarded for acts of conspicuous bravery in the face of the enemy. The initials also follow the names of the medal's recipients. James Dodd called old Colonel Emsworth "the Crimean V.C." (BLAN).

Vegetable alkaloid: see ALKALOID.

***Vegetarian Restaurant,** the restaurant which backed on to Jabez Wilson's pawnshop (REDH).

Vehmgericht *(faim′geh-richt),* one of the secret tribunals which flourished in Germany during the fourteenth and fifteenth centuries, a period of political turmoil and civil disorder. They at first afforded some protection from lawbreakers, since the official machinery of justice had become ineffectual, but later they misused their power and disappeared with the increasing strength of the regular governments. The *Daily Telegraph* alluded airily to the Vehmgericht in its editorial about the Drebber murder; and it was said that not even the Vehmgericht was ever able to put a more formidable machinery in motion than the Danites of Utah (STUD).

"Veiled Lodger, The Adventure of the" (VEIL), a chronicle which appeared originally in the *Strand* magazine for February 1927 and *Liberty* magazine of 22 January 1927 and was published in the collection entitled *The Case Book of Sherlock Holmes* the same year. It concerns the confession in the year 1896 of Eugenia Ronder to Holmes of the murder of her husband seven years earlier.

Veldt, in South Africa, an unforested or thinly forested tract of grassland (BLAN).

Velveteen, or *corduroy,* a strongly woven cotton fabric. One of Holmes's early clients was a railway porter in a velveteen uniform; John Ferrier wore a velveteen tunic (STUD).

Venetian, a variety of delicate ornamental glassware produced in Venice. Watson poured water for Mary Morstan from a Venetian carafe (SIGN).

Venezuelan loan, apparently a financial debacle which ruined the firm of Coxon & Woodhouse (STOC).

***Venner & Matheson,** the well-known firm of hydraulic engineers to whom Victor Hatherley had been apprenticed (ENGR).

Venomous lizard: see GILA.

Venucci, Pietro, a London cutthroat and Mafia member, murdered by Beppo. His sister **Lucretia Venucci** had been maid to the Princess of Colonna and had stolen the black pearl of the Borgias (SIXN).

Vere: see DE VERE.

Vere Street, a short street in the West End, opening into Oxford Street. A falling brick nearly struck Holmes as he walked down here (FINA). See Map III of LONDON.

*Vermissa Valley, a valley in the coal-mining and iron-working region of the United States, located within the Gilmerton Mountains. **Vermissa** was the chief town. It was here that the Scowrers waged their war with the coal and iron companies and the railroads (VALL).

Verner, the London physician and distant relation to Holmes who bought Watson's Kensington practice with money provided by the detective (NORW).

Vernet (*ver-nay'*), **Émile Jean Horace** (1789–1863), a French painter of martial pieces, which he executed with a realistic treatment. He was the last and greatest of several generations of noted artists. His sister was Holmes's grandmother (GREE).

*Vernon Lodge, the house near Kingston belonging to Baron Gruner (ILLU).

Vesta, a wax friction-match (SILV, TWIS).

Vestry: see PARISH.

Vibart, Jules, the fiancé of Marie Devine (LADY).

Vicar, in the Church of England, in general, the priest of a parish (BLAC, DANC, DEVI, RETI).

Victoria (1819–1901), the Queen of the United Kingdom of Great Britain and Ireland, and Empress of India. She ascended the throne upon the death of William IV in 1837 and was proclaimed Empress of India in 1877. In 1887 the people of the Empire celebrated the fiftieth year of her reign with the Golden JUBILEE, and the Diamond Jubilee followed in 1897. Holmes was born during the reign of Victoria and spent all but the last two years of his active practice in the Victorian Era.

Urgent representations concerning the theft of the Bruce-Partington plans arrived at the Cabinet from "the very highest quarter," and after the successful conclusion of the case Holmes spent a day at Windsor and received a present of an emerald tie-pin from "a certain gracious lady" (BRUC). Holmes chose to take pistol practice by adorning the wall of the Baker Street sitting room with a patriotic **V.R.** (*Victoria Regina*) done in bullet-pocks

Her Majesty Queen Victoria.

(MUSG). Watson writes that the documents of Holmes's cases provide "a perfect quarry for the student, not only of crime, but of the social and official scandals of the late Victorian era" (VEIL).

Victoria, formerly a British colony in the south-eastern part of Australia, since 1901 a state of the Australian Commonwealth, pop. 1,199,692. Old Turner and McCarthy had known one another here (BOSC).

Victorian architecture, the architectural style most prominent after the mid-nineteenth century. The most conspicuous manifestation of the so-called *Gothic revival* in the arts, the style is characterized by the GOTHIC ARCH and GROINED vaulting common to the Gothic fashion, adapted to modern tastes and requirements. The Houses of Parliament constitute perhaps the best-known example. Tuxbury Old Hall possessed what James Dodd called a Victorian portico (BLAN), and Caulfield Gardens, Watson writes, "was one of those lines of flat-faced, pillared and porticoed houses which are so prominent a product of the middle Victorian epoch in the West End of London" (BRUC).

Victoria Station, a railway station in Westminster, the West End terminus of the *South-Eastern and Chatham Railway,* and served also by the *London, Brighton and South Coast Railway* and four suburban lines. Opened in 1860, it was rebuilt early in this century. Holmes and his party left Victoria for Lamberley (SUSS) and for Birlstone (VALL), and he and Watson took the Continental express here (FINA). Mr.

Hansom cabs wait for fares at the main entrance to Victoria Station. At left the Grosvenor Hotel is seen behind the wooden portico leading to the booking-offices. The building on the right is a Metropolitan station.

Melas took a train for Victoria at Clapham Junction (GREE), and the train from Winchester arrived here (SILV). See also GROSVENOR HOTEL. See Map IV of LONDON.

Victoria Street, a street in Westminster, extending westward from Westminster Abbey to Victoria Station. Victor Hatherley had his professional chambers here (ENGR). See also GROSVENOR MANSIONS. See Map IV of LONDON.

"Vie de Bohème": see MURGER, HENRI.

View-holloa, the shout given by a huntsman upon sighting a fox break cover (CHAS, DEVI).

Vigor, the "Hammersmith wonder," an entry in Holmes's index (SUSS).

Villard, François le, a French detective who consulted Holmes and translated some of Holmes's monographs into French (SIGN).

Vincent Square, a square in Westminster, just off Rochester Row and the Vauxhall Bridge Road (SIGN). See Map IV of LONDON.

Violin. Holmes's own violin was a STRADIVARIUS (CARD), and Watson declared that he was a "very capable performer" (REDH) who played "well" (FIVE, STUD), though while his powers upon the violin were very remarkable they were as eccentric as all his other accomplishments (STUD). He was addicted to music, presumably violin music of his own making, at strange hours (DYIN), and would lie about with his fiddle during periods of lethargy (MUSG, STUD), as a solace and aid to thought during his cases (FIVE, NORW, SECO, STUD), or as a release after the conclusion of a problem (NOBL). He usually terminated these solos by playing in quick succession a whole series of Watson's favourite airs (STUD), and once he lulled the exhausted doctor to sleep (SIGN). Watson himself allowed that a well-played violin was a treat for the gods, while a badly played one was no more than a row (STUD).

Holmes's violin-case was kept in its accustomed place in a corner of the Baker Street rooms (EMPT, MAZA). He led Count Sylvius and Sam Merton to believe that he was playing the Hoffmann Barcarolle, which in fact was a recording (MAZA). At times he would talk about nothing but violins (CARD), and he prattled about CREMONA fiddles and the difference between a Stradivarius and an AMATI (STUD). Watson complained that he at last became an institution in Holmes's life like the violin and other (CREE).

See also NORMAN-NÉRUDA; PAGANINI; SARASATE; see also PEACE, CHARLES.

Viper, the name generally applied to poisonous serpents characterized by having no teeth in the upper jaw other than the two poison fangs. The common viper or *adder* is the only venomous snake in Great Britain.

Old Sherman threatened Watson with a "wiper" (SIGN). The box sent Holmes by Culverton Smith contained a poisoned spring "like a viper's tooth" (DYIN), and "Vipers" was an entry in Holmes's index (SUSS). See also SWAMP ADDER.

The distinctive poison-fangs of the viper have a wide hole in front, at the base, through which the venom is secreted.

Vitriol, sulphuric acid or one of its many compounds. There had been a vitriol-throwing committed for the sake of the blue carbuncle (BLUE). Kitty Winter was convicted of vitriol-throwing in the case of Baron Gruner (ILLU).

Vittoria, a "circus belle" entered in Holmes's index (SUSS).

Vixen Tor, a Dartmoor tor (HOUN).

Vizard mask, a mask worn across the eyes (SCAN).

Voilà tout, a French phrase meaning *that's all* (IDEN).

Volunteers, military bodies organized in 1863 within the English counties for the purpose of repelling invasion. The legislation was modified in 1900 to permit Volunteer regiments to take part in the South African War. Watson said that Cockneys made up crack Volunteer regiments (STOC). See also IMPERIAL YEOMANRY.

Von Bischoff, a man who was tried and presumably acquitted of a capital crime in Frankfort the year before the Drebber case because there was no reliable test for blood stains (STUD).

Von Bork, the German spymaster whose career of espionage in England 1910–14 was foiled by Holmes. His wife left England the day before his arrest (LAST).

Von Herder, the blind German mechanic who constructed Sebastian Moran's air-gun to the order of Professor Moriarty (EMPT).

Von Herling, Baron, the chief secretary of the German legation in London (LAST).

Von Kramm, Count, the King of Bohemia's incognito during his visit to London (SCAN).

Von Ormstein: see BOHEMIA, KING OF.

Von Saxe-Meningen: see SCANDINAVIA, KING OF.

Von und Zu Grafenstein: see GRAFENSTEIN.

Von Waldbaum, Fritz, a criminal specialist of Dantzig, who was associated with the case of the Second Stain (NAVA).

Voodoo, a common name in North and South America for certain secret rites of witchcraft and soothsaying which are tinctured with African superstitions and customs. The mulatto cook was a devotee of voodooism, which prompted Holmes to consult Eckermann's *Voodooism and the Negroid Religions* (WIST).

***"Voodooism and the Negroid Religions":** see ECKERMANN.

Vox populi, vox Dei, a Latin expression meaning *the voice of the people is the voice of God* (ABBE).

V.R., the abbreviation for *Victoria Regina* (MUSG); see VICTORIA.

Vulture. The BUZZARD is the vulture of the American West (STUD).

W

W. (*West London*), the designation given to the postal district embracing that part of London lying to the west of Westminster (3GAR). See the postal map of LONDON.

Wad, in American slang, money (LAST).

Wagner (*vahg'ner*), **Wilhelm Richard** (1813–1883), the most celebrated of modern composers. Holmes and Watson hurried from the Red Circle case to Covent Garden, where a Wagner night was in progress (REDC).

Wagonette, a four-wheeled pleasure-carriage, drawn by a pair of horses and having two seats at the back running lengthwise and facing each other (HOUN).

Wagonette.

Wahsatch Mountains: see WASATCH.

Wainwright, properly **Thomas Griffiths Wainewright** (1794–1847), a prominent English artist and man of letters who was transported to Tasmania for forgery in 1837. Well born and cultured, he was suspected, but never brought to trial, for the murder by poison of three of his relatives. Holmes said he was "no mean artist" (ILLU), an evaluation generally shared by his contemporaries; he exhibited at the Royal Academy and the British Institution.

Waiter, hotel servant: see BOOTS; HOTEL SERVANTS.

Waiting-maid, a diffusive term descriptive of no particular duties (BERY, BLUE). See SERVANT.

Waldron: see PRESCOTT, RODGER.

Wales, the principality in the south-west of Great Britain, conquered and united to England in the thirteenth

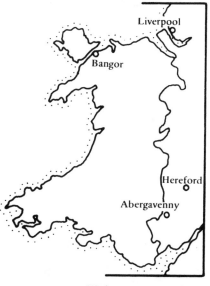

Wales.

century, pop. 1,720,600. The Duke of Holdernesse held mineral rights, granted by the Crown, in Wales, in addition to having his seat of Carston Castle at Bangor (PRIO). Cyril Overton had played Rugby for England against Wales (MISS), and Rachel Howells was of excitable Welsh blood (MUSG).

*Walker Brothers, a Vermissa coal-mining firm which paid to be left alone by the Scowrers (VALL).

Walking dress, a woman's dress intended to be worn when its owner appears in the street, as distinguished from a house-dress, a dinner dress, an evening dress, or others (SILV).

Walking-stick, a stick prepared for use as an assistance in walking, often affected rather by the dictates of fashion than by need. It is sometimes weighted at the head for use as a weapon.

Professor Coram had to use a stick in order to walk (GOLD), and Mr. Merryweather carried one (REDH). Trevor Senior had weighted his with lead (GLOR), Sir Robert Norberton carried a heavy stick (SHOS), and Arthur Charpentier threatened Enoch Drebber with what was described as a "stout oak cudgel" (STUD). Henry Baker attempted to defend himself with his stick against the street roughs who assaulted him (BLUE), Count Sylvius intended to assault Holmes with his stick (MAZA), and blood was found upon John Hector McFarlane's (NORW). Sticks were used in the sham fight before Briony Lodge (SCAN). Sir Eustace Brackenstall struck his wife with a stick (ABBE), and James Browner killed his wife and her lover with his (CARD).

Holmes sometimes carried a CANE (SPEC, THOR), as did Watson

(SHOS), Sir Henry Baskerville (HOUN), and the retired sergeant of Marines (STUD). Dr. Mortimer (HOUN), and the retired sergeant of (SILV) each owned a PENANG LAWYER. Holmes bore an ALPENSTOCK upon his walking-tour through Switzerland (FINA, EMPT).

Watson armed himself with his stick (LADY). Holmes too carried a stick (REDH) and was prepared to defend himself with it (MISS). His expertise at SINGLESTICK (STUD) enabled him to avoid the worst of the intended beating when he was attacked by two of Baron Gruner's hired ruffians wielding sticks (ILLU).

Wallenstein, Albrecht Eusebius Wensel von (1583–1634), a Bohemian nobleman and leader in the Thirty Years' War. He was suspected of treason and assassinated at Eger (SCAN).

Wallington, a small residential district in Surrey, lying just west of Croydon. Sarah Cushing lived here (CARD). See the back endpaper map.

Walsall, a town in the Midlands, pop. 86,430. Violet Hunter became head of a private school here (COPP).

Walsling, an obsolete word meaning *Welshman;* see NETHER WALSLING (WIST).

Walter, Sir James (d. 1895), head of the Submarine Department of the Admiralty, the man responsible for the Bruce-Partington plans. Their theft killed him. His younger brother **Colonel Valentine Walter** (1845–?97), who was in fact the thief, was taken by Holmes and died in prison toward the end of the second year of his sentence (BRUC).

Walters, the Surrey police-constable left in charge of Wisteria Lodge (WIST).

Wandsworth Common, a public

ground in the south-west of London. Mr. Melas was set at liberty here (GREE). See the front endpaper map.

Wandsworth Road, a thoroughfare of south London, running south-westerly from Vauxhall Bridge. Holmes's party passed along here on their way to meet Thaddeus Sholto (SIGN). In some editions the name is given erroneously as *Wordsworth Road.* See Map IV of LONDON.

Warburton, Colonel. Watson said that he was the means of introducing Holmes to the case of Colonel Warburton's madness (ENGR).

Ward, a curved ridge of metal inside a lock which serves to prevent the passage of an improper key. Holmes said that by the scratches upon the ward one could see that the lock to Beddington's room was forced with a wire (RESI).

Wardlaw, Colonel, the owner of Pugilist (SILV).

Warm, coarse or indelicate. The landlord of the country pub said that old Williamson's week-end visitors were "a warm lot" (SOLI).

Warner, John, the former gardener at High Gable who served as informant to Holmes (WIST).

Warren, a PRESERVE (BOSC, HOUN).

Warren, a timekeeper for Morton & Waylight's. He and his wife **Mrs. Warren** let rooms in their Bloomsbury house which were occupied by the mysterious lodger who prompted Mrs. Warren to consult Holmes (REDC).

Warrender, Minnie, an entry in Holmes's notebook about Count Sylvius (MAZA).

Warsaw, the capital of Russian Poland, pop. 756,426. Irene Adler had been prima donna of the Imperial Opera of Warsaw, where she met the King of Bohemia (SCAN).

Warships of the future: see ROYAL NAVY.

Wasatch or **Wahsatch Mountains,** a range in eastern Utah (STUD).

Washington, the capital city of the United States, pop. (1905) 323,123. Birdy Edwards claimed that the dollars he carried never passed the Washington mint; later he said he would not spend another three months among the Scowrers if he were set loose in the Treasury in Washington for it (VALL).

Washoe, a mountain range in western Nevada; also an American Indian tribe, now numbering some two hundred individuals in the neighbourhood of Carson City and Reno, Nevada, which once ranged across western Nevada and central California. The tribe is better known as the *Washoan.* Jefferson Hope alluded to himself as a "Washoe hunter" (STUD).

Water, formerly the transparency and lustre characteristic of a diamond. The *first water* once was the highest grade of quality in a diamond, and the phrase survives in popular use. Jonathan Small said there were 143 diamonds of the first water in the Agra treasure (SIGN).

Waterbeach, a village to the north of Cambridge, where Holmes sought Godfrey Staunton (MISS). See the map of the environs round CAMBRIDGE.

Waterford, a seaport on the southeastern coast of Ireland, pop. 26,769. The *May Day* stopped here (CARD).

Waterloo, a village in Belgium, about eleven miles north of Brussels, famous as the scene of the battle fought 18 June 1815 between Napoleon and the allied forces which finally put an end to his power. Holmes declared that the Brackenstall case was not his Waterloo but his MARENGO (ABBE).

Waterloo Bridge, a bridge spanning the Thames between Westminster and Lambeth, opened in 1817. Jefferson Hope's cab rattled across Waterloo Bridge in pursuit of Enoch Drebber (STUD), and John Openshaw met his death near here (FIVE). The bridge across which Holmes and Watson drove on their way to Bow Street (TWIS) most certainly was Waterloo. See Map II of LONDON and the photograph on p. 116.

Waterloo Road, also called **Waterloo Bridge Road,** a south London thoroughfare extending from Waterloo Bridge eastward through Lambeth. Holmes and Watson passed down the Waterloo Bridge Road on their way to Bow Street (TWIS), and Killer Evans shot Rodger Prescott in a night club here (3GAR). See Map IV of LONDON.

Waterloo Station, a railway station in Lambeth, terminus of the *South Western Railway,* constructed in 1848 and rebuilt in 1900. Trains to and from Horsham (FIVE), Woking (NAVA), Farnham (SOLI), and Leatherhead (SPEC) make use of Waterloo, where Holmes had supper upon his arrival from Aldershot (CROO). Sir Henry Baskerville arrived here, presumably from Southampton, and Stapleton was driven to Waterloo Station by John Clayton, whose cab-yard was nearby (HOUN). See Map IV of LONDON.

Waterman, a boatman or ferryman who plies his boat for hire (SIGN).

Water police: see RIVER POLICE.

Watson, John H., the friend and biographer of Sherlock Holmes.

Since he took his degree of Doctor of Medicine in 1878 (STUD), assuming him to have pursued his education at

the traditional ages, Watson would seem to have been born in the early 1850s. He would appear to have spent some of his early years in Australia (SIGN) and attended school in England (NAVA) before seeking his medical degree from the University of London (STUD). At about this time he served as a staff surgeon at St. Bartholomew's Hospital in London (STUD) and played Rugby for the Blackheath football club (SUSS).

Shortly before the outbreak of the Second Afghan War of 1878–79 he joined the ARMY MEDICAL DEPARTMENT, trained as a military surgeon at NETLEY, and was sent to Afghanistan, where he was severely wounded in the battle of MAIWAND (STUD); see MURRAY. His wound, or wounds (CARD,† NOBL, SIGN, STUD), combined with the general impairment of his health in the campaign (NOBL, RESI,‡ SIGN, STUD), earned him retirement and a wound pension (RESI, SHOS, SIGN, STUD). See also BERKSHIRES; FIFTH NORTHUMBERLAND FUSILIERS; INDIAN ARMY.

His chance introduction to Sherlock Holmes, as a result of their mutual need to share the expenses of the celebrated BAKER STREET flat (STUD), resulted in their first case together in March of 1881 or 1882 (FIVE, STUD). The association was a lasting one; of the twenty-three years Holmes spent in active practice 1878–91 and 1894–1903, Watson "was allowed to

† This allusion is inserted in "The Resident Patient" in many editions.

‡ This allusion appeared in the original magazine and book publications of "The Resident Patient" but was omitted from the 1928 omnibus volume and all subsequent editions.

Holmes and Watson.

coöperate with him and to keep notes of his doings" during seventeen of them (VEIL). See *Relationship with Holmes,* below. See also HOLMES, SHER-LOCK, subheaded *Untold Tales.*

Appearance. Watson was described as "a middle-sized, strongly built man" possessing a square jaw and a thick neck (CHAS) and a "modest" moustache (REDC—CHAS, LAST). While he was "as thin as a lath" following his Afghan experiences (STUD), his usual constitution made him a valuable Rugby player (SUSS). He remarked that he was "reckoned fleet of foot" (HOUN) and had held his own "in many a struggle" (LADY), though he lost his athletic frame in later life (SUSS) and was described as "heavily built" in 1914 (LAST). He apparently was quite handsome, for even Holmes remarked upon his "natural advantages" with the women (RETI); see *Character,* below.

Marriages. The course of Watson's married life is complex. While he plainly met Mary MORSTAN no earlier than July 1888 (SIGN), there is the clear implication of his being married in September 1887 (FIVE) and the explicit statement that he was married in March 1888 (SCAN), suggesting the possibility that Mary was his second wife. He alludes once to his impending marriage (NOBL) and often to his wife (CROO, FIVE, NAVA) or his marriage (DYIN, SCAN), or implies that he is married and not living with Holmes (BLUE, IDEN), without any indication that it is Mary Morstan Watson to whom he is wedded. In other cases, while Mary's name is at no time mentioned, it is certainly she who is his wife by implication (BOSC, STOC) or by virtue of Watson's dating the case between 1889 and 1891 (ENGR, FINA, REDH, TWIS). Mary apparently died between 1891 and

1894 (EMPT). Yet another marriage is suggested for 1903 (BLAN) and supported by Watson's once again living elsewhere (CREE, ILLU, MAZA, 3GAB). See also JAMES.

Practices. Three distinct practices are apparent in Watson's civil career. The earliest, which may be dated as having been established shortly after his marriage to Mary Morstan, was in Paddington (ENGR, STOC) and provided a "fairly long list" of patients (BOSC). By June 1890 (REDH) he had moved to Kensington (EMPT, NORW, REDH) and a "small" (NORW), "never very absorbing" (REDH) practice which he sold probably in 1894 or 1895 (NORW); see VERNER. An 1891 reference to MORTIMER STREET (FINA) is inconsistent with either location, and allusions to a practice prior to the Morstan marriage (FIVE, SCAN) are equally confusing. Elsewhere Watson mentions (CROO, IDEN, TWIS) or intimates (BLUE, DYIN, NAVA, 3GAB) a practice without a clue as to its location, nor does he explain his absence from Baker Street in 1896 (VEIL). A third practice (CREE, MAZA), which Watson says was "not inconsiderable" (CREE), apparently was located in QUEEN ANNE STREET in 1902 (ILLU) and would seem to be associated with the 1903 marriage (BLAN). Upon the outbreak of the German war he rejoined his "old service" (LAST), which was by then known as the *Royal Army Medical Corps.* See also ANSTRUTHER; JACKSON; also STETHOSCOPE.

CHARACTER

Almost all that is known of Watson's character is transmitted through the veil of his own writings and coloured by his unashamed admiration for Sher-

lock Holmes. Most apparent is his self-proclaimed slowness of mind, a pretence as often belied by his astute grasp of essentials as by his excellent literary abilities, and which must be discounted.

"If I have one quality upon earth it is common sense," he said of himself (HOUN), an assessment with which Holmes agreed, calling him logical (LADY) and "severely practical" (REDC). "You always keep us flat-footed on the ground" (CREE). He praised Watson's "zeal and intelligence" (HOUN), remarked upon his unselfishness (BLAN), and admired his "pawky" humour (VALL).

Watson's professed set of vices (STUD) would seem to include a certain laziness (STUD), a claim to keeping a BULL PUP (STUD)—that is, a quick temper—and a poor memory (VEIL). He confessed to a financial irresponsibility (STUD) evidenced in later years by his cheque-book being locked in Holmes's desk (DANC) and by a knowledge of the Turf acquired at the cost of "about half my wound pension" (SHOS), though he declined to engage in the equally uncertain gamble of the stocks market (DANC). He boasted of "an experience of women which extends over many nations and three separate continents" (SIGN), a claim Holmes would not dispute, alluding to his "natural advantages" (RETI) and telling him that "the fair sex is your department" (SECO).

Holmes remarked upon the doctor's "native shrewdness" and "that innate cunning which is the delight of your friends" (VALL), though he appears to have been indulging here in one of his frequent sarcasms. "Your best friends would hardly call you a schemer, Watson," he said elsewhere

(THOR), lamenting that "among your many talents dissimulation finds no place" (DYIN). He considered Watson's ideas "limited" but "exceedingly pertinacious" (BLAN) and complimented his "admirable tenacity" (HOUN). "I never get your limits, Watson. There are unexplored possibilities about you" (SUSS). "Good old Watson! You are the one fixed point in a changing age" (LAST).

See also BOHEMIAN; BURGLARY; CLUB; "REMINISCENCES"; STOCKS; TOBACCO; TURKISH BATH.

Friends and Acquaintances. Watson had no friends and "neither kith nor kin in England" when he arrived in London from India (STUD), and over the years he remained a man without intimate friends (HOUN). Aside from Holmes his acquaintances included his professional colleagues Anstruther (BOSC) and Jackson (CROO), Isa Whitney, the husband of his wife's old school-friend (TWIS), Lomax, the sub-librarian at the London Library (ILLU), his billiard-playing friend THURSTON (DANC), and young STAMFORD (STUD). His experiences with Holmes reunited him with his own former schoolmate Percy Phelps (NAVA) and Robert Ferguson, against whom he had played Rugby (SUSS), and of all Holmes's cases, he said, "there were only two which I was the means of introducing to his notice—that of Mr. Hatherley's thumb, and that of Colonel Warburton's madness" (ENGR).

Medical Abilities. Watson's professional skills are attested by his successes in civil practice (BOSC, CREE, FINA, STOC, TWIS) and by Holmes's emphatic expression of respect for his medical talents (DYIN). He assiduously read the *British Medical Journal* (STOC) and even when not in practice he kept up his studies, investing in a monograph upon obscure nervous lesions (RESI) or reading a recent treatise upon surgery (GOLD), though he admitted he had "lost touch" with the medical profession somewhat by the time of the Godfrey Staunton case (MISS).

RELATIONSHIP WITH HOLMES

The Holmes-Watson association was dominated by Watson's regard for Holmes as "the man whom above all others I revere" (THOR) and "the best and wisest man whom I have ever known" (FINA).

That their friendship, on Holmes's part, was based upon Watson's "position of partner and confidant" (3GAB) seems clear (BLAN). While Holmes's affection only occasionally showed itself (BRUC, DEVI, EMPT, 3GAR), Watson was his closest friend (ILLU) and in the early days his only one (FIVE), but the "intimate" relations between them (EMPT, FINA, YELL) became "to some extent modified" after Watson's marriage (FINA), and temporarily at least they drifted away from one another (SCAN). Though Watson wrote of the many cases they shared 1882–90 (FIVE) and referred in 1891 to "the seventy odd cases in which I have during the last eight years studied the methods of my friend" (SPEC), his marriage changed the detective's attitudes: "He still came to me from time to time when he desired a companion in his investigations, but these occasions grew more and more seldom, until I find that in the year 1890 there were only three cases of which I retain any record" (FINA).

Holmes's fondness for Watson as a partner appears motivated by the doctor's being someone upon whom Holmes could "thoroughly rely" (BOSC), his willingness to participate in illegal activities for a morally good cause (BRUC, SCAN) and to share danger (SPEC). "It is at the hour of action that I turn to you," Holmes asserted (HOUN), often reassuring him that he "should not dream of stirring" without him if danger threatened (NORW—BRUC, 3GAR, VALL, WIST). "Now, Watson, we'll just take our luck together, as we have occasionally done in the past" (LADY). He repeatedly invited Watson into his cases (BOSC, CARD, ILLU, SPEC, STOC, TWIS, VEIL) and most significantly sought him as a companion both in his flight to the Continent from Moriarty (FINA) and in his trapping of Sebastian Moran upon his return to London (EMPT).

"Several times during the last three years I have taken up my pen to write to you," Holmes confessed at the end of the Great Hiatus, "but always I feared lest your affectionate regard for me should tempt you to some indescretion which would betray my secret" (EMPT), a concern he had expressed before during the Baskerville case (HOUN). Their renewed intimacy after 1894 (NORW) would seem to be related not only to the fact of Mary Morstan Watson's death (EMPT) but also to Watson's publication 1891–93 of the *Adventures* and the *Memoirs* in the *Strand* magazine: "I hear of Sherlock everywhere since you became his chronicler," Mycroft Holmes said to him (GREE).

In the later years Watson's participation for the sake of publishable tales evidently balanced Holmes's desire for a companion, and their friendship took on a more pragmatic hue. The years following Holmes's return were crowded ones (BLAC, GOLD), and during 1894–1901 inclusive he handled hundreds of cases (SOLI). "The problem has always been not to find but to choose," Watson wrote (VEIL). "As I have preserved very full notes of these cases, and was myself personally engaged in many of them, it may be imagined that it is no easy task to know which I should select to lay before the public" (SOLI). The records of these investigations he preserved in "a travel-worn and battered tin dispatch-box" in the vaults of COX & CO. in Charing Cross (THOR—CREE, VEIL). See also DIARY; JOURNAL; NOTEBOOK; PORTFOLIO; SCRAPBOOK; YEARBOOK, also HOLMES, SHERLOCK, subheaded *Attitude to Watson's Writings*. See also DOYLE, SIR ARTHUR CONAN.

"The relations between us in those latter days were peculiar," Watson wrote. "He was a man of habits, narrow and concentrated habits, and I had become one of them. As an institution I was like the violin, the shag tobacco, the old black pipe, the index books, and others perhaps less excusable. When it was a case of active work and a comrade was needed upon whose serve he could place some reliance, my rôle was obvious. But apart from this I had uses. I was a whetstone for his mind. I stimulated him. He liked to think aloud in my presence. His remarks could hardly be said to be made to me—many of them would have been as appropriately addressed to his bedstead—but none the less, having formed the habit, it had become in some way helpful that I should register and interject. If I irritated him by a certain methodical slowness in my mentality, that irritation served only to make his own flame-like intuitions and impressions flash up the more vividly and swiftly. Such was my humble rôle in our alliance" (CREE).

"There is a delightful freshness about you, Watson, which makes it a pleasure to exercise any small powers which I possess at your expense," Holmes said, adding that Watson habitually underrated his own abilities: "It may be that you are not yourself luminous, but you are a conductor of light. Some people without possessing genius have a remarkable power of stimulating it" (HOUN).

"Speaking of my old friend and biographer," Holmes himself wrote, "if I burden myself with a companion in my various little inquiries it is not done out of sentiment or caprice, but it is that Watson has some remarkable characteristics of his own to which in his modesty he has given small attention amid his exaggerated estimates of my own performances. A confederate who foresees your conclusions and course of action is always dangerous, but one to whom each development comes as a perpetual surprise, and to whom the future is always a closed book, is indeed an ideal helpmate" (BLAN). "I was nearer him than anyone else," Watson confessed, "and yet I was always conscious of the gap between" (ILLU).

"An occasional week-end visit" was the most they saw of one another after Holmes's retirement (LION), and yet the detective once more called upon Watson to share the conclusion of the Von Bork affair, at the end of which they stood upon the terrace of the German's home above Harwich, "for it may be the last quiet talk we shall ever have," and "chatted in intimate converse for a few minutes, recalling once again the days of the past" (LAST).

See also HOLMES, SHERLOCK, subheaded *Character: Emotional Qualities.*

Watson's father, **H. Watson,** had been dead "many years" by 1888; his elder brother's life was not well spent, and he died of drink shortly before the Sholto case (SIGN).

*Watt Street Chapel, or **Watt Street Mission,** a Roman Catholic charity formed in connexion with the GUILD OF ST. GEORGE at Aldershot (CROO).

Waylight: see MORTON & WAYLIGHT.

Weald, an open, sparsely wooded countryside; e.g., HARROW WEALD (3GAB).

Weald, The, a district of south-eastern England lying across portions of Sussex, Kent, and Surrey between the North and South Downs. Formerly a region of forests and marshes, its 200,000 acres of woodland have now almost entirely disappeared as fuel for the ironworks which existed here from Roman times until the beginning of the nineteenth century. Woodman's Lee lay within the Weald (BLAC), and Birlstone was upon its fringe (VALL). See the map of SURREY.

Weald Station, properly **Harrow & Wealdstone Station,** the railway station serving Harrow Weald, located within the nearby town of *Wealdstone.* The Three Gables was within a short walk of here (3GAB).

Weasel. A stuffed weasel stood in old Sherman's window (SIGN). Holmes said that the footprints he found outside Lachine seemed to belong to an animal of the weasel or STOAT tribe (CROO).

Wei (*way*), a Chinese dynasty founded in A.D. 220 and ruling the northern portion of China until its collapse in the dynastic wars of the sixth century. Baron Gruner tested Watson's knowledge of Chinese pottery by asking what he knew of the Northern Wei dynasty and its place in the history of ceramics (ILLU).

Weiss & Co., properly **Weiss & Son,** a London manufacturer of cutlery. A delicate Weiss cataract knife was found in John Straker's hand (SILV).

Welbeck Street, a street in the West End. Holmes was nearly run down by a van at the corner of Bentinck and Welbeck streets (FINA). See Map III of LONDON.

Wellington Street, a street in Westminster, lying between Bow Street and Waterloo Bridge. Holmes and Watson's trap dashed up here on their way to the Bow Street police-court (TWIS). See Map II of LONDON.

*Wessex Cup, or **Wessex Plate,** the race meeting won at Winchester by Silver Blaze (SILV).

West, Cadogan: see CADOGAN WEST.

West Africa, that part of Africa lying south of the Sahara, west of the Sudan, and north of the Congo. The devil's-foot poison was native to West Africa (DEVI). The survivors of the *Gloria Scott* disaster pulled for SIERRA LEONE (GLOR), and Holmes recalled a case which occurred in SENEGAMBIA (SIGN).

Westaway, the founder of **Westaway's** agency for governesses (COPP).

Westbury, Violet, the fiancée of Arthur Cadogan West (BRUC).

*Westbury House, apparently an establishment of some social prominence, where Hatty Doran was introduced into London society (NOBL).

West End, that part of London lying west of the City (BERY, BRUC, COPP, RESI, SECO, 3GAB). See LONDON.

Western Morning News, one of the more important English provincial newspapers, published at Plymouth.

Holmes confessed that when he was young he once confused the type of the *Leeds Mercury* with the *Western Morning News* (HOUN).

Western Sussex: see SUSSEX; see also PARLIAMENT.

*Westhouse & Marbank, the London firm of claret importers, with French offices in Bordeaux, for whom James Windibank travelled (IDEN).

West India Docks, a series of three major docks lying to the north of the Isle of Dogs (SIGN). See the front endpaper map.

West Indies. Rear-Admiral Baskerville served under RODNEY here (HOUN).

Westminster, the heart of London's West End, pop. 183,011. Legally, since 1900, it is a distinct municipality within the administrative county of London. It is nearly as ancient as the City itself, and contains within its boundaries many of the metropolis's most famous landmarks, including the Houses of PARLIAMENT and WESTMINSTER ABBEY, the Government departments in and about WHITEHALL, royal palaces, CHARING CROSS and TRAFALGAR SQUARE, HYDE PARK, SCOTLAND YARD, and the foreign embassies.

The firm of Morton and Kennedy was in Westminster (SOLI), Adolph Meyer lived here (BRUC), and the newspaper account of Eduardo Lucas's death was headed "Murder in Westminster" (SECO). See the front endpaper map and Maps III and IV of LONDON.

Westminster Abbey, the great church of London, situated near the Thames, adjoining the Houses of Parliament, where takes place the coronation of the English Kings. It is distinguished as the burial place of many

Westminster Abbey.

English monarchs and for monuments to the great English warriors, statesmen, and poets. Godolphin Street lay between the river and the Abbey (SECO). See the map of WHITEHALL.

Westminster Bridge, a handsome iron and granite bridge spanning the Thames between Westminster and Lambeth, erected 1856–62. Holmes and Watson crossed it on their way to Poultney Square (LADY). See Map IV

The view across Westminster Bridge to the Houses of Parliament. Note the electric tram-car making its way toward the Surrey side.

of LONDON and the map of WHITEHALL.

Westminster Road, properly **Westminster Bridge Road,** a street in the north of Lambeth, extending from the Waterloo Road to Westminster Bridge. Holy Peters pawned one of Lady Frances Carfax's jewels in the "Westminster Road" (LADY). See Map IV of LONDON.

Westminster Stairs, properly **Westminster Pier,** a public pier located on the Victoria Embankment just below Westminster Bridge. Watson's allusion to it as *Westminster Stairs* (SIGN) is perhaps a confusion with *Whitehall Stairs* some two hundred yards downriver. See the photograph of New Scotland Yard accompanying SCOTLAND YARD and the map of WHITEHALL.

Westmorland, or **Westmoreland,** a north-west county of England, pop. 64,303. James Desmond was a clergyman here (HOUN). See the map of ENGLAND.

Westphail, Honoria, the aunt of Julia and Helen Stoner, their mother's maiden sister (SPEC).

*West Section Coaling Company, a Vermissa coal-mining firm which paid to be left alone by the Scowrers (VALL).

*Westville Arms, the only inn in the village of Birlstone, where Holmes and Watson stayed during their investigation (VALL).

*West Wilmerton General Mining Company, familiarly known as **General Iron,** a large company which bought up several ironworking properties in Vermissa Valley, and probably one of the five companies which joined to fight the Scowrers (VALL).

Whale. Peter Carey was a whaling-ship captain (BLAC).

Wharfinger, the owner or manager of a wharf (SIGN).

Wheat pit, in the United States, that part of the floor of an agricultural or other commodities exchange where business in wheat is carried on. Alexander Hamilton Garrideb was said to have made his fortune in the Chicago wheat pit (3GAR).

Wherry, a light, shallow rowboat, having seats for passengers and plying on rivers and harbors (SIGN).

Whip-poor-will, an American bird, so named because of its night call. The Danites used its cry as a recognition sign (STUD).

Whisky. Holmes treated himself to a whisky-and-soda following his first interview with Lord Robert St. Simon (NOBL) and after the taking of John Clay (REDH). He offered Lestrade a whisky-and-soda (NOBL), whisky and water to Jonathan Small (SIGN) and Inspector Gregson (STUD). There was a tantalus containing brandy and whisky in Peter Carey's cabin (BLAC).

Whisky-peg, in Anglo-Indian slang, a whisky-and-soda (SIGN).

Whist, a well-known game of cards. The best two of three games of whist constitute a *rubber.* Ronald Adair played a rubber of whist at the Bagatelle Club upon the night of his death (EMPT). Mr. Merryweather complained that the night of the vigil in the City and Suburban Bank vault was the first Saturday night in twenty-seven years that he had not had his rubber of whist (REDH).

Whitaker's Almanack, the most popular and best known of British almanacks. The coded message from Porlock to Holmes was keyed to Whitaker's (VALL).

White, Abel: see ABEL WHITE.

*White Eagle, a tavern in Nine Elms Lane (SIGN).

Whitehall, a short street in Westminster, extending southward from Charing Cross, in which many offices of the British Government are located and off which DOWNING STREET opens. The word *Whitehall* is often used in allusion to the Government itself. Mycroft Holmes worked in Whitehall (BRUC, GREE), in which Percy Phelps sought the thief who took the naval treaty (NAVA). The Mazarin diamond was apparently stolen from somewhere in Whitehall (MAZA). See the photographs on pp. 56 and 217.

Whitehall. The building at left is the Treasury.

*Whitehall Terrace, the street near the Government offices in which Trelawney Hope lived (SECO).

*White Hart, a public-house on John Rance's beat (STUD).

White jessamine: see JESSAMINE.

White Mason, the chief Sussex police detective, who was placed in charge of the Birlstone case and who sent for Scotland Yard (VALL).

Whitney, Isa, the friend whom Watson went to rescue from a London opium den upon the plea of his wife **Kate Whitney.** His brother **Elias Whitney, D.D.,** was principal of the Theological College of St. George's (TWIS).

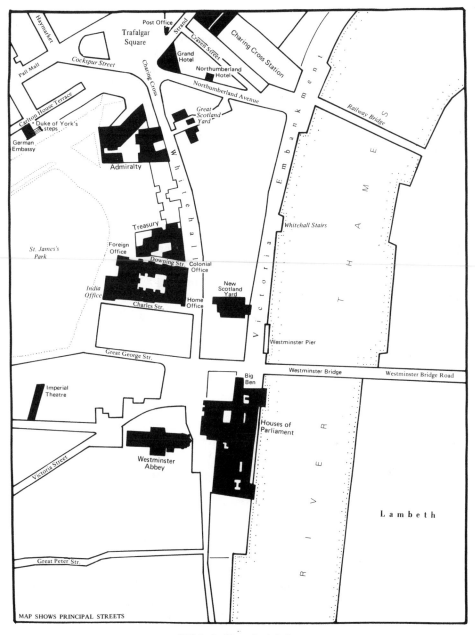

Whitehall and vicinity.

Whittington, Lady Alicia, an intimate friend of the Duke of Balmoral and his family (NOBL).

Whyte, Gulielmi, or **William Whyte,** the original owner of Holmes's copy of *De Jure inter Gentes* (STUD).

Wicket, in cricket, the object before which the batsman stands, consisting of two thin rods called *stumps,* twenty-two inches high, which are fixed into the ground six inches apart and over the tops of which is laid a small round piece of wood. Watson said that he and his playmates used to chase Percy Phelps with a wicket (NAVA), by which he no doubt meant the stumps.

Wicket-gate, a small gate (ENGR, HOUN).

Wide-awake, a soft, felt hat (YELL).

Wiggins, the spokesman for and apparently the leader of the BAKER STREET IRREGULARS (SIGN, STUD).

Wight, Isle of: see ISLE OF WIGHT.

Wigmore Street, a street in the West End, mostly of a residential character. Holmes and Watson passed through here on the way to the Alpha Inn (BLUE). Watson had been to the Wigmore Street Post Office (SIGN). In some editions this last allusion is to *Upper Seymour Street,* as it was formerly known. See Map III of LONDON.

Wigwam, the conical tent or lodge of an American Indian. Stapleton's allusion to neolithic stone "wigwams" may have been half jocular (HOUN).

Wilcox, Chester, a mine foreman whom the Scowrers tried unsuccessfully to kill on several occasions (VALL).

Wild, Jonathan (1683–1725), a central figure in London crime during the early part of the eighteenth century. Originally a buckle-maker, he became first a receiver of stolen goods and eventually controlled much of the London underworld before he was hanged. Holmes compared Moriarty to him (VALL).

Wilder, James, the illegitimate son of the Duke of HOLDERNESSE, whose scheme to abduct Lord Saltire was undertaken to force the Duke to break the entail upon his estates and leave them by will to Wilder (PRIO).

Willaby, Arthur, a Scowrer who, with his brother, sought vengeance

upon Birdy Edwards after their release from prison (VALL).

Willesden (*wil'ez-den*), a working-class residential suburb of London, lying in Middlesex immediately outside the metropolitan boundary, pop. 114,811. South of here *Willesden Junction* is an important railway junction and a station on the Outer Circle of the suburban railway system. Some of the rails near where Cadogan West's body was found were purely Metropolitan, and some "from Willesden and outlying junctions" (BRUC). See UNDERGROUND RAILWAY and the front endpaper map.

Williams: see MAWSON AND WILLIAMS'.

Williams, the prizefighter, once lightweight champion of England, who was hired as a bodyguard by Major Sholto and later was in the service of Thaddeus Sholto (SIGN).

Williams, Charlie, a victim of the Scowrers (VALL).

Williams, James Baker, a neighbour of Aloysius Garcia (WIST).

Williamson, the defrocked clergyman who performed the invalid marriage ceremony between Jack Woodley and Violet Smith (SOLI).

Willows, Dr., the doctor who attended John Turner (BOSC).

Wilson, the notorious canary-trainer whose arrest removed a plague-spot from the East End of London (BLAC). See CANARY.

Wilson (d. 1855), the partner of Jack Prendergast, who contrived to join the company of the *Gloria Scott* as chaplain (GLOR).

Wilson, one of the constables on duty at Yoxley Old Place (GOLD).

Wilson, the manager of a district messenger office whose good name, and perhaps whose life, Holmes had saved (HOUN).

Wilson, a sergeant in the Sussex Constabulary, who received the first alarm of the Birlstone tragedy (VALL).

Wilson, a Scowrer (VALL).

Wilson, Bartholomew, the district ruler in 1875 of the Ancient Order of Freemen in Chicago (VALL).

Wilson, Jabez, the London pawnbroker who was duped by John CLAY into accepting a position with the spurious RED-HEADED LEAGUE and who consulted Holmes when the organization was suddenly and mysteriously "dissolved" (REDH).

Wilson, Sir Archdale (1803–1874), a general in the Bengal Artillery, in command of the force which retook Delhi during the Mutiny (SIGN).

Wilson, Steve, the alias Birdy Edwards was said to be using in Vermissa Valley (VALL).

Wilton carpet, a variety of carpet possessing a lush, cut pile, so named from the town in south-western England where it was first made (SPEC).

Wimbledon, a city in Surrey, a residential suburb of London, pop. 41,652. The Ronder caravan was on its way here at the time of the Abbas Parva tragedy (VEIL). See the front endpaper map.

Wimpole Street, a street in the West End, noted for the residence of physicians and containing many literary associations. Holmes and Watson passed through here on their way to the Alpha Inn (BLUE). See Map III of LONDON.

Winchester, a historic city of Hampshire, pop. 20,929. The Copper Beeches was nearby (COPP). The Wessex Cup race meeting was held here (SILV), and here Grace Dunbar was gaoled

(THOR). The celebrated *Winchester Cathedral,* built 1070–1486, is one of the largest in England, and Holmes observed its tower from the approaching train (COPP).

Winchester, a brand of rifle, introduced in 1865 as one of the earliest examples of the magazine or repeating rifle. The Coal and Iron Police were armed with them (VALL).

Windibank, James, the stepfather of Mary SUTHERLAND, who in his disguise as *Hosmer Angel* courted her and then vanished upon the morning of their wedding in a plot to retain control of her income. His wife **Mrs. Windibank** was a willing accomplice to the scheme to deceive her daughter (IDEN).

Windigate, the landlord of the Alpha Inn (BLUE).

Windle, J. W., the division master of the Scowrers in Merton County (VALL).

Windsor, a town in the east of Berkshire, on the right bank of the Thames, pop. 14,130. *Windsor Castle* is well known as the ancestral residence of the English sovereigns since Saxon times. The present castle dates from the fourteenth century. The most recent restoration was begun in the reign of George IV and finished under Victoria, who much favoured it as a residence. See the back endpaper map and the engraving on the following page.

Some weeks after the successful conclusion of the Bruce-Partington case, Holmes spent a day at Windsor visiting, as he said, "a certain gracious lady" (BRUC).

Wine. James Windibank was a travelling representative for a wine importing firm (IDEN). Vamberry was a wine merchant (MUSG). The BEES-

Windsor Castle is famous the world over as the residence of the British sovereigns.

WING in the wine-glasses at the Abbey Grange provided an essential clue to unravelling the circumstances of Sir Eustace Brackenstall's death (ABBE).

See also BEAUNE; CHAMPAGNE; CHIANTI; CLARET; COMET WINE; MONTRACHET; PORT; SHERRY; TOKAY; also BRANDY.

Wine, spirits of: see SPIRITS OF WINE.

Wing, in Rugby, the position of the forwards on either side of the centre. Godfrey Staunton was the right-wing three-quarter for the Cambridge team (MISS), that is, was positioned behind the right-wing forwards.

Winter, James: see EVANS, "KILLER."

Winter, Kitty, the former mistress of Baron GRUNER; ruined by him, she took her revenge in a vitriol-throwing which left Gruner hideously mutilated (ILLU).

Wiper: see VIPER.

Wistaria, a variety of climbing shrub. Professor Presbury's house was covered with purple wistaria (CREE). A variant spelling apparently gave the name to WISTERIA LODGE; see also IVY.

*Wisteria Lodge, the house inhabited by Aloysius Garcia near Esher (WIST).

"Wisteria Lodge, The Adventure of" (WIST), a chronicle which appeared originally in the *Strand* magazine for 'September and October 1908 under the titles "The Singular Experience of Mr. John Scott Eccles" and "The Tiger of San Pedro" and in *Collier's Weekly* of 15 August 1908 as "The Singular Experience of Mr. J. Scott Eccles," and was published as "The Adventure of Wisteria Lodge" in the 1917 collection entitled *His Last Bow*. It concerns Holmes's interest in the strange adventure of John Scott Eccles and the murder of his host Aloysius Garcia by the infamous Don Juan Murillo.

Watson dates the case as having occurred in March 1892, an impossible date in that Holmes was believed to be dead between May 1891 (FINA) and March 1894 (EMPT), and estimates range between 1890 and 1902. Elsewhere, however, Watson states that the case of "the papers of ex-President Murillo" took place in the months following Holmes's return to active practice in 1894 (NORW).

Woking, a town in Surrey, pop. 16,244. The Phelps family home was here (NAVA). See the back endpaper map.

Wolf-hound, a large dog bred in Russia for the hunting of wolves (CREE).

Wombwell, George (1778–1850), an English showman, proprietor of a series of travelling menageries, who achieved remarkable success in the breeding of carnivorous animals in captivity. Ronder was the rival of Wombwell and Sanger in his fame (VEIL).

Wood, Dr., the Birlstone practitioner who examined what he believed to be John Douglas's body (VALL).

Wood, Henry, a British soldier, betrayed by his sergeant James BARCLAY into the hands of the Sepoy mutineers during the Indian Mutiny. Held prisoner and tortured for many years, he finally escaped and later made his way back to England, where the sight of him caused Barclay to fall dead of apoplexy (CROO).

Wood J. G. (1827–1889), an English writer and lecturer on natural history, well known as the author of a series of popular books upon the subject. His collection of essays *Out of Doors* (1874) helped Holmes solve Fitzroy McPherson's apparent murder (LION).

Woodcock. Holmes dined upon a woodcock the evening of the blue carbuncle case (BLUE) and served a couple of brace of cold woodcock to Mr.

and Mrs. Francis Hay Moulton (NOBL).

Woodhouse, one of fifty men who had reason for taking Holmes's life (BRUC).

Woodhouse: see COXON.

Woodley, Edith, formerly Ronald Adair's fiancée (EMPT).

Woodley, Jack, known as *Roaring Jack,* "the greatest brute and bully in South Africa," according to his partner Bob CARRUTHERS. He and Carruthers conspired to get at the fortune left to Violet SMITH, but the plan miscarried and Woodley was shot, though not fatally, by Carruthers (SOLI).

*Woodman's Lee, the name of Peter Carey's property in Sussex (BLAC).

Woolwich (*wool'ich*), a south-western metropolitan borough of London, pop. 117,178. It has many military establishments, and a large working population is employed in the Royal Arsenal. Part of the Bruce-Partington investigation was carried out here (BRUC), and the *Aurora* left her wharf with only enough fuel to take her to Woolwich and back (SIGN). See the front endpaper map.

The great **Woolwich Arsenal,** properly the **Royal Arsenal,** is one of the most imposing establishments in exist-

Woolwich as viewed from the Thames.

ence for the design, manufacture, and storage of war-materials. It covers an area of 593 acres and affords employment to over 14,000 men. The magazines, which extend along the Thames for a mile, contain enormous stores of war-materials. Arthur Cadogan West was a clerk here, where the Bruce-Partington submarine was designed, and from which the submarine's plans were stolen (BRUC).

Holmes and Watson detrained at **Woolwich Station** (BRUC), the name given by Watson to one of *Dockyard Station, Arsenal Station,* or *Plumstead Station,* each of which is a Woolwich railway station convenient to the town and the arsenal. Cadogan West and his fiancée were to have attended a performance at the **Woolwich Theatre** (BRUC), properly the **Woolwich Grand Theatre,** a suburban theatre located here.

Worchestershire (*woos'ter-shur*), a midland county of England, pop. 488,338. Jonathan Small said he was a Worcestershire man (SIGN).

Wordsworth Road: see WANDS-WORTH ROAD.

Workhouse, in Great Britain, a poorhouse in which able-bodied paupers are compelled to do labour in return for relief. Under the terms of the 1867 poor act each of London's metropolitan boroughs maintains its own workhouse and attendant facilities. Athelney Jones said that Holmes had the proper "workhouse cough" when disguised as an asthmatic old sailor (SIGN). Holy Peters found Rose Spender at the BRIXTON WORKHOUSE INFIRMARY (LADY).

***Worthingdon bank,** the institution robbed in 1875 (RESI).

Worthingdon Bank Gang, the name applied to five men who robbed the Worthingdon bank of £7,000 in 1875. Their names were *Biddle, Hayward, Moffat, Cartwright,* and BLESSSINGTON. Blessington turned informer, and on his evidence Cartwright was hanged and the other three received sentences of fifteen years each. Released some years before their full term, they set themselves to hunt down Blessington and avenge the death of Cartwright, following which they were believed lost at sea (RESI).

Wrack, properly **rack,** a mass of cloud being driven before the wind in the upper air (TWIS).

Wright, Theresa, the personal maid, formerly the nurse, of Lady Mary Brackenstall, who was an accessory to the scheme to cover up Sir Eustace's murder (ABBE).

X Y Z

XX.31, the private, emergency telephone number of Sir James Damery (ILLU).

Yard: see CAB-YARD.

Yard, The: see SCOTLAND YARD.

Yawl, a small, single-masted sailing-boat (SIGN).

Year-book. Watson kept a series of year-books concerning Holmes's cases (VEIL), and mentions specifically his records for 1887 (FIVE), for 1890 (FINA), for 1894 (GOLD), and for 1895 (SOLI). See also DIARY; JOURNAL; NOTEBOOK; PORTFOLIO; SCRAPBOOK.

Yeggman, in American underworld slang, a safe-cracker. The case of "Vanderbilt and the Yeggman" was entered in Holmes's index (SUSS).

Yellow-backed novel, a cheap sensational novel, so called from its yellow cover (BOSC, COPP).

"Yellow Face, The" (YELL), a chronicle which appeared originally in the *Strand* magazine for February 1893 and *Harper's Weekly* of 11 February 1893 and was published in the collection entitled *The Memoirs of Sherlock Holmes* the following year. It concerns Holmes's investigation of the mysterious behaviour of Mrs. Grant Munro, and is particularly notable as one of the half-dozen cases in which the truth was discovered even though Holmes himself erred. It has been dated to the early spring of nearly every year between 1882 and 1889.

Yellow fever, a highly infectious bacterial disease introduced through the bite of a mosquito, tropical in origin. Rodger Baskerville died of it (HOUN), as did John Hebron (YELL).

Yellowstone River, a river of the United States, the largest tributary of the Missouri (STUD).

Yeoman, in England, a freeholder (HOUN, SUSS).

Yeomanry: see IMPERIAL YEOMANRY.

Yew, a slow-growing and long-lived evergreen tree of moderate height. The yews of the YEW ALLEY were twelve feet high and impenetrable (HOUN). Holdernesse Hall was approached by a famous yew avenue (PRIO), Charlington Hall's park was surrounded by a yew hedge (SOLI), and Birlstone Manor was flanked by an old-fashioned garden of cut yews (VALL).

*Yew Alley, a pathway from Baskerville Hall to its summer-house, flanked by impenetrable yew hedges pierced by a single gate, where Sir Charles Baskerville met his death (HOUN).

York, the county-town of Yorkshire, pop. 77,914. Holmes possessed a photograph of the Stapletons taken here (HOUN).

York, Duke of: see DUKE OF YORK'S STEPS.

*****York College,** the college, presumably in the United States, where Jefferson Hope obtained the poison with which to murder Enoch Drebber (STUD).

Yorkshire, a north-eastern county of England, pop. 3,584,762. Much of the land is under cultivation, but there are also extensive manufactures and metal and chemical works. It is the largest county in England and is divided into three administrative divisions, the city of YORK being situated partly in each. The Stapletons' school was in the east of Yorkshire (HOUN).

See also BRADFORD; DONCASTER. See the map of ENGLAND.

Youghal, the Scotland Yard official to whom Holmes applied during the Mazarin diamond case (MAZA).

Young, Brigham (1801–1877), an American religious leader, the founder of the Mormon settlement in Utah and

Brigham Young.

for many years the almost absolute ruler of the sect (STUD). A painter and glazier by trade, he was converted to the Latter-Day Saints in 1832. He was a man of undoubted ability and strength of character, and upon the death of Joseph SMITH in 1844 he was unanimously chosen president and prophet. When the Mormons were expelled from Nauvoo he led them through toils and dangers over the plains and tablelands to the splendid valley of Utah, where they founded Salt Lake City in 1847. From 1851 to 1858 he was governor of the Utah Territory. Young was the founder of polygamy as an institution and was among the first to practice it. He was twice indicted for it but never convicted, and when he died in 1877 he left nineteen widows and fifty-four children.

*****Yoxley Old Place,** the Kentish home of Professor Coram (GOLD).

Yuan (*yoo-en'*), or *Yuen,* the Mongol dynasty of China which held power from the thirteenth to the fourteenth centuries. Watson read up on the ceramic wares of this dynasty (ILLU), which differ very little from those of the Sung dynasty which immediately preceded it.

Yung-lo (d. 1425), the son of HUNG-WU, and Chinese Emperor 1403–25. Watson read up on "the beauties" of his reign (ILLU), during which the egg-shell style seems to have originated.

Zamba, the junior partner of Tito CASTALOTTE (REDC).

Zeppelin, Count Ferdinand von (1838–1917), the German Army officer who invented and built the first dirigible airships 1900–6. Baron Von Herling mentioned the possibility of their use in war (LAST), a hope which was fulfilled by the air raids over England during the World War.

The Zeppelin airship in flight, 1900.

Zinc. Holmes was able to trace a counterfeiter by the zinc and copper filings in the seam of his cuff (SHOS).

Zion, figuratively the house or household of God, as consisting of the chosen people, or Israelites; among Christians, the theocracy of God or the church in general, or heaven as the final gathering-place of true believers, so called from Mount Zion, the holy hill of Jerusalem.

In the theology of the MORMONS, Zion is the location of the "mountain of the house of the Lord," separate from Jerusalem, which is to be established upon the American continent and from which Christ personally will reign over a renewed earth. In 1831 it was determined by revelation that Zion shall be located in the western part of the state of Missouri, centred near the town of Independence. In popular usage among Mormons, however, the word is extremely variable in meaning and often is applied in allusion to Utah (STUD).

Zoo, The, the popular name given to the *Zoological Gardens* in Regent's Park in London. Maintained by the Zoological Society, which was founded in 1826, the Gardens constitute one of the major zoological collections in Europe. Charles Augustus Milverton impressed Holmes, he said, in the same way as did the serpents in the Zoo (CHAS).

Zoology. The Stapletons had strong tastes for botany and zoology (HOUN). Trevor Bennett consulted a manual of zoology (CREE).

The Zoological Gardens, Regent's Park.

Bibliography

Sherlockian Reference Works

BARING-GOULD, WILLIAM S. *The Annotated Sherlock Holmes.* 2 vols. New York: Clarkson N. Potter, 1967. (The most comprehensive of Sherlockian works; the most reliable textual authority and an invaluable guide and inspiration for the whole of Sherlockiana.)

————. *Sherlock Holmes of Baker Street.* New York: Bramhall House, 1962. (Contains much valuable bibliographical material.)

CHRIST, JAY FINLEY. *An Irregular Guide to Sherlock Holmes of Baker Street.* New York: The Pamphlet House and Argus Books, 1947. (Said to be a classic; so rare that this writer has never laid eyes on a copy.)

DE WAAL, RONALD BURT. *The World Bibliography of Sherlock Holmes and Dr. Watson.* Boston: New York Graphic Society, 1974. (A genuine landmark in Sherlockian research, unhappily published too late to be of assistance in the preparation of this work.)

PAGE, ANDREW. *A Canonical Handbook.* New York: privately printed, 2nd edition 1972. (A mimeographed compilation of Sherlockian data; precise, practical, and of much use despite some minor errors and omissions.)

PARK, ORLANDO. *Sherlock Holmes, Esq. and John H. Watson, M.D.: An Encyclopædia of Their Affairs.* Northwestern University Press, 1962. (One of the most thoroughly worthless books ever published; included here for the sake of completeness.)

PECK, ANDREW JAY. *"The Date Being—?"* New York: privately printed, 1970; supplement 1973. (The authoritative compendium of Sherlockian chronology.)

General Works

"About Plover's Eggs," *Chambers' Journal,* Fourth Series, 19:189–91, 25 March 1882.

AMERY, L. S., gen. ed. *The Times History of the War in South Africa 1899–1902.* 7 vols. London: Sampson Low, Marston and Company, Ltd., 1900–9.

BAEDEKER'S *Austria-Hungary, with Excursions to Cetinje, Belgrade, and Bucharest.* 11th ed. Leipsig: Karl Baedeker, 1911.

BAEDEKER'S *Great Britain.* Leipsic: Karl Baedeker, 1897.

BAEDEKER'S *London and Its Environs.* 10th ed. Leipsic: Karl Baedeker, 1896.

BAEDEKER'S *Paris and Environs.* 12th rev. ed. Leipsic: Karl Baedeker, 1896.

BAEDEKER'S *Russia, with Teheran, Port Arthur, and Peking.* Leipsic: Karl Baedeker, 1914. Reprint, New York: Arno Press & *The New York Times,* 1970.

BAEDEKER'S *South-Eastern France*. 2nd ed. Leipsic: Karl Baedeker, 1895.

BAEDEKER'S *Southern Germany*. Leipsic: Karl Baedeker, 1896.

BAEDEKER'S *Spain and Portugal*. 2nd ed. Leipsic: Karl Baedeker, 1901.

BAEDECKER'S *Switzerland*. Leipsic: Karl Baedeker, 1895.

BALL, CHARLES. *The History of the Indian Mutiny*. 2 vols. London: London Printing and Publishing Company, n.d. [1858–59].

BARNES, R. M. *A History of the Regiments and Uniforms of the British Army*. London: Seeley Service & Co., Ltd., n.d. [1950].

BARTHOLOMEW'S *Reference Atlas of Greater London*. 11th ed. Edinburgh: John Bartholomew & Son, 1961.

BARTHOLOMEW'S *Survey Gazetteer of the British Isles*. 8th ed. Edinburgh: John Bartholomew & Son, 1932.

BARTLETT, JOHN RUSSELL. *Dictionary of Americanisms*. Boston: Little, Brown and Company, 1877.

BARTON-WRIGHT, E. W. "The New Art of Self-Defense," *Pearson's Magazine*, 7:268–75 and 7:402–10, March and April 1899.

BEADLE, J. H. *Polygamy; or, Mysteries and Crimes of Mormonism*. N.p. [Philadelphia: National Publishing Co.], 1870.

BELL, SIR CHARLES. *Portrait of the Dalai Lama*. London: Collins, 1946.

BESANT, SIR WALTER. *London North of the Thames*. London: Adam & Charles Black, 1911.

BIGELOW, S. TUPPER. "Sherlock Holmes and the Misprision of Felony," *The Baker Street Journal*, 8:139–46, July 1958.

BLAKENEY, T. S. "More Disjecta Membra," *The Sherlock Holmes Journal*, 5:55–56, Spring 1961.

BLEILER, E. F. Introduction to *Monsieur Lecoq* by Émile Gaboriau. New York: Dover Publications, Inc., 1975.

BOAZE, FREDERIC. *Modern English Biography*. 6 vols. London: Frank Cass & Co., 1965 (reprint of 1892 edition).

BOOTH, CHARLES. *Labour and Life of the People*. 8 vols. London: Williams and Norgate, 1892–96.

BOOTH, CHARLES, et al. *Life and Labour of the People in London* (Third Series: Religious Influences). 7 vols. London: Macmillan and Co., Ltd. 1902–3.

BOURNE, H. R. Fox. *English Newspapers: Chapters in the History of Journalism*. 2 vols. London: Chatto & Windus, 1887.

BROWN, JAMES D., and STRATTON, STEPHEN S. *British Musical Biography*. Birmingham: S. S. Stratton, 1897.

BURTON, SIR RICHARD. *The City of the Saints*. New York: Harper & Brothers, 1862.

The Century Cyclopedia of Names. 1897 and 1911 editions.

The Century Dictionary and Cyclopedia. 8 vols. New York, 1897.

Chambers's Encyclopædia. Rev. ed. 8 vols. New York, 1889.

CLARKE, RICHARD W. "On the Nomenclature of Watson's Ships," *The Baker Street Journal*, Old Series, 1:119–21, April 1946.

COLLINS' *Illustrated Guide to London and Neighbourhood*. London: William Collins, Sons, and Company, 1876.

The Columbia-Viking Desk Encyclopedia. 3rd ed. 2 vols. New York, 1968.

COOK'S *Tourist Handbook for Switzerland*. London: Thos. Cook & Son, 1905.

COPE, ZACHARY. *The Royal College of Surgeons of England*. London: Anthony Blond, 1959.

The Cyclopædia (Rees's Cyclopædia). 39 vols. London, 1819.

The Dictionary of National Biography. 22 vols. London, 1921–22.

Dictionnaire Historique & Biographique de la Suisse. 7 vols. Neuchâtel, Switzerland, 1921–33.

DUPUY, R. ERNEST, and DUPUY, TREVOR N. *The Encyclopedia of Military History*. New York: Harper & Row, 1970.

ELLISON, NORMAN. *The Wirral Peninsula*. London: Robert Hale Limited, 1955.

ELWORTHY, FREDERIC THOMAS. *The West Somerset Word Book: A Glossary of Dialectal and Archaic Words and Phrases*

Used in the West of Somerset and East Devon. London: for the English Dialect Society (Trübner & Co.), 1888.

The Encyclopædia Britannica. 8th ed. 21 vols. 1858–60.

The Encyclopædia Britannica. 9th ed. 25 vols. 1875–89.

The Encyclopædia Britannica. 11th ed. 29 vols. 1910–11.

FARMER, JOHN S., *Americanisms—Old and New.* London: Thomas Poulter & Sons, 1889.

FARMER, JOHN S., and HENLEY, W. E. *Slang and Its Analogues.* 7 vols. N.p., 1890–1904.

FARWELL, BYRON. *Queen Victoria's Little Wars.* New York: Harper & Row, 1972.

FELSTEAD, S. THEODORE. *Shades of Scotland Yard.* New York: Roy Publishers, n.d. [1953].

FORDHAM, MONTAGUE. *A Short History of English Rural Life.* London: George Allen & Unwin Ltd., 1916.

GEORGANO, G. N., ed. *The Complete Encyclopedia of Motorcars 1885–1968.* New York: E. P. Dutton & Co., 1968.

GOUGH, GEN. SIR HUGH. "Old Memories: Afghanistan," *The Pall Mall Magazine,* 17:389–404, March 1899.

Grand Dictionnaire Universal du XIX Siècle. 15 vols. Paris, 1865–76.

Le Grand Encyclopédie. 31 vols. Paris, 1886–1902.

Grove's Dictionary of Music and Musicians. 5th ed. 10 vols. New York: St. Martin's Press, Inc., 1954.

HALE, GEORGE W. *Police and Prison Cyclopædia.* Cambridge, Mass.: The Riverside Press, 1893.

Handbook and Guide to Bristol. Bristol: J. W. Arrowsmith, 1893.

HARBOTTLE, THOMAS. *Dictionary of Battles.* Revised by George Bruce. New York: Stein and Day, 1971.

HARRISON, MICHAEL. *In the Footsteps of Sherlock Holmes.* New York: Frederick Fell, Inc., 1958.

HARTNOLL, PHYLLIS. *The Oxford Companion to the Theatre.* London: Oxford University Press, 1951.

HOLLAND, GLENN S. "The 'Small, but Very Efficient, Organization' and Other Small Problems," *The Baker Street Journal,* 21:84–89, June 1971.

HOLMES, T. RICE. *A History of the Indian Mutiny.* 5th rev. ed. London: Macmillan and Co., Ltd., 1904.

HOSKINS, W. G. *Devon.* London: Collins, 1954.

HUGHES, RICHARD. Letter in *Sports Illustrated* (10 June 1963) 18:91–2.

The Imperial Dictionary. 4 vols. London, 1883.

The Imperial Gazetteer of India. New ed. 25 vols. Oxford: at the Clarendon Press, 1909.

"The Jacksonian Prize," *The Lancet,* 20 June 1835.

Johnson's Universal Cyclopædia. Rev. ed. 8 vols. New York, 1888.

JUDSON, RALPH. "The Mystery of Baritsu: A Sidelight Upon Sherlock Holmes' Accomplishments," *The Baker Street Journal Christmas Annual,* 1958.

KAHN, DAVID. *The Codebreakers.* New York: Macmillan, 1968.

KAYE, MARVIN. *The Histrionic Holmes.* Culver City, Calif.: Luther Norris, 1971.

KIRKLAND, JOHN. *Three Centuries of Prices of Wheat, Flour and Bread.* London: published by the author at the National Bakery School, Borough Polytechnic Institute, 1917.

KLOSS, C. BODEN. *In the Andamans and Nicobars.* London: John Murray, 1903.

LANGER, WILLIAM L. *An Encyclopedia of World History* Rev. ed. Boston: Houghton Mifflin Company, 1952.

LANGRIGG, ROGER. *The History of Horse Racing.* New York: Stein and Day, 1972.

L'ETANG, HUGH. "Some Observations on the Black Formosa Corruption and Tapanuli Fever," *The Sherlock Holmes Journal,* 4:58–60, Spring 1959.

LEWIS, SAMUEL. *A Topographical Dictionary of England.* 3rd ed. 5 vols. London: S. Lewis and Co., 1835.

LISTON, ROBERT. *Great Detectives.* New York: Mayflower, 1969.

LYSONS, DANIEL, and LYSONS, SAMUEL. *Magna Britannia; being a Concise Topographical Account of the Several Counties of Great Britain.* 6 vols. London: T. Cadell and W. Davies, 1806–22.

MARION, RODGER. "I Always Smoke 'Ship's' Myself," *The Baker Street Journal*, 24:146, September 1974.

MATHEWS, MITFORD. *A Dictionary of Americanisms.* 2 vols. Chicago: The University of Chicago Press, 1951.

MATTFELD, JULIUS. *Variety Music Cavalcade 1620–1969.* 3rd ed. Englewood Cliffs, N.J.: Prentice-Hall, Inc., 1971.

McLAREN, R. M. "Doctor Watson—Punter or Speculator?" *The Sherlock Holmes Journal*, 1:8–10, May 1952.

MEDVEI, VICTOR CORNELIUS, and THORNTON, JOHN L., eds. *The Royal Hospital of Saint Bartholomew 1123–1973.* London: [St. Bartholomew's Hospital], 1974.

MENKE, FRANK G. *The Pictorial Encyclopedia of Sports.* New and rev. ed. Chicago: Progress Research Corporation, 1955.

MLLER, RON. "Will the Real Sherlock Holmes Please Stand Up?" *The Baker Street Journal*, 22:232–36, December 1972.

Modern Roses V: A Concise Descriptive List of All Roses in Commerce or of Historical or Botanical Importance. Prepared in cooperation with the American Rose Society. Harrisburg, Penn.: J. Horace McFarland Company, 1958.

MOLESWORTH, COL. F. C. "The Diary and Letters of Arthur Moffat Lang," Part II, *Journal of the Society for Army Historical Research*, 10:69–108, January 1931.

MOYLAN, J. F. *Scotland Yard and the Metropolitan Police.* London: G. P. Putnam's Sons Ltd., 1929.

NEAVE, SHEFFIELD AIREY. *Nomenclator Zoologicus: A List of the Names of Genera and Subgenera in Zoology from the Tenth Edition of Linnaeus 1758 to the End of 1935.* 4 vols. London: The Zoological Society of London, 1939–40.

A New English Dictionary on Historical Principles. 10 vols. Oxford, 1884–1928.

The New International Encyclopædia. 20 vols. New York, 1905.

The New Practical Reference Library. 5 vols. Kansas City, 1910.

Nomenclator Animalium Generum et Subgenerum. 5 vols. Berlin: Im Verlage der Preussischen Akademie der Wissenschaften, 1926–38. (Incomplete.)

NORMAN, CHARLES. *The Genteel Murderer.* New York: The Macmillan Company, 1956.

PAGE, WILLIAM, ed. *The Victoria History of Hampshire and the Isle of Wight.* 5 vols. London: Constable and Company, 1900–12.

PARKER, JOHN. *The Green Room Book, or, Who's Who on the Stage, 1908.* London: T. Sealey Clarke & Co., 1908.

The Parliamentary Gazetteer of England and Wales. 4 vols. Edinburgh: A. Fullarton & Co., 1854.

PARTRIDGE, ERIC. *A Dictionary of the Underworld.* New York: The Macmillan Company, 1950.

A Pictorial and Descriptive Guide to London and Its Environs. London: Ward, Lock & Co., 1910.

PUGH, R. B., ed. *The Victoria History of the County of Cambridge and the Isle of Ely.* 5 vols. London: The Institute of Historical Research, 1938–60.

ROBERTS, B. H. *A Comprehensive History of the Church of Jesus Christ of Latter-Day Saints.* 6 vols. Salt Lake City: Church of Jesus Christ of Latter-Day Saints, 1930.

ROBERTS, S. C. *Doctor Watson.* London: Faber & Faber Limited, 1931.

RYAN, LIEUT.-COL. ERNEST. "Arms, Uniforms and Equipment of the Yeomanry Cavalry," *Journal of the Society for Army Historical Research*, 35:124–33, September 1957.

ST. JOHN, DAVID, ed. *A Regional History of the Railways of Great Britain.* 9 vols. Newton Abbot, Devon: David & Charles, 1963–76.

SEARS, MINNIE EARL. *Song Index.* New York: The H. W. Wilson Company, 1926.

SHERRING, CHARLES A. *Western Tibet and the British Borderland.* London: Edward Arnold, 1906.

SKENE MELVIN, DAVID. "Some Notes on the Name of the Brothers Moriarty," *The Baker Street Journal,* 21:90–96, June 1971.

SMITH, EDGAR W., ed. *Profile by Gaslight.* New York: Simon & Schuster, 1944.

SMITH, JOSEPH FIELDING. *Essentials in Church History.* Salt Lake City: The Deseret Book Company, 1966.

SOCIETY FOR ARMY HISTORICAL RESEARCH. *Journal of the Society for Army Historical Research: General Index 1921–1962.* Concordance of Numbered and Named Regiments [in the British and Indian Armies], 1969.

STANFORD'S *Geological Atlas of Great Britain.* London: Edward Stanford Ltd., 1964.

STARRETT, VINCENT, ed. *221b: Studies in Sherlock Holmes.* New York: The Macmillan Company, 1940.

STENHOUSE, MRS. T. B. H. *"Tell It All": The Story of a Life's Experience in Mormonism.* Hartford, Conn.: A. D. Worthington & Co., 1875.

SWINSON, ARTHUR, ed. *A Register of the Regiments and Corps of the British Army.* London: The Archive Press, 1972.

Tercentenary Handlist of English & Welsh Newspapers, Magazines & Reviews. London: The Times Publishing Company, 1920. Facsimile reprint, London: Dawsons, 1966.

THORNTON, RICHARD H., *An American Glossary.* 2 vols. Philadelphia: J. B. Lippincott Company, 1912. Supplement, Madison, Wisc.: The American Dialect Society, 1939.

Three Victorian Telephone Directories. New York: Augustus M. Kelley, 1970.

TIMBS, JOHN. *Curiosities of London.* Corrected and enlarged ed. London: Virtue & Co. [1867].

TRAILL, H. D., and MANN, J. S., eds. *The Building of Britain and the Empire.* 6 vols. London: The Waverley Book Company, 1909.

TRAYNOR, MICHAEL. *The English Dialect of Donegal.* Dublin: The Royal Irish Academy, 1953.

VESEY-FITZGERALD, BRIAN, ed. *The Book of the Horse.* Los Angeles: Borden, 1947.

VON STEINWEHR, A. *The Centennial Gazetteer of the United States.* Philadelphia: Ziegler & McCurdy, 1873.

Who Was Who 1916–1928. London: A. & C. Black, 1929.

WILDE, OSCAR, *Intentions.* London: Methuen & Co. [14th ed., 1921]; first published in 1891.

Willing's Press Guide, London (published annually).

YULE, HENRY, and BURNELL, A. C. *Hobson-Jobson: A Glossary of Colloquial Anglo-Indian Words and Phrases, and of Kindred Terms, Etymological, Historical, Geographical and Discursive.* London: John Murray, new edition 1903. Reissued, London: Routledge & Kegan Paul, 1968.

PICTURE SOURCES

The endpaper maps and the maps on pp. 5, 12, 18–19, 21, 36, 59, 74, 102, 118, 121, 151, 189, 194, 202–3, 218–19, 221, 222–23, 224, 225, 298, 319, 320, 338, 339, 351, 353, 369, 373, 375, 376, 383, and 395 are by the author.

The engravings on pp. xiii, 109 (bottom), 133, 159, 162, 166, 170, 173, 177, 246, 303, 365, and 387 are Sidney Paget's original illustrations for the Holmes tales as they appeared in the *Strand* magazine 1891–1904.

The engravings on pp. 3, 79, 110, 122, 154, 227, 230, 242, 357, 378, and 403 are from *Tallis's Illustrated London* by William Gapsey (London: John Tallis), 1851.

The photographs on pp. 7, 58, 65, 190, and 191 are from *Cities of India* by G. W. Forrest (Westminster: Archibald Constable), 1903.

The drawings on pp. 7, 26, 27, 37, 45, 51, 52, 58, 65, 87, 89, 95, 146, 152, 182, 197, 209, 235, 243, 244, 250, 344, 381, and 383 (left) are from *The Century Dictionary and Cyclopedia* (New York: Century), 1897.

The photographs on pp. 8, 47, 56, 75 (bottom), 88, 93, 113, 116, 151, 187, 220, 225, 227, 265, 271, 278, 302, 321, 323, 347, 356, 363, 364, and 380 appear through the courtesy of the Greater London Council.

The photograph on p. 22 is published through the courtesy of the Westminster City Libraries, London.

The photographs on pp. 25 and 306 are from *Pearson's* magazine for March 1899 and January 1897.

The drawing on p. 28 is from *The Encyclopædia Britannica,* 11th edition (Cambridge: At the University Press), 1910–11.

The engraving on p. 30 is from *A Biography of Rev. Henry Ward Beecher* by William C. Beecher and Rev. Samuel Scoville (New York: Charles L. Webster), 1888.

The engravings on pp. 33, 48, 73, 109 (top), 156, 216, 259, 277, 325, 345, and 393 are from *Old and New London* by Walter Thornbury and Edward Walford (London: Cassell, Petter, Galpin), 1873–78.

The drawings on pp. 43, 130, 207, and 236 are by the author.

The photograph on p. 49 is from *London South of the Thames* by Sir Walter Besant (London: Adam & Charles Black), 1912. Reproduced by permission.

The engraving on p. 50 is from *Rivers of Great Britain: Rivers of the East Coast* (London: Cassell), 1892.

The illustrations on pp. 59 (bottom), 83, 98, 350, and 372 were provided by the Radio Times Hulton Picture Library, London.

The photographs on pp. 68, 75 (top), 217, 226 (top and bottom), 393, and 394 are from *A Pictorial and Descriptive Guide to London and Its Environs* (London: Ward, Lock), 1910. Reproduced by permission.

The drawing on p. 86 is from *The New International Encyclopædia* (New York: Dodd, Mead), 1905.

The drawing on p. 92 is from *The Complete Sherlock Holmes* (Garden City: Doubleday), 1930.

The illustrations on pp. 103, 141, 200, 258, 287, and 379 are from the author's collection.

The photograph on p. 108 is from *Conan Doyle* by Pierre Nordon (London: John Murray), 1966. By courtesy of John Murray (Publishers) Ltd.

The photographs on pp. 117, 317, and 402 are published through the courtesy of the Utah State Historical Society, Salt Lake City.

The engravings on pp. 120, 143, 272, 315, 398, and 399 are from *Rivers of Great Britain: The Thames from Source to Sea* (London: Cassell), 1891.

The photograph on p. 127 is from *London City* by Sir Walter Besant (London: Adam & Charles Black), 1910. Reproduced by permission.

The drawing by Jay Finley Christ on p.

136 is from *The Baker Street Journal* for January 1946. By courtesy of The Baker Street Irregulars, New York.

The painting on p. 145 is reproduced by permission of the Trustees of the Wallace Collection, London.

The drawing on p. 155 is by Douglas Bergstreser.

The Sidney Paget drawing on p. 160 is published through the courtesy of Whitbread & Co., London.

The photograph on p. 199 is from *London in the Nineteenth Century* by Sir Walter Besant (London: Adam & Charles Black), 1909. Reproduced by permission.

The photographs on pp. 203 and 355 are from *From Bangkok to Bombay* by Frank G. Carpenter (Garden City: Doubleday, Page), 1924. Reproduced by permission.

The illustrations on pp. 213, 264, 360, and 403 (top) are from the *Strand* magazine for February 1904; March 1893; February 1904; and September 1900.

The photograph on p. 229 is from *The Playground of Europe* by Sir Leslie Stephen (New York: Putnam), 1909. Reproduced by permission.

The engraving on p. 239 is from *Alpenglühen* by Amand Freiherr von Schweiger-Lerchenfeld (Stuttgart: Union Deutsche), n.d. [1893].

The engraving on p. 248 is from *Stories of Sherlock Holmes* (New York: Harper), 1904.

The photographs on pp. 257, 274, 293, and 330 are from the *Pall Mall* magazine for March 1900; March 1897; October 1900; and March 1899.

The engravings on pp. 288 and 308 are from *England, Picturesque and Descriptive* by Joel Cook (Philadelphia: Porter and Coates), 1882.

The engravings on pp. 299 and 314 are from *Our Railways* by John Pendleton (London: Cassell), 1896.

The photograph on p. 300 is the frontispiece from *The Martyrdom of Man* by Winwood Reade, 19th edition (London: Kegan Paul, Trench, Tübner), 1910.

The photographs on pp. 312 and 313 appear through the courtesy of the Department of Medical Illustration, St. Bartholomew's Hospital, London.

H   e   r   t   f o   ...

Harrow
Weald

Pinner ○   ○ *Wealdstone*   *D   E*

○ Harrow-
on-the-Hill

Willesden

B u c k i n g h a m

D

Eton

Chiswick

D

Old
Deer
Park

Windsor

Richmond

L

BERKSHIRE   *M*

Wimbledon

Molesey ○   Kingston-
on-Thames

No

I

Esher

Wall

S   U   *R*   Oxshott ○   *R*   *E*

Woking   Leatherhead

Ripley ○

Guildford   t   h

Reigate

N   *o*   *r*